★ THE ENCYCLOPEDIA OF ★
REGGAE

★ THE ENCYCLOPEDiA OF ★
REGGAE

THE GOLDEN AGE OF ROOTS REGGAE
.BY MiKE ALLEYNE ★ FOREWORD BY SLY DUNBAR

STERLING
New York

STERLING
New York

An Imprint of Sterling Publishing
387 Park Avenue South
New York, NY 10016

Produced by Sideshow Media
Publisher: Dan Tucker
Project Editor: John Martin
Managing Editor: Megan McFarland

ISBN: 978-1-4027-8583-2

Distributed in Canada by Sterling Publishing
c/o Canadian Manda Group, 165 Dufferin Street
Toronto, Ontario, Canada M6K 3H6
Distributed in the United Kingdom by GMC Distribution Services
Castle Place, 166 High Street, Lewes, East Sussex, England BN7 1XU
Distributed in Australia by Capricorn Link (Australia) Pty. Ltd.
P.O. Box 704, Windsor, NSW 2756, Australia

For information about custom editions, special sales, and premium and corporate purchases,
please contact Sterling Special Sales at 800-805-5489 or specialsales@sterlingpublishing.com.

Manufactured in China

2 4 6 8 10 9 7 5 3 1

www.sterlingpublishing.com

"LIVICATION"

To my parents, the late John R. Alleyne, and Lauretto Alleyne, for always encouraging my love of music.

ACKNOWLEDGMENTS

It's been a long, difficult journey, filled with solitary hours of research and writing, without an assistant. I'd like to thank the Department of Recording Industry at Middle Tennessee State University (MTSU) for providing research time and support for the completion of this project. I'd also like to thank the following department colleagues: Charlie Dahan, for sharing his industry experiences and his record collection; John Dougan, for many reggae discussions; John Merchant, for crucial help acquiring some very rare documentary material; and Loren Mulraine and Amy Macy, for vital assistance with my teaching schedule.

Thanks to Soul Syndicate founder and bassist Fully Fullwood and his wife, Frances Fullwood, for generously providing historical details. The MTSU Center for Popular Music provided invaluable assistance in locating out-of-print research resources. Credit is especially due to Dicky Dixon, Grover Baker, Dale Cockrell, Lucinda Cockrell, and Martin Fisher. Research support recognition is also due to Dr. Richard James Burgess at Smithsonian Folkways Recordings for providing valuable Jamaican folk music archive recordings, reggae collector Milton Ellis for help with recordings and print sources, musician Jason Wilson for background on the Canadian reggae scene, and Elizabeth Watson at the Barbados campus of the University of the West Indies (UWI) for consultation on Jackie Opel. Thanks also to UWI colleagues in Jamaica at the Institute of Caribbean Studies and the Reggae Studies Unit, to Prof. Carolyn Cooper for early support in my academic analysis of reggae, to Dr. Dennis Howard for connecting me with key figures on the Jamaican scene, and all the musicians and producers whose work inspired this book. For consistent encouragement via long-distance phone calls, appreciation goes to to my old Tottenham school friend, Chris Devonshire, whose triumph over much greater challenges than this book was inspirational.

Special thanks to legendary Jamaican drummer Sly Dunbar for writing the dynamic foreword. I'd also like to mention the rigorous editorial and creative work of the staff at Sideshow Media, without which this encyclopedia would not have materialized, particularly Dan Tucker, project editor John Martin, and Megan McFarland. One of the encyclopedia's special aspects is its visual impact, and the credit for this goes to three people: the brilliant Phil Yarnall, responsible for the overall design concept and the cover; Jason Snyder, who dealt with the massive, tedious, and ever-changing page-by-page execution of the design; and Stacey Stambaugh, the photo editor at Sterling who researched and edited the entire enormous volume of photos. And finally, thanks to Nathaniel Marunas at Sterling Publishing for enthusiastic support of the project. To all others who contributed, this book proves that your effort was worthwhile.

TOP LEFT: Fans pack Jarrett Park at the first Reggae Sunsplash festival, Montego Bay, Jamaica, 1978.
BOTTOM LEFT: Singer and percussionist Herman ("Bongo Herman") Davis stirrin' it up, 1980.
ABOVE: Lord Flea (center), one of Jamaica's earliest recording artists, rode the calypso wave of the late 1950s.

ABOVE: The Congos (l–r: Roydel Johnson, Cedric Myton, Watty Burnett)
outside Lee Perry's Black Ark studio, Kingston, Jamaica, late 1970s.
OPPOSITE: Reggae speaks of "sufferation," but celebration also rules the Yard.

OPPOSITE: Lucky Dube, of South Africa, became Africa's top reggae artist in the 1990s.
ABOVE: Toots Hibbert performing with Toots & the Maytals, Amsterdam, 2009.

BOB MARLEY

CONTENTS

SIDEBARS

★ FOREWORD ★

The *Encyclopedia of Reggae* takes you back to a time when Jamaica's creative musical energy was reaching out to the world and making a real impact: it gives you the reggae vibe. That classic 1970s period was the most crucial time for Jamaican music. Reggae was deep within Jamaican culture; there was an energy that was going somewhere because everybody was signed to a label, everybody was releasing records, and everybody had a different sound. Acts like Justin Hinds and the Dominoes came from the ska period and into the reggae era. Even though sometimes the same musicians were playing on everyone's records, there was still a different frontier, a different philosophy of writing songs, and people just used to go for it.

This uniqueness is what really captured the audience outside of Jamaica, and the *Encyclopedia of Reggae* captures the uniqueness of the reggae music scene. This is one of the best books I've seen about the music. The high-quality research covers a broad range of reggae artists, and the visuals really make a strong statement. I used to see all of these artists perform—people like Big Youth, Max Romeo, Augustus Pablo—but I've never seen some of the pictures in this distinctive book. Looking back and viewing these photos of places like Channel One and the Black Ark studio brings back strong memories and the feeling of the whole roots reggae musical movement.

One of the first recordings I ever played on was "Double Barrel" by Dave & Ansel Collins (1971), when I was sixteen years old. It became one of the biggest records to come out of Jamaica, and it still sells. To give you an idea of the studio situation, it was recorded on a two-track machine. That night, we didn't have a drum set, so I had to use [session player] Winston Grennan's drum kit.

During the roots era, touring with Peter Tosh was a great experience because that's when Robbie [Shakespeare] and I were established, playing together as a complete rhythm section. At the One Love Peace Concert in 1978, in Kingston, we started playing, then Peter said "Hold on,

hold on. I want to talk to some people." We knew it would have been a concert of great magnitude because it took place for a reason. It wasn't a normal concert; it was a special event [editor's note: see page 246 for further information].

Today, it's vitally important to focus on the reggae era because it attracted international audiences to Jamaican music; it captivated people and made them very curious about how the music was performed and created. Reggae is the root that audiences have to keep coming back to musically, even from one generation to the next. In places like England, people have so many reggae records that their children are growing up listening to tracks from the golden age of roots. At the moment in Jamaican music there's a lot of energy, but no one is certain whether it will connect with people in the same way as reggae did in the 1970s because there's no one taking the music outside of Jamaica—like Island Records' former head Chris Blackwell did—to translate the energy into record sales. Blackwell signed all these reggae artists, got them front-page music-press coverage, and organized tours in the major international markets. Right now, there's room for someone to say, "Here's the new avenue for the music of Jamaica."

Looking to the future of Jamaican music, I think we can draw inspiration from the past. To me, a classic roots reggae song has a wicked bass line and wicked lyrics. One of my favorite roots reggae songs is Bob Marley & the Wailers' "Crazy Baldhead" (1976) because the rhythm drops like an H-bomb! There are many like that, including songs by Burning Spear, and Junior Byles's "Curly Locks." Among my own productions, there are Black Uhuru tunes like "Shine Eye Gal" and "Plastic Smile" (1982), and Junior Delgado's "Merry Go Round" (1981). Like those tracks, *The Encyclopedia of Reggae* has heavy impact, and it's the ideal history book for roots reggae fans: a true classic that every fan should own.

—Lowell "Sly" Dunbar, OD

Ace drummer Lowell "Sly" Dunbar during a sound check at the University of Miami, 1976.

OPPOSITE TOP: Micron Record Store, Kingston, Jamaica, 1975.
OPPOSITE BOTTOM LEFT: Pressing records at Sonic Sounds, Kingston, 2005.
OPPOSITE BOTTOM RIGHT: Record City, in Port Antonio, Jamaica, 1985.
TOP LEFT: A young fan in Sugar Minott's S&M record shop on Waltham Park Road, Kingston, 1987.
TOP RIGHT: The back room of Bob Marley's Tuff Gong records, Kingston.
BOTTOM RIGHT: Jamaican dancehall singer U U Madoo at Skateland, a dancehall venue in Kingston.

INTRODUCTION

If there were one all-embracing description that automatically determined the who, what, when, and where of roots reggae, then the task of writing this book would have been much easier, but popular music always has gray areas that don't lend themselves to easy definition or identification. With reggae in particular, formal boundaries were often blurred. As you turn the pages of this book, imagine a 1970s-era Kingston recording studio session, casual and chaotic, with shifting personnel and makeshift equipment, more often than not enveloped in ganja smoke. The resulting music had an impact on popular culture far beyond what anyone anticipated at the time, but the recordkeeping and individual memories pertaining to such sessions were inconsistent, to say the least—not to mention often contradictory. These are the rewards and the obstacles that any researcher on reggae music must face.

In this encyclopedia, the phrase "roots reggae" applies not only to reggae music and lyrics associated with cultural and religious philosophies. The descriptive phrase also refers to (mostly Jamaican) sound recordings within which the vocal, instrumental, and sound engineering elements collectively impact the listener on physical, emotional, and even spiritual levels.

The time frame centers on the roots reggae heyday of the 1970s, though inevitably this book addresses key figures from the earlier mento, ska, and rocksteady phases of Jamaican popular music evolution that led to reggae's emergence in the late 1960s. Musical and cultural aspects after the 1970s are also included to accommodate both the continuation of artists' careers and the emergence of newer acts embodying the roots style and ethos. Generally speaking, the alphabetical entries in the encyclopedia encompass artists, producers, record labels, and subgenres whose initial music industry presence or impact predates the 1990s. While there's no doubt that noteworthy roots-oriented acts emerged later, the goal here is to highlight key contributors and events on the scene before and during the emergence of reggae, while also referencing the aftermath of roots reggae's peak popularity.

Not everyone will agree with all of the choices, but I had to draw the line somewhere. In this book, as in many comprehensive surveys, space limitations affected how many artists could be included; and in some cases, the lack of reliable, verifiable information was a determining factor. As one example, accounts of the early history of the vocal group Wailing Souls either sharply contradict one another or share a severe lack of date-specific information—so you won't find that group among these pages. It has to be emphasized that in reggae literature, sources still vary widely on precise facts such as when or where an artist was born, or the year in which a given album was released. In some instances, I had to contact the artist or producer for firsthand clarification of such discrepancies. As a result, although every effort was made to ensure the accuracy of information in the respective entries, there are likely areas that remain open to debate or that await further research. The reggae genre is famous for its dub remixes that reconfigure the original identities of recordings, usually enhancing the listener's perspective in the process: perhaps it's useful to think of this encyclopedia as my dub reinterpretation.

In most cases, the cited discographies cover a limited number of works exemplifying an artist's style; for this reason, many compilations of reissued material were chosen, sometimes in favor of original album releases that are often rare or unavailable. It's also crucial to note that Jamaican records released in the 1950s and 1960s, in particular, rarely included the year of release in the label information, adding a further challenge to creating comprehensive discographies. Among other things, this means that writers of similar books dealing with rock, pop, R&B, and jazz instantly have a research advantage, since more detailed historical documentation has existed over a longer time span for those genres than it has for reggae.

On a similar note, reggae literature is rife with claims by various artists to have had a number one record in Jamaica, but this circumstance has to be placed in context. The Jamaican charts are impossible to verify, since during the roots reggae era there was (and still is) no standardized methodology for compiling the hit lists of either albums or singles, and each major radio station on the island had its own chart. There's also no evidence that record sales were consistently tabulated, or that they played a defined role in influencing the charts to provide an objective measurement of hit status. Even in the 2000s, multiple competing charts (including Internet listings) claim to represent the popularity of records in or from Jamaica, but the compilation strategies are not transparent enough for any given listing to have sufficient credibility. When artists speak of being on the charts in Jamaica, there's little doubt that the songs in question were popular, but that popularity can't be accurately quantified. Jamaican newspaper reports in 2011 suggested that payola is still an issue among the island's radio stations, further tainting the credibility of chart-ranking claims.

While some material for this encyclopedia was gathered from print and audio sources, I also used data from conversations and interviews I'd conducted over the past few decades with various artists and producers. These include (in no special order) Mykaell Riley of the Reggae Philharmonic Orchestra, solo singer-songwriter Eddy Grant, bassist Fully Fullwood from the legendary backing band Soul Syndicate, Wayne Jobson of the group Native, singer Cedric Myton of the Congos, and producer-artist Dennis Bovell, among other figures. I was born in London and grew up there in the late 1960s, when reggae arrived and the records first received mainstream airplay, so parts of the narrative are also drawn from my own firsthand recollection of the music's initial impact outside of Jamaica within London's West Indian communities.

The goal of the *Encyclopedia of Reggae* is to appeal to both the roots aficionado and newcomers to the genre, tracing the music's journeys mainly through the histories of individual artists, producers, engineers, and labels. It's impossible to satisfy every expectation of a volume like this, and there will surely be readers who feel aggrieved at the omission of a given artist, a historical angle, or emphases on particular records. However, I'm certain that there's more than enough historical value here to make the reading worthwhile, and to encourage readers to either continue or begin their own journeys into the music. As long as there's reggae, there will *always* be roots.

—Mike Alleyne

Reggae grew out of sound systems, like this Channel 7 system at a country dance in St. Catherine, Jamaica.

ABOVE: Jamaican police peruse the 1982 book
Reggae International.
OPPOSITE: Smoking herb with the chillum pipe
is a Rasta ritual in Jamaica.

through Treasure Isle or Studio One, the primary studio-label outlets of the era. This allowed him to retain ownership of the recorded material, which facilitated licensing of the songs to other labels years later. Although "Satta Massa Gana" was recorded in March 1969 at Dodd's Studio One, the sessions were financed by Collins, who hired the facility himself as opposed to acting as a hired hand in the recording process. Dodd failed to recognize the commercial potential of "Satta Massa Gana"—as well as of the other session recordings, including the brilliant and equally anthemic "Declaration of Rights"—leaving it unreleased until the band members were collectively able to buy the master tape in 1971 for £90, no small amount of money for sidelined material. The song was released that same year on Collins's own Clinch label, though it also appears to have been on sound-system turntables at least a year earlier as a dubplate (pre-release test mix) special.

Considered by many to be the roots reggae anthem representing African cultural and spiritual origins, the Rastafarian hymn uses the Ethiopian Semitic language of Amharic, linking the African past, present, and future as a continuum unbroken by slavery and imperialism. Vocalist Donald Manning—the Abyssinians' only Rasta member when the song was recorded in 1969—suggests that he subsequently sang "Satta Massa Gana" to correct what he believed was an inadequate translation.

Ironically, as "Satta Massa Gana" became a huge hit in Jamaica, Dodd rush-released instrumental versions of the song, notably one featuring former Skatalites saxophonist Tommy McCook. In fact, so

many competing versions were released that in 1973 the Abyssinians recorded "Mabrak" as a declaration of the group's role in creating the original song. Both "Satta Massa Gana" and "Mabrak" use the same rhythm track, with the latter song harshly chastising imitators of the Abyssinians' music and message in spoken word through selected biblical verses. Collins actually released a solo reinterpretation, "Satta Me No Born Yah," in 1976 on Clinch. As is typical in Jamaican popular music, scores of artists have subsequently created their own interpretations of the "riddim," ensuring the song's continued resonance.

Unlike bands in the pop-rock world, the Abyssinians were slow to record an actual album and didn't make their full-length debut until 1976, when they released *Forward on to Zion*, which included singles recently released by the group. The less-inspired *Arise* arrived in 1978 on Virgin Records, a UK label that had entered the reggae market following a whirlwind of signings, including Jamaican artists Culture, Peter Tosh (for the UK), the Mighty Diamonds, and U-Roy. This self-produced album was also released in Jamaica by Bob Marley's Tuff Gong Records.

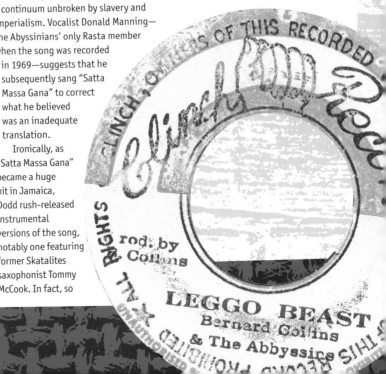

ABYSSINIANS
YEARS ACTIVE: 1968–1990s

The Abyssinians, a vocal group formed in 1968 in Jamaica, are best known for a single song, "Satta Massa Gana" (1971), which other reggae acts have recorded more than 400 times since. The title, which translates to "give praises," appears on the original 1971 Clinch Records vinyl 45 in Jamaica both as "Satta Massa Gana" and "Satta Amasa Gana." The spelling of the song title varies even within the group's later releases: one is titled "Satta-

Though not exactly one-hit wonders, the Abyssinians are best known for "Satta Massa Ganna," their enduring Rasta hymn.

Amassagana" (1976, with the group name misspelled) and another "Satta A Massagana" (1977). The song was partly influenced by 1968's "Happy Land," recorded by the pre-Abyssinians outfit Carlton & His Shoes as a B-side for Coxsone Dodd's Studio One.

In 1969, the Abyssinians' lead singer, Bernard Collins, opted to record his music independently rather than

The early 1980s compilation set *Forward* was issued by the US independent label Alligator Records. Following Collins's departure and replacement by Carlton Manning, the Abyssinians split in 1980. They have regrouped and disbanded several times since with a rotating cast of members. Few of the recordings since their heyday have had notable impact, though the 1998 album *Declaration of Dub* demonstrated that their best material had not lost any of its relevance.

MEMBERS: Bernard Collins (vocals); **Donald Manning** (vocals); **Lynford Manning** (vocals)

SELECT DISCOGRAPHY: "Satta Massa Gana" (Clinch, 1971); *Forward on to Zion* (various labels, 1976); *Arise* (Virgin Front Line, 1978); *Forward* (Musidisc, 1980); *Declaration of Dub* (Heartbeat Records, 1998); *Tree of Satta* (Blood & Fire, 2004)

College students and botanists were among those drawn to this 1978 Aggrovators dub collection.

BELOW: The cover of the Abyssinians' 1976 debut album linked Africa's past and present, suggesting a cultural continuum.

AGGROVATORS
YEARS ACTIVE: 1970s

The Aggrovators were a typically fluid, ever-shifting lineup of studio session musicians used by Jamaican producer Bunny "Striker" Lee. Among the better-known participants in the rotating cast of players were bassist Robbie Shakespeare and tenor saxophonist and arranger Tommy McCook, though the unit also occasionally featured less famous yet highly influential studio musicians such as bassist Jackie Jackson. In naming the group, Lee is thought to have adopted the term "aggro"—an altered abbreviation of "aggravation" favored by the white, middle-class British skinhead subculture—though Lee cites the Britain-based singer and hit producer Eddy Grant as the source who first exposed him to the word.

The Aggrovators were especially well known for the "flying cymbal" sound (created by alternately opening and closing the hi-hat) developed by Lee and drummer Carlton "Santa" Davis. The style was introduced in 1974, inspired by the protodisco releases from the US–based Philadelphia International record label, and Bunny Lee is credited with inventing the descriptive name. Davis's performance of the flying cymbal sound can be seen and heard in the documentary *Word Sound and Power* (1980), in which he drums with the Soul Syndicate band, another Jamaican studio session group. The rising mid-1970s popularity of dub and the B-side remixes of King Tubby brought this session unit into the limelight, as many record buyers became more interested in backup bands and engineers than in vocal artists. A handful of mid-1970s dub albums compiled from singles cemented the band's reputation among diehard reggaephiles, while compilations released in later decades (notably on such labels as Blood & Fire), including those released under the name of King Tubby, have introduced the Aggrovators' musicianship to new audiences.

MEMBERS: Robbie Shakespeare (bass); **Carlton "Santa" Davis** (drums); **Earl "Chinna" Smith** (lead guitar); **Tony Chin** (guitar); **Bernard "Touter" Harvey** (organ); **Ansel Collins** (piano); **Lennox Brown** (alto saxophone); **Bobby Ellis** (trumpet); **Vin Gordon** (trombone); **Tommy McCook** (tenor saxophone)

SELECT DISCOGRAPHY: *Jammies in the Lion Dub Style* (Love & Live, 1978); *Kaya Dub* (Attack, 1978); *Bunny Lee Meets King Tubby & the Aggrovators* (Culture Press, 1999)

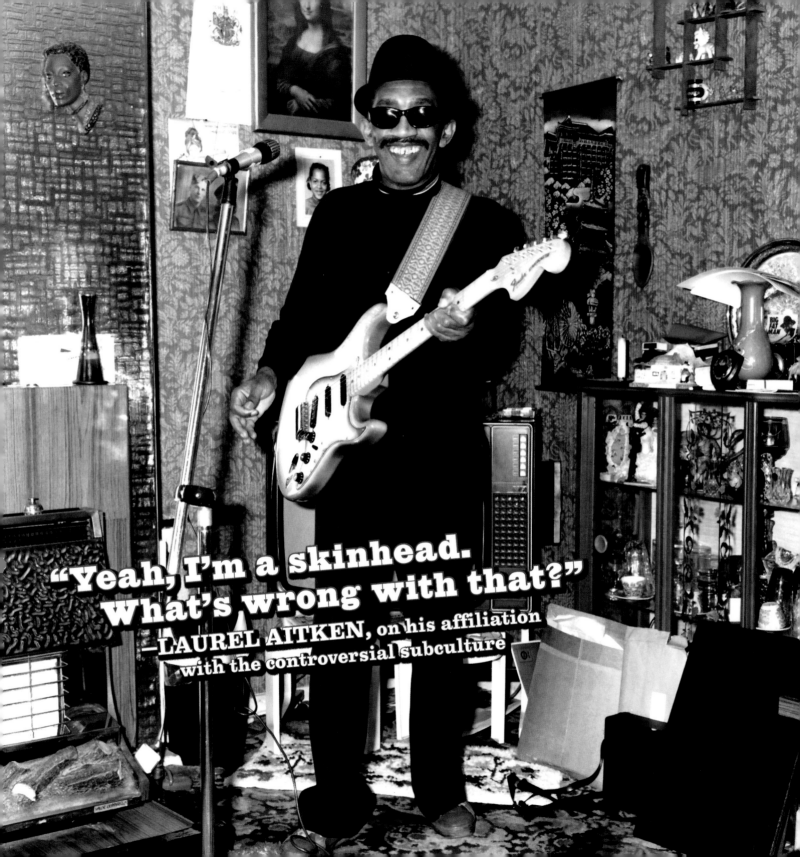

"Yeah, I'm a skinhead. What's wrong with that?"
—LAUREL AITKEN, on his affiliation with the controversial subculture

ECONOMY   MONO   ECO-8

PAMA

Scandal in a Brixton Market
GIRLIE and LAUREL AITKEN

LAUREL AITKEN
YEARS ACTIVE: 1950s–2005

Born Oliver Stephens on April 22, 1927, in Cuba (though the liner notes of one well-known compilation claim it was Panama), Laurel Aitken is known to many as the "Godfather of Ska." He is also one of the artists directly associated with the early Jamaican records of the late 1950s that were influenced by the American R&B style of Louis Jordan. Over the course of his career, Aitken covered subject matter ranging from liberation politics and societal survival to sex and skinheads, but like so many of his Jamaican contemporaries, his historical stature far outweighed any financial rewards he was able to reap.

Aitken made his debut in 1957 with "Roll Jordan Roll," recorded with Jamaican producer Dada Tewari's Caribou label but funded and produced by Aitken himself. Prior to that recording, he'd

gained experience as a frequent talent-competition winner in the early 1950s and released his first recordings—done in the Jamaican-folk mento style—for Stanley Motta's MRS label. One of his early MRS records was the single "One Night in Mexico," although the exact release date is not printed on the label. He also sang for the Jamaica Tourist Board, welcoming tourists as their boats docked.

Rasta drumming is heard on "Ghana Independence," one of the singles Aitken recorded and released in 1957, even though the 1960 song "Oh Carolina" by the Folkes Brothers is most often cited as the earliest intersection of roots culture with recordings of Jamaican popular music. Aitken was also responsible for "Boogie in My Bones," the first single released by Island Records. A major hit in 1959, the song was recorded at the Federal Studio in 1958 and represented Island head Chris Blackwell's debut release as a producer and music-business entrepreneur. "Boogie in My Bones" was

actually the B-side of "Little Sheila," and these two songs spent more than a year on the Jamaican charts, established in 1959. On these first Island Records releases Aitken was backed by a band of white Canadians about whom little seems to be known. Within a short period of time, Aitken had recorded not only for producer Duke Reid but also for the producers Ken Khouri and Leslie Kong.

Another early hit, "Boogie Rock," was released in the UK on Emil Shalit's Blue Beat label in 1960, typifying the dominance of the R&B boogie-style shuffles characterizing so many of Jamaica's post-mento records. In 1960, Aitken moved to London to capitalize on the developing market for Jamaican music; he released additional sides recorded in Britain with Blue Beat before brief stints at several other independent labels, as well as at EMI's Columbia imprint (not to be confused with the US label Columbia Records, owned by CBS) in 1964. He recorded for the Rio label until it went bankrupt around 1966, at which point he began making self-produced recordings for Pama Records. According to one account published in 1982, this deal developed when Aitken's past came back to haunt him. As the story goes, he was arrested after a show in Birmingham for defaulting on weekly child-support payments of £1.50. Confronted with the options of jail time or the payment of a £200 fine, Aitken came up with the appealing idea of using advance money from a new record deal to pay the fine. Really, though, he might have found it easier to have paid the child support on time rather than add another contractual obligation to his life. There was more than a touch of irony in the title of his Pama debut album, *Scandal in a Brixton Market* (1969).

As the 1960s unfolded, Aitken's music was

unexpectedly adopted by the mods and later the skinheads (both of them white, middle-class British subcultures), who became a devoted audience, making him a staple artist outside of Britain's West Indian communities. In the early 1970s, as the skinhead trend was fading, Aitken's attempts to revamp his reggae sound were not as successful. This phase featured the licensing of various one-off recordings to different labels associated with Pama, Trojan, and even EMI.

Despite his long-standing cult following, Aitken didn't score his first British chart hit until "Rudi Got Married," released in 1980 in the wake of the ska revival led by the 2 Tone record label. His resurgence continued with an appearance in the 1986 film *Absolute Beginners*, set in the 1950s and starring British rock icon David Bowie. While his career continued more quietly into the twenty-first century, Aitken toured frequently until he died in July 2005 at the age of seventy-eight. In October 2010, his adopted hometown of Leicester—located in England's Midlands region—held an interactive exhibition on his music.

SELECT DISCOGRAPHY: *Ska with Laurel* (Rio, 1966); *Scandal in a Brixton Market* (Pama/Economy, 1969); *The High Priest of Reggae* (Pama, 1970); *Live at Club Ska* (Sanctuary, 2004)

"Godfather of Ska" Laurel Aitken had plenty to smile about in the 1980s, a decade that began with his first British hit.

DOWN BEAT

CARIBBEAN RECORDING CO., LTD.

Time 2:14

45 RPM
HIGH FIDE.

CRC 2

COME BACK JEANNE
(R. Abrahams – L. Aitken)
LAUREL AITKEN
and the Boogie Cats

MADE IN JAMAICA

DENNIS ALCAPONE

YEARS ACTIVE: 1970s

As one of the contingent of Jamaican DJs who were making their own recordings in the early 1970s, when the DJ talk-over or "toasting" became a commercial phenomenon, Dennis Alcapone was a fixture with the El Paso sound system based in Kingston. The group derived its name from an unlikely source: a popular song recorded by country singer Marty Robbins about a city in Texas. As for Alcapone (born Dennis Smith in 1946), his moniker is explained by the popularity of Italian spaghetti westerns and Hollywood outlaw movies in Jamaica, where gangster heroes are prominent in the island's culture.

Alcapone was given his first studio break by producer and artist Keith Hudson. Although his first records—released under his birth name—were not successful, as Dennis Alcapone he succeeded the pioneering Jamaican DJ U-Roy in achieving popularity on record as the role of the DJ evolved from merely introducing sound-system records to vocally participating, or toasting,

over the songs. Alcapone rotated his services between two Kingston-based producers, Studio One owner Coxsone Dodd and rival studio boss Duke Reid, who owned the Treasure Isle label; between those stints he worked for a time with the prolific producer Bunny Lee. These were, after all, the owners of large stocks of hit "riddims" already loved by audiences.

One of Alcapone's best-known early hits was "Nanny Version," recorded in the early 1970s utilizing the "Nanny Goat" backing track that Larry Marshall had recorded for Studio One. Though it was not his first hit, "Guns Don't Argue" (1971) became a career-defining song for Alcapone, as did "Forever Version." He loved rocksteady grooves, and while at Treasure Isle he established one of reggae's first DJ duos, teaming up with fellow Jamaican DJ Lizzy to cut a series of singles.

Between 1970 and 1973 Alcapone was extremely prolific. According to one estimate, he recorded well over one hundred singles and worked with nearly as many producers. His popularity in Britain led to frequent UK tours and recording sessions, and in 1974 he

released the unappetizingly titled *Belch It Off* album, produced by Sidney Crooks of the Pioneers, a vocal group that was part of reggae's first international wave of success. This was a crucial phase in Alcapone's career, since his absence from Jamaica compromised his popularity there, allowing others to fill the void. Despite having spent a great deal of time in Britain, he never exploded there commercially, and he temporarily moved to the more mainstream Magnet label.

Alcapone's decline was almost as rapid as his burst onto the Jamaican sound-system scene, and he left the music business in 1979 when he moved to London permanently. Much was made of his well-received appearance in 1989 at the WOMAD (World of Music, Art and Dance) festival in England, but nothing could reestablish his early-1970s supremacy. Alcapone remains a prime example of the degree to which the early sound systems penetrated and influenced Jamaica's popular music culture.

SELECT DISCOGRAPHY: *Universal Rockers* (RAS, 1995); *Guns Don't Argue: The Anthology '70–77* (Trojan, 2005); *Forever Version* (Heartbeat, 2007)

ABOVE: Playing on Jamaica's love for outlaw heroes, Dennis Smith adopted the surname Alcapone and became one of the key "toasting" DJs of the 1970s.

RIGHT: Lest anyone find his stage name too subtle, Dennis Alcapone went full-on gangster for the cover of his career-defining 1971 single.

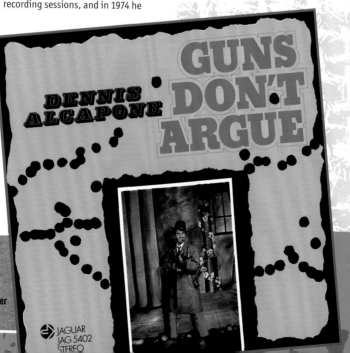

HORACE ANDY

YEARS ACTIVE: 1966–PRESENT

Born Horace Hinds in 1951 in Kingston, Jamaica, Horace Andy has sung in his distinctively soulful tenor voice with tremendous clarity and conviction for more than forty years. The Rasta consciousness and social awareness embedded in Andy's songs, however, connect to events that predate his singing career. As a teenager in the late 1960s, at the urging of a friend, he began to attend meetings of the Ethiopian World Federation; he recalls, "It was the Rastafarian faith that really open my eyes forming a consciousness, and that's why I sing those songs."

Producer Coxsone Dodd gave Andy his stage name, evidently feeling the singer was in the same league as Bob Andy, who had also recorded at Dodd's Studio One in Kingston. Under the production supervision of Phil Pratt, Horace Andy began his recording career with "Black Man's Country," cut in 1966 at the WIRL (West Indies Records Limited) studios in Kingston. It was also during this time that the young Andy learned how to play guitar under the tutelage of Pratt. It would be another four years before

King Jammy in the 1980s) at King Tubby's studio in Kingston. These two releases arguably represent the creative peak of Andy's solo career. His vocals undoubtedly make artistic and cultural statements on the original set, placing them in the context of dub. The impeccable musicianship on the rhythm tracks (including former Skatalite Tommy McCook on horns) and the skillful mixing take his sound to an altogether new level of roots reggae. *In the Light Dub* is quintessential dub that stands up to comparison with any of the subgenre's other landmark releases. Typically for the era, its basic cover art lends few clues to the apocalyptic dub explosion contained within.

Andy moved to Connecticut by the mid-1970s and worked on several albums in the 1980s for Lloyd Barnes's New York–based Bullwackies record label. This phase of his career included

the album *Dance Hall Style* (1982) and underlined the popularity of his vocal style beyond the roots reggae era. During this time, his recordings were continually issued on multiple labels in Jamaica, Britain, and the United States. They were not big sellers, partly because there was too much material on the market at once.

Andy's career took an unpredictable twist in the 1990s. Having relocated to Great Britain, he began working with Massive Attack—a collective from Bristol, England, known for pioneering the trip-hop sound—in time for the group's 1990 debut album, *Blue Lines*. He sang on subsequent Massive Attack releases and toured with the band in the late 1990s. Reggae artist Garnett Silk's 1994 cover version of "Skylarking," released before the young singer's tragic death, clearly shows how Andy's influence crosses generations of reggae fans and musicians.

SELECT DISCOGRAPHY: *In the Light* (Hungry Town, 1977); *In the Light Dub* (Hungry Town, 1977); *Dancehall Style* (Wackies, 1982); *Skylarking: The Best of Horace Andy* (Melankolic, 1997)

The ever-soulful Horace Andy at Channel One, 1984: a vision in blue.

Andy's next recording appeared, and during this hiatus he worked to improve his vocal skills: "I couldn't sing, man!" he recalled. "I could sing anybody's song but when it comes to mine."

In the early 1970s, Andy had a hit with "Got to Be Sure," soon followed by songs like "Skylarking" (1972), which became the title track of a compilation album comprising his Studio One hits. Over the next few years, Andy would record for Bunny Lee and several other major Jamaican producers. In 1977, Andy released *In the Light*, his debut for the Hungry Town label. A classic album with modest cover art, *In the Light* was recorded and coproduced with New York–based Everton DaSilva, also recored in Kingston. The collaboration marked the first stage in a productive partnership that ended when DaSilva was shot and killed in New York in 1979.

In 1995, the Blood & Fire reissue label combined 1977's *In the Light* (co-crafted with recording engineers like the talented Sylvan Morris) with its counterpart, *In the Light Dub*, brilliantly mixed by Prince Jammy (later dubbed

ASWAD

YEARS ACTIVE: 1975–2000s

Taking their name from the Arabic word for "black," Aswad was one of the groups on the frontlines of British reggae, persevering against the misguided notion that true roots reggae could only be made by Jamaicans—not by black, Britain-based, second-generation West Indians. Like their pioneering contemporaries Matumbi and Steel Pulse, Aswad built a hybrid sound that, while based on roots aesthetics, also expressed their experience of being "born and raised in Babylon / under lock and key," as the group sang on "Day by Day," from their 1994 album *Rise & Shine*.

Formed in 1975 in the Ladbroke Grove section of London, Aswad's original lineup featured Brinsley Forde (lead vocals), Angus Gaye (drums), Courtney Hemmings (keyboards), Donald Benjamin (guitar), and George Oban (bass). Two early independently released singles—"Back to Africa" and "Three Babylon"—and an eponymous debut album helped Aswad develop an underground following, though internal creative conflicts led to a split with Hemmings that later brought Tony "Gad" Robinson into the group in 1979. The 1976 self-titled debut album was licensed to Chris Blackwell's Island Records from Grove Music, making Aswad the first British reggae band signed to a major label. As Forde remembers, "In the early seventies, when we went to Island, they had no experience of having a reggae band that was based in England. So we had our ups and downs.

It was a learning period for everyone involved, but I think Chris [Blackwell] had faith in us. He signed us personally."

As Aswad's reputation grew, such high-profile Jamaican acts as Bob Marley and Burning Spear hired the group during UK tours. The 1978 album *Hulet* delivered the single "It's Not Our Wish," which Aswad performed in *Reggae in a Babylon*, a documentary released that year. At this point, musical differences led to Oban's departure. The group's mainstream notoriety was bolstered by its involvement in the Rock Against Racism concerts held in London in 1978, just a step ahead of the election of Margaret Thatcher as prime minister in 1979 and the ushering in of her administration's blatantly exclusionary race politics. Aswad gained further exposure from Forde's starring role in *Babylon* (1980), a film about the UK reggae industry that had an accompanying sound track album.

Babylon featured "Warrior Charge," which became not only one of Aswad's live staples but also one of British reggae's definitive artistic statements.

In late 1980, after Island released *Showcase*, a compilation of dub versions and remixes of previously released tracks, Aswad moved to CBS Records. During the band's Island stint, none of their records had been released in the United States—a market ripe for the emergence of new reggae stars following the success of Bob Marley—and this may have played some role in Aswad's decision to change labels. The simply titled *New Chapter* album emerged in 1981 as the first installment of the international deal with CBS to break new commercial ground. Hailed as a creative and influential landmark in British reggae, *New Chapter* was followed in 1982 by *Not Satisfied*, recorded in March and released in July. This was the first of Aswad's albums to break into the British charts, peaking modestly at #50. The record's title may have reflected the band's disenchantment with the new label, and by the end of the year, Aswad had returned to Island to release one of their strongest records, *A New Chapter of Dub*.

The following year brought *Live and Direct*, released on Island's Mango imprint. Aswad recorded the album live at London's Notting Hill Carnival with a band that included Barbadian guitarist Jimmy "Senyah" Haynes, who would produce Steel Pulse's Grammy-winning 1986 album *Babylon the Bandit*. One key figure in the British reggae community implied that *Live and Direct* was less live than most people thought and had been enhanced—like so many live rock albums—by strategic studio overdubs. Regardless, the record demonstrated

Aswad's trademark ability to incorporate dub elements into live performance, making their identity more authentic.

It wasn't until 1984 that Aswad landed their first single on the British pop charts, reaching #51 with the

philosophical "Chasing for the Breeze" from *Rebel Souls*, an album recorded in Jamaica. By the following year, Aswad had left Island again, this time to form their own label, Simba, on which their 1986 release *To the Top* was issued. This was by no stretch a hard-core roots album—the inclusion of "Nuclear Soldier" notwithstanding—and it was one of the group's most energetic and consistent collections. The album was more focused on dance and love than on the culture, truth, and rights political trinity that had previously defined so much of their character as a group.

Distant Thunder, Aswad's most commercially successful and crossover-focused album, arrived in 1988, issued on Mango as the band returned to Island for a third time. Although it was

eventually a top-ten record, achieving gold status in Britain (but only reaching #173 in the United States), its mainstream pop ambitions undermined the record's relevance to Aswad's former core roots following. And, while Aswad had proven their songwriting capabilities in earlier years, their breakthrough #1 British pop single, "Don't Turn Around," was written by two US-based songwriters, Albert Hammond and the prolific Diane Warren. In 1994, Sweden's Ace of Base also had a hit with the song. Polygram Records' $300 million acquisition of Island in 1989 presented Aswad with greater global opportunities but also made it increasingly important

to stick to a commercial pop-reggae formula. Though the 1990 album *Too Wicked* was cut in Jamaica with the talented producer Gussie Clarke, it seemed almost too commercial, aiming beyond the limited roots reggae audience. It even included a guest appearance by dancehall DJ Shabba Ranks.

A four-year recording hiatus preceded 1994's *Rise and Shine*, which Aswad followed a year later with *Rise and Shine . . . Again*, released on the Bubblin' label in Britain and Mesa/Bluemoon in the United States. The latter album was essentially the same as the former but with five bonus tracks thrown in—most of them remixes—thrown in. The UK top-five hit single "Shine" paid homage to black British athletes, making a cultural and political statement about the country in which the band had established itself and its reputation. Although Aswad was by now visibly a trio, they relied on session musicians in the studio.

The *Rise and Shine* releases marked the end of the group's commercial and artistic impact, and perhaps seeing the writing on the wall, Forde soon left the band. In a May 2009 interview with the leading British black newspaper *The Voice*, Forde said, "My way of life is Rastafarian and I think the time just came for me to tread a different path. It was just one of those things. . . . I signed over the rights [to the name Aswad] when I left, so it was all fine."

The 1999 album *Roots Revival*, released on Ark 21, practically disappeared without a trace. Since then Aswad's profile has been sustained almost entirely by reissues and compilations, including 2009's choice archival set *The BBC Sessions*. That same year, the two remaining members unexpectedly released *City Lock*, the first Aswad album of new material in a decade. One critic described the collection as suffering "from an identity crisis," since it attempted to be universally appealing. In many ways, Aswad's history—as underscored by *City Lock*—is one large paradox: the sound that brought them international success was also the sound that least reflected the roots from which their music had sprung.

Aswad (l–r: Angus "Drummie Zeb" Gaye, Brinsley Forde, and Tony "Gad" Robinson) backstage at the Raintree nightclub in Essex, England, 1984.

MEMBERS: Brinsley Forde (lead vocal, guitar, percussion), *Aswad* to *Rise and Shine*; **Angus "Drummie Zeb" Gaye** (drums, percussion), *Aswad* to *City Lock*; **Tony "Gad" Robinson** (keyboards, vocals, percussion), *Live and Direct* to *City Lock*; **Donald Benjamin** (guitar, vocals), *Aswad* to *Hulet*; **Courtney Hemmings** (keyboards), *Aswad*; **George Oban** (bass), *Aswad* to *Hulet*

SELECT DISCOGRAPHY: *Aswad* (Island, 1976); *Hulet* (Island, 1978); *New Chapter* (CBS, 1981); *Not Satisfied* (CBS, 1982); *A New Chapter of Dub* (Mango/Island, 1982); *Live and Direct* (Mango/Island, 1983); *Rebel Souls* (Mango/Island, 1984); *To the Top* (Simba, 1986); *Distant Thunder* (Mango/Island, 1988); *Too Wicked* (Mango/Island, 1990); *Rise and Shine* (Bubblin', 1994); *Rise and Shine . . . Again* (Bubblin'/Mesa, 1995); *Roots Revival* (Ark 21, 1999) *The Complete BBC Sessions* (Universal, 2009); *City Lock* (Absolute UK, 2009)

Aswad looks less than satisfied in London, 1981, a year before releasing the album *Not Satisfied*.

THEOPHILUS BECKFORD
YEARS ACTIVE: 1950s–1990s

Born in 1935 in Kingston, Jamaica, Theophilus Beckford was a versatile pianist and one of the architects of Jamaican music in the early 1950s. He began playing professionally in the middle of that decade and soon became one of producer Coxsone Dodd's Studio One session players. He was a member of the group Clue J and the Blues Blasters during the early 1960s dawn of ska. That group, led by Cluett Johnson, is perhaps best known for "Shuffling Jug" (1960), one of the first ska songs and also one of Dodd's earliest Studio One ska productions.

Beckford claimed that Johnson's exclamation of "skavoovie" was the root of the word *ska*, though this is just one of countless competing versions of the word's origin. In any event, Beckford was not only on the scene when crucial developments in the evolution of Jamaican popular music were taking place, but as one of the many freelance musicians drifting between rival producers, he also helped to create that scene. Some have described the sound of that era as "proto-ska," a product of the gradual fusion of mento with its historical antecedents and American R&B.

Beckford's shuffling, boogie-influenced "Easy Snappin'" single was reportedly recorded in 1956 and heard as a sound-system dubplate before its official release in 1959 on the Studio One label. Blue Beat Records later issued the song in Britain (as was typical at that time, many of the Jamaican and British record labels did not print the year of release on the records). The course of Jamaican musical history might have been altered if producers like Dodd had released such songs in the years they were actually recorded. Despite the historical importance of "Easy Snappin'"—a song that helped usher in a new era of locally recorded Jamaican music—Beckford apparently received no royalties for it or for his subsequent, less successful solo recordings of other songs.

In 1963, Beckford established his own label, King Pioneer Ska Productions, after becoming disillusioned with the financial inequalities of the business, but this enterprise failed to flourish. By the 1970s, he had become a session player at producer Lee Perry's Black Ark studio in Kingston, joining the shifting aggregation of musicians known as the Upsetters. After his stint with Perry, however, his profile remained low, as did his income. The onslaught of digital music in the 1980s meant far less work for piano players, unless they adapted their skills to include sequencing and programming, and Beckford could not make such a dramatic transition. Still, in 1991, when Studio One celebrated its history with The Beat Goes On: 35 Years in the Business, a concert held at Kingston's National Stadium, his participation led to a brief reemergence from oblivion.

After years of struggling for survival without the financial rewards that his work deserved, Beckford died in gruesome fashion in February 2001 when he received a fatal hatchet wound to the head while attempting to

intervene in a neighborhood dispute in Kingston. It was a sad and ignoble end for a man who made such invaluable contributions to Jamaican music.

SELECT DISCOGRAPHY: *Trenchtown Ska* (Jamaican Gold, 1999); *Trojan Battlefield: King Pioneer Ska Productions* (Sanctuary, 2004)

ABOVE: Theophilus Beckford in 1983. By this time session work had dried up for the influential pianist and ska architect.

BELOW: Released in 2004, after Sanctuary Records bought the Trojan catalog, *Trojan Battlefield* is one of many compilations that have introduced classic recordings to new generations of listeners.

BIG YOUTH

YEARS ACTIVE: 1971-PRESENT

Born Manley Buchanan in 1949 (some sources state 1955) in Kingston, Jamaica, the pioneering DJ known as Big Youth has been described as the first reggae star to display Rastafarian dreadlocks during a stage performance. He is said to have made this debut at Kingston's Carib Theatre in 1973, when Bob Marley's dreads were still at an early stage of cultivation. In the early 1970s, Rastas were still disregarded by Jamaica's middle and upper classes as dangerous, antisocial misfits, so the act of appearing on stage with free-flowing locks was a deeply sociopolitical statement.

Big Youth recorded his first album that same year, and eventually became one of the cornerstones of Jamaica's DJ culture. He was influenced by the improvisational genius of jazz legends John Coltrane and Charlie Parker, as well as by the pop songwriting craftsmanship of the Beatles. On paper, such influences might seem marginal at best, but on record, it's clear how the master DJ's vocal raps described in Jamaica as "toasting" translated the opportunities for free, fluid expression offered by jazz into a lyrical soundscape, all the while employing trademark verbal hooks to give his works shape and structure. Big Youth has also noted the influence of female soul singers, recalling how he practiced his vocalizations using records by Diana Ross and Dionne Warwick. His greatest influence, however, was his mother's skill as a church preacher, which prepared him for commanding the stage and projecting spiritual messages to audiences.

Before embarking on a musical career, Big Youth worked as an auto mechanic in what was then Kingston's Sheraton Hotel. After debuting on Lord Tippertone's sound system around 1971 and building a solid following as its resident DJ, he recorded his first two singles that year for the African Museum

> "This bling bling thing me start it; but me nuh follow hype, me just come fi do what I do."
> —BIG YOUTH, on hip-hop culture and his jewel embedded red, green, and gold teeth

Sporting red, green, and gold bejeweled teeth and dreadlocks, Big Youth embodied Rasta's antiestablishment stance.

ABOVE: Big Youth recorded 1972's "Chi Chi Run" on the same day he cut "S 90 Skank," named for a Rasta-approved Japanese motorbike.

As Big Youth tells it, the positive social-consciousness lyrics favored by some early toasters—himself included—accurately reflected daily ghetto realities and existed in the realm of sound systems long before actually making it onto records. But while U-Roy, another seminal DJ, had already scored large hits in the early 1970s, his were not songs that actively promoted Rastafari and its social politics of resisting the social establishment. This was a niche filled by Big Youth, and his fame was furthered by a sound-system culture that acted as a people's communication pipeline.

In the early 1970s, reggae producer Phil Pratt's "Tell It Black" offered Big Youth a chance to expand his audience by DJing over Dennis Brown's cover of "Black Magic Woman," a 1968 hit for the British blues-rock band Fleetwood Mac. Another of Big Youth's career-making early hits was 1972's "S 90 Skank" (title printed as "Ace 90" on early pressings), recorded with producer Keith Hudson, who had also worked with U-Roy. The Japanese S90 motorbike, a favorite mode of transportation for Rastamen of the time, inspired this reverb-laden toasting trip. (Big Youth himself had some frightening,

near-tragic experiences as a rider.) The equally successful "Chi Chi Run," produced by established singer and Jamaican music figure Prince Buster, was recorded on the same day, and these two hits put Big Youth firmly on the reggae map. A good indication of his popularity among producers and audiences is his claim to have had seven songs on the Jamaican charts at the same time.

Big Youth's debut album *Screaming Target* (1973) not only introduced him to a wider audience through its British release by Trojan Records but also typified Jamaican LPs of this era in its packaging. The hasty creation of many Jamaican album covers of the era imbued them with a sense of authenticity and immediacy that artists and fans alike could identify with. Members of the British punk-rock group the Clash later recalled how the cover and music of Big Youth's debut LP influenced them in the sense that both were more improvised than calculated. Typically, cover artists and designers reaped no royalties for their labor, despite its far-reaching cultural impact in markets like Britain, which offered potential financial rewards that were hard to come by in Jamaica. In an effort to correct this situation, Big Youth established his own record labels, one of which was Negusa Nagast (founded 1973), translated from Amharic as "King of Kings." Reaping more profits from his own recordings allowed the artist to "start eating some food," as he put it.

In 1974, Big Youth took a major artistic risk in self-releasing the double album *Reggae Phenomenon* (later re-released by Trojan in 1977), on which he branched out from solely toasting to actually singing on some

songs, though with uneven results. That album included his biggest hit, "Hit the Road Jack." The self-produced mid-1970s album trilogy *Dread Locks Dread* (1975), *Natty Cultural Dread* (1976), and *Hit the Road Jack* (1976) established Big Youth as a top toaster. The latter two albums were also released by Trojan in the United Kingdom and brought him closer to the attention of the mainstream. He signed with Virgin Records in the late 1970s, as that label leapt into reggae with its specialized Front Line imprint, and he rates *Isaiah First Prophet of Old*, released in 1978 on that label, as the best album of his career.

The records that Big Youth has released since his commercial peak in the 1970s have received little marketplace attention, and the DJ pathway he helped create is now populated by a host of dancehall and hip-hop candidates. Still, Big Youth's place in reggae history is undeniable.

SELECT DISCOGRAPHY: *Screaming Target* (Trojan, 1973); *Reggae Phenomenon* (Negusa Nagast, 1974); *Dread Locks Dread* (Klik, 1975); *Natty Cultural Dread* (Trojan, 1976); *Hit the Road Jack* (Trojan, 1976); *Isaiah First Prophet of Old* (Virgin Front Line, 1978)

label co-owned by singers Gregory Isaacs and Errol Dunkley. While those singles, "Movie Man" and "Black Cinderella," set the template for Big Youth's brand of DJing, neither was a major hit.

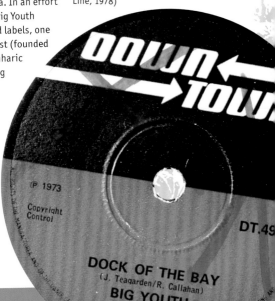

DOWN TOWN

℗ 1973
Copyright Control

DT.49

DOCK OF THE BAY
(J. Teagarden/R. Callahan)
BIG YOUTH
A DERRICK HARRIOTT PRODUCTION

BLACK SLATE

YEARS ACTIVE: 1974-1985; 2009-PRESENT

Black Slate was a six-man London-based outfit and one of Britain's first self-contained reggae bands. As was often the case with Britain-based reggae bands, not all of the members were of Jamaican descent, though reggae literature tends to overlook this reality. They formed in 1974 with the intention of backing touring Jamaican artists, but two years later their anti-mugging single "Sticks Man," which decried black-on-black crime, rose to prominence on the British reggae charts.

Black Slate first toured the United Kingdom in 1978 and formed their own label, TCD, on which their self-titled debut album was released in 1979. It was later remixed and reissued on the larger Ensign label and distributed through what was then the very major Phonogram label. In 1980, "Amigo," the title track

from their sophomore album, became their first British pop hit, reaching #9 in September. The light and catchy song was a stark contrast to the ominous dread Rasta atmosphere that characterized other group-based British reggae at that time. This proved to be the band's peak year, as they scored their only other minor hit, scraping the outskirts of the British pop charts with "Boom Boom," which reached #51. Black Slate managed to include some subversive ideology on the B-side of "Boom Boom" with "Legalise Collie Herb." With a different message, it might have made a great A-side and received airplay. A quality dub album, Ogima/Dub Slate, was issued in 1981, but that record rarely appears in any new or old reggae discographies.

Although Sirens in the City, recorded in Jamaica, was issued in 1981 (followed by another pair of collections in the mid-1980s), and the band continued touring, Black Slate's moment in the spotlight had passed. The 1982 album Six Plus One was released by both Top Ranking Sounds

and CBS Records and followed up with a dub version later the same year. The group's final record, 1985's Black Slate, disappeared into oblivion; the initial commercial momentum was gone.

Black Slate exemplified a brand of roots reggae that drew clear inspiration from Jamaica but evolved to become a more distinctly urban, British, instrumental and lyrical interpretation of the genre. The alienation experienced by black second-generation West Indians in Britain was different from British Caribbean-island colonialism because it occurred in the heart of so-called imperialist Babylon, and as Black Slate's lead singer Keith Drummond noted in a 1977 interview in Black Music magazine, "In this country, it doesn't matter who's in

ABOVE: This 1980 single reached #9 on the UK charts, marking the first pop hit for Black Slate, one of Britain's earliest self-contained reggae bands.

BELOW: Black Slate, creators of a distinctly British roots sound, hang tough in London's Brixton district, 1980.

power—if you're black, you're going to go through sufferation." Under Prime Minister Margaret Thatcher's Conservative party, elected to power in 1979, that "sufferation" would be magnified through racially oppressive policies, suggesting that it did matter somewhat who was in power. But Drummond's comment also provided evidence that in almost any social context, reggae draws its greatest strength when pushed into a corner or up against a wall. A new version of the band was unexpectedly formed in 2009.

MEMBERS: Anthony "Sir George" Brightly (keyboards); Keith Drummond (lead vocals); Desmond Mahoney (drums); Chris Hanson (lead guitar); Ras Elroy Bailey (bass, vocals); Cledwyn Rogers (rhythm guitar); Nicky Ridguard (trombone), Black Slate to Rasta Festival; Rudy Hymes (tenor saxophone), Black Slate to Rasta Festival

SELECT DISCOGRAPHY: Black Slate (TCD, 1979); Amigo (TCD, 1980); Ogima/Dub Slate (TCD, 1981); Rasta Festival (Alligator, 1981); Sirens in the City (Ensign, 1981); Six Plus One (Top Ranking Sounds/CBS, 1982); Six Plus One Dub (Top Ranking Sounds, 1982); Black Slate (Sierra, 1985)

"She played a big part in the group especially sound and image wise. She had a very powerful image and her sound was unusual in the reggae arena."

—DUCKIE SIMPSON on late Black Uhuru member Puma Jones

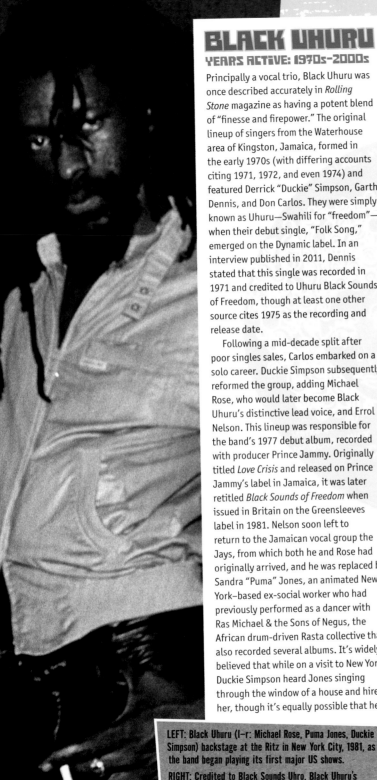

BLACK UHURU
YEARS ACTIVE: 1970s–2000s

Principally a vocal trio, Black Uhuru was once described accurately in *Rolling Stone* magazine as having a potent blend of "finesse and firepower." The original lineup of singers from the Waterhouse area of Kingston, Jamaica, formed in the early 1970s (with differing accounts citing 1971, 1972, and even 1974) and featured Derrick "Duckie" Simpson, Garth Dennis, and Don Carlos. They were simply known as Uhuru—Swahili for "freedom"—when their debut single, "Folk Song," emerged on the Dynamic label. In an interview published in 2011, Dennis stated that this single was recorded in 1971 and credited to Uhuru Black Sounds of Freedom, though at least one other source cites 1975 as the recording and release date.

Following a mid-decade split after poor singles sales, Carlos embarked on a solo career. Duckie Simpson subsequently reformed the group, adding Michael Rose, who would later become Black Uhuru's distinctive lead voice, and Errol Nelson. This lineup was responsible for the band's 1977 debut album, recorded with producer Prince Jammy. Originally titled *Love Crisis* and released on Prince Jammy's label in Jamaica, it was later retitled *Black Sounds of Freedom* when issued in Britain on the Greensleeves label in 1981. Nelson soon left to return to the Jamaican vocal group the Jays, from which both he and Rose had originally arrived, and he was replaced by Sandra "Puma" Jones, an animated New York–based ex–social worker who had previously performed as a dancer with Ras Michael & the Sons of Negus, the African drum-driven Rasta collective that also recorded several albums. It's widely believed that while on a visit to New York, Duckie Simpson heard Jones singing through the window of a house and hired her, though it's equally possible that her connection to Ras Michael led to a less dramatic introduction. Jones, a fixture of Black Uhuru's best-known lineup, was one of the few women in reggae to be represented as a genuine group member alongside male counterparts. Her introduction to the band followed the group's performance and production alliance with the drum-and-bass powerhouse duo Sly & Robbie on 1979's *Showcase*, released just prior to the group signing a contract with Island Records. *Showcase* was an appropriately titled collection of singles later reissued with at least two other titles on as many labels and with differing tracks.

The first full fruit of this collaboration with Sly & Robbie was 1980's *Sinsemilla*, seen (and heard) by some critics as the foundation of the quintessential Black Uhuru sound. The record demonstrated the development of the group's vocal and songwriting chemistries as well as just how integral Sly & Robbie (also known as the Riddim Twins) had become to the band's sound.

Sinsemilla was followed by the critically acclaimed 1981 album *Red* (included on Rolling Stone's list of the top one hundred albums of the 1980s), the band's first major tour dates in Britain and the United States, and 1982's *Chill Out*, on which Black Uhuru's collective creativity was becoming more cohesive. (Some critics, however, were unmoved by the digital experimentation.) *Chill Out* was one of only two Black Uhuru albums to cross over commercially and reach Billboard's Top 200 album chart in the US, though its modest #146 placement in no way did justice to the quality musicianship and production. On the other hand, *Chill Out* was the group's highest-charting record in the UK, reaching #28. The year 1982 also brought *Tear It Up–Live*, an album that actually delivered the artistic goods and wasn't made merely to fulfill contractual obligations. The live version of "Shine Eye Gal," a song that originally appeared on the *Showcase* LP, displays the considerable stylistic swagger, power, and energy that characterize that album.

In typical music-business irony, just when Black Uhuru's greatest success

LEFT: Black Uhuru (l–r: Michael Rose, Puma Jones, Duckie Simpson) backstage at the Ritz in New York City, 1981, as the band began playing its first major US shows.

RIGHT: Credited to Black Sounds Uhro, Black Uhuru's 1977 debut, *Love Crisis*, was renamed *Black Sounds of Freedom* upon release in Britain in 1981.

LOVE CRISIS
BLACK SOUNDS UHRO — TONEY — DUCKY — ERROL

was within reach, internal frictions and conflicts with their record label began to derail the group's upward trajectory. According to Duckie Simpson, one factor that contributed to the group's fracture was Rose's desire to dominate the songwriting; but Black Uhuru's relationship with Island was even more problematic. "The Island period was very rough," Simpson said in a late-1990s interview. "They tricked us into signing a bad contract. . . . So we had to work all those years for nothing, paid no royalties." Around the time that Black Uhuru's contract with Island expired, the label released two compilations. The first, in 1983, was part of the label's *Reggae Greats* series, while the following year's remix release, *The Dub Factor*, possessed an ominously apocalyptic digital sound perfectly captured by a black, gray, and white illustrated album cover, which further underscored the seriousness of Black Uhuru's Rastafari-centered sociopolitical messages.

Still, 1983's breakthrough album *Anthem*, their last studio album with Island, is both the apex and the axis of the group's history. The record won the first-ever Grammy Award for best reggae recording in 1985, showcasing both the vocal talents of the group as a whole and the rhythmic power of Sly & Robbie. Unlike so much of the reggae that later gained mainstream popularity in the United States, Black Uhuru's critical and creative (though sadly not commercial) breakthrough represented more than mere crossover compromise. Originally mixed by Jamaican engineer Steven Stanley and released in November 1983, *Anthem* was later remixed by Paul "Groucho" Smyrkle (also the engineer on *The Dub Factor*) with different versions for the British and American markets. The original release did not include "Solidarity," written by "Little Steven" Van Zandt, a member of Bruce Springsteen's E Street Band, though its popularity as a single after the album's first edition made it a necessary inclusion on later remixes. Ultimately, "Solidarity" became one of the band's best-known recordings.

This proliferation of multiple versions of the album left some fans unsure about which one they had heard. Adding to the confusion, at least three different album covers have been issued. The 2004 limited-edition compilation *The Complete Anthem Sessions* finally collected the various mixes, including a previously unreleased dub version. The deluxe edition capitalized on the group's most widely known record and demonstrated the post–Bob Marley sound of international reggae.

Rose's departure in 1985, after the end of the Island contract, revealed the turmoil brewing within the band and derailed the momentum its members had worked so hard to develop. Even though Sly & Robbie's participation didn't end with the termination of the Island deal (as demonstrated on 1986's *Brutal* LP and its solid dub counterpart *Brutal Dub*), the duo was no longer at Black Uhuru's production helm, and they only functioned on later releases as occasional

Released under the misprinted name Black Uhurie, "Plastic Smile" was produced and arranged by ace rhythm section Sly & Robbie, a key part of Black Uhuru's sound.

session musicians. The sound arguably became less focused and effective, despite Sly & Robbie's continued live performance with the band.

More lineup changes continued to affect the group's stability. Following Rose's departure, singer Junior Reid was introduced as his replacement at a Kingston press conference held on May 28, 1985. Reid debuted on lead vocals on the RAS Records release *Brutal* (nominated for a 1986 Grammy for best reggae recording) and continued on 1987's *Positive*—the first release that did not feature Puma Jones in the lineup since the year she had joined the band. Jones was diagnosed with breast cancer and was receiving medical treatment that forced her to leave the group. She was replaced on *Positive* by the Jamaican female singer Olafunke. Jones died in New York on January 28, 1990.

The group continued to shed vocalists as Reid left the group to resume his solo career following US visa problems and differences of direction, opening the door for the reformation of the original Black Uhuru with Simpson, Carlos, and Dennis.

This lineup resurfaced in 1990 on the Mesa Records label with *Now,* which became Black Uhuru's highest-charting album in the United States, peaking at #121. That same year they appeared with their touring band live in the studio on the then-progressive VH1 music television channel, performing their album-track cover of "Hey Joe," a song made famous by Jimi Hendrix. Reid was temporarily replaced by a vocalist called Rudo (also from the Waterhouse area of Kingston), who moved on to a solo career in the United States as the original lineup was about to record and perform again.

Between 1992 and 1994, other Mesa releases included *Iron Storm*, *Mystical Truth*, and *Strongg*, each of which had its dub duplicate, with *Strongg Dubb* arguably the strongest contender of the lot. During this phase the group integrated hip-hop elements into its sound and incorporated cover versions of non-reggae songs.

The original lineup splintered again in the late 1990s, and legal disputes arose over rights to the group name. Since Duckie Simpson was the only remaining original member, the rights to the Black Uhuru name resided with him, despite the sonic link between Rose's voice and the group brand. Eventually, in late 1998, a Duckie Simpson–led version of Black Uhuru emerged with *Unification*, clearly intended to revisit the group's most recognizable sound. With two new members, lead singer Andrew "Bees" Beckford and Jennifer "Nyah" Connally, the group opted for dancehall-flavored digital drum programming that had little in common with the more organic Sly & Robbie rhythm section of earlier years.

Since the mid-1980s the group has received less media attention and airplay in Jamaica than in Europe or the United States. Duckie Simpson attributes this to Black Uhuru's militant stance of not paying DJs for airplay and generally not playing the games of the promotional system. This, too, has meant staying away from the rhythms and lyrical "slackness" of dancehall, with its emphasis on sexual and/or violent themes, which for the most part has been the philosophical opposite of Uhuru's Rasta mission. According to Carlos, the group strongly preferred lyrics "that lick out against wrong and push consciousness on the people." In a 1990 interview, Duckie Simpson summed up the group's mission: "You see people have to realize say we are not entertainers. We are like soldiers, Jah soldiers." The group has not released any new material since 2001's *Dynasty* and appears to be dormant, if not officially dissolved.

MEMBERS: Don Carlos (vocals), "Folk Song" single, *Now* to *Strongg*; **Garth Dennis** (vocals), "Folk Song" single, *Now* to *Strongg*; **Puma Jones** (vocals), *Sinsemilla* to *Brutal*; **Errol Nelson** (vocals), *Love Crisis/Black Sounds of Freedom*; **Derrick "Duckie" Simpson** (vocals); **Junior Reid** (lead vocals), *Brutal* to *Positive*; **Michael Rose** (lead vocals), *Love Crisis/Black Sounds of Freedom* to *Anthem*; **Olafunke** (vocals), *Positive*; **Andrew "Bees" Beckford** (lead vocals), *Unification* to *Dynasty*; **Jennifer "Nyah" Connally** (vocals), *Unification*

Michael Rose of Black Uhuru onstage in 1982, a year before the release of *Anthem*, winner of the first-ever Grammy for best reggae recording.

SELECT DISCOGRAPHY: *Love Crisis/Black Sounds of Freedom* (Greensleeves, 1977); *Showcase* (Taxi/Heartbeat, 1979); *Sinsemilla* (Island, 1980); *Red* (Island, 1981); *Chill Out* (Island, 1982); *Tear It Up – Live* (Island, 1982); *The Dub Factor* (Island, 1983); *Anthem* (Island, 1983); *Brutal* (RAS, 1986); *Brutal Dub* (RAS, 1986); *Positive* (RAS, 1987); *Positive Dub* (RAS, 1987); *Live in New York* (Rohit, 1988); *Now* (Mesa, 1990); *Now Dub* (Mesa 1990); *Iron Storm* (Mesa, 1991); *Iron Storm Dub* (Mesa, 1992); *Mystical Truth,* (Mesa, 1993); *Mystical Truth Dub* (Mesa, 1993); *Liberation: The Island Anthology* (Island, 1993); *Unification* (Ryko, 1998); *Ultimate Collection* (Hip-O/Universal, 2000); *Dynasty* (Sanctuary, 2001); *The Complete Anthem Sessions* (Island, 2004); *Chicago 84* (Taxi, 2010)

ALPHA BLONDY

YEARS ACTIVE: 1983-PRESENT

Born Seydou Kone in the Ivory Coast on New Year's Day in 1953, Alpha Blondy insisted in a 1999 interview that his experience of popular music is more Westernized than most people would consider typical for an African: "So people ask why don't you sing like Salif Keita? I say, 'I wish I could!' But I grew up listening to Mick Jagger. . . . We come out of that new generation. That's how I got into reggae." Not surprisingly, his music embodies a Marleyesque fusion of rock and reggae. Blondy claims fluency in five languages, which is uncommon for a reggae artist and gives his work an authentic international character.

Blondy moved to New York to study English at Columbia University in 1976. During this phase of his life he worked as a part-time messenger (somewhat ironically, considering his later musical mission) and is thought to have visited Jamaica for the first time. He played some club gigs in New York, but a combination of academic, creative, and financial frustrations led Blondy to return to his homeland. His rejection of his country's social norms—underlined by his anti-Western adoption of dreadlocks—as well as conflicts with the local authorities led to a short spell in jail and admission to a psychiatric hospital.

Following Blondy's successful appearance on a television talent show in the Ivory Coast, his first album, 1983's *Jah Glory* (reportedly recorded in one day in his home country), sold well. After the formation of his backing band, Solar System, he signed a deal with EMI Records that resulted in 1984's *Cocody Rock*, recorded in Paris. In search of the authentic Rasta roots reggae sound, Blondy recorded his 1986 album, *Jerusalem*, in Jamaica with Bob Marley's backing band, the Wailers, at Kingston's Tuff Gong Studios. Even as he strove for a true Jamaican sound, however, Blondy has pointed out that Jamaican and African reggae differ in conceptual terms. Whereas Africa is portrayed mythically, as a kind of utopia, in Jamaican (or Jamaican-centered) reggae, African reggae artists like Blondy view their continent in less idealistic terms, focusing more directly on the continent's contemporary political and social realities.

Perhaps more so than with other reggae artists, Blondy's discography is complicated by numerous record labels and formats, as well as reissues of albums in territories where the originals never appeared in the first year of publication.

SELECT DISCOGRAPHY: *Jah Glory* (Celluloid, 1983); *Cocody Rock* (EMI, 1984); *Jerusalem* (Tuff Gong, 1986); *Apartheid Is Nazism* (EMI, 1987); *Masada* (EMI, 1992); *Akwaba: The Very Best of Alpha Blondy* (EMI, 2005); *Vision* (Zoom, 2011)

Alpha Blondy ignites the crowd at the Youth Festival in Algiers, 1985.

BLOOD & FIRE

YEARS ACTIVE: 1994-2007

Few reggae reissue labels have had the sweeping impact of Blood & Fire, based in Manchester, England. Founded by reggae biographer and former Trojan Records employee Steve Barrow; Mick Hucknall, a member of the pop band Simply Red; and three others, the label's journey began in 1994 with *If Deejay Was Your Trade*, a compilation of mid-1970s recordings of talk-over "toasters" that prefigured the starring role of the DJ in rap and dancehall. Hucknall's interest in reggae—perhaps surprising, given Simply Red's R&B-pop repertoire—and financial resources encouraged him to "put down a six-digit figure from his own pocket over the first five years of Blood and Fire," according to Barrow. The label's proclaimed philosophy was to raise reggae reissue standards to levels comparable with jazz and other genres while ensuring that the often neglected artists and producers received due compensation.

With this noble intent, Blood & Fire embarked on a reggae archaeological expedition, uncovering out-of-print roots-era classics and issuing previously unreleased dubplates and alternate versions of songs. Barrow acted as the label's A&R (Artists and Repertoire) man, while cofounder Bob Harding was the managing director. Combining an obvious passion for the music with attentive sound mastering, extensive liner notes, and distinctive, high-quality graphics, the label earned the respect—and the money—of reggae connoisseurs across the globe.

In 2007, one decade and more than forty-eight releases (excluding samplers) later, Blood & Fire closed its doors and ended trading after going bankrupt. Their best-selling releases are estimated to have sold between ten and twenty thousand copies each, but whatever the number of units shipped, the income was clearly insufficient to sustain the operation. The label's prospects may well have been dented by the timing of its establishment, coinciding with the early waves of rampant illegal music downloading. Initially it appeared that the company might emerge from bankruptcy and perhaps resume business in a different form, but nothing tangible materialized. The Blood & Fire website still exists, but only as an ironic historical artifact of a label that itself became defunct after having rescued so many works from obscurity. Meanwhile, today the Britain–based Pressure Sounds label is one of the few companies filling the void with precious reissues.

SELECT DISCOGRAPHY: *Pick a Dub* – Keith Hudson (1994); *In the Light/ In the Light Dub* – Horace Andy (1995); *Termination Dub* – Glen Brown & King Tubby (1996); *Heart of the Congos* – The Congos (1996); *Heavyweight Dub/Killer Dub* – Inner Circle & the Fatman Riddim Section (1999); *Ride On Dreadlocks 1975-77* – Linval Thompson (2000); *In the Dub Zone* – Ja-Man All Stars (2003)

BELOW: From 1994 to 2007, the good folks at England's Blood & Fire label played reggae archeologists, unearthing lost gems by such artists as Junior Byles, I-Roy, Horace Andy, and King Tubby.

REGGAE FESTIVALS

REGGAE SUNSPLASH

Launched in 1978, Reggae Sunsplash was the genre's first festival. As key acts participated in the Jamaican event and often recorded their live performances, it quickly earned a solid reputation. The enterprise eventually expanded into other regions, notably staging successful Sunsplash tours in Japan from 1985 to 1997. According to the Jamaican press, Reggae Japansplash, the banner for the Asian tours, hosted as many as eighty reggae artists on a tour of ten cities during the festival's last run in 1997.

The festival's beginnings were quite tentative: four individuals (Tony Johnson, Don Green, Ronnie Burke and John Wakeling) formed Synergy Productions based on the idea of creating a large-scale reggae concert that would attract international audiences. Lacking capital and enthusiasm from the Jamaica Tourist Board, the project could easily have fallen apart in its early stages. Instead, support from local audiences helped to get the event off the ground, and in late June 1978, Jimmy Cliff, Third World, Dennis Brown, Byron Lee & the Dragonaires, and the Heptones were among those to perform at the inaugural event, held at Jarrett Park in Montego Bay. A few years later, even after attendance had reportedly increased from four thousand to more than fifteen thousand, Reggae Sunsplash remained unprofitable. To accommodate its growing audiences, the organization intermittently shifted venues between Jarrett Park and the government-erected Bob Marley Entertainment Centre,

opened in 1983. Ongoing friction with government, additional venue changes, and limited sponsorship combined to undermine Reggae Sunsplash, resulting in dwindling finances, low attendance, and its eventual termination. Varying dates are given for the final Sunsplash Festival, though most concur that by the late 1990s the event had ended. Jamaican newspaper reports state that an unsuccessful attempt to revive Reggae Sunsplash took place in 2006. More than just a means of boosting Jamaican tourism with an internationally known cultural product, the festival was once a major vehicle for artists to gain exposure, and it resulted in many earning record contracts. The Sunsplash name still carries significant brand recognition, as is evident by the number of global reggae festivals that have incorporated "Sunsplash" into the title.

ABOVE: Good vibes abound at the weeklong Rototom Sunsplash festival in Benicasim, Spain, 2010.
RIGHT: Fans bask in the riddims as Reggae Sunsplash hits London's Crystal Palace, 1985.

REGGAE SUMFEST

Begun in 1993, this annual weeklong event held in Montego Bay drew an estimated thirty-eight thousand fans in 2009, and its success has been linked to the termination of rival Reggae Sunsplash. However, Sumfest's popularity has not come without controversy. After seven years of title sponsorship, the Red Stripe beer company withdrew its support in 2008 (though it returned in 2011) amid concerns regarding violent lyrics in dancehall songs. All artists were soon barred from using profanity during their performances.

Artists criticized for lyrics promoting gun violence include Vybz Kartel (arrested on murder charges in 2011), Mavado, and Bounty Killer. Red Stripe's decision was also influenced by complaints made by gay-rights organizations against dancehall performers such as Capleton and Beenie Man, who have both been accused of homophobia. Although more "cultural" reggae acts have been part of the festival lineups, their presence has not been strong enough to offset negative perceptions. In 2011, organizers were subject to local criticism for not having a Jamaican headlining act, since the bill was topped by American performers R. Kelly and Nicki Minaj. Some artists felt that Sumfest had become too reliant on such American hip-hop and R&B acts, placing them in the foreground even though none play reggae. Despite such issues, and unlike the now-defunct Reggae Sunsplash, Sumfest has been able to increase its corporate sponsorship. The festival remains a major event for reggae artists new and old, generating revenue of about US $2 to $3 million each year for the local economy.

STING

Billing itself as "the greatest one-night reggae show on earth," Sting celebrated its twenty-fifth anniversary in 2008. The show, which takes place on December 26 each year in the parish of St. Catherine, Jamaica, features dancehall DJs and therefore appeals to a less varied demographic than most other reggae festivals. While attracting large crowds, the event has sometimes been marred by bottle-throwing fans. Nonetheless, it remains a crucial venue for DJs seeking to either emerge from obscurity or consolidate their existing fan bases. During its history, Sting has staged clashes (onstage competition for crowd favor) among major dancehall acts including Mavado, Vybz Kartel, Ninja Man, Shabba Ranks, and Beenie Man.

ROTOTOM SUNSPLASH

The first Rototom Sunsplash festival took place in Italy in 1994. It moved to Benicàssim, Spain, in 2010, after Italian authorities accused the festival of promoting ganja use and effectively forced its relocation. Attracting more than one hundred thousand people each year to its annual weeklong gathering, Rototom aims for more than mere entertainment. In an attempt to educate fans, the festival conducts "Reggae University" panels that feature artists, producers, and other individuals behind the making of reggae music. Intellectuals also participate and analyze the industry and its performers. Rototom has also established a presence in Jamaica, where it holds press launches and brings contingents of journalists to experience the environment from which the music has come. The emergence of Rototom as arguably the largest international reggae festival has led some to question why Jamaica does not hold a comparable spectacle. The festival's 2011 lineup included established acts such as Inner Circle, Linton Kwesi Johnson, Jimmy Cliff, and Stephen Marley.

Big Youth checks the Sunsplash microphones, 1979.

REGGAE ON THE RIVER

One of the few reggae festivals with nearly three decades of history, Reggae on the River began in 1984 in Humboldt County, California. It was started by the Mateel Community Center, whose buildings had been severely damaged—and in some cases destroyed—by an arsonist a year earlier. Conceived as a fundraiser for the center's rebuilding efforts, the concert grew gradually in subsequent years, building a solid reputation and attracting top acts including Jimmy Cliff, Third World, Toots & the Maytals, and Culture. The event ran into trouble in 2006, when financial problems and conflict between the community center and the production company threatened its future. Both sides filed lawsuits, and following a legal conflict with the breakaway organizers of Reggae Rising, a rival event held in the same area between 2007 and 2009, Reggae on the River returned in 2011 and held its twenty-seventh concert.

OTHER INTERNATIONAL VENUES

Reggae festivals of various sizes and significance take place all over the world, and France has become a particularly lucrative market. That country is home to both the Reggae Sun Ska Festival, which held the fourteenth edition of its three-day event in 2011, and the roots-oriented Garance Reggae Festival, which has been drawing large summer crowds since 1989, with only two years' absence. Though it began in indoor venues, Garance is now a four-day outdoor event whose attendance tops thirty-five thousand. Other regular events include Sweden's Uppsala Reggae Festival, the Yokohama Reggae Festival in Japan, and the Montreal International Reggae Festival in Canada.

OPPOSITE: Coconut vendors benefited from a munchies pandemic at Reggae Sunsplash in Montego Bay, Jamaica, 1979.

ABOVE: Julian Marley does his late dad proud at Jamaica's inaugural Reggae Sumfest, 1993.

Come fly with me
FLY FLYING SKA

PRINCE BUSTER

SKATELITES, GAYNOR & ERROL.

OWEN GRAY, THE MAYTALS, DON DRUMMOND

MILLIE SMALL & ROY PANTON, ROLAND ALPHONSO

BLUE BEAT BBEP 302

MILLIE
AND
BLUE
BEAT

ABOVE LEFT AND RIGHT: In the early 1960s, Blue Beat cornered the market for ska in Britain, where the label's name became synonymous with the music.

LEFT: The star of the Blue Beat label, Prince Buster, reached the British top twenty with his 1967 smash "Al Capone."

BLUE BEAT RECORDS
YEARS ACTIVE: 1960-1967

In the early 1960s, when the export of Jamaican popular music became relatively consistent, the Blue Beat record label became so closely associated with ska in Britain that its name was often used there to describe the music. Its parent company was Emil Shalit's independent Melodisc Records, founded in the late 1940s in London (sources differ regarding the precise year). Melodisc released calypso and mento recordings, among other styles of black music, in the 1950s, a time when few British companies issued such material.

Blue Beat operated from 1960 to 1967 as Shalit aggressively pursued the licensing of records for British release from such early Jamaican producers as Coxsone Dodd, Ken Khouri, and Edward Seaga. Unlike other record company executives of the era, Shalit traveled to Jamaica, making the licensing deals in person and developing a good business reputation there. This was an exceedingly rare asset in an era of some of the most ruthless artist exploitation the industry has ever witnessed. By all accounts Shalit was a pure businessman with no special affinity for music; for him, it was just another commodity to be traded. Assisting Shalit with a deeper knowledge of the "Jamaican blues" was Siggy Jackson, who cofounded Blue Beat and was apparently responsible for conceiving the name.

While historical accounts of the development of Blue Beat's British market usually point to the arrival of Jamaican immigrants, it is often forgotten that non-Jamaican West Indians were also a substantial part of the audience. Laurel Aitken's "Boogie Rock" launched the label, followed by nearly thirty additional releases in its debut year. As part of Blue Beat's evolution, the design of the physical label on the singles went from blue print on a white background in 1960 to the more familiar and iconic silver-gray print on a blue background with a different logo starting in 1961. By aggregating hot releases that would otherwise have proved difficult to find, Blue Beat offered the best of Jamaica, at least until other independents like Chris Blackwell's Island Records and Sonny Roberts's Planetone Records began to make definitive market inroads.

Jamaican singing star and producer Prince Buster became Blue Beat's star artist around 1964, having done business with the label previously and reaped some success with the Folkes Brothers' "Oh Carolina" (1960). Buster's "Al Capone" single broke into the British top twenty in 1967, providing the label with one of its rare pop crossover hits. Buster had signed an exclusive recording deal with Blue Beat, following the ongoing malpractice of Jamaican labels leasing the same recordings to different British labels simultaneously, attempting to obscure the artist's

BLUE BEAT

All rights of the manufacturer and of the owner of the recorded work reserved   Unauthorised public performance, broadcasting

Copyright Control

Recording published
45/BB 3
(45/BB 375

SKA WAR
(Maytals)
THE MAYTALS

MELODISC RECORDS LTD.

identities with pseudonyms. In the mid-1960s, singer Derrick Morgan also signed an exclusive deal with Blue Beat but later rebelled, claiming undue restraint of trade. He overturned the contract with the assistance of former producer Edward Seaga, who had since become Jamaica's minister of development and welfare, a position he held from 1962 through 1967.

The Blue Beat imprint continued long enough to be part of the transition from ska to the slower-paced rocksteady, releasing one of the latter subgenre's earliest records, "Take It Easy," by Hopeton Lewis, in 1966. The following year, Blue Beat founders Shalit and Jackson parted company on unfriendly terms, and the label was shelved in favor of Melodisc's pop imprint, Fab. Given Blue Beat's overwhelming emphasis on singles (the label had only released nine LPs), it is interesting that the imprint was terminated just as the album format was beginning to dominate sales in the industry. Jackson left to help start Columbia Blue Beat, a British label run by EMI Records, which lasted until around 1970. Probably motivated by the desire to ensure control over his catalog, Buster eventually assumed majority ownership of Melodisc as Shalit receded from the frontline of the record business. When John Folkes of the Folkes Brothers won a 1994 lawsuit over the authorship of "Oh Carolina," Buster—who claimed he wrote the song—lost a valuable slice of music publishing revenue when a new version of the song by the dancehall DJ Shaggy became a hit across Europe. The Blue Beat imprint occasionally resurfaced in the late 1960s and early 1970s, primarily for reissues of its classic hits. Shalit died in 1982.

BOB & MARCIA

YEARS ACTIVE: 1968–1974

In commercial terms, Bob & Marcia were the biggest duo of the early reggae years, with their version of American singer Nina Simone's "Young, Gifted and Black" reaching #5 on the British pop charts in 1970. The duo formed when Bob Andy teamed up with longtime associate Marcia Griffiths after his protracted departure from the Paragons vocal group, who scored mid-1960s Jamaican hits such as "On the Beach" and "The Tide Is High." The hit song "Young, Gifted and Black" was initially an afterthought, as Andy added his vocal overdub to a preexisting backing track that Griffiths had cut with producer Harry Johnson (known as Harry J) at Dynamic Sounds, in Kingston—but it turned out to be a very fortuitous one.

Given the song's theme of black pride, it was perhaps unexpected that "Young, Gifted and Black" found an enthusiastic white audience in Britain, including among some skinheads. Since the song's message was not aimed at a white audience, its skinhead popularity was probably due to its immersive reggae rhythms. To cash in on the success of the single—which landed the duo on the all-important *Top of the Pops* television chart show—Bob & Marcia recorded a full-length *Young, Gifted and Black* album in London, licensed for British release in 1970 through Trojan by producer Harry

Johnson. That LP, however, appears to have had little impact outside of the reggae community. "Young, Gifted and Black" typified Trojan Records' commercial approach of adding heavy string arrangements to enhance a song's chances of earning airplay on pop radio. As such, the finished production would have sounded largely alien to the black audience, while white fans had yet to be fully convinced that reggae was music suitable for the album format.

The follow-up single, "Pied Piper," another cover version, reached #11 on the UK charts in 1971. The song had been a minor hit in America in 1965 for The Changin' Times; and in 1966 another version by singer Crispian St. Peters reached the top five in both Britain and America. But Andy became disillusioned by Trojan's apparent emphasis on individual records rather than on artist development. Bob & Marcia left Trojan for CBS Records in 1972, despite the fact that the former label had made them one of the top-selling reggae acts. By 1974, the duo had split to pursue solo careers.

MEMBERS: Bob Andy (vocals); Marcia Griffiths (vocals)

SELECT DISCOGRAPHY: *Young, Gifted and Black* (Trojan, 1970); *Pied Piper: The Best of Bob & Marcia* (Sanctuary, 2002)

KEN BOOTHE
YEARS ACTIVE: 1963–2000s

The soulful sound of Ken Boothe's distinctive voice brought him only sporadic success, yet he is one of Jamaica's most enduring singers. The youngest of twelve children, Boothe was born March 22, 1948, in Kingston. As a teenager, he served an apprenticeship writing and singing with artist and songwriter Stranger Cole, whom he credits with introducing him into the world of commercial recording. Boothe and Cole made their first recordings at Duke Reid's Treasure Isle studio in Kingston. After little success, they caught the attention of Coxsone Dodd, head of Studio One, and in late 1963 they moved to Dodd's studio. There, backed by the legendary ska group the Skatalites, they recorded "World's Fair." The single emulated the style of the popular Blues Busters, who were also Boothe's friends. This was the beginning of a string of ska successes that included "Artibella." Boothe credits Dodd with providing a studio apprenticeship and allowing him time to build confidence for a solo singing career. He was at first intimidated by the prospect of solo singing at a time when artists such as Jackie Opel, Owen Gray, Jackie Edwards, and Derrick Harriott were excelling at the art form. Dodd felt Boothe had similar soul-singer-style credentials and pushed him primarily in that direction, cutting ska tracks while maximizing the influence of American singers Wilson Pickett and Otis Redding.

In those days of two-track recording, and as the slower pace of rocksteady took hold of the Jamaican music market, many of Boothe's recordings for Dodd, such as "The Train," included backing vocals by the Wailers. Boothe first toured England in 1967 as part of a Studio One package that included fellow vocalist Alton Ellis, another premier talent during this phase in Jamaica's musical development. By the following year, Boothe's debut album *Mr. Rock Steady*, released by Studio One, set a career trend by featuring cover versions of songs.

Boothe's biggest breakthroughs arrived, however, after he departed Dodd's stable. *Freedom Street*, recorded with a variety of Jamaican producers in 1970, was a major reggae-market success on Beverley's Records, owned by Leslie Kong, who also produced the releases. Boothe signed with Britain's Trojan Records in 1971, cutting the socially conscious "Is It Because I'm Black," included on 1973's *Black, Gold & Green* album. At the other end of the musical spectrum, his cover of "Everything I Own," a 1972

FAR LEFT: Ken Boothe, one of reggae's most enduring singers, performs on the BBC television show *Top of the Pops*, 1974.

OPPOSITE: As the title of his 1968 debut album suggests, Ken Boothe survived the death of ska and remained successful during the rocksteady era.

TROJAN RECORDS

TR.792

EVERYTHING I OWN
(David Gates)
KEN BOOTHE
Producer Lloyd Charmers

TAXI

KEN BOOTHE

IPR 2067
IPR 2067-A

SHOW & TELL
(J. Fuller) 8.21

SIDE 1

45 RPM
STEREO

Produced by Sly Dunbar &
Robbie Shakespeare for
Taxi Productions

Pedro Music Ltd (Carlin)

℗ 1983 Original sound recording
by Taxi Productions

hit for the American rock band Bread, remarkably topped the British charts in 1974. (In comparison, Bread's original version reached only #32 in Britain but peaked at #5 in America.) By one estimate, "Everything I Own" had been a sound-system hit for as long as a year before it was released. Trojan Records reportedly paid £7,000 to producer Lloyd Charmers to release the song, and it was ultimately one of the label's biggest hits.

Although sustaining his breakthrough seemed likely, Boothe's timing was not ideal: Trojan's looming bankruptcy (even as they were pressing copies of "Everything I Own") became a harsh reality; Boothe blamed bad management for his inability to capitalize on the success of "Everything I Own"; and his rapidly declining fortunes eventually led to a cocaine habit. His career nosedived. He scored just one more British chart hit, "Crying Over You," which debuted in December

1974 and eventually peaked at #11. In the wake of Trojan's dissolution, Boothe became another wandering reggae singer, seeking out small-scale club gigs in Europe and North America. Without the benefit of a rehab clinic, he cured himself of his drug addiction around the time of his return to Jamaica in the 1980s.

He was later taken under the management wing of Specs-Shang, a Jamaican management and production company that brokered major-label record deals in the 1990s for dancehall stars Shabba Ranks and Patra. While occasional Jamaican hits, such as the much-celebrated "Don't You Know," emerged in the years that followed, Boothe's career never quite regained its earlier momentum.

SELECT DISCOGRAPHY: *Mr. Rock Steady* (Studio One, 1968); *Black, Gold & Green* (Trojan, 1973); *Let's Get It On* (Trojan, 1974); *Everything I Own: The Definitive Collection* (Sanctuary, 2007)

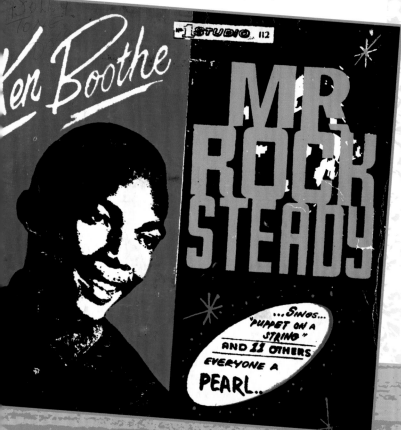

DENNIS BOVELL

YEARS ACTIVE: 1971-2000s

Few reggae producers based in the United Kingdom have been as influential as Dennis Bovell, one of the key figures in the development of the British reggae scene. Though he has had more impact as a producer than as an artist, Bovell co-founded the group Matumbi, released solo albums, and has collaborated for many years with the renowned dub poet Linton Kwesi Johnson.

Known earlier in his career as Blackbeard, Bovell was born in Barbados in 1953. He moved to England at age twelve, and in 1971 he cofounded Matumbi—a self-contained seven-piece outfit in which he played guitar—in South London. Their existence as a self-contained band was in sharp contrast to most of the Jamaican artists except the Wailers, whose *Catch a Fire* album (late 1972 in Britain, early 1973 in America) was a big influence. Matumbi was one of the few pre–*Catch a Fire* British reggae bands already headed in that same band-oriented direction. This was also a time when nascent British reggae bands received little support from UK sound systems, which were instead focused on Jamaican records. Matumbi had a rough baptism, choosing to play at clubs ruled by sound systems and to audiences interested in hearing a live DJ rather than a live band. Having resisted superimposing strings—a hallmark of many of the early reggae crossover records released by Trojan Records— Matumbi must have found it bitterly ironic that Trojan released their satirical version of pop band Hot Chocolate's "Brother Louie" as a single in 1973. Matumbi viewed the song, which

Influential UK-based producer and musician Dennis Bovell onstage with his band Matumbi, 1978.

had been recorded in leftover studio time, as a comical afterthought never intended for public exposure.

Instead of deserting the core reggae audience in Britain in favor of mainstream radio, Matumbi found ways to service both sectors with the same material. One strategy was to distinguish themselves from most Jamaican reggae acts by cleverly applying mainstream pop structures to their songs without diluting the reggae content, though the lovers rock style that they often adopted was innately commercial. Matumbi also provided exclusive "dubplates" (pre-release test mixes) to British sound systems, sometimes giving them enormous lead time ahead of the record's actual release. Bovell recalls that sometimes no information would be printed on their independently released singles to counter the prejudice against reggae not recorded in Jamaica. In one such example of a "white label," Matumbi's "After Tonight" was heard as an exclusive dubplate on the popular British sound system of Lloyd Coxson more than a year before it was actually released, and it become a huge hit with the British reggae audience. The track was issued in 1976 on the independent Safari label (marketed by EMI), while

Bovell's future as an independent producer was foreshadowed by his work on the second single by fellow black British reggae band Steel Pulse. Their collaboration with Bovell on the song "Nyah Love" led to an underground hit in 1977, and his production career took a major step forward in 1979 with the "Silly Games" single by Janet Kay, which reached #2 on the British pop charts (and charted again when reissued in 1990). Realizing that women constituted the majority of singles buyers in the black record shops—despite the fact reggae is a male-centered genre—Bovell set about targeting this

Bovell was still very much in touch with his "dread roots" side during this time, and he maintained his sound-system credibility and enhanced his production reputation by issuing dub albums. Two of these, *Blackbeard: Strictly Dub Wize* (1978) and *I Wah Dub* (1980), were underrated. By the late 1970s Bovell was also working with Linton Kwesi Johnson, a renowned dub poet. Their paths crossed when Johnson was working as a journalist and was assigned to interview Bovell—a meeting that turned into a long-term creative partnership. Their eventual album collaborations delivered arguably the most scathing, incisive indictments of British society, politics, and imperialist history in UK reggae, as evidenced in Johnson's coproduced 1979 set *Forces of*

included the 1979 debut album by the idiosyncratic female punk outfit the Slits.

Bovell's primary solo statement might very well be 1981's *Brain Damage*, a double album whose title track encompassed multiple dimensions of his soundscape: deep roots flavor with dub features and some DJ chatter thrown in alongside the catchy title refrain. Sadly, the album, recorded in full at Bovell's Studio 80 in London, was not released in the United States at the time. Also in 1981, Bovell was hired by Epic Records to produce reggae tracks for inclusion on a separate EP bundled with the *Escape Artist* album by American singer-songwriter Garland Jeffreys. Bovell's group the Dub Band, a collective of up to fifteen musicians, provided excellent backing, and one of the songs, "Miami Beach," featured Johnson's dub-poetry narration in conjunction with Jeffreys's vocals. The single's B-side, "Escape Goat Dub" (not released on the album until its reissue in 2007), is a virtual snapshot of the early-1980s moment in British reggae. Oddly, these superb productions are scarcely, if ever, mentioned in summaries of Bovell's work. He also recorded several singles with his Dub Band, including the creditable dub version of the pop-dance–accessible "Reggae High," released by EMI in 1983.

Beyond this early-1980s career apex, the Dub Band—with Bovell at the helm—has backed Johnson on global tours, and Bovell has continued to capitalize on his catalog of work and his eclectic musical palate. Additional solo albums were released on the LKJ Records imprint, though you'd have to be paying close attention to be aware of their presence in the market.

Trojan, which had arguably slowed the group's development, claimed they were still under contract. This situation was resolved only when Matumbi continued recording under a variety of names, forcing Trojan to eventually relent. (They later released "After Tonight" on their own label.) Following lineup changes, the band signed with EMI Records and scored a 1979 crossover hit single with "Point of View," from the acclaimed *Seven Seals* album. The band split up in the early 1980s, however, leaving little time to capitalize on their hard-earned success.

demographic with reggae-style love songs by female artists, thereby launching the lovers rock trend and creating a brand identity record label with that name. While lovers rock became a trend in Britain, it didn't fully cross over to a 1970s Jamaican market mired in escalating political violence and perhaps more interested in music that reflected the national states of urgency and emergency.

Victory. (In particular, the first two 1980s volumes of *LKJ In Dub* shed greater light on Bovell's construction of the music.)

Never content to stand still for long, Bovell also scored the 1980 film *Babylon*, which also reinforced his sonic imprint on British reggae, the movie's subject matter. His productions went beyond the traditional roots reggae realm and

SELECT DISCOGRAPHY: As **Blackbeard:** *Strictly Dub Wize* (Tempus, 1978); *I Wah Dub* (More Cut/EMI, 1980); As **Dennis Bovell:** *Brain Damage* (Fontana, 1981); *Decibel: More Cuts from Dennis Bovell 1976–1983* (Pressure Sounds, 2003); *Dub of Ages* (LKJ, 2007); As **Matumbi:** *Seven Seals* (EMI Harvest, 1978); *Point of View* (EMI, 1979); *Dub Planet* (Extinguish, 1980)

Vol. 1 No. 4

REGGAE *QUARTERLY*

$1.9

Dennis Brown:
*the Prophet
Rides Again!*
Leroy Sibbles
Josie Wales

Little John
Echo Minott
Toyan
cha

Prince Far-I — The Final
Encounter

Jackie
Edwards

DENNIS BROWN
SUPERSTAR

DENNIS BROWN

YEARS ACTIVE: 1969-1999

One of reggae's most distinctive and admired vocalists, Dennis Brown was a child prodigy whose father had been a dramatist and his brother a comedian, thereby preparing the singer for the limelight. Born in Kingston, Jamaica, in 1957, Brown's recording career began at about age twelve with "No Man Is an Island" (1969), tracked for producer Coxsone Dodd at Kingston's Studio One. Before long, he found himself split between attending school and playing local shows, and while his parents wanted him to pursue a more typically respectable path, he was convinced that music was his calling. Over time, Brown made sure that the love songs he sang were balanced with conscious lyrics promoting Rasta-infused black liberation and spiritual awareness.

When Brown began working with producer Joe Gibbs around 1972, he scored an instant hit with "Money in My Pocket," a song that he later rerecorded and that became one of his career calling cards. A newer version reached #14 on the British pop charts in 1979, pointing to a natural crossover potential that was never fully realized despite Brown's consistent string of Jamaican hits during a period of prolific—perhaps overly prolific—output. Considering the British origins of lovers rock, Brown surprisingly became one of the main proponents of that subgenre. By 1978 he had performed at the historic One Love Peace Concert in Jamaica headlined by Bob Marley, and established his very short-lived label, DEB.

Dennis Brown performs in Amsterdam at the Reggae Sunsplash Festival in 1986, midway through a prolific career that began in 1969 and ended with his death in 1999. Remembered for his soulfulness and versatility, he was awarded Jamaica's Order of Distinction in 2011.

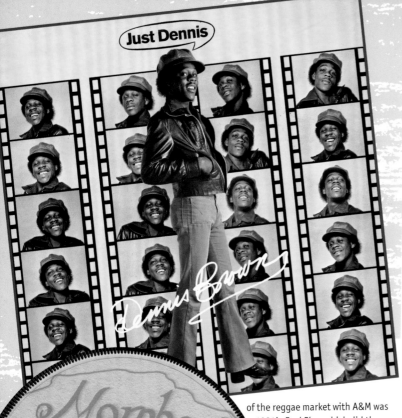

Just Dennis

Dennis Brown

Morpheus

45 RPM
Mor. 1001 A
P 1976
Dist. by
Morpheus Records

D.E.B. MUSIC

LIFE'S WORTH LIVING
(D. Brown)
Dennis Brown
Prod. by C. Brown & D. Brown

"Judge Not" and a rerecorded version of "To the Foundation," with singer Cocoa Tea, are excellent examples of both Clarke's finesse and Brown's vocal consistency. Brown allegedly began using cocaine in the 1980s, but any impact was not immediately apparent on his recordings. This phase of his career also inevitably included collaborations with DJs and other vocalists, such as Tiger. In the mid-1990s, as his seemingly endless recorded output continued, he recorded the *Three Against War* album with dancehall DJs Beenie Man and Triston Palmer.

In 1999, the longtime asthmatic and father of thirteen children was admitted to a hospital in his native Kingston, as a result of complications brought on by acute cocaine consumption. When Brown died later that year at the age of forty-two, reggae lost one of its most accomplished and soulful singers. A truly comprehensive retrospective collection of his work is yet to emerge,

no doubt complicated by the vast number of producers he worked with (notably including Derrick Harriott, Niney the Observer, and Sly & Robbie) and labels he recorded for. Factoring in actual releases and various compilations, his output is estimated to number hundreds of records. For his contribution to Jamaica's music industry, Dennis Brown was posthumously awarded the island's Order of Distinction in October 2011.

SELECT DISCOGRAPHY:

No Man Is an Island (Studio One, 1970); *Super Reggae & Soul Hits* (Trojan, 1972); *Visions* (Joe Gibbs, 1977); *Wolves and Leopards* (Blue Moon, 1978); *Joseph's Coat of Many Colours* (Laser, 1979); *Foul Play* (A&M Records, 1981); *The Prophet Rides Again* (A&M, 1982); *Three Against War* (VP, 1995); *Crown Prince of Reggae: Singles 1972–1985* (VP, 2010)

Although he was a longtime asthmatic, Dennis Brown puffed a pipe for the cover of this 1982 album—one of hundreds of records he's thought to have released over the years.

of the reggae market with A&M was 1981's *Foul Play*, which did the artist's talent little justice by reaching only #208, the very outskirts of the Billboard Top 200 album chart. The next year, the saccharine single "Love Has Found Its Way," from the album *The Prophet Rides Again*, became a minor British hit and reached the R&B singles chart in the United States. Brown then split with Gibbs, largely basing himself in London to capitalize on his popularity among lovers rock fans and to control his own creative destiny.

Brown wasn't an obvious fit in the digital dancehall environment that dominated reggae in the 1980s, but he eventually found his place in the latter half of the decade with the Music Works studio in Kingston, run by Gussie Clarke. Clarke brought to the table a polished production style that bridged the gap between high-tech sound and dub-inflected roots reggae.

By 1981, as major labels continued molding reggae to fit the mainstream, Gibbs had sealed a deal for Brown with A&M Records. Perhaps as a result of this crossover direction, the tracks selected for Brown's A&M releases lacked the roots-inspired urgency of his earlier work. In terms of chart success, the highest-ranking album he placed outside

STAGE COACH SHOWCASE DENNIS BROWN

THE USE OF GANJA ON THIS PREMISE, IS Strictly PROHIBITED By Order

...NGLES

PANTOMINE RECORDS
MUSIC AGAIN
G.L.B. Music

DIST BY:
52 AVENUE RD.
FOREST GATE
LONDON E.7
0181-555-1344
PROD & ARR
& PUB BY
GLEN BROWN
PUB: 1979

A SIDE
45 RPM
REDPR
20+936

YOUTH MAN
(G. BROWN MUSIC)
WAYNE JARRETT

ALL RIGHTS OF THE MANUFACTURER AND OF THE OWNER OF THE RECORDED WORK RESERVED UNAUTHORISED PUBLIC PERFORMANCE BROADCASTING AND COPYING IS PROHIBITED

GLEN BROWN AND KING TUBBY
Termination Dub (1973-79)

GLEN BROWN
YEARS ACTIVE: 1960s–1980s

A vocalist who became a producer, Glen Brown emerged from marginal roles in the 1960s to become a mainstay on Jamaican records in the following decade. He was behind the mostly instrumental melodica-centered 1972 hit "Merry Up," which, oddly enough, halts completely for a brief spoken-word interjection. Brown claims that the master tape with that vocal was stolen before a session at Dynamic Sounds in Kingston, requiring him to revamp it as primarily an instrumental piece.

His material was remixed regularly in dub form by the master engineer King Tubby, whose talents Brown utilized consistently. The high quality of the pairing shone through on Tubby's excellent and otherworldly remix of the 1970s track "Away with the Bad," which also demonstrated Brown's ability to create robust drum-and-bass centered rhythm tracks. He was one of the first artists to credit Tubby's work in print on his records. Brown also spurred the career of high-profile DJs such as Big Youth and U-Roy, and star vocalists like Johnny Clarke.

Brown is one of many 1970s Jamaican musicians whose presence diminished significantly by the 1980s despite his continuing production work. His scarce early recordings later became available on anthology CD collections, exposing newer reggae audiences to his work, though many of those same compilations are ironically now out of print. Brown's key contribution was helping to shape the roots sound on which countless vocal performances and dubs were built.

SELECT DISCOGRAPHY: *Termination Dub* (Blood & Fire, 1996)

TOP LEFT: Glen Brown shows his deep respect for Kingston's marijuana laws, 1979.

TOP RIGHT: Brown produced "Youth Man," a record for Wayne Jarrett. Initially a vocalist, Brown made his name as a producer.

ABOVE: Brown worked extensively with King Tubby and was one of the first artists to credit the pioneering dub engineer in print on his records.

"Well I would just like people to remember Spear as Spear. A man who would stand up for what he believes in, musically and otherwise." —BURNING SPEAR

BURNING SPEAR

YEARS ACTIVE: 1969–PRESENT

"I and, son the most high, Jah Rastafari / Our hearts shall correspond and beat in one harmony / Sounds from the Burning Spear." These words, spoken at the start of Burning Spear's debut single, "Door Peep," introduced the artist to the music world with a bold declaration of faith in Rastafari. The song's jazz-flavored reggae clearly drew on the prominence of horns in so much of the Jamaican music that preceded it, but because the single was released in 1969, fairly early in the days of reggae, its particular style was perhaps unexpected. Spear himself was aware of this: "I think 'Door Peep' create a newness musically in Studio One," he said, referencing the legendary Jamaican studio where he made his first recordings. "At that time, when I went there and do my thing, the music wasn't in that flavor or arrangement."

By his own account, Spear was born Winston Rodney on March 1st, 1945 in St. Ann's Bay, the same area of Jamaica that produced Bob Marley and black liberation icon Marcus Garvey. It is believed that Rodney's adopted stage identity echoed the name of Kenyan rebel leader and later president, Jomo Kenyatta, whose Mau Mau guerrillas loosened Britain's colonial grip on the country in the 1940s and 1950s. Spear's father was a farmer and his mother catered food for construction workers in St. Ann's Bay. A natural singer, Spear first came into contact with Garvey's teachings while working in his local community as a mechanic and clothes cleaner, among other jobs. Legend indicates that a 1969 meeting with Marley made Spear aware that producer Coxsone Dodd's legendary Studio One operation was a place where he might have a chance to make his first recordings. This led to the release of "Door Peep," a song that, in Jamaica, chastised the social establishment and laid the foundation for Spear's Rastafari-centered cultural focus, which emphasized the indignities historically suffered by black people and the icons that promoted black pride and nobility. Depending on whose account you read, the song either became a solid hit or simply disappeared without a trace.

Spear's early albums included *Studio One Presents Burning Spear* (1973) and *Rocking Time* (1974). The best of this early material was reissued on the American-based Heartbeat Records label in 2005 as *Creation Rebel: The Original Classic Recordings* from Studio One. In the typical exploitative fashion of the music industry, Dodd is listed as song co-writer on the album, an indication that money issues provided one of the motivations for Spear's departure from Studio One after a five-year spell.

Searching for further creative expression and exposure, Spear teamed up in 1975 with North Coast sound-system operator Jack Ruby, who became his new record producer while the artists also sought a new record label alliance. After Spear signed with Island

FAR LEFT: Burning Spear (Winston Rodney, far left) contemplates spiritual matters with harmony singers Delroy Hines (center) and Rupert Wellington (right) in Jamaica, 1975.

LEFT: Spear autographed this cover with his birth name, and offered a blessing: "Love to you / Jah live peace."

BURNING SPEAR

Records, which was fast developing international reggae credentials, his seminal *Marcus Garvey* album (1976) was released to critical acclaim and a measure of commercial success. The title track was one of the album's singles that—alongside the constantly covered "Slavery Days"—delivered a sharp reminder of Garvey's relevance. Spear recalled, "I run a research to see if anyone were there singing about Marcus Garvey, but no one was really hitting that point, so I decided to get into that musically." Joseph Hill of the group Culture also asserted that both he and Spear were at the forefront of the musical revival of Garvey's legacy.

Controversially, Island remixed the record for British release on the Mango imprint, perhaps conscious of the sonic readjustments the label had made for the Wailers' *Catch a Fire* a few years earlier. *Catch a Fire* represented the first serious attempt to internationalize a self-contained reggae band, and to achieve its commercial objective Island Records owner Chris Blackwell had rock guitar and keyboards added to the original Jamaican tracks in London. However, whereas the original mix of the Wailers record hadn't been widely heard, the Jamaican mix of *Marcus Garvey* had already found a public audience, so

the new remixing, which included speeding up some tracks, was an instant target of attack for critics. The *Garvey's Ghost* dub album, also released in 1976, lacked the sonic adventure of Jamaica's best engineers, featuring tracks remixed in London rather than B-side dubs created by King Tubby, and it consequently earned poor critical response.

In some accounts, Burning Spear is referred to as a group, since Spear was accompanied by two harmony vocalists soon after departing Dodd's Studio One: Rupert Willington, who also accompanied Spear for his first Studio One tracks, and Delroy Hines. Spear resumed his solo identity following the release of the critically successful 1976 album *Man in the Hills*, which was also produced by Ruby. Despite Spear's success with both Ruby and Island, which helped him gain an international profile, the roots reggae artist soon opted for self-produced independent releases.

By 1977, he had issued his first self-produced LP, *Dry & Heavy*; that year also marked his debut live appearance in Britain, where the British reggae outfit Aswad backed him. The

performance resulted in 1977's *Burning Spear Live!* His 1978 album *Social Living* also included contributions from Aswad members.

Hail H.I.M. (1980) is considered by some to be Spear's last major release. This was one of two albums issued during his brief early-1980s tenure with EMI Records, the other being 1982's *Farover* (released in the United States on the Heartbeat label). By this time, Spear had relocated to Queens, New York, as social and political fallout from Jamaica's violent 1976 elections continued. He established his own label, Burning Music, largely built on the recovered rights to his earlier catalog of recordings. Independent releases followed as major labels lost interest in roots reggae, yet Spear remained a frequent Grammy contender into the 1990s, earning best reggae recording nominations for the albums *Resistance* (1985), *People of the World* (1986), *Mek We Dweet* (1990), *The World Should Know* (1993), and *Rasta Business* (1995). It wasn't until 1999's *Calling Rastafari* that Burning Spear actually won the Best Reggae Recording award. Artists, critics, and fans alike have questioned the credibility of the

On songs like "Slavery Days," Delroy Hines, Rupert Willington, and Winston Rodney (l–r) sang of the historical injustices suffered by black people.

Grammy Award given for reggae, and Spear's success in the year that Steel Pulse was nominated for their superbly dynamic *Living Legacy* live album raised further eyebrows. Nearly a decade later, in 2009, *Jah Is Real* gave Spear another Grammy win. The mainstream recognition coincided with his adoption of a less militant, more commercially

MARCUS' CHILDREN

Burning Spear

ALL RIGHTS RESERVED

BURNING SPEAR

MARCUS CHILDREN BURNING SPEAR

Produced, Arranged & Written by: W. Rodney 4 Wharf Street, St. Ann's Bay, Jamaica W.I.

Published by: Blue Mountain Music Ltd.

(p) 1978 (c) 1978

Side One

1. Marcus' Children Suffer
2. Come
3. Social Life
4. Marcus Say Jah No Dead

Realizing that few of his reggae peers were singing about Marcus Garvey, Burning Spear made the late black leader and Rasta icon a major focus of his songwriting.

friendly sound, raising the question yet again of whether real roots Rasta radicalism loses its power once it reaches wider audiences.

Given the relatively noncommercial sound of Spear's voice and the uncompromising pro-Rasta political stance that has been a hallmark of his music since his first record, it is in some ways surprising that his audience became as large as it did. Nonetheless, whenever fans make lists of reggae's most roots-centered artists and albums from the music's 1970s heyday, Burning Spear inevitably crops up repeatedly.

SELECT DISCOGRAPHY: *Studio One Presents Burning Spear* (Studio One, 1973); *Rocking Time* (Studio One, 1974); *Marcus Garvey* (Mango/Island, 1976); *Garvey's Ghost* (Mango/Island, 1976); *Man in the Hills* (Mango/Island, 1976); *Dry & Heavy* (Mango/Island, 1977); *Burning Spear Live* (Mango/Island, 1977); *Social Living* (Island, 1978); *Hail H.I.M.* (Capitol, 1980); *Farover* (EMI/Heartbeat, 1982); *Resistance* (Burning Music, 1985); *People of the World* (Burning Music, 1986); *Mek We Dweet* (Mango/Island 1990); *The World Should Know* (Burning Music, 1993); *Rasta Business* (Heartbeat, 1995); *Calling Rastafari* (Heartbeat, 1999); *Live in Paris – Zenith '88* (Burning Music, 2004); *Original Living Dub. Vol.1* (Burning Music, 2004); *Creation Rebel: The Original Classic Recordings from Studio One* (Heartbeat, 2005); *Jah Is Real* (Burning Music, 2008)

JUNIOR BYLES
YEARS ACTIVE: 1967–1990s

Born in Kingston, Jamaica, in 1948, Junior Byles was the lead singer of the Versatiles, a vocal group that recorded for producer Joe Gibbs's Amalgamated label starting in 1967 and scored a Jamaican hit with "The Time Has Come" in 1968. Byles later became a successful solo artist, but by 1975, his time in the spotlight had ended—in quite tragic fashion.

Byles rose to prominence in Jamaica as one of the key acts produced by Lee Perry, who collaborated with Byles when they were both employees of Joe Gibbs. By 1970, Byles had become a solo act with a Rasta-centered political worldview that was evident in his recordings. In 1970, he released "What's the World Coming To" under the name King Chubby on Pama Records in Britain. As part of the musical groundswell of support for Michael Manley's 1972 campaign for Prime Minister of Jamaica, Byles recorded such politically focused hits as "Beat Down Babylon," further promoting the cause and language of Rastafari. Byles had no dreadlocks at the time, an interesting indication that not every artist who supported the Rasta cause adopted its typical appearance. With "Pharoah Hiding," he also cast the ruling Jamaica Labour Party leader Hugh Shearer in the unflattering light of capitalist establishment exploitation. Byles's debut LP, *Beat Down Babylon*, was released in 1972 on both sides of the Atlantic, as well as in Jamaica itself. Other early hits under Lee Perry's production supervision included "Curly Locks" (1973) and the repatriation-themed "Place Called Africa" (1974).

The most dramatic phase of Byles's life occurred when he experienced a mental breakdown and became largely reclusive following the 1974 death of Ethiopian Emperor and Rasta icon Haile Selassie. Several years of inactivity followed a meeting with Chris Blackwell, head of Island Records, at Lee Perry's Black Ark studio in Kingston, where Perry and Byles unsuccessfully attempted to convince Blackwell to support a collaborative album project. Little was heard or seen of Byles in the late 1970s, with only one commercially unsuccessful album of compiled new material, *Rasta No Pickpocket* (1986), released in the next decade among intermittent singles. Despite his potential, Byles became one of reggae's men in the margins.

SELECT DISCOGRAPHY: *Beat Down Babylon* (Dynamic/Trojan, 1972)

DL 5035A

Made in Ireland
Copyright Control

45 RPM

CURLEY LOCKS
Junior Byles
Arr. Prod. Lee Perry

Junior Byles at Channel One, 1984, a decade after the politically focused singer had suffered a mental breakdown and largely disappeared from public view.

CORNELL CAMPBELL

YEARS ACTIVE: 1960s–1980s

Noted for his distinctive falsetto, Cornell Campbell was born in Jamaica in 1948 and first came to attention recording in the early 1960s for Studio One producer Coxsone Dodd, though their business relationship disintegrated over the typical financial disputes. Campbell was initially discouraged by the criticisms he heard heaped on other prospective vocalists as he waited his turn at Dodd's famed auditions. During the rocksteady era in 1966, Campbell developed his skills as a member of the Uniques and as lead vocalist with the Eternals, who scored a 1969 hit with the soulful Campbell-composed single "Queen of the Minstrel." He abandoned prospects of a more traditional career in printing to record with the Sensations vocal quartet for Duke Reid's Treasure Isle Records, but despite these creatively fruitful group associations, his career did not take off.

Campbell began working with ace producer Bunny Lee around 1972, after

Cornell Campbell plays to the crowed at a beach gig in Negril, Jamaica, 1980.

Cornell Campbell

Press Along Natty

he had grown frustrated with other producers. His debut solo LP was issued in 1973, though one source claims that Campbell was unaware of the record's existence until four years later. During this phase, he performed on Lee's recordings as a multi-instrumentalist and singer in the Aggrovators studio session band and wrote perhaps his best-known song, the Rasta-roots-infused "Natty Dread in a Greenwich Farm" (1975). This came during Lee's "flying cymbal" phase, when his recordings featured disco-style cymbal playing by his drummers, who rhythmically opened and closed the hi-hat throughout songs. The record encouraged Campbell to adopt the more Rasta-oriented image he capitalized on with 1976's *The Gorgon* LP.

The transformation was to be short-lived, as Campbell returned to the more commercial lovers rock style for *Turn Back the Hands of Time* (1977). The alliance between Campbell and Lee ended in 1980, foreshadowing the singer's eventual withdrawal from the business by the middle of the decade after brief stints with other producers, including Niney the Observer.

SELECT DISCOGRAPHY: *Cornell Campbell* (Trojan, 1973); *The Gorgon* (Attack, 1976); *Turn Back the Hands of Time* (Third World, 1977); *I Shall Not Remove 1975–80* (Blood & Fire, 2000)

JP-814 A

HARRY HIPPY
(Lee)
CORNELL CAMPBELL
Produced by: Bunnie Lee

CHALICE
YEARS ACTIVE: 1980–PRESENT

Chalice is one of reggae's self-contained bands, with a wide range of pop influences woven into their roots sound. Enhancing their performances with tasteful use of digital music technology, Chalice is also renowned for their live shows. Despite their provocative name, which refers to a kind of pipe used to smoke marijuana, Chalice is a band that should have achieved much more commercial success than they ultimately did. Unfortunately, the pieces of their professional jigsaw never quite connected internationally. Formed in 1980 in Jamaica by former Byron Lee & the Dragonaires guitarist Wayne Armond, Chalice released their debut album, *Blasted*, in 1981. The album featured the future live mainstay "Good to Be There," which reappeared on three later records, as well as on a 2008 single collaboration with then-rising vocal star Tarrus Riley.

The group's performance skills soon generated a solid fan base in Jamaica, evidenced by the *Live at Reggae Sunsplash* release in 1982. The following year's *Standard Procedure* kept their digital roots sound in the spotlight but did not contribute to new levels of success. In a bid to globalize their audience, they signed a deal with Germany's Ariola Records and released *Good to Be There*, a compilation of tracks from the band's two previous albums, in 1984. That same year, they toured Turkey.

The band's studio performance skills have been somewhat underrated, as critics have focused on the live Chalice sound. As a result, typically Jamaican-style hits like 1986's "Revival Time," from the bold *Crossfire* LP, overshadowed the more ambitious reggae-rock fusion of "Caribbean Boy." By this point, Chalice had reached a career crossroads and were caught between anthologizing previous hits and reaching for growth in new directions. The 1987 album *Up Till Now* compiled tracks from 1980 through 1987 for American release on RAS Records, though arguably it didn't contain the band's best material. They remained functional, but only one additional album, *Tuff Enuff*, appeared in the 1990s. Chalice even appeared on a reggae tribute album to the Rolling Stones with a standout roots cover of "Paint It Black" (2002), underlining the band's unfulfilled potential and lack of critical recognition. During these years of sporadic activity, founding members Trevor Roper and Robi Peart withdrew from the music business, and keyboardist Mikey Wallace was murdered in 1999 by gunmen at his home in Jamaica.

After a lengthy break, the group returned to recording in 2010 and released *Let It Play*, recapturing the established Chalice vibe with four new members and three original players. Included in the lineup was Armond, who in a newspaper interview lamented the lack of originality from new bands. In 2011, *Billboard* magazine reported that Armond had received positive critical response for his scoring and production work on the film *Better Mus' Come* (2010), one of several recent films from Jamaica that highlight the complexity of the island's social history. It remains to be seen whether the new Chalice will influence the post-dancehall generation.

MEMBERS: Wayne Armond (lead guitar, vocals), *Blasted* to *Let It Play*; **Winston "Alla" Lloyd** (keyboards, vocals), *Blasted* to *Let it Play*; **Trevor Roper** (guitar, vocals); **Mikey Wallace** (keyboards, vocals); **Papa Keith Francis** (bass); **Desi Jones** (drums); **Robi Peart** (vocals); **Dean Stephens** (vocals), *Let It Play*; **Steve Golding** (guitar), *Let It Play*; **Wayne Clarke** (drums), *Let It Play*; **Chris McDonald** (keyboards), *Let it Play*

SELECT DISCOGRAPHY: *Blasted* (Pipe Music, 1981); *Live at Reggae Sunsplash* (Pipe Music, 1982); *Standard Procedure* (Pipe Music, 1983); *Good To Be There* (Ariola Records, 1984); *Stand Up* (CSA, 1985); *Crossfire* (CTS, 1986); *Up Till Now* (RAS, 1987); *Let It Play* (Tads International, 2010)

ABOVE: Bunny Tom Tom, aka Crucial Bunny, engineering at Channel One, 1984.
BELOW: Squningene Francis makes friends with the Channel One dub-cutting machine, 1984.

CHANNEL ONE
YEARS ACTIVE: 1972–1980s

One of the most revered and active studios of the 1970s, Channel One is also considered to have been highly influential in shaping the sound of reggae in its heyday. The studio, located on Maxfield Avenue in Kingston, Jamaica, was owned and run by the eldest and youngest of four brothers, Jo Jo (Joseph) and Ernest Hoo-Kim. Jo Jo had previously worked in the jukebox business, and Channel One was established as an alternative source of income for the brothers following the Jamaican government's 1970 ban on gaming machines.

A visit to Dynamic Sounds recording studio with singer John Holt drew Jo Jo Hoo-Kim into the world of recording, inspiring him to invest in outfitting his own studio operation. Channel One opened in 1972 as a four-track facility but struggled before developing its own distinctive sound and vibe. Cleverly, Jo Jo gave free initial studio session time to producers so he could learn how to run recording sessions and develop industry business relationships. His brother Ernest later became the active engineer.

The Hoo-Kims' previous business enterprises allowed them the luxury of buying top-grade equipment and assembling one of the island's best-ever studio bands, the Revolutionaries (which typically included members of other session groups). That crucial unit was formed after the Hoo-Kims hired the core of the Skin, Flesh & Bone group, which included drummer Sly Dunbar, who relished the brothers' attention to sonic detail and the freedom they gave to the musicians. It was at Channel One that Dunbar developed the double-drum sound featured on the Jamaican vocal trio Mighty Diamonds' 1976 album *Right Time* and molded the insistent "rockers" rhythm associated with the studio. Channel One also consolidated Dunbar's influential alliance with bassist Robbie Shakespeare, turning the duo into Sly & Robbie, one of reggae's principal rhythmic spearheads from about 1975.

By the time Channel One entered the scene, the dub B-side had become a standard feature in the industry, and the studio executed some excellent mixes in this format. Exemplary recordings included material from the Ja-Man All Stars session band, including *Ja-Man Dub* (1977) and *King's Dub* (1980), as well as the vastly underrated 1978 Inner Circle *Heavyweight Dub* LP.

The company soon had its own pressing plant and multiple label imprints, including Well Charge, Full Charge, and Channel One itself. The Hoo-Kims introduced the 12-inch single (played at 45 rpm) to the Jamaican scene, but they also attempted unsuccessfully to innovate with a long-playing 7-inch single (played at 33 rpm) featuring a song in several configurations. Labeled "economic packages," these were soon abandoned due to inferior sound quality. By 1979, Channel One had upgraded the studio facility for sixteen-track recording to capitalize on the technology's popularity among producers, and possibly to prevent loss of business to competition.

Jo Jo moved to New York at the end of the 1970s, following the death of their brother Paul in a robbery attempt. He set up a record pressing plant in Long Island City, New York, in 1982, but the sweeping arrival of digital music technology spelled the end of Channel One's reign. By the end of the 1980s, the operation had ceased to exist.

AQUARIUS Aq 001

Recorded by Herman Chin-Loy, *Aquarius Dub* has been called the first dub album, even though it lacked the spaced-out effects that would define the subgenre.

"Baby, I Love You So," voiced by Jacob Miller, and then the majestic "dubwise" incarnation "King Tubby Meets Rockers Uptown" (1976). Chin-Loy remixed "Cassava Piece" as "Jah Jah Dub" for *Aquarius Dub*, one of dub's earliest full-length albums. (It is thought to have been released in 1973, though sources vary widely.) Utilizing backing tracks from Chin-Loy's productions, *Aquarius Dub* was not heavy on the kinds of spacey echo, reverb, and delay effects that soon became dub trademarks. It was, however, one of several records that carried the reggae instrumental beyond mere "version" (meaning the song minus the vocals), altering the sonic terrain by subtracting and reassembling elements of the rhythm track. Chin-Loy believes that it was, in fact, the very first dub album, though the Clive Chin-produced Impact All Stars album, *Java Java Java Java* (1972) lays claim to being dub's first LP.

Chin-Loy scored a British pop hit on the Trojan Records label with Bruce Ruffin's "Rain," which reached #19 in 1971. (The song featured Trojan's typical overdubbed orchestral string flourishes.) In the mid-1970s, Chin-Loy installed Jamaica's first twenty-four-track studio, which was used by other producers. In the years that followed, his work had little impact until a few marginal proto-dancehall hits emerged at the end of the decade. Beyond this point, Chin-Loy seems to have faded out of the mix—much like the dub echoes his work had helped pioneer.

HERMAN CHIN-LOY

YEARS ACTIVE: 1969-1970s

Herman Chin-Loy is best known for creating one of dub's cornerstone recordings in the early 1970s: *Aquarius Dub*, mixed in a half hour at Dynamic Sounds in Kingston. Born in Jamaica in 1948, he was one of several Chinese Jamaicans to enter the music business and to play a key role in reggae. Chin-Loy experienced an unstable childhood in which he was shifted around from one relative to another. After his school days, which included a stint in a reform institution, his passion for music grew. He ran a variety of Kingston record shops in the early 1960s and was exposed to the Beverley's Records operation run by Leslie Kong, a relative (probably Chin-Loy's cousin).

By 1969, following further involvement in selling records and a spell as a discotheque DJ (spinning the records, not "toasting," or talking over the music), Chin-Loy had set up his own record shop, Aquarius, which included a record label. It was during this phase that he created an artist persona named Augustus Pablo—initially a fictitious name used on recordings by various session musicians. Then, in 1971, Chin-Loy encountered Horace Swaby, a master of the melodica, and gave him a chance to work in the studio. The rest is perhaps more mystery than history, as Swaby became Augustus Pablo and recorded a series of haunting records best reinterpreted in dub style. To create this sound, dub engineers remixed songs for sound-system use, eliminating most of the vocals in the standard version and focusing instead on the drum-and-bass-driven instrumentation spatially enhanced with echo, reverb, and delay.

Chin-Loy recorded Pablo's "Cassava Piece," which was the root of one of dub's most famous tracks, in either 1971 or 1972. In other skilled hands, the song later became

Geoffrey Chung (rear, in cowboy hat) with Ras Michael and the Sons of Negus, a year after they collaborated on the group's 1975 album, *Rastafari*.

GEOFFREY CHUNG

1970s-1995

Born in the early 1950s, Geoffrey Chung began his career as a keyboard player and became a successful reggae producer and songwriter, working with bands such as Ras Michael & the Sons of Negus, Inner Circle, and Steel Pulse, as well as the legendary Peter Tosh.

Chung spent some time in Hong Kong as a child before moving back to Jamaica as a teenager. He later drifted away from biochemistry studies at the Jamaican campus of the University of the West Indies and into the music business as a keyboard player. His first exposure came through preproduction work with the Peter Ashbourne Affair, a pop-reggae crossover act, prior to their recording

sessions with producer Herman Chin-Loy. Chung soon refined his own talents in production, arranging, and songwriting, working on singer Sharon Forrester's debut album, *Sharon* (1974). Although the album never broke through commercially, it provided Chung with vital experience.

Chung's credentials were elevated by his successful collaboration with the African drum-centered Rasta collective Ras Michael & the Sons of Negus on 1975's *Rastafari*, an album that once again brought him into contact with the cream of Jamaica's studio session players, many of whom he also played with in producer Lee Perry's Upsetters lineups. Chung also worked with the group Inner Circle a year later on their *Reggae Thing* album, released by Capitol Records at a time when major labels were beginning to recognize the

genre's commercial potential. Chung cemented his name in the reggae world by working with former Wailers member Peter Tosh, who had embarked on a solo career. His engineering and mixing on Tosh's *Bush Doctor* (1978), *Mystic Man* (1979), and *Wanted: Dread & Alive* (1981) albums boosted his reputation immeasurably. Chung was also selected to produce the 1980 Steel Pulse album *Reggae Fever* (titled *Caught You* in Britain) after the band had experienced problems with Island Records in finding a suitable producer.

Having established himself working with major artists, Chung shifted his base of production operations to Miami, setting up his own recording studio there in the late 1980s. He died in November 1995 after suffering kidney failure.

CIMARONS

YEARS ACTIVE: 1967-1980s

Considered Britain's first major reggae band (not just a vocal group), the Cimarons formed in 1967 in northwest London and built their career backing and recording with touring Jamaican rocksteady singers. When the Cimarons later emerged with their own records in the early 1970s, it was a time when British reggae suffered from an inferiority complex, dwelling in the shadow of Jamaica's musical authenticity. Ironically, the Cimarons' penchant for cover material—both reggae and pop—may have undermined their efforts to attain roots credibility.

The group was the backing band on many of Trojan Records' UK recordings, contributing to singer Ken Boothe's *Everything I Own* album (1974). They also scored national chart hits under alternate names: first in 1970 as Freddie Note & The Rudies, with a cover of Bobby Bloom's "Montego Bay," and again in 1973 as the Hotshots, with "Snoopy vs. the Red Baron," which reached #4. There is no clear explanation as to why the band opted for aliases.

It wasn't until 1974 that the Cimarons recorded their first album, *In Time*, released on Trojan. Since the collection was littered with pop and soul covers, it would appear that the Cimarons' affiliation with Trojan—a label renowned for watering down reggae with more commercial sounds—had truly affected their creative direction. The band was so unhappy with the musical compromise that they left the label. The inclusion of a cover of Jimmy Cliff's "You Can Get It If You Really Want" was notable considering that four years earlier, Desmond Dekker's version of the song for Trojan had been a chart hit.

The group's second album, 1976's *On the Rock*, is still considered to be their seminal statement and best release. Ironically, it was recorded mostly in Kingston, at Channel One and Randy's studio (so titled after the record shop owned by Vincent Chin), at a time when domestically recorded British roots-reggae was beginning to find a market and distinct sonic identity. With the rising commercial viability of reggae following Bob Marley's breakthroughs, the Cimarons signed to Polydor Records and became another of the 1970s major-label reggae acquisitions. The well-regarded *Live at the Roundhouse* (1978) captured the band's talent in live performance; it was followed later the same year by the positively rootsy *Maka*, on which the band sounded supremely confident. Despite their core following and consistently strong recordings made after their debut, the Cimarons never quite caught on like their British counterparts Steel Pulse, Aswad, or Matumbi. As a result, the group's shift to Virgin Records in 1980 (after the label's reggae Frontline imprint had been terminated) had little impact on the market.

The 1982 album *Reggaebility*, released on the very mainstream Pickwick label, was a collection of pop covers (including "Mull of Kintyre," written by Paul McCartney, who instigated the project) that was naturally seen as a major step backward for a band that had shown its reggae originality and creativity within and beyond the studio. Though the Cimarons continued touring following the release of *Reggaebility*, the record ended a crucial phase in their career, dashing their dreams of British reggae glory.

MEMBERS: Franklyn Dunn (bass, percussion); **Carl Levy** (keyboards, percussion); **Sonny Binns** (keyboards), *Freedom Street*; **Locksley Gichie** (guitar, percussion); **Maurice Ellis** (drums, percussion), *In Time* to *Freedom Street*; **Jah "Bunny" Donaldson** (drums), *Freedom Street* and *Reggaebility*; **Winston Reid** (vocals, percussion)

SELECT DISCOGRAPHY: *In Time* (Trojan, 1974); *On the Rock* (Vulcan, 1976); *Live at the Roundhouse* (Polydor, 1978); *Maka* (Polydor, 1978); *Freedom Street* (Virgin Records, 1980); *Reggaebility* (Pickwick, 1982); *The Best of the Cimarons* (Culture Press, 1999)

LEFT: In their 1970s heyday, the Cimarons, who hailed from northwest London, demonstrated the viability of British reggae.

ABOVE: Recorded mostly in Kingston, *On the Rock* (1976) is considered the Cimarons' definitive musical statement.

THE CLARENDONIANS
YEARS ACTIVE: 1965–1968

Formed in 1965 by prominent Jamaican producer Coxsone Dodd, the Clarendonians quickly became popular when ska began to wane, leaving a void partially filled by songs following the "rude boy" theme of "Simmer Down," a 1963 release by the Bob Marley–fronted Wailers. The "rude boys" (Jamaican gangsters) were a phenomenon of Kingston's urban ghetto, and their violence and virtues became common subject matter for songs. The Clarendonians were one of the groups that chronicled the development of this criminal underclass, though love was an equally prominent theme in their music.

The founding members of the Clarendonians, Ernest Wilson and Peter Austin, came to Dodd's attention after their successes in various talent competitions. At some point, Dodd added a third member, seven-year-old Freddie McGregor. The group's "Rude Boy Gone a Jail" (1966) was one of the records that seemed to capture the transition in Jamaican popular music from ska to rocksteady. The song had ska's animated rhythmic accents, but the pace was somewhat slower than most of its predecessors. Similarly, their "Rudie Bam Bam," considered a Clarendonians classic, speaks of rude-boy transgressions and their legal consequences.

Some of the Clarendonians' singles were licensed to Island Records for release in Britain, but their commercial impact is difficult to measure. After leaving Studio One at some point between 1967 and 1968, the group briefly recorded for producer Ken Lack's Caltone label; their first (and possibly only) Caltone single, "Baby, Baby," was released in 1968.

After the Clarendonians split up around 1968, Wilson began recording as a solo artist. Austin eventually left the business, lamenting the rampant dishonesty of the people involved, and became an aviation supervisor. Neither he nor the other Clarendonians had received any royalties. As he put it, "We got a lot of fame, but no fortune." After initial solo struggles, McGregor went on to a distinguished music career as a solo artist.

MEMBERS: Fitzroy "Ernest" Wilson (vocals); **Peter Austin** (vocals); **Freddie McGregor** (vocals)

SELECT DISCOGRAPHY: *The Best of the Clarendonians* (Studio One, 1968)

Johnny Clarke in Jamaica, 1975, the same year his "Move Out of Babylon" summed up the Rastafarian rejection of the political system.

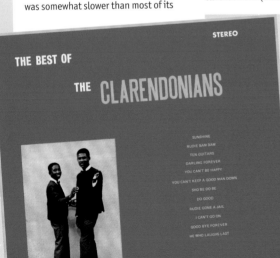

STEREO

THE BEST OF

THE CLARENDONIANS

SUNSHINE
RUDIE BAM BAM
TEN GUITARS
DARLING FOREVER
YOU CAN'T BE HAPPY
YOU CAN'T KEEP A GOOD MAN DOWN
SHO BE DO BE
DO GOOD
RUDIE GONE A JAIL
I CAN'T GO ON
GOOD BYE FOREVER
HE WHO LAUGHS LAST

STUDIO ONE
SOL 1122

Popular as ska transitioned into rocksteady, the Clarendonians are best remembered for songs about "rude boys," young Kingston gangsters who captured the national imagination.

JOHNNY CLARKE
YEARS ACTIVE: 1973–PRESENT

Born in Jamaica in 1955, Johnny Clarke played in a school band at Kingston's Jamaica College with future members of the bands Inner Circle and Third World. His recording career got off to a difficult start in 1973 when material recorded at Federal Studio in Kingston went unreleased. His debut with producer-artist Clancy Eccles, "God Made the Sea and Sun," was issued only on a blank-label test pressing, without any identifying information or official release. His work finally received some attention when Clarke recorded "Everyday Wondering" for producer Rupie Edwards. While it was not a great success, "Everyday Wondering" found a large audience when it was recut by Edwards as "Ire Feelings

Produced by Bunny Lee, Clarke's "We're Going to a Ball" arrived via the Weed Beat label in 1975.

(Skanga)," a single that reached #9 on the British charts in 1974.

Clarke's breakthrough hit was "None Shall Escape the Judgement" (1974), produced by Bunny "Striker" Lee and written and originally recorded by singer Earl Zero. Mixed by King Tubby, that song included the disco-influenced "flying cymbal" sound, made by the continual rhythmic opening of the hi-hat cymbal, which for a time became an integral part of Clarke's records. He began touring internationally in late 1974, playing first in the United States before continuing to Canada and England (possibly backed by the band Matumbi) with Augustus Pablo and the Heptones. In 1975, Clarke scored his biggest hit, "Move Out of Babylon," which summed up the Rastafarian rejection of the political establishment, though the song's popularity among reggae audiences did not translate into pop chart success. His debut album, *Enter into His Gates with Praise* (1975) was released in Britain by Trojan Records on the Attack imprint. Trojan went bankrupt soon after, prompting Virgin Records to approach Clarke.

By 1976, Clarke had signed with Virgin in the United Kingdom, joining a host of other reggae acts as the label stepped forward to claim its share of the growing market. In the same year, Virgin released two Clarke albums: *Rockers Time Now* and *Authorized Version*. He briefly moved to the Britain-based Greensleeves Records before returning to Jamaica, where he found a changed scene that was focused on rhythm recycling to a greater degree than he had previously experienced. Clarke was largely inactive during the 1980s, as digital dancehall music gained popularity, and it became clear that his peak had passed. Like so many Jamaican artists of his generation, Clarke feels various producers robbed him of profits, but his 1970s hits have kept him an "oldies" show fixture.

SELECT DISCOGRAPHY: *None Shall Escape the Judgement* (Justice, 1974); *Enter into His Gates with Praise* (Attack, 1975); *Rockers Time Now* (Virgin, 1976); *Authorized Version* (Virgin, 1976)

GUSSIE CLARKE
YEARS ACTIVE: 1971-PRESENT

Born in Kingston, Jamaica, in 1953, Augustus "Gussie" Clarke gained his first exposure to the music business as a budding entrepreneur who imported records for sound systems. He soon became an established producer, eventually owning a studio, publishing company, and CD-pressing plant.

As was often the case in Jamaica during the early 1970s, Clarke's studio involvement stemmed from his ownership of a sound system, a unit he called King Gussie's Hi-Fi. After 1971, Clarke acquired a record-cutting machine from the Treasure Isle studios in Kingston and began cutting dubplates for other sound systems.

Clarke was responsible for crafting the seminal Big Youth album *Screaming Target* (1973) while still a teenager. He attracted attention for a distinctly polished production style that would eventually yield international rewards, especially with Britain-based singer Maxi Priest. His early work also included DJ I-Roy's debut album, *Presenting I-Roy* (1973), as well as releases by Mighty Diamonds, Augustus Pablo, Dennis Brown, and Leroy Smart. Selected rhythms were compiled and remixed for *Black Foundation Dub* in 1976.

Clarke established his own Music Works label (part of his Anchor Recording Company) in Kingston in 1987. Unlike many of his dancehall-era contemporaries, Clarke's production fused a harmonic musical sensibility with the newly emergent digital technologies, creating a sound that was both progressive and commercial. Gregory Isaacs's single "Rumours" laid down the new template in 1988, and its influence endured with Clarke's use of the rhythm as the basis for J.C. Lodge's "Telephone Love," which was a transatlantic smash hit in reggae markets later that year.

Demonstrating his ability to spot creative talent, Clarke employed the songwriting and arrangement skills of Mikey Bennett to help create the Music Works style as other producers and artists sought access to the new sound.

Clarke began the 1990s by working with British reggae group Aswad on the highly commercial *Too Wicked* album and reached the sales pinnacle of his career producing tracks for Maxi Priest's *Bonafide*, which was certified gold in the United States. Since the mid-1990s he has been less visible, though he is still actively involved in record production. His Anchor company currently claims to own Jamaica's largest professional recording studios, attracting international clients that include Sting and the Jewish reggae artist Matisyahu.

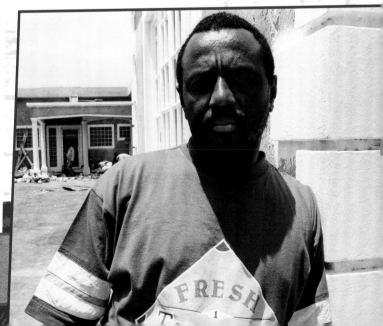

Gussie Clark outside of his Anchor Music facility in Kingston, 1992. Said to be Jamaica's largest professional studio, Anchor has played host to artists like Sting and Matisyahu.

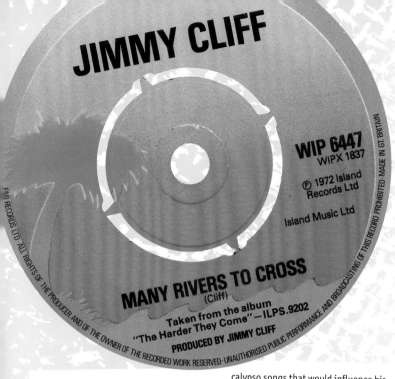

JIMMY CLIFF

YEARS ACTIVE: 1962–PRESENT

Born James Chambers in Jamaica on April 1, 1948, Jimmy Cliff is one of reggae's true survivors. The singer-songwriter is also one of the few Jamaican artists to have launched a career during the ska era of the early 1960s and continued to make a major impact on reggae long thereafter. For more than four decades, and with varying degrees of success, Cliff has projected his own soul-pop-reggae hybrid of commercially accessible message music, designed to reflect both the anguish and aspirations of his audiences. In a 1981 interview, he described himself as "the live and living African ambassador," and to fulfill this mission, he's created a suitably radio-friendly sound.

In 1962, at the age of fourteen, Cliff moved to Kingston from the neighboring parish of St. Catherine. By this time, he had begun singing the mento and calypso songs that would influence his musical development. Recalling his transition into city life, Cliff once asked, "What was I supposed to do with my life? Work in a banana field? Cut cane?" Clearly, he had bigger things in mind. Cliff's first break came via Leslie Kong, a Kingston businessman whose enterprises included a combination ice cream parlor and record shop. After seeing Cliff in an impromptu audition, and because he was interested in making records himself rather than just selling those made by others, Kong invested in the young singer's vocal talent.

By Cliff's own recollection, the first recording sessions with Kong began in either "late 1961 or early 1962," with the second session producing Cliff's first hit, "Hurricane Hattie." Additional ska hits he recorded with Kong included "King of Kings" and "Miss Jamaica" in 1962. That year, as an informal A&R man for Kong's fledgling Beverley's Records, Cliff also made it possible for the future stars Desmond Dekker and Bob Marley to cut their first recordings. Few record executives have unearthed two talents of this caliber in such a short span of time.

Two years later, Cliff traveled to New York as part of the Jamaican musical contingent organized by music promoter and politician Edward Seaga for the 1964 World's Fair. The traveling artists were backed by the polished middle-class, mainstream group Byron Lee & the Dragonaires. For Cliff, the trip yielded an appearance in the film *This Is Ska* (1964) and—perhaps most important—a meeting with Island Records head Chris Blackwell, who encouraged the singer to further his career in England. Cliff followed Blackwell's advice in 1965, though he initially had to settle for work as a backup vocalist before recording again as a solo artist.

Cliff made no impact with "Pride and Passion," his 1966 single for Fontana Records, but by 1968 he had made his Island debut with the prophetically titled *Hard Road to Travel* (not released in the United States). The album included the single "Give and Take," which failed to reach the British pop charts despite receiving some airplay. In 1968, frustrated with his seemingly stalled career, Cliff represented Jamaica at the International Song Festival in Brazil, performing "Waterfall," which had flopped as a UK single. He got a much warmer response in the Southern Hemisphere, where the song became a hit. Cliff remained in Brazil for nine months after the festival to perform and write.

By this time, none of Cliff's five singles on Island had charted. "Wonderful World, Beautiful People," his biggest single, was released in 1969 on Trojan Records (established with Blackwell) in the United Kingdom, where it reached #6, and on A&M Records in the

ABOVE: "Many Rivers to Cross," featured on the sound track to *The Harder They Come*, was later covered by the UK pop-reggae band UB40.

RIGHT: Jimmy Cliff played the semiautobiographical lead role in the 1972 cult film *The Harder They Come*, which hipped international audiences to the exploitative practices of Jamaica's recording industry.

United States, where it hit #25. Notably, the song was overlaid with string arrangements designed to satisfy the BBC (British Broadcasting Corporation) radio's preferences for pop norms and to appeal to pop consumers—goals that accurately represented Trojan's commercial strategy in Britain. Cliff's only other British top-ten hit followed shortly after, in 1970, with his cover of Cat Stevens's "Wild World." The single came out on Island but was not released in the United States, despite the original's top-twenty success.

By now Cliff's songs were beginning to attract attention from mainstream artists. Although his single "Vietnam," Cliff's social commentary on the era's key military conflict, got no further than #46 on the UK charts, Bob Dylan described

it as the best protest song he'd heard—high praise from one of popular music's prime lyrical architects. Paul Simon was apparently so inspired by the sound of that single that it led him to record the 1972 hit "Mother and Child Reunion" in Jamaica with the same musicians who had backed Cliff on "Vietnam" (they were best known as the studio session band for Leslie Kong's Beverley's Records). The same band that backed Cliff on his *Wonderful World, Beautiful People* album was also employed on hits by Johnny Nash, an American singer who, like Paul Simon, fused reggae and pop, helping the music cross over to the mainstream on both sides of the Atlantic.

Cliff's songs were so good that other reggae artists wanted to cover them. In 1970, he released "You Can Get It If

You Really Want" as a single, though it was Desmond Dekker's version that was a hit in Britain reaching #2 on the pop charts. Cliff's recording was later included on the iconic sound track album *The Harder They Come* (1972). The Pioneers, a Jamaican vocal trio, also scored a hit on the British charts in 1971 with another of Cliff's songs, "Let Your Yeah Be Yeah," which remarkably reached #5. The sudden death of Cliff's mentor, Leslie Kong, in 1971, posed potential problems, but unlike Dekker, who was also one of Kong's stars, Cliff managed to keep his career on track after the loss.

The artist returned to Island after his spell with Trojan and recorded the controversial album *Another Cycle* (1971). The album raised some eyebrows, as it included no reggae and instead consisted

entirely of R&B, suggesting Cliff's reluctance to be pigeonholed as solely a reggae artist. In addition, the album was not recorded in either Britain or Jamaica but rather the United States, at the famed Muscle Shoals Studios in Alabama. Some have viewed this record as a major artistic and commercial miscalculation that eroded Cliff's fan base instead of broadening it. Fortunately, his next project—a film—dramatically restored his credibility.

Released in 1972, *The Harder They Come* stars Cliff in the semiautobiographical role of a singer struggling for success within the exploitative record industry. His character included elements of a Jamaican outlaw figure from the 1940s known as Rhygin, who Cliff described as "a kind of Robin Hood." In an interview published in the 1977 book *Reggae Bloodlines*, he explained, "I could identify with him in certain ways. I read the script and said, yeah, I'd like to do it." *The Harder They Come* offered Cliff an opportunity to portray the realities of Jamaica's impoverished underclass and, of course, it gave him a stage on which to display his musical talents.

Cliff figures prominently on the film's sound track, which also features songs by various artists; among his own four songs was the classic "Many Rivers to Cross," later covered by UB40. The film was a cult hit more so than a mainstream box office phenomenon, and the sound track wasn't released in the United States until 1975—but it became reggae's biggest-selling record by the end of that year. Still, by 2010, *The Harder They Come* sound track had sold fewer than five hundred thousand copies, a fact that demonstrates the steep hurdles that have tempered reggae's commercial success. (The album has since been dwarfed by the 1984 Bob Marley & the Wailers compilation *Legend*, which has sold more than ten million copies in America.) Although *The Harder They Come* reached only #140 in the United States, it sowed countercultural seeds that would soon bear fruit for other reggae artists tackling the largely resistant

American market. Cliff's subsequent solo albums were musically varied efforts, and he fought an uphill battle to lift his career from star to superstar status. He became frustrated by Island's focus on rock acts such as Traffic, and he left the label in 1973. His departure disappointed Blackwell, who had hoped to take both Cliff and reggae to the next level.

After leaving Island, Cliff continued in his musical-chairs experimentation with record companies. He signed to EMI Records in the United Kingdom and Warner Bros. Records in the United States. *Unlimited* (1973) was his first album released under the new deals, and it advanced his efforts to create a reggae-pop middle ground. The set included the social-commentary song "Commercialization," which unwittingly underscored a key challenge in much of Cliff's career as a recording artist: how to remain true to his creative impulses while building a clear and authentic identity from album to album. Describing this spiritual phase in his career, which lasted until 1977, Cliff said, "I changed. I went into a heavy spiritual and cultural thing which I felt was more important. . . . My interest wasn't 100% into music." He converted to Islam and visited Africa to strengthen his ancestral connections. As

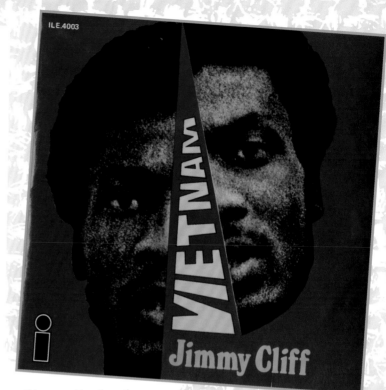

part of his personal transformation, he also became a Muslim steeped in the philosophies of Malcolm X; though by 1981, things had changed. "I don't belong to any religion," he said that year in a *Rolling Stone* interview. "All religions belong to I."

In 1974, Cliff staged his first full US concert tour and released two studio albums: *Struggling Man*, featuring equal measures of reggae and R&B, and *House of Exile*, which received considerable airplay in the Caribbean. However, while Cliff was now an established star in both Africa and Brazil, neither of these albums charted in the United States or Britain.

By the mid-1970s, since Cliff was contracted to different major labels on both sides of the Atlantic, several of his album releases—such as 1974's *Music Maker* (possibly the only one that does not feature Cliff on the cover)—were hampered by a lack of promotional coordination that led to poor sales. His first completely solo album to chart in the United States was 1975's *Follow My Mind*, on the Warner Bros. Reprise

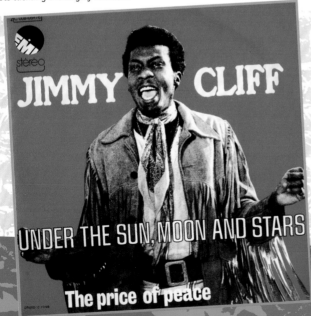

OPPOSITE: Jimmy Cliff in Trench Town, the rough-and-tumble Kingston ghetto he managed to escape through music.

ABOVE: From Trench Town to Carnegie Hall: Jimmy Cliff lives it up in New York City, 1974.

Records label. Despite some positive reviews, it had little effect on advancing reggae in the United States and only reached #195 on the *Billboard* Top 200 album chart. Cliff followed a 1976 live album with *Give Thankx*, released two years later. By this time, he had settled on one label, Warner Bros., for international distribution. *Give Thankx* was greeted with critical acclaim, and one reviewer called it his best work since *The Harder They Come*, but it was a commercial failure, peaking only at #209 in America.

By late 1980, Cliff had moved to MCA Records for *I Am the Living*. (The move probably pushed him into the category of reggae artist with the largest number of major-label affiliations to date.) Most of the songs on the album were recorded in California, with a sound targeting the black American audience. Similarly, its 1981 follow-up, *Give the People What They Want*, reinforced Cliff's trademark fusion of soul- and pop-influenced reggae without quite fulfilling the commercial crossover promise of his few albums to ever show up on the US charts.

1982's *Special*, his Columbia Records debut, reached #186. That the album was recorded with rock producer Chris Kimsey perhaps says a lot about Cliff's commercial ambitions at the time. His 1983 effort *The Power and the Glory* was one of several collections during this era that diluted his "roots" credibility among listeners who were less enthusiastic about the singer's ongoing pop crossover pursuit.

Reward finally came when Cliff won the second reggae Grammy ever awarded, for 1985's *Cliff Hanger*. (Oddly, the singer didn't actually attend the ceremony.) Despite—or for some listeners, because of—production work by Khalis Bayyan of the funk group Kool & the Gang, *Cliff Hanger* lacked major commercial impact. In fact, each of Cliff's Columbia albums seemed to mirror the same crossover template without significantly advancing his career. Ironically, his highest rank on the US album chart was in the form of another sound track album, as he contributed seven tracks to *Club Paradise* (1986), a comedy in which he also had an acting role. The sound track peaked at #122 on the *Billboard* charts.

Hanging Fire, released in 1988 and partly recorded in the Congo, largely followed formula, but the strong title track demonstrated creative confidence and a renewed militant edge. A series of low-profile independent releases followed, but just as it seemed that no further hits would arrive, Cliff's 1994 remake of Johnny Nash's 1972 hit "I Can See Clearly Now"—included on the sound track for the film *Cool Runnings* (1993)—reached #23 in the United Kingdom and #18 in the United States.

A short-lived 1998 return to Island brought *Higher & Higher*, a mix of old and new material. Both that record and *Journey of a Lifetime*, issued in the same year, went unreleased in America. Reverting to the indie route, in 2004 Cliff released *Black Magic*, one of his more notable albums in recent times. In a clear crossover thrust, it featured guest appearances from pop stars Sting, Wyclef, and Annie Lennox, as well as an appearance from Joe Strummer, formerly of the punk band the Clash, recorded before Strummer's death in 2002.

Cliff has come a long way from the meager earnings of his career beginnings in the early 1960s. In a 1981 interview, he insisted that "reggae is not a fad music—something that's big this year and gone the next. It's a music of the people." Cliff's induction into the Rock & Roll Hall of Fame in 2010 proved that point. It also represented a reward for survival, perseverance, and commitment to his creative mission. In August 2011, he embarked on a new challenge, collaborating with Tim Armstrong from the ska- and reggae-influenced punk rock band Rancid.

SELECT DISCOGRAPHY: *Hard Road to Travel* (Island, 1967); *Wonderful World, Beautiful People* (Trojan/A&M, 1969); *Another Cycle* (Island, 1971); *The Harder They Come* (Island, 1972); *Unlimited* (EMI/Warner Bros., 1973); *Struggling Man* (Island, 1973); *House of Exile* (EMI, 1974); *Music Maker* (Reprise, 1974); *Follow My Mind* (Reprise, 1975); *In Concert: The Best of Jimmy Cliff* (Reprise, 1976); *Give Thankx* (Warner Bros., 1978); *I Am the Living* (MCA, 1980); *Give the People What They Want* (MCA, 1981); *Special* (Columbia Records, 1982); *The Power and the Glory* (Columbia, 1983); *Cliff Hanger* (Columbia, 1985); *Hanging Fire* (Columbia, 1988); *Breakout* (JRS, 1992); *Higher & Higher* (Island, 1998); *Journey of a Lifetime* (Island, 1998); *Humanitarian* (Eureka, 1999); *Black Magic* (Artemis, 2004); *Better Days Are Coming: The A&M Years 1969–1971* (Hip-O Select, 2006)

RIGHT: Jimmy Cliff at the Greek Theatre in Los Angeles, 1986.

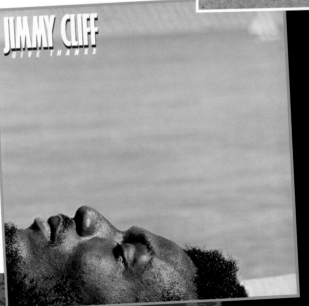

"I grew up economically poor, spiritually rich. Even though I had this condition, that kind of balance made me always take the downside and put an up to it."

—JIMMY CLIFF

REGGAE ON FILM

The ten years spanning 1972 to 1982—a period that saw Bob Marley rise to fame and introduce reggae to audiences around the world—brought the rich cinematic harvest of *The Harder They Come* (1972), *Rockers* (1978), and *Countryman* (1982), three feature films that captured to varying degrees the realities of Jamaican music, culture, and society. It's worth noting that all three were preceded by *Reggae*, a 1971 documentary by black British filmmaker Horace Ové. His film focused on the Caribbean Music Festival held at London's Wembley Stadium on April 26, 1970, and featured a combination of interviews and performances by artists including the Pioneers, Desmond Dekker, Toots and the Maytals, and Millie Small. Unfortunately, Ové's crucial contribution to reggae's filmography is no longer available, though fragments can be found on the Internet.

The Harder They Come, produced and directed by Perry Henzell and supported by Island Records founder Chris Blackwell, who released the movie's soundtrack on his label, set the foundation and yardstick for reggae-related dramas. Henzell, who died in 2006, recalled, "Jamaicans had never ever seen themselves on the screen, their lives represented on the screen." This sense of reality—conveyed by both the lack of professional actors and the authentic sounds of the street—attracted audiences within and beyond Jamaica. Although the film was more a cult phenomenon than it was a mainstream commercial hit, its story of ruthless music-business exploitation in the midst of poverty both shocked and compelled viewers, many of whom had imagined Jamaica as an island paradise. Singer Jimmy Cliff plays the lead role, that of a ripped-off singer who becomes an outlaw. Casting him directly connected the film and the sound track, giving his songs in the movie a greater weight and sense of truth. As Henzell expressed it, Cliff "had lived the experience." Part of the dramatic impact of *The Harder They Come* arises from the singer's identification with his character. "I was a

ABOVE: The gold standard of reggae films, this 1972 cult classic conveyed the harsh realities of Jamaican life.

OPPOSITE: Leroy "Horsemouth" Wallace feels the wind through his dreads in 1978's *Rockers*.

The Harder They Come star Jimmy Cliff identified with his rebellious singer-turned-outlaw character.

as director Francis Ford Coppola's epic *Apocalypse Now*. In some ways, the reggae scene, with its predominant messages of truth, rights, and love, constituted an apocalypse of its own, bringing a distinctive type of quasi-religious consciousness into popular music. In addition, singer Burning Spear's (a cappella) scene was apparently filmed on July 7, 1977, a date some Rastafarians believed would bring about the apocalypse. Jamaican black liberation advocate Marcus Garvey had allegedly prophesied it as the day the "two sevens clash"—an idea echoed in the album of the same name by the band Culture. But far from being a doom-and-gloom affair, *Rockers* was essentially a celebration of music and life in the midst of challenging odds.

Countryman, directed by Dickie Jobson—a longtime colleague of Blackwell—centers on an American couple that survives a plane crash in Jamaica. When the couple's ill-advised, ganja-smuggling mission fails under army surveillance, the Jamaican government seizes the opportunity to claim that the flight involves Central Intelligence Agency (CIA) agents collaborating with the Jamaican political opposition. In a case of fact meeting fiction, the 1970s were characterized by bloody political and social turmoil in Jamaica, and the CIA was responsible for importing arms

bit of a rebellious youth, so I was kind of always on the side of the underdog when I was growing up," Cliff said. "So I kind of liked those kind[s] of rebellious character[s]." Released in the immediate aftermath of the hippie era, the film resonated with a generation of American college students bent on social rebellion. The movie's inevitable abundance of ganja on screen also contributed to its appeal. The underground impact of *The Harder They Come* was one of the cornerstones on which the wider reggae market was built. Underlining the film's importance, a remake headed by Justine Henzell—the original filmmaker's daughter—was scheduled for release in 2012.

Jeremy Marre's 1977 documentary *Roots Rock Reggae: Inside the Jamaican Music Scene*, which was shot in Kingston, captures the critical moment when reggae went from an obscure novelty to a Rastafarian-driven social force. As the music was beginning to reach a global audience, Jamaica was beset by increasingly violent political rivalry. Much of the documentary's value stems from the direct commentary of the musicians, including Bob Marley, Jimmy Cliff, Lee Perry, and Inner Circle,

among others, who discuss their creative and spiritual philosophies and motivations. By sharing their perspectives, they communicate what reggae means in the context of Jamaican society.

The rootsy *Rockers* revealed the clear influence of *The Harder They Come* on producer Patrick Hulsey. The project began as a documentary and mushroomed into a feature film; according to its Greek director, Theodore Bafaloukos, "It is authentic; it's for real. It's something that really came from the scene." The film establishes its musical credentials from the outset, as the title sequence fuses the live vocals of the Abyssinians and the Nyabinghi drumming of Ras Michael & the Sons of Negus on the Rasta anthem "Satta Massa Gana" (1971). Starring session drummer Leroy "Horsemouth" Wallace, the film required subtitles for audiences unfamiliar with the cadences and nuances of Jamaican English.

Rockers debuted at the Cannes Film Festival in France on the same night

ABOVE: Aubrey Reid stars in 1997's provocative *Dancehall Queen*.
RIGHT: A spiritual scene from 1972's *The Harder They Come*.

to undermine Prime Minister Michael Manley's left-leaning administration. The film's premise, therefore, draws directly on the political realities of the era, as violence, race, class, and the CIA's ties to political corruption are all key elements. The couple's rescue by the Jamaican lead character, Countryman, is somewhat reminiscent of an event from Blackwell's own life. In the late 1950s, after he became lost in a Jamaican swamp following a speedboat malfunction, a group of Rastas saved his life. Made by Blackwell's Island Pictures, *Countryman* features an undercurrent of mystical spirituality that is also significant to the film. Michael Thomas, one of the film's writers, noted in *Rolling Stone*, "It could have hung together a lot better than it did. There was something wrong with the story. But there was nothing wrong with the idea."

The film also showcases music from Island Records artists, chief among them Marley, who is cited in the closing credits as the inspiration behind the film. The sound track's reggae focus was no doubt an effort to enhance the film's authenticity. This was also achieved by shooting entirely on location in Jamaica and, following in the footsteps of *The Harder They Come*, having the local actors, who made up the bulk of the cast, speak in their own distinctive patois. Credit for the film's excellent score belongs to Wally Badarou, who is perhaps best known for his production work with British pop-funk outfit Level 42.

Released the year after Marley's death, *Countryman* in some ways marked the end of the roots heyday in Jamaican popular music. As dancehall rose to prominence, the marijuana-laced utopianism and consciousness of 1970s reggae would be replaced in the 1980s by a much harsher, cocaine-driven sound. The music was propelled by digital technology, and its lyrics promoted a more materialistic agenda. This shift is visually and sonically evident in such films as *Kla$h* (1995),

The documentary, released on DVD in 1999, is particularly insightful in its examination of the commercial objectives of the album and the ways in which the music and packaging were used to advance them. Despite the hours of film material already available on Marley, a comprehensive documentary containing insights from all of the surviving key participants in his career, directed by Scotsman Kevin Macdonald, best known for

from Tosh, whose voice is heard mainly in intense audiotape excerpts. The film also includes interview and performance footage, but the audiotapes of the singer speaking—the *Red X* tapes, found at the home where Tosh was murdered in 1987—are particularly affecting. Recorded by the singer between 1983 and 1987 and intended for use in an autobiography, they effectively link his life and death. The term *Red X* arose from Tosh's self-perception; justifiably, he viewed himself as a truth-telling, persecuted man, and he would often see red *X*'s next to his name in official government documents. The movie trailer uses only Nyabinghi drumming and the recurring sounds of gunshots, foreshadowing the film's exploration of Tosh's psyche and the harsh injustices he experienced— and challenged—without compromise.

Several early reggae documentaries have resurfaced on DVD in recent years, expanding on some sparsely recorded historical phases with rare archival footage and interviews. *Reggae in a Babylon* (1978) was filmed in Britain in the 1970s and chronicles the music's development in England's West Indian communities. It contains key performance footage of Aswad and Steel Pulse, two of the first British reggae acts to sign major record contracts. Among the films more

Dancehall Queen (1997), *Third World Cop* (1999), and *Shottas* (2002), all of which arguably magnified the violence and corruption addressed in the narratives of the earliest reggae films.

In addition to those higher-profile feature films, several quality documentaries have been made about Marley, focusing on the life, music, influences, and Rastafarian worldview of reggae's greatest superstar. *Time Will Tell* (1992) and *Rebel Music* (2000) do not simply present a romanticized image of the singer but rather allow Marley and those close to him to tell their own stories, either through interviews or audio commentary. Also notable is an episode of the *Classic Albums* documentary series devoted to Marley's Island Records debut, *Catch a Fire* (US release in 1973).

directing the Oscar winning film *The Last King of Scotland* (2006), was scheduled for a 2012 release.

Beyond the realm of Marley lies perhaps the most haunting biographical reggae documentary of all, *Stepping Razor: Red X* (1993), a look at the ultimate roots rebel, Peter Tosh. Co-executive-produced by musician, filmmaker, and friend Wayne Jobson, the film is built around narration

ABOVE LEFT: Featuring numerous reggae stars, 1978's *Rockers* was a celebration of life and music amid challenging circumstances.

ABOVE: *Rockers* debuted at the Cannes Film Festival in 1979 and is known for its realistic representation of the reggae world during its late-1970s peak.

centered on Jamaica are *Deep Roots Music* (1983), *Land of Look Behind* (1982), and *Word Sound Power* (1980).

More recently, *Made in Jamaica* (2006) attempted to bridge gaps between the worlds of roots reggae and dancehall. The film features a wide array of artists, from dancehall's Lady Saw to roots reggae band Third World. Fans interested in dub and the history of its influence welcomed Bruno Natal's *Dub Echoes* (2007), which includes interviews with musicians and producers in Jamaica, Britain, the United States, and South America to trace the international underground impact of what is arguably popular music's most powerful subgenre.

Many other noteworthy documentaries are not actually focused on reggae but contain subject matter inextricably linked to the music. *Life and Debt* (2001) examines the negative impact that globalization and international financial institutions have had on developing countries, Jamaica in particular. If you have ever wondered what caused much of the suffering referenced in the music of the 1970s (and beyond), look no further. The reggae songs on the *Life and Debt* sound track speak directly to the plight addressed in the film. The PBS documentary *Marcus Garvey: Look for Me in the Whirlwind* (2000), offers an in-depth look at the Jamaican black civil rights crusader and

ORISHA DISTRIBUTION
Sanvi PANOU
Présente

nova 101.5

orisha

La vie et la Mort de Peter Tosh

(STEPPING RAZOR-RED X)

LE FILM
SORTIE NATIONALE LE 25 MAI

Nicolas STILIADIS et Syd CAPPE present pour 5C ENTERTAINMENT INTERNATIONAL
Un film de Nicholas CAMPBELL : La vie et la mort de Peter Tosh/ Stepping Razor RED X.
Avec Peter TOSH et la participation de Bob MARLEY et Mick JAGGER.
Editeur Trevor AMBROSE–co-Producteur Exécutif Wayne JOBSON.
Producteur Exécutif Nicolas STILIADIS et Syd CAPPE. Produit par Edgar EGGER.

Rastafarian icon. Curiously, its formal orchestral score features only the occasional flash of reggae, the music that has kept Garvey's name alive more than any other. *Coping with Babylon* (2007) sets out specifically to illuminate key aspects of Rastafarianism for mainstream audiences.

As the twenty-first century entered its second decade, three films emerged that addressed Jamaica's recent political and musical histories. *A Dance for Grace* (2010), by Jamaican director and actor Orville Matherson, tells the story of dancehall reggae teenagers and is aimed at a mainstream cinematic demographic. *Rise Up* (2009), shot entirely on location in Jamaica, proposes to shed light on

"stories from Jamaica's music underground," as performers otherwise on the margins get to speak for themselves. Interestingly, while Argentinean native Luciano Blotta directed the award-winning film, Justine Henzell coproduced it.

The historical narrative embedded in *Better Mus' Come* (2010), an incendiary film directed by Kingston native Storm Saulter, is even more compelling. The film is set amid the sociopolitical conflicts that ripped Jamaica apart in the late 1970s—an era that simultaneously brought horrendous acts of violence and some of the island's best music. Wayne Armond, a member of Chalice, a group best known for its 1980s releases, created much of the movie's musical sound track.

Thanks to advances in filmmaking technology that have led to greater cost-effectiveness, more perspectives connecting Jamaican life and popular music are rapidly emerging, and the Jamaica Film Festival, which began in 2008, is an important venue for their initial exposure.

TRUTHS & RIGHTS

STRANGER COLE

YEARS ACTIVE: 1960s–1970s

Wilburn Cole, born in 1945 in Jamaica, is one of the unheralded artists whose work laid the foundations for others throughout the ska and reggae eras. He acquired his nickname from his family, who initially felt that Cole bore little resemblance to his musically talented relatives—hence the moniker "Stranger." In the early 1960s, his brother Leroy, a recording engineer who worked for producer Duke Reid, took Stranger to audition for the "Trojan," as Reid was known

to sound-system fans. Reid was initially hesitant to record Cole, but he softened his stance after discovering the newcomer's songwriting skills. In 1963, Cole scored hits with the ska blockbuster "Rough and Tough," and "When You Call My Name," a duet with singer Patsy Todd. It is believed that Reid's unauthorized use of Lee Perry's lyrics on one of Cole's songs led to Perry's defection to rival Coxsone Dodd's camp, where he would become a star producer. Cole's additional hits included "World's Fair," a duet with singer Ken Boothe that was recorded for Dodd.

By the mid-1960s, Cole had drifted between producers as a freelancer, and

in 1968, he scored a major hit with "Bangarang," which Cole claims was the first reggae record ever made in Jamaica, though like many declarations of historical milestones in Jamaican music, this is difficult to verify. He eventually sought greener pastures, moving first to England in 1971 and then to Canada in 1973. There, he set up his own label and released several albums, but it is his 1960s music that earned him his place in history.

SELECT DISCOGRAPHY: *Bangarang: The Best of Stranger Cole 1962–1972* (Sanctuary, 2003)

DUTCHESS

ROUGH AND TOUGH
(Copyright Control)
STRANGER COLE
SIDE A

TOP: Stranger Cole at his Toronto record store, 1982. Shoplifters, beware!

ABOVE: Among Cole's early hits was the 1963 ska blockbuster "Rough and Tough."

DAVE & ANSEL COLLINS
YEARS ACTIVE: 1971

Dave Barker and Ansel Collins formed an unlikely duo that helped to create one of reggae's biggest (mostly) instrumental hits in 1971. That song, "Double Barrel," also played a role in popularizing DJ rapping, or "toasting," at a time prior to the commercial explosion of American rap music.

Both artists were born in Kingston, Jamaica, in 1948. (The name they performed under gives the misleading impression that the two were brothers with the same last name.) Collins worked as a performing vocalist and drummer in the early 1960s before learning to play piano and putting his keyboard skills to work, initially in sessions for producer Bunny Lee and later on record for producer Lee Perry. Dave Barker (born David Crooks), meanwhile, had worked with producer Harry Johnson (known as Harry J) and with Perry, cutting the soulful reggae-market hit "Prisoner of Love" around 1969. Barker's exuberant, soul-influenced, spoken-word intro to Perry's "Shocks of Mighty," as well as his James Brown–style grunts and screams, set the template for the 1971 UK hit single "Double Barrel."

The duo became known for "Double Barrel" and "Monkey Spanner," both released on the Techniques label, run by Winston Riley. "Double Barrel" is also notable for being one of the first records to feature future drumming ace Sly Dunbar. Collins and Dunbar arranged the track independently, but since they didn't have the money to release it, Collins passed it on to Riley, who enlisted Barker to add vocals to the track. Barker initially struggled with the two-track recording of "Double Barrel" at producer Joe Gibbs's studio in Kingston; he couldn't find working ideas to accompany the rhythm track until he adopted an exaggerated soul DJ persona. But the

recording earned him the princely sum of twenty dollars for his vocal work at a time when he was completely broke. "Double Barrel" topped the British pop charts in 1971, while "Monkey Spanner" peaked at #7 that same year.

As a result of the remarkable chart success of "Double Barrel," Barker and Collins were suddenly summoned to England from Jamaica by Trojan Records to appear on *Top of the Pops*, the influential weekly television chart show. Barker had to acquire a passport, and neither he nor Collins had clothing suitable for England's cold weather. Some of the other musicians who took part in that lip-synced television appearance (but didn't actually play on the record) wore grass skirts, diminishing the creativity behind the song and demeaning the artists. Shortly thereafter, as themes of black identity and liberation moved to the fore, no self-respecting reggae act would be seen anywhere near such garb.

The top-ten success of Dave & Ansel Collins's next single, "Monkey Spanner," led to further UK touring, at the conclusion of which Barker chose to remain in the country. He was completely caught off guard by the British chart success that occurred about a year after the Jamaican recording of "Double Barrel" took place; in later years, he recalled his deep disillusionment over the lack of money that he and Collins netted while they were a hot item. Riley's promises of good living conditions were never fulfilled; instead, the duo traveled all over England, cramming in three shows a night and earning a mere forty pounds a week (minus airfare deducted by Riley).

The duo split up after cutting a single album, also predictably titled *Double Barrel* (1971), which was really a rushed assemblage of tracks. Collins later returned to Jamaica and became an in-demand session musician, playing with the now-legendary house band at the renowned Channel One studio in Kingston. Known as the Revolutionaries, this group helped define the 1970s roots reggae sound. Barker joined the hotly tipped group Chain Reaction in the mid-1970s in his conventional singing role, but the band's relationship with Gull Records collapsed, and they broke up.

Dave & Ansel Collins staged an unsuccessful comeback in 1981, and it is not known whether this reunion yielded any new recordings. Barker's subsequent bitterness regarding music-industry exploitation, detailed in the 2011 documentary *Reggae Britannia*, is understandable, considering the business once promised him so much.

MEMBERS: **Dave Barker** (vocals); **Ansel Collins** (organ)

SELECT DISCOGRAPHY: *Double Barrel* (Trojan, 1971)

BTS 2005
double barrel
Dave and Ansell Collins

LEFT: "Double Barrel" (1971) popularized DJ rapping long before the rise of hip hop.

BELOW: Dave Barker (left) and Ansel Collins formed the unlikely duo Dave & Ansel Collins, who topped the UK charts with "Double Barrel."

demonstrated that another kind of apocalypse had already arrived. This simply made Culture's lyrical focus on justice and spiritual righteousness— "truth and rights"—all the more relevant, as reflected by an appearance at 1978's One Love Peace Concert, a national unification effort headlined by Bob Marley to help quell Jamaica's social unrest.

Culture moved to Sonia Pottinger's Kingston-based stable of Jamaican artists, and the resulting product, *Harder Than the Rest* (1978), was licensed for international release to Virgin Records' specialist reggae label, Front Line. Backed by the Revolutionaries studio session band, which included the drum-and-bass combination of Sly & Robbie (drummer Sly Dunbar and bassist Robbie Shakespeare), Culture toured Britain; they released *Cumbolo* and their last

Front Line album, *International Herb*, in 1979. The previously stable lineup dissolved around 1982, coinciding with the digital mutation of reggae culture during the dancehall era. Despite a definite loss of marketplace momentum, the original configuration of Culture temporarily reunited in 1985 before fracturing again in the 1990s. Later releases filled out the catalog and shuffled personnel, and overall, they did little to enhance Culture's reputation.

Hill released his final album with Culture, *World Peace*, in 2003. He died on August 19, 2006, after suffering liver failure and collapsing onstage in Berlin, Germany.

MEMBERS: **Joseph Hill** (vocals), **Albert Walker** (vocals), **Kenneth Paley** (vocals)

SELECT DISCOGRAPHY: *Two Sevens Clash* (Lightning, 1977); *Cumbolo* (Virgin, 1979); *International Herb* (Virgin, 1979)

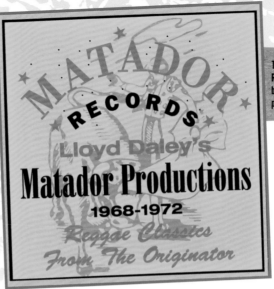

This 1992 reissue by Heartbeat Records collected key works by the skilled electrician and producer Lloyd Daley.

LLOYD DALEY
YEARS ACTIVE: 1956-1975

Born in Kingston, Jamaica, sometime between the late 1930s and early 1940s, Lloyd "the Matador" Daley was one of the first Jamaican sound-system operators to start selling locally recorded records. Capitalizing on his youthful fascination with technology, Daley became an electrician and built his own sound-system amplifier, which he used to play small party gatherings starting in 1956. Daley challenged the sound-system icon (and later, Studio One producer) Coxsone Dodd to a "clash," or public DJ "battle" around 1956 or 1957, though the outcome is unknown. He chose the title "Matador" to differentiate himself from such sound-system rivals as Duke Reid, Dodd (often called Sir Coxsone in his sound-system work), and King Edwards, who had all adopted aristocratic names. Daley's nickname also suggested the idea of a successful Spanish matador who kills his opponent, the bull, in a public combat arena, in this case the Jamaican dance hall.

Daley began recording in 1958 out of sheer necessity, as he lacked quality material and found rivals reluctant to trade valued discs with him. He first worked with such artists as singer Owen Gray, trombonist Rico Rodriguez, and

tenor saxophonist Roland Alphonso, all of whom later played crucial roles in developing Jamaica's own musical styles. The sound quality of the Matador's system was significant enough that in 1960, a young King Tubby (later a master dub remix engineer) requested a reverb circuit diagram from Daley that he later used to build his own unit. During this phase, Daley also built and repaired amps for other sound systems. By 1966, he had sold off his own system, focusing instead on recording activities. He scored a major hit in reggae markets in both Jamaica and Britain with singer Little Roy's "Bongo Nyah" (1969), still one of the most recognizable songs of the time. A healthy portion of the songs he chose to record addressed consciousness of Africa as a recurring theme: the Abyssinians' "Y Mas Gan" (1969) and Alton Ellis's "Back to Africa" (1971) are key examples.

Feeling burned by his experiences in the music business, Daley withdrew from the industry altogether around 1975. He cited the ruthless battles for supremacy and the difficulties of financial survival in a disorganized Jamaican business lacking copyright protection and compensation. He asserts that he never made any money from his recording enterprises, though happily for him, his electrical skills gave him a viable career alternative that was not available to many others in the industry.

SELECT DISCOGRAPHY: *Lloyd Daley's Matador Productions 1968-1972* (Heartbeat, 1992)

OPPOSITE: Culture lead singer Joseph Hill shakes his dreads at the Omni in Oakland, California, 1989.

ABOVE: The title of Culture's landmark debut, *Two Sevens Clash*, refers to the Rasta belief that July 7, 1977, would bring about the apocalypse.

DESMOND DEKKER
YEARS ACTIVE: 1963-2006

Though most people think of Bob Marley as the first reggae artist to have reached a wide white audience, Desmond Dekker had the genre's first major hit singles in the UK and US markets, cowriting the songs, and was the first reggae act to top the British charts. Born Desmond Dacres in Kingston, Jamaica, he deliberately cited three different birthdates in various interviews, though July 16, 1941 is thought to be accurate. His distinctively Jamaican accent and patois created an extremely unlikely sound on mainstream British and American radio in the late 1960s and became many listeners' first encounter with reggae outside of Jamaica.

Dekker began his singing career in Jamaica as the frontman of the Aces, a studio group assembled by producers Duke Reid and Lloyd Daley. Dekker achieved his eventual hit status

"Because of my accent, a lot of people ask me many times what do I say? Do I say 'get up in the morning, baked beans for breakfast?'"
—DESMOND DEKKER,
on people misunderstanding the lyrics to his hit song "Israelites"

LEFT: Desmond Dekker keeps it snappy in London, 1985. His 1969 single "Israelites" was the first reggae record to make an impact in America.

ABOVE: Desmond Dekker's "rude-boy" anthem "007 (Shanty Town)" cracked the British top twenty in 1967, much to the singer's surprise.

Initially rejected by the BBC for its lack of production quality, "Israelites" topped the British charts and hit #9 in America.

under the guidance of Leslie Kong, the Chinese Jamaican businessman who ran Beverley's Records in Kingston. One of Dekker's earliest chart-topping records in Jamaica was 1963's "Honour Your Mother and Your Father," released on Chris Blackwell's Island Records in Britain the following year.

Dekker's initial international success came with the 1967 release of "007 (Shanty Town)," credited to Desmond Dekker & the Aces, which penetrated the UK top twenty during the "rude-boy" era when Jamaican artists sang about the country's criminal underclass. That same year, Dekker made his first visit to Britain. He was amazed that the song had become a hit there, since he "thought people wouldn't understand the lyrics," that were sung in Jamaican patois with a distinctive local accent. However, his real breakthrough came in 1969, as "Israelites" topped the British charts in March. In June, it peaked at #9 in the United States. The song sold more than five million copies,

also topping the charts in Canada, Holland, Belgium, and Germany. These were new global heights for a reggae record up to that point, and it was even a hit in apartheid-era South Africa—a more than slightly ironic fact given the song's themes of poverty and oppression. Dekker recalled that "Israelites" was a commentary on Jamaica's social and economic problems: "I just wrote what I saw happening, but people in the UK liked the tune, even if they didn't really understand what the song was all about."

The public may have embraced the single, but its path to mainstream airplay wasn't smooth. The British Broadcasting Corporation (BBC) initially rejected the record, claiming it lacked production quality, but was later forced to play it due to growing public demand at the club level. In fact, "Israelites" reentered the British charts in rerecorded form in 1975, reaching #10. What's especially puzzling, particularly in the United States, is how the song achieved this

success with a vocal intonation, patois delivery, and rhythmic syncopation that must have been incredibly foreign to mainstream white audiences.

Despite the single's success, reggae was far from becoming an album-oriented force in these markets: the *Israelites* LP, for example, peaked only at #153 on the US charts during its brief three-week stay. Nonetheless, the title track was the first reggae record to have any real commercial impact in the United States, preceding Jimmy Cliff's first hit single there ("Wonderful World, Beautiful People") by six months and Cliff's first hit album by four years. By contrast, Bob Marley never had an American pop hit single and did not crack the album charts until 1975.

Dekker's follow-up singles "It Mek" (1969) and the Jimmy Cliff–composed "You Can Get It If You Really Want" (1970) were both top-ten hits in Britain but had no impact at all in the

United States. Despite having moved to England to advance his career in 1969, Dekker was still collaborating with Kong, his mentor, who organized the recording of backing tracks in Jamaica for vocal overdubs by Dekker in London. Following Kong's sudden death in 1971, Dekker's career declined and never truly recovered, despite partially reigniting during the British 2 Tone ska and rocksteady revival of the late 1970s and early 1980s. As a result, he recorded two unsuccessful albums for punk–New Wave label Stiff Records and declared bankruptcy in 1984, following years of mismanagement. He died of a heart attack in 2006 at age sixty-four, his permanent place in reggae history secure.

SELECT DISCOGRAPHY: *Action!* (Beverley's, 1968); *This Is Desmond Dekker* (Trojan, 1969); *You Can Get It If You Really Want* (Trojan, 1970); *Black and Dekker* (Stiff, 1980); *Compass Point* (Stiff, 1981)

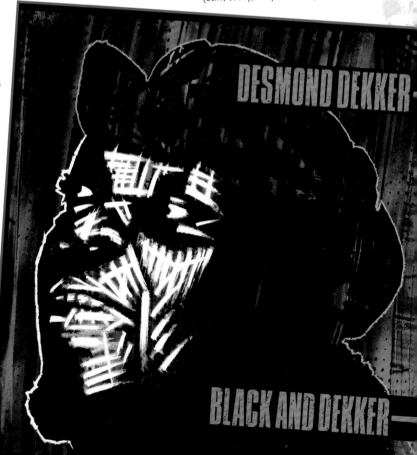

DESMOND DEKKER

BLACK AND DEKKER

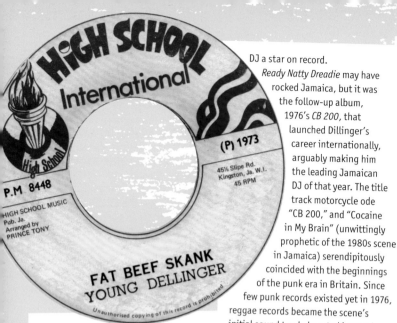

High School International

(P) 1973

P.M 8448

45⅓ Slipe Rd.
Kingston, Ja, W.I.
45 RPM

HIGH SCHOOL MUSIC
Pub. Ja.
Arranged by
PRINCE TONY

FAT BEEF SKANK
YOUNG DELLINGER

Unauthorised copying of this record is prohibited

DILLINGER
YEARS ACTIVE: 1972–2000s

Kingston, Jamaica native Lester "Dillinger" Bullocks, born in 1953, was an early-1970s "toaster" (a Jamaican DJ rapper before the existence of rap) whose talents were first noticed by DJ Dennis Alcapone of the Kingston-based El Paso sound system. His discovery led to studio work at Kingston's two leading reggae studios: Channel One, headed by the Hoo-Kim brothers; and Studio One, owned by Coxsone Dodd. Bullocks was encouraged by producer Lee Perry to adopt the gangster name "Dillinger" rather than label himself Alcapone Jr. after his mentor. An unsuccessful recording spell with Perry in 1973 was followed by work with producer-artist Yabby You a year later, and the single "Freshly" placed Dillinger on the reggae map. Numerous other single experiments occurred in the early 1970s with producers Phil Pratt, Bunny Lee, and Augustus Pablo.

On his 1975 debut, *Ready Natty Dreadie*, recorded with Dodd, Dillinger drew inspiration from such recent predecessors as U-Roy and Big Youth, whose early 1970s recordings made the DJ a star on record.

Ready Natty Dreadie may have rocked Jamaica, but it was the follow-up album, 1976's *CB 200*, that launched Dillinger's career internationally, arguably making him the leading Jamaican DJ of that year. The title track motorcycle ode "CB 200," and "Cocaine in My Brain" (unwittingly prophetic of the 1980s scene in Jamaica) serendipitously coincided with the beginnings of the punk era in Britain. Since few punk records existed yet in 1976, reggae records became the scene's initial sound track, boosted in part by the dreadlocked, British-born Don Letts (later a documentary filmmaker), the DJ at the Roxy, a London punk club. As with many Jamaican artists of the era, Dillinger's output was often split between his local Jamaican releases and those that appeared to target the global mainstream. Although Dillinger's album had been recorded at Channel One, Island Records picked it up for international distribution.

In 1976, a prolific year, Dillinger followed his breakthrough record with *Bionic Dread*, featuring the trademark "Ragnampiza," and then with *Clash*, a collaboration with DJ Trinity, which included the song "Rizla Skank." By the time "Marijuana in My Brain" was released in 1979, the extended drug themes sounded increasingly contrived, though not surprisingly, the song was a smash hit in Holland. ("LSD in My Brain" would emerge in the 1980s.)

Finding himself at a creative crossroads in 1981, Dillinger signed to A&M Records, but the resulting *Badder Than Them*, released later that same year, lacked the energy and power of his earliest releases. The album suffered from a pop-oriented production approach that greatly diluted its impact. Once again, a major label's effort to harness and enhance reggae's commercial potential had actually undermined it, and Dillinger was promptly dropped. Ironically, the synthesizer technology liberally used on the record would soon drive the new decade of Jamaican music in its digital dancehall form. Dillinger remained an active performer in the 1980s and 1990s, even recording live albums to service his ongoing British following, but he had peaked in the 1970s. Artistically or commercially he rarely threatened to challenge recordings like "War Is Over" (1978), which has become a toasting classic. The hollow title of Dillinger's album *Say No to Drugs* (2001) suggested that his career was in need of reinvention.

SELECT DISCOGRAPHY: *Ready Natty Dreadie* (Studio One, 1975); *CB 200* (Island, 1976); *Bionic Dread* (Island, 1976); *Clash* (Burning Sounds, 1976); *Talkin' Blues* (Magnum, 1977); *Answer My Question* (Third World, 1979); *Marijuana in My Brain* (Burning Sounds, 1979); *Badder Than Them* (A&M, 1981); *King Pharoah* (Blue Moon, 1984)

ABOVE: Recording as Young Dellinger, Dillinger served up "Fat Beef Skank" in 1973.

RIGHT: Pioneering toaster Dillinger was a lyrical gangster, not a literal one, but in 1975, he still didn't want you searching his trunk.

DR. ALIMANTADO

YEARS ACTIVE: 1971-1980s

Kingston-born Winston Thompson became Dr. Alimantado (a name he bestowed on himself) in 1973, when he established his Vital Food label and ventured into self-production. Earlier, he had begun his career as a DJ with Kingston's Tippertone sound system, and ace producer Lee Perry invited Thompson to record with him in 1971. He found creative success vocalizing over old rhythm tracks and using a series of identities, but he didn't achieve commercial success until he began to produce as Dr. Alimantado.

Some sources suggest that Alimantado's atmospheric dub-flavored 1977 single "Born for a Purpose" sold more than fifty thousand copies in Britain as a result of prime-time airplay on a Capital Radio show hosted by Johnny Rotten, lead singer of the seminal British punk group the Sex Pistols.

(If the figures are accurate, it's unclear over what time span these sales occurred.) One of the first singles released on the London-based Greensleeves Records label, "Born for a Purpose" never reached the pop charts, but the sales-reporting system in Britain at that time was slanted toward mainstream outlets rather than the ignored specialist reggae outlets. Regardless, as a result of the song's popularity, Alimantado's British audience multiplied, justifying his relocation to Britain.

More than most of Alimantado's songs, "Born for a Purpose" resembled the shape of a traditional pop song and featured vocals rather than DJ chat and chants. Alimantado had originally called the self-produced song "Reason for Living," since the song's inspiration was a near-death incident in which he was hit by a Kingston bus. (The song was recorded at Channel One studio and released in Jamaica on the studio's record label, so co-owner Jo Jo Hoo-Kim

insisted on changing the title.) Alimantado had almost drowned in the sea off the coast of downtown Kingston on the morning of the accident and required a rescuer to pump water out of his stomach. The bus collision occurred just as he was leaving the site of this aquatic mishap, and incredibly, it wasn't the last of his troubles that day. After being admitted to the hospital after being hit by the bus, he suffered food poisoning. The physically impaired artist hobbled to Channel One to lay down tracks without any money. Jo Jo Hoo-Kim let him use the facilities for free, making his massive hit a humanitarian exercise. In this sense, "Born for a Purpose" was a true statement of survival, and Alimantado's vocals on the record were infused with a new level of urgency that was further accentuated by an excellent dub mix.

Alimantado had unsuccessfully negotiated with both Virgin Records and Island Records for the UK release of his material, and he chose Greensleeves when they agreed to help him establish his own company. He became a punk favorite with Greensleeves's very first album release, 1978's *Best Dressed Chicken in Town*. Here, Alimantado benefited from marvelous timing and one of reggae's most idiosyncratic album covers: it depicts the artist ironically shirtless, standing in the middle of a (presumably) Kingston street about to make a transaction. While the album title was apparently inspired by a poultry advertisement, the cover and the song seem to have no literal reference point. After connecting with the album's cool roots groove, no one would have cared much about this or the fact that it

Dr. Alimantado in Kingston, 1977: the best-dressed leopard in town?

was actually recorded in 1974 at Perry's Black Ark studio in Kingston.

Alimantado's 1980s output included the *In the Mix* three-installment series (1985–1986), followed rapidly by six other albums before the end of the decade. Virtually invisible in the 1990s, Alimantado is an artist whose first album stands as arguably his best and best-known work, and this has forced him to compete with his own success thereafter. He is currently thought to be living in West Africa.

SELECT DISCOGRAPHY: *Best Dressed Chicken in Town* (Greensleeves, 1978); *Sons of Thunder* (Greensleeves, 1981); *Born for a Purpose* (Greensleeves, 1987)

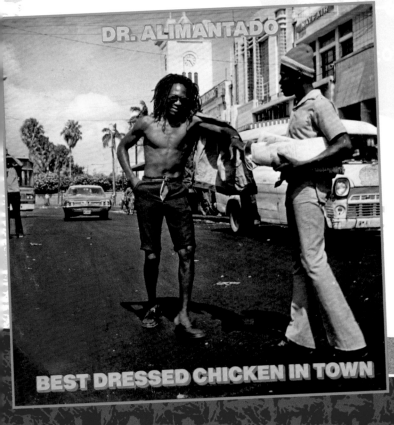

DR. ALIMANTADO

This 1978 album made Alimantado a favorite among UK punk rockers.

BEST DRESSED CHICKEN IN TOWN

CLEMENT "COXSONE" DODD

YEARS ACTIVE: 1954-2004

Considered "the root of Jamaican music" by Island Records founder Chris Blackwell, Clement "Coxsone" Dodd was born on January 26, 1932, in Kingston, Jamaica. He first traveled to the United States as a farm laborer at about age 17, and there began collecting American R&B records to play for the customers of his mother's liquor store on East Queen Street in Kingston. The rise of rock 'n' roll in the United States pushed R&B to the margins, limiting availability of the records on which Jamaica's sound systems survived. Satisfying the appetites of local audiences meant making special original Jamaican recordings, or "dubplates," which would suit audience taste and still provide systems with exclusive material.

Dodd began his own Sir Coxsone Downbeat sound-system operation around 1954, with Count Machuki as his pioneering DJ. Machuki, whose real name was Winston Cooper, had been a "selector" (spinning records) beginning around 1950 in the crew of Tom the Great Sebastian (Tom Wong), one of Jamaica's earliest sound-system operators. After joining Coxsone's sound system some time in the middle of the decade, Machuki began "toasting" (rapping) on the microphone, making witty comments to complement the records, and he became the first star DJ of the Jamaican dance halls. During this time Dodd also began to face off against the dominant Jamaican operator, Duke Reid, in the proverbial "sound clash," pitting his system against his rival's to see which would receive greater public acclaim.

One of Dodd's key American sources of rare R&B records for the Downbeat system was Randy's, a record store in Gallatin, Tennessee. The owner, Randy Wood, who died in April 2011, formed Dot Records in 1951; ironically, that label specialized in making white cover versions of songs originally recorded by black artists. As such, Wood's Dot releases were an incredibly unlikely catalyst for the development of Jamaican popular music.

By the early 1960s, Dodd had introduced at least six record labels; but the first, World Disc, had perhaps the greatest historical significance. Seminal early releases on World Disc included 1959's "Easy Snappin'" by pianist-singer Theophilus Beckford, which fused American R&B influences with Jamaican rhythmic accents. After Dodd set up his own studio equipped with a one-track machine acquired from Kingston's Federal Studio, he introduced the Studio One label. (Some sources cite late 1962 as the date of the label's introduction, while others suggest 1963.) Prior to his founding of Studio One, located at 13 Brentford Road in Kingston, Dodd's only studio options were Federal and the Jamaica Broadcasting Corporation (JBC). The idea of actually selling records to the public was initially an afterthought, but the burgeoning studio owner quickly realized its commercial potential.

Dodd's empire was officially known as the Jamaica Recording and Publishing Company. As he developed Studio One—widely considered the "university" of reggae—his work signified the Jamaican music industry's transition from sound systems to recording, as well as the vital relationship between both spheres. Studio One might also be considered a university in another sense, since it gave many artists their first lessons on the inequities of the business. As a result, Jamaican popular-music history is littered with stories of artists engaging in financial disputes with Dodd and being forced to seek new alliances in their quests for success and fair compensation. Some artists were reportedly signed to five-year contracts as the norm, earning twenty pounds per side, while all recording, publishing, and management rights resided with Dodd. Other accounts confirm Dodd's overall control but suggest that no artist contracts existed at all.

Studio One's musical reputation was built on the Heptones, the Wailers, Alton Ellis, the Maytals, Horace Andy, and countless other artists who constituted a vital part of Jamaica's musical identity, particularly in the 1960s. Equally important were the various session musicians, who performed on so many records that even the members couldn't accurately state how many recordings there were.

In early 1980 Dodd's Kingston studio was robbed, and Dodd subsequently made New York his base of operations. Another factor in the move was the fact that Jamaica's stringent currency restrictions made it difficult to buy the basic raw materials from which records were pressed, so that even those records that could be produced in Jamaica were only available in limited quantities.

In 1991 Jamaica's government awarded Dodd the Order of Distinction for his contribution to the island's music industry. Dodd returned to Jamaica in 1998, following his mother's death, and reopened the original Brentford Road studio site. He died in May 2004, having played one of the most crucial roles in developing Jamaica's music and shaping the careers of many of reggae's leading lights.

Clement "Coxsone" Dodd, considered "the root of Jamaican music" by Island Records founder Chris Blackwell, mans the controls at his Brooklyn, New York, studio, 1992.

Coxsone RECORDS

CS 7014
CSMX 5022 A

EVERY BODY RUDE NOW
(K. McCarthy)
KEITH McCARTHY
Produced by: Coxson Dodd

BANANA

BA 338A

℗ 1971
Harrisongs
Essex Int.

MY SWEET LORD (Instrumental)
(Harrison)
CYCLONES
Prod. C. S. Dodd

ERIC DONALDSON

YEARS ACTIVE: 1964–PRESENT

Born in 1947 in the parish of St. Catherine, Jamaica, Donaldson has been relegated to the margins of reggae history, perhaps because of his high-pitched voice, the fact that none of his albums were truly outstanding, and the inclusion of pop covers in so much of his repertoire.

Donaldson began his career in 1964 in Kingston, at producer Coxsone Dodd's Studio One, recording music that wasn't released. By the middle of the decade he'd become the lead singer of a group called the West Indians, who scored one Jamaican hit in 1968 with "Right on Time" (produced by J.J. Johnson, whose best-known work was with the Jamaican vocal group the Ethiopians on their 1968 single "Everything Crash") and recorded with legendary producer Lee Perry. A lack of success led the West Indians to abandon working with Perry and change its name to the Kilowatts. Similar failure with at least two other producers led to the band's dissolution, and Donaldson went solo, finally achieving success with "Cherry Oh Baby," the winning song in the 1971 Jamaica Festival Song Competition. The song was reportedly a huge seller in Jamaica on the Dynamic Sounds label, with one source claiming the song moved more than fifty thousand copies, but no truly reliable figures exist.

Despite subsequent festival wins into the 1990s, Donaldson never made the wider mainstream impact that initially seemed possible, though it can be argued that his best song is now known by millions of people thanks to covers by other artists. "Cherry Oh Baby" appeared as the opening track on *Labour of Love*, the 1983 album of covers by the British reggae band UB40. Even the iconic Rolling Stones cut a version, included on 1976's *Black and Blue*. Donaldson's later recordings were not exceptionally appealing, and he's lacked a major hit to lift him from the nostalgia circuit. In recent times, the spotlight, unfortunately, has focused less on his music than on his drug and legal problems. In August 2005, he was arrested on the Eastern Caribbean island of St. Vincent for marijuana possession, and in June 2011 he faced similar charges in Jamaica, reportedly paying a fine of one hundred Jamaican dollars.

SELECT DISCOGRAPHY: *Eric Donaldson* (Dynamic Sounds, 1971); *The Very Best of Eric Donaldson* (Rhino, 2001)

Eric Donaldson's "Right on Time" was a Jamaican hit in 1968, when he was lead singer of the group West Indians.

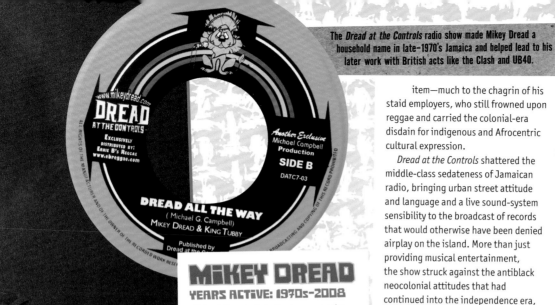

DREAD ALL THE WAY
(Michael G. Campbell)
MIKEY DREAD & KING TUBBY

MIKEY DREAD
YEARS ACTIVE: 1970s-2008

Michael Campbell, better known as the influential radio DJ, artist, and producer Mikey Dread, was born in Port Antonio, on the northern coast of Jamaica, on January 1, 1954. In the decade that followed, his involvement with sound systems and his school's radio station foreshadowed his reggae future. After gaining further exposure to radio on a school tour of a popular local station, Campbell became infatuated with the chemistry of voice and electronics and pursued his scientific education at the College of Arts, Science, and Technology in Kingston.

After being turned down by one of the island's two major stations, Radio Jamaica Rediffusion (RJR), for being overqualified, he secured an internship as a technical operator at the Jamaica Broadcasting Corporation (JBC) in Kingston. During this initial stint, he successfully negotiated with his bosses to extend the station's traditional midnight sign-off point and continue transmitting until 4:30 a.m. Campbell points out that when his show, *Dread at the Controls,* began in 1976 (some sources cite 1977), he was not allowed to speak on air, since his principal role was as an engineer. To combat this obstacle, he injected his personality and voice into the customized show jingles he inserted between the exclusive pre-release sound-system "dubplates" (soft wax acetate recordings). The combination of style and specialization made the show a hot

item—much to the chagrin of his staid employers, who still frowned upon reggae and carried the colonial-era disdain for indigenous and Afrocentric cultural expression.

Dread at the Controls shattered the middle-class sedateness of Jamaican radio, bringing urban street attitude and language and a live sound-system sensibility to the broadcast of records that would otherwise have been denied airplay on the island. More than just providing musical entertainment, the show struck against the antiblack neocolonial attitudes that had continued into the independence era, and the negative views of reggae and local culture in general. Broadcasting six nights a week and playing only Jamaican music—instead of the imported pop music that dominated the nation's airwaves during the daytime—the show was nothing short of a revolution.

At the time, Dread did not have dreadlocks. With them, he probably wouldn't have been able to get a job at any station, in any capacity. Yet he already possessed the Rastafarian attitude that rejected Jamaican establishment norms. Despite predictable resistance to Dread's cultural innovation from radio authorities, the show was a sensational hit. It was regularly recorded on cassettes by fans craving the dubplate exclusives that he featured, and Dread claimed that Jamaica Defence Force personnel supplied him with food and drinks, since his late-night broadcasts reduced the crime rate by keeping people indoors! Dread was so popular that he won Jamaica's award for radio personality of the year in 1977 and 1978. He had the legendary producer King Tubby mix his original promotional radio jingles, and acting on Tubby's encouragement, Dread turned one jingle into a full-length song, "Love the Dread." Dread credited Tubby with providing an unparalleled education in sound.

By 1979, when administrative opposition at JBC increased (despite—or because of—his international popularity through cassette bootlegs), Dread had become respected enough to leave radio and transition into the roles of a live DJ and producer of other acts. That year, he released his appropriately titled debut album, *Dread at the Controls*, which featured a title track produced by Lee Perry. The album was released by Trojan Records along with his dub-oriented *African Anthem* (1979), which penetrated the British underground scenes.

Dread's stock in Britain's punk rock community rose when he appeared on the Clash's 1980 album *Sandinista!* He also produced the group's "Bankrobber" single (originally released by CBS only in its Dutch market), the dub version of which was as close to authentic reggae as any punk band was likely to sound at the time. Beyond studio collaborations, he also toured Europe and the United States with the group. Less well known is the fact that he narrated *Deep Roots Music* (1982), a documentary series about reggae broadcast on British television. The project demonstrated Dread's passion for the music and its creators, as well as his consciousness of the history from which they emerged. He subsequently worked with British reggae band UB40, touring Europe and Japan, and then migrated to Miami to serve as program director for the Caribbean Satellite Network. Following the expiration of album deals and contracts, he assumed control of his back catalog in the late 1980s and reissued the material on his own Dread at the Controls record label.

In the summer of 2007, Dread was diagnosed with a brain tumor, and on March 15, 2008, he died at the age of fifty-four. He was survived by his wife and at least six children, and is remembered for the major part he played in reggae's internationalization.

SELECT DISCOGRAPHY: *Dread at the Controls* (Dread at the Controls, 1979); *African Anthem* (Big Cat, 1979); *World War III* (Dread at The Controls, 1980)

DUB

The roots of all contemporary electronically driven dance music can be traced to dub, and yet despite its enormous influence, this reggae subgenre has never produced its own million-seller. Using the drum-and-bass emphases of roots reggae, dub effectively creates newly textured soundscapes from preexisting rhythm tracks. Words do little to convey the music's impact on receptive listeners, but it is perhaps best described as a studio-centered, remixed manipulation of sound, time, and space.

This sonic art form is the result of accidents, acumen, and artistic brilliance. As the late DJ Mikey Dread once put it in *The Story of Jamaican* Music, a 2004 TV documentary, "Dub is . . . an artistic expression of internal, molecular energy." Part of dub's magic is that revolutionary soundscapes were created by using minimal equipment and money, and the remixing was driven by vibrant imagination and musicianship as well as by a close relationship with the target audiences. Dub would not have been possible without harnessing and manipulating electronic sound-processing equipment capable of reconfiguring the sonic signals that were fed into it. Reverb, echo, and delay were radically and innovatively applied to refashion the musical terrain, with equipment often being electrically retrofitted to suit the customized purposes of the engineer. Dub thus gave rise to an uncommon popular-music phenomenon in which the engineer rather than the original performing artist became the star: fans of dub generally are more concerned with who did the mixing on any given record than with who played the instruments.

Essentially, dub is about soundscapes rather than song form. The word itself can be primarily linked to the process of copying, or "dubbing," a recording, as well as to the Jamaican practice of making copies of exclusive song recordings—acetates called "dubplates"—for live use by the sound systems that

King Jammy's studio was a haven for artists looking to create dub masterpieces in the 1970s, Red Stripe beer and all.

DUB 73

VITAL DUB

Well Charged

ABOVE: While most dub engineers shied away from ganja at work, the wisdom weed still often found its way onto album covers.

RIGHT: This 1974 album was the first dub release in UK history, opening up the international market to the genre's spacious sounds.

KEITH HUDSON & FAMILY MAN

PICK A DUB
PICK A DUB
PICK A DUB

KEITH HUDSON & FAMILY MAN

a sound-system staple. Initially, mixing the "version" did not involve any of the studio techniques that later became primary dub features, such as warping the sound with echo, reverb, and delay effects or dropping vocal and instrumental fragments in and out of the mix.

Initially a DJ would chant, or "toast," over the instrumental version as part of a live dancehall phenomenon. Once sound systems adopted the "versions," commercially issued singles began including them. This practice was propelled into the Jamaican recorded-

tracks would become even more important with the arrival of dub, as more of the toasters themselves, such as Tappa Zukie (a hit DJ whose first success was in Britain in 1975), recorded albums—many of which had the phrase "in Dub" in their titles. This "in Dub" description is still applied by some artists and DJs in the twenty-first century.

By 1973, the first dub albums had appeared in Jamaica, though they were issued in very limited quantities. Among them was Herman Chin-Loy's *Aquarius Dub* (1973), a fairly conservative effort if viewed by later experimental standards, though songs on the collection were reportedly tracked as early as 1971. But producer Clive Chin claims that the *Java Java Java Java* album (1972), sometimes credited to the Impact All Stars, was dub's first album. In 1974, *Pick a Dub* by Keith Hudson became the first UK dub release in history, propelling this remixing style into international markets, mainly through urban Caribbean communities.

Although there is debate as to whether the first dub album was Chin-Loy's *Aquarius Dub* or songwriter-producer Lee Perry's *Blackboard Jungle Dub* (both 1973 releases), the emergence of the radically remixed reggae instrumental is most closely linked to the early 1970s work of engineer Osbourne Ruddock, better known as King Tubby. Tubby initially used a very basic four-track home studio facility—this at a time when major studios in Europe and the United States had already graduated to sixteen and twenty-four-track machines. The popularization of dub versions on B-sides soon led the producer and engineer to become more important than the artist whose work was being remixed. In 1976, following his crucial full-length dub expeditions *The Roots of Dub* (1974) and *Dub from the Roots* (1975), Tubby remixed songs by the iconic Jamaican melodica player Augustus Pablo for the landmark album *King Tubby Meets Rockers Uptown* (1976), recognized as one of the best dub albums ever. Its title track was the seminal single B-side remix of "Baby, I Love You So" featuring singer Jacob Miller. The rhythm track for that song came from "Cassava Piece," one of Pablo's 1971 recordings with Chin-Loy.

Tubby, Lee "Scratch" Perry, and Prince Jammy (later King Jammy) were among the leading figures

have been present in Jamaica since the 1940s. These sound systems entertain the public by playing records, often outdoors, with DJs and formidable arrays of speakers creating larger-than-life volume.

The birth of remixing can be traced to the late 1960s, though the exact moment when dub was born is open to speculation. The specialized needs of sound systems helped develop the "version," the instrumental B-side of a single containing the song's rhythm track—usually minus the vocals. Legend has it that the version arose from a 1967 error in which engineer Byron Smith inadvertently omitted the vocals from the Paragons' 1966 Jamaican hit "On the Beach" at producer Duke Reid's Treasure Isle studio. Smith was transferring a dubplate of the song for sound-system operator Ruddy Redwood, and when Redwood played the mix on his system, the absence of vocals (which the dance hall crowd could sing instead) made the instrumental version

music

mainstream in the early 1970s by U-Roy (whose "Wake the Town" on the Treasure Isle label was an early hit), who was then working with King Tubby's Home Town Hi-Fi sound system. U-Roy himself was building on the live interjections made popular by Count Machuki and King Stitt on Coxsone Dodd's Downbeat sound system decades earlier. Both were veteran "selectors" (they chose which records were played) and DJ innovators, performing their banter on top of songs, but U-Roy was the first to make commercially successful records on which the DJ was the star. The DJs' vocal improvisations over rhythm in dub's late-1970s heyday. Perry's Black Ark studio projected the sonic equivalent of a dense African forest. Perry moved from collaborating with Tubby on such groundbreaking records as *Blackboard Jungle Dub* to exploring soundscapes at Black Ark, which Tubby had helped to build. Jammy became one of Tubby's protégés around 1976 and, thanks to his brilliant remixing intuition, he created such first-class records as Horace Andy's *In the Light Dub* (1977), a timeless classic. Lesser-known but highly influential engineers at the time included Errol Thompson, Sylvan Morris, and King Tubby understudies Philip "Prince Philip" Smart and Overton Brown, better known as Scientist, whose outstanding creativity in recording and remixing reggae left an indelible imprint on dub. Individually and collectively, these figures contributed to a general peeling away of the version's more conventional musical components, deconstructing songs to their elemental rhythmic drum-and-bass centers while fragmenting and expanding the sonic presence of vocals and other instruments. In effect, a good dub version required at least two layers of creative performance: the musical rendition and the engineering reinterpretation, which could—and did—produce numerous dub incarnations of the same song.

Dub's elevation of the Jamaican recording engineer to spotlight status soon began occurring in other dance-oriented genres of popular music in the 1970s. Dub also directly influenced the disco remix, and key engineers in that genre, among them François Kevorkian and Larry Levan, recalled in interviews the impact of Jamaican dub. It must also be mentioned that excellence

in creating dub mixes wasn't restricted to Jamaica. Such British-based innovators as Dennis Bovell and Mad Professor helped shape sonic environments with distinct tonal and spatial dimensions.

The 1980s witnessed a decline in dub releases as dancehall ushered in a digital era less concerned with ambient spatiality and traditional notions of musicianship and stylistic innovation. Ironically, many of the electronic dance subgenres emerging at the time in Europe and the United States employed dub's textures, tones, and tactics to reap commercial success. In the Eastern Caribbean, *dub* often applies to dancehall, and is almost completely detached from the mixing concept that brought the word into popular use in the first place. In addition, while the British electronic dance-music hybrid known as dubstep achieved enough commercial notoriety to become the subject of a *Billboard* magazine article in 2010, the story never once mentioned or alluded to dub. Sadly, dub albums are not released as frequently or valued as highly in the twenty-first century as in their heyday, but classic reissues are now widely available, keeping the echo of dub alive.

ABOVE: King Jammy perfecting his craft behind the soundboard, 1984.
TOP RIGHT: This Prince Jammy (later King Jammy) album cover could easily double for a kung fu movie poster.

LUCKY DUBE

YEARS ACTIVE: 1984–2007

One of Africa's biggest and most commercially successful reggae stars was Lucky Dube, born in South Africa in 1964. Dube clearly drew influence from Jamaican star singer-songwriter and former Wailers member Peter Tosh as he established his global fan base. Many observers have noted that while he mirrored Tosh's tone and articulation, Dube wrote lyrics that were by no means as militant. Though dreadlocked, Dube was not a stereotypical Rasta—he was a complete nonsmoker of marijuana, considered a holy sacrament within Rastafari—and reggae wasn't his first form of recorded musical expression. Even so, his emergence as a reggae artist during the apartheid era in his native South Africa gave his messages of resistance immediate political relevance and resulted in censorship from the government.

One of Dube's early musical experiences was as a choir leader, but he only began playing reggae and singing in English in 1984, recording the solo EP *Rasta Never Dies* that year. Despite an indifferent response from both audiences—the record sold a mere four thousand copies—and from his record company, as well as a government censorship ban, Dube maintained his direction and reaped rewards when his first full-length reggae album, *Slave*, arrived in 1987, selling more than a half a million copies worldwide. The rapid sales success of what would be his biggest album, 1989's *Prisoner*, opened up new opportunities for touring, especially in the European and American markets.

In 1991, he became the first South African act to perform at Jamaica's Reggae Sunsplash—reggae's premier annual festival event at the time—and in 1992 he served as the supporting act for rock and world music icon Peter Gabriel, underlining a phenomenal ascent from

obscurity a decade earlier. During the 1990s, he solidified his status as Africa's top reggae artist, outselling the Ivory Coast's revered Alpha Blondy and Nigeria's Majek Fashek both on record and in concert. His appearance onstage in Johannesburg in 2005 as part of the globally telecast Live 8 concert—singer Bob Geldof's global humanitarian aid and awareness event—was a career highlight, demonstrating the high regard in which he was held. Tragically, Lucky Dube was shot dead in a carjacking on October 8, 2007, in Johannesburg. The killing took place in front of two of his seven children. He was just forty-three.

SELECTED DISCOGRAPHY: *Rastas Never Die* (Gallo, 1984); *Think About the Children* (Gallo, 1985) *Slave* (Shanachie, 1987); *Prisoner* (Shanachie, 1989); *House of Exile* (Shanachie, 1992); *Victims* (Shanachie, 1993); *Together as One* (Zoom, 1994); *Trinity* (Motown, 1995); *Taxman* (Shanachie, 1997); *Respect* (Gallo, 2006); *Retrospective* (Rykodisc, 2008)

ABOVE: Lucky Dube's 1987 debut album sold more than half a million copies worldwide.

RIGHT: Wardrobe aside, Lucky Dube shows no signs of fatigue at Reggae Sunsplash, 1991, when he became the first South African to play the festival.

"The stage keeps me happy. I'm happy when I'm on stage. I don't think of anything; all I think about is the people and the music and the vibe."

—LUCKY DUBE

CLANCY ECCLES

YEARS ACTIVE: 1960–LATE 1970s

One of reggae's most underrated yet influential producers, Clancy Eccles is also known for a handful of hit releases as an artist, as well as for his socialist political outlook. Eccles helped shift Jamaican popular music from rocksteady to reggae and noted that the session contributions of guitarist Ernest Ranglin led to the new rhythm. Some even suggest that Eccles himself was responsible for the name *reggae*, extracting it from *streggae*, which describes a loose woman, though there are many others who lay claim to this honor. The sound he developed on songs like Lord Creator's "Kingston Town" (1970) (later covered by British pop-reggae group UB40) featured rhythmic accents that would rarely be played in the same style after the early years of reggae had passed.

Eccles was born in the Jamaican countryside in 1940. After working for a time in the mid-1950s as a hotel singer on Jamaica's north coast, he was discovered by sound-system operator and new producer Coxsone Dodd in a talent contest in either late 1959 or early 1960. As the eventual runner-up, he signed a three-year contract with Dodd, though money issues led to his departure from Dodd's stable of artists at Studio One in late 1961. His repatriation-themed song "Freedom," recorded at Ken Khouri's Federal Studio in Kingston, was co-opted in 1961 by the then-opposition Jamaica Labour Party (JLP), as it agitated for Jamaica's independence and separation from the other islands of the short-lived West Indies Federation. The political use of the song occurred despite the fact that Eccles was not yet associated with either of Jamaica's two main parties.

Having moved temporarily into concert promotion after leaving Dodd, Eccles made his production debut with "Say What You're Saying" by Monty Morris in 1966

clan disc

Produced by: Clancy Eccles

(P)(C) 1970
MADE IN
JAMAICA

ALL RIGHTS OF THE MANUFACTURER AND OF THE OWNER OF THE RECORDED WORK RESERVED · UNAUTHORISED PUBLIC PERFORMANCE BROADCASTING AND COPYING OF THIS RECORD PROHIBITED

ETERNALLY
(C. Eccles/D. Simpson)
THE DYNAMINTES

Distributed by:
New Beat
Records
7 Retirement
Road
Kingston 5.
Jamaica W.I.
Ph:- 929-1748

SIDE 1

or 1967, using studio time provided by top producer Duke Reid at his Treasure Isle studio in Kingston. Eccles owned at least two record labels, New Beat and Clandisc, and scored hits with such vocalists as Alton Ellis. Eccles was also instrumental in launching the careers of Lee Perry and Winston "Niney" Holness, producers whose work became integral to Jamaican music in the 1970s. By 1969 the UK Trojan Records label had begun releasing material from Eccles's Clandisc imprint, and Eccles's own *Freedom* arrived via Trojan that same year. The album cover depicted Eccles on a motorbike in a landscape seemingly far from the urban scene within which his work gained popularity. His studio house band, the Dynamites, was at the rhythmic core of Clandisc's output, crafting the groove of Eccles's lurid 1969 single "Fatty Fatty," which, oddly enough, was adopted by the British skinhead subculture.

In 1972, Eccles became actively involved in supporting the election campaign and democratic socialist ideals of prime minister candidate Michael Manley's People's National Party (PNP). He organized the party's "Musical Bandwagon," a promotional caravan mixing entertainment with sociopolitical ideology in the song lyrics, and which featured performances by such reggae artists as Inner Circle and the Wailers. After Manley won the election, Eccles was appointed as an unpaid unofficial adviser to the music industry, and this firmly shifted his focus away from music production and toward politics. He died of complications from a stroke in 2005, and his full value as a producer is perhaps only now being recognized.

SELECT DISCOGRAPHY: *Freedom* (Clandisc/Trojan, 1969); *Herbsman Reggae* (w. the Dynamites) (Clandisc/Trojan, 1970); *Freedom (The Anthology: 1969–1973)* (Trojan, 2005)

Clancy Eccles (center, denim jacket), one of the most underrated producers in reggae history, takes five with the better-known Lee Perry (in black tank top), whose career he helped launch, 1976.

Jamaica's ambassadors of song VOL.1

Jackie Edwards

Jackie and Millie

Millie Small

Millie Small
KILLER JOE
MY BOY LOLLIPOP
WHAT A PRICE

Jackie Edwards
L.O.V.E.
SOMEBODY HELP ME
THINK TWICE

Owen Gray
YOU DON'T KNOW LIKE I KNOW
SHOOK, SHIMMY AND SHAKE
GONNA WORK OUT FINE

Jimmy Cliff
LET'S DANCE
PRIDE AND PASSION

Jackie and Millie
THIS IS MY STORY

Owen Gray

Jimmy Cliff

JACKIE EDWARDS

YEARS ACTIVE: 1950s–1970s

Born Wilfred Edwards in Kingston, Jamaica, singer-songwriter Jackie Edwards grew up on Maxfield Avenue as a neighbor of singer Alton Ellis, a star of the mid-1960s rocksteady era. Edwards made his public debut on the *Vere Johns Opportunity Hour*, a widely heard radio show that offered many of Jamaica's future singing stars their first chance to gain exposure and provided them with a gateway to recording. After scoring a series of hit singles in Jamaica and debuting as a songwriter, he was brought to England in 1962 by Island Records founder Chris Blackwell. Edwards initially recorded a gospel EP for Decca Records, which he followed in 1964 with a full-length gospel LP, *Stand Up for Jesus*, for Island. Edwards even became a part of Blackwell's small-scale distribution system and delivered boxes of singles to record stores by bus.

The move to England turned out to be crucial for Edwards, as his songwriting talents made him one of the few Jamaican artists in the 1960s to succeed commercially beyond the confines of the island's musical styles. Most notably, he wrote "Keep on Running" (1965) and "Somebody Help Me" (1966) for the rock band the Spencer Davis Group, and both singles reached #1 on the British pop chart. Edwards recorded a series of seven soul, gospel, and reggae albums for Island (including one with singer Millie Small who scored the 1964 global hit, "My Boy Lollipop"), but despite their positive critical reception, those records were overshadowed by his work for other artists. His singles, which were released on a variety of Island's subsidiary labels, also made little

impact. After 1969's *Put Your Tears Away*, Edwards left Island and moved to CBS Records for his 1970 LP *Let It Be Me*. He moved back to Jamaica in the 1970s, and while his performance and songwriting skills remained intact, his musical direction was out of step with the heavy Rasta rhetoric and the sociopolitical subject matter that was occupying more of reggae's lyrical and rhythmic space. Edwards never matched the success of his major pop-songwriting achievements. Unlike most of his contemporaries, however, he at least reaped the financial rewards of his work, receiving ongoing royalty payments until his death in August 1992 from a heart attack.

SELECT DISCOGRAPHY: *Stand Up for Jesus* (Island, 1964); *The Most of Jackie Edwards* (Island, 1965); *Come On Home* (Island, 1965); *The Best of Jackie Edwards* (Island, 1966); *By Demand* (Island, 1966); *Pledging My Love* (by Jackie and Millie) (Island, 1966); *Premature Golden Sands* (Island, 1967); *The Best of Jackie & Millie* (Island, 1967); *Put Your Tears Away* (Island, 1969); *This Is My Story* (Trojan, 2005)

OPPOSITE: Jackie Edwards is surrounded by sound at his home in Kingston, where he returned in the 1970s after achieving success as a songwriter in Britain.

JACKIE EDWARDS
i must go back
baby i want to
be near you

ALTON ELLIS
YEARS ACTIVE: 1959-2008

Commenting on the Jamaican music business, Alton Ellis was once quoted as saying, "You have to be God blessed to pick up any royalties . . . but there wasn't a lot of money in it." Sadly underappreciated, his music was clearly characterized by messages of love and unity. Born in Kingston, Jamaica, in either the late 1930s or early 1940s, and himself blessed with a distinctively expressive vocal character, Ellis began his musical career in the R&B duo Alton & Eddy with singer Eddy Perkins in 1959, after changing his original plan to become a professional dancer. The duo soon signed with then-upcoming producer Coxsone Dodd and scored their first hit single, a ballad titled "Muriel" (1960). Ellis recalled that in 1959, when there was only one microphone in the Federal Studio, musicians were strategically positioned depending on the instrument, and recording in one take was the norm.

Alton & Eddy split up after Perkins immigrated to America, and both members then pursued solo careers. Ellis's 1966 single "Rock Steady" was the first hit recorded in its titular style, and he even claims to have named the genre in 1965. As one of the stars of rocksteady, Ellis occasionally performed duets with singer Phyllis Dillon or his sister, Hortense. He also recorded hits as Alton Ellis & the Flames. In 1966, partially for financial reasons, Ellis joined Duke Reid's artist roster at Treasure Isle Records, where he recorded "Cry Tough," a classic of the rude-boy era. During this period Ellis sang songs opposing the urban gangster violence that arose out of Kingston's poverty, but he later switched his focus to love songs, reportedly due to

LEFT: Alton Ellis, who claimed to have given rocksteady its name, looking stoic in 1984.

OPPOSITE: In the pre-reggae era, Jamaican album covers were heavily influenced by American R&B.

threats from "rude boys" unhappy with Ellis's lyrical criticisms of them.

Ellis wrote the mid-1960s hit "I'm Still in Love with You," which became the basis for Althea & Donna's 1977 pop-reggae crossover single "Uptown Top Ranking," a #1 UK hit by reggae's first female DJ "toasting" duo. He later recorded some intriguingly Afrocentric material, such as the single "Back to Africa" (1971), with producer Lloyd Daley and worked briefly with singer-producer Keith Hudson. After spending a few years in Canada, Ellis moved to London around 1973, adopting it as his home base and sporadically making records, some of which were created in Jamaica for producer Sonia Pottinger.

Ellis was acutely disheartened by the growing dominance of "slackness"—a performance style focused on sex and materialism and influenced by the American rap scene—during the dancehall era. Although he never achieved the international chart impact with own releases that Althea & Donna did with his material, and he received little financial reward for his work, he asserted his presence indirectly through hits that were adapted from his music. In 1994, Ellis received Jamaica's Order of Distinction for his musical contributions to his country. Better known for individual songs than for entire albums, he continued performing despite health concerns and even collapsed onstage at a show two months before his death in 2008.

SELECT DISCOGRAPHY: *Mr. Soul of Jamaica* (Treasure Isle, 1966); *Sunday Coming* (Studio One, 1970); *Be True to Yourself: Anthology 1965–1973* (Sanctuary, 2004)

This 1969 album featured the controversial "Everything Crash," a commentary on Jamaica's economic woes.

THE ETHIOPIANS
YEARS ACTIVE: 1960s–2000s

The Ethiopians were led by Leonard Dillon, who had recorded as a solo artist at producer Coxsone Dodd's Studio One in Kingston under the name Jack Sparrow—with The Wailers as background vocalists. Despite rehearsing as a trio for about a year, the Ethiopians did not carry on in that format for long. After they recorded the ironically titled "Owe Me No Pay Me" (1966), Dodd apparently did not pay much of what he owed the band, causing co-vocalist Aston "Charlie" Morris (cited as Morrison in some sources) to leave in a state of disillusionment. The remaining duo of Dillon and Stephen "Tough Cock" Taylor left Studio One as Dillon moved into self-production and found independent financial backing for "Train to Skaville" (1967), recorded with the Supersonics session band in the measured rocksteady tempo. Released on the Rio label in England, the single reached #40 on the pop charts and led to the Ethiopians' first British tour. By 1968, they had recorded another signature song, "Everything Crash," a commentary on Jamaica's social and economic decline. The song resonated with listeners despite being banned by the ruling Jamaica Labour Party (JLP) administration. Cut with producer Carl "Sir JJ" Johnson, "Everything Crash" was another in a series of transient associations leading mostly to singles rather than albums, and the group splintered in 1974.

Tragically, Taylor died in 1975 after being hit by a van. Dillon dissolved the Ethiopians until in 1977, when original member Morris was persuaded to return to the fold for the *Slave Call* LP. In later years, pushed to the fringes by dancehall, the Ethiopians evolved into a group generally consisting of Dillon and whichever male or female vocalists he preferred, although he also recorded solo under his own name. While always appreciated by critics and hard-core reggae fans, the records constituting the Ethiopians' career output rarely sold well, and royalties certainly didn't flow freely. Dillon died of cancer in September 2011.

MEMBERS: Leonard Dillion (vocals); **Stephen "Tough Cock" Taylor** (vocals); **Aston "Charlie" Morris** (vocals)

SELECT DISCOGRAPHY: *Slave Call* (Heartbeat, 1977); *Train to Skaville: Anthology 1966–1975* (Sanctuary, 2002); *Everything Crash: Best of the Ethiopians* (Sanctuary, 2003)

FOLKES BROTHERS

YEARS ACTIVE: 1960s; 2011–PRESENT

It has often been said in the music industry that one song is all it takes to change your life and career, but no one guarantees that all the change will be good. The Folkes Brothers' place in popular-music history revolves around a single song, "Oh Carolina," released in Jamaica in 1960, after which they vanished from the scene. The indigenous style of the record, which featured Rasta drumming led by Count Ossie's Afro-Combo, was a peculiarity in the Jamaican market. Count Ossie (Oswald Williams) was a Rastafarian master drummer whose 1950s gatherings at Rasta camps around Kingston attracted other musicians, including future members of ska giants the Skatalites. Ossie's percussion group played on traditional African drums, creating a sound that was relevant to the Afro-Jamaican cultural experience and which was the very opposite of British colonial musical ideals.

American R&B and its local equivalents were still dominant at the time, as homegrown ska music had yet to fully take hold. As such, "Oh Carolina" was the record that drew greater attention to the use of African drumming on local records and the cultural significance of those drums being played by Rastafarians, who were socially marginalized at the time. Released by Blue Beat Records in Britain in 1961, the record made an impact on many different types of listeners. If the story had ended there, the song would be a simple historical footnote, but there was more intrigue to follow.

The authorship of "Oh Carolina" became a major point of contention

The authorship of this 1960 single has been disputed, but its place in history is secure.

when dancehall star Shaggy scored an international hit with his version in 1993, released in the UK by Greensleeves Records. The original Jamaican release of the record lists "C. Campbell" as the writer—Cecil Campbell, better known as Prince Buster, the song's producer and a Jamaican sound-system operator. But singer John Folkes, one of the three Folkes brothers who made up the eponymous group, claimed that he was the real author. While Shaggy's record lacked the cultural significance of the original, using fairly bland digital drum programming without the percussive verve of Count Ossie's group, it generated more money in the year of its release than the Folkes Brothers' version had in the previous thirty. Greensleeves Records and its publishing arm sued Melodisc (parent company of the Blue Beat Records label) and Prince Buster over the right to receive publishing royalties from "Oh Carolina." Prince Buster had become Melodisc's majority shareholder, owning a 99 percent stake in the company, according to reports.

According to conflicting versions of the events, the Folkes Brothers received either sixty pounds, as they claimed, or one hundred pounds, as Buster recalled, for making the record.

On November 4, 1994, the British High Court upheld John Folkes's claim that he, not Buster, had written the song. Folkes, who had since become a literature professor in Canada, said that he had penned the song in twenty minutes while sitting on his doorstep in 1958. He further stated that it was about his girlfriend Noelena, but since he had not wished to name the song after her, he used "Carolina" instead. Buster, on the other hand, claimed that he had written the song about a former girlfriend named Caroline. Dissatisfied at the court's decision, Buster felt it should be appealed, but nothing seems to have come of that idea.

Mico and Junior Folkes, the other two brothers who performed on "Oh Carolina," apparently didn't pursue the matter in court, but in another highly bizarre twist, they released the Folkes Brothers' debut album, *Don't Leave Me Darling*, in May 2011 without their brother John. (Their remake of "Oh Carolina" is best avoided by those with fond memories of the original.)

MEMBERS: John Folkes (vocals); **Junior Folkes** (vocals); **Mico Folkes** (vocals)

BORIS GARDINER

YEARS ACTIVE: 1960s–2000s

Born in 1946 in Kingston, Jamaica (though there are conflicting published dates), Boris Gardiner became a bass player, arranger, and singer—all skills that served him well during his long career. Gardiner began as a regular on the Jamaican hotel circuit, which focused on bands playing mainstream pop for tourists. He used these limitations to his advantage, becoming a reliable session musician whose wide musical vocabulary enhanced performances that turned up on recordings across the reggae spectrum.

Gardiner played at Studio One in Kingston on singer Larry Marshall's "Nanny Goat" (1968), one of the late-1960s songs frequently identified with the transition from rocksteady to reggae, though few would regard Gardiner's style as even vaguely revolutionary. His 1969 instrumental hit single "Elizabethan Reggae," a reggae adaptation of the 1950s light-music favorite "Elizabethan Serenade," typified an uptown, gentrified reggae sound quite reminiscent of Byron Lee & the Dragonaires, a band in which Gardiner had played. In fact, initially the recording was mistakenly credited to Lee, who also produced Gardiner's debut album. By early 1970, Gardiner's song had peaked at #14 on the British pop charts. The song's success foreshadowed the somewhat unexpected mainstream breakthrough he would experience sixteen years later. With a clean pop-style production, "Elizabethan Reggae" was well suited to challenge the prejudices of the British Broadcasting Corporation (BBC) radio gatekeepers. It was also exactly the kind of commercialized reggae that Britain's Trojan Records would soon champion. It was no surprise, then, that a year later, Gardiner was the bass player on "Young, Gifted and Black," the singing duo Bob & Marcia's top-five hit for Trojan.

In the 1970s, in a move that typified Jamaica's persistent class divisions, Gardiner sacked vocalist Earl Sixteen from his band, the Boris Gardiner Happening, for having dreadlocks visible under his hat during a formal-dress live show. In light of this firing, it seems odd that the same Boris Gardiner was a member of Lee Perry's very roots-oriented Upsetters session band, having joining around 1969 after brothers Aston and Carlton Barrett left to become the Wailers' full-time bass-and-drum rhythm section. It was quite a shift from middle- and upper-class uptown to the creative but less economically prosperous environment at Perry's Black Ark studio in Kingston.

In 1986, Gardiner called on his ballad-style vocal skills and remarkably scored three hit singles on the British charts. Among them was the #1 smash "I Want to Wake Up with You," a song influenced by the lovers rock style of reggae.

The fact that Gardiner's style was the very anthesis of the digital dancehall onslaught was perhaps a catalyst for his reinvention; nevertheless, his renewed solo commercial success in Britain was one of the least likely occurrences in reggae history. While none of his records had any mainstream impact in the United States, Gardiner is now able to enjoy the financial fruits of his labor with regular royalty checks from other markets. Gardiner was awarded the Order of Distinction by the Jamaican government in 2006 for his contribution to the island's music.

SELECT DISCOGRAPHY: *Reggae Happening* (Dynamic, 1970); *I Want to Wake Up with You* (Revue, 1986); *The Very Best of Boris Gardiner* (Music Club, 2004)

Singer and session ace Boris Gardiner in London, 1986, the same year he embraced his inner balladeer and scored three British hits.

MARCUS GARVEY
(1887–1940)

Marcus Garvey is a major icon of Rastafarianism. He is viewed by many as a visionary and a prophet—a figure who was able to unite the black world by moving his people from oppression to liberation and, in the process, make Africa a recognized world power. Garvey never visited Africa, yet no other black revolutionary leader has the equivalent of his long-term galvanizing effect on the global black population, imprinting ideas of Pan-African pride, independence, unity, and self-sufficiency. Some of the contradictions in his life have made him a controversial figure: At least one observer described him as a "supreme egotist," while others noted his financial mismanagement. In the context of Garvey's high cultural and political aspirations, both of these factors became liabilities exploited by his opponents.

Like Bob Marley, Garvey was born in the parish of St. Ann, Jamaica. As part of his anticolonial quest, he launched the United Negro Improvement Association (UNIA) in August 1914 in Kingston, and left for the United States in 1916 to promote the organization, eventually traveling across the country. The first UNIA convention was held in New York City in 1920. Garvey had to establish his political profile outside of Jamaica, since his worldview challenged the island's white-centered power structure and was not embraced by the aspiring black middle class. As several writers have noted, both Garveyism (the collective philosophies of Marcus Garvey) and Rastafarianism found receptive audiences beyond Jamaica before gaining acceptance on the island. In 1918, Garvey began publishing *The Negro World*, a newspaper he remained involved

with until the early 1930s. Unlike other African American newspapers of the era, *The Negro World* didn't run advertisements for hair-straightening products or skin-lightening products. Garvey refused to publish them, most likely because they would undermine the fundamental thrust of the newspaper and Garvey's sociopolitical objectives.

These objectives were focused on eventually uniting the many branches of the African diaspora under one political umbrella and raising black consciousness and pride, which were under constant psychological assault from the colonial powers. He saw repatriation as a crucial element in this process, and he felt that the dignity of African history should be truthfully represented. This was evident in seemingly small matters as well as large ones. For example, the UNIA advertised and sold black dolls. According to one newspaper ad, this strategy was the "easiest way to teach race pride," while another ad posed the question "Why should a Negro child play with a white doll?" Clearly Garvey felt that black pride had to be instilled in black children from the earliest possible age to counteract society's racist assaults.

His 1919 formation of the Black Star Line steamship company also signaled his determination to translate theory into action. Garvey formed this enterprise, an entirely black-owned shipping company, as an example of the black economic independence he preached, though its symbolic importance was perhaps just as relevant as its commercial potential. In theory, the Black Star Line would spur trade within the African diaspora, acting as a catalyst for self-reliance. The company's name has taken on mythical proportions in reggae, and "Black Star Liner," a 1978 single by the UK band Reggae Regular, is one of the many liberation narratives that have made Garvey a legend. The Black Star Line

"The Black skin is not a badge of shame, but rather a glorious symbol of national greatness."
—MARCUS GARVEY

Garvey's teachings were a great ideological influence on the Nation of Islam, and particularly distinct echoes were evident in the black nationalist rhetoric of Malcolm X. Moreover, African leaders seeking to break the yoke of colonialism adopted Garvey's themes. Yet his virtual deification by Rastafari is sometimes seen as a contradiction. In 1935, for example, following the Italian invasion of Ethiopia and the exile of emperor Haile Selassie, Garvey described Selassie as cowardly. Garvey also rejected ganja, or marijuana, as a critical threat to black society, and he had an overall distaste for Rastafari ritual that challenged prevailing Christian ideologies. In addition, his preference for Western-style attire and deportment meant that the idea of dreadlocks was abhorrent to him.

In 1935, after declaring bankruptcy in Jamaica, Garvey immigrated alone to England, struggling to survive on speaking engagements. He had suffered a stroke early that year, and in a bizarre turn of

events, his horrified reaction to reading his prematurely published obituary on June 9, 1940 led to another stroke and his death the following day. He died in England at the age of fifty-three. While he may have died under ignoble and impoverished circumstances, and never set foot in Africa, his visions of and efforts to achieve black independence successfully fueled later movements across the African diaspora. Ultimately, the nobility of his ideals, embodied in his pronouncement "Africa for the African at home and abroad," was more powerful than his business mishaps and personal flaws. In 1964, his body was returned to Jamaica from England, and the previously marginalized figure was declared a national hero in recognition of his contributions to Pan-Africanism. Demonstrating Garvey's continuing resonance, in August 2011 the Jamaican government approved the compulsory acquisition of his birthplace at 32 Market Street in St. Ann's Bay, with the intention of preserving it as a historic site.

proved to be a short-lived episode, however, largely undermined by the strength of opposing forces eager to eliminate its economic and political potential. It also fell victim to Garvey's own mismanagement, as he delegated unreliable personnel to positions for which they were either unqualified or ill-suited.

Garvey's potential to mobilize black masses worried white authorities everywhere. In the United States, Federal Bureau of Investigation director J. Edgar Hoover was determined to end Garvey's ascent and used undercover informants to advance this agenda. One of Garvey's more controversial and less palatable moves in these years was his July 1922 meeting with the head of the racist Ku Klux Klan to discuss repatriation for displaced Africans. This alienated him from other black leaders in the United States—some of whom called for his deportation—and he was vigorously denounced as a traitor. In early 1922, Garvey and other UNIA officers were arrested and charged in the United States with federal mail fraud in connection with the ambitious

Black Star Line enterprise, and the following year he received a five-year prison sentence. (Garvey's poverty became clear when, upon imprisonment, his only assets were useless Black Star Line stocks and forty dollars.) This was the beginning of a long series of ongoing health issues that arose in America during his imprisonment, including heart disease, asthma, and bronchitis. It was in part because of these physical ailments that Garvey was pardoned, released, and deported to Jamaica in late 1927: the American government feared that his dying in custody would inflame the situation it sought to diffuse in the first place.

OPPOSITE: Revolutionary leader Marcus Garvey preached black unity, pride, and self-sufficiency, despite his traditional Western image.

ABOVE: Garvey fought for the truthful representation of African history and even favored repatriation, or a return to the continent.

RIGHT: Garvey formed his Black Star Line shipping company in 1916 to promote trade and foster self-reliance within the African diaspora.

No. 26830   Shares 2

INCORPORATED UNDER THE LAWS OF THE STATE OF DELAWARE
BLACK STAR LINE, INC.
CAPITAL STOCK $10,000,000
SHARES $5. EACH

This Certifies that Ephram Giblou trustee for John Gibbou is the owner of _____ Shares of the Capital Stock of

BLACK STAR LINE, INC. full paid and non-assessable

transferable only on the books of this Corporation in person or by Attorney upon surrender of this Certificate properly endorsed

IN WITNESS WHEREOF the said Corporation has caused this Certificate to be signed by its duly authorized officers and its Corporate Seal to be hereunto affixed this _____ day of _____ A.D. 19 __

Secretary-Treasurer   President

RASTAFARIANISM

Reggae has taken the Rasta message across the world, making a formerly marginal religious practice an integral part of popular culture. Considering the Caribbean's history of slavery and the roles that race and color have played in the region's societies since emancipation in the nineteenth century, it's not surprising to see the emergence of an Afrocentric doctrine focused on anti-imperialist ideas. By affirming belief in a black—rather than white—god, Rastafarianism posed a major threat to colonialism's brand of Christianity, which was based on racial hierarchy.

In Jamaica, Rastafarianism has been crucial in redefining and reinforcing ancestral, spiritual, and cultural links to Africa, and it has consolidated international antiestablishment sentiments. The Rastafarian refusal to accept any of the foundations of colonial ideology placed its followers in direct opposition to the system, making them targets for brutal oppression. The early core followers were based in such urban slum areas as Back-O-Wall and the Dungle, both located in Kingston. These areas housed the city's dispossessed and dissidents, with Rastas living alongside criminals, former prisoners, and squatters in a zone that was eventually bulldozed by the Jamaican government in 1966. Yet by the late 1960s, Rastafarianism was also becoming a middle-class phenomenon.

Much of the Rasta culture of resistance can be linked to the Maroons, the rebellious slaves who, beginning in the mid-seventeenth century, fled Jamaican plantations for secluded mountain hideouts and consistently wrought revenge on their former masters. Following the hurried departure of the Spanish from Jamaica in

1655 (they were themselves under siege from the marauding English), the Maroons began terrorizing sugar planters with their continual attacks, eventually forcing the British to agree to a peace treaty in 1738. After this, the Maroons were not the same anticolonial force they had been, but rebellion against slavery was far from over. This was evident in the Sam Sharpe Rebellion of 1831, an uprising based on the belief that plantation owners were withholding freedom that the king had granted. This revolt resulted in the mass executions of slaves. Similarly, the 1865 Morant Bay Rebellion ended with the hangings of its leaders, preachers Paul Bogle and George William Gordon. (The incident was memorialized in Jamaican band Third World's 1977 song "96° in the Shade.") These disturbances also roughly coincided with the Great Revival, an era that spanned 1860 to 1861 and witnessed a resurgence of African religious culture in the midst of orthodox Christianity. The period marked a split between missionary church ideology and Afro-Jamaican religious practices. From this phase came Revival religion, whose rituals

LEFT: A Rasta family in Moore Town, Jamaica, 1971. The area has been a center of Maroon culture since the eighteenth century.

ABOVE: The Lion of Judah is a powerful symbol for Rastafarians.

(including Kumina) included many of the vocal and rhythmic features later so prominent in reggae.

By the early 1900s, Pan-Africanists (who promoted the interests of black people internationally) were active within the Caribbean. In 1889, physician and clergyman Dr. Robert Love began publishing the influential *Jamaica Advocate* newspaper, which rejected colonialism and the racial hierarchy that came with it. Before the establishment of Rastafarianism, this was one of the strands of conscious resistance that created a suitable platform for the emergence of Marcus Garvey, whose philosophies of black liberation and pride became central to the Rasta ethos.

The Rastafarian movement began in the early 1930s and was built on the idea that its followers and all African people displaced outside of the continent would eventually be repatriated to "Zion"—Africa, or more particularly, Ethiopia—after exile and captivity in "Babylon," the world of exploitation. This is the philosophical reality behind Bob Marley's lyric "movement of Jah people," expressed in the title track from his 1977 album *Exodus*. There are many sects and versions of Rastafarianism, and as a result, practices vary. Similarly, not every Rasta or Afrocentric individual embraces the concept of repatriation or even wears dreadlocks, though achieving psychological

liberation from colonialism is a common goal. Marley's exhortation to "emancipate yourself from mental slavery" in 1980's "Redemption Song" speaks to this goal.

The establishment of Rastafarianism coincided with a sharp decline in peasant landownership, which naturally resulted in further poverty and destitution. While Garvey's name has become familiar through reggae, other important early anticolonial crusaders include Alexander Bedward and Leonard Howell (described as a follower of Garvey). Born in 1859, Bedward was a fiery revivalist preacher who, just before the turn of the twentieth century, was held on sedition charges for his opposition to white oppression. He was later committed to

a mental asylum in Kingston; after his release, he clashed with the authorities again in 1921 while participating in a protest march. He and his followers were imprisoned, and he was later sent back to the mental asylum, where he died in November 1930. Despite some eccentric behavior—he apparently thought himself to be Jesus Christ—Bedward is seen as a founding hero by Rastafari, and he is believed to have prophesied the rise of Ethiopian emperor Haile Selassie, whose crowning in 1930 was seen as a divine intervention on behalf of blacks. While one of the central precepts of Rastafarianism was to shift the iconic objects of religious devotion from white to black, Bedward became an actor lost in his own role. He cast himself not merely as a pathway to salvation but as the supposed savior himself.

Born in 1898, Leonard Howell, like Bedward before him, is considered one of the first individuals to have preached the divinity of the iconic Selassie. In addition to achieving notoriety for his anticolonial preaching, Howell had the unusual distinction of being Jamaica's first known ganja farmer, practicing his cultivation in the early 1940s on the Pinnacle plantation commune just outside Kingston. Growing and harvesting ganja as a staple crop did not sit well with the authorities, and this farming quite literally laid the seeds for the plant's future as a symbol

A PROCLAMATION.

By His Excellency SOMERSET LOWRY, EARL of BELMORE, Captain-General and Governor-in-Chief of this our Island of Jamaica, and other Territories therein depending in America, Chancellor and Vice-Admiral of the same, &c. &c.

WHEREAS it has been ascertained that certain Incendiaries have been employed to poison the minds of the Slaves in some parts of the Island, and to induce them to be guilty of acts of outrage and insubordination:—And whereas it is necessary that the Ringleaders of this disturbance should be brought to condign punishment, I do hereby, in his Majesty's name, offer a reward of *Three Hundred Dollars* to any person or persons who shall apprehend either of the following slaves:—

A slave calling himself COLONEL GARDINER, belonging to Greenwich Estate, Hanover.
A slave calling himself CAPTAIN DOVE, belonging to Belvidere Estate, St. James's
A slave calling himself CAPTAIN JOHNSON, belonging to Retrieve, St. James's—and
GENERAL RULER, SAMUEL SHARP, or THARP, *alias* DADDIE RULER SHARP, or THARP, director of the whole, and styled also, Preacher to the Rebels, belonging to Croydon Estate, St. James's.

And in order to afford encouragement to such Slaves who may be disposed to assist in apprehending the aforesaid Rebels, I do hereby promise his Majesty's most gracious Pardon to any slave or slaves who may assist in such purpose, except those who have been actually guilty of setting fire to the works or houses on different Properties, or attempted the life of any peaceable inhabitant.

Given under my Hand and Seal at Arms, at St. Jago de la Vega, this third day of January, Annoque Domini, one thousand eight hundred and thirty-two, and in the second year of our reign.

BELMORE.

By His Excellency's Command,
W. BULLOCK, Sec.

GOD SAVE THE KING.

Heb. 3. 13.

PHŒBE.
Jamaica Royal Gazette, Oct. 7, 1826.

35—42   Spanish-Town Workhouse.

Notice is hereby given, that unless the undermentioned Slave is taken out of this Workhouse, prior to Monday the 30th day of October next, she will on that day, between the hours of 10 and 12 o'Clock in the forenoon, be put up to Public Sale, and sold to the highest and best bidder, at the Cross-Keys Tavern, in this Town, agreeably to the Workhouse Law now in force, for payment of her fees.

PHŒBE, a Creole, 5 feet 4½ inches, marked NELSON on breasts, and I O on right shoulder, first said to one Miss Roberts, a free Black, in Vere, secondly, to Thomas Oliver, Esq. St. John's, but it is very lately ascertained that her right name is Quasheba, and she belongs to Salisbury-Plain plantation, in St. Andrew's; Mr. John Smith is proprietor.   May 11

Ordered, that the above be published in the Newspapers appointed by Law, for Eight Weeks.

By order of the Commissioners,
T. RENNALLS, Sup.

" To admit *Slave-evidence* (of course cautiously and properly guarded) and to abolish the *whipping of women*, are two desirable points, and would destroy topics used with much effect against the Colonies."
Letter of J. R. Grossett, Esq (a West India Proprietor,) to the Editor of the Jamaica Journal and Kingston Chronicle, August 1, 1826.

associated with Jamaica. Accounts cite different dates for the key events in Howell's life, but it's known that he gained American citizenship in the early 1920s and served in the army before a stint as a construction worker in New York City. Howell was confronted by deep racism in the United States, but this only strengthened his ideological resolve. He later returned to Jamaica—possibly in the 1930s, shortly after Selassie's accession to the Ethiopian throne—and began spreading the message of Rastafari. In early 1934, Howell was arrested for, charged with, and convicted of sedition, which meant that he had publicly challenged the British colonial status quo in all of its forms. Howell served a two-year sentence, and other leaders of the movement were also arrested and jailed, but the seeds of revolution had already been sown and were nurtured by surviving members.

Inevitably, given the colonial climate of the times, police raids often led to evictions, and authorities used such offenses as the cultivation of ganja to push Rastas off of the communes. One such raid occurred in 1941 on the Pinnacle plantation and resulted in the jailing of twenty-eight Rastas. Howell was also soon arrested again after initially eluding the police, and he served an additional two years in prison for his ganja cultivation. It's thought that the growing of dreadlocks at Pinnacle followed this period of police harassment. The members of the commune not imprisoned after its 1954 destruction inhabited the Kingston slums that would later become some of popular music's most fertile grounds—as well as centers of political strife. Howell was imprisoned in a mental institution in 1960, and after his eventual release, he died in 1981.

In the early twentieth century, many of these promoters of black consciousness worked simultaneously, and as the movement gradually gained strength, it benefitted from having multiple advocates. Best remembered among these is Marcus Garvey, who has been immortalized repeatedly in reggae. Despite Garvey's rejection of ganja and the idea of Selassie as god, numerous Rasta artists have carried awareness of his presence and ideas to new generations. He established the United Negro Improvement Association in Jamaica in 1914 and developed a philosophy based on black pride. A key foundation of his beliefs was the unbreakable connection between blacks

everywhere and the ancients of Ethiopia and the African continent, where civilization was created long before the Greeks and Romans arrived. This idea predates Garvey by several centuries, but his positive representation of African history and reinterpretation of biblical verses acted as powerful motivations for the continent's displaced victims of racial discrimination. He is also considered the first Jamaican to have made public reference to Selassie. In 1916, in what is perhaps his most frequently cited quotation, Garvey reportedly said, "Look to Africa when a black king shall be crowned, for the day of deliverance is near." That directive references the biblical passage Psalm 68:31, and the Rastafarian movement drew upon key passages from both the Old and New Testaments. With the ascent of Selassie—whose title was Ras (King) Tafari—to the throne in Ethiopia in 1930, Garvey's declarations

assumed greater importance, heralding a new era for Africa and the black diaspora.

Selassie was hailed as a living deity—a new messiah descended from the biblical King Solomon. Arriving amid the harsh economic conditions of the Great Depression and lingering brutality associated with colonialism, the pro-black revelations from biblical scriptures provided a meaningful ray of hope. Italy's fascist invasion of Ethiopia in 1935 led to a phase of exile for Selassie, but this also further fanned the black world's opposition to colonialism. The 1938 establishment of a Jamaican branch of the Ethiopian World Federation (a black liberation organization founded a year earlier in New York City) led to local distribution of that organization's *Voice of Ethiopia* newspaper, from which many principles of Rastafarianism are thought to have arisen.

In its early days, Rastafarianism was mainly preached in Kingston, where many rural migrants first became exposed to the doctrine and its practices. Among these, the wearing of uncut beards dates back to the early days of the movement, while the adoption of dreadlocks has been traced to the late 1940s (although some Rastafari followers may have grown locks much earlier). The first adoption occurred in Jamaica's remote hills, and the look may have been partially inspired by pictures of Kenya's Mau-Mau guerrillas, dreadlocked warriors who helped Kenya gain independence from Britain in 1956. A debate developed within the Rastafarian community in the 1950s over whether dreadlocks should be combed or not, though by the 1960s, the issue had been resolved. Police victimization of Rastas often involved shaving off their locks and beards as a physical removal of the "dreadness" they embodied.

In the early 1950s, the drums that are now so

characteristic of Rastafarian ritual were not yet used in meetings. The percussive rhumba box employed in mento music was played instead. When drumming became an integral part of the Rasta soundscape in the 1940s, it mirrored the sound of the heavily African-influenced Kumina. Rasta drumming famously found its way onto record in 1960, thanks to the performance of Rasta musician Count Ossie on the Folkes Brothers' hit "Oh Carolina."

Rastafarian use of language has been another widespread means of challenging Babylon, an attempt to overturn the oppressors' linguistic rules and thus the means through which their ideologies are imposed. Since colonizers devalued any language beyond the boundaries of formal English, alternative speech was an act of bold defiance. Rasta language features numerous inversions of perspectives; as a common example, "oppression" becomes "downpression," reflecting the plight of the downtrodden Rastas. The inversions highlight the ways in which subordination (in this case, to the colonial mindset) is often embedded in Standard English. The "dread talk" is said to originate from the Kingston Rastafarian camp known as the Youth Black Faith in 1949, though Rastas in other camps may have been developing their own variations. One of Rastafarianism's more glaring contradictions is its gender hierarchy. Women are considered subordinate to men, and this has arguably impacted on the overall profile of women in reggae.

When Jamaica's independence from Britain, granted in 1962, failed to deliver prosperity, social disillusionment among the impoverished in the ghettoes accelerated the spread of Rastafari. The accusation that Rastas committed a murder during a gas station disturbance in 1963 led to social unrest, and the group was further marginalized when the army was called in. As the decade progressed, however, the Rastas established a presence in Jamaican popular music, and 1964 saw the emergence of the Skatalites, a group whose jazz musicianship challenged the establishment's negative stereotypes. By the end of the decade, the Abyssinians had cut one of the reggae era's most important anthems of African repatriation, the single "Satta Massa Gana," released in 1971 but recorded in 1969.

Selassie's 1966 state visit to Jamaica proved a major turning point for Rastafarian acceptance in Jamaica, as Rastas were part of the official welcoming delegation. Upon his arrival, Jamaican followers eager to pay homage with deference and ganja-filled chalices fervently surrounded Selassie's plane. According to some accounts, the Ethiopian emperor denied his divinity in private, but either way, the visit magnified his mythical status and the growing profile of Rastafari. Selassie's death in August 1975 (following a military coup the previous year) was disregarded by Rastas, since death has no place in their worldview and Selassie

which social practices and cultural codes vary. Dreadlocks are a common factor, as are the recognition of Selassie's divinity, the desire for repatriation, and the spiritual significance of ganja. The widespread Rasta rejection of pork (since pigs are considered dirty) reflects a general avoidance of the dead and a preference for a salt-free diet. Somewhat ironically, the otherwise inspirational Maroons are credited with the creation of the "jerk pork" seasoning. The vegetable-centered "Ital" food (related in both sound and meaning to *vital*) of the Rastafarian represents yet another

LEFT: Jamaican soldiers survey the crowd awaiting the arrival of Haile Selassie in Jamaica, 1966.
ABOVE: Dreadlocks and a spiritual reverence for ganja unite many Rastas.

was considered immortal. Bob Marley, who asserted Selassie's immortality on the 1975 single "Jah Live," was quoted in 1979 as saying, "I don't believe in death neither in flesh nor spirit." Funerals are also shunned by Rastafarians, perhaps because attending them would in some way confirm the presence of death's shadow.

Like many religions, Rastafari has distinct branches or sects—among them Bobo Ashanti, Twelve Tribes of Israel, and Nyabinghi—within

rejection of Babylon. In keeping an Ital diet, Rastas oppose the use of chemicals found in imported foods and fight the economic and nutritional dependency often felt by small countries like Jamaica. Long before organic food became trendy, Rastafarians promoted natural foods and ways of living. Consumption of meat in any form is usually viewed negatively, and processed liquids like alcohol, coffee, and milk are also rejected. Tea is permitted, but it must come from a natural herbal source, and fruits are among the staple items. Many

Rastas consume fish—generally the smaller, nonpredatory, and/or scaleless varieties—and even make their livings through fishing.

The role of reggae in awakening international awareness of Rastafari cannot be underestimated. Marley's global commercial success in the 1970s took the philosophy—and ganja along with it—to places it probably otherwise would not have reached. Through his records, as well as those made by other artists, Rasta symbols, sounds, and language assumed a global presence. The declaration "Jah Rastafari" (asserting that Selassie is god) signals the antiestablishment leaning of whoever makes the spiritual proclamation. While Rastas are predominantly Afro-Jamaican, Jamaica—and indeed, the world—now has Rastas of all ethnicities. This diversity has helped sustain the popularity of reggae.

JOE GIBBS
YEARS ACTIVE: 1960s–1980s

Joe Gibbs, born Joel Gibson in either 1940 or 1943 in Montego Bay, Jamaica, trained as an electronics engineer in the United States before returning to Jamaica to work as a producer. He made his production debut in 1966 with singer Roy Shirley's "Hold Them," released during the island's rocksteady era. As was typical of Jamaican producers at the time, he played little or no creative role in the music but rather funded and facilitated recordings while reaping the bulk of the profits.

Gibbs opened a two-track studio in Kingston in 1967, and the following year founded his own Jamaican label, Amalgamated Records, named after his Beeston Street television repair shop from which he also used to sell records. Amalgamated also became a custom imprint designated by the Britain-based B&C Company that ran Trojan Records, reggae's major international distribution pipeline from the late 1960s into the early 1970s. At his Kingston studio, Gibbs recorded the Versatiles, a vocal group led by Junior Byles, who would make an impact as a solo artist in the first half of the 1970s. Oddly, the Versatiles' first Jamaican hit, 1968's "The Time Has

Come," included the kind of syrupy string arrangements that soon helped to land Trojan releases on the British charts, but this production approach is rarely associated with Jamaican music.

Gibbs attained international success in a variety of forms. He is known for his many productions for the Pioneers—one of the first Jamaican reggae acts to chart in Britain—and for Jamaican singer Nicky Thomas's "Love of the Common People," a top-ten UK hit in 1970. The song was arranged by another talented and, later, independently successful employee, Winston Holness, better known during his career as Niney the Observer. As with "The Time Has Come," the original Jamaican mix of "Love of

the Common People" was overlaid with incongruous string arrangements for British release on Trojan. With lyrics about cold weather and snow that were irrelevant in the island context, the song is a clear example of a Jamaican recording that directly targeted the West Indian migrant market.

It was at Gibbs's studio that the duo Dave and Ansel Collins recorded the major 1971 international hit "Double Barrel." In 1972, coinciding with the establishment of a new studio, Gibbs formed a production alliance with Errol

A window-shopper checks out what's new at producer Joe Gibbs's Kingston record store, 1974.

Gibbs's name became associated with such breakthrough early dub releases as *Dub Serial* (1973) and the influential multivolume *African Dub* series, which spanned the latter half of the 1970s. In reality, these records, which featured remixed rhythm tracks originally released with vocals, resulted from Thompson's engineering creativity and intuition, and his role in the success of Gibbs's releases should not be underestimated.

As was typical for major Jamaican producers of the 1960s and 1970s, Gibbs found himself the object of considerable resentment among artists, many of whom accused him of financial misconduct concerning royalties. One such artist was former employee Lee Perry, who recorded the song "People Funny Boy" (1968) as an insult to Gibbs (the song commented on Gibbs's lack of appreciation for people who aided his quest for success). In 1978, Gibbs responded to journalist Vivien Goldman's question about such alleged improprieties by punching her in the face. The assault, which took place in his Kingston studio, certainly did his reputation no favors. It was therefore bitterly ironic that failure to pay royalties would ultimately lead to Gibbs's financial downfall in the music business.

He was essentially put out of business by a copyright infringement lawsuit involving a 1980 Jamaican recording of the song "Someone Loves You Honey" by female singer J.C. Lodge. The song was first previously recorded by the American country singer Charley Pride in 1978 with little commercial success. Lodge reinterpreted the song in the lovers rock style, which often adapted syrupy love songs from other genres, aimed at the female market. There's no data suggesting that the Lodge version ever reached Britain's pop charts, though it likely became a hit in the UK reggae market. The single found audiences elsewhere after being licensed to Arista Records for wider release, while Lodge later scored a major reggae market hit in 1988 with "Telephone Love" produced by Gussie Clarke. Gibbs paid a high price for duplicating an originally obscure song, and his inability to pay the court settlement led to the collapse of his music operation.

As the Jamaican economy went into free fall in the early 1980s, Gibbs relocated to Miami as part of an ongoing exodus of producers, artists, and others who could afford to leave the island. His involvement in the music business from his new base centered on exploiting the rich catalog of releases that had been issued on a variety of labels he owned. Gibbs died of a heart attack on February 21, 2008.

Thompson known as the Mighty Two. Gibbs's session band, the Professionals, included the talents of the future Rhythm Twins Sly Dunbar (drums) and Robbie Shakespeare (bass), as well as ace guitarist Earl "Chinna" Smith. This exceptional lineup made them one of the most appropriately named outfits in reggae history. The unit became one of the genre's sonic foundations, imprinting its style on Gibbs-produced records by Jamaican vocal trio the Mighty Diamonds, and singers Gregory Issacs and Dennis Brown (notably on Brown's 1979 top twenty UK hit "Money in My Pocket"), among others.

Gibbs upgraded to a sixteen-track console in 1975, and established his own pressing plant. A highlight of the prolific Mighty Two's career came with the 1977 album *Two Sevens Clash* by Culture. British punk rockers adopted the title track as one of their reggae anthems, immortalizing the record's cultural impact. That same year, Gibbs produced Althea & Donna's "Uptown Top Ranking," another chart-topping British hit. The song was based on Alton Ellis's "I'm Still in Love with You," a 1960s hit that typified the rocksteady era in which Gibbs first emerged.

TOP LEFT: "All Night Long," credited to Joe Gibbs & the Professionals and released on the producer's Globe label.

LEFT: In the disco era, Gibbs got a bit cheeky with his sleeve designs.

EDDY GRANT

YEARS ACTIVE: 1960s-PRESENT

Eddy Grant's position in the reggae world is not straightforward. Much of his success was built on fusing reggae elements with rock, R&B, and funk, and yet in 1988, he released *File Under Rock*, an album aimed at discouraging retailers from automatically filing his records in the reggae section just because he wears dreadlocks.

Born in 1948 as Edmond Montague Grant in Guyana, the future star immigrated to London in 1960 with his family. At school he showed a talent for woodworking, and he crafted a guitar before he learned to play the instrument. The inevitable jamming with schoolmates eventually led to the formation of a multiracial group, the core of which became the Equals in 1965. Their first major hit arrived in 1968 with the Grant-composed "Baby Come Back," which topped the British charts (and others across Europe). The song would again reach #1 in 1994, when it was covered by reggae "toaster" Pato Banton (assisted by members of British pop-reggae band UB40). That single also propelled the album *Unequalled Equals* to #10 on the British album charts, foreshadowing Grant's future success as a solo act. The 1968 follow-up album *Equals Explosion* didn't fare as well, but the group later returned to the charts with the utopian theme of the funky "Black Skin Blue Eyed Boys," which gave the Equals their third top-ten single in early 1971. Grant would later describe this song in a 1995 interview as "the only pop song that Rastamen danced to" at that time, and he controversially identified it as the beginning of soca, calypso's more commercial, rhythm-driven counterpart.

In 1971, at the age of twenty-three, Grant first encountered serious heart problems that weren't helped by his role as the band's creative and organizational linchpin. In 1972, after seven Equals albums, Grant decided to move on. He had planned to produce the band while opting out of touring, but that idea collapsed, leaving him to explore solo options. He established the Ice Records label in the mid-1970s, though not in time for his self-titled solo debut, an album that—contrary to some accounts—was actually released in 1975, before

BERES HAMMOND

YEARS ACTIVE: 1970s-2000s

Jamaican vocalist Hugh Beresford Hammond began his career in the late 1960s, but it wasn't until the mid-1990s that he hit his most productive recording stride. Born in 1955 in the Jamaican parish of St. Mary, Hammond was one of ten children. He refined his vocal talents in his church choir and at age thirteen even recorded a song, "Wanderer," produced by Clancy Eccles. Hammond had a wide range of local and international musical influences, from Jamaican singer Alton Ellis to American soul great Marvin Gaye. After winning a talent contest in 1972, he began playing on the hotel circuit, performing for tourists, an experience he found especially discouraging. Around 1975, he briefly formed the vocal trio Tuesday's Children with singers Calman Scott and Ferris Walters, and simultaneously joined Zap Pow, a group of Jamaican session musicians that released an album on Island Records the following year. Hammond noted that Zap Pow's musical direction was more political in nature than was his own work—which focused on personal relationships—and that contrary to his expectations, the Island deal did not raise the group's profile.

He eventually recorded his first solo album, *Soul Reggae* (issued only in Jamaica on the Aquarius label), in 1977. Around this time, although the R&B style in which he performed was popular, Hammond became disillusioned by his lack of income and began work as a session vocalist. He established his own Harmony House Music label in the mid-1980s and achieved some solo success in Jamaica with such hits as "What One Dance Can Do" and "Groovy Little Thing" in 1985. He even pressed and distributed the records himself.

In 1986, Hammond was tied up and robbed by armed thieves at his house in Jamaica. Not surprisingly, he left the country, retreating to New York for a time. He continued recording during this period, working with producer and guitarist Willie Lindo, who coproduced "How Can We Ease the Pain," a duet with British pop-reggae singer Maxi Priest, in 1988. By 1990, Hammond had signed a deal with Penthouse Records, releasing the Jamaican hit singles "Tempted to Touch" and "Putting Up Resistance," produced by the hit 1970s DJ Tappa Zukie.

Hammond's 1994 Elektra Records debut, *In Control,* became his best-selling record, moving more than sixty-seven thousand copies in America. Hammond wrote the album largely in the studio, allowing for some spontaneous inspiration. Surprisingly, it was his only album with Elektra, as he soon fell into a dispute with the label over what it alleged was the slow pace at which he completed material. He struck out on his own again before signing a licensing deal with VP Records that has led to his most productive recording spell. His 2001 album, *Music Is Life,* earned a Grammy nomination and ranked among the top-ten best-selling reggae albums of the year. By late 2008, it had sold more than forty-six thousand copies in the United States. Hammond's career has likely been hampered by the constant label shifts earlier in his career, but that hasn't prevented him from developing a devoted fan base that attends his live performances.

Beres Hammond at Jamaica's famous One Love Peace Concert, 1978.

SELECT DISCOGRAPHY: *Soul Reggae* (Aquarius, 1977); *A Love Affair* (Penthouse, 1992); *Sweetness* (VP, 1993); *In Control* (Elektra Records, 1994); *Love from a Distance* (Harmony House, 1996); *Getting Stronger* (Heartbeat, 1997); *A Day in the Life* (VP, 1998); *Music Is Life* (VP, 2001); *Can't Stop a Man: Best of Beres Hammond* (VP, 2003); *Love Has No Boundaries* (VP, 2004); *A Moment in Time* (VP, 2008)

extensively before pressing copies for release on the Duke Reid label in Jamaica about a year later, while Blue Beat Records in England also issued the record in 1960.

At this point, Harriott established his own label, Crystal Records, putting him steps ahead of his contemporaries. As he recalled, he founded the label in 1960, becoming "the first artist-producer in Jamaica," though others claim he started Crystal in 1962. At the time of his debut solo hit "I Care" (1962), the label's home address was notably in New York, perhaps suggesting something about Harriott's perception of the lack of economic fairness in the Jamaican music business. This entrepreneurial instinct would be a major factor in securing his longevity in a ruthless business where talent alone is not enough to ensure survival. Harriott, for example, was one of many label owners who benefitted in the early 1960s from licensing deals with the UK-based Blue Beat Records, whose head Emil Shalit was hungry for hot new material. Harriott secured a similar deal with Chris Blackwell's Island

DEREK HARRIOTT
YEARS ACTIVE: 1950s-1980s

Derek Harriott is one of only a handful of musicians to have survived Jamaican music's many transitions on the road to reggae. He has also functioned in several industry-related roles simultaneously throughout his lengthy career. Born in Kingston, Jamaica, in 1942, he entered a talent contest as a singer in 1957, inspired by sound systems, Jamaica's high-volume hi-fi operators. The following year he formed his first group, the Jiving Juniors, who cut a "dubplate"—a sound-system acetate—of a song called "Lollipop Girl" at producer Stanley Motta's studio. It became a sound-system smash and was adopted by both Coxsone Dodd and Duke Reid, two of the island's biggest sound-system operators and later, major studio owners. In fact, Reid insisted on having his own exclusive recording of "Lollipop Girl" and cut a new version with Harriott in late 1959. He used it on his system

Records, gaining another pipeline into the growing British market.

In the midst of these business activities and solo releases, Harriott was still singing with the Jiving Juniors, who rotated among producers as they looked for a better opportunity. In 1961, they left Reid to record with Dodd at Studio One in Kingston. The mid-tempo ska treatment of 1961's "Over the River" took off in Jamaica, boosting the youngsters' confidence. Harriott spent time briefly in New York in the late 1950s and returned there in 1962 to record "Sugar Dandy" with a different group lineup. He soon went solo, spending more time on producing other acts and developing other label imprints.

During the rocksteady era Harriott scored a solo hit in Jamaica with "The Loser" (1967), a song that underlined the characteristic R&B styling of the records he made both for himself and for the artists he produced, such as the Jamaican duo Keith and Tex. He was able to fuse those influences into subsequent hits—among them, 1970's "Psychedelic Train," recorded with the Chosen Few (a Jamaican group discovered by Harriott in 1968)—that were distinctly reggae but possessed unmistakable soul and funk traces. Harriott's seamless transition into the new reggae era not only showed his versatility but also foreshadowed the long-term influence of the rocksteady rhythms that fuelled his growing business empire.

Harriott had a busy start to the decade. He maintained record-shop enterprises alongside his record label productions and crafted hits with the Kingstonians ("Sufferah" in 1968) and DJ Dennis Alcapone, among others. With his studio backing band, the Crystalites, he

recorded *The Undertaker* (1970), a lively instrumental set on which Harriott wrote or cowrote all but one of the twelve songs, further demonstrating self-sufficiency at every level of the business. Harriott would advance this instrumental protodub style in the 1970s with *Scrub-a-Dub* (1974) and *More Scrubbing the Dub* (1975). In a further indication of his creative vision, *Scrub-a-Dub* was one of the first albums to employ the skills of a not-yet-famous dub remix engineer named King Tubby.

Harriott was one of the Jamaican producers who ventured boldly into the British market in the 1960s and 1970s, exploiting the significant presence of Jamaican expatriates as a source of steady sales. While his productions didn't grace the mainstream pop charts, many records were sold through obscure channels not yet recognized by the formal industry. Since the late 1970s, Harriott has released new solo material sporadically and perhaps paid more attention to highlighting his legacy with reissues, many of which were licensed to other labels.

SELECT DISCOGRAPHY: *The Undertaker* (Trojan, 1970); *Scrub-a-Dub* (Crystal, 1974); *The Donkey Years: 1961–1965* (Jamaican Gold, 1995); *For a Fistful of Dollars* (Jamaican Gold, 1996)

The self-professed "first artist-producer in Jamaica," Derek Harriott targeted the British market in the 1960s and 1970s, licensing material to numerous labels.

HARRY J
YEARS ACTIVE: 1968–PRESENT

Former insurance salesman Harry Johnson, born in 1945 in Kingston, Jamaica, is best known for heading Harry J's All Stars, the studio band behind the 1969 UK instrumental hit "Liquidator." The 1972 worldwide smash single "I'll Take You There" by the Staple Singers featured the rhythm "borrowed" from Johnson's composition. He also produced the duo Bob & Marcia's top-five British single "Young, Gifted & Black" (1970), which was licensed to Pama Records in its original Jamaican form and later to Trojan Records, which added strings to create the popular hit version.

Johnson's production career began in 1968 with Jamaican vocal trio the Beltones at producer Coxsone Dodd's legendary Studio One in Kingston, but his most important record, "Liquidator," reached #9 in Britain on his custom Harry J label, distributed through Trojan. The song featured Winston Wright's memorable organ line, and its success, coupled with the two landmark Bob & Marcia pop hit singles ("Young, Gifted and Black" and "Pied Piper") gave Johnson the financial base to establish his own Harry J studio in 1971. It was there that the Wailers, featuring future superstars Bob Marley, Peter Tosh, and Bunny Wailer, recorded several of the original Jamaican tracks for their *Catch a Fire* album in 1972 with engineer Sylvan Morris, before rock guitar and keyboard overdubs were added in London under the supervision of Island Records chief Chris Blackwell.

Johnson's role in reggae's internationalization was underlined when American singer Johnny Nash recorded his 1972 covers of Bob Marley's "Stir It Up" and "Guava Jelly" at the Harry J studios. Johnson was also a key advisor to Blackwell regarding early reggae signings (Toots & the Maytals, and Joe Higgs, among others), and his studios

were used again by Marley for the *Burnin'* (1973), *Natty Dread* (1974), and *Rastaman Vibration* (1976) albums. Further crossover hits included singer Sheila Hylton's "The Bed's Too Big Without You," a 1981 cover of a track from the 1979 *Reggatta De Blanc* album by the reggae-influenced rock band the Police. The newer recording by a reggae artist said a lot about how the mainstreaming of reggae had turned the genre on its head.

More than forty years after it first became a hit, "Liquidator" remains an integral part of UK popular-music culture. (The rereleased original version even returned to the charts in 1980). In late 2010 the British music press announced that the publishing company administering the rights to "Liquidator" planned to market it to hip-hop acts. The news came after the Johnson-produced Lloyd Robinson single "Cuss Cuss" (1968) had been sampled more than a hundred times by hip-hop artists, among them Jay-Z, Beyoncé, and Kanye West. The wealthy English Premier League football team Chelsea F.C. also uses "Liquidator" for home matches, broadcasting it as the players take the field. Clearly, the rhythm and melody that first made the song popular in 1969 still resonates strongly in the twenty-first century. Harry Johnson remains active in his Kingston recording studio, collaborating with fellow ace Jamaican producer-engineer Steven Stanley.

SELECT DISCOGRAPHY:
Liquidator: The Best of the Harry J All Stars (Sanctuary, 2003)

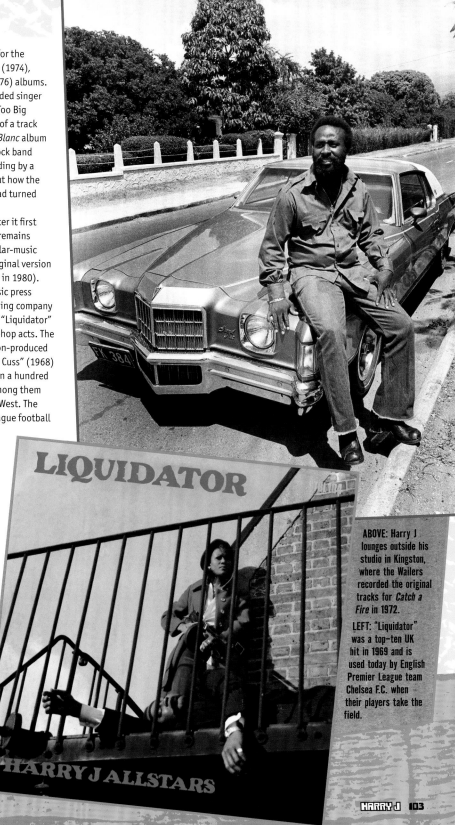

ABOVE: Harry J lounges outside his studio in Kingston, where the Wailers recorded the original tracks for *Catch a Fire* in 1972.

LEFT: "Liquidator" was a top-ten UK hit in 1969 and is used today by English Premier League team Chelsea F.C. when their players take the field.

SISTER CAROL

HEARTBEAT RECORDS

Heartbeat Records was established in Boston in 1981 as a reggae subsidiary of independent roots music label Rounder Records, which also specialized in bluegrass and country. The label aimed to release a vintage reggae-related catalog along with new albums by active reggae artists, such as former Black Uhuru member Michael Rose, and Jamaican singers Everton Blender and Richie Spice. Rounder Records distribution manager Duncan Browne founded the operation with Bill Nowlin, and by the end of the 1980s, Chris Wilson—who grew up in Jamaica—had begun to generate quick results in his talent-spotting A&R (Artists and Repertoire) role. The label gained access to the classic Studio One releases that have become synonymous with Jamaican popular music of the 1960s, and it eventually released about sixty-five records.

Through extensive licensing deals with top Jamaican producers, Heartbeat filled many gaps in reggae archives, issuing rare and out-of-print records and providing detailed liner notes to give listeners historical context. The label's first record was a 1981 reissue of Linton Kwesi Johnson's landmark dub-poetry album *Dread Beat an' Blood*, originally released in 1978. However, as compilations were issued, the crises of copyrights that had both plagued and stimulated creative activity in the Jamaican market came back to haunt Heartbeat. In one particularly notable example, disputes over ownership and royalty payments threatened to derail the potentially lucrative Studio One reissues of early Wailers and Bob Marley recordings. Marley was a minor at the time the Wailers signed their original agreements with Studio One owner Coxsone Dodd, and therefore questions arose regarding their legality. Further confusing matters, Danny Sims, the owner of Cayman Music, which had signed Marley around 1967, claimed Dodd did not hold all of the publishing rights. With Dodd also frequently receiving songwriting credits on Heartbeat releases, such conflicts were inevitable.

To boost record sales and promote its artists, the label also sponsored the Heartbeat Culture Splash tour of the United States in 1996, which included singer Michael Rose and DJ Sister Carol. When Burning Spear's *Calling Rastafari*, a Heartbeat release, won the Grammy award for best reggae album in 2000, it seemed a bright future lay ahead. But by 2011, the label had seemingly been placed on indefinite hiatus by Rounder—shelved, presumably, until the economic downturn of the 2000s improved.

THE HEPTONES

YEARS ACTIVE: 1960s-2000s

The Heptones produced some of the richest vocal harmonies in reggae, a genre never short of them. While they might not have fulfilled their commercial potential on an international level, there is no doubting their influence on other artists. Member Earl Morgan has said that the group was formed as far back as 1958, even though no records were made until 1966. Leroy Sibbles, on the other hand, suggests that it was 1962 or 1963 when the Heptones entered the scene. Still other sources cite 1965. One thing that is certain is that they auditioned for producer Ken Lack in 1965, after an introduction was made by Sydney Crooks of the Pioneers, a Jamaican group that became one of the first to score pop hits with reggae in Britain .

The Heptones' debut single, "Gunmen Coming to Town," was released on Lack's Caltone Records label in 1966. The record wasn't a smash hit, possibly because it used parts of the *William Tell Overture*, and it marked an inauspicious beginning to their career. The band then signed a five-year contract with producer Coxsone Dodd at Studio One. The Heptones scored Jamaican hits for Dodd near the end of the rocksteady era, and the sexually suggestive "Fattie Fattie" (1967) won

Jamaican harmony kings the Heptones, whose career has spanned more than forty years, stroll the streets of London, 1979.

Greensleeves

℗ 1979 Greensleeves Publishing Ltd.
© Greensleeves Records Ltd.
44 Uxbridge Rd., London W12
01-749 3277

A SIDE
GRED 13
45 RPM

ALL RIGHTS OF THE MANUFACTURER AND OF THE OWNER OF THE RECORDED WORK RESERVED · UNAUTHORISED PUBLIC PERFORMANCE BROADCASTING AND COPYING OF THIS RECORD PROHIBITED.

GOOD LIFE
(B. Llewellyn)
THE HEPTONES
Produced by Joseph Hoo Kim

them popularity and boosted Studio One's profile among artists at a time when rival producer Duke Reid's Treasure Isle studio was dominant. "Fattie Fattie" has been adapted repeatedly over the years by other artists, but at the time, it got the Heptones banned from Jamaican radio. The trio showed that it also had a definite sociopolitical consciousness with the song "Equal Rights" (1968).

During their Studio One stint, Sibbles began playing bass at the suggestion of gifted keyboardist Jackie Mittoo and quickly demonstrated skill with the instrument. Also a skilled arranger, Sibbles eventually took charge of the studio band and played on practically every important Studio One record released between about 1968 and 1971. He also functioned as an A&R (Artists and Repertoire) man and producer. The Heptones did not release an actual album until *On Top* in 1970, a strange circumstance for a group featuring Studio One's most valuable session man at the time. Poorly paid and underappreciated, Sibbles and his fellow Heptones split with Dodd in 1971. The perception in the reggae community is that their movement toward songs of protest and resistance clashed with Dodd's more commercial agenda.

Freed from Studio One's contractual constraints, the Heptones worked with multiple producers, including Augustus Pablo and Joe Gibbs, to make their next batch of recordings in the early

1970s. Sibbles temporarily departed for Canada in 1973, and though he returned to fight for success with the group, he would head north again years later in search of a solo career. It wasn't until the Heptones signed with Island Records in 1975 that they became known for releasing more than just singles. On 1976's *Night Food*, the band revisited some of its earlier Jamaican hits, among them "I've Got the Handle" (perceived by many as misogynistic) and "Fatty Fatty" (the same song as the one they had recorded the previous decade but

During the Heptones' Studio One days, singer and bassist Leroy Sibbles led the label's studio band and played on just about every important record cut between 1968 and 1971.

with an altered spelling). In a 1976 issue of *Rolling Stone*, American reviewer Dave Marsh described the songs as "first-rate evocations of Jamaican experience," which was also a reflection of the mature harmonic chemistry the Heptones displayed. Their high-water mark with Island was the

1977 *Party Time* album, produced by Lee Perry and one of their best-selling records. Given the Island Records graphic treatment, the album cover sidestepped the stereotypical use of red, green, and gold in favor of a more rock-style abstractionist approach that still conveyed the energy of reggae in the sound-system arena.

When international sales failed to match the Heptones' overall critical acclaim, Sibbles went solo, leaving after 1978's ironically titled *Better Days*. His former Heptones colleagues continued working the marketplace with a new member, Naggo Morris, but without the pivotal Sibbles, who had been the main songwriter, vocalist, and producer, things would never be the same. The original trio reunited and sounded

reinvigorated on 1995's *Pressure*, produced by Tappa Zukie. On that album, guest musicians including production teams Sly & Robbie and Mafia & Fluxy carried the group instrumentally into the digital age while enhancing the Heptones' trademark vocals. The years following the brief reunion primarily saw reissues, though the original members reunited for a concert in Toronto, Canada, in January 2011. Unfortunately, the death of original Heptones singer Barry Llewellyn in Jamaica later that year laid to rest any hopes of further activity from the group's best-known lineup.

MEMBERS: **Leroy Sibbles** (vocals, bass); **Barry Llewellyn** (vocals); **Earl Morgan** (vocals)

SELECT DISCOGRAPHY: *On Top* (Studio One, 1970); *Freedom Line* (Studio One, 1971); *Night Food* (Island Records, 1976); *Party Time* (Island, 1977); *Better Days* (Third World, 1978); *In Love with You* (United Artists, 1978); *Pressure* (RAS, 1995); *Peace & Harmony: Anthology* (Trojan, 2004)

JOE HIGGS
YEARS ACTIVE: 1950s-1990s

The song "Stepping Razor" was so closely associated with Peter Tosh that it became his nickname, but Joe Higgs is the man who wrote it. He was a skilled songwriter who was brilliant at passing along his knowledge, but his greatest strength was creating harmonies for vocal groups. Higgs is the person who took the raw talent of the Wailers—the group that launched Tosh, Bob Marley, and Bunny Wailer—and taught them how to blend their voices harmonically. He refined their vocal synthesis through rigorous rehearsal and training, yet never received the public recognition he deserved.

Higgs was born in 1940 in Kingston, Jamaica, and learned music from his choir-singing mother. In 1958 he was spotted at a talent contest—along with his singing partner Delroy Wilson—by music enterpreneur and future Jamaican prime minister Edward Seaga, who was looking for artists to record for his WIRL (West Indies Records Limited) label. At one of the local Jamaican radio stations, RJR (Radio Jamaica Rediffusion), Higgs & Wilson, as the duo was known, cut "Manny Oh" in 1959. Written by Jamaican singer and songwriter Jackie Edwards and falling somewhere between Southern R&B and rock 'n' roll, "Manny Oh" was also released in England on the Blue Beat label.

Audiences were already familiar with the song from contest performances, so the record did well, although there's no way to confirm how many copies were sold. The duo had other hits, but Higgs's most crucial role was providing musical mentorship in the impoverished Trench Town section of the parish of St. Andrew, Jamaica, where he gave instruction in voice and guitar. The Wailers are among the best-known examples of students who successfully applied Higgs's lessons and reaped international rewards.

Higgs actually toured briefly as one of the Wailers in the United States following Bunny Wailer's departure in 1973. He also worked with the Jamaican vocal group Wailing Souls and toured with Jimmy Cliff before releasing his own solo debut, *Life of Contradiction*, in 1975. The albums he released periodically from the 1970s through the 1990s were usually met with critical enthusiasm, but unfortunately, that never translated into significant record sales. Despite his talent, Higgs's reluctance to take center stage in the music business perhaps hampered his solo career. He was highly respected among musicians, however, and recorded material with Irish band Hothouse Flowers shortly before his death.

In his later years, Higgs was based in Los Angeles, and it was there that he died from cancer at age fifty-nine on December 18, 1999. His work is indelibly woven into the fabric of popular music, and while the threads seem barely visible at times, they have helped hold Jamaica's popular music together.

SELECT DISCOGRAPHY: *Life of Contradiction* (Grounation, 1975); *Unity Is Power* (Island, 1979); *Triumph* (Alligator, 1985); *Family* (Shanachie, 1988); *Blackman Know Yourself* (Shanachie, 1990); *Roots Combination* (Macola, 1995)

Joe Higgs, the master songwriter who taught Bob Marley and his fellow Wailers to harmonize, is all smiles in Kingston, c. 1980.

JUSTIN HINDS

YEARS ACTIVE: 1950s–2005

In his autobiography, Rolling Stones guitarist Keith Richards referred to Justin Hinds as "Sam Cooke reincarnated." Richards came to know and respect Hinds through their loose collaboration in the Wingless Angels—an unlikely assembly of African drum-centered Rasta music and blues musicians that gathered informally for more than twenty years, beginning in the early 1970s, in the north coast town of Ocho Rios, Jamaica, where Richards maintained a home. While Hinds's voice and phrasing were quite different from Cooke's, there is no doubt that, within Jamaica, Hinds's impact was comparable to the American soul legend's.

Hinds was born in rural Steer Town, Jamaica, in 1942. As a teenager he sang on the beach for tourists in Ocho Rios while working at a water-sports business. He formed the Dominoes with Dennis Sinclair and Junior Dixon in 1958, and over the next several years the group gradually built their reputation as performers. In late 1963, following advice from his friend Charlie Babcock, a radio DJ, Hinds moved to Kingston on his own with the intention of meeting with and auditioning solo for producers Coxsone Dodd and Duke Reid. His attempt to meet with Dodd proved unsuccessful, but he had better luck with Reid. Hinds's fellow Dominoes joined him in Kingston after they learned of his move to the capital. An eventual group audition led to the recording of "Carry Go Bring Come" (1964), the group's first major Jamaican hit. Reputedly recorded in a single take at Federal Studio, the track featured a Treasure Isle studio session band led by saxophonist Tommy McCook (of Skatalites fame) and produced by Reid. The precise subject matter of the song is open to interpretation, though it seemed to admonish gossip and lack of spiritual righteousness. Hinds's association with

Reid's Treasure Isle label would last for nearly a decade, ending in 1972—an uncommonly long time for a producer-artist alliance at this stage in Jamaican music business history.

The Dominoes' vocal style conveyed a rural revivalist energy—a dose of Jamaica's essence transmitted through an R&B framework. Reid was betting on the potential appeal of "Carry Go Bring Come," but the song's success probably exceeded his and the group's expectations. Unfortunately, neither Reid nor Hinds ever fully capitalized on that success by following up with enough songs of comparable commercial appeal. Hinds rerecorded "Carry Go Bring Come" several times as Jamaican popular music transitioned from ska to rocksteady to reggae. Later ska hits such as "Botheration" (1964) and "Rub Up, Push Up" (1965), both also released in Britain by Island Records, maintained the group's popularity, while the slower rhythmic pace on "The Higher the Monkey Climbs" (1966) clearly signified the arrival of rocksteady. Even when the instrumental backdrop changed, Hinds's voice was always the key feature. By the time he recorded "Drink Milk" around 1969 (credited to Justin Hinds & the Waves), the arrival of reggae, with its slower rhythm, offered him more musical space than ever to project his Jamaican country-accented messages of moral and spiritual instruction.

"Drink Milk" prefaced one of Hinds's periodic withdrawals from the business, as he seemed more concerned with maintaining his spiritual well-being and connections to his rural roots in farming than with chasing stardom or riches. In 1972, the Dominoes finally split with Reid, and a few years passed before Hinds resurfaced, working with Jamaican producer and sound-system figure Jack Ruby on two albums later released on Island. The label's founder, Chris Blackwell, had heard the Ruby recordings and sought out Hinds, which led to the roots reggae–styled Dominoes album *Jezebel* in 1976. Hinds—whose name was printed as "Hines" on his Island releases—

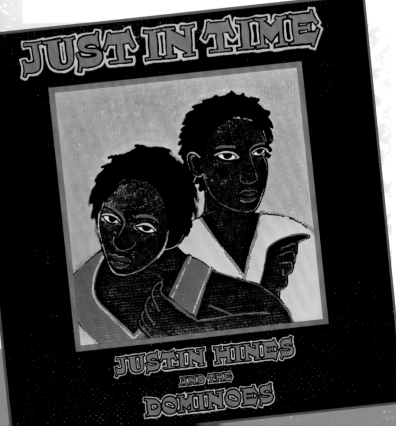

felt that the album lacked promotion, and it certainly was not generating any income. Once again he retreated, leaving the business for about seven years by his own estimation. However, in 1978, he recorded singles for female producer Sonia Pottinger, who had taken over Duke Reid's business after his death in 1975. But Hinds's relationship with Pottinger was similarly disrupted by his retreat from the music business.

Even after he reemerged on the American independent Nighthawk Records label in 1984 and released the critically well-received *Travel with Love*, promotion problems persisted, prompting him to pull back once again. It wasn't until 1992 that he recorded another studio album, *Know Jah Better*, on the same label, and another decade passed before two live albums surfaced. Despite Hinds's sporadic output across the decades, reggae fans appreciated what he had to offer, particularly as his vocals always carried an aura of authenticity. His role as a messenger of Jamaica's musical heritage was cemented on the Jamaica All-Stars albums *Back to Zion* (2003) and *Right Tracks* (2004).

Hinds died of cancer on March 16, 2005, in Steer Town, in his home parish of St. Ann, Jamaica. Despite his ambivalent view of the music business, he found creative motivation in delivering musical messages of morality to the Jamaican people. He wrote songs continually throughout his career, even when he was not actively recording or touring.

SELECT DISCOGRAPHY: *Jezebel* (Island, 1976); *Just in Time* (Mango, 1978); *Travel with Love* (Nighthawk, 1984); *Know Jah Better* (Nighthawk, 1992); *Let's Rock Live* (Sanctuary, 2002); *Live at the Grassroots* (I-Town, 2003); *Carry Go Bring Come: Anthology '64–'74* (Trojan, 2005)

By 1976, Justin Hinds and the Dominoes—Dennis Sinclair and Junior Dixon—had found success as a trio and were releasing albums on Island Records.

"The Rastaman don't matter what color, creed or race you may be, as long as your conscious within yourself. Love everybody like you love yourself.
—JUSTIN HINDS, on morality and his deep cultural roots

WINSTON "NINEY" HOLNESS

YEARS ACTIVE: 1960s-2000s

Winston "Niney" Holness is an underrated producer-artist who has worked with a *who's who* list of Jamaican singers, DJs, and instrumentalists, and yet his name is little known to fans not inclined to read album credits—or books like this. Also known as Niney the Observer, he was born George Boswell in 1944 in Montego Bay, Jamaica; for reasons that are unclear, he became Winston Holness after his parents separated. He lost his thumb in a work-related accident, and his nickname derives from his nine remaining fingers.

He began his career plugging songs in the mid-1960s, promoting recordings produced by Joe Gibbs, initially collaborating with legendary producer Lee Perry but moving to the fore after his partner's acrimonious split with Gibbs in 1968. (He would link up again with Perry after both had become freelancers.)

Niney established his own Observer label in 1970 and set out to record himself and other artists. His earthy debut single, "Blood and Fire," was released in December 1970. Featuring musical backing by the Jamaican band Soul Syndicate, who would soon be in great demand for studio sessions, the song placed Niney on the reggae map, revealing him to be an independent force. "Blood and Fire" was perceived as important not only because it was a hit but also because it laid down a thematic cornerstone of Niney's work, demonstrating a Rasta worldview.

Niney's production work on singer Dennis Brown's "Westbound Train" (1973), a smash single in Jamaica, ensured that additional collaborations with star-quality acts would follow. He made multiple recordings with singer Max Romeo, cut the original 1972 version of the hit "Guess Who's Coming to Dinner" with Michael Rose (later of Black Uhuru), and scored legions of hits with Gregory Isaacs, Freddie McGregor (whose 1980 debut LP he produced), and Horace Andy, among others. It should also be remembered that Niney was equally capable of working with the new generation of DJs, and such artists as U-Roy and Big Youth figured prominently in his career. Niney was also one of the first producers to utilize the mixing skills of ace dub engineer King Tubby. The 1975 album *Dubbing with the Observer* (credited to the Observer All Stars and King Tubby) was released in Britain on Trojan Records to a warm reception just prior to the label's bankruptcy.

Despite his tremendous track record of success, Niney practically disappeared in the late 1970s. He reinserted himself into the music scene by the early 1980s, largely through his work with the hit-producing studio Channel One in Kingston. Like most hit producers of the 1970s, Niney has occasional but limited involvement with the contemporary scene, though Sanctuary's 2009 comprehensive compilation of his work has placed his productions in the ears of reggae fans who were either too young to remember the songs or not yet born when Niney was at his peak in the studio. As he amassed his catalog of quality work, he remained ideologically consistent in his lyrics, which placed the spiritual before the material.

SELECT DISCOGRAPHY: *Blood & Fire: Hit Sounds from the Observer Station 1970–1978* (Sanctuary, 2009)

JOHN HOLT
YEARS ACTIVE: 1950s–2000s

Kingston-born John Holt is another example of talent groomed on the *Vere Johns Opportunity Hour*, a Jamaican radio show for aspiring performers. He competed on the show between 1958, when he was just twelve years old, and 1962. By the time he became the lead singer of the Paragons, a vocal group that first recorded for producer Coxsone Dodd's Studio One label based in Kingston, and later hit its stride at Duke Reid's Treasure Isle label, he had recorded several solo and duet singles for producer Leslie Kong. Holt's rich, expressive vocal tone effectively became the Paragons' trademark on such major hits as "Wear You to the Ball" and "The Tide Is High," both released in 1967. After the group dissolved in 1970, he committed himself to a solo career that had actually begun in 1968 with records produced by Bunny Lee. Holt's cover of "Stick By Me," originally recorded by American R&B vocal group Shep & the Limelites and released in 1963, was a massive hit in Jamaica in 1972, foreshadowing the mass-market mainstream success that awaited him.

Holt's 1973 album *1,000 Volts of John Holt* was released by Trojan Records in the United Kingdom, where it sold well for a reggae record. The album broke into the British mainstream charts in early 1975, reaching #42, driven by Holt's cover version of country singer Sammi Smith's 1971 hit "Help Me Make It Through the Night," which reached #6 on the pop singles chart. The album exemplified the marketing challenges then facing reggae artists, even those whose music was laden with typical pop trappings. Although originally recorded by white independent British record producer Tony Ashfield as a special acetate item, the record was later overlaid with the kind of string orchestration that Trojan often used to court crossover success from the reggae realm into the pop market. The next album, predictably titled *2,000 Volts of John Holt* (1976), followed Trojan's winning formula, but the Bunny Lee–produced third installment of the trilogy, *3,000 Volts of John Holt* (1977), was a more stripped-down recording that dispensed with the orchestral template. Although the "Volt" series electrified Holt's solo career, he never enjoyed the same degree of pop crossover appeal afterward.

In 1982, he scored a Jamaican hit with "Sweetie Come Brush Me," a collaboration with hot dancehall producer Henry "Junjo" Lawes. From a career standpoint, however, 1983's "Police in Helicopter" represented a virtual reinvention. Now dreadlocked, Holt adjusted his pristine, crooning vocal style to accommodate the edginess of the dancehall era. "Police in Helicopter" also tackled controversial subject matter—the organized American-sponsored destruction of ganja in Jamaica—rather than the previously typical themes of love or heartbreak that he was best known for in the 1970s. His new roots-rasta rebel image—representing his native Jamaican culture—was the polar opposite of the clean-cut pop-crossover icon he had once been.

Holt's output has been prolific since the 1980s, and *40 Greatest Hits* (2011), a fairly comprehensive compilation of his work, ensures that listeners will know exactly why Holt's voice has been so important in reggae history.

SELECT DISCOGRAPHY: *1,000 Volts of Holt* (Trojan Records, 1973); *Time Is the Master* (Creole, 1974); *2,000 Volts of Holt* (Trojan, 1976); *3,000 Volts of Holt* (Trojan, 1977); *Police in Helicopter* (Greensleeves, 1983); *40 Greatest Hits* (Justice, 2011)

John Holt (left) was the most famous—and perhaps the most easily amused—member of the Paragons.

KEITH HUDSON

YEARS ACTIVE: 1960s–1984

Keith Hudson was one of reggae's more business-conscious producer-musicians as well as one of the earliest adopters of the dub subgenre. Born in Kingston, Jamaica, in 1946, he was trained as a dentist. He established his own Imbidimts record label in 1967, funding the enterprise with money from his dental work. The Hudson-composed Ken Boothe hit "Old Fashioned Way" (1969) launched the label, though it's not known what sort of revenue was generated by the single. His early production work also included DJ Big Youth's 1972 single "S 90 Skank," for which he recorded a motorcycle in the studio, launching Big Youth's career into orbit.

More of Hudson's own recordings followed soon after, with albums like 1974's *Flesh of My Skin* possessing a spirit of soulful experimentation. The title track is one of the few in reggae to have no drum kit evident at all, though Rasta-style percussion fills the rhythmic role. His 1974 album *Pick a Dub* is thought to be the first dub album released in Britain (on the independent Atra label) and is rightly recognized as a dub classic. On it, the instrumental tracks of previous hits he had produced were remixed in dub (which stripped recordings to their elemental core, but made them more ambient with effects). The album features such top-shelf performers as melodica master Augustus Pablo and Soul Syndicate guitarist Earl "Chinna" Smith, as well as the pivotal Wailers band instrumentalists Aston "Family Man" Barrett and his brother Carlton on bass and drums, respectively.

Hudson signed a four-year deal with Virgin Records in 1976 as that label sought a piece of the reggae market, and in the same year he released the uncharacteristic *Too Expensive*. The title proved prophetic, as Hudson was promptly dropped by the label. The album had found him shifting away from his hard roots style and moving toward a type of reggae-pop-R&B middle ground that included entirely nonreggae tracks, such as the synthesizer-accented funk workouts of "Civilization" and "Too Expensive."

By 1976, Hudson had relocated to New York City, and he soon released the excellent 1977 dub album *Brand* (titled *The Joint* in the United States) and its 1978 conventional vocal version *Rasta Communication*. Both records would have thrilled Virgin if that relationship had not already collapsed. It was rather unorthodox to release the dub version first, when normally it would be a sequel to a standardly structured album, but this decision highlights Hudson's intuitive spirit of innovation and commitment to making his own musical statements.

Sadly, Hudson died of lung cancer on November 14, 1984, at the age of thirty-eight, leaving many to mourn the loss of a creative leader whose peak had not yet been reached.

SELECT DISCOGRAPHY:

Entering the Dragon (Imbidimts, 1974); *Flesh of My Skin* (Imbidimts, 1974); *Pick a Dub* (Atra, 1974); *Torch of Freedom* (Imbidimts, 1975); *Brand* (Pressure Sounds, 1977); *Rasta Communication* (Greensleeves, 1978); *Playing It Cool & Playing It Right* (Joint International, 1981); *Studio Kinda Cloudy* (Trojan, 1988)

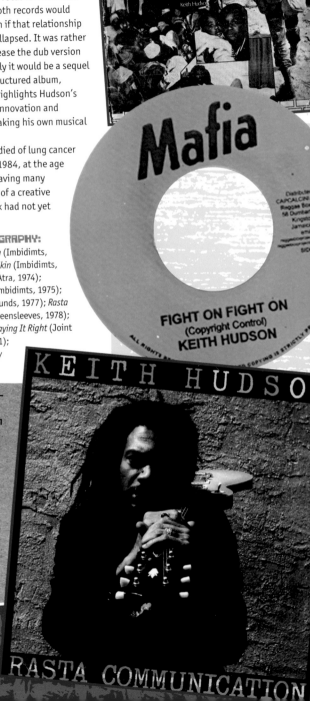

TOP LEFT: A business-savvy performer and producer, Keith Hudson was responsible for 1974's *Pick a Dub*, thought to be the first dub album released in Britain.

RIGHT: Reversing the usual reggae trend, Hudson released this 1978 album a year after its dub companion, *Brand*, known in America as *The Joint*.

i-ROY

YEARS ACTIVE: 1960s–1980s

Roy Samuel Reid, born in 1944 in the Jamaican parish of Saint Thomas, capitalized on the commercial success of such DJs as U-Roy (no relation) and Big Youth with confident, animated vocalizations, feeding an appetite among audiences in the 1970s for the improvised rapping monologues described as "toasting."

He got his start as a DJ with Ruddy Redwood's SRS (Supreme Ruler of Sound) operation before rotating through many other local sound systems (among them King Tubby's Home Town Hi-Fi), just as he would later work with multiple producers. Reid adopted the name I-Roy around 1969 and recorded his first album, *Musical Pleasure* (1970), for producer Harry Mudie. I-Roy split with Mudie over financial issues, and on the follow-up album, 1973's *Presenting I-Roy*, he worked with a very young Gussie Clarke, who became one of Jamaica's most successful producers in the 1980s. I-Roy opted to self-produce *Hell & Sorrow*, released the same year, and by this time, he had become popular enough in the United Kingdom to tour that country. He did not return to Jamaica until 1975.

One of the many artists signed by Virgin Records during the mid-1970s, the prolific I-Roy released material too quickly for the marketplace to assimilate it. Sources differ on how many records he made during the late 1970s, but between his first and last albums for Virgin and its Front Line subsidiary label—a time spanning 1976 to 1980—he released as many as seven albums. His final record for Virgin, *Whap'n Bap'n* (1980), was produced by UK-based dub master Dennis Bovell; but by this time, critics had perhaps begun to greet his constant output with some degree of indifference. After a few early 1980s albums, I-Roy appeared to be swept aside by the tide of dancehall DJs that signaled the arrival of the digital era. He did not fare much better in the 1990s.

Things took a turn for the worse in 1996, when he developed serious heart problems and collapsed at London's Heathrow Airport as a result. Compounding this misfortune was I-Roy's homelessness on the streets in Jamaica as he became trapped in destitution by his poor health. He collapsed and died in Jamaica after hospitalization on November 27, 1999. I-Roy came from a generation of musicians who gave much but generally received very little compensation for their artistry, as became starkly apparent in his final years.

SELECT DISCOGRAPHY: *Musical Pleasure* (Trojan, 1970); *Presenting I-Roy* (Trojan, 1973); *Hell & Sorrow* (Trojan, 1973); *Many Moods of I-Roy* (Trojan, 1974); *Crisus Time* (Virgin Records, 1976); *Musical Shark Attack* (Virgin, 1976); *Heart of a Lion* (Front Line, 1978); *Whap'n Bap'n* (Virgin, 1980); *Don't Check Me with No Lightweight Stuff 1972–75* (Blood & Fire, 1997)

DJ and hat lover I-Roy cuts a sharp figure in Kingston, 1977, midway through his prolific stint with Virgin Records.

I-THREES

YEARS ACTIVE: 1970s–2000s

After Peter Tosh and Bunny Wailer left the Wailers in 1974, remaining founder Bob Marley recruited the female vocal trio the I-Threes to sing harmonies that added a new dimension to the band's overall sound. The I-Threes consisted of Rita Marley, Marcia Griffiths, and Judy Mowatt. Ironically, the suggestion for the group's name came from Bunny Wailer. As Mowatt recalled, the trio had resolved to call itself "We Three," but Wailer proposed the more Rasta-relevant alternative. Among other things, the use of "I" by Rastas signifies a subversion of what they see as the establishment's oppressive use of the English language.

Rita Marley was recording with the Jamaican female vocal group the Soulettes in the mid-1960s when she married Bob, and Marcia Griffiths had recorded as a solo artist at Studio One in Kingston and as one-half of the duo of Bob and Marcia (with singer Bob Andy), who enjoyed brief international success. Both Griffiths and Rita Marley are credited with providing backing vocals on the Wailers' *Catch a Fire* (1973) album—recorded when Tosh and Wailer were still in the band—so Bob Marley had some idea of their singing chemistry. Judy Mowatt had been a backing vocalist with the Gaylettes, who were house studio singers at Kingston's Federal Studio, before going solo around 1970.

The I-Threes made their album debut with Bob Marley & the Wailers on *Natty Dread* in 1974, though their first actual recording was on the group's single "Jah Live," released in early 1976. With their singing, choreography (directed by Mowatt), and African attire, the I-Threes provided a visual and tonal contrast to the Wailers' instrumentalists. They also established what has likely been the most consistent high-profile female presence in a globally recognized reggae group. They scored their own Jamaican hit "Many Are Called" in 1978 on the Bob Marley–owned Tuff Gong label.

After Bob Marley's death in 1981, the I-Threes' members resumed their respective solo careers and did not release much material as a group. Their 1986 debut album, *Beginning*, is now out of print, and though singles were occasionally issued after that release, the trio did not release a full-length follow-up until 2007's *Songs of Bob Marley*.

MEMBERS:
Rita Marley (vocals);
Judy Mowatt (vocals);
Marcia Griffiths (vocals)

SELECT DISCOGRAPHY:
Beginning (EMI America, 1986); *Songs of Bob Marley* (Universal Music, 2007)

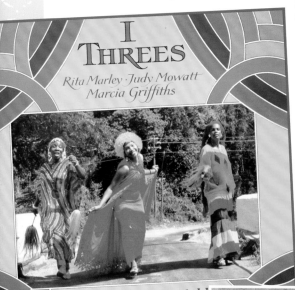

I THREES
Rita Marley · Judy Mowatt
Marcia Griffiths

*Music for the World,
Many Are Called*

GIANT EXTENDED PLAY 12"45 RPM SINGLE

As background singers for Bob Marley, the I-Threes (l-r: Marcia Griffiths, Rita Marley, and Judy Mowatt) were known for their choreography and African-inspired attire.

IJAHMAN LEVI

YEARS ACTIVE: 1970s–2000s

The father of thirteen children and a spiritual emissary of Rastafari, Ijahman Levi has recorded more than forty albums, but none have had the distribution or impact on audiences achieved by his first two, *Haile I Hymn* (1978) and *Are We a Warrior* (1979), both of them distinctly spiritual, roots reggae works.

Ijahman was born Trevor Sutherland in the mid-1940s in Jamaica and was deeply inspired by the legendary Joe Higgs, who taught him and other young people to play music in Kingston's economically deprived Trench Town area. Moving to England in 1963 in the midst of the chilling racism that pervaded Britain in the early 1960s, he taught himself guitar, struggling alongside fellow English youths to learn their instruments in London. American soul was a major influence, as it had been for most of Jamaica's major acts, and that musical genre would surface later on in his work.

His life took a radical turn when, after an incident involving his first wife, he received a three-year prison sentence for assault and resisting arrest. This challenging phase, which spanned 1972 to 1974, saw prisoner 266701 turn to the Bible, and he rechristened himself Ijahman Levi after his spiritual transformation. Upon his release from prison, he returned to Jamaica before independently recording the 1976 single "Jah Heavy Load" in England. His major break arrived when Chris Blackwell, the head of Island Records, heard his recording and sent him back to Jamaica with money to record additional tracks. Accounts vary regarding what resulted from those sessions. Ijahman says he initially cut four songs for inclusion on a single, but that they instead became his first album. Another version of the story suggests that he returned to England with eleven songs—recorded with producer Geoffrey Chung—from which his first two albums were created. It might be slightly misleading to call his first two works full-length albums, since overall lengths are relatively short, but the records are of high artistic quality.

At just over thirty minutes long, the first record, *Haile I Hymn* (1978), is "a lost masterpiece," according to Tony Wright, who designed its cover. Ijahman's early music was in the mold of laid-back roots reggae with a distinct spiritual flavor. His Island debut featured both first-rate session players from the Kingston studio scene and rock superstar Steve Winwood, who was also signed to Island at the time.

Ijahman's second album, 1979's *Are We a Warrior*, was a deeply felt roots meditation on life and connection to Jah, the higher cosmic force. The album seemingly has little to do with the world of entertainment but rather targets something more quintessentially human, almost as if the listener is overhearing Ijahman's prayers being made directly to his maker. More than just meaningful music, *Are We a Warrior* is virtually a religious experience in itself. Again designed by Wright, the illustrated cover purposefully incorporates the art from *Haile I Hymn*—visible on Ijahman's T-shirt—and establishes creative and thematic links between the two records. Wright also designed the cover of Bob Dylan's 1980 album *Saved*, and he has said that the legendary musician based his directions for creating the cover on Ijahman's *Haile I Hymn* sleeve and Bob Marley's *Natty Dread* (1974).

Conflicts soon arose between Ijahman and Island, resulting in a split between the parties. Uncharacteristically for a reggae artist, Ijahman retained his publishing rights, since Island had apparently never established contractual control over them. His first post-Island record, 1982's *Tell It to the Children*, released on the Tree Roots International label, followed the soulful roots path of its predecessors. Neither of Ijahman's first two albums were officially released in the United States in the 1970s, but they are now readily available.

SELECT DISCOGRAPHY: *Haile I Hymn* (Island, 1978); *Are We a Warrior* (Island, 1979); *Tell It to the Children* (Tree Roots International, 1982)

Ijahman Levi (left) has nothing but love for Freddie McGregor at Reggae Sunsplash in London's Brockwell Park, 1987.

Inner Circle's Ian Lewis (left) and Jacob Miller work up a sweat in London, 1979.

INNER CIRCLE

YEARS ACTIVE: 1960s–PRESENT

Inner Circle was formed around 1968 by brothers Roger and Ian "Munty" Lewis, who came up with the band's name after playing a show with a group called Outer Limits and inverting that moniker. They were drafted as the backup band by ace Jamaican reggae producer Bunny Lee on the recording of singer-songwriter Eric Donaldson's "Cherry Oh Baby" (1971), the winner of the 1971 Jamaican Festival Song Contest, a competition started in 1966 to promote national pride and creativity with original songs. They received greater recognition as a unit in 1972, when they provided instrumental support for the so-called Musical Bandwagon, the collective name given to the touring artists supporting the election campaign of People's National Party (PNP) leader Michael Manley. At the same time, Inner Circle held down a regular gig as an American top 40 cover band at the Tunnel Club in Kingston, Jamaica. By 1973, however, they had splintered apart; some members—Stephen "Cat" Coore, Michael "Ibo" Cooper, Milton "Prilly" Hamilton, and Irvin "Carrot" Jarrett—formed Third World, successful beyond Jamaica from the mid-1970s as an eclectic reggae band. The remainder continued as Inner Circle, adding additional session work to their activities.

Jacob Miller, born in 1955 in Jamaica, was invited to join Inner Circle as lead vocalist in early 1974. He had recorded the unsuccessful single "Love is a Message" as a teenager in 1968 for producer Coxsone Dodd's Studio One label, but the 1970s would prove to be far more fruitful for Miller's musical success. That year, Inner Circle appeared in San Francisco as a backing band for Jamaican singer Dennis Brown and Toots & the Maytals, a stint that revealed international possibilities for performing original reggae material rather than adapting pop songs. The group soon cut two albums—*Rock the Boat* (1974) and *Blame It on the Sun* (1975)—issued by Trojan Records in the United Kingdom, though both records were released under different titles in Jamaica.

By 1976, the band's solid reputation had earned them a contract with Capitol Records in the United States. Their debut for Capitol, *Reggae Thing* (1976), earned a decidedly cold critical response, as one *Rolling Stone* magazine reviewer

accused them of being "faceless" and "without distinguishing characteristics." It's curious that one song, "Love Is a Drug," featured guitar work from Neal Schon of future rock superstars Journey (who shared the same management), a group that would endure precisely the same criticism. Despite having proven musical capability and the charismatic and obviously gifted singer Miller fronting the band, Inner Circle's top 40 pop leanings often led to them being disregarded as an anonymous, throwaway outfit. At the time, there were also many stereotypical ideas about how a reggae band should sound, and Inner Circle's professional sound and versatility didn't meet many critics' roots reggae expectations. *Reggae Thing* did, however, yield the Jamaican hit "Forward Jah Jah Children," which Miller had previously cut as a solo artist in 1974.

The group's performance vitality and attention to songcraft were clearly evident in the closing segment of the 1977 documentary *Roots Rock Reggae*, which featured top reggae acts in performances, interviews, and studio activity. Inner Circle's inclusion confirmed their high standing in the reggae scene at the time. That same year, a lack of commercial response, promotion, or both for the album *Ready for the World* suggested that many major labels, including Capitol, simply didn't know how to break reggae albums into the mainstream market.

Both *Reggae Thing* and *Ready for the World* failed to make a dent in the United States, but Inner Circle's domestic credibility remained intact with a well-received live appearance at Bob Marley's 1978 One Love Peace Concert, a gathering that challenged the political violence sweeping Jamaica at a time of deepening economic woes. By the

next year, Inner Circle had migrated to Island Records. Thanks to a roster that included Bob Marley & the Wailers, Third World, Burning Spear, and Bunny Wailer, Island had become the reggae label with the greatest international credibility. Meanwhile, in 1978 the group unleashed two of the strongest albums in their entire catalog: *Heavyweight Dub* and *Killer Dub*, on which the Lewis brothers dubbed themselves the "Fatman Riddim Section," a subsidiary unit on future Inner Circle releases. With rhythm tracks from Jacob Miller's two late-1970s solo albums, *Killer Miller* (1977) and *Wanted* (1978), these records made a forceful, combined statement about the inscrutable depth of Inner Circle's reggae roots. It didn't hurt that *Heavyweight Dub* and *Killer Dub* were mixed at Channel One and King Tubby's studio in Jamaica, respectively, or that the latter was mixed by Tubby's apprentice Prince Jammy. All of these associations linked Inner Circle with reggae's highest production qualities and sound. The albums proved beyond any doubt that this music, which they decided wasn't in the major-label mold, was as fit as any reggae for top-class "dubwise" treatment. Dub may be an engineer's art, but even the best mixer must have something to work with, and Inner Circle provided plenty.

Everything Is Great (1979) got a promotional push in Britain thanks to a positive critical response and Inner Circle's tour with the Average White Band, the improbable Scottish funk band. However, Inner Circle had once again become victims of their wide musical vocabulary. They tapped into straight-ahead disco on the album's title track, while other songs brought rock elements to the fore. Despite their reggae credentials, the overt infusion of pop may have confused the same crossover audiences they were trying to reach, creating an identity crisis. Nonetheless,

Members of Inner Circle on the streets of Kingston during the filming of *Roots Rock Reggae* (1977), a documentary featuring top reggae acts.

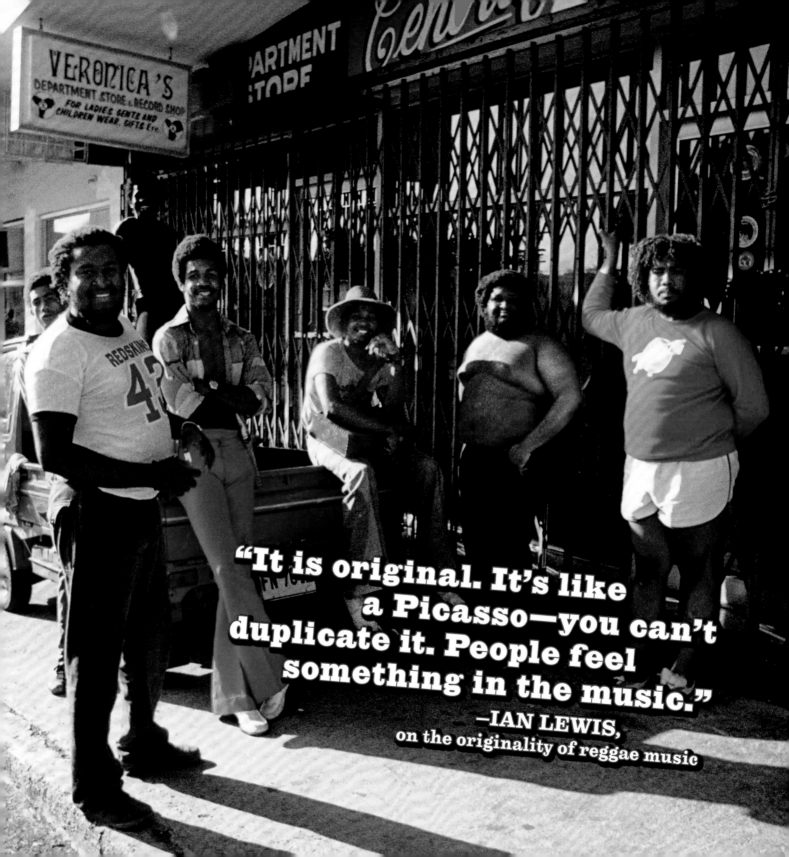

"It is original. It's like a Picasso—you can't duplicate it. People feel something in the music."

—IAN LEWIS,
on the originality of reggae music

both "Everything Is Great" and "Stop Breaking My Heart" made the top fifty of the British singles chart in 1979. It would be another thirteen years before they scored another UK pop hit.

Tragedy struck in March 1980, when Miller was killed in a car crash, curtailing a career with a very bright future. Miller's death marked a major turning point, as Inner Circle collapsed and the Lewis brothers responded to the setbacks by decamping to Miami and establishing a new base there. They appeared to be searching for a new direction when the less inspired, pop-centered *New Age Music* (so titled before the term was used to describe a genre) emerged later in 1980 as Miller's final contribution to the band's legacy. The pop-flavored *Something So Good* hit the shelves in 1982 with an unidentified lead singer. Magnifying the band's lack of definition at that time, the record was later issued with a wide variety of cover designs.

Their next vocalist, Jamaican Carlton Coffie, debuted on the *Black Roses* album (1986) and appeared on 1987's *One Way*, as the band reaffirmed its existence. Although the LP wasn't a big hit, it contained the original version of "Bad Boys," later known as the theme song for the long-running US television series *Cops*. A lean phase then ensued in the band's long reconstruction process and lasted until 1993, when the band finally capitalized on the "Bad Boys" television exposure. The song became Inner Circle's biggest international hit, selling more than a million copies in the United States and breaching the top ten. The 1993 album of the same name also became their only platinum release, aided by the success of the follow-up single, "Sweat" (originally "Make U Sweat" on the 1992 *Bad to the Bone* album), which helped them secure a Grammy Award for the best reggae album in 1994. This was sweet reward for Inner Circle's persistence against the odds, as

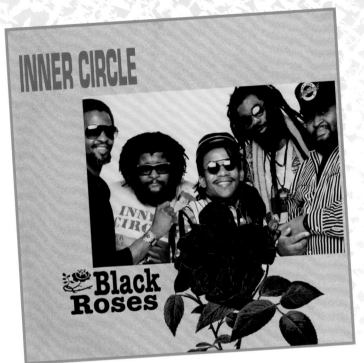

INNER CIRCLE

many had written them off after Jacob Miller's death thirteen years earlier.

Inner Circle's next record, *Reggae Dancer* (1994), was not nearly as commercially successful, although it earned them another Grammy nomination. Lead singer Carlton Coffie fell ill in 1995 and was replaced—first temporarily, then permanently in 1996—by Kris Bentley, former lead singer of the Jamaican group Skool. The commercial breakthroughs, awards, and personnel adjustments established a solid platform for Inner Circle's global touring marathon that continues today across Europe, Latin America, and Asia. (However, to highlight one of reggae's occasional global obstacles, the song "Sweat" was banned in the predominantly Muslim country of Malaysia because of its sexually suggestive lyrics.) They were unable to achieve international chart success with any of their records after *Bad Boys*, but the demand for live reggae at festivals around the world means Inner Circle will continue performing for some time to come.

MEMBERS: Jacob Miller (vocals), d. 1980; Roger Lewis (guitar); Ian "Munty" Lewis (bass, guitar, percussion); Calvin McKenzie (drums, percussion), 1973 to present; Bernard "Touter" Harvey (keyboards), 1973 to present; Charles Farquharson (keyboards) 1973 to present

SELECT DISCOGRAPHY: *Dread Reggae Hits / Rock the Boat* (Starapple/Trojan, 1974); *Heavy Reggae/Blame It on the Sun* (Starapple/Trojan, 1975); *Reggae Thing* (Capitol, 1976); *Ready for the World* (Capitol, 1977); *Barry Biggs & Inner Circle* (Trojan, 1977); *Heavyweight Dub* (Top Ranking Sounds, 1978); *Killer Dub* (Top Ranking Sounds, 1978); *Everything Is Great* (Island, 1979); *New Age Music* (Island 1980); *Something So Good* (Carrere, 1982); *One Way* (RAS, 1987); *Black Roses* (RAS, 1990); *Identified* (Vision, 1991); *Bad to the Bone* (RAS 1992); *Bad Boys* (Big Beat/Atlantic Records, 1993); *The Best of Inner Circle: The Capitol Years 1976–1977* (Capitol, 1993); *Reggae Dancer* (Atlantic, 1994); *Da Bomb* (Soundbwoy, 1997); *Speak My Language* (Uptown/Universal Records, 1998); *Jamaika Me Crazy* (Eureka, 1999); *State of Da World* (Shanachie, 2009)

GREGORY ISAACS

YEARS ACTIVE: 1960s-2010

Few singers with nasal deliveries have attracted the rabid adoration of audiences, but Gregory Isaacs is one of the exceptions. That respect also extended to a community of first-class producers and engineers who worked with him—King Jammy, Lee Perry, King Tubby, Sly & Robbie, and Gussie Clarke, to name a few. Isaacs didn't invent lovers rock, but he is one of the singers most commonly associated with that mellowed-out style of reggae. Known as the Cool Ruler, he specialized in tortured tales of romantic need, and while many of his songs also had a distinct sociopolitical focus, they weren't among his more popular recordings.

Isaacs was born in Kingston, Jamaica, in 1951 and raised by his mother, along with his younger brother, Sylvester, after his father left Jamaica for America. Isaacs was influenced early on by such local stars as the Melodians and Alton Ellis, as well as American giants Sam Cooke and Otis Redding. His first recording was "Another Heartbreak" (1968), a song he cut at age seventeen as a duet with singer and friend Winston Sinclair on a blank label (a white label without printed artist or song title information). In the absence of any kind of promotion, the song had no commercial success. In 1969, Isaacs formed his first group, the Concords, a vocal trio on producer Rupie Edwards's Success record label. Having made little headway with the group, Isaacs left around 1970 to pursue a solo career, which he felt was his natural direction. Around this time (1970 by some estimates), Isaacs, in partnership with singer Errol Dunkley, established the African Museum combined record label and record shop in Kingston. The venture

Even without a throne, reggae's Cool Ruler, Gregory Isaacs, exudes smoothness, 1977.

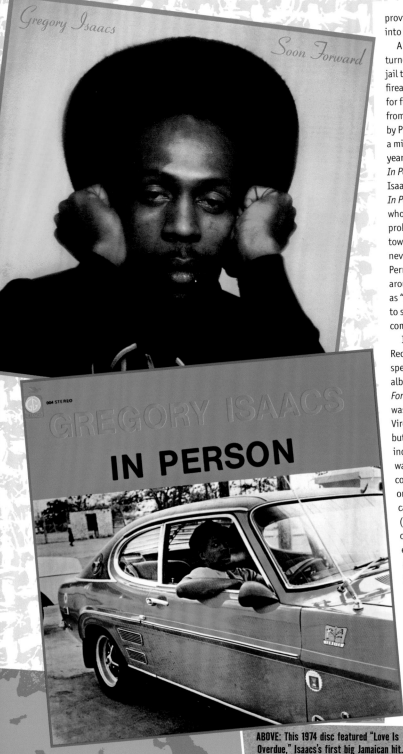

Gregory Isaacs

Soon Forward

GREGORY ISAACS

004 STEREO

IN PERSON

provided Isaacs with valuable insights into the business side of music.

A police raid on his house in 1972 turned up a gun and led to Isaacs serving jail time for the possession of an illegal firearm, setting an unfortunate precedent for future events. After being released from prison, "All I Have Is Love," produced by Phil Pratt and released in 1973, became a minor Jamaican hit, but the following year's "Love Is Overdue," from Isaacs's *In Person* album, had greater impact. Isaacs had a turbulent relationship with *In Person* producer Alvin "GG" Ranglin, who he felt was dishonest, and this was probably an incentive for him to move toward occasional self-production. He nevertheless worked with producer Lee Perry at the Black Ark studio in Kingston around 1975, recording such hit singles as "Mr. Cop," on which he urged police to show more humanity and sense of community.

In 1978, Isaacs signed to Virgin Records' Front Line label, which specialized in reggae, and released two albums, *Cool Ruler* (1978) and *Soon Forward* (1979). He felt that *Cool Ruler* was one of his best releases, and that Virgin did a good job promoting it, but since he was still cutting tracks for independent labels in Jamaica, there was soon a glut of his material. It's a controversial statement to make, but one of the strongest albums in his catalog, *Slum: Gregory Isaacs in Dub* (1978), is one on which his vocals are only partially present. Mixed by dub engineer extraordinaire Prince Jammy and repeatedly reissued throughout the years, the record brings out the roots reggae depth of Isaacs's music while also providing an aural snapshot of the tense social atmosphere in Jamaica during the late 1970s.

His appearance as a criminal character in the film *Rockers* (1979) may have kept him in the public eye, but the context was unflattering, even though he was shown onstage performing. Isaacs was imprisoned again around 1981, this time for cocaine possession,

after the police searched him while he was walking home one night. That same year, his album *More Gregory*, released on the short-lived Pre Records label, landed on the lower reaches of the British album charts.

On 1982's *Night Nurse*, Isaacs was backed by the rising Jamaican studio outfit the Roots Radics band and Paris-born ace keyboardist Wally Badarou. This was the first product of a two-album deal that Isaacs's manager signed with Island Records, and Isaacs later left the label on good terms, happy with his heightened international profile. *Night Nurse* crossed over to the mainstream in Britain, reaching #32 on the album chart. Isaacs was still in jail when the record started getting airplay, and his incarceration left him unable to capitalize on his biggest hit. It's justifiably argued that drugs were the only real obstacle between Isaacs and a higher level of stardom. He eventually suffered lost teeth and reduced vocal capability, as well as lost gig opportunities, as a result of his drug habit. To make matters worse, he was once again detained and imprisoned for six months in 1982 on a weapons charge. The 1983 album *Out Deh!* was largely a prison autobiography and reflection.

After a lean spell, "Rumours," produced by Gussie Clarke in 1988, represented a reggae market comeback for Isaacs. It was released during the digital dancehall era, which threatened to engulf many of the previous decade's reggae crooners. Unfortunately, Isaacs's drug problems persisted, as did their physical and legal consequences.

Isaacs's appearance in the 2006 reggae documentary *Made in Jamaica* is especially revealing. In the film, he describes the hard-core world of violence, poverty, and social injustice from which he emerged as an artist. It's ironic that an individual so aware of his surroundings and of the need for financial and creative independence in the music business would allow his talent to be so easily tarnished by a drug addiction that siphoned away so much of the money he had worked so hard

FRICAN MUSEU

to earn. His flashy style of dress was counterbalanced by his use of cocaine, but few will remember that undesirable aspect of his life the next time they hear "Night Nurse."

His final studio album, *Brand New Me* (2008), showed real signs of creative resurgence and renewed performance capability. Unfortunately, on October 25, 2010—after a life marked by countless arrests and album releases estimated to be in the hundreds—the Cool Ruler died of lung cancer at age fifty-nine in London, England.

SELECT DISCOGRAPHY: *All Have Is Love* (Tad's, 1973); *Mr. Isaacs* (Shanachie, 1977); *Cool Ruler* (Front Line, 1978); *Slum: Gregory Isaacs in Dub* (Burning Sounds, 1978); *Soon Forward* (Front Line, 1979); *More Gregory* (Pre, 1981); *Night Nurse* (Mango/Island, 1982); *Out Deh!* (Mango/Island, 1983); *Private Beach Party* (Greensleeves, 1985); *Red Rose for Gregory* (Greensleeves 1988); *Brand New Me* (African Museum, 2008)

Gregory Isaacs (center) steps away from the cash register at his African Museum record shop in Kingston, 1983.

African Museum

Produced by:
G. Isaac
Museum

Produced &
Arranged by:
Gregory Issacs

Ja, W.I.

RUB A DUB
(G. ISSACS)
GREGORY ISSACS

ALL UNAUTHORISED COPYING OF THIS LABEL IS STRICTLY PROHIBITED

HARD ROAD TO TRAVEL
JIMMY CLIFF

ISLAND RECORDS

Island Records is uniquely important among all of the labels involved in reggae's penetration of the global pop mainstream. Best known for releasing landmark albums by Bob Marley & the Wailers, Island became inseparably linked to reggae's peak commercial years in the 1970s and 1980s, when founder Chris Blackwell was at the helm. Without Island's international success, it's anyone's guess where reggae would be today.

Blackwell was born on June 22, 1937, in England, but spent his childhood in Jamaica, where his family had accumulated wealth and property. He was sent to England for private education in his home country. Following his expulsion from the Harrow School in northwest

London for selling alcohol and cigarettes to his classmates, Blackwell worked briefly as an accountant with Price, Waterhouse & Co., and later enjoyed an apparently more successful spell as a racetrack and card game gambler, developing sensibilities that would serve him well in the music business. He returned to Jamaica and served brief stints in various jobs, including assistant to the country's governor general, a representative of the British monarchy in states associated with the British empire. Such conventional vocations did little to nurture Blackwell's business intuition, however. While in Jamaica, his awareness of consumer behavior was also sharpened by his jobs renting motor scooters and teaching water-skiing.

An often-recounted story describes how, at age nineteen, Blackwell was rescued and nursed back to health by Rastamen after his motorboat ran out of gas and was stranded in an isolated swamp on the south coast of Jamaica. After searching fruitlessly for help for four to five hours and suffering from extreme thirst, Blackwell came upon a hut belonging to the Rastamen, who provided him with water and a place to rest. He fell asleep and awoke to find himself in the presence of Rastas, who read him Bible passages and returned him by boat to the Port Royal coastal area. This early exposure to the Rastas' "ital" food (a vegetarian diet devoid of processed food) and Bible-based philosophies was the complete opposite of what Blackwell had been taught to expect, as Rastas were portrayed as demonic in colonial Jamaica. The incident established within Blackwell a deeper link to Jamaican culture and gave him a greater understanding—or "overstanding," in Rasta-speak—of how it should be represented.

Blackwell formed Island Records in 1958, as the Jamaican music scene was still developing. The label's first LP—an album of jazz standards by Lance

Aswad's Tony "Gad" Robinson (left) and Angus "Drummie Zeb" Gaye admire the Island Records studio in St. Peter's Square, London, 1985.

Haywood, a blind hotel pianist from Bermuda—was released that year, when Blackwell was still based in Jamaica. By 1960, Island had scored its first hit single by a Jamaican artist, "Boogie in My Bones" by Laurel Aitken. The next year Blackwell worked as a production assistant on the first James Bond film, *Dr. No*, following a recommendation to the film's director from Ian Fleming, the author of the Bond novels.

After receiving a permanent job offer from the film company Eon Productions, Blackwell consulted a fortune-teller in Kingston, who suggested that he stick to his own independent path. Blackwell heeded this advice, and in 1962, after he'd established Island in England with a mere $5,300, the label issued its first albums in Britain by Jamaican artists. By this point, Island had licensed rights to Jamaican recordings from sound-system operators and record company entrepreneurs such as Duke Reid and Coxsone Dodd. Blackwell's departure from Jamaica roughly coincided with the country gaining its independence from Britain. In one interview with reggae historian David Katz, Blackwell noted, "I felt that in view of my complexion, I'd be more associated with the past than the future of Jamaica." It's a highly ironic statement, given that his subsequent roles in the music business would give Jamaica a firm international profile.

The very first Island LP was the self-explanatory *Keith and Enid Sing* by Jamaican singers Keith Stewart and Enid Cumberland. Through these first releases, Blackwell was primarily servicing relocated West Indians in such English cities as London, Birmingham, and Manchester. Island also sold records on subsidiary labels, such as the calypso-focused Jump Up imprint.

The 1964 licensing of Jamaican singer Millie Small's version of the R&B song "My Boy Lollipop" to Fontana Records was a major turning point. The single became a global chart hit, selling more than six million copies and confirming Blackwell's commercial instincts. However, by the mid-1960s, as his involvement in the Jamaican scene decreased, he had turned his attention to the growing rock LP market, focusing on British acts. Still, in 1967 Island released its first Jimmy Cliff album, *Hard Road to Travel*, the opening chapter of one of reggae's most important artist and record label relationships, and one that would help define the genre in the early 1970s. By 1968, Island's subsidiary reggae labels were sold to the B&C (Beat & Commercial) company, which had been founded in England by Jamaican businessman Lee Gopthal. The new joint label was called Trojan Records, a partnership with Island Records. Following the creation of Trojan, as Island transitioned into the rock market, such releases became increasingly sporadic. By 1972, Island had split from the

ABOVE: Island Records founder Chris Blackwell in 1977, at the height of Island's heyday and the year he built Compass Point studio in the Bahamas.

NEVER GROW OLD b/w IRENE by THE VIKINGS

partnership over business conflicts and left B&C in sole charge of Trojan.

By this time, Blackwell had made a deal with independent label A&M Records to get Island material released in the United States. In 1971, he attempted to boost Cliff's career through this channel. Although the title track from Cliff's *Wonderful World, Beautiful People* album reached #25 on the American singles chart, the commercial failure of the album signaled the need for other strategies to break reggae in the US market. Two other landmark albums would eventually draw American audiences toward Island's reggae acts. The first was the sound track to the 1972 Jamaican cult film *The Harder They Come*, which was not released in America until 1975. It peaked at only #140 on the album chart but laid the foundation for reggae's future, arguably helping to open the American market for Bob Marley.

The next album involved a group that came to Chris Blackwell's attention just as he and Cliff parted ways over how the artist's career should be developed. Following the collapse of other record and tour deals, Bob Marley, Peter Tosh, and Bunny Wailer—then collectively known as the Wailers— found themselves stranded in England and approached Blackwell about recording a new album. This became the iconic 1972 release *Catch a Fire*. This album is the touchstone of Island's internationalization of reggae, as both its musical content and packaging were designed to reach rock audiences. Blackwell recalled in an interview, "I really felt the best way to break the Wailers was as a Black rock group . . . to make the record more accessible to a rock audience. . . . " This meant adding rock guitar and keyboard overdubs in London after the basic tracks had been cut in Jamaica, and for some listeners this was a controversial move. But the memorable Zippo lighter album cover, the inclusion of liner notes, and the photography of the band combined to create a statement of intent: This was music to be taken seriously.

By the late 1970s, concurrent with the commercial emergence of Bob Marley & the Wailers, Britain's own second-generation reggae acts had begun to demand attention. Aswad and Steel Pulse, two of Island's earliest signings from the burgeoning domestic scene, added to a prestigious roots roster that now included such Jamaican acts as Burning Spear, Lee Perry, Toots & the Maytals, and Third World. With the abundance of widely distributed, high-quality releases—many of them accompanied by some of the genre's best album covers (such as the Wailers'

(l–r): Ex-Beatle George Harrison hangs backstage with Island USA head of publicity Jeff Walker, Bob Marley, and Island USA president Charley Nuccio.

Burnin' in 1973, and Rasta singer Ijahman Levi's *Haile I Hymn* in 1978)—the 1970s constituted a classic era not only for Island but for reggae in general. The rebellious photo of Bob Marley on the back of the *Burnin'* album sleeve was taken by one of his many lovers, actress Esther Anderson, who claimed in a 2012 interview that she hadn't been paid by Island for that creative work. (Disillusioned by this and a general lack of acknowledgment of her developmental roles with Island, she sued the label's current owner, Universal Music, for compensation.)

In 1977, Blackwell built the idyllic Compass Point studio in the Bahamas, a facility that essentially functioned as the label's house recording center, freeing up more time for acts to perfect their creative visions. Marley's death in 1981 was, in commercial terms, both a blow and a boon to the label, as three years later, Island released what would become reggae's best-selling album, *Legend*. More than twelve million copies have been sold in the United States alone, taking it past platinum status (more than one million copies) and into diamond territory (more than ten million copies).

The label's continued successful involvement in the rock world made it a valuable takeover target, and in 1989, Blackwell sold the label for $300 million to what was then Polygram Records. Through other mergers and acquisitions, the buyer of Island had become Universal Music by the mid-1990s. Blackwell initially stayed on at the label as an advisor but soon tired of the corporate restrictions and sought out his next challenges. These included establishing the short-lived Island Jamaica record label and the Palm Pictures film company. Island's reggae profile soon dwindled, as it became little more than a label imprint without the direction, identity, or purpose of its heyday. The world was reminded of the label's valuable contribution to reggae when Island celebrated its fiftieth anniversary in 2009, though it now exists in the shadow of its rich past.

Famous Jamaican actress Esther Anderson was involved in development at Island Records in its early days.

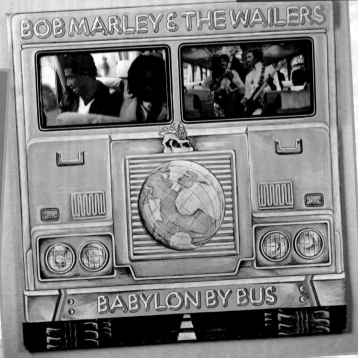

REGGAE ALBUM COVERS

As the cliché goes, you can't judge a book—or in this case, a record—by its cover, and yet we make such judgments all the time. In *Stir It Up* (1999), perhaps the only major book devoted to reggae album art, American author Chris Morrow suggests that the golden age for cover designs began in the 1960s, during the ska and rocksteady eras of Jamaican music. That may be so, but some of the genre's most memorable artistic and political images emerged in the period roughly spanning 1973 to 1983. Prior to the reggae era and even in its early phase, jacket designs were rudimentary and generic, as evidenced on records released by Jamaica's Studio One label and Britain's Trojan Records. Many of the early Island Records releases—albums that introduced such Jamaican artists as Jackie Edwards, Ernest Ranglin, and Jimmy Cliff to UK audiences—had no design credits at all.

The first reggae covers created in Jamaica were usually rushed affairs, since album art was typically the least of a producer's concerns. As with the music, much of the initial inspiration for the covers was drawn (pun intended) from the American R&B scene, as demonstrated on the Wailers' pre-reggae *Wailing Wailers* (1965) record jacket. The cover shows Bob Marley, Peter Tosh, and Bunny Wailer in slick suits, trying their best to look like the American soul vocal group the Impressions. Those early covers shared much in common with the similarly unimaginative jackets adorning the era's calypso records, and a distinctive genre identity was yet to be established. As Morrow notes, unlike their higher-profile counterparts in the rock world, the producers or labels that financed the releases also excluded early reggae artists from licensing and packaging decisions.

The evolution of reggae as an art form is well reflected in the ambitious album covers produced by Island Records, especially during the roots reggae era of the 1970s. Though other labels made noteworthy contributions, Island was the most influential in reshaping people's perceptions of reggae and transforming its visual presentation. It wasn't always this way at Island, however. Much of the label's cover art for Jamaican music in the 1960s is typified by the rather basic artwork of Jamaican singer Joyce Bond's 1967 *Soul and Ska* album. Attempting to capitalize on the similarity of the singer's name with the popular fictional movie spy James Bond, that cover featured a circular inset black and white photo of Joyce Bond posing with two guns drawn. Set against a sharply contrasting bright red cover background, with mauve lettering superimposed, its overall effect is not compelling.

With the success of Bob Marley & the Wailers, Island's records and their cover images achieved widespread global distribution. While Island founder Chris Blackwell's push to commercialize the sound of reggae has long been a point of controversy, there is no doubt that Island's

design savvy helped the music break through to international markets in the 1970s. Blackwell brought his rock-market sensibility and a clear awareness of the critical relationships between sound and visuals in popular music. In the 2009 book *Keep On Running: The Story of Island Records*, Blackwell concludes, "I was always very interested in artwork. If you felt the artwork was intriguing then there must be something going on inside. There's some thought, there's some creativity.

LA BOSTELLA ● WALK AWAY ● MORE & MORE AMORE ● BLOWING IN THE WIND ● SPANISH EYES ● ARCHIE ● WHAT NOW MY LOVE? ● LEMON TREE ● YOU WON'T SEE ME ● BORN FREE ● FELICIA ● SOMEWHERE MY LOVE

Artwork was very important to Island's life . . . always seeming a reflection of the larger world."

British and American designers and art directors hired by Island had access to stylish printing, typography, and photography, and as a result they produced work that was far more polished—though not necessarily more relevant to the music. The original cover and packaging for the Wailers' international debut, *Catch a Fire* (released in the US in 1973) was designed by Rod Dyer Inc., in the United States, where visual artists employed by major labels had access to a wide range of creative resources. The record's flashy cigarette lighter visuals were in keeping with the rock-oriented commercial transformations heard in the music.

In major contrast, because Jamaican designers had limited technical options and finances, their covers focused mainly on illustration. The *Catch a Fire* cover was developed as part of a larger packaging concept. The two halves of the jacket were riveted together by hand, and this made the manufacturing process very expensive. Only twenty thousand copies were made before this sleeve was

and marijuana subsequently became both the visual signposts and stereotypes of reggae, leading many record buyers to assume that they coexist *only* in the context of reggae. This, of course, is not true, and today, musicians working in various genres wear dreadlocks. Interestingly, while the packaging for 2001's *Catch a Fire* deluxe edition CD recreates the original LP cover,

Island emphasized the substitute photo in its promotional campaign.

As the tide of reggae and Rasta consciousness gathered momentum, the genre became defined by a handful of visual signifiers that echoed the social, political, and economic spheres within which the music was made. The collective red, green, and gold color scheme of the Ethiopian flag became a key element, and this was often used in conjunction with other major symbols of Pan-Africanism, among them the lion, Ethiopian Emperor Haile Selassie (considered a living god by some Rastas), the continent of Africa, and military uniforms and weaponry tied to armed struggle and revolution. The popularity of Hollywood westerns was reflected in both artists' names—Clint Eastwood, for example—and the attire they chose for album covers, whether illustrated or photographed. In the case of the often radically remixed dub records, mixing desks sometimes figured into the artwork, indicating the star role of the remix engineer. The *Tighten Up* compilation series launched by Trojan Records in the late 1960s featured scantily clad women. Considering Trojan's role as a leading British reggae label in the late 1960s and early 1970s, anyone interested in the genre

replaced. There are also accounts of the jacket rivets scratching the record, both during the shipping process and in the hands of consumers. The original jacket has become a major collector's item, and copies often sell for more than one hundred dollars on the Internet.

The substitute *Catch a Fire* cover, featuring a photo of Marley smoking a joint (or spliff), remains somewhat controversial. Whereas the original used artfully executed metaphor to convey the fiery urgency of Marley's music, the replacement was far less subtle. In a sense, the rebellious image of Marley smoking marijuana is more consistent with the aesthetics of immediacy and directness that had characterized most reggae album covers up to that point. However, the countercultural elements of dreadlocks

OPPOSITE: In the 1960s, Jamaican albums such as this one by Ernest Ranglin tended to be fairly generic.

ABOVE LEFT: For the cover of this 1965 LP, Bob Marley and his fellow Wailers took style cues from American soul singers the Impressions.

RIGHT: Boasting a flashy, high-concept sleeve whose cardboard halves are riveted together, the original version of this 1973 album has become a collector's item.

would likely have encountered this imagery. This did reggae no favors among feminists, and it was not until the emergence of notable female roots reggae artists like Rita Marley that more regal representations of women became commonplace. As roots gave way to dancehall and album artwork centered increasingly on illustrated portrayals of gritty sexuality, the sex symbol poses that had characterized earlier records returned with a vengeance.

Of course, one of the strongest anti-establishment symbols associated with reggae was ganja, and there was little commercial value in hiding its presence. Instead, artists and labels capitalized on the college audience's cravings for "collie"—one of marijuana's numerous pseudonyms—by blatantly advertising. High-profile examples include the back cover of the Wailers' *Burnin'* (1973), which features a large spliff, and the even bolder Peter Tosh album *Legalize It* (1976), whose cover photo shows the artist sitting in an herb field and smoking from a chalice.

When assessing the history of reggae album covers, it's useful to examine the work of Neville Garrick and Tony Wright. By no means are they the only significant art directors and designers of reggae covers, but they are two of the best known. Trained at the University of California, Los Angeles, Garrick has worked with numerous reggae legends. His illustrations and designs adorn the widely familiar Bob Marley & the Wailers albums spanning 1976's *Rastaman Vibration* to Marley's posthumous 1983 collection *Confrontation*. His cover for Bunny

Wailer's 1975 *Blackheart Man* album led to his work with Marley, and he later created covers for Tosh's *Wanted Dread & Alive* (1981) and *No Nuclear War* (1987) albums. Garrick is also responsible for the cover of top British reggae band Steel Pulse's 1984 album *Earth Crisis*. On more than one hundred covers, he has drawn inspiration from both album titles and his personal knowledge of the artists. Garrick also occasionally performed onstage with Marley as a percussionist, and he received a percussion credit on *Blackheart Man*, marking one of the few instances when a cover designer actually helped to shape the sound of a record.

It may be common knowledge among reggae fans that *Time* magazine named Marley's *Exodus* (1977) the "album of the century," but the story of how the lettering on the cover came into being is not as well known. In a 2008 interview in Jamaica, Garrick explained how he arrived at a new concept: "I had Ethiopian books, alphabets, and I started playing around, and I basically used letters from the Amharic alphabet

ABOVE: The popularity of Hollywood westerns in Jamaica led many artists to adopt cowboy themes on their record covers.

RIGHT: For this 1977 cover, talented designer Neville Garrick repurposed letters from Ethiopia's Amharic alphabet.

BOB MARLEY & THE WAILERS

. . . turning them in different angles from where they're normal to read English. It turned out to be brilliant." This refashioned lettering demonstrates how deceptively simple reggae album art often incorporates the past, present, and future—particularly as they relate to African people. Some artists are able to capture more facets of history and culture in their images than entire books convey.

Tony Wright was also prominent in Island's history. He began designing covers for the label's rock albums in 1969 and later became the in-house art director. In this role, he oversaw the production of covers for countless reggae albums, including Black Uhuru's *Sinsemilla* (1980). His better-known work includes Bob Marley & the Wailers' 1974 album *Natty Dread*.

Inspired by a nineteenth-century painting, the *Natty Dread* cover depicts the cataclysmic destruction of New York City. In what amounted to a minor concession, the label cropped the image to exclude most of the toppling building in the top right-hand corner. By this time, Tosh and Wailer had left the Wailers, and Blackwell insisted that Marley appear on the cover. The label opted for an illustration, not a photograph, and as Wright explained to me in a 2007 interview, this was another calculated move. "If you wanted to make a record look as if it was serious music—not just something released by EMI, [but instead] it was released by a label that cared—you'd put a painting on a cover or a piece of artwork rather than a photograph," he said. "It was very standard in those days." Instead of specifically criticizing EMI, Wright likely meant to highlight the tendency among major labels to create neutral covers that did not always represent the philosophical or artistic dimensions crucial to an artist's identity. While it was designed with the marketplace in mind, the *Natty Dread* cover presented apocalyptic imagery that implied the overthrow of "Babylon," the Rasta term for the establishment and the imperialist mindset—something Marley aimed for with his music.

Wright's work was a major reason that Island made such an impact in the reggae market. On the series of covers he designed for Jamaican reggae band Third World (1976's *Third World*, *96° in the Shade* in 1977, *Journey to Addis* in 1978, and 1979's *The Story's Been Told*) he actually told a continuing story, using the group's logo and recurring characters to create a narrative link between albums. Those first four Island Records covers for Third World, all designed by Wright, represent some of the most resonant visual statements in reggae history. Rather than give in to commercial concerns, Wright created an aura of cultural authenticity. While the covers are known for their narrative arc, Island did not initially plan on such continuity. Based on a Haitian painting brought to Wright by Blackwell, the art for Third World's self-titled 1976 debut was initially conceived of as a one-off.

Wright also designed and illustrated the 1978 and 1979 Island album covers for reggae singer Ijahman Levi. In search of a final defining image to complement otherwise finished work for *Are We a Warrior* (1979), Wright cleverly incorporated the previous album cover into the current one, illustrating the name and central image of *Haile I Hymn* (1978) on Ijahman's shirt. Largely due to Island's push for crossover success,

LEFT: The cover of this 1978 LP was part of a four-album visual narrative devised by artist Tony Wright.

ABOVE: On this cleverly illustrated 1979 cover, Ijahman Levi's shirt features the artwork from his previous album.

these types of covers garnered widespread attention. Before long, rock covers began to bear distinct signs of reggae packaging. As Wright recalled, "When Bob Dylan asked me to make an image for his album *Saved* (1980), it was an amalgamation of this [Ijahman] cover and *Natty Dread* that he asked for. By 1980 all those originally obscure reggae releases had got through to a diverse number of people." The early albums of the punk era are prime evidence of this influence, and members of the iconic British group the Clash have spoken of how they gathered inspiration from looking at Jamaican covers. Wright's reggae-related work extended into film, as he also did the graphic design for the 1982 movie *Countryman*, shot on location in Jamaica.

Another label that has created notable reggae album art is Blood & Fire. With its reissues of vintage recordings, the UK label has created a unique style that links each artist to the company's overall identity. Although this has inevitably involved replacing the original covers, Blood & Fire has done so in a manner appropriate for the music.

In reggae, perhaps more than in any other genre, it's crucial for album artwork to convey cultural authenticity. The best covers, like the most powerful songs, need to communicate on multiple levels simultaneously, fusing roots sensibilities with artistic sophistication.

(l–r) Cecil "Skelly" Spence, Lacelle "Wiss" Bulg[in]
and Albert "Apple" Gabriel Craig overcame polio [and]
poverty to find success as Israel Vibration.

ISRAEL VIBRATION

YEARS ACTIVE: 1960s–1982; 1988–PRESENT

Overcoming obstacles with spiritual aid is a recurring theme in reggae, but few Jamaican groups have confronted the challenges faced by Israel Vibration. All three members of this roots reggae vocal trio were afflicted with polio as children during the 1950s and first met at what was then the Mona Rehabilitation Center in Kingston, Jamaica. In the 1960s, they each individually adopted Rastafari only to be treated as social outcasts.

Albert "Apple" Craig was deprived of the Center's rehab assistance, while Cecil "Skelly" Spence was booted from the Jamaican wheelchair sports team. Lascelle "Wiss" Bulgin, who had been working as a tailor's apprentice, was suddenly fired from his job after returning one day to find his work space cleared away. Craig studied for a time at the Alpha School in Kingston, through which so many Jamaican musicians passed, but he found the institution's rules and regulations too restrictive. He began living on the streets, singing for money at age fourteen.

Meeting again in Kingston a few years later as Rasta brethren, the three young men began literally singing for survival, the harshness of their circumstances between 1969 and 1975 informing their lyrics. Their poverty affected their physical appearance and therefore their ability to acquire financial backing once they began seeking a record deal and named themselves Israel Vibration. After an unreleased studio recording for the Channel One label, renowned for its sonic clarity and its Revolutionaries house session band, Israel Vibration scored their first Jamaican hit in 1977 with the spiritually focused, Spence-penned composition "Why Worry." The recording was funded by the Rasta organization Twelve Tribes of Israel and released on the Orthodox label, which was this sect's recording imprint. "The Same Song"—recorded with the band Inner Circle's Fatman Riddim Section (principally guitarist Roger Lewis and his bassist brother Ian Lewis) —became the title track of Israel Vibration's 1978 debut album, produced by Jamaican music industry entrepreneur Tommy Cowan, head of the Top Ranking Sounds label. A dub version of the record followed, and remarkably, thanks to Cowan, Israel Vibration immediately attracted major-label attention. EMI licensed the album for UK release on its Harvest label, a formerly progressive-rock–oriented imprint also home to the British reggae band Matumbi.

On 1980's *Unconquered People*, Israel Vibration actively pursued a roots direction in which they all shared lead vocals, receiving musical backing from top Jamaican session musicians including four members of the Wailers.

For the album's follow-up, they worked with Henry "Junjo" Lawes, putting their sound in the hands of one of dancehall's leading producers. This decision alarmed some fans, and the resulting album, *Why You So Craven* (1982), reportedly involved creative conflicts with Lawes that may have affected the impact of the finished product. Dissatisfied with their career, the band split up in 1982, just as dancehall's popularity was growing—and bringing racy sex-based topics and increasingly digital music to the forefront. Despite their apparent separation, all three members wound up in Brooklyn, New York, recording solo singles and occasionally performing individually. The group eventually reunited for the 1988 album *Strength of My Life*, released on the American RAS Records label.

Israel Vibration's consistent—though not earth-shattering—output in this second phase of their career was supplemented in 1995 by *Reggae in Holyland*, a film chronicling their 1993 tour of Israel. The film presents a rather curious spectacle, as three Rastamen and their Roots Radics band members (producer Lawes's Jamaican studio band for his early dancehall records) negotiate a decidedly foreign environment. Craig quit for the second time in 1997, leaving Spence and Bulgin to continue Israel Vibration as a duo focused on live international gigs.

MEMBERS: **Lascelle "Wiss" Bulgin** (vocals); **Cecil "Skelly" Spence** (vocals); **Albert "Apple" Craig** (vocals)

SELECT DISCOGRAPHY: *The Same Song* (Top Ranking Sounds, 1978); *Unconquered People* (Greensleeves, 1980); *Why You So Craven* (RAS, 1982); *Strength of My Life* (RAS, 1988); *Praises* (RAS 1990); *Israel Dub* (RAS, 1996); *Free to Move* (RAS, 1996); *Pay the Piper* (Sanctuary, 1999); *Dub Combo* (Sanctuary, 2001); *Live & Jammin'* (RAS/ Sanctuary, 2003); *Cool & Calm* (RAS, 2005); *Stamina* (Tafari Music, 2007)

LINTON KWESI JOHNSON
YEARS ACTIVE: 1970s–2000s

Linton Kwesi Johnson—also referred to as LKJ—is perhaps the most widely known and commercially successful dub poet in reggae history. Dub, a remixing concept that reveals a reggae song's basic instrumental and vocal elements while adding spacy effects, was the ideal backdrop for antiestablishment spoken word denunciation. While there is a tendency among listeners to group all revolution-focused reggae artists under a single ideological Rastafari banner, however, Johnson breaks the stereotype. He considers himself to be an atheist and doesn't embrace the idea that Haile Selassie is god or that large-scale repatriation of Caribbean people to Africa is a viable concept. Even so, his work echoes the steadfastly antiestablishment stance of Rastafari.

Johnson was born in Chapelton, Jamaica, on August 24, 1952, and raised in an environment where the absence of electricity ruled out television, radio, and even streetlights. He discovered the Bible at an early age, learning the power of the written word. His life was drastically altered in 1963, when he left the Jamaican countryside to join his mother in Brixton, a densely populated urban section of London, England. The social discomfort he experienced there led him to join the British arm of the Black Panthers, a militant group engaged in armed opposition to authorities in the US in a quest for African-American civil rights. That association laid the foundation for the revolutionary perspectives on black culture and history that would surface in Johnson's writing.

Long before he began recording, Johnson incorporated musical elements in his poetry. Driven by his involvement

Dub poet Linton Kwesi Johnson at New York City's Iroquois Hotel, 1981, the year after Johnson's album *LKJ in Dub* was released by Island Records.

in black social movements and his need to express his feelings about the racism, police victimization, and economic marginalization he witnessed in his Brixton community, Johnson began performing locally at a young age with Rasta drummers, who would accompany him during his readings. He cites the ambitious 1973 triple album *Grounation* by Ras Michael & the Sons of Negus as one of his prime musical influences, partly for its combination of poetry and drumming. Other influences were many: Various African American, African, and Caribbean writers who shaped his approach to language (Barbadian poet Edward Kamau Brathwaite was an especially influential figure); the recorded work of Jamaican poet Louise Bennett, in which she uses the island's dialect; and the pioneering reggae DJ Big Youth and other storytellers who favored a talking-singing style.

Johnson's studies in sociology at London's Goldsmiths College provided additional ammunition for his work, leading to the publication of his first volume of poetry, 1974's *Voices of the Living and Dead*.

After performing regularly and participating in poetry workshops within the West Indian community, Johnson began to find an audience for his material through radio and television appearances. His next printed volume of poetry, *Dread Beat an' Blood*, was issued in 1975. It continued to address themes of racism, politics, and crises of the black human condition, foregrounding his use of Jamaican patois and an authentic accent seemingly untouched by his time in Britain.

Johnson's recording debut came in 1978, when his critically acclaimed printed poetry

volume from three years earlier was set to roots rhythms and recast as the album *Dread Beat an' Blood*, originally released under the pseudonym Poet and the Roots on Virgin Records' Front Line label. His deal with Virgin came about partly through his work as a copywriter for print ads that the company used to sell reggae releases following the establishment of Front Line. Ironically, Johnson's facility with language in another context had helped him reach a wider audience even as the album was

representative of reggae's resistance to political exploitation.

Johnson's stylistic approach extended Afro-Caribbean traditions of oral expression, and his fusion of spoken word with reggae rhythms effectively created a new genre. In a 2008 radio interview, Johnson said, "The term 'dub poetry' was a phrase I coined way back in the midseventies to describe the art of the reggae DJ." In a poetry review essay in the British political periodical *Race Today*, Johnson also used the term to describe the prison poems of Oku Onuora (then known as Orlando Wong), a Jamaican writer jailed for involvement in an armed robbery who himself went on to record albums that were less well-known than Johnson's. Johnson credits Onuora with popularizing the term "dub poetry."

Johnson moved to Island Records for his second album, *Forces of Victory* (1979), continuing his powerful alliance with Dennis Bovell, whose production provided the appropriate rhythmic soundscape for the poetry. The following year, Johnson translated his 1980 poetry collection *Inglan Is a Bitch* into the *Bass Culture* album, a musical indictment of the former colonial mother country. *LKJ in Dub* was also released on Island in 1980. The album caught Bovell at a creative peak, after his years as a sound-

ABOVE: Linton Kwesi Johnson's 1978 debut was based on a volume of poetry he had released three years earlier and that earned high marks from critics.

LEFT: LKJ sets the record straight with fellow activist Darcus Howe, 1991.

system operator, a member of British reggae group Matumbi, and a solo artist and producer. His varied skills merged perfectly to reinforce Johnson's messages. Johnson's spoken word contribution combined with Bovell's production at the dawn of the 1980s bolstered "Miami Beach" (1981), a caustic reggae commentary on police brutality from American artist Garland Jeffreys.

In 1984, Johnson clashed with Island over *Making History* after the label had remixed the album despite his objections. This friction led to Johnson's departure from the label in 1985 after a remarkably fruitful phase. Fortunately, he had formed his own LKJ Records label in 1981. In a 2007 magazine interview, Johnson asserted, "Starting my label was just practicing what I was preaching. It gave me a measure of independence from record companies. I can set my own agenda." Freed from the mechanical restraints of typical record companies—which tend to require cyclical recording and touring schedules almost regardless of their artists' creative moods—he released material at his own pace.

The following two decades witnessed the release of *LKJ in Dub: Volume 2* (1992) and *LKJ in Dub: Volume 3* (2002). Showcasing his diversity as an artist, he wrote and presented the British Broadcasting Corporation Radio documentary series *From Mento to Lovers' Rock* in 2005. The dub poet is committed to creative excellence but recognizes the difficulty of transcending earlier work.

SELECT DISCOGRAPHY: *Dread Beat an' Blood* (Virgin Front Line, 1978); *Forces of Victory* (Island Records, 1979); *Bass Culture* (Island, 1980); *LKJ in Dub* (Island, 1980); *Making History* (Island, 1984); *LKJ Live in Concert with the Dub Band* (LKJ Records, 1984); *LKJ in Dub, Vol.2* (LKJ, 1992); *LKJ in Dub, Vol.3* (LKJ, 2002)

JUDGE DREAD

YEARS ACTIVE: 1970s-1998

Alex Hughes, better known as Judge Dread, was born in England in 1945 and scored a series of British hits in the 1970s, effectively becoming reggae's longest-running novelty act. At the time, few could have predicted his commercial success, given that he was a white English reggae DJ whose songs were essentially risqué monologues. What's more, he had come to music from an unlikely background, having worked as a professional wrestler, a bodyguard for the Rolling Stones, and a nightclub bouncer. Rumor has it that for a time he was also a debt collector for the British reggae label Trojan Records. Judge Dread took his name from the title of a 1967 single by Jamaican singer Prince Buster and based much of his subject matter on another Buster track, the blatantly lewd "Big Five." In fact, Judge Dread's series of "Big Five" sequels—ultimately banned in Britain—formed the basis of his career.

The sexually themed hits began with "Big Six" (so named at the suggestion of his producers at Trojan), which reached #11 on the UK pop charts in 1972, selling three hundred thousand copies. Predictably, he followed this initial success with "Big Seven," another smutty song that made the top ten the same year. After moving from Trojan's Big Shot imprint to the EMI Records–distributed Cactus label, he released the single "Je T'Aime" in 1975. An odd spoken-word reggae parody of a song whose original pop version by Jane Birkin & Serge Gainsbourg had already been a UK hit three times between 1969 and 1974, the cover single sold four hundred thousand copies. It was quickly banned by the British Broadcasting Corporation (BBC) for its sexual content, in which Judge Dread referred to his genitals as "Big Nine," continuing the numerical sequence theme. The song's absurd narrative involved a misadventure with a transvestite, and

Judge Dread is gone, but his smutty novelty tunes will live on forever.

despite the unconventional subject matter, people actually bought the record. Although "Je T'Aime" marked Judge Dread's second and final top-ten hit—and perhaps the point at which his concept began to run out of steam—his 1975 *Bedtime Stories* LP reached #26 on the UK album chart.

While it may seem that Judge Dread's music has little to do with traditional roots reggae, there are some connections. For one, his backing tracks contained authentic flavor, as they were either cut in Jamaica or tracked in Britain with reggae musicians. However, the sexual content of his lyrics certainly didn't represent the political, religious, and cultural themes permeating the reggae community. Some might argue that Dread is not a vital figure in reggae history, but he helped to maintain the genre's commercial profile in

Britain, offering an alternative to the inevitably serious politics of domestic reggae bands and the Rasta-centric social consciousness of Jamaica's natty dreads.

Over the three years following the release of *Bedtime Stories*, Judge Dread's increasingly tiresome formula continued playing itself out—yes, there was a "Big Ten," released in 1975—and his singles fared progressively worse on the UK charts. After his final single—a hollow double A-side comprising "Hokey Cokey" and "Jingle Bells"—peaked at #64, Judge Dread became a part of the nostalgia circuit and even wrote a local newspaper column. He died of a heart attack playing a concert on March 13, 1998.

SELECT DISCOGRAPHY: *Bedtime Stories* (Cactus, 1975); *Big Seven: The Best of Judge Dread* (Sanctuary, 2003)

INI KAMOZE
YEARS ACTIVE: 1980s–PRESENT

Born Cecil Campbell on October 9, 1957, Ini Kamoze—meaning "mountain of the true god" in Swahili and Amharic—was virtually unknown beyond the reggae world until 1994, when "Here Comes the Hotstepper," a crossover single from the Rastaman, blazed its way across the international charts.

Kamoze's career began after he independently recorded the 1981 single "World Affairs," when he came to the attention of the legendary Jamaican drum and bass production partners Sly & Robbie (reportedly via Jimmy Cliff, a reggae legend in his own right). The drum-and-bass duo recorded an eponymously titled six-song EP with Kamoze that was licensed from Sly & Robbie's Taxi Records label to Island Records. The collection included the catchy "Trouble You a Trouble Me," a Jamaican hit that featured a high-tech roots sound and polished production similar to Sly & Robbie's work with Grammy award-winning reggae band Black Uhuru.

Despite making two additional credible Island albums, *Statement* (1984), and *Pirate* (1986), Kamoze was dropped in 1988 when the label cleared its roster of acts that had not found large enough audiences. He returned later that same year with the *Shocking Out* set (released in America by RAS Records and in England on the Greensleeves label), which moved distinctly closer to the digital dancehall sound in vogue at the time. He followed the album with occasional singles on his own Selekta label.

The commercial pinnacle of Kamoze's career, however, came in 1994, when "Here Comes the Hotstepper" became a million-selling #1 record in the United States. Influenced by pop and hip hop, the single included song samples from disco tracks and borrowed part of its vocal hook from the 1960s pop-R&B hit "Land of a Thousand Dances," which had reached the American pop charts in versions by seven other artists, including soul singer Wilson Pickett. Remarkably, "Here Comes the Hotstepper" had been recorded in 1992—more than two years before its chart ascent—and several major labels had passed on the opportunity to release it. The song was first released in March 1994, a year after Columbia Records had licensed it for inclusion on the *Stir It Up* dancehall crossover compilation album. Columbia apparently had a one-year "first shot" contract option to sign Kamoze, but the deal expired as the song became a hit, proving that timing really is everything.

Reggae's presence was secondary to hip hop on "Here Comes the Hotstepper," and Kamoze's reliance on sampled loops raised questions for fans of his earlier work about his creative direction. Nevertheless, once the song took off, six record labels began courting Kamoze, who remained unsigned as late as November 1994. Due to the multilabel bidding war, it would have cost Columbia nearly $1 million to sign Kamoze, and there was reluctance to do so, since his commercial longevity was uncertain. In the immediate wake of the single's success, it became the opening track on the sound track to director Robert Altman's film *Ready to Wear (Prêt-à-Porter)* (1994), released by Columbia.

The single was so hot that Columbia felt obliged to cash in by including it on a compilation of Kamoze's earlier Island work titled *Here Comes the Hotstepper* (1995). Kamoze eventually signed with Elektra Records to release 1995's *Lyrical Gangsta* album, which did not include the international hit. Although Kamoze had scored a major hit song, neither

Ini Kamoze in 1984, a decade before "Here Comes the Hotstepper" made him an international star.

album charted on either side of the Atlantic. This was partly due to the major labels diffusing his sales by overlapping releases and confusing music buyers. Ironically, while his solo albums faltered, the *Ready to Wear* soundtrack went gold in the United States, peaking at #29. Since no other major hits were on that album, at least part of its success should be attributed to the inclusion of "Here Comes The Hotstepper." Kamoze was no doubt frustrated, and he was quoted as describing Island and Columbia as "vampires." Still, in another interview, he said that he came from the world of farming and could return anytime if necessary. Instead, he recorded additional reggae-centered singles with *Lyrical Gangsta* collaborator Xterminator, also known as Philip "Fattis" Burrell.

In the midst of the label conflict, Kamoze disappeared for a decade, returning in 2006 with *Debut*, a series of remakes of earlier tracks. Undoubtedly, his career heat had long since cooled off, and few listeners were aware of the record or the original albums at its roots.

SELECT DISCOGRAPHY: *Ini Kamoze* (Island, 1984); *Statement* (Island, 1984); *Pirate* (Island, 1986); *Shocking Out* (RAS/ Greensleeves, 1988); *Here Comes the Hotstepper* (Columbia, 1995); *Lyrical Gangsta* (Elektra, 1995); *Debut* (9 Sound Clik, 2006); *51 50 Rule* (9 Sound Clik, 2009)

KEN KHOURI
YEARS ACTIVE: 1940s–1970s

"I am the complete pioneer of everything"—according to Ken Khouri, a Lebanese Jamaican who claimed to have made the island's first musical recordings, initially advertising the service in 1947. Research on the early days of Jamaica's recording industry carried out by scholars such as Daniel T. Neely have shed further light on the trailblazing developments in the Jamaican recording industry. On a trip to Miami around 1946 or 1947, Khouri acquired a disc cutter and purchased hundreds of blank discs before returning to Jamaica. He initially installed the equipment at his home, but when this proved inconvenient, he relocated to 129 King Street in Kingston, near the Times Furniture Store, which was an early distribution point for records in the city. Comprising "just one microphone, one track," as Khouri recalled, the assembled equipment hardly resembled a real studio.

While Khouri's studio was certainly one of the earliest on the island, it should be noted that American ethnomusicologist Helen Heffron Roberts made the first recordings of Jamaican music in 1921. At the time, she was assisting anthropologist Martha Beckwith, whose early work on the island's musical traditions is widely known. Furthermore, the first recordings of mento, Jamaica's calypso-styled folk music, reportedly occurred as early as 1924 in New York, as calypso became part of the record industry's growing global catalog.

Khouri's studio services initially included plain voice recordings for Jamaicans sending messages to relatives abroad. But only the elite, who had no interest in promoting indigenous music, could afford to make such recordings. Perhaps partially because of the limited income those records generated, Khouri did not produce his first commercial release until 1951: *Calypsos from Jamaica*, a multiartist compilation LP. The album featured the singing of Lord Flea, a Jamaican performer who later appeared in the Hollywood movie *Bop Girl Goes Calypso* in 1957. After attaining success as a Kingston nightclub act, Lord Flea became one of Jamaica's earliest recording artists, working with Khouri in the early 1950s before being discovered by a Miami nightclub owner in 1954 and becoming a part of America's short-lived calypso boom in the middle of the decade.

Coincident with Khouri's recording enterprise, the island's first radio station, WZQI in Kingston, occasionally allowed some musicians to make recordings for broadcast. In addition, businessman Stanley Motta began advertising and providing commercial recording services in his Kingston studio in November 1950, claiming this was a new service. Khouri had clearly preceded Motta, but his focus had been more on location recording than on studio recording.

In 1954, Khouri established Federal Records, Jamaica's first record-pressing plant, and his own Kalypso label. He also secured a licensing deal with the American label Mercury Records (and later with RCA Records) to distribute and sell their records in Jamaica. By 1957, following Federal's move from King Street to Marcus Garvey Drive, sound-system operators Coxsone Dodd and Duke Reid had begun producing records at Khouri's newly established operation. Some writers suggest that when the sound-system operators began cutting their first productions, Khouri's Federal Records was the island's only studio, and that before Dodd and Reid opened their own recording facilities, Khouri's studio was their only practical option. By the early 1960s, thanks to a licensing deal with Britain's Melodisc label that released calypso and later promoted ska with the Blue Beat label, Khouri's own productions had become more readily available beyond Jamaica.

In the decades that followed, Federal's recording studio continued to thrive, though little is known about Khouri's latter-day career. In the 1970s he left Jamaica for America with his wife during the island's social and political upheavals. He lived in Miami from 1977 to 1980, during which time his sons ran the business in Jamaica. Khouri returned in 1980, and, after his company had incurred large debts, he sold it in 1981 to Bob Marley's Tuff Gong Records. He died in 2003, and was given a posthumous government award for his contribution to Jamaica's music industry.

Khouri's Federal Records had a number of subsidiary labels, including Kentone, which released this record by The Hammond Sauce Works Band in 1977.

KING JAMMY

YEARS ACTIVE: 1970s–PRESENT

King Jammy is easily one of Jamaica's most important creative assets. As a top-class engineer and eventual producer, he not only played a crucial role in the reggae scene of the 1970s—especially with his dub mixes and other recordings—but also ushered in the digital dancehall era in the 1980s. Throughout his nearly forty-year career he has worked with reggae's greats, including King Tubby, Bunny Lee, Horace Andy, Inner Circle, Gregory Isaacs, and Black Uhuru. Moreover, he remains active in the business at a time when many of his contemporaries are either in some stage of retirement or dead.

Born Lloyd James in 1947 in Montego Bay, Jamaica, Jammy was interested in electronics from an early age. He established a sound system in Kingston's Waterhouse area in 1962, and built equipment for other sound systems. He established his credentials under the name Prince Jammy before leaving for Canada in 1969, where he provided live and studio engineering for different Jamaican artists based there. During this time away he resumed running his sound system, apparently importing all of the original equipment from Jamaica. When he arrived back in Kingston in January 1976, he set up a basic studio and formed his own Jammy's label. He also became part of dub maestro King Tubby's engineering crew. While he worked on a number of Bunny Lee productions, he distinguished himself on other records as well. Jammy's remix work on 1977's *In the Light Dub* transformed Horace Andy's original album (*In the Light*) into a dub masterpiece. The quality of his dub remix reinterpretations is also clear on Inner Circle's *Killer Dub* and Gregory Isaacs's brilliant *Slum (In Dub)*, both released in 1978. He worked with Black Uhuru early in their career, creatively refashioning their *Love Crisis* album as 1977's *Prince Jammy's in Lion Dub Style*.

Although Jammy was operating then as an independent entity, he remained connected to King Tubby's studio until about 1982. Meanwhile, his own label recordings targeted the more lucrative British market, which he felt was better organized, and he believed that payola was necessary to top the Jamaican charts. By 1985, the digital dancehall revolution he created with Wayne Smith's "Under Mi Sleng Teng" would give him undisputed public popularity in both Jamaica and Britain.

"Under Mi Sleng Teng" was initially built around a preset rhythm in a Japanese Casiotone keyboard. Jammy slowed the speed of the automated Casio rhythm, added lyrics and vocals, and gave the song its acid test on his sound system, where it met with great success. Unfortunately, many of the producers and artists who jumped on the bandwagon immediately afterward were not prepared to be as innovative, and the result was as many as two hundred songs using what became known as the "Sleng Teng" rhythm. Since that song had no bass line, the use of the digital technology often meant that one of reggae's critical rhythmic and sonic foundations was missing also from the recordings of many other artists who copied the style. The frequent absence of bass has been one of the central criticisms of dancehall leveled by audiences raised on roots and dub.

During this phase of unprecedented success, Jammy elevated himself from Prince to King. His own apprentices, Bobby Digital and Steely and Clevie later successfully struck out on their own. King Jammy has managed to prosper across several decades and was responsible for a massive number of releases in the dancehall-dominated 1980s. But his 1970s sessions have been the focus of reissue releases, which have made otherwise rare or obscure material available again.

SELECT DISCOGRAPHY: *Prince Jammy's in Lion Dub Style* (Jammy's, 1977); *Umoja: 20th Century Dubwise* (Blood & Fire, 2004); *Evolution of Dub: Volume 6* (Greensleeves, 2011)

BELOW: King Jammy (front) hangs with Junior Murvin and promotes himself in the process, 1986.

TOP RIGHT: The cover of *King Jammy's*, a 1989 book on the dub extraordinaire. The book, by Beth Lesser, is considered a reggae literature essential.

King Jammy's

Beth Lesser

Still the best book ever written about reggae.
Dave Hendley
Reggae photographer and journalist

Beyond his mastering of the dub soundscape, King Tubby was also known for building his own amplifiers and mixing consoles.

KiNG TUBBY
YEARS ACTIVE: 1960s-1989

Without the genius contributions of King Tubby, the reggae remixing art known as dub—stripping down tracks to their basic elements while infusing them with ambience through effects devices—arguably would not have become as important or influential. Tubby's work in the live arena influenced and inspired his best studio creations, which were informed by the remixing strategies he used to move dancehall crowds into varying states of frenzy while simultaneously leaving other sound men in awe. More than a tinkering engineer, Tubby built his own amplifiers and later

mixing consoles, joining a rare class of technologically innovative music producers. He took a marginal trend and—as far as reggae or even electronic pop is concerned—made it as mainstream as possible without compromising its avant-garde sensibility.

Tubby was born Osbourne Ruddock in 1941 in Kingston, Jamaica. At a young age, he developed an interest in electronic equipment, occasionally repairing radios to generate income and expanding the knowledge that would make him a full-time electrician. By the mid-1950s, his family had moved to Waterhouse, the area of west Kingston

Black & White

Produced by
G Patterson

45 R.P.M.

COPYING OF THIS RECORDING IS STRIC-LY PROHIBITED

Booby Trap
King Tubby's

he would later make the home base of his musical activities.

Tubby established his Home Town Hi-Fi sound system in 1968, enlisting U-Roy as its DJ. Tubby's work as a disc cutter for producer Duke Reid at the Treasure Isle studio and label in Kingston gave him firsthand exposure to the tape vaults of Treasure Isle and opportunities to experiment with remixing versions of sound system hits. This innovative remixing took on still newer dimensions as Tubby added reverb, echo, and tape delay to the songs he played on his sound system, treating audiences to proto-dub explorations.

Despite the outer space soundscapes created within, Tubby's studio was originally a cramped bedroom space at the back of his house. It was a far cry from the comparatively plush multitrack facilities found in Europe and the United States, but its lack of standardized studio sterility—coupled with Tubby's unconventional mind—led to the unusual song deconstructions created there. Eventually, the whole house became Tubby's studio and electronics workshop. Reggae record producer Bunny Lee helped Tubby buy two four-track recording machines owned by Byron Lee's Dynamic Sounds when that studio upgraded its multitrack facilities. Tubby also acquired a four-track mixing console from Dynamic, which he duly customized to suit his own needs, reportedly replacing the sliding faders with more responsive, less resistant ones. Fundamentally, he ran a remix operation, refashioning previously recorded material from other producers by pushing the drums and bass to the front of the mix and occasionally overdubbing vocals. Tubby was also known to physically hit his effects units to coax new sounds from

the devices. He was also an engineering-mixing collaborator on one of dub's earliest albums, Lee Perry's *Blackboard Jungle Dub* in 1973, and soon released his own albums, *Dub from the Roots* and *The Roots of Dub* in 1974.

By 1976, the rising climate of violence in Jamaica had taken its toll on Tubby, who withdrew from the sound-system frontline after his equipment was repeatedly damaged. Despite the invaluable income he derived from such performances, he shifted his focus toward his studio work, providing apprenticeships for many of dub's future engineering stars, including Prince Jammy (now known as King Jammy), Philip Smart, and Scientist.

In 1985, Tubby opened Firehouse Studios and began what was to be the next phase of his dub adventures. This new enterprise was cut short, however, when on February 6, 1989—Bob Marley's birthday, ironically—Tubby was shot and killed by an unknown assailant in an apparent attempted robbery outside his Kingston home. The king of dub was gone, though thanks to the prodigious talent he either directly nurtured or indirectly inspired, he has retained his sonic throne. His passing marked the end of an era, as dancehall DJs rose to prominence, propelled in the next decade by digital technologies that somehow never produced soundscapes more imaginative than the ones Tubby had created. Indeed, his innovations are all the more remarkable given the limited gear he used to take listeners to new galaxies of sound and space.

SELECT DISCOGRAPHY: *Dub from the Roots* (Total Sounds, 1974); *The Roots of Dub* (Total Sounds, 1974); *Dub Gone Crazy: The Evolution of Dub at King Tubby's 1975–1979* (Blood & Fire, 1994); *Dub Gone Crazy 2: In Fine Style 1975–1979* (w. Prince Jammy) (Blood & Fire, 1996); *Freedom Sounds in Dub* (w. Soul Syndicate) (Blood & Fire, 1996)

KINGSTON

There is not another capital city in the world comparable in size and population to Kingston that has produced so much music over a long period of time with such widespread global impact. At just over 8 square miles, the city was home to 123,000 people in 1960, and currently counts more than 500,000. As the primary recording site for the music that placed Jamaica on the map, Kingston has been the starting point for a never-ending series of audio adventures. The fact that musicians were in close proximity to one another and, eventually, to recording studios within the island's dense urban space does not completely explain Kingston's creative productivity over the decades. For many artists, whether they grew up there or migrated from the countryside, Kingston promised much but delivered little beyond more time on the survival treadmill. The poor economic and social conditions under which most artists lived were also catalysts for a kind of musical exorcism out of which remarkable work arose.

The impact of colonial rule affected Jamaica on every level, beginning in 1494 with the Spanish, who virtually wiped out the native Arawaks, and continuing with the English, who assumed power in 1655 and began enslaving Africans and importing them to the island. Established around 1692, Kingston became the nation's capital and the main trading port in 1872, displacing Spanish Town. The legislative foundations for the social injustice that impoverished so many

Jimmy Cliff's touring chef "Taco" cooks up Ital stew (a Rastafarian dish) for a hungry crowd outside of Channel One, Kingston, 1984.

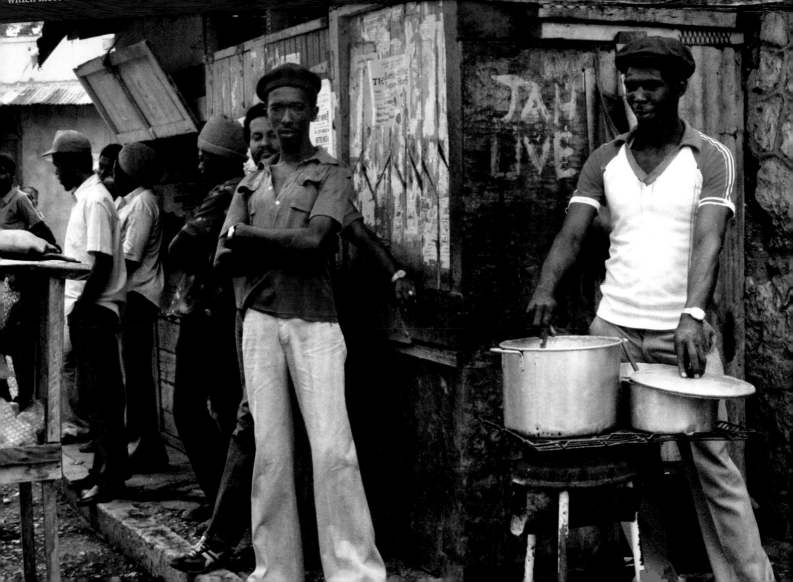

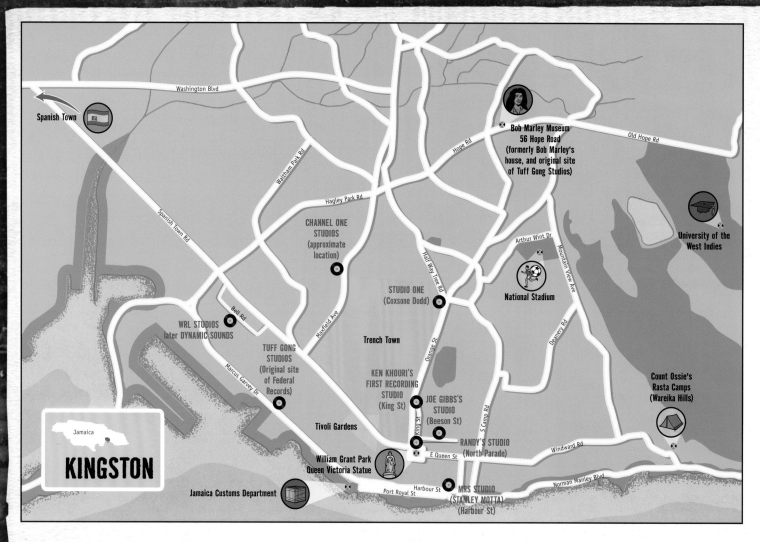

Jamaica

KINGSTON

Jamaicans in the twentieth century were firmly laid in Kingston during the seventeenth century, when under British rule Jamaica became a world leader in sugar exportation.

The colonial exploitation of the laboring underclass that kept the sugar industry thriving led to serious unrest and a series of 1938 riots that shut Kingston down. The death and turmoil ultimately created by political circumstances and racial hierarchies foreshadowed the crises of later decades. The economics of survival within a largely unemployed workforce practically forced people to migrate to the capital city, and Kingston's population grew substantially by 1960. The poverty that existed in Kingston's urban enclaves sparked inevitable competition for resources, leading to recurrent violence that became increasingly evident during the island's general elections.

In the early twentieth century, Rastafarianism became a potent, long-term source of resistance once preaching of the faith began in Kingston. Although Jamaican black liberation icon Marcus Garvey (1887–1940) was not himself a Rasta, Kingston was the site of many of his major pronouncements promoting the black nationalism and independence that intersected with the Rastafarian worldview. Rastafarianism also had followers outside of the city who were practically forced into Kingston after the 1954 police raid of the ganja-cultivating Pinnacle commune, located in the parish of St. Catherine to the west of Kingston. This event is believed to have left more than a thousand people homeless and penniless, and many drifted into Kingston's urban slums. The district unofficially known as Back-O-Wall, on the city's west side, became one of the key locations in which the Rastafarian musical dimension developed, emphasizing African practices, rituals, and philosophical consciousness. More famous were drummer Count Ossie's Eastern Kingston camps—zones of Rasta philosophical reasoning and artistic expression—that attracted such prime musicians as the legendary Don Drummond and Tommy McCook, whose later work in the Skatalites was a cornerstone of Jamaican popular music.

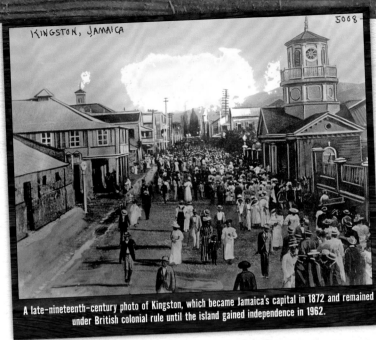

A late-nineteenth-century photo of Kingston, which became Jamaica's capital in 1872 and remained under British colonial rule until the island gained independence in 1962.

Jamaica's cultural roots in African spiritual drum and dance rituals such as Kumina, Burru, and Pukkumina were critical seasonings in the city's musical melting pot. Other ingredients included jazz, R&B, English folk, and even country music—elements that combined to create something new. The Dungle and Trench Town sections became the province of squatters but also produced artists whose work was infused with survivalist urgency. The political decision to turn part of that area's coastal zone into a rubbish dump in the mid-1960s instantly destroyed what had been a site of relative refuge for the city's many strugglers.

Western Kingston was the core of Jamaica's music business. In the 1950s and 1960s, to have any hope of being recorded on the island, an artist had to be in Kingston, home to a concentration of studios, producers, and musicians who knew how to get results. Informally known as Beat Street, for obvious reasons, Orange Street was initially the headquarters for producers Coxsone Dodd, Prince Buster, and Bunny Lee, among many others. Auditions, studios, labels, and even record shops were concentrated in a relatively small area of the city that also included King Street (running roughly parallel to Orange Street), Beeston Street, Chancery Lane, and North Parade (home to the Randy's operation that became VP Records). Joe Gibbs, the Hoo-Kim brothers (later of Channel One

fame), Clancy Eccles, Derrick Harriott, and countless other producers and artists literally occupied the same space, competing against and sometimes collaborating with one another to create the next hit. While the business did not remain limited to this area as time progressed, Kingston itself continued to be vital. It was the core of Jamaica's creative explosion in popular music, aided by the cluster of major sound systems on which "dubplates" (soft wax acetate pre-release discs) could be tested on audiences.

In more instances than there is space in this book to recount, the recordings themselves were infused with a distinct sense of place, making Kingston not merely the place where the work was created

but also a literal part of the musical narrative. On "Trenchtown Rock" (1971), Bob Marley makes sure everyone knows the ghetto is in the Kingston 12 district of the capital. Later, on his 1975 song "Natty Dread," Marley lyrically maps out parts of the city's urban geography and takes the listeners on the same journey. On the other hand, Trinidadian singer Lord Creator's "Kingston Town," produced by Clancy Eccles and released in 1970, idealizes the city as magic rather than tragic. Even instrumentally, the Rasta vibes surface in trombonist Rico Rodriguez's *Man from Wareika* (1976), as he affirms his link to Count Ossie's Rasta camp in the hills and the inspiration it provided. And one reason for the artistic success of the 1972 movie *The Harder They Come*, starring singer-songwriter Jimmy Cliff, is that it encapsulates much of Kingston's twentieth-century history and reputation. The narrative is partly based on the story of Rhyging, a gangster gunman who ran riot in the city in 1948 before being killed there by police. Cliff's character also typifies the rural peasant who migrates to Kingston in search of a better life but finds only further hardship and poverty, as well as rampant criminality, in a dehumanizing and uninspiring physical setting.

A view of Chestnut Lane in Trench Town, one of Kingston's poorest areas, but one rich with reggae history.

Record shops like this one studded the Kingston streets during reggae's heyday.

Kingston has also been a horrific political battleground as agents of the two parties, the People's National Party (PNP) and the Jamaica Labour Party (JLP), have struggled for both power and physical territory in the city. Scores of lives have been lost in the process, as each general election reignites simmering tensions. While this was especially true in the 1970s, the year 2010 brought sharp reminders of such turmoil, as Jamaican soldiers embarked on a quest to capture alleged gangster and drug kingpin Christopher "Dudus" Coke for extradition to the United States. The hunt for Coke led to roadblocks, barricades, destruction, claims of police misconduct, and a significant death toll. The event also provoked musical reactions against the extradition assault, with Bunny Wailer's "Don't Touch the President" emerging as one of the notable records. Moreover, the conflict made Kingston appear nightmarish in international news coverage, further diminishing prospects for the survival of its residents, who rely so heavily on the tourism industry.

Kingston is a cultural collision point of past, present, and future in which the creativity of its residents has taken the city's ghettos to global greatness. People who might have no idea where to find Trench Town still sing and dance to songs about it. There is no doubt that Kingston places high on the list of international cities that are also creative cauldrons for music.

ABOVE: A billboard in Trench Town, where growing up was tough for many reggae superstars, like Bob Marley, Peter Tosh, and Bunny Wailer.

RIGHT: The Channel One Recording Studio on Maxfield Avenue, a frequent hangout for Kingston residents.

THE HISTORIC REGGAE RECORDINGS 1968-1970

THE "KING" KONG COMPILATION

beverley's

LESLIE KONG
YEARS ACTIVE: 1960s-1971

Leslie Kong was a Chinese Jamaican businessman who had no apparent ties to the music industry before a teenaged Jimmy Cliff showed up at his Kingston variety store, Beverley's, sometime around 1961. This was not unusual: in the 1950s and 1960s, when being a producer in Jamaica mostly meant funding and facilitating recording, artists might approach any successful entrepreneur in the hope of a break. Cliff's impromptu audition inspired Kong to finance his recordings and start Beverley's Records despite being advised against it by his two brothers. Under these circumstances, it's quite a paradox that Kong, who was born in 1933 in Kingston, turned out to be one of Jamaica's most successful record producers in the 1960s.

Cliff became an official A&R (Artists and Repertoire) man for the label and brought in a certain young singer named Bob Marley. Kong produced his first record, "Judge Not," in 1962. That single was followed in the same year by "One Cup of Coffee." Cliff's own single "Miss Jamaica," produced by Kong, was a major 1962 hit. Kong wasn't a musician, but according to Cliff, he had clear ideas about what the songs should sound like.

Kong made an exclusive licensing deal with Island Records owner Chris Blackwell in England to release many of his Beverley's Records productions in the United Kingdom. Many Jamaican producers had access to the British market through the same or similar channels, but sales were typically limited to the West Indian immigrant communities in England. This began to change when another of Kong's artists, Desmond Dekker, made the British top twenty with "007 (Shanty Town)" in 1967, demonstrating that, despite limited airplay, Jamaican artists could reach the pop market.

Kong was behind a host of hits, among them "Do the Reggay" (1968) by the legendary reggae group Toots & the Maytals, the first song to use the genre's name in its title (though

the spelling with the "y" cropped up in those days). Kong was also responsible for one of the most important songs in reggae's early internationalization, Desmond Dekker's "Israelites" (1969), which became a massive hit across Europe, reaching #1 in Britain and even making the top ten in the notoriously reggae-resistant United States. By late 1969, the Pioneers, a Jamaican vocal trio, had given the producer additional leverage, as their single "Long Shot Kick De Bucket" reached #21 on the UK charts.

By the late 1960s, Kong had begun licensing material to the British reggae label Trojan Records. His roster at the time included Ken Boothe ("Freedom Street"), Toots & the Maytals ("54-46"), Delroy Wilson, the Melodians (whose "Rivers of Babylon" would later be turned into a million seller by the German reggae group Boney M), and of course, the Wailers, who recorded for Kong in 1969. After the Wailers had recorded a series of singles that had no commercial impact at home or abroad, Kong proposed releasing *The Best of the Wailers* in 1970. Group singer-songwriter Bunny Wailer was disgusted and allegedly threatened to place a curse on Kong, telling him he would die if he issued the record. Kong released the collection, and the following year, despite having no history of heart problems, he died of heart failure at the age of thirty-eight. One can only guess at whether he would have remained successful when the Rasta-influenced tone of reggae took hold in the mid-1970s.

BUNNY LEE
YEARS ACTIVE: 1960s-1980s

Because of the vast number of influential records he was associated with from the late 1960s to the late 1970s, Bunny Lee's name is inextricably linked to the roots reggae era. Like Coxsone Dodd and Duke Reid (of Studio One and Treasure Isle fame, respectively), the Jamaica-born Lee was not a producer in the traditional musical sense. He functioned more like a film producer, funding projects without having any direct hands-on creative role in the sound of the finished product. His productions often enhanced preexisting rhythms instead of originating new ones. Yet the consistent quality of Lee's output and the deals he negotiated in England were instrumental in establishing the international reach of Jamaican popular music.

Edward O'Sullivan Lee, later known as Striker as well as Bunny, was born in 1941 in Kingston, Jamaica. He began his music industry career as a record "plugger" for producers Duke Reid and Leslie Kong in his hometown during the early 1960s. His job entailed pushing singles to radio stations to gain airplay. In 1967, Reid gave Lee a block of free studio time, launching his career in record production. Lee's early work included records by singers Jackie Edwards, Derrick Morgan, Slim Smith, and Delroy Wilson.

Weed Beat

P 1978 Dynamic Sounds Less Music

WB 069

VERSION
(The Aggrevators)
THE AGGREVATORS

MANUFACTURED BY DY... ...15 BELL ROAD

Following a short stint with producer Ken Lack's Caltone Records label, Lee traveled to England in 1967 to make distribution connections. Not long afterward he produced Stranger Cole's 1968 single "Bangarang," which Lee claimed was the first reggae release. Issued on the Unity label, "Bangarang" was among the initial fruits of a

licensing deal Lee had made with Britain's independent Pama Records that lasted until about 1970. The following year, singer Max Romeo's smutty "Wet Dream" gave Lee a top-ten hit on the British pop charts. The song remained on the charts for about six months, thanks in part to its popularity among skinheads and the notoriety that came with a ban from the British Broadcasting Corporation (BBC).

In any event, Lee was one of the new movers on the Jamaican scene who pushed reggae to the fore and created commercially appealing records. His key recordings from this period include "Stick By Me" (1972), one of several hits with John Holt; and Eric Donaldson's 1971 Jamaica Song Festival winner "Cherry Oh Baby," later covered by the British pop-reggae group UB40. While Lee was the producer behind many hit songs of this era, he was also one of several Jamaican producers directly or indirectly involved in licensing individual Jamaican records to more than one British label—a practice that eventually contributed to the erosion of the commercial strength of reggae in the UK market.

Few figures in the Jamaican music scene were able to shield themselves completely from the rampant political violence that swept through the island in the 1970s, and Lee was no exception. His production of Delroy Wilson's popular "Better Must Come" (1971), adopted by the opposition People's National Party (PNP), was surely perceived as a subversive act. As the 1972 election approached, Lee was shot in the hand at home in alleged retaliation for recording songs that supposedly criticized the Jamaica Labour Party's (JLP) rule.

Musically, Lee was a major supporter of the early exploits of dub remix pioneers King Tubby and Lee Perry, encouraging both to follow their creative instincts. As a result, Tubby created some excellent dub mixes that are still very much ahead of their time. Chief among these is his debut album, *Dub from the Roots* (1974), which he crafted from Lee's studio master tapes. Lee made particular use of Tubby's skills while pushing the so-called flying-cymbal sound, a disco-influenced, rhythmic opening and closing of the drum's hi-hat, typified by singer Johnny Clarke's "Move Out of Babylon." This trend didn't last long, however. Channel One, the influential Kingston studio headed by the Hoo-Kim brothers, assumed supremacy in the mid-1970s with the more aggressively syncopated, percussive rockers style promoted by session band drummer Sly Dunbar that was more in tune with the militancy characterizing the era. Nevertheless, the flying cymbal constituted a rather one-dimensional sound, and Lee did a good job of maximizing its potential.

Lee has been far less active since the 1980s, when he bought producer Joe Gibbs's Kingston studio and began focusing on reissues from his own catalog of recordings, but he remains one of reggae's last surviving elder statesmen.

SELECT DISCOGRAPHY: *Sly & Robbie Meet Bunny Lee at Dub Station* (Jamaican Recordings, 2002); *Creation of Dub* (Jamaican Recordings, 2011)

Bunny Lee in 1975, midway through a decade in which he would produce countless recordings and establish himself as one of the key figures of the roots era.

CHINESE JAMAICANS

The narratives found in reggae music tend to focus on social and economic injustices characteristic of the Afro-Jamaican experience. But various other ethnic groups (European, Middle Eastern, Asian) make up the rest of the island's population, and they also played key roles in shaping the music. In particular, Chinese Jamaicans made critical contributions, both in and out of the recording studio. They exerted their influence in a variety of ways, including financing and forming labels, selling and distributing records, and in some instances, becoming directly involved in performances and studio engineering. The impact of Chinese Jamaicans may surprise some reggae fans, as poster and album artwork generally features Afro-Jamaican and Rastafarian imagery, but the Asian cultural presence on the island dates back to the nineteenth century.

Following explorer Christopher Columbus's arrival in Jamaica in 1494, the Spaniards colonized the island, wiped out the indigenous Arawak Indian population, and imported African slaves. The British seized control in 1655, and following the abolition of slavery on the island in 1838, a shortage of workers on sugar plantations led to the arrival of other ethnic groups. In response, the British government imported East Indian and Chinese laborers. The first Chinese contingent to arrive in Jamaica in 1854 comprised a mere 472 workers. They came from the territory of Panama in Central America, where they had worked in railroad construction. Later, the British relocated Chinese

workers to Jamaica from Hong Kong and British Caribbean colonies.

The Chinese workers were initially hired by the British government on three-year contracts, often living under harsh conditions. After their period of indentured labor was completed, the Chinese set out to make their own living on the island, concentrating on retail trade. Distrust of the British colonial government and a vulnerability to exploitation due to lack of fluency in English made the Chinese in Jamaica insular, and they focused on making money from their own small businesses. This entrepreneurial legacy partly explains the financial roles Chinese Jamaicans played in reggae history.

In the 1940s and 1950s, Tom Wong became one of the first Chinese Jamaicans to make a name in Jamaican entertainment. Born to a Chinese Jamaican father and a mother of African descent, he founded the sound system known as Tom the Great Sebastian. Since Jamaica's homegrown recording industry had not yet taken off, Wong played mostly American R&B and Latin records. His remained one of the island's top sound systems until the mid-1950s, when the gang violence that had become part of the music business forced him to move his sound system operation to the Silver Slipper nightclub in Kingston. The venue had a reputation for being "uptown," and it tended to draw a more middle-class clientele.

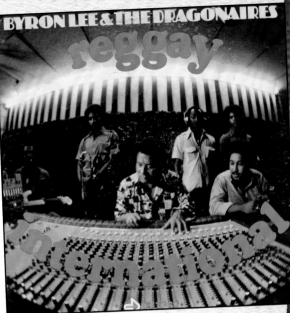

Vincent "Randy" Chin, born in Kingston in 1937, was the son of a father who arrived in Jamaica from China in the 1920s. Chin started his first record store, Randy's Record Mart, around 1959. With the help of his wife, Patricia—a woman of mixed Chinese and Indian ethnicity—he moved the shop from its original Kingston location and launched a recording operation above the store in 1968. That spawned the prolific Randy's Records label, which scored hits with such Jamaican artists as Lord Creator, Dennis Brown, the Maytals, the Heptones, Augustus Pablo, and Black Uhuru. One of Randy Chin's sons, Clive, began producing records in 1972, and up until about 1977, many leading reggae producers created hits at Randy's. By 1978, competition from rival studios—among them Black Ark studio, run by former client and renowned producer Lee Perry, and the Hoo-Kim brothers' Channel One studio—and deteriorating political and economic conditions in Jamaica led the Chin family to relocate to New York City. They resumed recording and retail operations in 1979, and in the early 1990s those enterprises merged into VP Records, the world's largest independent reggae label. Clive's son Joel kept the family tradition alive as the label's director of A&R (Artists and Repertoire) until he was tragically shot and killed in 2011. Remaining Chin family members continue to run the label, which now dominates the reggae landscape.

The Hoo-Kim brothers set up the Channel One studio in 1972, with Ernest Hoo-Kim working there as a recording and mixing engineer. By the mid-1970s, after initially struggling to make an impact on the Jamaican music scene, Channel One became a Kingston studio hotspot. This was due in part to technical improvements made to the studio itself, as well as the establishment

of the Revolutionaries as the studio's session band. DJs Tappa Zukie and Dillinger, vocal group the Mighty Diamonds, and singer John Holt were among a long list of artists whose recordings at the studio became hits on the Channel One label.

Another Chinese Jamaican, Leslie Kong, is notable for having produced the first-ever recordings by eventual superstar and reggae ambassador Bob Marley. Kong cut these landmark songs—"Judge Not" and "One Cup of Coffee"—in 1962, the same year he established Beverly's Records to record material by the singer Jimmy Cliff. Prior to getting involved in music, Kong had been in business with his brothers and ran a record shop and ice cream parlor and traded in real estate. In 1962, after leaving Jamaica earlier that same year, Chris Blackwell established Island Records in London with Kong as one of four investing founders. By the 1970s, Island would become the standard-bearer for reggae's international thrust, with Bob Marley & the Wailers at the spearhead. Following the immediate Jamaican success of Cliff's debut single, "Hurricane Hattie" (1962), Kong scored a series of hits with other artists, including Jamaican singer Desmond Dekker, whose records began crossing over into the British charts in 1967. In 1969, Kong again worked with Marley and recorded his group the Wailers, which also featured Peter Tosh and Bunny Wailer. This partnership yielded little in the way of commercial success, and Kong suffered a fatal heart attack in 1971.

OPPOSITE: Randy's Record Mart in Kingston, 1972. Vincent "Randy" Chin opened the original store in 1959, moving it to this location in 1968 and launching a recording studio upstairs.

LEFT: Chinese Jamaican producer Leslie Kong cut Bob Marley's first-ever singles in 1962, including "One Cup of Coffee."

ABOVE RIGHT: Musician, producer, and businessman Byron Lee brought ska and reggae to mainstream audiences.

Bandleader, producer, promoter, and label and studio owner Byron Lee was born to a Chinese father and black Jamaican mother, and also played a vital role in reggae history, especially in the 1960s. After his group, Byron Lee & the Dragonaires, recorded their Jamaican debut single, "Dumplins," in 1959, they quickly built a strong reputation. In 1964, they recorded as the Ska Kings for the American label Atlantic Records, though they achieved no commercial success. In 1968, Lee made perhaps his most significant move and acquired the West Indies Records Limited (WIRL) studio from producer-turned-politician Edward Seaga. After completing anthropology studies at Harvard in 1952, Seaga began recording and distributing Jamaican folk songs, and ventured into record production by accident, scoring a major Jamaican hit in 1960 with "Manny-O" by singing duo Higgs & Wilson. Lee renamed WIRL as Dynamic Sounds, and it quickly became Jamaica's top studio, even playing host to a series of rock acts, among them Paul Simon, who recorded his 1972 international hit "Mother and Child Reunion" there. Lee also established a Dynamic Sounds label imprint as an outlet for his own group's recordings and material by other Jamaican acts. He died in 2008, and while his name remains synonymous with a middle-of-the-road reggae style that lacked the intensity of genuine roots, his entrepreneurial activity helped put Jamaica on the global musical map.

Perhaps not as well known as Lee, producer Herman Chin-Loy made at least two important contributions to reggae history. He helped launch

ABOVE: Operated by Byron Lee, Dynamic Sounds hosted such rock artists as Paul Simon and grew to become Jamaica's top studio.
RIGHT: Patricia Chin, matriarch of VP Records, at the label's headquarters in Queens, New York, 2009.

the career of melodica player Augustus Pablo in the early 1970s; and, under his own name, Chin-Loy released one of the most influential early dub albums, 1973's *Aquarius Dub*. However, due to Jamaica's turbulent social and political climate, he had moved his Aquarius Studio to Miami by the mid-1970s.

Brothers Geoffrey and Mikey Chung feature prominently among the Chinese Jamaicans who became directly involved in the writing, arranging, performing, and production of reggae music. Geoffrey, a keyboardist, worked as a session musician and producer with such reggae bands as Inner Circle and Britain's Steel Pulse. He is best remembered for his work with former Wailers singer Peter Tosh, whose *Bush Doctor* (1978), *Mystic Man* (1979), and *Wanted: Dread & Alive* (1981) albums he engineered and mixed. Nearly two decades after Geoffrey's death in 1995, Mikey remains a highly regarded session guitarist. He's played lead and rhythm on numerous albums, including Black Uhuru's Grammy-winning 1983 set *Anthem* and a series of Tosh albums dating from the late 1970s to the early 1980s. In 2010, he appeared on *Legacy*, an album by Andrew Tosh, Peter's son. Another group of Chinese Jamaican brothers, Justin and Philip Yap were behind the Top Deck label (established in the early 1960s), which released classic ska records in the early to mid-1960s by such artists as top-rated session instrumentalists the Skatalites and singer Jackie Opel.

Since many Chinese Jamaicans left the island during the political turmoil of the 1970s, they have not been as influential on the music scene in recent decades. Nevertheless, their contributions have left an indelible imprint on the sound of reggae.

BYRON LEE
YEARS ACTIVE: 1950s–2008

Byron Lee is not the most popular man in the reggae world, but he may be among the most prolific. Despite the multiple roles he played in developing Jamaica's music industry (artist, producer, and promoter), he has been accused of overly commercializing reggae by smoothing out its rough edges for wider mainstream consumption.

A Chinese Jamaican born in the rural Jamaican parish of Manchester, Lee formed his group the Dragonaires at some point in the 1950s. Accounts differ regarding the exact year the group came together, but the Dragonaires' original purpose was to service the hotel circuit, playing to tourists and providing backup for foreign (usually American) singers performing in the Caribbean. These included everyone from calypso legend Harry Belafonte to rocker Chuck Berry. The Dragonaires' sound was in demand, however, and the group also performed as an independent act.

Lee purchased an electric bass in 1959 and is said to have been the first Jamaican musician to own one. This is likely true, given the poverty experienced by most Jamaican musicians at the time. Later that year, West Indies Records Limited (WIRL) owner and future Jamaican prime minister Edward Seaga produced the Dragonaires' first single, "Dumplins," a kind of rock 'n' roll-R&B instrumental featuring saxophone and bass. The record came out just as the Blue Beat Records imprint was launched in the United Kingdom, and through a licensing agreement, "Dumplins" became that label's second-ever record. The Dragonaires appeared as background musicians in the debut James Bond film, *Dr. No* (1962), performing in a bar and playing what sounds more like calypso than the ska that was popular in Jamaica at the time. Interestingly, the founder of Island Records, Chris Blackwell, worked as a Jamaican consultant on that film.

Lee represented Jamaica as part of a music promotion package organized by Seaga for the 1964

BYRON LEE AND THE DRAGONAIRES
plays **JAMAICA**
SKA
SENSATIONAL NEW BEAT
JAMAICA'S NO. 1 BAND

ABOVE: Byron Lee and the Dragonaires were accused of watering down Jamaica's gritty urban sounds for "uptown" audiences.

LEFT: This Atlantic Records release coincided with the 1964 World's Fair in New York City, where many felt the Skatalites, not the Dragonaires, should have represented Jamaica.

OPPOSITE: The cover of Disco Reggae (1975) became a perfect promotional tool for Jamaican tourism.

World's Fair in New York City. Some in Jamaica criticized the idea of sending a light-skinned Chinese Jamaican musician to promote a sound that had originated in the predominantly black urban ghettoes. As Lee himself recalled in the book *Reggae Routes*, "Nobody uptown knew what the music was about, they couldn't relate to it." Moreover, the very popular Skatalites, who were the archetypal ska band and therefore an obvious choice in many people's minds, appear to have been overlooked despite their impeccable credentials as ska originators and ambassadors. Meanwhile, Ahmet Ertegun, then the head of Atlantic Records, had become interested in the island's popular music and the *Jamaica Ska* album was released in America by Atlantic to coincide with the World's Fair. The singers were backed by Lee's band, credited as the Ska Kings on some versions of the LP. The album failed commercially, foreshadowing the fate of ska in the American market. By the mid-1960s, after ska had faded, the Dragonaires had begun

playing the increasingly popular and slower rocksteady rhythm on such albums as *Rock Steady Explosion* (1968), which came packaged with illustrated dance steps. Lee bought WIRL from Seaga in 1968 and eventually renamed it Dynamic Sounds around 1969. This bolstered Lee's profile, as Dynamic became Jamaica's top recording studio, playing host to American singer Johnny Nash's first ventures into the realm of reggae-pop crossover. Since Dynamic's equipment was up to international standards, Paul Simon chose the studio to record his 1972 reggae hit "Mother and Child Reunion." The studio attracted other top-level acts in the early 1970s, including Cat Stevens and the Rolling Stones.

From the late 1960s through the early 1970s, the Dragonaires continued releasing albums on Dynamic with the word "reggay" in their titles. But from the mid-1970s onward, although he continued playing reggae, Lee focused his attention on developing an annual calypso carnival in Jamaica. This was influenced by his touring experiences in calypso's homeland, Trinidad. Byron Lee and the Dragonaires appeared at Jamaica's annual Reggae Sunsplash festival on at least five occasions in the 1970s and 1980s, but during and after this phase, they were primarily identified with soca, calypso's more rhythm-driven commercial offshoot.

In 1982, the Jamaican government awarded Lee its Order of Distinction for his music industry contributions, and gave him the Order of Jamaica in 2008 while he was in the hospital with cancer. In recent years, reggae historians and Caribbean music artists have reexamined Lee's role in Jamaican popular music. Whereas he had been typically portrayed as diluting the music for commercial purposes, newer books present multiple sides to his contribution. He died in Jamaica in 2008 at the age of seventy-three.

SELECT DISCOGRAPHY: *Rock Steady Explosion* (Trojan, 1968); *Reggay Blast Off* (Trojan, 1970); *Reggay Round the World* (Dragon, 1973); *Reggay International* (Dynamic, 1976)

HOPETON LEWIS

YEARS ACTIVE: 1960s–PRESENT

With a voice soulful enough to sell millions of records, Hopeton Lewis, born in 1947 in Kingston, Jamaica, became stylically stranded somewhere between reggae and pop, never fully satisfying fans of either genre. Like many others—most notably Alton Ellis, the singer behind 1966's "Rock Steady"—Lewis says he invented rocksteady, the popular mid-1960s midtempo style that followed the frenetic pace of ska. During a 1966 recording session for "Take It Easy," Lewis wanted the band to slow the tempo in order to enhance his vocal expression. His hit "Sound and Pressure," released in the same year, typified the rocksteady sound.

Lewis's 1970 single "Boom Shaka Laka," produced by Duke Reid, won the annual Jamaica Festival Song Competition that year, when the event was part of Jamaica's independence celebrations. He became a vocalist with top studio and show band Byron Lee and the Dragonaires, and Lee produced Lewis's solo single "Grooving Out on Life" (1971), which was a big hit in the West Indian community

This song won Hopeton Lewis the Jamaica Festival Song Competition in 1970.

in London. It was also the title track of the solo album Lewis recorded, produced by Byron Lee at Dynamic Sounds in Kingston after the single's success. The song, which never quite crossed over to the pop charts despite some airplay, was a cover of a 1969 single by the American pop trio the Newbeats. (Lewis's reggae interpretation was itself rerecorded by British pop-reggae band UB40 in 1989.) After spending about four years fronting the Dragonaires, Lewis left the group around 1977 and sang at hotels around the Caribbean.

Lewis' career has taken an interesting turn in recent years as he turned to singing gospel music and set up a record label, Rockstone Music Productions. Despite claiming to be rocksteady's originator, he has moved in a different direction from the traditional reggae world.

SELECT DISCOGRAPHY: *Grooving Out on Life* (Trojan, 1971); *Dynamic Hopeton Lewis* (Dragon, 1975)

LOVERS ROCK

According to black British dub master Dennis Bovell, "Lovers rock *is* the British sound of reggae." Curiously bereft of an apostrophe in its name, the style centers on love songs with suitably syrupy rhythms and none of the instrumental or lyrical cutting edges of militant roots reggae. Many prominent lovers rock artists (and audience members) were women, but typically men were the key producers behind the music. Male performers such as Dennis Brown, Gregory Isaacs, John Holt, and Sugar Minott had vocal styles that easily matched the lovers rock romantic framework, and they became associated with the style even though most of them had begun their careers before its debut. As a subgenre, it was one of the early signs that the British reggae scene was maturing fast enough to influence Jamaican artists. A few years earlier, Jamaican reggae was the only kind deemed truly authentic by British sound-system operators.

One of the pivotal singles that typified the UK-based lovers rock trend was "Caught You in a Lie" by Louisa Marks on Safari Records (1975). Bovell's establishment of the Lovers Rock record label around 1977 also helped define the genre's identity. With the exception of Janet Kay's "Silly Games," a Bovell production that reached #2 on the British charts in 1979, the lovers rock genre operated outside of the pop mainstream and was essentially the province of sound systems and their community audiences. "Silly Games" featured a distinctive and complex offbeat hi-hat cymbal pattern played by Drummie Zeb, a member of the British reggae band Aswad, while Bovell himself played guitar and keyboard. Janet Kay never had another pop hit, suggesting that lovers rock did not have a reliable pop audience.

As crossover history repeated itself, British pop group Culture Club's massive 1983 global single "Do You Really Want to Hurt Me?" was a pastiche of lovers rock that emphasized its most commercial rhythmic elements and gave the music a white pop identity. It's slightly surprising that lovers rock wasn't more successful in the pop market, with its middle-of-the-road crossover appeal. In an interview decades later, Culture Club lead singer Boy George described lovers rock as "reggae that didn't frighten white people!"

Unfortunately, lovers rock also became an arena for an endless string of reggae covers of pop and R&B songs, disconnecting it from the reggae innovations that preceded it. It also failed to have any impact on the United States beyond West Indian audiences. The style, however, did play a major role in reviving the solo career of Jamaican session bassist Boris Gardiner, whose vocals and rhythms on "I Want to Wake Up with You" took a quintessential lovers rock song to #1 on the British pop charts in 1986.

Audiences with militant Rasta politics and more roots reggae–oriented tastes often found themselves at odds with the lightweight subject matter and pop-friendly instrumentation of lovers rock, but neither man nor woman can live on antiestablishment protest alone. Every now and then, reggae's ruminations on the apocalypse would have to be delayed in favor of amorous pursuits.

Beres Hammond demonstrates the perks of being a lovers rock artist, 1979.

TOMMY McCOOK

YEARS ACTIVE: 1940s–1980s

The list of Jamaican instrumental maestros responsible for building the island's popular music must include Skatalites tenor saxophonist and arranger Tommy McCook, born in Kingston, Jamaica, in 1927. In the first years after Jamaica attained political

independence from Britain in 1962, he was one of the catalysts in establishing a more definitive Jamaican musical identity. McCook was also one of the many musicians who participated in the Rastafarian music sessions of Count Ossie, whose robust African drumming helped shape the sound of Jamaican popular music.

A product of the strict Catholic Alpha School for Boys in Kingston, McCook began playing in jazz bands as a teenager. He left Jamaica to work the hotel circuit in the Bahamas in 1954 but returned in 1962 because he wanted to play something other than dance music. After forming a jazz quartet, he caught the attention of Studio One producer Coxsone Dodd, who quickly hired him for

studio work. As McCook later recalled, Dodd's equipment at the Federal Studio sessions in Kingston (before the producer had his own studio) was very basic, with just a two-track machine recording the singer on one track and the instrumentalists—crammed around one microphone—on the other.

McCook became a founding member of the Skatalites, a group renowned then and now for its studio work. Partially as a result of freelancing with other producers, which he did in order to make a decent living, McCook played on most of the influential ska hits by other artists, including the Wailers, featuring the legendary vocal trio of Bob Marley, Bunny Wailer, and Peter Tosh. But he also helped the Skatalites create their own identity on record, and such songs as "Guns of Navarone," a 1967 pop hit in Britain, emerged after the group's demise.

After the group dissolved in 1965, McCook formed the Supersonics, another top-flight studio session unit with a fluid line-up that occasionally included some former Skatalites (Johnny Moore, Lloyd Knibb, Roland Alphonso, Lester Sterling) and the ace guitarists Ernest Ranglin and Lynn Tait. The Supersonics worked for Duke Reid's Treasure Isle operation into the early 1970s and were integral in molding rocksteady and reggae—slower rhythms that emerged after the mid-1960s transition from the frenetic ska beat. They were the backup band on the Paragons' original hit version of "The Tide Is High" (1967), which later became an international pop smash in 1980 for the American new wave group Blondie. After the Supersonics broke up in the early 1970s, McCook played on numerous records produced by Bunny Lee and in the studio at Channel One. Later, after the peak of the roots reggae era, his emphasis switched from studio work to live gigs. His 1970s solo albums, *Blazing Horns* (1977) and *Tenor in Roots* (1978), set a high standard for instrumental roots reggae. Although McCook reformed the Skatalites in the early 1980s, recurrent illness affected his ability to play with subsequent versions of the group.

McCook bitterly lamented the absence of royalties over the years for some of his best instrumental work, particularly the rhythm tracks used by seminal DJ U-Roy on his first hits—tracks that made "toasting" (rapping) a fixture of reggae culture. McCook died in May 1998 at the age of seventy-one, but his work lives on in a series of comprehensive anthologies.

SELECT DISCOGRAPHY: *Brass Rockers* (Striker Lee, 1975); *Cookin'* (Horse, 1975); *Horny Dub* (Grounation, 1976); *Top Secret* (w. the Supersonics) (Beatville, 1999); *Blazing Horns/Tenor in Roots* (Blood & Fire, 2004); *Real Cool Anthology 1966–1977* (Sanctuary, 2005)

Saxophonist Tommy McCook (top right) was best known as a founding member of the Skatalites, the top-flight studio crew that virtually invented ska in the 1960s. He went on to perform with numerous artists, among them Jimmy Cliff (foreground).

FREDDIE McGREGOR

YEARS ACTIVE: 1960s–PRESENT

Thanks in part to his rich vocal texture and early experience in the music business, Freddie McGregor has enjoyed an unusually long career. Born in the Jamaican parish of Clarendon in either 1955 or 1956, he first recorded at Studio One at the age of seven, and later described his experiences in that environment over several years as an invaluable informal musical education. He began his performing career as a member of the Clarendonians after Studio One producer Coxsone Dodd suggested that the group add a third member (the vocal duo of Fitzroy "Ernest" Wilson and Peter Austin recorded for Dodd from about 1965 to 1968). McGregor also recorded the single "Why Did You Do It" in 1966 as part of the duo Fitsy and Freddie. In 1972, McGregor joined the Generation Gap, one of several self-contained bands emerging in Jamaica at the time. The group split up in 1975, the same year that McGregor teamed up with studio session backing group Soul Syndicate, whose presence permeated the decade's Jamaican roots reggae recordings.

Following the dissolution of Generation Gap, McGregor began recording with producer Niney the Observer and released a series of singles, including 1975's "Bobby Bobylon," which later became the title track of his first Studio One album, released around 1980. In between those releases McGregor had mostly been a session vocalist at Studio One. Although he had learned a great deal working with Dodd and had become a multi-instrumentalist during his Generation Gap stint, McGregor's long-term affiliation with the producer was not financially satisfying. McGregor's years waiting in the wings had not been wasted, however: he applied his studio knowledge and worked as a drummer and songwriter on the 1979 *Black Woman* album self-produced by Judy Mowatt, a member of the I-Threes vocal trio that performed in reggae's premier band, Bob Marley & the Wailers. His 1980 single "Jogging" was an early contender for best product placement in a reggae song, referencing such athletic-apparel brands as Puma, Adidas, and Nike.

McGregor's solo breakthrough came in 1982 with *Big Ship*, produced by Jamaican singer Linval Thompson. McGregor then signed a deal with RAS Records in the United States and later established his own Big Ship record label. This allowed him to license material to RAS for American release and issue his own recordings in Jamaica. McGregor's 1986 album *All in the Same Boat*, featuring the single "Push Come to Shove," earned him some attention in the British reggae market, but he did not cross over to the UK pop charts until 1987, when his lovers rock version of the 1970s Ronnie Dyson R&B hit "Just Don't Want to Be Lonely" reached #9. In a 1989 interview, McGregor claimed the single had sold more than two hundred thousand copies in Britain alone. Another song released in 1987, "That Girl (Groovy Situation)," proved less successful, peaking at #47. That single came out on Polydor Records, a major label he had signed with earlier that year, when he astutely aligned himself with Big Life, a management company run by Jazz Summers, who also handled the massively successful pop group Wham!

Although it was never released, his 1988 album *Toughen Up* revealed further crossover potential. It was to include the single "And So I Will Wait for You," penned by ace British songwriter and producer Simon Climie, then half of the hit pop duo Climie Fisher. The single failed to chart in Britain, and Polydor shelved the album. In a 1991 interview, McGregor discussed the tendency of the major labels to alter reggae music and make it more commercial for the American market, noting that he would prefer to see the music reach audiences "in its more natural form."

His twenty-four-track Big Ship studio in Kingston opened in December 1995, granting McGregor the luxury of recording at his own pace and in his own space. Since establishing himself as a solo artist, McGregor has blended themes of righteousness and romance and recorded mostly in the roots reggae and lovers rock styles, rarely diverging from his signature sound. He received a 2003 Grammy nomination for best reggae album for *Anything for You*, and at a time when dancehall DJs often lack an appreciation for melody, he is a living echo of the songcraft, vocal performances, and production techniques that typified an earlier era. The release of the 2011 DVD *John Holt & Freddie McGregor: Living Legends—Live in Concert* acknowledged his status as a successful Jamaican music veteran.

SELECT DISCOGRAPHY: *Bobby Bobylon* (Studio One, 1979); *Mr. McGregor* (Observer, 1979); *Big Ship* (Greensleeves, 1982); *Come on Over* (RAS, 1983); *Across the Border* (RAS, 1984); *All in the Same Boat* (Greensleeves/RAS, 1986); *Freddie McGregor Sings Jamaican Classics* (Jetstar/VP 1991); *Freddie McGregor Sings Jamaican Classics 2* (Jetstar/VP 1992); *Push On* (Big Ship, 1994); *Zion Chant* (Heartbeat, 1994); *Forever My Love* (RAS, 1995); *Masterpiece* (VP, 1997); *Anthology* (VP, 1999); *Anything for You* (VP, 2002); *Comin' in Tough* (VP, 2005)

FREDDY McGREGOR I AM READY

MAD PROFESSOR

YEARS ACTIVE: 1970s–PRESENT

Directly inspired by the 1970s dub pioneers, Neil Fraser, better known as Mad Professor, is one of the producer-engineers who carried roots reggae aesthetics into the digital era in uncompromising fashion. Fraser was born in Guyana in 1955 and moved to England as a teenager in 1970. Like many of his studio heroes, he came from an electronics background, building and customizing equipment to suit his needs. He recorded parts of his first dub album using low-tech equipment indicative of his do-it-yourself ethos. Friends gave him the nickname Mad Professor as a child, when his obsession with electronics kept him away from more typical juvenile pursuits.

Mad Professor began operating the independent Ariwa Sounds studio in 1979. By the early 1980s, after several rapid upgrades, he had established a commercial twenty-four-track facility that he also used for releases on his Ariwa Sounds label, established in 1982. Though Mad Professor is best known for his outrageous dub albums,

the more commercial and sentimental lovers rock subgenre has also helped him pay the bills in a career defined by blending both elements. This combination of lovers rock and dub has worked with artists who fit neither mold, as demonstrated on his 2006 remix of "Get Used to It" for the British jazz-funk band the Brand New Heavies. Mad Professor also began collaborating with dub legend Lee Perry in the early 1980s, briefly touring with him and doing live dub mixing during the shows. Before long, Perry's legendarily erratic behavior fragmented the touring unit, and they stopped working together for a time. Mad Professor gained additional credibility in both Jamaica and Britain when such artists as singer Johnny Clarke (*Yard Style*, 1983) chose to work in his studios.

Mad Professor's most crucial commercial moment arrived when Massive Attack, a trip-hop (ambient electronic) group from the city of Bristol in England, hired him to mix the *No Protection* album (1995)—a dub version of the band's 1994 *Protection* album. Sales registered on the British charts as one collection instead of two separate works, and the combined sales took the album to #4 and platinum (more than three hundred thousand copies sold) in the United Kingdom. Such success is a key example of dub's influence on the mainstream, even if it was filtered through a pop façade.

Mad Professor's massive recorded output mirrors that of Jamaica's vintage roots reggae producers. He has released several series of dub albums, most of which are variations of his debut album,

Mad Professor busies himself with lab work at Slim's in San Francisco, 1991.

Dub Me Crazy, released in 1982, which has at least twelve volumes. More recently, he's released multiple chapters of *Black Liberation Dub*. In 2004, he attempted to bridge the gap between dub and dancehall audiences with *Dancehall Dub*, but the result of this ambitious project was music stranded in a neutral zone between the two subgenres. In one *Reggae Report* magazine interview, he admitted that he was "not really into dancehall," calling it an aspect of reggae he could not readily identify with. Perhaps *Dancehall Dub* was an effort to upgrade dancehall-style instrumentation by placing it in a dub context.

Never restricted to the studio, Mad Professor has partially maintained his global cult following by playing live DJ shows, both with and without singers and musicians. Given his large catalog of more than sixty albums, there's presumably much more dub on the way.

SELECT DISCOGRAPHY: *Mad Professor—RAS Portraits* (RAS, 1997); *Afrocentric Dub: Black Liberation Dub—Chapter 5* (Ariwa/RAS, 1999); *Dub Revolutionaries: Sly & Robbie Meet the Mad Professor Featuring Dean Fraser* (Ariwa/RAS, 2004)

BOB MARLEY

YEARS ACTIVE: 1962-1981

No artist has had a greater effect on reggae's long-term international profile than Bob Marley, who emerged from marginal status in the early 1960s to become the world's most well-known reggae artist in the 1970s, and then died tragically in 1981, at the age of thirty-six. Early singles like "Get Up, Stand Up," "No Woman No Cry," and "I Shot the Sheriff," which Marley recorded as a member of the Wailers with Peter Tosh and Bunny Wailer, morphed from reggae anthems into mainstream classics. His 1977 solo album *Exodus* was hailed by *Time* magazine in 1999 as the album of the century.

For many people, Marley's multiracial heritage played a role in facilitating his later international appeal. He was born on February 6, 1945, in the parish of St. Ann, Jamaica, to a black mother, Cedella, and a white army captain, Norval Marley, who died when his son was very young. In 1962, after moving to Kingston and trying his hand at welding (a career that was cut short when a piece of metal landed in his eye), Marley recorded the unsuccessful singles "Judge Not" (as Robert Marley) and "One Cup of Coffee" (as Bobby Martell) for producer Leslie Kong's Beverley's Records. These songs

were also licensed for UK release in the early 1960s by Island Records head Chris Blackwell, whose later business dealings with Marley in the 1970s would transform reggae into an international phenomenon. Marley's relationship with Kong, meanwhile, dissolved over the producer's refusal to pay him for other songs he had recorded.

Marley's initial success in Jamaica came in late 1963 as a member of the R&B-inspired Wailing Wailers, a group consisting of vocalists Bunny Wailer, Peter Tosh, Junior Braithwaite, Beverley Kelso, and Cherry Smith. Backed by the leading ska band of that era, the Skatalites, Marley's group recorded "Simmer Down" at producer Coxsone Dodd's Studio One in two takes after extensive rehearsals. The single was released on the Studio One label and became a chart-topping ska hit in Jamaica. By 1965, the Wailing Wailers had become the trio of Marley, Tosh and Wailer, and despite their Jamaican popularity, by 1966 they had departed Studio One due to disputes over financial issues.

Following his 1966 marriage to Rita Anderson, a singer in the Jamaican female vocal group the Soulettes, Marley spent a brief time in the United States that year, initially heading to Delaware to visit his mother, who had immigrated there three years earlier with plans to bring Bob over permanently. While this stint in America temporarily put a halt to Marley's recording career, it influenced his antiestablishment social, political, and musical viewpoints. However, he found the United States too intense and chaotic for his liking. After working several jobs—including assembling cars for Chrysler—Marley returned to Jamaica in 1967. He adopted the Rastafarian faith, partly through the influence of the Rasta elder Mortimer Planno, who briefly acted as the Wailers' manager in 1967. Ironically, during Marley's absence from

LEFT: The Wailers (l-r: Bunny Wailer, Bob Marley, and Peter Tosh) in the mid-1960s, when American R&B influenced the group right down to their snazzy outfits.

RIGHT: Bob Marley jammin' on stage, c. 1975.

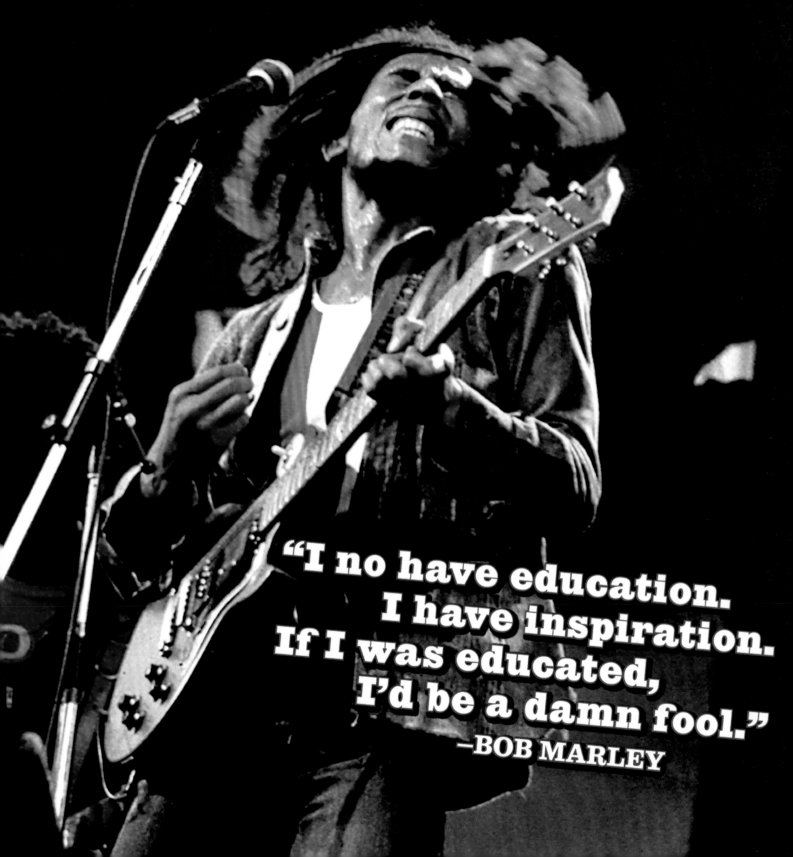

"I no have education.
I have inspiration.
If I was educated,
I'd be a damn fool."
—BOB MARLEY

Jamaica, the island had been visited by Ethiopian Emperor Haile Selassie, the Rastafarian icon who would inspire so many of his songs.

After returning to Jamaica, Marley ambitiously established the Wail 'N' Soul 'M' record label and store in 1967 in an effort to secure greater independence, and financial reward for his music. Despite a handful of moderately successful Wailers singles on the new label, none of the group members were fully prepared to run the business, and its existence proved relatively brief. Marley simultaneously signed a solo recording and publishing deal with American manager Danny Sims. Marley had come to Sims's attention thanks to American singer Johnny Nash, whose own hits (some written by Marley) would popularize the emerging reggae sound. Nash's version of Marley's composition "Stir It Up" reached the top twenty in both Britain and the United States in 1973. Since Marley's deal with Sims did not include the Wailers, the group—including Marley—began to work once again for Leslie Kong and, in 1969, for producer Lee Perry, tracking such songs as "400 Years," which Marley would rerecord during his commercial rise in the 1970s. Eventually Perry licensed the tapes to Trojan Records for release in Britain without consulting the group, and this unauthorized material would appear continually even after the Wailers had formed new relationships with other record labels.

Marley went to Sweden in 1971 to work with Nash on a film score, but the movie (which also starred Nash) subsequently failed commercially, and a planned tour also fell through. Meanwhile, Marley had signed with CBS, and that deal resulted in the gritty but unsuccessful Nash-produced single "Reggae on Broadway." To promote the record, the other members of the Wailers joined Marley in London, where the band became disillusioned. Many accounts state that Nash and Marley's manager, Danny Sims, suddenly returned to America without informing the band, leaving them stranded in London; but in a 2011 interview with the *Jamaica Gleaner* newspaper, group member Bunny Wailer dismissed that version of events as "fictitious garbage." Regardless, the group was in despair,when Marley met with Chris Blackwell, the Island Records head who had licensed some of his earliest releases for sale in Britain.

Blackwell's decision to sign the Wailers to Island in 1972 marked a critical turning point for reggae. The genre had not yet been taken seriously by the recording industry, and it was not seen as album-oriented music made by self-contained bands, as had been the case with rock. While some saw the Wailers as potential trouble, perhaps because of their rebellious image, Blackwell was likely encouraged by their solid musical reputation, as well as by the success of the cult reggae film *The Harder They Come* (1972) in the United States.

The first fruit of the Wailers-Island collaboration was *Catch a Fire*, the reggae genre's first serious international concept album. Released in Britain in 1972 and in the United States in 1973, the album targeted the rock audience. *Catch a Fire* was initially a commercial failure, selling only fourteen thousand copies in its first year, but it set the stage for reggae's future commercial growth. Controversially, it featured rock guitar and a flashy sleeve package in the shape of a Zippo cigarette lighter, with a hinged top that opened to reveal a cardboard flame and the album inside. The package also included liner notes, which were uncommon on reggae releases. The original Jamaican master tapes had been overdubbed and mixed in London, and the resulting sound—a more treble-oriented brand of reggae with bass no longer dominant in the mix—represented yet another way the album catered to rock audiences. Decades later, questions linger regarding the album's reggae authenticity, as well as the decision to hire American session musicians who were inexperienced at playing reggae. For his part, however, Marley saw their inclusion as part of an opportunity to reach larger audiences with his music and Rasta message. He was evidently ready, willing, and able to adapt the Wailers' sound on record, and the positive critical reaction to the album was one factor that led to tours of Britain and the United States.

The Wailers' next album, *Burnin'*, was released in 1973, a mere six months after *Catch a Fire*. *Burnin'* contained the anthems "Get Up, Stand Up" and "Burnin' and Lootin'," and yielded Marley's "I Shot the Sheriff," which was a transatlantic hit for British rock legend Eric Clapton in 1974. Segments of the Wailers' audience saw *Burnin'* as a less calculated, more authentic and organic expression of the group's identity—a perception reinforced by the album cover, which was less flashy than its predecessor. Tosh and Wailer left the group soon after the release of *Burnin'* to pursue solo careers, prompted by

OPPOSITE: The Wailers on their way to a gig in London in the early 1970s.

TOP: This 1975 live album, recorded in Britain, helped further Marley's mainstream success.

ABOVE: *Natty Dread* was the Wailers' first studio album after Peter Tosh and Bunny Wailer left the group in 1973, and is best known for "No Woman, No Cry."

evident that the mix is more refined and spacious than on the earlier works, and that the synthesizers assume more central melodic and rhythmic roles. In effect, "Positive Vibration" introduces an album that is sonically cleaner and crisper than its predecessors. *Rastaman Vibration* has a different overall texture, and the original burlap-sack album cover, with its raised surfaces, acts as a kind of visual allusion to the revamped sound. Of course, the canvas cover also served more practical purposes.

to rock fans. Meanwhile, such songs as "Who the Cap Fit" and "War" continued to promote the worldview and political conscience of Rastafari.

It was during his rise to mainstream prominence in the early 1970s that Marley also became involved in Jamaican politics. He performed on the People's National Party (PNP) Musical Bandwagon, a vehicle for promoting the 1972 election campaign of the socialist-leaning Michael Manley, whose egalitarian rhetoric and association with Ethiopian emperor Haile Selassie attracted potential Rastafarian votes. Marley's public support of Manley would lead some to brand him politically partisan, and it may have contributed to the December 3, 1976 assassination attempt on Marley. Despite the armed attack, which occurred at Marley's 56 Hope Road compound in Kingston, he performed at the free Smile

ABOVE: Tuff Gong's headquarters at 56 Hope Road in Kingston. Today the complex is home to the Bob Marley Museum.

RIGHT: A young Bob Marley (second from left) and Rasta brethren in Kingston's Trench Town.

disagreements over the Wailers' musical path as well as discomfort with the low-budget processed food on tour and the cold weather they encountered in Europe.

After Tosh's and Bunny Wailer's departures, the band was billed as Bob Marley & the Wailers on 1974's *Natty Dread*. (The album was originally titled *Knotty Dread*, a phrase with distinct downtown ghetto connotations.) Although it contains several gems, *Natty Dread* is probably most famous for the studio version of "No Woman, No Cry," which quickly became a live staple. Later that year, *Live!* reinforced Marley's growing reputation among audiences, both black and white, particularly in Britain, where it was recorded. But his real commercial breakthrough came with 1976's *Rastaman Vibration*, which became a top-ten album in the United States and reached #15 on the UK charts.

Over the years, the response to *Rastaman Vibration* has varied widely. While some fans have declared it a reggae masterpiece, others—such as the authors of *Reggae: The Rough Guide*, who describe it as "weaker than any of the preceding Island albums"—take the opposite stance. What is certain is that Marley's sound and image targeted a more mainstream audience, and it's notable that *Rastaman Vibration* became his highest-charting studio release in the United States. From the opening bars of the first track, "Positive Vibration," it's

As its designer, Wailers art director Neville Garrick, recalls, Marley was excited to find that a sample of the jacket kept the herb he was rolling in place while the seeds rolled away. "Ratit boy, dis [cover] good fe cleaning herb," Marley said. Blackwell insisted that this statement (in standard English form, "This album jacket is good for cleaning herb") be included in the album, appearing on the inner panel. It may well be that Marley's fans were already using his covers for the purpose of rolling joints, even without a textured surface! The cover also underscores the rebellious Rasta image that would appeal

Jamaica concert three days later. Some speculate that the attempt on Marley's life was motivated by the misperception that his hosting of a peace-and-unity concert in the run-up to the 1976 elections was an endorsement of Manley's PNP. In fact, the purpose of the event was to heal Jamaica's political divisions. In light of Jamaica's unstable political climate and the tangible danger facing his family at this time, Marley decided to leave the island until things cooled off. Following a stop in the Bahamas, he spent most of his 18-month exile in London, where much of his next album was recorded and mixed.

Exodus, released in 1977 and later hailed by *Time* magazine in 1999 as the "album of the century," confirmed Marley's ascendance to commercial superstardom, showcasing both the political and personal sides of his music. Some critics felt that *Kaya*, recorded during the same sessions as *Exodus* but released in 1978, was too romantically focused, as evidenced by songs like "Is This Love." Blackwell assumed responsibility for placing the Wailers' album tracks in sequence, as he had done since *Catch a Fire*, and it had been his decision to separate the songs from the London recording sessions into two distinct albums. Meanwhile, Marley had also recorded the single "Punky Reggae Party," produced by Lee Perry amid the rise of British punk rock in 1977. Featuring musical backing by members of Jamaica's Third World band and the British reggae outfit Aswad, "Punky Reggae Party" celebrated the similarities between Rastas and punks—both social outcasts in the United Kingdom. That unifying sentiment reached the British top ten as part of a double–A-side single that also included the *Exodus* album track "Jamming." It was at the end of the successful European tour in support of *Exodus* in 1977 that Marley was diagnosed with a cancerous toe and forced to cancel the American leg of the tour.

The 1978 One Love Peace Concert brought Marley back to Jamaica and the island's political turmoil as he adopted the role of musical peacemaker. The event is usually remembered for Marley's ability to bring the heads of Jamaica's two rival parties, Manley and Edward Seaga, onstage to shake hands in an all-too-brief symbolic gesture of unity that unfortunately did nothing to quell the election-related violence. Nonetheless,

it resulted in Marley receiving the United Nations Peace Medal that year.

The live double album *Babylon by Bus* (1978), recorded in several different countries, demonstrated reggae's global impact, while the politically focused collection of songs on 1979's *Survival* dispelled any notions that Marley had lost his political or musical direction. The single "Zimbabwe" was adopted by that country's freedom fighters, and Marley was invited to perform the song at Zimbabwe's independence day celebrations in 1980. Later that year, Marley released his final studio album, the triumphant *Uprising*. Marley's ascent was not without some friction within his camp. Various members of the Wailers have recounted Marley

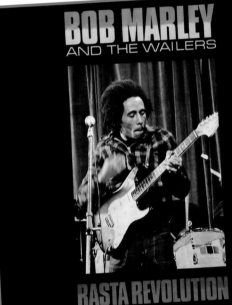

physically attacking manager Don Taylor for stealing money from the group and, perhaps more importantly, for betraying Marley's trust.

In the fall of 1980, Bob Marley & the Wailers performed at Madison Square Garden in New York City, opening for the American R&B-pop band the

Commodores as part of a tour that, sadly, would never be completed. The renowned venue signified the tremendous journey Marley had made from Trench Town to the top of the music business while delivering messages of peace and spiritual salvation. Similarly, in Milan, Italy, the band drew a capacity crowd of one hundred thousand to San Siro stadium in an unmistakable demonstration of commercial success. But by September 1980, Marley's cancer was spreading throughout his body, and he collapsed while jogging in New York City's Central Park. Following a variety of unsuccessful treatments—including some in Austria overseen by Dr. Josef Issels, a reputed former officer in the German SS—Marley died in Miami on May 11, 1981, at the age of thirty-six. Symbolizing his importance to the Jamaican people, he was given a state funeral—unprecedented for a Rastaman yet

quite fitting for a man who successfully highlighted the plight of the African diaspora and the interconnection of all races. He had also been awarded Jamaica's Order of Merit shortly before his death.

Marley's passing led to a seemingly endless string of compilations—including *Legend* (Island Records, 1984), the top-selling reggae album in history, with more than 20 million copies sold worldwide. Conspiracy theories surrounding his death are plentiful, and not surprising considering Marley's political significance and ability to motivate millions of people.

The subsequent mass marketing of Marley's image and music has led to numerous lawsuits over who controls the rights to profit from them. According to a Marley family legal representative, between 2000 and 2011 the family initiated thirty lawsuits in the United States and issued more than four hundred cease-and-desist letters to halt the illegal production and sales of merchandise. Given that the family reportedly paid $11 million to secure

LEFT: This 1974 compilation album was one of many released by Trojan Records without Bob Marley's and the Wailers' blessings.

BELOW: The single "Zimbabwe" was adopted by Zimbabwe's freedom fighters and led to a performance by the group in that country in 1980.

rights to Marley's identity—a payout made necessary by the fact that he left no will—it is perhaps not surprising that his relatives would seek to block such infringement.

The consolidation of the record industry has also complicated matters. Island Records was purchased by PolyGram Records in 1989; in turn, in 1998, PolyGram became part of the Seagram empire, which built on its original success in the alcoholic beverage industry to own multiple entertainment subsidiaries by the 1990s, including MCA and Universal. Seagram renamed

its music operations the Universal Music Group, effectively creating the world's largest record company. In September 2010, the Marley family's effort to secure copyright to the run of studio albums from *Catch a Fire* to *Exodus* was rejected by a New York judge, who defined the recordings as works for hire. This left Universal Music Group free to exploit the catalog further and to sell Marley's songs in various formats, including phone ringtones.

Rare or "lost" Marley recordings, photos, and film footage continue to emerge virtually every year and are eagerly consumed by a public still hungry for Marley material. Despite the anguish that characterizes much of Marley's work, the best-selling *Legend* album contains few of the artist's sociopolitical

narratives. Further, the covers of most authorized retrospective albums show Marley in distinctly non-threatening poses. Blackwell recalls that even though he refused to participate in the *Legend* compilation project, the final track selection and choice of a benign cover photo followed extensive market research aimed at creating the most commercially viable collection possible.

The musical catalog is the center of the Marley empire, and while a vast number of nonmusical products now bear his name and likeness, they would have little economic value without the commercial success of his recordings and the broad appeal of his messages.

SELECT DISCOGRAPHY: *The Wailing Wailers* (Studio One, 1965); *Soul Rebels* (Trojan/Upsetter, 1970); *Soul Revolution* (Trojan/Upsetter, 1971); *The Best of the Wailers* (Beverley's, 1970); *African Herbsman* (Trojan, 1973/1974); *Catch a Fire* (Island, 1972; *Burnin'* (Island, 1973); *Rasta Revolution* (Trojan, 1974); *Natty Dread* (Island, 1974; *Live!* (Island, 1975); *Rastaman Vibration* (Island, 1976); *Exodus* (Island, 1977); *Babylon by Bus* (Island, 1978); *Survival* (Island, 1979); *Uprising* (Island, 1980); *Confrontation* (Island, 1983); *Legend* (Island, 1984); *Songs of Freedom* (Island, 1992); *Live Forever* (Island/Universal, 2011)

The Wailers and company (including Lee "Scratch" Perry in the background) congregate before a performance.

MARLEY FAMILY

As the indisputable king of reggae, Bob Marley did not just make good music with the Wailers, the pivotal reggae band that included singers Peter Tosh and Bunny Wailer. He also ensured that there were many children to carry the Marley name and genes into the future. While some children were born to his wife, Rita, Bob applied his "One Love" credo liberally, fathering as many as twenty-two children by one estimate. There are many mothers of his children, and more than a few of his offspring are involved in making music.

Bob's mother, Cedella Marley Booker, is the real root of the Marley musical dynasty. Her singing of songs and hymns at home directly influenced the young Bob, who would join in. Much later, his mother's passion for music would become recorded reality, as she made a few albums before her death in 2008. The post–Bob Marley musical generation in the family began with the Melody Makers, whose lineup featured Ziggy (b. 1968), Stephen (b. 1972), Sharon (b. 1964), and Cedella (b. 1967), all children of Bob and Rita. They were initially signed to Bob Marley's Tuff Gong Records and recorded his composition "Children Playing in the Street" as their first single around 1979. A decade later, they became the first Marleys to collect Grammy Awards, taking top reggae honors with their 1988 album *Conscious Party*. The collective went on to record ten studio albums through 2007, after which time the Melody Makers name no longer appeared on records featuring leader Ziggy, and brother Stephen began a solo career. Brothers Ziggy and Stephen were also prime movers behind the formation of Ghetto Youth International in 1989, an unusual amalgam of a record company and registered charity designed to uplift Jamaica's underprivileged youths.

Having served his musical apprenticeship from age six, Stephen initially focused his solo efforts on production, becoming most visible with the hip-hop–reggae Bob Marley tribute album *Chant Down Babylon* (1999). This controversial record featured the late Bob "collaborating" with contemporary artists (Erykah Badu, Busta Rhymes, and The Roots, to name a few) and drew fire from those who felt it was commercially diluted, as well as ethically questionable to overdub new vocal performances onto the work of a deceased artist. However, plenty of fans loved the album, which targeted a younger generation of listeners that might not otherwise be exposed to Bob's music. The gold record it earned in the United States suggests that the album met its objective.

When Stephen embarked on his full-fledged solo career in 2007, his well-received *Mind Control* album peaked at #35 on the *Billboard* pop chart and won a Grammy for best reggae album in 2008. In 2010, he won the best reggae album Grammy again, this time for the acoustic version of *Mind Control*, released the previous year, and

became the first artist in the history of the reggae category to reprise a complete album of songs from an earlier award-winning release. His 2011 album *Revelation Part 1: The Roots of Life* extended the roots echoes of his late father's music while also demonstrating Stephen's growth as a solo act. Stephen's son, Jo Mersa Marley, has begun performing with his father, bringing the next generation of offspring into the musical arena.

Damian "Jr. Gong" Marley is the product of Bob's sensationalized relationship with the Jamaican Miss World 1976, Cindy Breakspeare, during his British exile, a period that followed an assassination attempt in Jamaica in late 1976. Born in 1978 and just two years

ABOVE: Bob Marley's children (l–r: Steven, Sharon, Cedella, and Ziggy) formed the Melody Makers in 1979 and went on to record ten studio albums.

RIGHT: Like father, like son: Damian Marley, burnin' in New York City, 2004.

old when his father died, Damian first performed with the Shepherds, a short-lived group featuring children of reggae artists that also included bassist Shiah Coore (now bassist in the pop supergroup SuperHeavy and son of Third World guitarist Cat Coore). He then assumed a DJ persona, releasing his debut single "Deejay Degree" on his father's Tuff Gong label in 1993 and contributing the dancehall song "School Controversy" to Sony Records' 1995 *Positively Reggae* compilation.

The 2005 album *Welcome to Jamrock* won a best reggae album Grammy and went gold in America, taking Damian to a higher commercial level. The album cover raised some interesting questions, however, as it shows him standing amid the galvanized sheet metal of an inner-city ghetto—a setting that sharply contrasts with his privileged position as a Marley on a major label. *Distant Relatives*, his 2010 album with rapper Nas, aimed to capitalize on the not-so-distant musical and commercial relationships between hip hop and reggae. Many critics hailed the album as an innovative and landmark record, but Marley and Nas weren't above sampling "Love Fire," a 1982 track by the British reggae group Aswad, on "Land of Promise." Although Damian's releases always have major impact on the reggae charts, *Welcome to Jamrock* and *Distant Relatives* have been his only albums to reach the *Billboard* 200. By 2011, he had sold 1.3 million albums, and that same year, his inclusion in the pop supergroup SuperHeavy—formed by Rolling Stones singer Mick Jagger and the British musician and producer Dave Stewart, formerly of the group Eurythmics—confirmed his star status.

As another one of the later arrivals to the music scene, Miami-raised Ky-Mani Marley, born in 1976 to Jamaican table-tennis champion Anita Belnavis, brought a definite R&B-infused urban vibe to his music. His 2007 set *Radio* was predominantly a hip hop album and contained only a few traces of reggae. This was in complete contrast to 2001's *Many More Roads*, a start-to-finish reggae album that brought him a Grammy nomination for best reggae album. The shift in musical emphasis roughly coincided with his move into acting and his appearance in the Jamaican crime film *Shottas* (2002). In 2010, Ky-Mani began collaborating in a roots reggae style with Andrew Tosh, son of the late Wailer and solo artist Peter Tosh. Their nostalgic acoustic version of "Lessons in My Life" evoked the roots era of their fathers' heyday.

Julian Marley, born in London in 1975 to Lucy Pounder, adopted Rastafarianism as a teenager and has few surviving memories of his father performing, only recalling watching him in London at Crystal Palace in 1980. His older half brothers have been involved in developing his career, which began with *Lion in the Morning* in 1996. Julian has yet to emerge as a breakout artist, with *A Time & Place* (2003) and the stronger *Awake* (2009) yet to capture large audiences.

For each Marley in the music business, the challenge has always been finding the balance between reflecting the inevitable influence of their father and expressing an individual identity. Results may vary, but the public's appetite for music from Bob's children isn't disappearing any time soon.

RITA MARLEY
YEARS ACTIVE: 1960s–2000s

Rita Marley, born Alpharita Anderson in Cuba in 1946, was a Sunday school teacher and lifelong resident of the Trench Town section of St. Andrew, Jamaica, in the early 1960s when she became an original member of the Soulettes, a female vocal trio modeled in sound and image after such American acts as the Supremes. After the Soulettes successfully auditioned for Kingston record producer Coxsone Dodd at Studio One, Rita's future husband, Bob Marley, was given the A&R (Artists and Repertoire) duties of developing the group by providing them with original songs (Bob's own group, the Wailers, were also recording for Dodd). Bob and Rita were married in 1966, shortly before Bob's spell in the United States with his mother. That year, Rita witnessed Ethiopian Emperor Haile Selassie's arrival in Jamaica, an event that had an immediate spiritual and cultural effect on her, leading her to embrace Rastafarianism.

The Soulettes broke up in 1967, and soon after Rita scored a few solo Jamaican hits. Although she had backed the Wailers in the 1960s, performed with Bob on the pre-1972 election Musical Bandwagon (a collection of various reggae artists that supported Michael Manley's People's National Party),

and provided background vocals on the Wailers' 1973 *Catch a Fire* album, it took the formation of the female vocal trio the I-Threes to make her a consistently visible force. The I-Threes made their album debut with Bob Marley & the Wailers on *Natty Dread* (1975), and Rita's collaborative role with fellow members Judy Mowatt and Marcia Griffiths effectively made her one of the most powerful women in reggae.

In 1976 Rita survived an assassination attempt against Bob at his home in Jamaica, although she sustained a gunshot injury to the head as part of the incident. Following Bob's death in 1981, Rita achieved her biggest hit that year with "One Draw," a catchy dedication

to marijuana. While some listeners might not have initially recognized the references to marijuana, the British Broadcasting Corporation (BBC) banned the song.

It's believed that the numerous legal battles surrounding the Marley estate limited Rita's career development, and after *Who Feels It Knows It* (1981), she released no albums in the early 1980s to capitalize on the popularity of "One Draw." A decade later, she received a best reggae album Grammy nomination for *We Must Carry On* (1991), but in a sign of how times were changing in reggae, the award

went to the dancehall DJ Shabba Ranks. Lately, Rita has focused on preserving her late husband's musical legacy, recording a 2003 solo tribute album and one with the I-Threes in 2007.

SELECT DISCOGRAPHY: *Who Feels It Knows It* (Shanachie, 1981); *Harambe* (Shanachie, 1988); *We Must Carry On* (Shanachie, 1991); *One Draw: The Best of Rita Marley* (Varese Sarabande, 2002); *Rita Marley Sings Bob Marley...and Friends* (Shanachie, 2003)

Bob Marley's widow, Rita, keeps her husband's memory alive, c. 1985.

ZIGGY MARLEY

YEARS ACTIVE: 1970s-PRESENT

As far as audience perception is concerned, being Bob Marley's eldest son has been a mixed blessing for David "Ziggy" Marley, born in Kingston, Jamaica, in 1968. From his point of view, however, it has been completely positive. Arguably, he has fluctuated between standing in his father's shadow and asserting his own musical identity, and he has also faced the typical reggae dilemma of balancing good-time party songs with political missives aimed at "Babylon"—the Rasta designation for the social and political establishment—and pronouncements of peace and love. When the major labels went looking for successors to the reggae throne following Bob Marley's death, Ziggy and his siblings were seen as likely candidates.

Ziggy began his career at age 11 as part of the Melody Makers collective, teaming with the three other children (Stephen, Sharon, and Cedella) that Bob had fathered with Rita Marley. However, from the outset, Ziggy was the main songwriter and musical force, and the group's records prominently feature his performances. There are competing accounts of how they came to be called the Melody Makers. In one version, they derived their name from the model of Bob Marley's first guitar, while another narrative suggests that Britain's weekly *Melody Maker* music magazine was the source of inspiration. Critical reaction to the group's existence as a recording act was decidedly mixed; some welcomed seeing the Marley legend extended by his children, while others questioned their validity, credibility, and musical value. Ziggy repeatedly dismissed claims that the group's profile and image were due only to their famous father. In 1979 they donated royalties from their debut single, a cover of their father's "Children Playing in the Streets," to the United Nations, and their performance at Bob's 1981 state funeral further imprinted them on the public's consciousness.

The Melody Makers' early singles were released on Bob Marley's Tuff Gong label between 1979 and 1984, and despite the distinctly youthful voices on the popular 1982 song "What a Plot," the anguished tone and message implied that the group might be heading in a deep roots direction. In 1984, they made their first attempt at cutting an album, completing a full-length record for EMI Records with

Steve Levine, a producer known for his work with the British pop group Culture Club. But the label was allegedly dissatisfied with the pop focus and shelved the album project. Nonetheless, the initial singles that were released got airplay in Britain, including "Met Her on a Rainy Day" (1984). The lack of enthusiastic public response may have persuaded EMI to go back to the drawing board.

On the group's 1985 official debut album, *Play the Game Right*, released on EMI and subsequently nominated for a Grammy Award for best reggae album, Ziggy displayed the songwriting skills on which a solo career could be built. Renowned Jamaican session players Ashley "Grub" Cooper and Rocky Walters, who were presumably enlisted to restore a more Jamaican sound, produced the album. While the 1986 album *Hey World!* did not advance the Melody Makers' creative agenda dramatically, it turned out to be more important as a transitional stepping-stone toward greater musical maturity. The first two albums failed to reach the mainstream album charts, and for many listeners, the underlying theme of revolting against the system was initially a hard sell coming from the artistic and financial inheritors of a man who had actually challenged the establishment.

After signing a new deal with Virgin Records, the group finally took off with *Conscious Party* (1988), an album produced by Chris Frantz and Tina Weymouth, the husband-and-wife rhythm section behind the rock band Talking Heads. The album was certified platinum in America for selling over a million copies, and the group won the Marley family's first-ever Grammy Award in 1989 for best reggae recording. The single "Tomorrow People" became the first—and so far only—song featuring Ziggy to crack the American Top 40. In later interviews, Ziggy would maintain that an audience for reggae exists, but that radio's musical segregation is an obstacle to reaching people. More cohesive than the previous records, *Conscious Party* showed a sharp focus and soaring self-assurance. The next album, 1989's *One Bright Day*, was less commercially successful, achieving only gold sales (over 500,000 copies), and sounded slightly pedestrian compared to the previous record, but it nevertheless earned the group another Grammy for best reggae recording. Given the strength of his global live following, Ziggy has not appeared overly concerned with industry politics or chart placements. His lowest-charting album in the United States, 1993's *Joy and Blues*, which reached only #178, was arguably his most progressive, vibrant, and creatively ambitious. He shifted to Elektra Records for *Free Like We Want 2 B* (1995) and returned to Tuff Gong for *Dragonfly* (2003), neither album producing any notable movements in musical direction. *Family Time* (2009) was the first album credited solely to Ziggy Marley and indicated his priorities as a married father of two. *Family Time* won the Grammy award for the best children's music album and featured such collaborators as reggae great Toots Hibbert, country singer Willie Nelson, and folk-rock legend Paul Simon. The album wasn't his first recording suited for children, as over a decade earlier, in 1996, he and the Melody Makers had recorded "Believe in Yourself" as the theme song to the long-running PBS children's television cartoon series, *Arthur*.

Released in 2011, *Wild and Free* revealed an artist simply happy to be making music without trying to satisfy anyone but himself. As the once-precocious youth moves into the role of reggae elder statesman, it's questionable whether Ziggy will again scale major commercial heights. If not, chances are it will not bother him—just as long as he finds audiences willing to share his vision of modern roots reggae.

SELECT DISCOGRAPHY: as **Ziggy Marley & the Melody Makers:** *Play the Game Right* (EMI, 1985); *Hey World* (EMI, 1986); *Conscious Party* (Virgin, 1988); *One Bright Day* (Virgin, 1989); *Jahmekya* (Virgin, 1991); *Joy and Blues* (Virgin, 1993); *Free Like We Want 2 B* (Elektra, 1995); *Spirit of Music* (Elektra, 1999); *Dragonfly* (Tuff Gong, 2003); *Love Is My Religion* (Tuff Gong, 2007); *Best of Ziggy Marley & the Melody Makers* (Virgin, 2008); as **Ziggy Marley:** *Family Time* (Tuff Gong, 2009); *Wild and Free* (Tuff Gong, 2011)

OPPOSITE: Ziggy Marley and the Melody Makers shooting a music video for their single "Tumblin' Down," 1988.

RIGHT: Chris Frantz (left) and Tina Weymouth (right), producers of Ziggy Marley's Grammy-winning *Conscious Party* (1988), with the singer, 1987.

CULTURAL ROOTS

The Afro-Jamaican roots of reggae lie in musical forms and local communities that are usually little known to audiences beyond the Caribbean. Generally speaking, song-and-dance rituals associated with religion have been the driving forces behind the island's recorded music. Jamaica's cultural roots are many and varied, and what follows is an overview of the key elements that have influenced the reggae soundscape. At the trunk of the tree is the importance of communal celebration and interaction, exemplified in modern times by the sound system (a mobile setup featuring massive speakers through which records and DJs are heard by the public) and its figurative and literal power to attract people to sites of sonic intensity.

The stage for cross-cultural collision was set when the Spanish colonized Jamaica in 1494, and followed this with the virtual extermination of the indigenous Arawak population. According to historical accounts of the Spanish arrival, the Arawak played drums and wind instruments when their chief met Christopher Columbus, the explorer vilified centuries later in the music of reggae singers Peter Tosh ("Can't Blame the Youth" in 1972) and Burning Spear ("Columbus" in 1980). The Spanish had brought sugar to the Caribbean, and after they had depleted the indigenous Indian population, they began importing and enslaving Africans in the 1500s to provide agricultural labor. In doing so, however, the Spanish unwittingly planted the seeds of colonial rebellion: runaway slaves merged with remnants of the Arawaks and formed a new group known as the Maroons, occupying remote inland areas, especially hills and mountains. The Maroons established a culture of resistance that became an integral part of Jamaica's twentieth-century reggae philosophy.

The British eventually captured the island in 1655 and assumed colonial rule. Maroon opposition to slavery continued under British rule in the seventeenth and eighteenth centuries,

as other African laborers imported by Jamaica's new colonial rulers escaped the plantations and joined the Maroon ranks. As part of their campaign of active resistance, these fugitives waged guerrilla warfare against plantation owners, foreshadowing the steadfast opposition to exploitation later associated with reggae and Rastafari. The Maroons' assaults on their former masters forced the British to sign peace treaties in the 1730s and grant them a degree of independence. According to some sources,

ABOVE: Pukkumina spiritual gatherings combine ancient African and Christian traditions.
RIGHT: Mystic Revelation of Rastafari, headed by legendary Rasta drummer Count Ossie, brought African musical traditions to the foreground of roots reggae.

the British also enlisted some Maroons as bounty hunters to prevent more runaway slaves from joining their ranks. Maroon communities continue to exist in Jamaica, and while they were once found in other Caribbean and Latin American territories (with some still existing in Suriname in South America, for example), few such groups can be linked so directly to forms of music still vital in the twenty-first century.

Specifically, the Maroon style of drumming has impacted most, if not all, of the forms associated with Jamaica's musical roots. Beyond entertainment purposes, the drums were used to summon ancestral spirits and facilitate communication among Maroon communities during their sustained anti-plantation warfare. Due to the presence and enforced cultural dominance of the British, some less rhythmically fluid, tonally flat European influences also became part of the musical fusion.

African oral traditions, including storytelling in song, have contributed directly to the DJ culture and what some have termed the "sing-jay" style, in which performers use a vocal style that blends talking and singing. Although this practice became an established element in Jamaican musical entertainment via the sound systems in the 1950s, it only became a commercial recorded phenomenon in the early 1970s. The rhythmic patterns and call-and-response features of vocal expression in the African diaspora are also branches from the same trees.

The importance of religion in the development of Jamaican cultural identity should not be underestimated. One of the first acts of European colonization was the attempt to replace ancestral African spirituality and religious rituals with Christianity. The British effort to psychologically subdue slave laborers in Jamaica with such ideology was only partially successful, and the African practices were never fully eliminated. Instead, the enslaved persisted in Jamaican versions of the African religious experience,

ABOVE: Maroons— descendants of Jamaica's indigenous Arawak and runaway slaves—at a dance in the mountainous Accompong region, 1946.

OPPOSITE: Maroons in rural Jamaica, c. 1908–09. The Maroons cultivated a spirit of resistance that carried over into reggae music.

in Revivalist practices such as Pukkumina and Kumina, which combine aspects of African tradition with Christianity.

The Great Revival was an era of Jamaican history that spanned 1860 to 1861 and witnessed a resurgence of African religious aspects in the midst of orthodox Christianity. This period marked a split between missionary church ideology and Afro-Jamaican religious practices, and it's from this period that the African-Christian cult of Revival originates. Listening to the polyrhythmic percussive syncopation of revivalist drumming, it's easy to hear how reggae echoes its punctuation and emphases. Religious hymns and hand clapping are also prominently featured in modern-day Jamaican music.

Jonkanoo (also spelled as Jonkunnu, Junkanoo, or John Canoe, among the many alternatives) is a term associated with carnivalesque role-playing dance rituals, and these practices have spread throughout the Caribbean in one form or another. More than just another component in the cultural jigsaw, it emerged as an emblem of roots in reggae on the 1978 album *Jonkanoo Dub,* by the Revolutionaries, best known for their work as the Channel One studio session band.

The prominence of Ethiopia and the African continent in Jamaican lore—as well as the significance attributed to both—is described as Ethiopianism. It asserts Ethiopia's status as the birthplace of civilization and rates the country's achievements alongside those made by the black ancient Egyptians. Such views run contrary to negative and historically inaccurate accounts made for centuries by white historians, who often portrayed Africa as an uncivilized, savage continent. Ethiopia became a visible force in black religious life in Jamaica as early as 1784, with the emergence of the Ethiopian Baptist Church.

Despite the oppression associated with colonialism, European music and dance filtered into Afro-Jamaican culture. This initially occurred as slaves performed for the entertainment of white masters, but the cultural cross-pollination continued in slave communities. Ethnomusicologists see the French quadrille style of music as an ancestor of the Jamaican folk style known as mento, with dance being an integral common factor.

The emergence of Rastafarianism in the 1930s was propelled by a reinterpretation of biblical passages from which directives to smoke marijuana and grow dreadlocks were directly derived. Rastafarian drumming, representing another link to African heritage and beating down oppression (or "downpression" in Rasta-speak), assumed greater popular importance in Jamaica when leading Rasta drummer Count Ossie backed the singing Folkes Brothers on their 1960 hit "Oh Carolina." This set the stage for the gradual emergence of Rasta rhythms in Jamaican popular music, with antiestablishment reggae providing the ideal expressive outlet. The music was set against a backdrop of ruthless exploitation under British colonialism until Jamaica attained independence in 1962, and then against the social and economic instability that followed. Reggae's musical messages of spiritual and political liberation were a natural extension of Jamaica's religious influence and cultural experience.

Like many of the 1950s and 1960s American R&B artists who inspired them, Jamaican vocalists based their styles and rhythmic foundations on church experiences. Singers Justin Hinds (of Justin Hinds & the Dominoes) and Toots Hibbert (of Toots & the Maytals) are two prominent examples. In studio performances, the two artists often sounded as though they were interacting with a religious congregation rather than just laying down vocals in a recording booth. One of reggae's most commercially successful albums of the 1970s, Bob Marley & the Wailers' *Rastaman Vibration* (1976), included biblical scripture, "The Blessing of Joseph," printed on the back of its original jacket. This underscored the religious motivation behind the music.

Part of the impact of reggae music lies in its spiritual call, which is derived from Jamaica's rich and often tormented past. Rhythms resonating from the African experience have translated themselves into reggae's hypnotic syncopation, connecting the cultural past, present, and future through recorded sound.

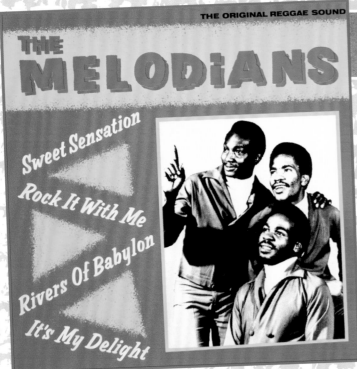

THE MELODIANS

Sweet Sensation

Rock It With Me

Rivers Of Babylon

It's My Delight

The Melodians hit #41 in the UK with "Sweet Sensation" (1970), yet reaped few rewards from their most popular song, "Rivers of Babylon," recorded with Leslie Kong in 1969.

THE MELODIANS
YEARS ACTIVE: 1960s–1980s

The Melodians' story is sadly familiar, one chapter in a history of the Jamaican music industry replete with bad deals for artists, including low one-off payments for recordings, no royalties, and the naïve surrender of publishing rights. In this particular narrative, the Melodians, a respected reggae vocal group consisting of Brent Dowe, Tony Brevett, and Trevor McNaughton, has its most popular song, "Rivers of Babylon," covered by a pop outfit. The song is a massive global hit and goes platinum, yet the writers and original performers reap next to no financial rewards. In this case, the success raised questions about the industry's exploitation of musicians—particularly those in Jamaica—whose limited knowledge of the business and persistent poverty often force them to make costly decisions.

The Melodians formed around 1965 and are said to have first recorded unreleased sound-system specials for producer and artist Prince Buster as a quartet, with Renford Cogle as the fourth member. The group began recording singles with Studio One producer Coxsone Dodd the following year, though little material was released and there were no hits. With the exception of a few sessions at producer Duke Reid's Treasure Isle studios in the mid- to late 1960s, their output was not prolific. They did, however, contribute to Reid's commercial success with rocksteady hits such as "Expo 67." The group was paid better under Reid than they were in Dodd's stable, receiving ten pounds each for their recordings as opposed to the six to ten pounds—to be shared among all the members—offered by Dodd. The Melodians also relied on live performance for income, which was often far from certain when it came to recording.

Seeking better pay, the Melodians migrated to producer Sonia Pottinger's Gay Feet label around 1968 and recorded the Jamaican hit "Swing and Dine." Their fortunes further improved when they moved to Leslie Kong's Beverly's Records label and cut "Rivers of Babylon" in 1969. Although this version never crossed over to the British pop charts, it was a sleeper hit in the reggae market. One source suggests that a decade after its release, the single had sold more than seventy-five thousand copies in Britain. As is typical in reggae literature, another source claims that the Melodians had sold eighty thousand copies in Britain before 1978. Either way, those figures were completely dwarfed when Germany-based pop group Boney M (featuring a lineup of all Caribbean vocalists, ironically enough) scored a massive international hit with their cover version in 1978. It topped the British charts, becoming a platinum single there, and conquered Europe, though it barely made the Top 40 in the United States.

The success of Boney M's version of "Rivers of Babylon" should have created some financial windfall for the Melodians. However, singer Brent Dowe was allegedly paid to share writing credit on the song with Boney M producer Frank Farian (who later created the pop group Milli Vanilli, famous for their lip-syncing scandal in 1990). Lacking business savvy or suitable advice, Dowe signed away what would have been substantial income from a million-selling song with enormous publishing value, thus exposing the Melodians to one of the consequences of involvement in the exploitative, survival-oriented Kingston music scene.

Dowe recalled that Kong was the first producer to pay them publishing money; ironically, Kong initially dismissed "Rivers of Babylon" and did not want to record it. Once it was cut, due to its Rastafarian lyrical references, the song was briefly banned in Jamaica until Kong protested. While that spell with Kong led to a few more hits in Jamaica, "Sweet Sensation" was the Melodians' only single to reach the British charts, briefly peaking at #41 in 1970 on the Trojan Records label. The song was covered by the British pop-reggae group UB40 on their US and UK platinum album *Labour of Love* (1983).

The Melodians' association with Kong ended with the producer's sudden death in 1971. The group returned to Reid in 1972, but lack of success led the group to split temporarily in 1974. During this time the members released solo singles in Jamaica. They briefly reunited in 1976 for *Sweet Sensation*, a collection comprising new versions of their early songs produced by Harry J, the Jamaican studio owner behind the British 1969 instrumental pop hit, "Liquidator." They made further attempts at album success with *Pre-Meditation* (1978) and *Irie Feeling* (1983), but neither made a commercial impact, making the Melodians an item for reggae nostalgia.

MEMBERS: **Brent Dowe** (vocals); **Tony Brevett** (vocals); **Trevor McNaughton** (vocals)

SELECT DISCOGRAPHY: *Sweet Sensation* (Harry J, 1976); *Pre-Meditation* (Sky Note, 1978); *Irie Feeling* (RAS, 1983); *Sweet Sensation: The Best of the Melodians* (Sanctuary, 2003)

THIS BEAUTIFUL LAND
(Brevitt — Cogle)
MELODIANS

MENTO

Mento was Jamaica's first indigenous form of popular music, and as with many of the styles that followed, its evolutionary process involved a fusion of sounds from Africa, Europe, and other places, as it played a foundational role in Jamaican popular music. It existed long before recording began on the island and remained visible through the 1950s. It was one of the cultural forms that kept melodic, rhythmic, and percussive elements of Africa alive during the colonial era, when the authorities tried to push such things to the margins, fearing they would incite rebellion. In a British Broadcasting Corporation (BBC) radio documentary series, the dub poet Linton Kwesi Johnson accurately described mento as "the seed of the basic rhythmic orientation of today's reggae music." Since mento was a musical expression rooted in the slavery era, work songs and folk traditions played pivotal roles in shaping its sound.

Mento was also influenced by the rhythms and customs of the Jonkanoo masquerade (alternatively spelled "Junkanoo" or "John Canoe"), which involved groups of musicians roving the streets in costumes at Christmastime and soliciting contributions from their audiences. Another key influence was the quadrille, a dance-oriented black rural reinterpretation of nineteenth-century European musical forms. Largely concentrated in rural areas, mento first appeared in the late nineteenth century and featured a variety of percussion instruments—most of them improvised—alongside the ever-present guitar, rhumba box, and flute. However, the first mento recordings did not appear until the 1950s, as entrepreneurs such as Stanley Motta and Ken Khouri acquired gear to establish extremely basic studios.

Some writers have tried to make clear-cut distinctions between mento and calypso, but the two genres are very similar stylistically. Both also peaked in popularity during the 1950s. The recording of mento and calypso singer Lord Fly that Motta produced in the early 1950s for MRS Records label—short for "Motta's Recording Studio"—has been called both the first mento recording and Jamaica's first domestic commercial release. But even that record is linked to mento's alter ego, as it bears the title "Medley of Jamaican Mento – Calypsos." MRS Records also issued the *Authentic Jamaican Calypsos* album series, beginning in the early 1950s. Jamaican performer Lord Flea (not to be confused with Lord

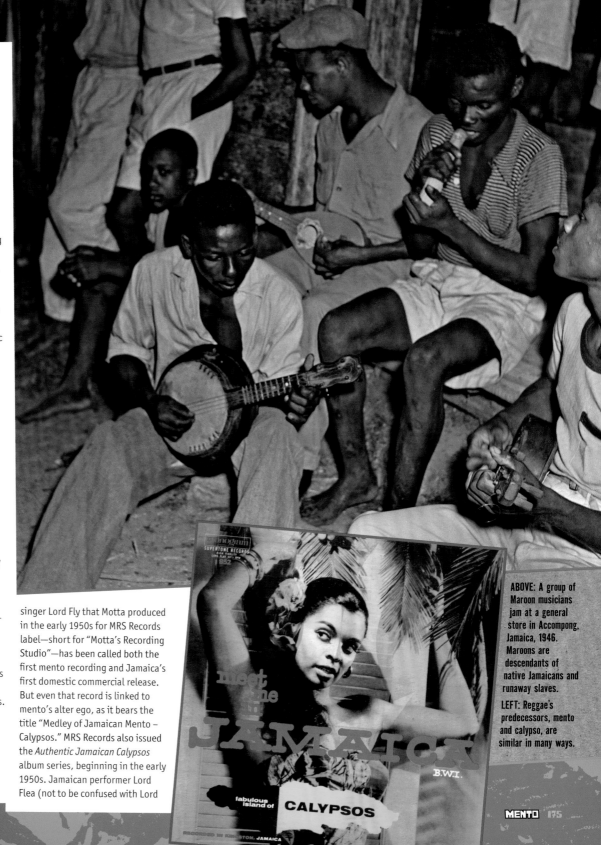

ABOVE: A group of Maroon musicians jam at a general store in Accompong, Jamaica, 1946. Maroons are descendants of native Jamaicans and runaway slaves.

LEFT: Reggae's predecessors, mento and calypso, are similar in many ways.

Fly) benefited from the United States' brief mid-1950s flirtation with calypso and appeared in two movies, *Calypso Joe* and *Bop Girl Goes Calypso,* both in 1957. That same year, in the wake of American singer Harry Belafonte's million-selling RCA Records *Calypso* album, Capitol Records released Lord Flea's *Swingin' Calypsos* LP. Although Lord Flea effectively became the first Jamaican artist to cross over into the American major-label and movie mainstream, the use of the word *calypso* in the album and film titles suggests that few people outside of Jamaica knew of or would become familiar with mento as a separate style. Other notable mento artists include Count Sticky and Lord Tanamo.

Many 78 rpm mento records were released in Britain on the Melodisc Records label, but mento remained in a decidedly niche market. Although Belafonte scored two top-five UK singles in 1957, the calypso fever that briefly gripped the United States never crossed the Atlantic to the same extent. In the late 1950s, as sound systems gained ground in Jamaica, mento was viewed as outdated folk music suitable solely as a sound track for tourists seeking a calypso-style exotic experience. Even before the turn of the next decade, mento was heard almost

exclusively in hotels, although its musical accents permeated ska, rocksteady, and reggae, the new Jamaican genres that followed it. Even in the digital dancehall era, as old songs and melodies are repackaged for newer audiences, mento continues to wield influence.

In one of the stranger turns of events in the post-mento era, 2010 witnessed the rise of one of few groups keeping mento alive, the Jolly Boys. Allegedly named by Hollywood actor Errol Flynn in 1946, this group of veterans (whose members are all older than seventy) found a new global audience through the Internet. Their somewhat bizarre 2010 version of British soul singer Amy Winehouse's 2007 hit "Rehab" gave them a bridge to a younger generation of listeners for whom mento was essentially new. While the Jolly Boys can deliver the genuine article at a moment's notice, what they play today is not really mento but rather another calculated hybrid. It's more than a little ironic that even mento has had to be commercially diluted to reach wider audiences, as has been the case with reggae. Beyond the Jolly Boys, mento remains an important relic of Jamaica's musical past and a cornerstone of the house on which reggae was built.

MIGHTY DIAMONDS
YEARS ACTIVE: 1970s– PRESENT

One of the most soulful reggae vocal trios of the 1970s, the roots-oriented Mighty Diamonds are perhaps best known outside of the reggae world for a hit they did *not* have in the 1980s. Their herb-praising track "Pass the Kouchie" (1981)—whose title refers to a kind of pipe used to smoke marijuana—was altered to become "Pass the Dutchie," a ganja-free international hit for the kid-fronted British group Musical Youth in 1982.

Formed in late 1969 in the Trench Town area of Kingston, the Mighty Diamonds initially made the rounds of Jamaican producers, working with Stranger Cole, Lee Perry, Rupie Edwards, Bunny Lee, and Jah Lloyd, among others. While they recorded numerous singles—some of which made an impact in Jamaica—it wasn't until they connected with Channel One studios in Kingston, run by the Chinese Jamaican Hoo-Kim brothers, and were picked up by a major label that it

seemed possible they might establish a global following.

In 1975, the group signed with Virgin Records as the label reached into the reggae market. *Right Time* (1976), recorded at Channel One and produced by Jo Jo Hoo-Kim, was their most commercially and critically successful album. It was released on two Jamaican labels before being issued internationally by Virgin in 1976. Many would argue that *Right Time* represents the Mighty Diamonds' finest contribution to reggae's greatest decade. Regrettably, 1977's *Ice on Fire,* coproduced by famed New Orleans musician Allen Toussaint, was an ill-advised and deeply unsatisfying pop-crossover effort. On it the group smoothed out most of its roots reggae edges and became a shadow of its former self. It's hard to imagine that anyone at Virgin thought this album—recorded in New Orleans with American rather than Jamaican musicians—held much appeal for the Mighty Diamonds' core following. In a 1994 *Reggae Report* magazine interview, the members later acknowledged, "It wasn't us." However, their appearance in 1978 as one of the many supporting acts at the anti-violence One Love Peace Concert in Jamaica

restored a measure of street credibility. While their albums (particularly *Right Time*) invoked the memory of iconic black liberation activist Marcus Garvey, it was the starkly aggressive cartoon characters on the cover of *Stand Up to Your Judgment* (1978) that visually underlined their pro-Rastafarian political stance.

On *Planet Earth*, recorded at Compass Point studios in the Bahamas in 1978, Virgin actually billed the group as the Diamonds, unwittingly confirming that the major-label connection and quest for mainstream recognition had eroded the group's musical might. A more reggae-focused album than its predecessor, *Planet Earth* lacked incisiveness despite production by the well-regarded Karl Pitterson, who was probably following orders from Virgin to aim for a crossover hit. Despite the commercial compromises made during their time with Virgin, the Mighty Diamonds claim that, due to bad contracts and an absence of tour support from the label, they earned no money from the deal.

The following year, returning to Jamaica's Channel One studio, the group benefited from the top-flight musicianship of the Soul Syndicate band, and cut the more inspired *Deeper Roots*, which was later accompanied by a compelling remixed companion, *Deeper Dub*; both albums were released in 1979. The Mighty Diamonds might have enjoyed a more successful career had they tracked more of their recordings at Channel One, where the sound, musicians (both resident and hired), and production were all superbly suited to enhancing their harmonic spectrum and vocal urgency. The 1979 release date of *Deeper Roots* coincided with the end of the dominance of roots reggae and the sociopolitical culture in which it flourished. The era had been punctuated by rampant economic instability, poverty, and violent death, as Jamaica's political parties fought for power. In some ways, *Deeper Roots* summarizes a decade of fluctuation for both the country and the group itself.

They recorded "Pass the Kouchie" for 1981's *Changes*, one of a series of 1980s albums produced by Gussie Clarke, who became one of the decade's top reggae producers. After topping the British charts and reaching #10 in the United States, Musical Youth's hit adaptation of the song should have delivered major financial rewards for the Mighty Diamonds, but they later described the experience as a "financial disaster." Like the ganja that was the subject of the Mighty Diamonds' original version, their prospects for profits went up in smoke. Mighty Diamonds members Lloyd "Judge" Ferguson and Fitzroy "Bunny" Simpson had written the song's lyrics, but many people laid claim to the instrumental authorship. Making matters worse, the group failed to register the song's copyright in a timely fashion and was hamstrung by numerous one-sided contracts. They claimed to have paid $20,000 for the first three months of legal representation and had to wait an additional three years for a legal resolution that left them no better off than when the problems began. The members subsequently resolved to complete copyright registration for all of their works before recording them.

Their releases with Gussie Clarke's Music Works label, *The Real Enemy* (1987) and *Get Ready* (1988), raised the group's profile in the digital dancehall decade while retaining their trademark vocal style. Some fans may have felt that the tasteful digital backdrop heard on these albums lacked the roots texture of their 1970s sound; but overall, Clarke's production infused new energy when it was greatly needed.

Unlike many 1970s reggae acts, the Mighty Diamonds have maintained a stable lineup and consistently released albums of new material, including twelve since the late 1980s. However, while those records have their bright moments, they remain overshadowed by the group's best 1970s tracks. Given that they are still actively touring, there is perhaps hope that these Diamonds will again dazzle reggae audiences—provided all the elements materialize at the right time.

MEMBERS: Fitzroy "Bunny" Simpson (vocals); **Donald "Tabby" Shaw** (vocals); **Lloyd "Judge" Ferguson** (vocals)

SELECT DISCOGRAPHY: *Right Time* (Virgin, 1976); *Ice on Fire* (Virgin, 1977); *Planet Earth* (Virgin, 1978); *Stand Up to Your Judgment* (Channel One, 1978); *Deeper Roots* (Virgin, 1979); *Deeper Dub* (Virgin, 1979); *Changes* (Music Works, 1981); *The Real Enemy* (Music Works/Greensleeves, 1987); *Get Ready* (Music Works/Greensleeves, 1988); *Reggae Street* (Shanachie, 1990); *Bust Out* (Greensleeves, 1993); *Speak the Truth* (RAS, 1994); *Reggae Legends* (VP, 2009)

ABOVE: The pro-Rastafarian Mighty Diamonds ironically are best known for their single "Pass the Kouchie," the basis for "Pass the Dutchie," a 1982 international hit for the British group Musical Youth.

SIDE TWO STEREO
℗ 1975 Virgin Records Ltd
Virgin Music (Publishers) Ltd

VS 137
VS 137-B
© 1975 Virgin Music (Publishers) Ltd

THEN NEVER LOVE POOR MARCUS (2.45)
(Mighty Diamonds)
MIGHTY DIAMONDS
Produced by JOSEPH HOO KIM

JACOB MILLER
WHO SAY JAH NO DREAD

THE CLASSIC AUGUSTUS PABLO SESSIONS 1974-75

LEFT: Jacob Miller, tragically killed in 1980, lives on through compilations such as this one, released in 1992.

RIGHT: Jacob Miller holds nothing back at the Marquee in London, 1979.

JACOB MILLER

YEARS ACTIVE: 1974-1980

One of Jamaica's most popular vocalists in the late 1970s, singer Jacob "Killer" Miller enjoyed only six short years of a bright career before he was killed in an automobile accident while still in his twenties. He was a successful soloist as well as the charismatic lead singer of Inner Circle from 1974 to 1980, the year of his death. Miller's birthdate is an unresolved issue, with competing estimates of 1952, 1955, and 1960. Regardless of the exact year, he was no older than a teenager when his career got off to a rocky start with 1968's "Love Is a Message," a single that Studio One hit producer Coxsone Dodd recorded but did not actively promote. On the track, Miller's voice sounds obviously young

and lacks the vibrant texture that would become his hallmark in the next decade. Miller was not an overnight success. In 1974, after constantly hanging around Kingston's studios, Miller joined the Rockers International label founded by reggae melodica player Augustus Pablo and his brother.

As a solo artist, Miller was not credited for his lead vocal on Pablo's hit single "Baby I Love You So" (1975), and as a result, uninitiated listeners might have mistakenly thought that Pablo was the singer. While "Baby I Love You So" is arguably one of the most important songs in reggae history, much of the single's significance comes from its B-side dub reformulation "King Tubby Meets Rockers Uptown." It quickly became the A-side when Island Records, which released the record in Britain, realized the dub version was more

popular among reggae audiences. Although neither the dub nor the vocal versions of the song reached the British pop charts, the remix by the now-legendary dub engineer King Tubby created a significant underground buzz.

During his stint at Rockers International, Miller recorded other notable singles, including "Who Say Jah No Dread" (1975), but he needed another vehicle to fulfill his creative ambitions. Inner Circle provided that opportunity when they asked him to fill their vacant lead singer slot around 1974, while he was still launching his solo profile. The band was as adept at American Top 40 covers as with reggae, and Miller's vocal versatility was well suited to the task. Although Inner Circle had first formed in 1968, Miller joined in time for their debut album, 1974's *Blame It on The Sun* (also known as *Heavy Reggae*).

Miller's job as a reggae front man did not stop him from releasing new solo work, which included backing by his Inner Circle bandmates. *Tenement Yard*, *Killer Miller*, and *Wanted* were all the fruit of a highly productive solo phase spanning 1976 to 1978. The deep roots vibe on Miller's LPs was sometimes at odds with Inner Circle's more pop-oriented sound. Both before and after the group signed with Capitol Records in 1976, elements of disco and rock played significant roles in their music. However, Miller's "Peace Treaty Special" single (1978), coupled with

Inner Circle's headlining set at the 1978 One Love Peace Concert—a unification effort in the wake of rampant political violence in Jamaica—affirmed the group's social awareness and proved that their music was about more than mere entertainment.

Further proof of Miller's growing star power came with his appearance in the 1978 reggae film *Rockers*, in which he performs with Inner Circle and has a small acting role. Inner Circle's two hit singles in Britain in 1979 augured well for their collective future, but the success story was cut short. On March 23, 1980, two days after returning from Brazil, where he had joined Island Records founder Chris Blackwell and Bob Marley & the Wailers on an promotional trip, Miller died in a car crash in Jamaica. According to some accounts, he was returning from a jam session at Bob Marley's Tuff Gong studio in Kingston.

Oddly, the record that may be doing more than any other to keep the voice of Jacob "Killer" Miller alive is his 1978 album, *Natty Christmas*. Throughout the Caribbean and in West Indian communities in metropolitan cities across Europe and North America, fans dust off the record annually and spin it as though Miller had never left. Although Inner Circle reached their commercial peak in the early 1990s, fans continue to speculate about what the band might have achieved had Miller not died so young.

SELECT DISCOGRAPHY: *Tenement Yard* (Arab, 1976); *Killer Miller* (Top Ranking, 1977); *Wanted* (Top Ranking Sounds, 1978); *Natty Christmas* (Joe Gibbs, 1978); *Mixed Up Moods* (Top Ranking Sounds, 1979); *Who Say Jah No Dread* (Greensleeves, 1992)

Sugar Minott says "cheese" at his home studio in London.

Minott's 1978 solo debut, *Live Loving,* has been called the first dancehall album, though within a few years the onslaught of digital music technology would alter the character of the genre's sound. Despite his love for Studio One's rhythms and history, Minott felt compelled to leave the label in search of better financial rewards. He established the Black Roots label in 1979 and used his aptly titled Youth Promotion sound system to test the talent of aspiring ghetto performers. Notably, though, his vocal style on such hit singles as "Vanity" (1977) was quite soulful and melodic—a far cry from the atonal, aggressive deliveries favored by some later dancehall DJs.

The reggae audience response in the UK to "Hard Time Pressure" from his *Black Roots* album (1979) encouraged Minott to relocate to Britain to boost his career. He

BLACK ROOTS RECORDS
BRST 1002

SUGAR MINOTT

Dance Hall Showcase VOL. II

SUGAR MINOTT
YEARS ACTIVE: 1969-2010

When taking stock of Jamaica's music history it can often be difficult to pinpoint the precise moments of change from one genre to another. However, the late 1970s emergence of Lincoln Barrington "Sugar" Minott clearly sowed seeds for the dancehall reggae subgenre that exploded in the digitally dominated 1980s.

Born on May 25, 1956 in Kingston, Jamaica, Minott made his debut as a recording artist with the vocal trio the African Brothers in 1969, cutting a few singles but achieving little success and

earning even less money. The group split in 1974 after recording "No Cup No Broke" for Studio One producer Coxsone Dodd. Studio One subsequently launched Minott as a solo artist by adding new vocals to existing backing tracks from the label's extensive catalog. While the concept of recycling a rhythm track certainly wasn't new in Jamaica, this method of making records became a major catalyst for the dancehall movement. Describing the pre-digital proto-dancehall situation, Minott recalled, "We only had to play the version from a Studio One record and make up our own song. That's how it started, and nobody was doing it before."

arrived during the lovers rock era, and, adopting a romantic, laid-back singing style typical of the genre's commercial flavor, he became one of the vocalists most closely associated with that British style of reggae. The 1979 *Ghetto-Ology* album, later reissued with dub mixes of the album tracks by the renowned Jamaican engineer King Tubby, marked a creative highpoint in Minott's career. Listeners are sharply divided on the record, perhaps because it represents a transitional phase in Minott's artistic growth and is much more artistically ambitious than the lovers rock recordings that followed soon after.

Minott scored his biggest international hit in 1981, reaching #4 on the British charts with a lovers rock cover of Michael Jackson's 1972 Motown track "Good Thing Going." The single had been released independently, but its sales activity caught the attention of RCA Records, prompting the major label to handle the record and its distribution. The 1984 track "Wicked a Go Feel It," recorded with America-based producer Lloyd "Bullwackie" Barnes, expanded the scope of Minott's sound and material, proving he could do more than just lovers rock. By 1985, he had adopted the more muscular, digitally programmed sound heard on "Herbman Hustling," released on famed drum-and-bass duo Sly & Robbie's Taxi Records label. The soulfully delivered song dealt with searching for good marijuana to make a living and resonated with listeners, helping to set the tone for the imminent high-tech dancehall explosion.

The surge of new digitally focused DJs and singers made Minott less influential as the decade ended. After rampant (though undistinguished) studio activity in the 1990s and a subsequent period of less frequent recording, Minott achieved a major renaissance with the 2008 album *New Day*. The collection found Minott in fine vocal form, sounding fresh, inspired, and motivated, reaping the benefits of his extensive experience. He also made a guest appearance on the Easy Star

All-Stars' 2006 album *Radiodread*, which featured songs by the British alternative rock group Radiohead reinterpreted in reggae.

A consistent touring artist, Minott experienced chest pains in 2010 and was forced to cancel live appearances in Canada. When he died at the age of fifty-four in July 2010, his wife of fourteen years, Maxine Stowe—a niece of Coxsone Dodd and herself a former Sony Music A&R (Artists and Repertoire) executive—blamed heart problems for his demise. Oddly, numerous obituaries referred to *New Day* as an album about to be released, even though it had emerged two years earlier.

In a moving but rather chaotic funeral service, many musicians paid tribute to Minott in song, including veteran singer Derrick Harriott and dancehall star Triston Palmer. Following a tradition among reggae artists started by Bob Marley and continued by Peter Tosh and Dennis Brown, Minott left no will. Financial and legal issues surrounding his estate were unclear. While he was alive, his significant assets—including a recording studio and control of many items in his catalog—had suggested that his musical enterprises were on solid financial ground; however, a different picture emerged in the wake of his death, when his wife disclosed that there were money problems. Profiting from Minott's catalog was further complicated by the dispersion of his work among multiple record labels in Jamaica, Europe, and Japan. The precise number of albums he recorded is unknown, but his discography is thought to contain about forty albums. In addition, two albums reportedly awaited release before his death, so perhaps we may still hear more from Minott.

SELECT DISCOGRAPHY: *Live Loving* (Studio One, 1978); *Black Roots* (Black Roots, 1979); *Ghetto-Ology Plus Dub* (Easy Star, 2000); *Sugar Minott at Studio One* (Soul Jazz, 2004); *New Day* (Stop, Look & Listen, 2008); *Reggae Legends* (Indie Europe/Zoom, 2010)

ABOVE: Regarded as the first dancehall album, *Live Loving* (1978) predated the subgenre's move toward digital rhythms.

phase welcomed the group's return with *Roots Controller*, which was reminiscent of their 1970s work. At its peak, the band was particularly popular in Europe, and it sought such popularity on its own terms rather than by following the major label path of its British reggae contemporaries.

LEFT: Misty in Roots at a Rock Against Racism concert in London, 1979.

BELOW: The UK group began its recording career with a live album in 1979.

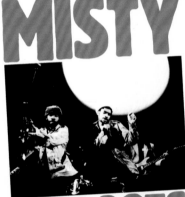

MISTY IN ROOTS

LIVE AT THE COUNTER EUROVISION 79

MiSTY IN ROOTS

YEARS ACTIVE: 1970s-2000s

A large collective with a frequently rotating lineup, Misty in Roots formed in London around 1975. The band initially backed Jamaican singer Nicky Thomas, best known for his 1970 British hit "Love of the Common People." Alongside such better-known counterparts as Aswad and Steel Pulse, the group was part of the 1970s British reggae revolution. These three self-contained bands, whose members were all raised in the United Kingdom, arrived at a time when most popular Jamaican reggae artists relied on session musicians in the studio and makeshift local bands when touring foreign markets. Misty in Roots was Rastafarian and political to the core, and participated in such causes as Britain's Rock Against Racism movement in the late 1970s.

Around 1978, Misty in Roots became one of the last early British reggae bands to release their debut album. It is uncommon for reggae acts to start their recording careers with a live album, but Misty in Roots released *Live at the Counter Eurovision* in 1979. The studio follow-up, *Wise and Foolish*, didn't emerge until 1982, by which time Britain's political landscape had shifted toward greater conservatism under the social and economic policies of Prime Minister Margaret Thatcher, whose administration provoked musical criticism from both reggae and rock bands.

While British reggae bands like Aswad, Steel Pulse, and Matumbi had all sold noteworthy numbers of records on major labels by this time, Misty in Roots opted for a less mainstream path by making recurring trips to Africa to perform. Helping them remain in the public ear was John Peel, the most adventurous and respected DJ at the British Broadcasting Corporation (BBC). Peel championed their music, and they recorded many exclusive sessions for the DJ from 1979 into the first decade of the 2000s. Beginning in the early 1980s, recording on their own fiercely independent People Unite label, the group made a series of albums inspired by African landscapes. This string of releases, all with very limited distribution, began with *Earth* (1983), recorded in Germany, and extended through *Forward* (1989). The group's progress was disrupted in 1992, when singer Delvin Tyson drowned while swimming in Ghana.

After an extended hiatus, Misty in Roots returned to action as an eight-piece unit in 2001, releasing *Roots Controller* the following year. Consisting largely of remastered versions of tracks the band had recorded in the 1980s, as well as six new tracks, the album surfaced—surprisingly, perhaps—on rock musician Peter Gabriel's Real World Records. Although that label has always been a home for global music, it has rarely been a venue for artists making comebacks, let alone ones who have spent more than a decade away from the business. Roots reggae fans who had witnessed Misty in Roots' first

MEMBERS: Delvin Tyson (vocals); Delbert McKay (vocals, guitar); Walford Tyson (vocals, trumpet); Lawrence Crossfield (lead guitar); Chesley Sampson (guitar); Dennis Augustin (rhythm guitar); Anthony Henry (bass); Deford Briscoe (keyboards)

SELECT DISCOGRAPHY: *Live at the Counter Eurovision* (People Unite, 1979); *Wise and Foolish* (People Unite, 1982); *Earth* (People Unite, 1983); *Musi-O-Tunya* (People Unite, 1985); *Forward* (People Unite, 1989); *Chronicles: The Best of Misty in Roots* (Kaz, 1994); *The John Peel Sessions* (BBC, 1995); *Jah Sees, Jah Knows* (Recall Records, 1998); *Roots Controller* (Real World, 2002)

JACKIE MITTOO
The Keyboard King at Studio One

JACKIE MITTOO

YEARS ACTIVE: 1960s–1990

It may never be known exactly how many Jamaican records included the Hammond organ riffs and arrangements of Jackie Mittoo, but his musical influence is indisputable. He is one of the few players whose performances on ska, rocksteady, and reggae records influenced each stage of Jamaica's popular-music development. Best known for his role as keyboardist in the Skatalites, the prime instrumental exponents of ska in the early 1960s, Mittoo developed a reputation among Jamaica's musicians as a first-class session player and arranger.

Mittoo was born Donat Roy Mittoo in 1948 in Kingston. Even before he was a teenager he displayed skills far beyond his years, applying knowledge from the piano lessons he had received from his grandmother. After brief spells with local bands in his home city, he became a record producer and A&R (Artists and Repertoire) man for the Studio One label. Mittoo began working with Studio One head Coxsone Dodd in 1961, before

the label had its own studio and when it recorded at one of the island's first recording venues, Kingston's Federal Studio. Bursting with potential, Mittoo became one of the musicians who built Studio One's reputation, joining one of Jamaica's most musically powerful instrumental units, the Skatalites, at age fifteen. That house band, established in 1964, embodied and defined the rhythm of Jamaica as the country reveled in optimism after gaining independence from Britain in 1962. Mittoo played on practically every Studio One record after Coxsone Dodd moved his operation to Brentford Road in the early 1960s.

After the Skatalites dissolved in 1965 following trombonist Don Drummond's murder of his common-law wife, a few of the members, including Mittoo, formed a new Studio One house band, the Soul Brothers, which later became the Soul Vendors. Mittoo also recorded solo instrumental albums, debuting with *In London* in 1967, the same year the Soul Vendors toured England. Following more than a decade of sterling contributions, Mittoo left Studio One in the 1970s, immigrating to Canada. While there, he

worked with the Canadian Talent Library to ensure that radio stations met their quota of playing Canadian music. He recorded the *Reggae Magic* album in 1972, and the record received a great deal of radio airplay in his new homeland.

Despite living in Canada, Mittoo continued doing session work in both Jamaica and England, notably with singer Sugar Minott, whose early dancehall sound was built on the Studio One rhythms that Mittoo had helped create. His work's commercial value was affirmed under convoluted circumstances when "Full Up," an influential instrumental he had recorded in 1968 with Studio One session band Sound Dimension, became the unlikely basis of a global hit single. First, the Mighty Diamonds used the "Full Up" rhythm in "Pass the Kouchie" (1981), a song that the British group Musical Youth then utilized to create their international pop-reggae hit "Pass the Dutchie" (1982). Legal disputes arose over the song's authorship, and Mittoo filed a lawsuit in Britain, successfully securing ownership of and rights to his composition. During Mittoo's time in Canada, he routinely

complained about the copyright crisis that allowed others to use his original musical ideas without granting him any financial compensation.

The recycling of Mittoo's 1960s session recordings continued into the dancehall era, confirming that he was truly part of Jamaica's musical fabric. Neither Mittoo's music nor his ability to adapt to the times ever evaporated, and his work on producer Gussie Clarke's *Music Works Showcase 89* (1989) updated his sound for the digital era. In 1990, he died in Canada of cancer at the age of forty-two.

SELECT DISCOGRAPHY: *In London* (Coxsone, 1967); *Now* (Studio One, 1969); *Macka Fat* (Studio One, 1970); *Tribute to Jackie Mittoo* (Heartbeat, 1995); *Champion in the Arena 1976–77* (Blood & Fire, 2003)

LEFT: Throughout the 1960s, Jackie Mittoo was a mainstay of Studio One's house bands and played on virtually every recording.

BELOW: Mittoo's train kept rolling well beyond the ska years, and he remained influential during the rocksteady and reggae eras.

DERRICK MORGAN

YEARS ACTIVE: 1950s–PRESENT

Born March 27, 1940, in Clarendon, Jamaica, singer Derrick Morgan became a long-term Kingston resident at the age of three, when he was sent to the city by his family for treatment of a rare eye disorder. His professional career began when he performed at age seventeen on the radio talent show *Vere Johns Opportunity Hour*, a program that gave many singers in Jamaica their first public exposure. Morgan won first prize by imitating American rock legend Little Richard. He eventually auditioned successfully for sound-system operator and producer Duke Reid, making his recording debut with Reid in 1959, when he cut "Lover Boy" and "Oh My" as sound-system dubplates (soft wax pre-release recordings). As was typical of the Jamaican music business in those years, the entire process of auditioning, rehearsing with a band, recording the material, and finally hearing one of the songs on the radio took about one week.

Beverley's RECORDS

135ᴬ
ORANGE
STREET

MADE IN
JAMAICA

KINGSTON
JAMAICA
W.I.

COPYING OF
THIS RECORD
IS PROHIBITED

FORWARD MARCH
(D. MORGAN)
DERRICK MORGAN
BEVERLEY'S ALL-STARS

A dapper Derrick Morgan brings a touch of class to Reggae Sunsplash, 1984.

Best of DERRICK MORGAN

By 1960 Morgan had become one of the island's most popular recording stars: he had recorded a steady stream of Jamaican hit singles and performed for hit artist and producer Prince Buster on the ska song "Shake a Leg" (1961). That year Jamaican audiences also embraced his duet with Patsy (Millicent Todd), "Housewife's Choice." He soon moved to Chinese Jamaican producer Leslie Kong's Beverley's Records and became an unofficial A&R (Artists and Repertoire) man and arranger there. Although Morgan wasn't making much money, he was likely better paid by Kong than by Prince Buster.

One of the singer's best-known hits was "Forward March," a ska song celebrating Jamaica's 1962 independence from Britain. His debut album, also titled *Forward March*, was released in 1963, the same year he toured England with Prince Buster.

The two maintained an ongoing feud, probably designed to boost record sales, and when Morgan moved to Beverley's, Buster poked fun at Kong, recording "Black Head Chinaman," a song banned by Jamaican radio for its racist content.

At this point in his career Morgan was so successful that the Britain-based Blue Beat Records, a subsidiary of Melodisc Records, signed him to an exclusive contract after Prince Buster—also on the label—encouraged the deal. About six months later, however, Morgan enlisted then–government minister Edward Seaga to free him from his obligation to a single company. Besides being a politician, Seaga was also a Harvard-trained ethnomusicologist and the founder of the WIRL label (West Indies Records Limited). As such, he was a logical person for Morgan to consult on legal matters related to the music business.

Morgan flourished during the mid-1960s emergence of rocksteady, recording the iconic "Tougher Than Tough" (1967), which dealt with the phenomenon of "rude boys," Jamaican gangsters who were vilified in the day's popular music. Morgan did miss out on one big hit, becoming one of several singers who refused to record the smutty "Wet Dream" (1969) for producer Bunny Lee. Singer Max Romeo took on the task and landed in the British top ten, despite the fact that the British Broadcasting Corporation (BBC) banned the song.

Capitalizing on reggae's rising profile and popularity among skinheads, Morgan scored his only British pop hit with "Moon Hop," reaching #49 in 1970. The record was also immensely popular in Britain's West Indian communities. Meanwhile, Morgan had set up his Hop label and scored a massive Jamaican hit with "Let the Power Fall on I," a 1971 single he produced for Max Romeo. This was one of the songs adopted by the People's National Party (PNP) in Jamaica during the election campaign that brought Michael Manley to power in 1972.

By 1975 Morgan had moved to Canada, where he lived until the end of the decade, when he relocated to Miami. He continued to be occasionally involved in production, including on the eponymous 1994 album *Tony Rebel Meets Garnett Silk in a Dancehall Conference*, released on the American label Heartbeat. Morgan's deteriorating vision has left him blind, and he has not received the flow of royalties due to him from his vintage recordings. Despite these hardships, he continues to perform live, and his daughter, singer Queen Ifrica, who is one of reggae's high-profile female artists of the past decade, is extending his Jamaican musical legacy. In October 2001 Morgan received Jamaica's Order of Distinction in recognition of his music.

SELECT DISCOGRAPHY: *Forward March* (Island, 1963); *Seven Letters* (Trojan, 1969); *Moon Hop: Best of the Early Years 1960–69* (Trojan, 2003)

Forward MARCH!

SIDE 1
1 Forward March
2 The Hop
3 Look before You Leap
4 Don't You be a Fool
5 It's True My Darling
6 Housewife's Choice

SIDE 2
1 The Blazing Fire
2 I've found a Queen
3 Teach My Baby
4 Angel with Blue Eyes
5 Last Chance
6 Don't You Worry

DERRICK MORGAN

Derrick Morgan

feel so good

SYLVAN MORRIS

YEARS ACTIVE:
1960s-PRESENT

It's no exaggeration to say that the skilled work of legendary music engineer Sylvan Morris superbly enhanced the sound of Jamaica's popular music from the late 1960s through the 1970s; certainly, Morris played a crucial role in the development of the distinctive sound of Studio One, the renowned Kingston studio run by Coxsone Dodd. Morris worked with the major Jamaican producers and studios of the era and engineered landmark albums by Bob Marley & the Wailers, Burning Spear, and Horace Andy, among other artists.

Born in Kingston in 1946, Morris grew up in Trench Town, an impoverished area that was nonetheless rich in musical talent. From an early age he displayed a curiosity about electronics, and he worked with a local establishment repairing VHF two-way radios before entering the music business. Morris became a technician at WIRL (West Indies Records Limited) around 1965, operating briefly under the tutelage of Australian recording engineer Graeme Goodall, whose mentorship was crucial to Morris's development. After leaving WIRL, Morris worked for producer Duke Reid's Treasure Isle studio in Kingston, but within a year he became disenchanted and joined rival Dodd's Studio One around 1967. Moving beyond engineering, Morris soon took on an unofficial production role, directing studio work in conjunction with such resident session musicians as Leroy Sibbles, a vocalist, bass guitarist, and arranger.

Morris spent eight years at Studio One, an era that defined both the studio's sound and Morris's career as an engineer. When the studio acquired a pair of two-track tape machines, Morris employed track-bouncing strategies that made overdubs possible on songs where additions could not otherwise be made without compromising the sonic quality. Known for dancing while operating the recording console, an inanimate Morris was a sure sign that something was missing in the music.

He left Studio One to join producer Harry Johnson's twenty-four-track studio, Harry J's, in Kingston, where his early engineering work included the Jamaican tracking sessions for *Catch a Fire*, the 1973 Island Records debut by Bob Marley's group, the Wailers. (Rock guitar and keyboards were later overdubbed on the tracks in London.) Morris also engineered on the Wailers' 1973 album *Burnin'*, though some erroneously claim that he first worked with Marley on *Natty Dread*, released the following year. Morris went on to co-engineer Marley's American commercial breakthrough, *Rastaman Vibration* (1976), and his approach to sound became a key part of reggae's international imprint. The polished veneer of that album represented one of the genre's more readily identifiable sonic upgrades.

Morris is perhaps best known for his work with roots reggae act Burning Spear during successful mid-1970s recordings with Island. During this time, such Burning Spear releases as *Man in the Hills* (1976) achieved critical success internationally. Like other Jamaican engineers of the 1970s whose names were relatively familiar to reggae audiences, Morris also released collections of remixes under his own name, such as *Morris on Dub* (1975) and *Cultural Dub* (1978). He has noted that sound-system operators were crucial catalysts for the roots of dub, as they constantly requested remixed versions of songs. In another prime example of his work, Morris's underappreciated engineering on Horace Andy's *In the Light* (1977) created the platform for ace engineer Prince Jammy's dynamic dub version of the album, *In the Light Dub* (also 1977).

By the 1980s, Morris had returned to Dynamic Sounds studio (formerly the WIRL studio where he made his engineering debut); but since that time, he has become far less visible and active as an engineer-producer. Nonetheless, he has continued at Dynamic into the twenty-first century, and given his monumental contributions to music, he will remain a legend even if he never goes near a mixing board again.

SELECT DISCOGRAPHY: *Morris on Dub* (Harry J, 1975); *Cultural Dub* (Harry J, 1978)

Sylvan Morris (center) at Tuff Gong, one of the many studios to benefit from his engineering talents.

MORWELLS

YEARS ACTIVE: 1973-1980s

With a name created by fusing the first syllables in founder Maurice Wellington's name, the Morwells—initially a duo featuring cofounder Eric "Bingy Bunny" Lamont—formed in 1973 in Kingston, Jamaica, where Wellington was born in the Trench Town area. They founded the Morwells Esq. label in 1974 as the main outlet for their work, and in the same year they expanded to a trio with the arrival of Louis Davis. Despite the odds facing their small, new, independent Jamaican label, they secured British distribution that allowed them to score a reggae-market hit with "Bit by Bit" in 1975. Their debut album, *Presenting the Morwells*, and its counterpart, *Morwell Unlimited Meet King Tubby's—Dub Me*, remixed by the electronics and engineering maestro King Tubby, were both released that year as the band established its roots reggae credentials.

Bassist Errol "Flabba" Holt joined the band in 1975. *Crab Race* followed in 1977, with somewhat misleading liner notes claiming it was the group's first album. The Morwells' *Cool Runnings* LP (1979), featuring the excellent and urgent roots single "Give It to Me," should have reached a larger audience, given its Channel One sound and the musicianship of the Revolutionaries, who backed the vocalists. But neither that record nor the subsequent albums *A1 Dub* and *Kingston 12 Toughie*, both

released in 1980, earned the Morwells the attention they deserved. Lamont left the group in the early 1980s to form what became the Roots Radics studio band with Holt.

Lamont died in 1994 of prostate cancer at age 37 (though some accounts state that he died at the end of December 1993). Wellington migrated to the United States in the 1980s before returning to Jamaica in the late 1990s. He was diagnosed with cancer (as well as lupus) and died in 2000 at the age of fifty. Much of the group's repertoire exists only on singles, and a comprehensive anthology is yet to appear.

MEMBERS: Maurice "Blacka" **Wellington** (vocals); Eric "Bingy Bunny" **Lamont** (vocals, rhythm guitar); **Louis Davis** (vocals); Errol "Flabba" **Holt** (bass)

SELECT DISCOGRAPHY: *Presenting the Morwells* (Morwell Esq., 1975); *Morwell Unlimited Meet King Tubby's—Dub Me* (Morwell Esq., 1975); *Crab Race* (Burning Sounds, 1977); *Cool Runnings* (Bushranger, 1979); *A1 Dub* (Trojan Records, 1980); *Kingston 12 Toughie* (Carib Gems, 1980); *The Best of the Morwells* (Nighthawk, 1981)

FAR RIGHT: Morwells founder Maurice "Blacka" Wellington in 1983, after releasing a string of albums that should have brought wider acclaim.

MORWELLS ESQ

Producer by:
Morwell Records
(C) 1977
(P) Morwell
Arranged by:
M. Wellington
Bingy Bunny
Brian C. Davis
Exec. Producer
Dhaima Wellington

Distributed by:
Morwells
Lot 20
Torrington Park
Kingston 5
Side A
Made in
Jamaica
(P)(C)1999

M 001

KINGSTON 12 TUFFY
(M. Wellington /E. Lamont)
MORWELLS ESQ

UNAUTHORISED COPYING IS PROHIBITED

STANLEY MOTTA'S RECORDING STUDIO

MRS

Made in England

SM.194 SERIAL Nº

DSM.59

ONE NIGHT IN MEXICO
(Laurel Aitken)
LAUREL AITKEN AND HIS
AFRO-CUBAN BAND
(Vocals by Laurel Aitken)
R.P.M. 78 R.P.M.

STANLEY MOTTA LT. KINGSTON, JAMAICA. B.W.I.

Stanley Motta's 1950s releases marked the start of Jamaica's recording industry.

STANLEY MOTTA

YEARS ACTIVE: 1950s

The Jamaican record industry had to start somewhere, and Stanley Motta was one of the founders. Primitive recording facilities did exist at Jamaica's radio stations before Motta, a businessman, entered the fray, but his interest in catering to tourists while selling records to the secondary local market created new opportunities for early mento artists. Mento is a form of Jamaican folk music with definite stylistic similarities to the more widely known calypso, and in the 1950s it was rarely considered to be a separate style or genre.

Little definitive information exists about Motta's origins. He was born in 1915 in Jamaica; according to one account, his Sephardic Jewish family had lived on the island for centuries. Motta's music career began when he recorded the guests at his son's bar mitzvah sometime in 1950; by November of that year he was advertising his recording services to the public.

At the time, he claimed it was a new service in Jamaica, even though Ken Khouri, Jamaica's other early recording pioneer, was already making records that contained personal messages and that documented family events rather than music. These recordings by Khouri, however, were primarily made on location. Motta was apparently the first to provide a consistent studio environment—though by today's standards it was extremely basic. When Motta's first musical recordings emerged in December 1950, they placed him several months to a year ahead of Khouri in this regard. (Khouri produced his first commercial release, *Calypsos from Jamaica*, in 1951, and established Federal Records in the mid-1950s.) The initial absence of mastering and pressing capabilities in Jamaica meant that the master tapes or acetates of these early recordings were sent to Decca Records in England for manufacturing.

Motta made most of the early recordings for his MRS (Motta's Recording Studio) Records label in his Hanover Street studio in Kingston. These were geared toward the tourist market, featuring performers from Jamaican hotel nightclubs who conformed to the tropical calypso stereotype. In fact, by 1956 Motta was both a local calypso competition judge and the chairman of the Jamaica Tourist Board. His son, Brian, claims that in 1951, mento performer Lord Fly recorded the first Jamaican mento record in Motta's makeshift studio, which according to Brian was "twelve or fourteen feet square." There was no separation in Motta's studio between the musicians and the recording gear, and the disc-cutting machine had but a single knob. Motta later acquired a mono reel-to-reel tape recorder, which he also used during the 1950s. In 1954 he recorded the vocal duo Bunny & Skully, whose song "Till the End of Time" was a hit on the Jamaican dance hall sound systems playing at public venues. This song signaled the movement away from mento by local acts.

By 1958, Motta had stopped making records, a decision presumably precipitated by the decline of calypso-oriented music (due in part to the vigorously imposed censorship of lurid lyrics), and by the much stronger emergence of American R&B and the rising popularity of sound systems at the expense of live music. Motta shifted his focus toward his successful electrical goods business, which he sold in 1986. He died in Jamaica in 1993.

JUDY MOWATT

YEARS ACTIVE: 1960s–2000s

As a member of the I-Threes vocal trinity, Judy Mowatt became one of reggae's most visible women and maintained a solo artistic presence while serving as part of Bob Marley & the Wailers' performance entourage. Mowatt's 1979 *Black Woman* LP is considered to be the first album recorded at Marley's Tuff Gong Studios. She made history again in 1986 when her album *Working Wonders* (1985) was nominated for a Grammy in the best reggae album category, marking the first time a female vocalist had been nominated for the prize.

Mowatt was born in 1952 in Kingston, Jamaica. In 1967, she became a member of the Gaylettes, an R&B-influenced female trio that regularly provided backing vocals on sessions at Federal Studio in Kingston. After the group's other two members, Beryl Lawrence and Merle Clemenson, left to pursue other opportunities in the United States, Mowatt began a solo career. Due to contractual issues she released some singles under aliases; her cover version of rock singer-songwriter Van Morrison's "I Shall Sing" (1974) was the first record bearing her own name (actually credited to Judy Mowatt & the Gaytones).

Her talents were thrust into the spotlight when Bob Marley hired her, Rita Marley, and Marcia Griffiths in 1974 to provide backing vocals and stage presence for the Wailers, effectively creating the I-Threes. The trio made its recording debut on "Jah Live," a single released in 1976 following the death of former Ethiopian emperor Haile Selassie the previous year. The Wailers' *Natty Dread* (1974) marked the I-Threes' first album appearance. Mowatt's first solo album, *Mellow Mood*, appeared in 1975. The title track was a cover version of a Bob Marley–composed Wailers song from the 1960s. It was during this phase that Mowatt became a Rastafarian, joining the Twelve Tribes sect founded in Kingston in 1968.

In December 1976, while at Marley's compound at 56 Hope Road in Kingston, the then-pregnant Mowatt fell sick and was driven home by artist and designer Neville Garrick. In leaving the site that day she very narrowly escaped an unsuccessful attempt on Marley's life during which gunmen—believed to have been politically motivated—injured several members of the Wailers entourage. Five years later, Mowatt recalled that just before she heard the radio report of Marley's death in 1981,

Judy Mowatt dresses for success in 1987, a year after the former I-Threes singer became the first female vocalist nominated for a reggae Grammy.

loud thunder erupted and she saw a massive bolt of lightning.

The I-Threes disbanded after Marley's death. In the years that followed, as the three members concentrated on solo work, they made only occasional live appearances and recorded even less frequently. Later releases tapped reggae's niche market, but her records since the Grammy nomination have rarely been as successful. She has been active in staging concerts at Jamaica's Fort Augusta women's prison, and she converted to Christianity in 1995. Mowatt now considers herself a reggae gospel singer. She has released little new studio material since the turn of the century, and her records are now more overtly spiritual.

SELECT DISCOGRAPHY: Mellow Mood (Tuff Gong, 1975); Black Woman (Ashandan, 1979); Only a Woman (Shanachie, 1982); Working Wonders (Shanachie, 1985); Love Is Overdue (Shanachie, 1986); Look at Love (Shanachie, 1991); Rock Me (Pow Wow, 1993); Something Old, Something New (Judy M, 2002); Sing Our Own Song (Shanachie, 2000)

HUGH MUNDELL
YEARS ACTIVE: 1970s–1983

Jamaican singer Hugh Mundell had a promising but tragically brief career: in the five short years before his murder in 1983, he produced the debut single by future Black Uhuru vocalist Junior Reid, collaborated on his own album with producer Prince Jammy, and worked with reggae melodica player and dub instrumental icon Augustus Pablo.

Born in 1962 in Kingston, Mundell was spotted at about the age of twelve by Pablo at producer Joe Gibbs's studio. He had been hanging around Kingston's recording studios constantly in search of a break. Sensing the potential of the young singer's distinctive voice and songwriting, Pablo made Mundell a DJ in the Rockers International sound system, and a solo studio act.

In 1978 Mundell recorded his own, most popular song, "Africa Must Be Free by 1983." He produced Junior Reid's first single, "Speak the Truth," in 1979. Accelerating his creative activity, Mundell then collaborated on his 1980 *Jah Fire* album with Prince Jammy, who engineered and produced the record. He then coproduced his own *Time and Place* LP with Pablo in 1981. His life and career were cut short in 1983 when he was fatally shot in the back of the head in a car in Kingston following a petty dispute (accounts of the actual events vary). Reid, who witnessed the dreadful incident, credits Mundell with laying the foundation for his highly successful career.

SELECT DISCOGRAPHY: *Africa Must Be Free by 1983* (Message, 1978); *Jah Fire* (J & F, 1980); *Time and Place* (Killer Price, 1981); *Mundell* (Greensleeves, 1982); *Arise* (Atra, 1987); *Blackman's Foundation* (Shanachie, 1988)

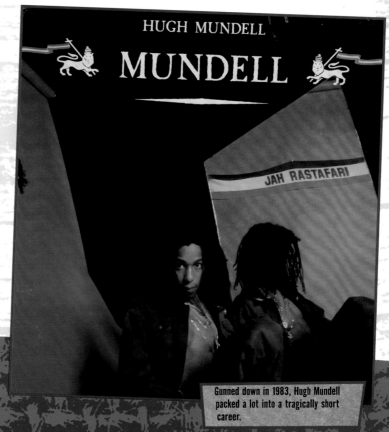

Gunned down in 1983, Hugh Mundell packed a lot into a tragically short career.

on. As a teenager, he was given his first guitar by an aunt living in America. Soon he began singing with the Hippy Boys, a group that included brothers Carlton and Aston Barrett (on drums and bass respectively), who would later go on to greater success as members of the Wailers. Murvin made a few solo recordings for the Jamaican producer and label owner Sonia Pottinger in the mid-1960s and auditioned unsuccessfully for Studio One producer Coxsone Dodd. His first local commercial success came with "Solomon" (1972), recorded under the name Junior Soul for producer Derrick Harriott's Crystal label.

Murvin wrote "Police and Thieves" in the mid-1970s, following the dissolution of Young Experience, a Jamaican band he had fronted. The recording, produced by Lee Perry, had major impact in both Jamaica and Britain, where it became a sleeper hit after its 1977 release. It reached #23 on the pop chart three years later, in 1980. The song made the Rastafarian antiestablishment label of

Gardiner. The *Police and Thieves* (1977) album contained other strong tracks, such as "Tedious," whose arguably more compelling dub version wasn't included on the original record but occupies a spot on the 2010 deluxe reissue. But it's the title track that made Murvin's name as endless alternative versions of the song were released by both him and others. British punk rockers the Clash covered the song on their 1977 self-titled debut, and although their jagged version completely removed the song from its reggae context, it caught Perry's attention, leading to the producer's eventual collaboration with the Clash—and brought Murvin some additional notoriety. Unfortunately, Perry's erratic behavior meant that he and Murvin were not able to build on the success of "Police and Thieves," and they failed to produce any further material together.

In subsequent years, Murvin recorded occasional singles and tried unsuccessfully to rekindle his spark with such producers as Joe Gibbs and Mikey Dread. Alluding to his biggest hit, he released *Muggers in the Street* in 1984, using the "Police and Thieves" rhythm on the title track. Murvin was backed on this album by the Roots Radics studio session band. The album was produced by Henry "Junjo" Lawes, who by this time was maestro of the newly emergent dancehall sound. Dancehall featured DJs and often recycled rhythms that had been successful in Jamaica in previous decades. After releasing sporadic dancehall recordings in Jamaica, in 2007 Murvin released the largely acoustic *Inna De Yard* (reissued in 2009), which inevitably included another version of "Police and Thieves," as well as remakes of "Roots Train" and "Solomon," all of which had appeared previously on the *Police and Thieves* album. Murvin remains one of those artists who have had to stand in their own shadow after an early career peak.

SELECT DISCOGRAPHY: *Police and Thieves* (Island, 1977); *Badman Possee* (DATC, 1982); *Muggers in the Street* (Greensleeves, 1984); *Inna De Yard* (Believe, 2007)

JUNIOR MURVIN

YEARS ACTIVE: 1970s–2000s

Not to be confused with the Bob Marley & the Wailers guitarist with a similar name (Junior Marvin), Junior Murvin is recognized largely for one song, "Police and Thieves" (1977), which has virtually overshadowed all of his other recordings. It was the right song at the right time, released when both Jamaica and Britain were experiencing political and social turmoil. The song's international popularity was a testament to its infectious rhythm and powerful lyrics, which reflected Jamaica's growing social instability and resonated with victims

ABOVE: Junior Murvin in 1973, four years prior to releasing "Police and Thieves," a tune the Clash would make a punk classic.

RIGHT: Produced by Lee Perry, this 1977 album remains Murvin's best-known work.

of racially motivated police brutality and harassment in Britain.

Junior Murvin was born Murvin Junior Smith in 1949 in Port Antonio, Jamaica. From around the age of six, Murvin emulated the vocal greats of the era, among them Nat King Cole, and developed the falsetto style that he would put to memorable use later

"Babylon" anything but abstract. Murvin recalled having a vision that directed him to take his song to Perry, who fortunately had access to such star session players as Sly Dunbar, Ernest Ranglin, and Boris

MUTABARUKA

YEARS ACTIVE: 1960s–2000s

Reggae has a strong tradition of striking out against imperialism and the political and social injustice that comes with it. But few artists have been as steadfastly militant and outspoken as the revolutionary Rastafarian dub poet Mutabaruka, whose chosen name is a Rwandan word meaning "one who is always victorious." Mutabaruka has said that his objective is to provoke thought with his words, and that he sees himself as an Afrocentric poet rather than a musician or entertainer. Placing his philosophical poetry and spoken word into a reggae setting, however, he extended the artistic approaches of the late Jamaican poet Michael Smith and the more widely known Britain-based Jamaican dub poet, Linton Kwesi Johnson.

Born Allan Hope in 1952 in Kingston, Jamaica, Mutabaruka was trained as an electrician and then hired by the Jamaica Telephone Company. He worked on his word craft in his spare time, performing his poetry publicly in the 1960s, until he decided to concentrate fully on creating and transmitting his messages around 1971. At a time when neocolonial concepts ruled the nation, Mutabaruka's poetry aimed to reinforce Afrocentric consciousness among Jamaicans. Deeply influenced by the progressive and radical 1960s narratives of such black Americans as Malcolm X and Eldridge Cleaver, he began a journey that eventually led him to Rastafarianism. He left Kingston and retreated to nearly the other end of Jamaica, settling in the parish of St. James. He published his first poems under the name Allan Mutabaruka in July 1971, in the Jamaican magazine *Swing*.

Following Jamaica's severe economic crises of the 1970s, Mutabaruka emerged in the 1980s with a decidedly political voice. He recorded his debut album, *Check It*, at Tuff Gong Studios in Kingston with guitarist and producer Earl "Chinna" Smith, who founded the High Times label around 1980. Released in 1983, *Check It* created a stir in Jamaica, becoming popular at a time when roots reggae rhythms and ideals were arguably becoming scarce on the reggae scene. Emphasizing his Jamaican accent, Mutabaruka established on record the themes he had already pursued in poetry: the plight of Africa and the lack of collective black consciousness, marginalization of ordinary people in society, religious hypocrisy, technological tyranny, the cultural importance of women, and all forms of exploitation. This was heavy subject matter for the dancehall era, when songs initially featured materialistic, misogynistic, and often violent lyrics that Mutabaruka later criticized as a means of cultural brainwashing. His *Dub It* remix album, also issued in 1983, may be one of dub's more underrated records, not only because of its roots-centered spacey echoes, but also because it further highlights Chinna Smith's excellent guitar work, arrangement, and production.

Mutabaruka's later releases are more than albums—they are mission updates from the front line of his continuing assault against the sociopolitical establishment—referred to by Rastas as "Babylon"—and the absence of spiritual righteousness. His philosophies appear in the 1982 documentary film on Jamaican culture, *Land of Look Behind*, providing an ideal introduction to his work. Perhaps surprisingly, he has been able to take his combative critiques of the system to the Jamaican airwaves, hosting both a television program (*Simply Muta*) and a radio show (*The Cutting Edge*) on Irie FM, Jamaica's first all-reggae station.

The demands of his many media activities, coupled with his duties as owner of a Kingston health food store, contributed to a lengthy hiatus, and he released no albums between 1994 and 2002. He returned to music with *Life Squared* (2002), demonstrating he had not lost his edge. Others have also remixed his work, including Beat Pharmacy (New York–based artist Brendon Moeller), whose release of the ambient dub-flavored electronic remix of "Wata (Water)" in 2006 gave Mutabaruka's dub poetry a twenty-first-century context without watering down the song's antiestablishment sentiment. Mutabaruka is one of the main reasons that roots reggae fans seeking artistic confrontations with the system should look beyond Bob Marley and Peter Tosh.

SELECT DISCOGRAPHY: *Check It* (High Times, 1983); *Outcry* (Shanachie, 1984); *The Mystery Unfolds* (Shanachie, 1986); *Blakk Wi Blak...k...k...* (Shanachie, 1991); *Ultimate Collection* (Shanachie, 1993); *Melanin Man* (Shanachie, 1994); *Muta in Dub* (Lethal, 1998); *Life Squared* (Heartbeat, 2002)

Dub poet Mutabaruka recites his incendiary verse in London, 1983.

MYSTIC REVEALERS

YEARS ACTIVE: 1980s–1998

According to an oft-repeated cliché in popular music, you don't know what you've got until it's gone. This is certainly the case with the Mystic Revealers, who formed in Bull Bay, Jamaica, in the late 1970s and whose absence from the reggae scene today is more significant than many people realize. The compelling reggae-rock guitar style and distinctive use of digital technology heard on the group's records of the 1990s were just two indicators of their greater creative ambition. Yet in a dancehall market filled with mostly generic clones, this distinctiveness probably worked against the Mystic Revealers.

The group chose a name that showcased both their recognition of music's mystical, intangible nature and their desire to "reveal Rastafari word, sound, and power," according to a 1994 *Reggae Report* magazine interview with their frontman and main songwriter, Billy "Mystic" Wilmot—better known as Billy Mystic. The self-contained group released

their early single "Mash Down Apartheid" in Jamaica in 1986 on the Oneness label. Soon, Mystic Revealers established itself as an internationally viable live act and made a number of superbly performed and produced records.

In what amounted to a coup for the band, in 1988 the Mystic Revealers landed a spot on the bill for Jamaica's annual Reggae Sunsplash concert, which in turn led to an appearance on Japanese television. The group's 1991 debut album, *Young Revolutionaries*, made little commercial impact despite promising songwriting. As Mystic later said in an interview, the recordings on that album were demos not intended for release, but limited time and money had forced the group's hand.

In 1992, they took their live show to Spain, performing in Seville at Expo '92 (an odd appearance for a reggae band, since the Expo commemorated the 500th

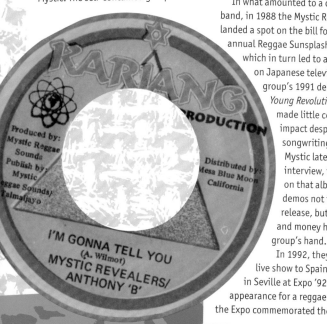

anniversary of Christopher Columbus's trip to the Americas), and later made two trips to Cuba. The band took a major step forward with 1993's *Jah Works*. One of the decade's most complete and progressive reggae albums, it was deserving of far more attention than it received. Such tracks as "Got to Be a Better Way" and "Religion"—the latter attacking anti-Rastafari attitudes—were probably the most popular, but one of the album's strongest songs was "Remember Romeo," a contemplation on an unnecessary death. Musically, the song's overall mix, production, and haunting synthesizer chords made it sound surreally futuristic—twenty-first-century reggae well before the millennium arrived. Mystic's vocal delivery infused "Remember Romeo" with an emotional urgency and realism that were among the band's artistic trademarks. Although the music was as digital as any dancehall of the time, the application of the technology was startlingly different. Unfortunately, such distinctiveness was underappreciated. Mystic Revealers soon became more popular abroad—especially in Europe—than they were in

The woefully underappreciated Mystic Revealers bring their rock-reggae fusion to Jamaica's Reggae Sunsplash festival, 1993.

Jamaica. By the mid-1990s, the band had signed a deal with RAS Records to release its albums in America. They had also established their own production company, Kariang, and an independent publishing company.

Several lineup changes accompanied the release of *Space and Time* (1995), whose sparsely beautiful single "Righteous" featured foregrounded acoustic guitar, piano, and Rasta drumming. Recording the album, the band returned to more organic studio techniques that reflected improved instrumental capability and signaled a break from the digital programming that—however successfully—had dominated *Jah Works*. For some listeners, the companion *Space and Dub* album, issued a year later, delivered greater sonic impact and revealed much more of the artful musicianship embedded in the recordings. The group left RAS for Mesa/Bluemoon Records to record what became the final Mystic Revealers studio album, *This One's for Jah* (1997), featuring dancehall star Anthony B on the single "I'm Gonna Tell You." The back cover of *RAS Portraits: Mystic Revealers* (1997); the RAS Records retrospective, included the quote, "The Mystic Revealers are destined to become a major force in reggae." But perhaps because their emergence coincided with the less musically adventurous dancehall era, their musicianship was both an asset and a crucial liability. Although the group was on the threshold of wider international success, they soon disbanded. *Crossing the Atlantic*, released in 1998 on the group's own Mystic Reggae label, compiled remixes of some of their best tracks.

Since the band's demise, Mystic himself has taken on a second career as an actor, including work on the Jamaican soap opera *Royal Palm Estate*. He also became president of the Jamaica Surfing Association. In March 2012, Mystic announced the regrouping of the Mystic Revealers with two of its other original members (bassist Leroy Edwards and drummer Nicky Henry).

MEMBERS: **Billy "Mystic" Wilmot** (vocals, guitar); **Leroy "Lion" Edwards** (bass, backing vocals); **Nicky "Cymbal" Henry** (drums); **Steve "Metal" Davis** (guitar, keyboards {*Jah Works*}, backing vocals); **Earl "Maestro" Fitzsimmons** (keyboards), *Jah Works* to *Space and Time*; **Noel Davey** (keyboards), *Jah Works* to *Space and Time*; **Paul "Scooby" Smith** (keyboards), *Space and Time* to *This One's for Jah*; **Nikita Chin** (keyboards), *This One's for Jah*; **Clarence Charles** (guitars), *This One's for Jah*; **Willigan** (percussion), *This One's for Jah*; **Christopher "Sky Juice" Burth** (percussion), *Space and Time* to *This One's for Jah*; **Sojan** (DJ), *This One's for Jah*.

SELECT DISCOGRAPHY: *Young Revolutionaries* (RAS, 1991); *Jah Works* (RAS, 1993); *Space and Time* (RAS, 1995); *Space and Dub* (RAS, 1996); *This One's for Jah* (Mesa/Bluemoon, 1997); *RAS Portraits: Mystic Revealers* (RAS, 1997); *Crossing the Atlantic* (Mystic Reggae, 1998)

JOHNNY NASH
YEARS ACTIVE: 1950s–1970s

There are two key reasons that any comprehensive history of reggae must include the American singer Johnny Nash: First, he was one of the artists responsible for landing reggae—or at least an approximation of reggae—on pop radio, particularly in the United States, where it had previously been marginalized. Second, if Nash had not recorded many of Bob Marley's compositions, a significant part of the reggae story would have been altered.

Born in 1940 in Houston, Texas, Nash had to overcome the era's racial prejudice to break through as a teenage singing star and sign a record deal with ABC-Paramount Records in the 1950s. Certainly, his middle-of-the-road music and image made him a safe contrast to more outrageous black performers like American rock 'n' roll act Little Richard. Nash first gained exposure on the radio and TV variety shows of host Arthur Godfrey, broadcast on the CBS network, becoming one of the few highly visible black personalities in mainstream American entertainment. Retaining a white audience inevitably meant that Nash would have to maintain a clean-cut image, typified by his series of maudlin singles that charted from 1957 to 1966.

By 1965, he had begun recording for the JODA and JAD record labels, which he founded in New York in collaboration with Danny Sims, who became Nash's manager and promoted the singer and other artists in the Caribbean. JODA was an amalgam of the first two letters of Nash's and Sims's first names, while JAD combined the initials of their first names with the *A* of producer Arthur Jenkins. Sims's frequent forays into the Jamaican market had alerted him to the island's creative and financial possibilities, and his decision to shift his operation there explains how Nash became a pop-reggae star in the late 1960s. Nash's *Hold Me Tight* album, its sound clearly influenced by reggae, was recorded at

Byron Lee's WIRL Studios (later Dynamic Sounds) in 1968. The commercial title track became Nash's biggest hit to date, reaching #5 in both Britain and the United States. It was somewhat ironic that a non-Jamaican artist had scored a bigger pop hit with a reggae-tinged song than most Jamaican acts had managed up to that time—the notable exception being Desmond Dekker, the singer behind 1967's "007 (Shanty Town)."

Nash met Bob Marley while attending a Rasta "grounation"—a gathering devoted to praise and "reasoning" (philosophical dialogue)—and soon introduced him to Sims. The Wailers (including Marley, Peter Tosh, and Bunny Wailer) were literally instrumental in creating the tracks on Nash's next album, *I Can See Clearly Now* (1972), in London, as Nash recorded several of Marley's original songs. Although the million-selling title track was not penned by Marley, the album's opening song, "Stir It Up," was a Marley composition that became a hit single for Nash in its own right in 1973.

Nash was now at the peak of his career, but while he had helped to popularize the concept of reggae, his mainstream sound took it further from the ragged aspects of its roots. He even used Jamaican musicians in the process, including session bassist Jackie

American singer Johnny Nash in 1973, when "Stir it Up" became a hit single.

Jackson, guitarist-arranger Lynn Taitt, and the band Fabulous Five, though none of these were credited on his albums. Nash's version of "Tears on My Pillow," which hit #1 in Britain in 1975 (written by Jamaican singer-songwriter Ernie Smith), marked the end of a run of lightweight reggae hits for the singer—songs that in some ways prefigured the commerciality of the romance-centered lovers rock style. It was perhaps not coincidental that Nash's decision to retire gradually from performing came at the same time that a dreadlocked and Rasta-inspired Marley began to penetrate the market with his harder-edged political messages.

SELECT DISCOGRAPHY: *Hold Me Tight* (JAD, 1968); *I Can See Clearly Now* (JAD/CBS, 1972)

INTERNATIONAL REGGAE

Today, artists on every continent are playing reggae and singing about their respective societies. In the first half of the 1960s, reggae's immediate predecessors—ska and rocksteady—accelerated the global spread of Jamaican popular music. Immigration also played a role, as many West Indians relocated and settled into urban enclaves in British cities. As the music evolved during the decade, British record labels gradually emerged. Capitalizing on demands from white youth subcultures—first the scooter-riding mods and later the racist and often violent skinheads—these labels helped push the music that would become reggae into an initially resistant mainstream. While Jamaican singer Millie Small's ska-pop record "My Boy Lollipop" was a global hit in 1964, it failed to generate ongoing success for Jamaican music in the pop market. Likewise, the adoption of ska by Britain's mod subculture had little effect. The top instrumental exponents of ska, the Skatalites, reached #36 on the British pop charts in 1967 with "Guns of Navarone," but since it had been recorded in 1964, when ska was still popular in Jamaica and the United Kingdom, it hardly heralded a new era.

In 1967, as the slower rocksteady rhythm transitioned into reggae, singer Desmond Dekker's "007 (Shanty Town)" made it to #14 on the UK charts. It was the first in a string of hit singles that helped Jamaican popular music reach a wider audience than ever before. Britain's white, middle-class successors to the mods, the skinheads, championed such 1969 reggae recordings as Dekker's chart-topping UK hit "Israelites" and fellow Jamaican singer Derrick Morgan's "Moon Hop," which became a minor British hit in early 1970. However, the music was perceived solely as a singles genre, and as such, it was neither warmly received nor taken seriously by the UK music press or mainstream media. This was true even as the world's ultimate pop icons, the Beatles, dabbled in reggae with "Ob-La-Di, Ob-La-Da," a song from their 1968 self-titled album, better known as the *White Album*. Throughout the 1970s, Chris Blackwell, head

of London-based Island Records, strove to reach the rock audience. His rock-style promotion, album packaging, and production clearly heightened reggae's profile, and the Wailers' *Catch a Fire* (first released in Britain in late 1972) still represents one of the bolder marketing moves in reggae history, even if the record's initial audience was small. The ambitious cigarette lighter sleeve concept, and its symbolic ties to the record's title, took reggae-related visuals into new territory.

Many pop fans were first introduced to reggae via British rock legend Eric Clapton's 1974 cover of Bob Marley's "I Shot the Sheriff." Clapton's version was an international hit and topped the charts in America. While there were always some listeners who heard such reggae approximations and sought out authentic roots music, they were relatively few in number. Pop artists who integrated reggae elements into their repertoires and released singles utilizing the style sold far more records than the Jamaican artists who inspired them. Nevertheless, these records played a key role in

reggae's internationalization, stimulating mainstream curiosity about the music. Paul Simon traveled to Jamaica to record the rhythm tracks for his 1972 single "Mother and Child Reunion," one of the era's many reggae-influenced hits.

Other examples of rock and pop acts turning diluted reggae interpretations (or related song titles) into chart success include Paul McCartney & Wings' "Jet" (1973), Stevie Wonder's "Boogie On Reggae Woman" (1974), the Eagles' "Hotel California" (1976), and various singles released by the Police. However, the pop-reggae scene coincided with and was inspired by the gradual emergence of Jamaican artists such as Marley (still the genre's biggest star), Burning Spear, and Peter Tosh. The reggae subgenre known as dub, characterized by spacey remixes of songs, also left its mark on the 1970s, influencing the evolution of extended disco remixes.

As reggae spread around the globe, it proved particularly resonant wherever people identified with narratives of "downpression" (the Rastafarian

OPPOSITE LEFT: Despite the title, Stevie Wonder's "Boogie on Reggae Woman" was actually a funk song.

OPPOSITE RIGHT: Eric Clapton topped the charts in America with this 1974 Bob Marley cover.

LEFT: This spacey 1979 single was one of many reggae-inspired Police tunes.

BELOW: Reggae-loving UK punk band the Clash rocks the Jamaica World Music Festival, 1982.

THE POLICE

Walking on the Moon

inversion of *oppression*) and injustice. By the mid-1970s, another UK subculture, the punk rockers, had followed in the footsteps of the mods and skinheads and adopted Jamaican music. Their fervor helped spread the music even further, and in 1977, the British punk group the Clash teamed up with legendary reggae producer Lee Perry to record "Complete Control." By 1980, when the Clash toured with Jamaican DJ Mikey Dread, reggae had street credibility and commercial value. Overlapping with punk's rise and fall was the brief British ska revival spearheaded by the 2 Tone Records label. Throughout the label's run, which spanned 1979 to 1985, such groups as the Specials, the Selecter, Madness, and the Beat (known as the English Beat in America), just to name a few, fused 1960s Jamaican music with the anarchic energy of contemporary punk. 2 Tone's chart success brought renewed interest in older music, and Jamaican singer Laurel Aitken, best known for his late 1950s and early 1960s singles, was among the artists to win a new generation of fans.

The Jamaican DJ and its attendant culture, which rose to prominence on the island in the early 1970s through recordings by artists such as U-Roy and Big Youth, was a key influence on urban American rapping styles. The extent to which hip hop derives from the Jamaican tradition of sound-system "toasting"—a form of improvised rapping—is perhaps not acknowledged often enough. The 2010 album *Distant Relatives*, a collaboration between American rapper Nas and

Damian Marley, one of Bob Marley's many musically inclined children, demonstrated the connection between hip hop and the dancehall sound that emerged in the 1980s.

ABOVE: Fusing punk and ska, the Beat were at the forefront of the 2 Tone ska revolution.

RIGHT: Amid rising violence and sagging economic conditions, "Ghost Town" topped the UK charts in 1981, becoming a 2 Tone classic.

Hip hop's utilization of Jamaican DJ styles was not the only factor that contributed to reggae's heightened mainstream presence after the roots era. In the mid-1980s, when roots-influenced records by the multiracial British pop-reggae band UB40 began receiving airplay in America, the group offered a new avenue of discovery for potential reggae fans in the US pop market. Between 1983 and

1997, UB40 charted nine albums (three of which sold more than a million copies) and scored four top-ten hit singles in America, outselling all other living reggae artists during that time. Similarly, by assimilating the vocal nuances and accents of Jamaican dancehall DJs, white Canadian rapper Snow scored his only million-selling album in the United States with 1993's *12 Inches of Snow*. On the strength of his chart-topping US hit "Informer," Snow overshadowed and outsold most pop-friendly Jamaican dancehall DJs in the 1990s, including Shabba Ranks, who had previously scored two gold albums in the United States.

Snow's short-lived success coincided with the rapid rise of Ace of Base, a Swedish group whose sugary, digitally driven pop-reggae sound proved massively popular in Europe and especially in America. "All That She Wants" (1993) and "The Sign" (1994) were both platinum-selling top-five hits (selling over a million copies each), while the follow-up, "Don't Turn Around" (1994), went gold (selling over half a million copies). The latter song was also a chart-topping hit in the United Kingdom in 1988 for the British reggae group Aswad as they pursued their own crossover path. Ace of Base's debut album, *The Sign* (1993), sold an incredible nine million copies in the United States, demonstrating that the right visual appearance coupled with a knack for weaving pop hooks into reggae rhythms could take the music to new audiences. Certainly, no Jamaican group could match Ace of Base's global commercial impact at that time.

While roots reggae fell out of favor in Jamaica itself during the dancehall-dominated 1980s and 1990s, it remained appealing to relatively small but enthusiastic audiences in other countries who adopted the music as their own. This created an international touring market for the genre's Jamaican acts.

One of the more commercially successful non-Jamaican reggae artists in the twenty-first century has been American Hasidic Jewish singer and rapper Matisyahu. He rose to prominence when his sophomore effort, 2005's *Live at Stubb's*, an album he recorded for a mere $8,000, reached #30 on the *Billboard* 200 and topped the reggae album charts in 2006. That record and its studio follow-up, *Youth* (2006), were certified gold in America. *Youth* debuted on the *Billboard* 200 at #4, a rare feat for a reggae album and an even more unusual accomplishment for a relatively new act in the genre. The fact that the record's dub version, *Youth Dub* (2006), did not chart at all signifies the difficulty that reggae artists—even popular ones—face in maintaining high sales. Despite landing on the reggae charts, Matisyahu's subsequent records, including the 2011 album *Live at Stubb's, Vol. 2*, have not reached the levels of his early career successes.

Hawaiian group the Green debuted at the top of the *Billboard* reggae charts in 2011 with their second album, *Ways & Means*. The four-man band plays what is known to some as "Jawaiian" reggae—a mix of Jamaican and Hawaiian sounds—and demonstrates the influence of Jamaican music far from its island of origin. Reggae's 1970s following in the Pacific region was invigorated by Bob Marley's 1979 tour of New Zealand. The presence of roots reggae's most successful international artist was a key factor in the emergence of reggae bands in the area in the 1980s.

In Holland, Canadian-born producer Ryan Moore records under the name of the Twilight Circus Dub Sound System. The multi-instrumentalist also runs his own M Records label (established in 1995), and in his catalog of more than twenty Twilight Circus albums, *Volcanic Dub* (2001) is one of the highlights. Clearly influenced by the vintage mixes of such Jamaican dub exponents as engineer King Tubby and producer-engineer Lee Perry, the Twilight Circus records echo the atmospheric sounds of the 1970s. By also working with Jamaican vocalists—among them former Black Uhuru front man Michael Rose—and such session musicians as legendary drummer Sly Dunbar, Moore has given his productions an aura of roots-era authenticity that some newer international reggae lacks.

A vibrant reggae scene has emerged in Cologne, Germany (home of the German-language reggae magazine *Riddim*), and in 2008, the studio group DubXanne released the intriguing *Police in Dub*. Featuring the four-man backing band Okada Supersound, the album consists of covers of songs by the Police. It's interesting that music from one of the acts that helped bring elements of reggae into the pop mainstream has found itself repeatedly reinterpreted by reggae acts around the world.

Damian Marley (left) and rapper Nas blur the lines between reggae and hip hop, 2010.

American Hasidic Jewish reggae star Matisyahu feels the support of his fans, 2009.

native

No average roots band, Native (l-r: Warren Mendes, Wayne Jobson, Brian Jobson) crossed reggae with rock and pop.

NATIVE

YEARS ACTIVE: 1970s-MID-1990s

Like their contemporaries Inner Circle and Third World, Native was a multigenre Jamaican band born in the 1970s that boasted both a wide musical vocabulary and a penchant for playing roots reggae. While purists have sometimes frowned upon the "uptown" (middle or upper class) backgrounds of such groups, claiming that they don't represent the typical Jamaican "sufferer's" reality, reggae's creativity has come from many sources.

Native's lead singer, Wayne Jobson, was a cousin of both Bob Marley's longtime lawyer Diane Jobson, and former Wailers manager Dickie Jobson. The young Wayne Jobson's musical direction was greatly influenced by the time he spent with the Wailers in their early days, listening to and jamming with the group before their rise to fame. His friendship with Peter Tosh began at this time, and led to him

eventually serving as co-executive producer on the posthumous, award-winning Tosh documentary *Stepping Razor: Red X* (1994). Prior to forming Native, Jobson had been a member of a group called Little Madness, which had released a single, "Mother Country," in Jamaica as early as 1975 on the Arab label owned by producer and promoter Tommy Cowan.

Wayne Jobson apparently connected with producer Lee "Scratch" Perry in August 1977. Brought to Perry's Black Ark studio in Kingston by bassist and vocalist Boris Gardiner, Jobson successfully auditioned material on acoustic guitar for Perry, who mistakenly believed that Jobson was an Arawak descended from Jamaica's indigenous inhabitants. Native recorded their first demos at Black Ark with help from the legendary Jamaican vocalist and arranger Joe Higgs and session players Sydney Bennett (bass) and Ray Levy (drums). Jobson then went to law school in London, earning his degree

there in 1979. The five songs that Native recorded at Black Ark led to a deal in late 1978 with the English branch of Arista Records. The signing came after the group had attracted some industry buzz thanks to positive comments made in the press by Johnny Rotten, former lead singer of the infamous British punk group the Sex Pistols.

After signing the Arista deal, Jobson returned to Black Ark in May 1979, intending to turn the original five-song demo collection into a full-length Native album, even though the band had yet to form officially. Unfortunately, Jobson's efforts coincided with Perry's spell of acutely erratic behavior—as Jobson put it, Scratch had "gone mad." Perry, also known as the "Upsetter," had embarked on a destructive streak that would ultimately contribute to a thirty-year delay in the release of that ambitious Native album.

Despite his various ties to the Wailers and Chris Blackwell, the head of Island Records, Jobson felt it was essential for Native to secure their record deals independently, so that the music would succeed on its own strength. They had signed with RCA Records by 1980, completing their self-titled debut that year; but the album was insufficiently promoted by RCA. Against the odds, in 1980 Native landed a slot opening for Jamaican reggae star Burning Spear at the Whisky a Go Go club in Los Angeles, a gig that prompted RCA to take the group more seriously. Now seven members strong, Native enthusiastically embarked on recording their second album, *In a Strange Land* (1981), considered by many to be their definitive record. Its cover, featuring the band members posing like a typical rock group without any visual hint of their reggae influence, was indicative of the multicultural direction of their sound. Native was frustrated by continual delays in the album's release, however, and the record company's

internal coordination was poor. When Jobson finally secured a guarantee that RCA would release the album within a few months, he shocked the label's product manager by revealing that he had just bought a copy of the record at a store; RCA had somehow released the record without informing Native. Due to the nonstop turnover of A&R (Artists and Repertoire) staff at RCA and the other major labels they subsequently signed with, Native always struggled to find the kind of promotion necessary to reach wider audiences. Nevertheless, *In a Strange Land* offered a potent blend of rock and reggae that was different from Bob Marley's sound, and arguably ahead of its time. The gritty "Make No Mistake" was released as a single, and the album also contained "Super Dread," a tribute to Marley, who had recently died. Still unavailable on CD, *In a Strange Land* may eventually gain recognition as a highly progressive classic that was lost in the shuffle of major labels hustling to fill Marley's space.

Amid Native's frustration with a lack of promotion, in late 1982 or early 1983 Lee Perry the "Upsetter" lived up to his nickname by burning down the Black Ark studio, destroying Jobson's master tapes in the process. Luckily, a satisfactory mix had already been made and transferred. The album had to be completed with several other engineers at Dynamic Sounds, and its twenty-first century debut as *Rockstone: Native's Adventures with Lee Perry at the Black Ark* (2007) on the archival Pressure Sounds label was warmly received. In 1984, Native cut the independently released single "Love Ain't No Holiday," produced by James Mtume, whose eponymous group had scored a massive R&B-pop hit a year earlier with "Juicy Fruit." The collaboration was somewhat ironic given Jobson's reservations about R&B and its dilution of reggae, which he discussed in a 2007 interview. Also in 1984, Native released *R&B, Rock &*

Reggae, so titled as if to unequivocally represent what the band was about. By this time, Native had shed members and become a trio comprising Wayne Jobson, his brother Brian, and Peter Couch. In the stretch of inactivity that followed, partly due to lack of commercial success, Jobson decided that the only way to avoid the constant instability of record companies was to sign with someone whose label mirrored Blackwell's Island model, which he greatly admired. Trumpeter Herb Alpert—the "A" in A&M Records—heard Native's new material and signed them to his label for the *No Boundaries* album (1989). According to Wayne Jobson's logic, the owner of the label (in this case Alpert) could not be fired, so stability was guaranteed—and Herb Alpert even played on the album. Meanwhile, Couch left the group, while multi-instrumentalist and original member Warren Mendes rejoined, having left after *In a Strange Land*. The band covered the Sam Cooke hit "What a Wonderful World," a song the legendary soul singer had cowritten with Alpert and *No Boundaries* veteran producer Lou Adler. A promotional copy of the single was included in editions of *Radio & Records*, an influential American industry magazine, taking Native's profile to new heights. Things seemed to be falling into place, but shortly after the single's release, PolyGram Records stepped in, bought A&M, and removed Alpert. (PolyGram itself would later be absorbed into Universal Music Group.)

No Boundaries was a lighter, more laid-back and pop-friendly record than *In a Strange Land*, but both attempted to balance crossover appeal with distinct reggae identity. Native's eclectic sound may have kept them from being perceived as solely a reggae act, and the excellent lyricism and confident performance on the pop-rock track "Did She Fall or Was She Pushed," from *No Boundaries*, clearly suggested that this was no average roots band.

With the impact of *No Boundaries* limited by A&M's ownership changes, Native disintegrated further, eventually leaving Wayne Jobson as the sole member, just as he had been in the beginning. A rebound seemed possible when "Here Comes the Night" (a cover of a 1965 hit by Irish group Them) was selected as the lead single on the film sound track for *Ace Ventura: When Nature Calls* (1995). Chrissie Hynde, lead singer of the rock band the Pretenders, was originally slated to provide vocals, but her label withheld single release rights, killing off another potential success. (Katrina Leskanich of the pop group Katrina & the Waves replaced Hynde.)

This was one disappointment too many for Jobson, who turned his attention fully toward other media activities, including making films and running a reggae radio show at KROQ in Los Angeles. He later became a consultant for XM Satellite Radio. In a 2007 interview, he lamented the inability of the major labels to market reggae effectively, citing Island as the key exception. Particularly in the case of Native—a band with brown-skinned, mixed-race personnel and eclectic musical influences—the A&R impulse to place all reggae artists into the R&B category due to their blackness seriously undermined the group. Jobson prefers Blackwell's vision, which involved marketing Bob Marley and the Wailers to rock audiences. By contrast, the major labels that signed such reggae bands as Steel Pulse and Third World tried to dilute their reggae identities and cultivate more conventional R&B sounds and images.

Jobson did not completely exit the music business in later years. He served as executive producer on *Rock Steady*, the Grammy-winning 2001 album by reggae-influenced rock band No Doubt, and he has worked with other acts in both creative and business capacities.

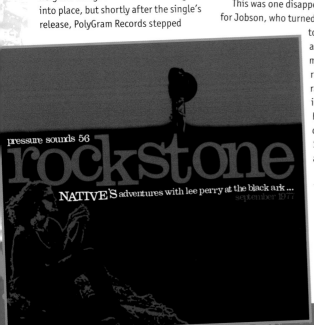

pressure sounds 56
rockstone
NATIVE's adventures with lee perry at the black ark ...
september 1977

ABOVE: Native lead vocalist Wayne Jobson at the LA Film Festival premiere for the film *What We Do Is Secret*, 2007. The film chronicles the late Darby Crash, lead singer of the 1970s punk band the Germs.

MEMBERS: **Wayne Jobson** (lead vocals, guitars, percussion, background vocals); **Brian Jobson** (bass, vocals, keyboards, percussion); **Peter Couch** (keyboards, flute); **Warren Mendes** (lead vocals, guitars, saxophone, harmonica, background vocals); **Chris Lopez** (lead vocals, guitars, percussion, background vocals), *In a Strange Land*; **Perry Tole** (lead guitar); **Richie Sinclair** (drums, percussion, vocals)

SELECT DISCOGRAPHY: *Native* (RCA Records, 1980); *In a Strange Land* (RCA, 1981); *R&B, Rock & Reggae* (Jamaica, 1984); *No Boundaries* (Ode/A&M, 1989); *Rockstone: Native's Adventures with Lee Perry at the Black Ark* (Pressure Sounds, 2007)

JACKIE OPEL

YEARS ACTIVE: 1960s

Listeners unfamiliar with Jackie Opel and his remarkable vocal range might be surprised by the prices of his vinyl recordings on the Internet. Many of his singles sell for more than $200, and in auctions, his records have fetched even greater amounts. These high asking prices highlight the major disparity in the value that record collectors and reggae historians have accorded his work.

Although many reggae reference books mention his name sporadically, there's a serious lack of reliable information on Opel's life and career in the 1960s, the decade when he rose to prominence. An unpublished University of the West Indies doctoral thesis by researcher and writer Elizabeth Watson has filled crucial gaps in Opel's biography, and is a key source. Opel was born in Barbados, not in Trinidad or Jamaica, as many books have often suggested. (Some publications place him in all three countries, although there's no evidence to suggest that he ever assumed citizenship in any country but

his homeland.) It is certain, however, that he lived in Trinidad, and in Jamaica—the home of reggae—where he made his greatest impact as a musician.

According to his birth certificate—and contrary to other published dates—he was born Dalton St. Clair Bishop in Bridgetown, Barbados, on August 27, 1937. At some point he assumed the name Jackie Opel, derived from the onstage histrionics of American singer Jackie Wilson and the high-quality reputation of the German-made Opel automobile. One account suggests that he was influenced in his early years by radio broadcasts from Nashville, but those signals would not have reached Barbados. The singer first visited Jamaica in either the late 1950s or early the 1960s, but the exact date is not known. Formerly a part of the entourage of the Trinidadian calypsonian the Mighty Sparrow, Opel was brought over by Jamaican musician and promoter Byron Lee to sing with the Dragonaires, Lee's group.

In 1962, during Jamaica's ska era, Opel settled in Kingston with a woman reputed to be his wife. (During Opel's

lifetime, several women claimed to be his wife, but to date, no supporting documentation has surfaced.) Shortly after the introduction of television to the island in 1963, he recorded "TV in Jamaica" with producer Leslie Kong. That single was released in England on the Jump Up label. According to vocalist Desmond Dekker, Opel "just come and dominate the scene." Dekker also commented that this occurred to such an extent that other singers on Kong's Beverley's Records label, including Bob Marley, sought different producers. Opel's subsequent reputation was built largely on his dynamic James Brown–style live performances and on the recordings he made for producer Coxsone Dodd's Studio One label in Kingston during his tenure in Jamaica.

Until 1966, Dodd licensed many of Opel's singles to Chris Blackwell's Island Records for sale in England. It's been stated elsewhere that Opel relocated to England to boost his career, but unlike such contemporaries as Jamaican hit singer Laurel Aitken, he never actually took up residence in Britain. There are rumors that he might have toured there at some point, however. At least one promotional single, "You Gotta Cry" (c. 1965)—an alternate title for his song "Cry Me a River"—was issued on MGM Records in the United States.

During this time, Opel performed both on record and live with such later icons as Marley and the prime ska instrumentalists, the Skatalites. The documentation of his work with Bob Marley on *Wailers and Friends*, a 1999 collection released on the Heartbeat Records label, demonstrates that he influenced others in the Kingston musical community. The founding members of the Skatalites allegedly formed the band while backing Opel on a Studio One session, and in concert, the musically versatile singer sometimes served as a stand-in bassist for the group. He also performed duets with

singer Doreen Shaffer on records made for Dodd's Ska-Beat offshoot label. After the Skatalites dissolved in 1965, Opel reportedly performed and recorded with Tommy McCook & the Supersonics, a session group partially formed from remnants of the Skatalites. He also recorded at Studio One for producer Justin Yap, who funded the sessions and released the recordings on his own Top Deck Records label in 1965. Several songs featuring Opel from those Top Deck sessions were reissued on the 2003 various artists compilation *Ska Down Jamaica Way: Vol. 2*, released on BMG Records.

In the mid-1960s, Opel moved back to Barbados before recording *The Memorable Jackie Opel* at Caribbean Sound Studios in Trinidad in 1967 (though the record wasn't released until 1970). This solo album ultimately became his final—and definitive—musical statement, as he died in a car crash in Bridgetown, Barbados, in March 1970 at the age of thirty-two. Shortly before his death, he was said to be working on a new rhythmic style intended to be as distinctive to Barbados as reggae was to Jamaica. Other Barbadian musicians promoted the late singer's "spouge" rhythm, which featured a percussive cowbell. Spouge attained some Caribbean popularity in the 1970s when artists mostly from Barbados began recording songs in that style. But spouge rapidly faded from the spotlight despite attempts to resurrect it over the decades, and it remains almost unknown beyond the Eastern Caribbean.

Opel's funeral was supposedly the largest ever in Barbados up to that time. Some of his recordings have never been issued, and forty years after his death, a truly comprehensive anthology of his work has yet to be compiled or released.

SELECT DISCOGRAPHY: *The Memorable Jackie Opel* (WIRL, 1970); *Cry Me a River* (VP, 1997); *Top Sounds from Top Deck: Vol. 2 - Jackie Opel & Ferdie Nelson* (Westside, 1998); *The Best of Jackie Opel* (ERNI, 2009)

A LOVE TO SHARE

In Memory of Jackie Opel

Decades after his death in 1970, Jackie Opel remains a favorite of reggae collectors, who pay big bucks for his soulful recordings.

AUGUSTUS PABLO

YEARS ACTIVE: 1969-1999

Augustus Pablo released some of the most iconic records of the roots reggae era, using his multi-instrumental talents to craft songs that formed an essential backdrop to the rise of Rastafari. Born Horace Swaby around 1953 in the Jamaican parish of St. Andrew, Pablo got his stage name from Herman Chin-Loy, the producer best known for the 1973 album *Aquarius Dub*. Not surprisingly, his parents did not encourage his involvement in a musical style that, at the time, was associated with ghetto-class Jamaicans. Chin-Loy had already used the name on recordings featuring organist Glen Adams, but after the introverted and relatively unknown Swaby became Pablo (perhaps as early as 1969), what had originally been a floating identity for session musicians took on a specific face and sound.

Augustus Pablo unleashes the mystical sounds of the melodica, his instrument of choice, onstage in London, 1980.

Pablo's signature instrument, the melodica—a wind instrument that has a small keyboard attached to a mouthpiece—was an unlikely musical weapon in an era featuring electrical rather than acoustic instruments, but its sonic texture complemented the rhythms, philosophies, and ethereal dub mixes that characterized roots reggae. Pablo's introduction to the instrument was rather accidental. Already a piano player, he found his musical curiosity further awakened when he met a friend's girlfriend who owned a melodica. He promptly requested to try it, and since the girl did not need the instrument, she gave it to him. He began recording with it following a 1969 visit to Chin-Loy's Aquarius record shop. Chin-Loy arranged for a session at Randy's studio in Kingston, which was initially run by Vincent "Randy" Chin and owned by the Chin family, who later established the well-known VP Records label. That session resulted in "Iggy Iggy" and "East of the River Nile," though Pablo's first hit did not arrive until "Java Java Java" in 1972 (though some sources cite both 1971 and 1973 as the release date).

Pablo set up a Kingston-based sound system, Rockers International, run with his brother, Garth, starting in the late 1960s, and began producing his own records around 1972, initially drawing influence from the records on Coxsone Dodd's Studio One label in Kingston. Like many Jamaican artists of the day, Pablo took his recordings to ace engineer King Tubby for special dub remixing, and it soon became evident that a creative chemistry existed

AUGUSTUS PABLO 45
EL ROCKER'S

COLECCION

PERMISO N 2 0 4
25 LUCES

MARCA REGISTRADA
DE LA CENTRAL

PRESSURE SOUNDS 29

era, interweaving echoed fragments of melodica, guitar, and vocal over an insistently kinetic drum-and-bass rhythm track. Compared to the more radically remixed "King Tubby Meets the Rockers Uptown," "Jah Jah Dub"(Chin-Loy's earlier remix) sounds more like a conventional instrumental version with additional keyboard overdubs and a few applied effects than it does a proper dub track.

Released in 1976, the seminal dub album *King Tubby Meets Rockers Uptown* featured twelve dub remixes of Pablo's self-financed recordings mixed by Tubby with assistance from renowned Kingston studio engineer Errol Thompson. Thanks to the pairing of Pablo and Tubby, the album became one of reggae's most highly regarded releases of all time. It fared especially well in Britain, where it was an underground sensation. Although the album did not enjoy such a high profile in Jamaica, it ensured that Pablo would have an international audience.

When dancehall arrived in the 1980s, Pablo embraced the new style, despite its initial distance from the sound and philosophical ideals that had characterized the roots era. Even when his later records were not selling well in the 1980s and 1990s, he was able to attract live audiences across the world, particularly in Japan, where he had an enthusiastic fan base.

After recurrent spates of poor health, Pablo died in 1999 from myasthenia gravis, a rare nerve disorder. Although his name will forever be associated with dub, his musicality transcended the genre and was one of the key reasons that his recordings were so suitable for a variety of dub treatments.

SELECT DISCOGRAPHY: *This Is Augustus Pablo* (Tropical, 1973); *King Tubby Meets Rockers Uptown* (Island, 1976; *East of the River Nile* (Message, 1978)

ABOVE: (l-r) Mike McKenzie, Jah Bull, and Augustus Pablo at Pablo's Rockers International Store, Kingston, 1983.

RIGHT: A version of an earlier Pablo single, this crucial 1975 cut exemplifies the decade's echo-drenched dub sound.

KING TUBBY
MEETS THE ROCKERS UPTOWN
AUGUSTUS PABLO

(H. Swaby)

MS 2001-A
2:31

produced by
A. PABLO
A ROCKERS
PRODUCTION

arranged by
A. PABLO

published by
Ackee Music
Inc. (ASCAP)

© 1974 Island
Records Ltd.

MANGO

Mfg. and Distributed by
Island Records Inc.
7720 Sunset Blvd.
Los Angeles, Calif. 90046

between the artist and the engineer. At about age twenty, Pablo mixed his debut album, *This Is Augustus Pablo* (1973) at Randy's studio and record-label operation. As the artist later noted, an error resulted in "Java" being left off of the record.

Pablo established his own Rockers label (sometimes printed on singles as Rockers International) in 1972, naming it after his sound system. During the mid-1970s, the word *rockers* also became associated with a distinctive style of roots reggae featuring a rhythmic drumming style introduced by Sly Dunbar. Pablo nurtured the talents of the young vocalist Hugh Mundell, developing his unique style and giving him his first studio sessions in 1975. This led to the release of Mundell's well-known *Africa Must Be Free* album in 1978. Unlike most reggae musicians of the time, Pablo was considerably shrewd in business matters. In addition to setting up his Rockers International sound system and record-shop operation in Kingston, he established record labels that were more than mere vanity projects and retained

full control over his publishing.

Pablo's best-known recording, the dub single "King Tubby Meets the Rockers Uptown" (1975), went through several earlier incarnations, and the same song was remixed several times by different producers and engineers during the 1970s. The single was actually a revised version of Pablo's own instrumental "Cassava Piece," recorded for Herman Chin-Loy in 1972, and then remixed and presented as "Jah Jah Dub" on the producer's *Aquarius Dub* album. Another version based on the original "Cassava Piece" rhythm, utilizing the same instrumental tracks but adding vocals, appeared as the A-side of singer Jacob Miller's single "Baby, I Love You

So." The B-side dub remix of "Baby, I Love You So" by King Tubby was "King Tubby Meets the Rockers Uptown"—and with this version, Pablo fully established his place in reggae folklore. Miller's version was relegated to the B-side when the dub remix became more popular. Released in Britain by Island Records, "King Tubby Meets the Rockers Uptown" typifies the classic 1970s dub

PAMA RECORDS

Rocksteady channeled the intense rhythmic pace of ska into a slower musical style, and by the late 1960s, rocksteady had materialized into reggae—which was often even slower, but usually with more varied rhythmic accents. Pama Records was one of the Britain–based companies ready to supply a domestic West Indian market hungry for the new style of music; the label also provided a soundtrack for the skinhead subculture of shaven-head, white, working-class British youths who rejected mainstream lifestyles. Pama played a crucial role as one of the key British independent reggae labels of the late 1960s and early 1970s, and was one of the few real rivals to Trojan Records, Britain's leading reggae label.

Jamaican brothers Harry, Jeff, and Carlisle Palmer established Pama in Britain in 1967. Their involvement in the music business began around 1962 with the Happy Sounds record shop, which later burned down. The brothers then ventured into real estate and ran a nightclub, all in the same Harrow Road area of London. Before establishing the Pama label the Palmer brothers were also involved in artist management and worked to promote singer Joyce Bond. After they tried unsuccessfully to interest such major British pop record labels as Philips and Pye, Island Records agreed to release Bond's singles "Tell Me What It's All About" (1966) and "Do the Teasy" (1967). Island also released Bond's *Soul and Ska* album in 1967, though by this time, ska had already metamorphosed into rocksteady. That album is probably best known for its cheesy cover photo, which depicts Bond playing on the image of her well-known male on-screen namesake, James Bond, and posing with two guns.

The record label was something of an afterthought and was not intended to become the brothers' core business enterprise. The label aimed to compete effectively with Island, which up to that time was the chief UK source of Jamaican popular music. For its first two years, Pama also issued soul recordings licensed from independent American labels. However, one of Island's associated labels (at least until 1972 when Island withdrew all involvement), Trojan, soon outstripped all rivals to become the nation's top reggae label, which it remained until its 1975 bankruptcy.

Sources differ regarding which record marked Pama's first actual release, but Jamaican singer Clancy Eccles's "What Will Your Mama Say" (1967) was among the earliest. The label developed working relationships with many major Jamaican record producers, including the relative newcomer and former record plugger (a promoter working to get radio airplay for songs) Bunny Lee, with whom the Palmers established the subsidiary label Unity as a showcase for his recordings. Among the key records released on the Unity label was Stranger Cole's "Bangarang" (1968), which Lee and Glen Adams, who played organ on the single, both describe as the first reggae song.

By 1969, Pama had effectively challenged Trojan's dominance in the marketplace, having licensed singer Max Romeo's salacious but enormously successful single "Wet Dream" (1969). The song was banned by the British Broadcasting Corporation (BBC), but even without airplay, it stormed the charts and reportedly sold more than 250,000 copies. That year, former Jamaican ska star Laurel Aitken, who had relocated to Britain, began licensing commercially viable material to Pama. (It has been suggested that his connection to the label began after he was arrested in Birmingham, England, for falling behind on child-support payments and needed an advance to pay the fine.) Many releases were issued on Pama's numerous subsidiary labels, which had the side effect of obscuring the full extent of the company's market impact. Pama established its commercial presence in the reggae market mainly through singles. Many of these, such as Derrick Morgan's "Moon Hop" (1970), only grazed the outer edges of the pop charts and were bundled on a variety of album compilations.

But just as Pama appeared to be gaining ground, its growth seemed to start working against it. Artists began defecting to other labels, complaining about lack of payment (if they had not received large advances) and inadequate promotion and distribution. Consequently, Pama's business connections with Jamaican producers looked increasingly unstable. By 1973, the Palmer brothers had become frustrated with double-dealing Jamaican producers who consistently licensed the same records to both Pama and Trojan. As a result, Pama switched its focus to British reggae, thereby avoiding the problems associated with long-distance business transactions. Despite the change in strategy, in 1973 the company went bankrupt and withdrew from the market. The withdrawal may have been due to uncertainty about the direction of the reggae marketplace. Harry Palmer also suggested that a growing conflict between his religious beliefs and reggae's rowdy recording artists and rude lyrics forced him to reevaluate what he was doing. The fact that some Jamaican artists either threatened him with violence or assaulted him over what they felt were underpaid royalties only hastened his retreat from the business.

Oddly, Pama releases resurfaced briefly in 1975. Jet Star Phonographics, primarily a distribution company that rose from Pama's ashes, emerged in 1977 or 1978. Under the Palmer brothers, Jet Star became a major reggae music outlet as both a label and distributor, not only in Britain but also across Europe, until it went out of business in 2009.

Established in 1967 by three Jamaican brothers, Pama Records briefly challenged Trojan for UK reggae supremacy. The British label focused on singles.

THE PARAGONS

YEARS ACTIVE: LATE 1950s-1970

The Paragons lived up to their name by being one of the jewels in the crown of Jamaican vocal groups, setting the standard by which many others would be measured. The group formed in Kingston in the late 1950s, when the founding duo known as Andy and Ronnie (Bob Andy and Garth "Tyrone" Evans) were still teenagers. Before long, they recorded a dubplate (a soft wax pre-release recording) for producer Duke Reid. After trying out several vocalists, the Paragons became a quartet with the inclusion of Junior Menz and Leroy Stamp. In 1964 Menz and Stamp left the group. Stamp was replaced as lead vocalist by John Holt, and around that same year this new lineup of the Paragons signed with Coxsone Dodd's Studio One label. Holt, who would become a successful solo artist, soon left following internal clashes. He returned shortly thereafter, but this personnel reshuffle revealed friction between the two lead singers and led directly to the departure of Andy in 1965.

Following a recording hiatus as the group reorganized, the Paragons returned as a trio that capitalized on the emergence of rocksteady, a style whose rhythm was slower than the high-speed intensity of the declining ska sound. In 1966, they left Studio One and joined Duke Reid's Treasure Isle roster. It was the pinnacle of the rocksteady era, and thanks to such Jamaican hits as "Happy Go Lucky Girl" (1967), the much-covered "Wear You to the Ball," and the even more famous "The Tide Is High"—a song that would later become a transatlantic #1 single when covered by the new wave group Blondie in 1980—both the Paragons and Treasure Isle prospered.

In late 1967, the Paragons' recording of "On the Beach" played an unintended role in the development of the "version" (a song's instrumental rhythm track)—and subsequently of dub. As legend has it, when sound-system operator Ruddy Redwood had a dubplate made of the song at Reid's Treasure Isle studio in Kingston, the engineer mistakenly excluded the vocal track. Nevertheless, the instrumental version became an enormous hit in Jamaica's dance halls, leading others to recognize the potential popularity of such recordings. The Paragons' distinctive harmonies survived the transition into reggae, as the singers seemed to grow in vocal confidence and chemistry.

After the Paragons split up in 1970, singers Garth Evans and Howard Barrett moved to the United States, where both had relatives. Blondie's success with "The Tide Is High" led to a brief reformation and an album release with 1981's The Paragons Return.

MEMBERS: **John Holt** (vocals); **Garth "Tyrone" Evans** (vocals); **Bob Andy** (vocals), left in 1965; **Junior Menz** (vocals), left in 1964; **Leroy Stamp** (vocals), left in 1964; **Howard Barrett** (vocals)

SELECT DISCOGRAPHY: The Paragons Return (Island, 1981); On the Beach: The Best of the Paragons '66–'82 (Trojan, 2007)

TOP RIGHT: Throughout the 1960s, few groups sang or dressed better than the Paragons.

RIGHT: "The Tide Is High" became a transatlantic smash in 1980, when it was covered by Blondie.

Treasure Isle RECORDS

ON THE BEACH
with the PARAGONS

A Treasure Isle Production

TILP 100/1A

1. ON THE BEACH
2. ISLAND IN THE SUN
3. WHEN THE LIGHTS ARE LOW
4. THE TIDE IS HIGH
5. SO MUCH PAIN

ALL RIGHTS OF THE MANUFACTURER AND OF THE OWNER OF THE RECORDED WORK RESERVED UNAUTHORISED PUBLIC PERFORMANCE BROADCASTING AND COPYING OF THIS RECORD PROHIBITED

LEE "SCRATCH" PERRY

YEARS ACTIVE: 1960s–PRESENT

Lee "Scratch" Perry is arguably the most eccentric figure in reggae history. Over the years, his erratic behavior has been offset by an artistic instinct that has added fresh dimensions to the sound of reggae—especially dub. His career output, which peaked between the late 1960s and the late 1970s, exceeds sixty albums and reaches almost four hundred singles—as both a solo act and a producer. Many songs have yet to appear on albums.

Perry was born Rainford Hugh Perry in 1936 in the northwestern Jamaican parish of Hanover. In his twenties, he operated a bulldozer on a construction site, an experience that made him acutely aware of the power of sound. Perry's introduction to the music business began with producer Duke Reid, who, according to Perry, would not let

him record but stole some of his lyrics and gave them to another artist, singer Stranger Cole, offering Perry neither credit nor financial compensation. Perry wasn't entirely new to entertainment, having been a champion of many informal dance competitions in the 1950s, when he excelled at the "yank," a trend that supposedly often resulted in other dancers dislocating hips. The song that gave Perry the first of his widely known nicknames was "Chicken Scratch," which, according to some sources, was never actually released on vinyl and achieved its popularity solely as a "dubplate" (a pre-release soft-wax acetate disc) around 1961. We can only speculate about what type of career Perry might have had as a solo artist if his later sonic experimentations as a producer-engineer had not taken prominence. While he often delivered his vocals with conviction, his voice was fairly thin and shaky. It lacked the texture of such conventional lead vocalists as former Paragons singer John Holt, whose R&B-influenced delivery had far greater commercial appeal. In any event, Perry leaned toward instrumental pieces that led him down a path toward sonic innovation.

Perry later established a connection with Studio One producer Coxsone Dodd, working first as a record "selector" for Dodd's Downbeat sound system and later taking on a variety of creative roles at the Studio One label. Principally, Perry functioned at Studio One as an A&R (Artists and Repertoire) man, songwriter, and producer, though he often did not receive credit for his work. Perry connected Dodd with a string of artists who would become central to the label's sound and therefore to Jamaican popular music. Perry also recorded singles as a solo artist, sometimes under the name King Perry. The virtually X-rated singles "Rub & Squeeze" and "Doctor Dick," both released in 1966, extended Perry's lewd calypso-style lyrics into

ABOVE: Lee Perry, reggae's mad genius, stands proud at his legendary Black Ark studio, 1975.

RIGHT: The cover of this 1975 dub curio contains a clue to Perry's nickname, "The Upsetter."

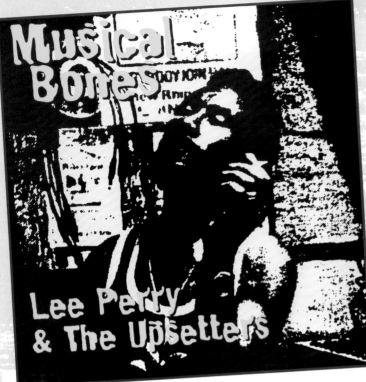

Musical Bones

Lee Perry & The Upsetters

the realm of Jamaican popular music. At the time, few would have guessed that Perry had been a married family man briefly in the late 1950s, seemingly headed for a sedate and unspectacular existence. Perry's disillusionment with this failed relationship left him with a cynical view of women and perhaps of life in general, which could help to explain the erratic behavior he displayed throughout his career.

Having received little money up front and no royalties at all from Coxsone Dodd, as was typical of the island's industry practices of the era, Perry left the Studio One camp sometime between 1966 and 1968 to work with several other producers, including Prince Buster and Joe Gibbs. In 1968, he worked for a time as an independent producer at West Indies Records Limited (WIRL), but according to ace Jamaican producer Bunny Lee, Perry was fired for failing to generate hits. One of Perry's better-known records from this WIRL phase was

"Set Them Free" (1969, recorded as Lee Perry & the Defenders), a call for understanding on behalf of Jamaica's misbehaving "rude boys," ghetto youths whose response to economic deprivation was violence and intimidation. The single was a response to Prince Buster's fictitious Judge Dread, a character who chastised the rude boys in song, regularly handing down four-hundred-year prison sentences.

Perry occasionally recorded incisive attacks against his former employers, among them Prince Buster, Coxsone Dodd, Joe Gibbs, and Bunny Lee. The 1968 single "I Am the Upsetter," which prompted yet another of Perry's enduring nicknames, was thought to have been aimed squarely at Dodd, whose lopsided business dealings aggravated and alienated many of the artists and

producers he worked with. Perry's first self-produced hit, 1968's "People Funny Boy," dealt specifically with Gibbs—though it might have described any number of unsatisfactory relationships in which his artistic contributions were grossly and callously undervalued. Perry had worked with Gibbs as a producer and arranger until financial disputes—then a hallmark of the Jamaican industry—led to his departure. "People Funny Boy" sold more than thirty thousand copies, according to one estimate. That Perry invested so much energy in attacking the business tactics of others is ironic considering that he himself would later allegedly engage in questionable dealings while working with the Wailers, the band featuring future reggae superstars Bob Marley, Peter Tosh, and Bunny Wailer. Such dealings occurred because the ability to license material to multiple foreign labels was an issue of financial necessity.

In 1969, prior to his conflicts with the Wailers, Perry scored an international hit with his best-known studio band the Upsetters, formerly known as the Hippy Boys, proving that his eccentricity also had widespread commercial value. The unit's claim to fame, the instrumental hit single "Return of Django," was inspired by the era's spaghetti westerns, gun-laden Italian outlaw films that screened

often enough in Jamaica to become part of the culture. "Return of Django" broke into the British pop charts, peaking at #5 in late 1969 on Perry's own Upsetter Records label, an imprint distributed by Trojan Records, which had begun charting reggae records on a regular basis. The song's success was partially due to its adoption by British skinheads, shaven-head, white, working-class youths who rejected mainstream lifestyles. During this time, Perry also produced some of the earliest recordings to feature U-Roy, the pioneering DJ who would soon carve out his own space in Jamaican music lore.

It was under Perry's direction that the Wailers' vocalists first recorded with their future drum-and-bass rhythm section, the brothers Aston and Carlton Barrett.(The Barretts had been in the early Upsetters lineup but became full-time members of the Wailers by the time Perry opened his Black Ark studio in 1973; they did not play on later recordings credited to the Upsetters.) The 1970 track "Duppy Conqueror" was one of the earliest hit collaborations between Perry and the Wailers. The multiple sessions, tracked at Studio One, produced key songs in the Wailers' future live and recorded repertoire, including "Sun Is Shining," "Small Axe," and "Kaya," all recorded between 1970 and 1971. In fact, the sessions resulted in several albums' worth of unauthorized material released in Britain by Trojan Records, including *Soul Rebels* (1970), *Soul Revolution* (1971), and *African Herbsman* (1974). This is just one example of the complex relationship between Perry and the Wailers; the producer frequently did not pay the group money it was owed.

Perry's first album to include attempts at dub was *Cloak & Dagger*, issued in either 1972, 1973, or 1974, depending on the source. *Cloak & Dagger* featured

Lee Perry dances to his own beat at Black Ark, 1978. By 1983, the erratic producer would burn his studio to the ground.

"I expect artists to do exactly as I say. I teach them everything. How to play, how to move, everything. I am a dictator!"

—LEE PERRY, on his style as a producer

previously used rhythm tracks he had produced with his session band, the Upsetters. To complicate matters, there were different versions of the full-stereo LP for the British and Jamaican markets. Perry may have referenced the undead on the cover, appearing in vampire-like garb, but through his selective mixing process he infused a great deal of life into the recordings. Although *Cloak & Dagger* was not a full-fledged dub release, it was one of the first steps in that direction for reggae. It may well have been too innovative for its time, since the dub tracks from the original Jamaican release were deleted from the UK version, which found distribution through EMI Records and was a commercial failure. Perry's next album, *Rhythm Shower* (1973), was released solely in Jamaica and remains a rare item.

Perry soon joined the ranks of producers like Bunny Lee, employing the four-track studio and sonic skills of engineer King Tubby for dub remixing. Perry's *Blackboard Jungle Dub* (1973) was one such collaboration. (Despite their collaborative relationship, Tubby and Perry approached dub quite differently, and in later years, their individual recordings grew increasingly distinct.) A rare reggae concept album initially pressed in limited numbers, it eventually became one of the classic early dub LPs. Perry reportedly sold copies in England direct to consumers for the princely sum of twenty pounds each. Even though the record had no British mainstream chart profile, it presented Perry with the kind of profit margin enjoyed by few artists in any genre.

Prior to 1973, Perry did not yet have his own studio. He recorded at Randy's studio and at Dynamic Sounds in Kingston before establishing the Black Ark studio, which he set up at the back of his house in the middle-class Washington Gardens area of Kingston late that year. One major catalyst for Perry founding his own studio was his alarm and disgust at the prospect of Randy's upgrading its gear and replacing its existing console with a new twenty-four-track unit. To Perry, this meant that the sound he had created there would be completely altered. Having his own studio empowered him to shape his own creative destiny. According to some accounts, Perry's four-track setup was custom built by Tubby, who was an electronics wizard as well as an excellent engineer. Other equipment was installed by Errol "E.T." Thompson, a Jamaican recording engineer who remains underrated despite the enormous volume of influential work he produced at Randy's.

Black Ark also became a visual canvas for Perry's ideas. The studio's walls were plastered with seemingly unrelated photos and handwritten symbols and statements—ephemera that fueled speculation about Perry's mental state. More than just a studio, it became a Lee Perry audio-visual museum, though as former Island Records head Chris Blackwell recalls, the studio was much more organized and free from graffiti in its early days. Still, Perry's business sense remained intact, and he sold many tracks in exclusive dubplate form to top-ranking London sound systems. He also bartered records for clothes and other supplies.

In addition to acquiring his own studio, Perry's 1976 licensing deal with Island helped him reach wider audiences with his music. By the mid-1970s, Island had positioned itself at the vanguard of reggae. Prior to this, Perry was almost solely responsible for the production, recording, pressing, distribution, and sale of his studio's product. Perry's influential 1976 album *Super Ape* was one of the first releases to benefit from the Island production and distribution deal. While it found a global audience thanks to Island, other Black Ark releases showcasing Perry's eccentricity lingered in relative obscurity.

The Island alliance also enabled Perry to upgrade his studio equipment and create more experimental and multilayered recordings. But in some instances, his experimentation did not always suitably enhance his mixes. Case in point: "Know Love," a 12-inch single released in 1977 by the Twin Roots, singing siblings Keith and Kenneth Thompson. Clocking in at over nine minutes, the midtempo Perry-produced roots groove is a song of two sharply contrasting sonic halves. The standard vocal segment is crudely spliced into the dub version after about three and a half minutes, and at times, the dense distortion of the remixed recording undermines its conceptual brilliance. The sonic inconsistency reflects much of what appears to have been going on in Perry's life, foreshadowing his crucial loss of focus.

Even so, he remained actively engaged in successfully producing other acts. Jamaican singer Junior Murvin's "Police & Thieves," one of Perry's more memorable productions in this era, reached #23 on the British pop charts in 1976, while "Hurt So Good" by Brtish reggae singer Susan Cadogan breached the top five a year earlier, selling more than 250,000 copies. He had other reggae-market hits with such vocalists as

Junior Byles—who released "Place Called Africa" in 1972 and "Curly Locks" in 1973—and more notably Max Romeo, whose *War Ina Babylon* album was released by Island in 1976. But it's likely that Perry was more readily recognized as a producer among reggae fans than in the pop mainstream— at least before he produced material on the self-titled debut album by British punk rockers the Clash in 1977. That same year, he teamed up with Bob Marley at Island Studios in London to record the single "Punky Reggae Party," a symbolic statement of unity aligning the antiestablishment ideals of British punk rockers and dreads. Also in 1977, Perry reinforced his pop production credentials on material performed by the Upsetters for *Wide Prairie*, an album by Paul McCartney's then-wife, Linda. (The record was not issued until 1998, following her death.)

Another 1977 project produced by Perry, the Congos' *Heart of the Congos* LP featuring singer Cedric Myton, came to be recognized as a reggae classic, but its availability was severely limited, since Island passed on the option to release it, along with three other Perry projects. This further limited Perry's ability to pierce the mainstream market and effectively ended his relationship with Island.

Perry's successes in breaking sonic boundaries while simultaneously receiving commercial recognition diminished as the Black Ark sound became increasingly impenetrable and obscure. The inaccessibility of his music may also have reflected his psychological battles. Despite his deals with Island, the label marginalized his work, and many of

Thanks to Lee Perry's distribution deal with Island Records, this 1976 album found a worldwide audience.

his solo recordings—music in which he was financially and creatively invested— went unreleased internationally. The mid-decade collapse of Trojan Records, the label through which he had funneled much of his material, did not help his situation. There were undoubtedly other factors contributing to his turbulent behavior, and his productivity declined in the late 1970s as Black Ark gradually disintegrated.

By early 1983, the studio had been consumed by a fire set by Perry himself, marking an end to one of Jamaica's original temples of dub. Some have speculated that Perry developed a madman persona to deflect the attention of criminal characters in the rising sociopolitical heat of Jamaica, while others insist there were genuine signs of psychic implosion—a real-life equivalent of his often dramatic dub creations. Perry asserts that his reasons for burning down Black Ark related to the intoxicants he used during the making of his dubs and recordings. He cites cigarettes, meat, alcohol (specifically rum), and ganja as the key chemical contributors, claiming that when he changed his consciousness by giving up those substances, he could

no longer identify with the space in which the music had been made. Instead, he reverted to what he describes as "simple clean music"—sounds unpolluted by what he perceived as negative stimulants impacting the mind and body. Although this renunciation of vice suggested a new mental clarity, Perry's responses in interviews would remain thoroughly enigmatic and cryptic, defying anyone to decode their real meaning.

His work since the end of the Black Ark era has been inconsistent, both in terms of quality and direction, perhaps mirroring his feelings of restlessness and dislocation following his departure from Jamaica. After leaving the island for an extended time in 1984, he shuttled between London and New York before settling down to family life in Switzerland around 1989, far removed from the environment that gave rise to his best work in the 1970s.

SELECT DISCOGRAPHY: *Cloak & Dagger* (Rhino, 1973)*; Blackboard Jungle Dub* (Upsetter, 1973)*; Double Seven* (Trojan, 1974); *Kung Fu Meets the Dragon* (DIP, 1975)*; Super Ape* (Island, 1976)*; Lee Perry: I Am the Upsetter* (Trojan, 2005)

THE PiONEERS
YEARS ACTIVE: 1962-1970s

The Pioneers were originally a vocal trio formed in 1962 in the Trench Town section of Kingston, Jamaica, by Winston Hewitt and brothers Sidney "Luddy" and Derrick "Joe" Crooks. The group's first single was released on producer Ken Lack's Caltone Records label, and their first single, "Good Nannie" (1966), was independently financed following initial rejection from both of Jamaica's top record producers of that era, Coxsone Dodd and Duke Reid. By this time, the Pioneers had already shown up on the 1965 single "Sometime," released in England on Island Records as the B-side of pianist Theo Beckford's "Trench Town People." At this stage, Island was mostly licensing its British releases from Jamaican producers, having only begun UK operations in 1962. After the early departures of Hewitt (who moved to Canada and was temporarily replaced by Glen Adams) and Derrick Crooks, the sole remaining member, Luddy Crooks, connected with producer Joe Gibbs and recorded "Give Me Little Loving" (1968) at the WIRL (West Indies Records Limited) studio. The song featured vocals from Jackie Robinson, a young aspiring singer who provided harmonies on the record; eventually, Robinson became the Pioneers' lead vocalist.

Their work at Gibbs's studio and label later came under the direction of the eccentric producer and songwriter Lee Perry, who was still a long way from establishing himself as an independent creative force. He oversaw the recording of "Jackpot" (1968), which featured a trumpet intro later used by the group on one of their most famous singles, "Long Shot Kick De Bucket" (1969).

The song was adapted from the group's "Long Shot," a less polished 1968 recording for Joe Gibbs. "Long Shot Kick De Bucket" recounted an actual recent event in which a horse died during a race in Jamaica. This single peaked at #21 on the British charts after the Pioneers moved to producer Leslie Kong's label, Beverley's Records, though their tracks made with Kong were licensed for British release to the Trojan Records label. "Long Shot Kick De Bucket" reentered the British singles chart after re-release in 1980, perhaps due to the commercially successful revival of ska and vintage reggae by new acts like the Specials on the British 2 Tone label, though it reached only #42. Although Kong was credited as producer, Luddy Crooks actually supervised the recording. He and Robinson later hired a third singer, George Agard—brother of singer Desmond Dekker—but Kong was not in favor of the move.

The Pioneers' highest-charting single came in 1971 with "Let Your Yeah Be Yeah," written by top Jamaican singer-songwriter Jimmy Cliff, which reached #5 on the British charts. The Pioneers went on to score one more British hit, "Give and Take," released in 1972. Having achieved some success, the band moved to Britain after touring with Lee Perry's session band, the Upsetters, in 1969, but their pop focus and Trojan's crossover objectives did not help them to immediately reach the charts again. As the Pioneers sought to redefine themselves, Robinson was quoted in Britain's *Melody Maker* newspaper in 1971 as saying, "We're trying to get away from being tagged a reggae group." They continued to stage international tours, traveling as far as Egypt and Thailand, and in 1975 they signed to the British branch of Philips Records and began releasing material on the subsidiary Mercury label. *Feel the Rhythm* (1976) contained songs written and produced entirely by Eddy Grant, and was clearly crafted to capitalize on the disco trend. Grant had written many hits for the British multiracial band Equals in the late 1960s, and he'd also produced one of their biggest hits, "Black Skin Blue Eyed Boys" (1970), their only chart success in the 1970s. Grant had already begun a solo career that included producing his own records by the time he started working with the Pioneers. Their two Mercury albums yielded no hits, and in subsequent years, they recorded sporadically for the resurrected version of Trojan Records (restarted by Saga Records), which first folded in 1975.

In the 1990s, Luddy Crooks worked as an arranger at Gibbs's studio in Jamaica, and according to one biographer he has since relocated to Brazil. Meanwhile, another incarnation of the Pioneers, including Crooks, has been making successful festival appearances in Brazil. Robinson has enjoyed acting success, both on television and in film, where he appeared in *Superman III* (1983) and *IV* (1987), as well as *Out of Africa* (1985). After years of occasionally participating in Pioneers comeback tours, Robinson, who now lives in South Florida, finally left the group by 2010. In 2011, he released *Have a Little Faith*, an album featuring reggae covers of soul songs.

MEMBERS: Sidney "Luddy" Crooks (vocals); **Derrick "Joe" Crooks** (vocals); **Winston Hewitt** (vocals); **Jackie Robinson** (vocals); **George Agard** (vocals)

SELECT DISCOGRAPHY: *Feel the Rhythm* (Mercury, 1976); *Give and Take: The Best of the Pioneers* (Trojan, 2009)

LIQUIDATOR - HARRY J. ALLSTARS
LONG SHOT KICK DE BUCKET - THE PIONEERS

THE ORIGINAL RECORDINGS

TROJAN

LEFT: "Long Shot Kick de Bucket," a hit in 1969, was a Pioneers classic that reentered the UK charts in 1980, during the ska revival.

OPPOSITE: In the 1970s, the group dabbled in disco and its dubious fashions.

Pablo, and Steel Pulse, Pitterson has been deeply involved in making reggae history. Still, his name might be familiar only to fans who read credits and liner notes. Pitterson entered the studio scene around 1970. His most famous clients were Bob Marley & the Wailers, for whom he recorded not just *Exodus* but also *Kaya*, released in 1978. By that time, he had already worked on former Wailers singer Bunny Wailer's 1976 album *Blackheart Man*, playing bass on that record in addition to performing his recording and mixing duties. A year later, Pitterson worked as a guitarist with another former Wailer, Peter Tosh, contributing to *Equal Rights* (1977) and later *Bush Doctor* (1978). Much of his Jamaican work was done at Dynamic Sounds in Kingston, but he also tracked his artists at several of the island's other studios, including Aquarius and Harry J, both also in Kingston. Partly because he had been associated with Island Records through their release of the Bunny Wailer album he engineered, he was able to apply his skills in England and gain a level of experience that most Jamaican engineers did not have.

Apart from his Marley connection, Pitterson is best known for laying the foundations for the sound and career of the UK-based Steel Pulse. He produced their first two albums, *Handsworth Revolution* (1978) and *Tribute to the Martyrs* (1979), on Island; both reached the British pop album charts. He was unavailable when Steel Pulse recorded their third album, *Caught You/Reggae Fever* (1980), and

KARL PITTERSON

YEARS ACTIVE: 1970s–PRESENT

Jamaican-born Karl Pitterson engineered what *Time* magazine hailed in 1999 as the "album of the century": Bob Marley & the Wailers' *Exodus* (1977). That accolade alone makes him one of the key record engineers of the roots reggae era, but as both a producer and engineer Pitterson has contributed to a long list of major recordings by other reggae (and pop) artists, as well as others by Marley. Unlike most engineers whose talents graced that era's music, he is also an accomplished musician who often played on the albums he recorded and mixed.

Through his work with such artists as the Abyssinians, Aswad, Big Youth, Burning Spear, the Mighty Diamonds, Augustus

TOP LEFT: Recording engineer Karl Pitterson, who worked with the biggest names in reggae.

LEFT: Despite Pitterson's sonic contributions, he was often not credited by name on records.

Produced by
G Patterson
L Smith

Black & White

45 r.p.m.

NOT RESPONSIBLE
CARLTON & LEROY

COPYING OF THIS RECORDING IS STRICTLY PROHIBITED

his absence was so apparent that Steel Pulse reunited with him for *True Democracy* (1982), arguably their most definitive album. Group leader David Hinds credits Karl Pitterson's skills and special chemistry with Steel Pulse for the quality of that record, as well as for the cohesion of their first two efforts. The veteran Jamaican hit singer Dennis Brown also had high praise for Pitterson's production skills and musicianship, describing him as a "maestro" who personifies the essence of a true producer. While Pitterson is primarily known for his studio work, he has also showcased his talents in the live setting. In 1978, he engineered the One Love Peace Concert, a multiartist initiative headlined by Bob Marley & the Wailers to end Jamaica's rampant political violence.

By working with a wide range of reggae artists, Pitterson appeared on many critically acclaimed records that were not major sellers. He played bass on some of the tracks on *Termination Dub:(1973–79)*, a compilation of songs credited to singer Glen Brown and dub remix engineer King Tubby, released on the Blood & Fire reissue label in 1996. Pitterson was also one of the engineers on former Skatalites trombonist Rico Rodriguez's *Man from Wareika* in 1977.

By 1987, Pitterson had amassed one of reggae's most extensive résumés and even released a single, "Been a So Long," under his own name on the Tuff Gong Records label. He moved to South Florida in 1988 and has run the thriving South End Studio business there, despite a brief interruption following Hurricane Andrew in 1992.

SONIA POTTINGER
YEARS ACTIVE: 1960s–MID-1980s

Jamaica's first female record producer, Sonia Pottinger, born in 1931 in the parish of St. Thomas, combined her business capabilities with a love of music and an ability to get the best out of the musicians who recorded for her in the 1960s and 1970s. She married chartered accountant Linden Pottinger, and together, they ran the Tip Top record store and distribution operation on Orange Street in Kingston.

Around 1961, before Coxsone Dodd opened Studio One, Linden Pottinger began recording artists in the family's Kingston house, effectively becoming the first black owner of a studio in Jamaica. Singer Derrick Harriott and the vocal group the Maytals were among the early artists to record for such custom Pottinger imprints as Gaydisc. After releasing many records, Linden Pottinger sold his equipment to the Jamaican producer Duke Reid in 1964 and left the business. After Sonia and Linden separated in 1965, Sonia followed her instincts

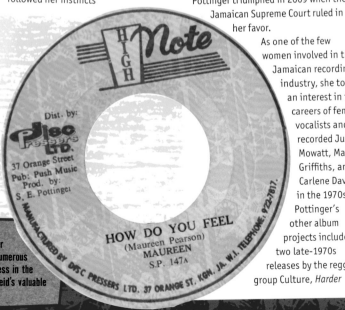

and became a producer herself. The first record she released, "Every Night" by Joe White & Chuck, became a hit in 1965 and was followed by a string of successful mid-1960s rocksteady singles, including the Melodians' "Swing and Dine" and the Gaylads' "It's Hard to Confess," both released in 1968. As Pottinger's production business flourished, her list of Jamaican label imprints grew to include High Note, Tip Top, Gay Feet, Excel, Pep, and Rainbow, though the different names did not represent significant differences in musical styles.

Pottinger acquired the commercially valuable Treasure Isle label catalog from Duke Reid in 1974, shortly before he died of cancer. A long-term legal dispute arose over her ownership of and rights to the Treasure Isle catalog. The defendants included rivals Coxsone Dodd and Bunny Lee, as well as Reid's son Anthony, but Pottinger triumphed in 2009 when the Jamaican Supreme Court ruled in her favor.

As one of the few women involved in the Jamaican recording industry, she took an interest in the careers of female vocalists and recorded Judy Mowatt, Marcia Griffiths, and Carlene Davis in the 1970s. Pottinger's other album projects include two late-1970s releases by the reggae group Culture, *Harder*

Than the Rest (1978) and *Cumbolo* (1979), which were licensed to Virgin Records following the group's falling out with producer Joe Gibbs. By 1985, as dancehall dominated the reggae scene, Pottinger had left the business and turned her attention to other activities, including a ceramics business. Like many Jamaican producers of her time, she was arguably more of a financial facilitator with some musical sensibility than she was a hands-on participant in crafting material.

While Pottinger's entrepreneurial longevity and efforts to nurture artists are worthy of recognition, she was still very much a product of the ruthless record business in which she operated. Following typical Jamaican music business practice in the 1960s and 1970s, Pottinger was frequently listed on records as the author of works she did not actually compose. Despite the questionable business ethics of that time period, her work in the Jamaican record industry was rewarded in 2004, when she received the country's Order of Distinction. After suffering from Alzheimer's disease, Pottinger died on November 3, 2010, at the age of seventy-nine.

Groundbreaking female producer and entrepreneur Sonia Pottinger scored her first hit in 1965. She went on to run numerous imprints, and before leaving the business in the 1980s, she assumed control of Duke Reid's valuable Treasure Isle catalog.

WOMEN IN REGGAE

To date, no solo female artist has won a Grammy Award in a reggae category, and only three—Judy Mowatt (1986), Rita Marley (1992), and Sister Carol (1997)—have been nominated. These are merely statistics, but they speak volumes about how males have historically dominated reggae. With a few notable exceptions, women in reggae have enjoyed relatively limited commercial visibility and career self-determination. At the same time, they have struggled with the kind of industry-wide exploitation that has also plagued their male counterparts. Few women have been able to liberate themselves from supporting singing roles and become artists recognized in their own right. Many have also encountered sexual harassment on the path toward success.

One of the first locally recorded solo singles by a Jamaican female artist was Marguerita Mahfood's "Woman a Come," released in 1964 on Duke Reid's Treasure Isle label. With its choppy rhythmic accents and the singer's idiosyncratic, frequently off-pitch delivery, it ranks as one of the oddest records of the ska era. Tragically, Mahfood's common-law husband, legendary Skatalites trombonist Don Drummond, murdered her on New Year's Day in 1965.

Keith and Enid (Keith Stewart and Enid Cumberland) were among the earliest male-female Jamaican singing duos to make a record. They scored a local hit with "Worried Over You" (1960) and continued releasing singles until the mid-1960s. Their 1962 album, *Keith and Enid sing* [sic], was one of

the first albums pressed by Island Records in Britain as the label began its journey from obscurity to become a major force in reggae in the 1970s. Despite this success, Enid Cumberland suffered a fate typical of female performers of the time. After experiencing difficulties scoring hits and problems getting paid for her recordings, she disappeared from the scene, leaving behind a sparse catalog of recordings.

In the days of ska, a teenage Millicent "Patsy" Todd got her first break in the duo Derrick & Patsy (sometimes listed as Derrick Morgan & Patsy), recording "Feel So Fine" (1961) and a host of other singles that were licensed to the Blue Beat Records label in Britain. Although she is listed as a cowriter on two of the songs, Patsy recalls having no say in the recording sessions, which were produced by Reid. She claims she was given instructions to follow, and in one account, she describes the members of the backing band, the Skatalites, as being egotistical, rude, and disrespectful. Perhaps the most successful Derrick & Patsy collaboration was "Housewife's Choice" (1962), which had been licensed to Island for UK release. Derrick Morgan's 1963 tour of England with singer-producer Prince Buster created a rift between Derrick & Patsy that was never healed. During Morgan's absence from Jamaica, which left Todd unexpectedly without a vocal partner, she began recording duets with singer Stranger Cole, scoring quick Jamaican success with "When I Call Your Name" (1963). On returning to the island, Morgan viewed Patsy's recording alliance with Cole as a treacherous act, and the resulting tension meant the end of Derrick & Patsy as a team. Although records bearing the duo's name continued to be

released through at least 1968, they had ceased working together on a consistent basis well before that.

Besides working with Stranger Cole, Patsy recorded in other duos, including Patsy and Desmond (Dekker, in 1963 before his late-1960s success in Britain), and she occasionally cut solo tracks during the rocksteady era (such as "A Man is Two-Faced," a 1968 B-side with session band Lynn Taitt and the Jets). Despite hit records, years of hard work, and mentoring from the island's lone female producer of the era, Sonia Pottinger, Patsy struggled financially. She became understandably disillusioned with the exploitative Jamaican music business, migrated to America in 1968, and abandoned the entertainment world for years. She returned with a one-off performance at a nostalgia concert in 2002 in Toronto, Canada, and in 2011 she sang at the Tribute to the Greats awards show in Jamaica. After the latter performance, she spoke to the press and lamented that she had nothing to show for her career despite making (by her estimate) over one hundred recordings.

OPPOSITE: Sister Carol, one of only three female artists to have earned a Grammy nomination in a reggae category.

ABOVE: This 2005 compilation features such artists as Hortense Ellis, a top female vocalist in the rocksteady era.

RIGHT: Jamaican teenagers Althea & Donna scored their first and only UK hit with 1977's "Uptown Top Ranking," a #1 smash that paved the way for subsequent female DJs.

Hortense Ellis, the sister of vocalist Alton Ellis, debuted as a singer at a Kingston talent contest in 1959. By 1962, she had toured the Caribbean with top Jamaican band Byron Lee & the Dragonaires, and she was considered one of Jamaica's best female vocalists in the 1960s. She began recording duets with her brother as early as 1963, and then ricocheted between producers, enjoying one of her more productive spells at Coxsone Dodd's Studio One label in Kingston. Like her brother, she peaked during the rocksteady era, and afterward she immigrated briefly to Canada in the early 1970s before returning to Jamaica. By 1976, she had married, given birth to five children, and divorced, and these major life events disrupted her career. Her first solo album, the appropriately titled *Jamaica's First Lady of Song*, did not appear until 1977. Prior to that release, she scored what some consider her most popular Jamaican hit single with "Unexpected Places" (1976), produced by Gussie Clarke in the less rootsy and more commercial lovers rock style. She moved to Miami in the 1980s, returning to Jamaica at the end of the decade. She was diagnosed with throat cancer in the 1990s, and died from the disease in 2000 at the age of fifty-nine.

Millie Small was the first Jamaican female singer to achieve a truly international profile, though she, too, emerged from a duo, Roy & Millie, with vocalist Roy Panton. Having recognized her talent, Island Records founder Chris Blackwell brought her to England to record the 1964 pop-ska single "My Boy Lollipop." It went on to sell more than six million copies around the globe and put both Small and Jamaica on the map, albeit temporarily. Ska soon transitioned into the slower rhythm of rocksteady, and she never had another major hit. The pair of Jackie & Millie albums she recorded with Jamaican songwriter Jackie Edwards in 1967 did not halt her career decline, and she eventually vanished into oblivion. In 2011, however, the Jamaican government recognized her

Althea Forrest and Donna Reid, teenage "toasters," in the late 1970s.

contributions to the island's music and presented her with the Order of Distinction.

Singer Phyllis Dillon's story is as sad as any female singer's in the early days of Jamaican popular music. Between 1967 and 1972, she recorded for Reid's Treasure Isle label and was one of the few Jamaican artists to work with only one producer. She, too, became frustrated with the endless exploitation that, despite her hits—including "Don't Stay Away" and "Perfidia" in 1967—left her with little money. Oddly enough, the most dramatic events in her career unfolded after she had moved to America and decided to leave the business

permanently. After being coaxed out of retirement in 1991 and agreeing to perform in Jamaica at a rocksteady nostalgia show, she embarked on a decade-long string of gigs to fund her retirement in her homeland. However, her comeback turned sour when, after returning to Jamaica to live in a newly built house, she was allegedly threatened with extortion and acts of violence by what a local newspaper described only as "unscrupulous persons" who assumed Dillon was wealthy. Bitterly disillusioned, she fled the island, put the house up for sale, and returned to America. She died of cancer in April 2004, and according to newspaper reports, her family insisted that she would not be buried in Jamaica. During the rocksteady period of the mid-1960s, there were other singles-oriented female artists on the scene, but like Dillon, such artists as Cynthia Richards and Joya Landis were unable to make their marks on the subsequent reggae soundscape.

Joyce Bond was hardly known in Jamaica, but her releases on Pama Records, Island Records, and Trojan Records between 1966 and 1971 earned her the attention of the reggae market in Britain, where she was based. The 1967 *Soul and Ska* album she recorded for Island featured an unusual red-bordered cover with a black-and-white picture of Bond flashing two drawn pistols. The image was no doubt meant to evoke her fictional movie namesake, James Bond. While few would describe her as particularly influential, she was nevertheless one of the female artists to maintain a presence on record during and after the transition from ska to rocksteady and into reggae.

Sharply contrasting the stereotypical role of women in reggae as singers, Sonia Pottinger blazed a new trail on the production and administration side of the business between 1965 and 1985. Her

success on the multiple labels she owned attracted the interest of both vocal groups and solo acts, and perhaps not surprisingly, she undertook active roles in assisting prominent female vocalists with their careers. She effectively outlasted many of her male peers, opting out of the business only when dancehall tightened its market grip, signaling an end to the roots era in which her business had flourished.

Major success and visibility for women in reggae in the 1970s came with the I-Threes, the vocal trio comprising Judy Mowatt, Marcia Griffiths, and Bob Marley's wife, Rita. As members of the Bob Marley & the Wailers entourage, both onstage and on record, they were well known to audiences around the world. Singing and dancing in their signature African-style clothing, they became key members of reggae's biggest act. Performing as Rastas at a time when the world was just coming to terms with the religion, the I-Threes represented the front line of the push for gender equality, staking a place for women in reggae's notoriously patriarchal realm. From 1975 to Bob Marley's death in 1981, they were effectively reggae's principal female presence, and all three singers released solo records during this time. They had all paid their dues in the studios of Kingston and, before joining forces, experienced the frustration of poor reward for persistent work.

Mowatt began releasing solo albums soon after she joined the group, and she received her first Grammy nomination in 1986 for the previous year's *Working Wonders* album. Speaking in 1992 about the situation then facing female reggae artists, Mowatt stressed that it was very difficult for them to succeed, noting that male artists still received priority from record companies, and better promotion. She also said that raising a family had altered her career momentum, and that like many female reggae artists, she had made childrearing a priority in her life.

Griffiths's initial taste of international success came as a member of Bob & Marcia, with singer and songwriter Bob Andy. The duo hit the British charts with "Young, Gifted and Black" (1970) and "Pied Piper" (1971), leading to tours and television appearances before that phase of their collaboration had run its commercial course. In a 1988 interview, she recognized her own influence on a new generation of emerging female reggae artists.

Following Bob Marley's death, Rita Marley took charge of her husband's Tuff Gong Studios and record label, shifting her focus from making music to working behind the scenes. She was not finished

As both a solo artist and member of the I-Threes, Rita Marley has staked a place for women in reggae.

yield the first Grammy Award for best reggae recording in 1985 for their 1983 album, *Anthem*. The group's lone female member, the US-born Sandra "Puma" Jones, actively sang harmonies and was not merely a background vocalist. The group's digital instrumentation gave international reggae a much more penetrating sonic edge, and Puma became one of the first Rasta women of the 1980s to play in a self-contained reggae band. Tragically, she died of cancer in 1990.

Beyond the heyday of roots reggae from the 1970s through to the early 1980s, few female reggae artists have achieved international chart success. Female acts have also encountered legal problems, as demonstrated by the case of singer Dawn Penn's "You Don't Love Me (No No No)," which reached #3 on the British charts in 1994. The song's success was overshadowed by copyright infringement accusations. Her recording co-opted melodies, lyrical ideas, and structure from songs by early rock 'n' roll artist Bo Diddley (1955's "She's Fine, She's Mine") and bluesman Willie Cobb (1961's "You Don't Love Me").

In the 1990s, reggae singer Diana King joined the ranks of internationally successful reggae women with the 1995 hit "Shy Guy," which reached #2 in Britain and #13 in America, although her career stalled after 1997. Among female dancehall acts of the 1990s, Jamaican singer Patra enjoyed the greatest international commercial success, scoring a gold album in America on Epic Records with *Queen of the Pack* (1994). While Patra attracted attention with her tales of female sexual power and autonomy, the narratives of Jamaican DJ Lady Saw proved far more controversial. Echoing the lyrical "slackness" (raunchy lyrics) of her male counterparts, Lady Saw achieved Jamaican hits with lewd

songs that challenged patriarchal dominance in and out of the bedroom. She soon developed a kind of creative schizophrenia, and her songs swung like a pendulum between sex and religious supplication. Her guest appearance on American pop-rock act No Doubt's 2002 single "Underneath It All," made her the first female dancehall DJ to win a Grammy. (Interestingly, it came in the category of best pop performance by a duo or group.) The song, produced by reggae studio session veterans Sly & Robbie, reached #3 on the US singles chart and brought her to the attention of audiences that might otherwise be out of reach.

In the twenty-first century, the question of whether women in reggae have truly made sufficient progress remains open to debate. None have rivaled the international longevity of the I-Threes, and few have carried comparable philosophical and spiritual presence in their music though singers Queen Ifrica and Etana offer future hope.

performing, however, and *We Must Carry On* garnered a Grammy nomination in 1992.

During the years of Bob Marley's ascent to superstardom, other female reggae performers, the crooning singers associated with the Britain-based lovers rock style, also rose to prominence. Unlike the I-Threes, they sang songs whose subject matter was usually far removed from the sociopolitical consciousness of roots reggae. While women were prominent during the lovers rock era, male producers and musicians dominated the scene. According to British lovers rock singers Carroll Thompson and Janet Kay, female artists were discouraged from voicing opinions about any aspect of the recording process. The teenage Jamaican schoolgirl duo Althea & Donna (Althea Forrest and Donna Reid) became sensations with the release of 1977's "Uptown Top Ranking," one of the earliest successful instances of female DJ "toasting," or rapping, on record. Based on Jamaican DJ Trinity's "Three Piece Suit" (1977), the record was a hit in both Jamaica and Britain, where it reached #1. Althea & Donna were soon snapped up by Virgin's Front Line label, the fledgling reggae imprint launched by Virgin Records, but their novelty value quickly evaporated, and "Uptown Top Ranking" proved their only hit. Nevertheless, they had opened the door for the generation of female DJs that would emerge fully in the next decade.

As the 1970s ended, reggae group Black Uhuru was building momentum that would

Singer Deborahe Glasgow, whose "Champion Lover" became the basis for dancehall star Shabba Ranks's 1992 hit "Mr. Loverman."

PRINCE BUSTER

YEARS ACTIVE: 1950s–1990s

In what turned out to be a historic year for Kingston, Jamaica, 1938 saw the outbreak of major labor riots, ignited by the social injustices of British colonial rule and massive unemployment. Another force was unleashed that year when Cecil Bustamante Campbell, later known as Prince Buster, was born. He grew up in the vicinity of Orange Street, a center of Kingston's music scene, and became a devoted fan of Tom the Great Sebastian, one of the island's first sound-system operators. Early exposure to the entertainment business came when he took a job as a bouncer for Coxsone Dodd's Downbeat sound system. Competition between sound systems in the 1950s often involved using violence against rivals, so each system hired its own henchmen for protection against disruption and sabotage. Buster graduated to helping identify songs played by rival systems—a key role at a time when DJs scratched off the titles of records to keep them exclusive. Around 1959, he left Dodd's setup to form his own Voice of the People sound system. According to one well-known account, thugs working for rival operator (and later producer) Duke Reid went searching for Buster shortly after he had established his system, and in the ensuing fight, Buster's skull was split open with a rock. Such was the extent of the rivalry among sound-system operators at that time.

Buster soon provided serious competition for his more established rivals. He founded the Voice of the People record label around 1960, and set up the Record Shack store. Buster was also a catalyst for direct Rastafarian involvement in Jamaican popular music. It was he who brought Jamaican Rasta drummer Count Ossie to the recording sessions for the Folkes Brothers' 1960 track "Oh Carolina," which later became a hit for Jamaican dancehall singer Shaggy in 1993. Following Shaggy's success, a legal dispute erupted between John Folkes—the lead singer on the original recording—and Prince Buster over the song's ownership. The battle ended in November 1994, when a British High Court verdict affirmed Folkes's claim that he was the song's writer. The case underlined the difficulties in accurately determining who wrote a popular song in Jamaica, when producers frequently assumed total ownership of the song, including writing credits, to earn publishing revenue. Nonetheless, in 1960, "Oh Carolina" helped establish Buster's credentials as a producer, and he licensed the song for British release on Emil Shalit's Blue Beat Records.

The early 1960s also witnessed the start of Buster's ongoing rivalry on record with hit Jamaican singer Derrick Morgan. The rivalry began with Buster's ska song "Black Head Chinaman" (1963), which mocked Morgan's musical alliance with Chinese Jamaican producer Leslie Kong. Depending on the source, this verbal jousting was either lighthearted combat, during which Buster and Morgan remained on good personal terms, or more sinister and divisive. Either way, it helped both singers sell enough records to support a joint tour of England and receive offers for exclusive recording contracts from Blue Beat. The label eventually focused on Buster as its main artist and continued to do so until it developed an identity crisis in 1967. (Blue Beat had been so closely identified with ska that when it was replaced by the slower rocksteady beat in the mid-1960s, the label was scrapped.) As a producer and artist well known both inside and outside of Jamaica, Buster was also part of the promotional tour party sent by the Jamaican government to perform at the 1964 World's Fair in New York City.

The emergence of the slower paced style of rocksteady and the outlaw "rude boys"—violent urban males—in Jamaica presented Buster with an opportunity to chastise the nation's gangster youth on record while also boosting his career. The 1967 single "Judge Dread," the first in a series of thematically related tracks, was both topical and entertaining, and it was a hit with the United Kingdom's West Indian communities, though it never reached the pop charts. That same year, Buster scored his first UK pop hit with "Al Capone," which reached #18. (His next British hit single would not arrive for another thirty-one years!) Also in 1967, one of the most significant years in his career, he cracked the *Billboard* Hot 100 and scored a minor US hit (#81) with "Ten Commandments," which had been released in Britain by Blue Beat in 1963 and 1965. Though the Philips label released the single, the song was the title track of a full-length album, *Prince Buster Sings His Hit Song "Ten Commandments,"* released that year by RCA Records. The religious subject matter was perhaps appropriate given that he had become a minister in the Nation of Islam; by some accounts, he attained this title as early as 1961. It remains a mystery how Buster reconciled this role as a minister

with the unfiltered sexual salaciousness of his notorious "Big Five" single (1967) and the other songs he recorded about female anatomy and copulation. While the dancehall era was later criticized for depraved lyrics, lewd songs had existed in Jamaican popular music since recording took off in the 1950s, and the verbal tradition goes back much further.

Buster remained popular in Britain after his first tour there, and as groups of young white hipsters—the mods in the mid-1960s and the skinheads later in the decade—gravitated toward his music, he was repeatedly drawn back to the country. By the early 1970s, however, he had become more visible as a producer than as a solo artist. DJ "toasting" (improvised rapping over instrumental tracks) and roots reggae began to dominate Jamaican popular music, and their arrival marked the start of a long period of inactivity for Prince Buster. This hiatus was interrupted only by the release of the reggae single "Finger," issued by Arista Records in 1981, and a series of sporadic international live appearances in the late 1980s.

Following these live appearances and a 1992 Japanese tour, Prince Buster returned to the

British charts in 1998, reaching #21 with a new version of his classic "Whine & Grine" (originally released in 1967). The song had been covered by the Beat (known as the English Beat in America) in 1980

during Britain's commercially successful 2 Tone label ska revival when new bands and audiences became captivated by Jamaican music from the 1960s. Despite numerous reissues, much of Buster's early repertoire went out of print decades ago and remains unavailable.

SELECT DISCOGRAPHY: *Fabulous Greatest Hits* (Diamond Range, 2001); *Prince Buster Sings His Hit Song "Ten Commandments"* (Reel Music, 2009)

OPPOSITE: In the 1960s, artist and producer Prince Buster was king of Britain's Blue Beat label.

LEFT: Peaking at #18 in 1967, "Al Capone" was Buster's first UK pop hit.

PRINCE FAR I
YEARS ACTIVE: 1970s–1983

Michael Williams was born in Spanish Town, Jamaica, in the parish of St. Catherine around 1944 and was working as security muscle for producer Coxsone Dodd at Studio One in Kingston when he unexpectedly received his first recording opportunity. Allegedly, veteran DJ King Stitt failed to turn up for a studio session, prompting Dodd to give his bouncer a chance. Williams recorded his early singles as King Cry Cry—a less-than-imposing stage name given to him by Dodd—before being renamed Prince Far I by Jamaican singer and producer Enos McLeod, with whom he worked in the early 1970s. This was a more impressive name for a man who informally referred to himself as the "voice of thunder."

On his debut 1976 album, *Psalms for I*, recorded for the UK independent label Carib Gems, Prince Far I established the sound that would define his career. He blended the persona of a powerful religious orator with the half-spoken, half-sung vocal delivery of DJ "toasting," demonstrating the similarity between the two. His tales of spiritual guidance found critical acclaim and earned him a larger audience, and the 1977 album *Under Heavy*

LEFT: Fiery roots orator Prince Far I in 1982, a year before he was gunned down in his Kingston home.

Manners reflected Jamaica's alarming social crises as economic disaster threatened, bringing a proportionate rise in violent crime. The artist benefited from the largesse of Virgin Records as it entered the reggae market, and in 1978, the label released *Message from the King* and *Long Life*, which took Prince Far I's style of moral reprimand to reggae fans in the rock market. In 1976, he had also begun releasing a series of *Cry Tuff Dub Encounter* albums. These albums were recorded with the young and later influential English reggae enthusiast Adrian Sherwood, who subsequently formed On-U Records, the Pressure Sounds reissue label, and several different reggae groups such as Dub Syndicate. This mid- to late-1970s phase arguably represents the creative peak of Prince Far I's career; after he left Virgin, the albums he recorded for Trojan Records (based in the UK) were sketchier and less convincing overall. As he spent more time in Britain in the late 1970s and early 1980s, he collaborated further with Sherwood and recorded material with the global music collective, the Suns of Arqa.

Prince Far I had a lengthy prison record dating back to his early DJ years. He had shown himself quite capable of finding trouble, but few were prepared for the consequences of it finding him. On September 15, 1983, he was shot dead in his Kingston home. The various accounts attempting to explain the event range from a botched burglary attempt to a financial dispute with a dance promoter. The gruesome murder silenced Prince Far I's deeply textured voice and robbed the roots reggae audience of one of its favorite artists.

SELECT DISCOGRAPHY: *Psalms for I* (Carib Gems, 1976); *Under Heavy Manners* (Joe Gibbs, 1977); *Message from the King* (Front Line, 1978); *Long Life* (Front Line, 1978); *Voice of Thunder* (Trojan Records, 1981); *Heavy Manners: Anthology 1977–83* (Sanctuary, 2000); *Cry Tuff Dub Encounter: Chapter One* (Pressure Sounds, 2005); *Dubwise* (Virgin Records, 2005)

RANDY'S RECORDS

Initially run by Vincent "Randy" Chin as part of a family-owned operation, Randy's Records in Kingston followed a typically Jamaican template, functioning as both a recording studio and record label and selling records through its own retail outlet. Randy's studio was founded in 1968, following the establishment of Randy's Record Mart, and was built directly above the shop located at 16–17 North Parade in Kingston.

From the early to mid-1970s, Randy's studio was one of a select number of hit factories utilized by the hot producers of the day. The engineering skill of Errol Thompson was a major draw, since he had previously earned a solid reputation working with artists at producer Coxsone Dodd's recording location, Studio One in Kingston. Thompson's presence at Randy's attracted Bunny Lee and Lee Perry, two of the many producers associated with the studio's success. At the dawn of the 1970s, Perry brought the Wailers, featuring Bob Marley, to record at Randy's, and the sessions yielded recordings—such as the *Soul Rebels* (1970) and *African Herbsman* (1973) albums—that still constitute a large part of that group's perpetual reissue catalog. The early dub music coming out of Randy's during this era was quite conservative and transitional, lacking the liberal use of effects and the ambitious exploration of sonic space that would soon become standard features of the genre. Nonetheless, with its fluid studio band, the Impact All Stars, Randy's was a hothouse of reggae rhythm.

Producer Clive Chin, Vincent's son, scored a hit early in his studio career with only his second production, melodica player Augustus Pablo's "Java" (1971, but also listed as 1972 in some sources), which became one of the artist's trademarks. In addition to working with such marquee vocalists as Alton Ellis, Clive Chin produced Pablo's *Java Java Dub*. Released in 1972, this was one of the earliest dub albums (Chin maintains it was the very first), and it is believed that only one thousand copies were made. Clive's good ears and instincts fostered hits with such legendary reggae singers as Gregory Isaacs and Dennis Brown. Reflecting its connection with reggae's Rasta-influenced sound, Randy's was also the recording venue for *Man in the Hills*, the 1976 album by archetypal roots artist Burning Spear.

In 1976, Thompson left for producer Joe Gibbs's studio. His apparently sudden departure not only left an engineering void but also changed the energy and mood at Randy's. By the mid-1970s, Perry—once a frequent Randy's client—had begun recording at his soon-to-be-legendary Black Ark studio. This facility increased the studio options available to Jamaican producers in Kingston, as did the far more competitive and widely influential Channel One operation started by the Hoo-Kim brothers, which became one of the major reggae studios of the decade. Amid this emerging competition, which led to the defection of session musicians to rival studios, Randy's closed down in 1977, and the Chin family moved to New York City. This relocation coincided with Jamaica's declining economic conditions, rising political violence, and overall social turmoil.

After moving to the United States, the family remained involved in record retail and distribution. The Chins started VP Records in New York in the early 1990s (possibly as early as 1991), seeking to further service the Jamaican immigrant market in the United States and explore crossover possibilities. The label soon established offices in Florida and expanded into Britain. In 2008, they bought one of Britain's major reggae companies, Greensleeves Records. This helped solidify VP Records as the dominant independent reggae label of the early twenty-first century, but its origins lie in Randy's Records.

Bobby Melody was one of many artists to record at Randy's Records, a reggae hothouse in the 1970s.

ranglin roots

ERNEST RANGLIN

**YEARS ACTIVE:
1940s–PRESENT**

The self-taught musician Ernest Ranglin participated in creating many of the key milestones of the ska and reggae era, working with such legendary names as Coxsone Dodd, Duke Reid, Prince Buster, the Wailers, Jimmy Cliff, and Clancy Eccles, among many others. Ranglin is one of the few artists who can truly claim to have been instrumental in the birth of ska, helping to create the style in sessions at producer Dodd's Studio One in Kingston. Ranglin was greatly influenced by artists such as the American jazz guitarist Charlie Christian, and Jamaican player Cecil Houdini.

Born in Manchester, Jamaica, in 1932, Ranglin began playing in the Val Bennett Orchestra when he was about fifteen and later moved to the Eric Deans Orchestra, where he gained experience touring the Caribbean. Both orchestras were hotel groups, playing for tourists, and also occasionally performed at clubs in Kingston.

In the mid-1950s, Ranglin became a regular session player and arranger on early recordings made by Dodd, joining such key studio regulars as bassist Cluett "Clue-J" Johnson. Although he did not play on the released version, he is credited with creating the arrangement for pianist Theophilus Beckford's "Easy Snappin'" (1960), a song whose combination of American R&B and Jamaican rhythms is said to have launched the ska era. Like most Kingston studio musicians, Ranglin divided his time among the city's leading producers and recorded for Duke Reid and Prince Buster, among others. Ranglin also performed on one side of *Lance Haywood at Half Moon*, the 1959 live LP that was Island Records' first-ever release. Ranglin arranged recordings made by the vocal group the Wailers (whose members included future reggae stars Bob Marley, Peter Tosh, and Bunny Wailer) in the early 1960s, long before they were connected to Island. Having established himself as a first-rate musician in both live and studio settings, Ranglin answered a call from Island founder Chris Blackwell and went to England around 1963 to advance his career by making recordings there.

In 1964, Ranglin was voted jazz guitarist of the year in the annual reader's poll conducted by the British popular-music periodical *Melody Maker*. Around this time, he recorded two jazz albums, *Wranglin'* (1964) and *Reflections* (1965), for Island (released only in Britain) and arranged singer Millie Small's massive international hit "My Boy Lollipop" (1964). More than any other song up to that time, "My Boy Lollipop" created mainstream awareness of Jamaica's music, though it certainly did not represent the ska sounds emerging from Kingston at the time. Recorded with British musicians, the single lacked ska's inherent fluidity between the upbeats and was devoid of rough instrumental or vocal edges. But it was exactly what Blackwell wanted in order to break into the pop market.

During the rocksteady years of the mid-1960s, during which time the overall tempo of Jamaican popular music slowed down from ska's intensity, Ranglin was the musical director, or chief musician, at Duke Reid's Treasure Isle studio, a Kingston venue where some of Jamaica's most pivotal recordings were made. He also played on what he says were the first-ever reggae recordings: Clancy Eccles's "Feel the Rhythm" and Monty Morris's "Say What You're Saying" (both 1968). In the 1970s, Ranglin toured for three and a half years with star reggae singer-songwriter Jimmy Cliff and played on countless studio sessions in Jamaica.

Ranglin's busy schedule was partially to blame for his lack of solo material in the 1970s and 1980s, though he likely earned more money from live work than he would have recording his own music. (Ranglin has noted that he has never made any real money from his solo albums or studio work.)

In 2000, after a string of releases in the 1990s on Blackwell's Island Jamaica Jazz and Palm Pictures labels, Ranglin signed to the Telarc Records label and released *Modern Answers to Old Problems*. The record found him again playing a brand of heavily jazz-accented, African-inflected world music that only occasionally involves reggae. Ranglin has received Jamaica's Order of Distinction (1973) for his major contributions to the island's music and an honorary degree from the Kingston campus of the University of the West Indies. Despite these honors, he has never stopped searching for new musical directions.

SELECT DISCOGRAPHY: *Wranglin'* (Island, 1964); *Reflections* (Island, 1965); *Below the Bassline* (Island, 1996); *Memories of Barber Mack* (Island Jamaica Jazz, 1997); *In Search of the Lost Riddim* (Palm Pictures, 1998); *Modern Answers to Old Problems* (Telarc, 2000); *Gotcha!* (Telarc, 2001)

Guitarist Ernest Ranglin in 1982, decades after his innovative arrangement on Theophilus Beckford's "Easy Snappin'" (1960) launched the ska era.

RAS MICHAEL & THE SONS OF NEGUS

YEARS ACTIVE: 1960s-2000s

Following in the footsteps of Count Ossie, Ras Michael (also known on some records as Dadawah) helped maintain the presence of Rastafarian drumming in Jamaica's popular music. Chant-like vocals and funde and repeater drums dominated his soundscapes in a style known as Nyabinghi drumming, although he also used such standard instruments as bass, drums, keyboards, and guitar. He was also influenced by the teachings of such 1930s Jamaican anticolonial leaders as Marcus Garvey and Leonard Howell. Ras Michael's strong cultural philosophies centered on black consciousness and liberation and were shaped by his Rastafarian belief in the divinity of Ethiopian Emperor Haile Selassie, whose crowning was seen by Afrocentric advocates as confirmation of biblical prophecy. His group, Ras Michael & the Sons of Negus, provided a musical vehicle for the promotion of peace and spiritual elevation through Rastafari.

Ras Michael was born Michael George Henry in Kingston in 1943 and grew up in the city's Trench Town ghetto area, where he was surrounded by creative individuals, among them legendary Wailers members Bob Marley and Bunny Wailer. Formed in the early 1960s, the Sons of Negus never had a fixed lineup and usually consisted of a fluid collective of studio session players led by Ras Michael. These included guitarists Earl "Chinna" Smith and Peter Tosh, drummer Carlton "Santa" Davis, keyboardist Geoffrey Chung, and bassist Robbie Shakespeare, all of whom played on the group's 1975 set, *Rastafari*. The group's debut single, "The Lion of Judah," was recorded at WIRL (West Indies Records Limited) in 1967 and released on Ras Michael's own Zion Disc label. No album appeared until 1974's *Peace & Love* began a spurt of activity. The record was the first of three releases that year that together practically defined the sound

of roots reggae. Trojan Records released *Nyabinghi*, produced by Tommy Cowan, internationally, while the six-song set *Freedom Sounds* was credited simply to the Sons of Negus. The versatile reggae journeyman guitarist Earl "Chinna" Smith played on *Freedom Sounds*, infusing the drum-driven Ras Michael sound with funk, rock, and blues, especially on the opening track, "Watch & Pray."

Rastafari, one of the group's better-known releases, at least visually, featured a cover photo of the young Haile Selassie and gained wide release in 1975, although it had been previously released in Jamaica as early as 1972. It sheds fresh light on the evolution of Ras Michael's music, and its companion dub album, *Rastafari Dub* (1975), was a powerful statement that placed him on reggae's musical and ideological cutting edges.

In addition to the high-quality session musicians who played on Ras Michael's records, dancer and future Black Uhuru vocalist Puma Jones briefly joined the fold and appeared on 1978's *Movements*. One could argue that by the end of the decade Ras Michael had already marked his sonic and ideological borders, and that his subsequent albums offer mere variations on the same Rastafarian themes. But ultimately, Ras Michael placed spiritual consciousness ahead of commercial concerns. On 2007's *Medicine Man*, his acoustic Rasta singer-songwriter persona suggested that even in the realm of folk-centered music, there could be many dimensions to an artist's personality.

Greetings in The Name of H.I.M. Emperor Haile Selassie I

Saturday November 30th

AT

The Uhuru Sasa (Armory)
357 Sumner Ave.
Brooklyn, N.Y.

LIVE IN CONCERT
IN
BROOKLYN

BRING
THE
YOUTH

RAS MICHAEL
The Sons of Negus

MUTABARUKA

DOORS OPEN
7:30 P.M.
SHOWTIME — 9:00 P.M.

FREE
I

AFRIKAN MERCHANTS WELCOME !

ABORTION
IS
MURDER

NYABENGHI ORDER
Freedom by any means necessary

TICKETS: $12.00 IN ADVANCE
$15.00 AT THE DOOR

POSITIVE VIBES ONLY
JAH IS LOVE

THE BLACK FAMILY IS
ONLY AS STRONG AS THE
BLACK WOMAN IS !

TELL THE CHILDREN
THE TRUTH

AFRIKA IS
ON THE RISE !

STOP APARTHEID

AN AFRIKA HOUSE PRODUCTION
FOR INFO (212) 862-6209 or (212) 491-7202
TAXI SERVICE AVAILABLE FROM A TRAIN (Kingston Ave.)

SELECT DISCOGRAPHY: *Peace & Love* (Wildflower, 1974); *Nyabinghi* (Trojan Records, 1974); *Freedom Sounds* (Dynamic, 1974); *Rastafari* (Grounation, 1975); *Tribute to the Emperor* (Trojan, 1976); *Irations of Ras Michael & the Sons of Negus: Volume One* (Top Ranking Sounds, 1977); *Movements* (w. Sons & Daughters of Negus) (Dynamic, 1978); *Kibir Am Lak* (Talent Music, 1978); *Love Thy Neighbour* (Live & Learn, 1979); *Promised Land Sounds* (Lion's Gate, 1980); *Disarmament* (Trojan, 1981); *Revelation* (Trojan, 1982); *Rally Round* (Shanachie, 1985); *Zion Train* (SST, 1988); *Know Now* (Shanachie, 1989); *Try Love* (Vista Ave., 2007); *Medicine Man* (Inna De Yard/ Makasound, 2007)

RAS RECORDS
YEARS ACTIVE: 1979-2003

RAS—short for "Real Authentic Sound"—Records was established in Washington, D.C., in 1979 by Gary Himmelfarb, whose producer moniker, Doctor Dread, originated with his reggae radio show that aired in the capital, Himmelfarb's hometown. The independent label began as a record import and distribution business operating out of a basement. Himmelfarb visited Jamaica regularly to purchase records and meet with music makers, and on one such visit, he had a chance encounter with vocalist Peter Broggs. This led to the first RAS Records album release, Broggs's *Rastafari Liveth*, recorded in Jamaica at Channel One studio and released in 1982.

The label released more than three hundred records by such high-caliber roots artists as Black Uhuru, Augustus Pablo, Sly & Robbie, and Mystic Revealers, as well as albums by

dancehall DJs, and reggae records specifically made for the children's market. RAS was also bold enough to look beyond Jamaica for its reggae, releasing, for example, *Stranger* by Barbadian artist David Kirton in 1999.

RAS won a best reggae album Grammy award in 1996 for Bunny Wailer's *Hall of Fame: A Tribute to Bob Marley*. While the label was already on the radar of regular reggae consumers, the Grammy win raised its profile and arguably its economic value. After carving out its own niche in the international reggae market, RAS was bought by UK-based Sanctuary Records in 2003. Sanctuary merged the RAS catalog with the Trojan Records library that it already owned, enhancing the parent company's reggae assets while making RAS defunct.

Launched in a basement in Washington, D.C., RAS Records released more than three hundred records.

REGGAE PHILHARMONIC ORCHESTRA
YEARS ACTIVE: 1980s-2000s

The Reggae Philharmonic Orchestra (RPO) demonstrated that orchestral string arrangements and roots reggae could comfortably coexist. The music of the British RPO was significantly different from the string-laden, pop-crossover reggae singles released by Trojan Records during the late 1960s and early 1970s. These Trojan recordings featured superimposed orchestral arrangements that were not part of the songs' original concepts, while the RPO offered a fusion style of roots reggae that actually integrated orchestral elements into the production instead of using them as afterthoughts. Importantly, the Orchestra achieved this by using a group of mostly black, classically trained musicians, many of whom were women. It's difficult to think of another reggae outfit with at least five active female instrumentalists at any one time.

Described as Britain's first black orchestra, the RPO was the brainchild of Mykaell Riley, one of the original members of the successful reggae group Steel Pulse, founded in the 1970s. Riley was ejected from that band after a clash over his unwillingness to accept Ethiopian emperor Haile Selassie's iconic Rastafarian status as a living god without further historical investigation. In the late 1980s, Riley developed an orchestral reggae vision while working for London Weekend Television and doing research and booking for *Club Mix*, one of the first black shows on British television. He eventually assembled a group of musicians who had been recommended repeatedly by different sources. A performance on *Club Mix* drew enthusiastic audience responses and resulted in Island Records offering a recording deal. Since the group contained roughly eighteen people

at the time, Island opted to make a solo deal with Riley, who would serve as the group's representative and finance the debut album with money paid by the label. RPO scored a minor 1988 hit in Britain with an adaptation of Cab Calloway's 1931 song "Minnie the Moocher." Although it reached only #35 on the pop charts, it was a major achievement, considering the group's unusual stylistic and racial characteristics. With its commercially appealing approach, RPO was in effect invading orchestral territory previously thought to be an exclusively white domain.

RPO's self-titled debut album was released in 1988 and featured a nascent fusion sound the group would take a step or two further the following year. Though not often acknowledged, RPO played and was credited on the hugely successful debut album by the British R&B collective Soul II Soul (released in 1989), which used Riley's groove-appropriate string arrangements. Soul II Soul was heavily influenced by reggae sound-system culture, so the alliance with RPO was built on reggae vibes, although not that many listeners or radio programmers recognized this connection. The album collaboration was nonetheless an international triumph for black British musicianship that had emerged from city spaces steeped in reggae vibrations. The year after Soul II Soul's debut, RPO released its second album, *Time* (1990). "Lovely Thing" grazed the outer reaches of the UK singles chart, but the group's mainstream visibility didn't fully translate into record sales.

The first fracture in RPO's foundation appeared in 1990 when some female members were hired by Soul II Soul as part of the touring band in America, which affected rehearsals for other imminent gigs slated for the complete orchestral group. A significantly different lineup played on the *Marley Classics* tribute record (1991), which has become exceedingly rare. Parts of the album were cut in Jamaica at Bob Marley's Tuff Gong

Part Mozart, part Marley, the Reggae Philharmonic Orchestra skanks with strings, 1988.

Studios and included vocals from the I-Threes (Marcia Griffiths, Rita Marley, and Judy Mowatt) and saxophone from highly regarded British Jamaican player Courtney Pine.

RPO bassist Winston Blissett and session drummer Andy Gangadeen later surfaced in the band that backed 1990s white British soul diva Lisa Stansfield. Riley is currently Director of the Black Music Research Unit at the University of Westminster in London, where he also lectures on music production. While it appears RPO never formally disbanded, as they still performed occasionally in Britain in the 2000s, they have not released any new recordings.

MEMBERS: Mykaell S. Riley (vocals, drums); **Ellen Blair** (violin, viola); **Johnny T** (violin), *Reggae Philharmonic Orchestra, Time*; **Steve Bradshaw** (violin, viola), *Reggae Philharmonic Orchestra*; **Simon Walker** (violin), *Reggae Philharmonic Orchestra*; **Pam Crawford** (viola), *Reggae Philharmonic Orchestra, Time*; **Everton Nelson** (violin), *Marley Classics*; **John Taylor** (violin), *Marley Classics*; **Steven Hussey** (violin), *Marley Classics*; **Andrew Tait** (viola), *Marley Classics*; **Faye Clinton** (cello); **Ivan Hussey** (cello), *Time, Marley Classics*; **Sara Loewenthal** (double bass); **Yolisa Phahle** (keyboards), *Reggae Philharmonic Orchestra, Time*; **Deirdre Pascall** (keyboards), *Reggae Philharmonic Orchestra*; **Jenny Adgyayan** (cello), *Marley Classics*; **Mark Edwards** (organ), *Marley Classics*; **Izumi Kobayashi** (piano), *Marley Classics*; **Wayne Batchelor** (bass guitar, double bass); **Winston Blissett** (bass guitar); **Tim Atkins** (drums), *Reggae Philharmonic Orchestra*; **Kushite** (saxophone), *Reggae Philharmonic Orchestra, Time*; **Marc D'Aieur** (acoustic guitar), *Reggae Philharmonic Orchestra*; **Nick Page** (acoustic guitar), *Reggae Philharmonic Orchestra*; **Joe Asghar** (acoustic guitar), *Marley Classics*; **Ciyo** (guitar), *Marley Classics*

SELECT DISCOGRAPHY: *Reggae Philharmonic Orchestra* (Mango/Island, 1988); *Time* (Mango/Island, 1990); *Marley Classics* (w. I-Threes and Courtney Pine) (Mango/Island, 1991)

REGGAE REGULAR

YEARS ACTIVE: 1976–PRESENT

The seven-piece Reggae Regular was among the self-contained British reggae bands that emerged in the 1970s, and in 1977 they became the first group to release a single on the newly formed Greensleeves Records, a company that soon became Britain's leading independent reggae label. Formed in London in 1976, they began as a live tour-backing band for Jamaican group the Morwells and the more commercially friendly, female lovers rock trio 15-16-17 before deciding to take their own music more seriously and carve out an independent identity.

Reggae Regular's Greensleeves debut, "Where Is Jah" (1977), made a clear statement about their philosophical and musical direction, but they had greater impact the following year with "Black Star Liner," referencing the shipping enterprise that Jamaican black liberation icon Marcus Garvey founded in 1919 to repatriate displaced Africans and foster black economic self-sufficiency. "Black Star Liner" could easily be considered a definitive statement of the group's Rastafarian crusade against "Babylon" (a Rasta description of the social establishment), and the peak of their commercial success. The track was issued in 1978 as a 12-inch record containing the original song and its dub version spliced together. The commercial value of the record was enhanced by the inclusion of a similarly extended version of the previously released single, "Where Is Jah," on the B-side.

Their style of dub-infused roots did well in the domestic reggae market, and like contemporaries Steel Pulse, Aswad, and Black Slate, Reggae Regular drew from Jamaican influences and created sonic representations of urban experiences unique to England. As record companies looked to capitalize on reggae's growing popularity in the late 1970s, Reggae Regular was among the bands to sign with a major label. By 1978, they had gone into business with the UK branch of CBS Records, which changed their name to the Regulars, a more pop-friendly identity. The label's removal of the word "reggae" from the group's name was not a positive sign. Despite extra promotional spending that included a pop-styled album cover for *Victim* (1979) and flashy picture discs for the singles "Victim" and "Fools Game," the album the Regulars released on CBS never took off commercially. The musicianship, thematic focus, and production were still there, but by incorporating the more lightweight lovers rock style and adopting a glossier new image, the group might have alienated its earlier hardcore roots reggae followers.

The *Victim* illustrated album cover featured the band in the foreground waiting at an improvised London bus stop. Sandwiched uncomfortably between the musicians is a "Babylon" businessman in a derby hat and three-piece suit. The contrast between this scenario and the image's background, a Caribbean coastal village landscape, was one of the most literal representations of the cultural poles defining British reggae.

In the wake of the album's failure and CBS's effort to push the band toward a more commercial sound, the Regulars released 1980's *I & I* on the independent Sound Off label, achieving a deeper roots sound on such songs as "Marcus the Prophet." After rigorous touring in support of higher-profile pop and reggae acts, the band temporarily split up in 1980. They reformed at a London gig in 1981 as Rebel Regular, soon rejoining the Greensleeves label where they began. By 1982, they had practically become the Greensleeves house band, backing such dancehall DJs as Clint Eastwood. In 1984, they went back to their roots in both sound and name: as Reggae Regular, they released the rootsy and dub-flavored *Ghetto Rock*, mixed by British reggae producer Mad Professor.

After an extended hiatus, the five-piece band released a new album (as Reggae Regular), *If Only*, in 2011, that included a remake of "Black Star Liner" featuring British DJ Tippa Irie.

MEMBERS: **Allan King** (lead vocals); **Tony Rookwood** (lead vocals); **Patrick Johnson** (lead vocals, 2009–present); **Norman Ebanks** (lead guitar); **Trevor Salmon** (bass, vocals); **Derek Demondo** (bass, 2009–present); **Weston Salmon** (vocals, 1982–present); **Patrick Donegan** (rhythm guitar, vocals); **George Clarke** (keyboards); **Brian Campbell** (keyboards, 1982–present); **Errol Francis** (drums); **Winston Wayne Williams** (drums, 1982–present)

SELECT DISCOGRAPHY: *Victim* (CBS, 1979); *I & I* (Sound Off, 1980); *Ghetto Rock* (Greensleeves, 1984)

The Regulars' 1979 album, *Victim*, literally illustrated the cultural divide between Rastas and the British establishment.

REGGAETÓN

YEARS ACTIVE: 2000s

Reggaetón is an urban Latin Caribbean phenomenon with roots in Panama and Puerto Rico, though arguments continue about exactly where and when it first emerged. A close relative of dancehall reggae, it features digitally programmed drums, bass-heavy rhythms, and the braggadocio lyrics of mostly male rappers. Its rhythms share as much with Trinidad's soca—a commercial fusion of soul and calypso that originated in the early 1970s—as they do with dancehall. The Panamanian connection stems from El General, who has fused Latin rap with dancehall reggae since the early 1990s, creating a reggae *en español* sound that predates the emergence of reggaetón.

Like their Jamaican dancehall counterparts, reggaetón artists have made commercially viable crossover recordings by collaborating with more mainstream performers. Non-reggaetón Hispanic and English-singing artists frequently commissioned custom remixes to broaden their commercial appeal to younger audiences. By 2005, the year that reggaetón exploded out of the underground music scene, the estimated cost of such remixes had climbed to between $20,000 and $50,000 per track. Though several songs contributed to this trend, the momentum can be traced primarily to the chart success of two 2004 singles. One was "Oye Mi Canto" by N.O.R.E. (American rapper Victor Santiago), which featured guest rappers and singers, including Puerto Rico's Daddy Yankee, who scored a somewhat unexpected international breakout success with the year's other major reggaetón single, "Gasolina." Remarkably, Daddy Yankee's track peaked at #5 on the British charts, broke into the American Top 40, and charted in a number of less likely markets, including Switzerland. Daddy Yankee carried reggaetón into previously uncharted territory and even achieved platinum sales in the United States with his 2004 album, *Barrio Fino*. However, while other reggaetón acts such as Puerto Rican rappers Tego Calderón and Don Omar had hits among Hispanic communities in the United States, they were not as successful elsewhere. By 2006, some had come to fear for the genre's business independence as major labels—especially Universal Music—moved in to reap the potential commercial benefits from a Latin musical style that had demonstrated some brief global appeal.

Crossover collaborations continued to fuel the growing reggaetón fever. For example, the popular duo Wisin y Handel teamed with R&B-pop vocalist R. Kelly for "Burn It Up" (2006), while artist and producer Hector "El Bambino"— better known as El Father—recorded the compilation album *Los Rompe Diskotekas* (2006). That album included a collaboration with American hip-hop superstar Jay-Z ("Here We Go Yo"), whose Roc La Familia Records imprint released the record.

As has long been the case with both rap and dancehall, there are relatively few female reggaetón rappers and MCs, and Puerto Rican singer-rapper Ivy Queen is the leading female act in the genre. Reggaetón's rise has coincided with increased branding consciousness in popular music, and its best-known artists have endorsed footwear, soft drinks, alcohol, and other products.

Thanks to the bilingual capabilities of many of its hit artists, reggaetón has enjoyed a cross-cultural market reach that dancehall reggae arguably lacks. *Billboard* magazine's top reggae album charts at the end of March 2005 featured eleven reggaetón albums out of the fifteen titles listed. The inclusion of several reggaetón songs in the *Grand Theft Auto* video game series has helped strengthen the genre's market muscle in the face of repeated predictions about its imminent demise.

Kicking off his first US tour, Daddy Yankee prowls the stage at New York's Madison Square Garden, 2005.

SOUND SYSTEMS

Vinyl singles and albums made Jamaican popular culture a global force, but without the sound systems, the island's distinctive music—and perhaps even this book—might not exist. In the early 1950s, economic conditions in Jamaica were such that owning a record player was an upper-middle-class luxury beyond the reach of most people. A more affordable entertainment alternative was the sound system—an electronic sound reproduction setup that some writers have described as a mobile discotheque. A DJ, or "selector," would play the current hits through massive custom-made speakers and powerful amplifiers to attract an audience, and the sound-system equipment would be packed onto a truck after each session, to move to the next night's venue. In Jamaica, sound systems are often simply described as "sounds."

Chinese Jamaican who performed under the name Tom the Great Sebastian. His system featured Duke Vin (who started the UK's first sound system in 1954) as the selector, and the grandiose titles adopted by both men spoke to the power and expectations of respect associated with this brand of entertainment. Wong began performing as Tom the Great Sebastian as a means of luring customers into his hardware store. It has often been reported that on this system, DJ Count Machuki took to the microphone on December 26, 1950, and introduced the concept of adding spoken-word improvisations over records, thus heralding

While sound systems were the heart of Jamaican music, jukeboxes played an underdocumented role in exposing the largely disenfranchised Jamaican audience to American R&B. By the end of the decade, American radio stations had also become influential, and much larger local audiences could pick up their signals. As Jamaicans traveled to the United States and took on short-term contracts as migrant workers cutting sugar cane there, many returned with R&B records. This quickly created a wider local demand for the music, which came to dominate the early sound systems. In a sense, these mobile units bridged the gap between the local and global—in this case American—audiences, providing imported music in a communal setting and at a low price.

By the late 1950s, homegrown material had begun to displace the imports. As the first proto-ska recordings began to emerge, they had a stronger impact on Jamaican audiences than the calypso-oriented mento music heard on the island's first commercially released discs earlier in the decade. The rise of rock 'n' roll in America interrupted the supply of the R&B on which the sound systems had built their reputations, forcing them to become catalysts in developing a viable Jamaican substitute.

The sound-system dance hall arenas, referred to as "lawns," were generally enclosed outdoor areas attached to Kingston rum shops. The music was a central attraction, but sound systems were also intended to generate cash from food and drink sales. Simultaneously social and economic in nature, they therefore caught the attention of some of Jamaica's political power brokers, who realized that they could harness the public's love of music in electoral campaigns. The sheer sonic power of these systems demanded public attention, and each operation sought to outdo the competition not only with its selection of records but also with the volume from its massive speaker columns.

One of the first commercial sound systems to emerge in the 1940s was run by Thomas Wong, a

ABOVE: DJs, or "toasters," are integral parts of the sound-system experience.
RIGHT: Many sound systems in Jamaica were literally attached to vehicles to bring the music to any available dance hall area.

the start of another dimension in Jamaican popular music: the DJ who did not merely play records, but also chatted or "toasted."

In a 1994 Jamaican newspaper interview, Machuki emphasized that "No one else was doing it at the time and I really did it

Sound systems brought the latest hit songs directly to the people of Jamaica.

in 1952, pitting Tom the Great Sebastian against Count Nick the Champ, another early sound-system operator. Many system owners were typically armed, and they would often dispatch gangs to vandalize and damage the equipment of rivals and break up their public sessions. The credits were often scratched off of record labels to conceal song titles and artist names, thus thwarting attempts by rivals to identify and acquire the same records. In this era, the systems continued to play mostly American R&B records.

The late 1950s saw the balance of sound-system power swing away from Tom the Great Sebastian and toward the so-called Big Three: Duke Reid's Trojan (established in the early 1950s), Dodd's Downbeat, and the Giant system of King Edwards, which began in 1955. Wong moved his Tom the Great Sebastian operation uptown to the Silver Slipper Club as an era of violence set in, characterized by the destruction of rivals' equipment by Reid's henchmen. Wong later committed suicide in 1971, apparently as a result of financial problems. The fearless Prince Buster (once a follower of Tom the Great Sebastian), whose Voice of the People system surfaced sometime around 1958, eventually disrupted the dominance of the sound-system trinity. A former boxer, Buster had worked in Dodd's operation as an enforcer and occasional DJ until financial disputes caused a split. Buster's business strategy was to create what were essentially local exclusives—

recordings made by aspiring artists and accomplished session musicians. Reid and Dodd also began recording local talent to meet the demand for exclusive new material. As new record producers, they used their sound systems as proving grounds for test pressings of their own recordings, gauging audience reaction.

As a wave of immigration brought Jamaicans to other countries—most notably Britain—the sound-system concept continued to thrive and meet immigrants' cultural demands. The UK's first Jamaican sound-system operator, Duke Vin, likely left Jamaica in part because the business had become increasingly cutthroat—literally— and violence had become an intrinsic part of the culture. Count Suckle soon emerged in the same area, boosting the entertainment options for West Indians across England.

By the 1960s, a new crew of DJs was looking beyond the sound systems and beginning to make records. As one example, Sir Lord Comic recorded "Django Shoots First" with the Upsetters in 1965. Filled with fairly indistinct groaning and exclamatory sounds from Comic, the record shares little in common with what people came to recognize as DJ records in the early 1970s, when

to take away the drabness, to make the sound system sound different from a jukebox." Other accounts vary on when Count Machuki began his microphone chanting, with sources suggesting that it might have been 1951, or as late as 1953, after he had joined Coxsone Dodd's Downbeat system. At that time, Dodd, who later became the influential founder of the Studio One label and recording operation, was still in the early days of his sound-system activity. DJs like King Stitt, who joined the Downbeat system in the late 1950s, soon became key parts of sound systems' identities, and their improvised "toasting" (rapping) extended African oral communication traditions into an electronic realm.

Sound-system supremacy was determined by "clashes" between rival operations, and crowds at these events would determine the outcomes. The first such audio showdown is said to have occurred

ABOVE: A scene from the Volcano sound system, founded in 1983 by Henry "Junjo" Lawes, one of the most important producers of the dancehall era. Volcano was Jamaica's top sound system in the 1980s.
OPPOSITE: Sound systems remained an integral part of the Jamaican music scene in the 1980s, despite the new influence of dancehall.

U-Roy and Big Youth rose to prominence. Nevertheless, it represents the impact that sound systems were making on recorded music in Jamaica.

For much of the 1960s, the trio of owners dominating the Jamaican sound-system scene consisted of Buster, Reid, and Dodd (King Edwards bowed out of the business in the early 1960s, disliking the volatility of the scene). They were also the prime forces in the recording industry, and unlike Reid or Dodd, Prince Buster was also able to boost his popularity as a recording artist. Sound-system culture was directly responsible for the instrumental-only performances of songs, known as "versions," that became omnipresent in the late 1960s. In one account, the first such record

was created when Treasure Isle studio engineer Byron Smith erroneously omitted the vocal track from a test pressing or "dubplate" created for Ruddy Redwood's SRS sound system. By the early 1970s, the exclusive version had led to the creation of dub, a subgenre whose leading exponents—among them producers King Tubby and Lee Perry—derived their creative instincts and sonic sensibilities from the sound-system environment. Their studio mixing styles were directly influenced by their desire to elicit reactions from live audiences.

Concurrent with the rise of dub in the early 1970s was the full-fledged emergence of DJ voice-

over, or toasting, recordings. The live spoken improvisations made a special impact on recorded music, and U-Roy's "Wake the Town" (1970), cut for Reid, opened the door for such DJs as Big Youth, Dillinger, and Tappa Zukie. "Wake the Town" and the rise of toasting in Jamaica also created the template for American rap music. Through sound systems, the DJ's role had been redefined and brought into the performance foreground. Rather than merely acting as sonic accompaniment, DJs played an active role: toasting, not simply hosting. As the roots reggae era gave way to dancehall, and the political militancy and spiritual emphases of

the 1970s were replaced by a more materialistic worldview, the sound system was once again the vehicle of transformation. By the mid-1980s, digital production had come to characterize the vast majority of releases.

As Jamaican politicians recognized years ago, the island's recorded music is a gauge for the public's temperament at any given time. Even so, it has always been the sound system that has allowed artists to convey their messages to the people.

DUKE REID
YEARS ACTIVE: 1950S-1975

Arthur "Duke" Reid was born in 1915 in Portland, Jamaica, and his activities as a sound-system owner and later record-label producer and entrepreneur made him one of the most influential figures in the development of Jamaican popular music. Reid's legendary Trojan sound system, its name a reference to the brand of imported British truck he used, began as an extension of the Treasure Isle liquor store he opened in the early 1950s. The system played obscure American R&B records and was the sponsor of a radio show. His operation later evolved into the Treasure Isle record label, and some of his early productions gained international recognition through a licensing deal with the UK record label Blue Beat.

A former police officer, Reid had a reputation for being constantly armed. He tended to carry at least two guns—usually worn openly in holsters—and like other sound-system operators, he assembled an intimidating group of enforcers to violently disrupt the dances thrown by his rivals. Along with King Edwards the Giant, another sound system with its own gang of violent enforcers, Trojan was a dominant force. Before long, however, the emergence of Coxsone Dodd's Downbeat system in the mid-1950s led to an intense, ongoing rivalry that extended into both Reid and Dodd's later recording enterprises. At the same time, singer Prince Buster's Voice of the People system also posed a threat. Accounts suggest that Reid was literally prepared to go to war in the battle for sound-system supremacy, and that his henchman would raid rival dances and wreak havoc on patrons and equipment to end an evening's entertainment.

Reid ventured into recording as early as 1957, working at Federal Studio, which had recently opened in Kingston. Initially, Reid assembled local musicians to record R&B instrumentals for his sound system. He was reluctant to embrace the early prototypes of ska, the uptempo fusion of American R&B and Jamaican rhythms that became popular in the early 1960s, and instead made mento (calypso-styled folk music) the focus of his more Jamaican-flavored releases. But as a businessman with an eye and an ear for what the public wanted, it was not long before he, too, became a ska merchant and began working with such artists as the now-legendary Skatalites, the instrumental group that defined the ska genre by playing on countless Jamaican recording sessions backing other artists, as well making their own records.

Reid founded his own label, Treasure Isle, in the early years of the decade, and in 1965 opened a studio above his liquor store in Kingston. This setup enabled him to be virtually in two places at once, as he could monitor the recording activities through a speaker box while conducting business downstairs. According to musician and producer Brent Dowe, Reid would run upstairs anytime he heard a mistake or an otherwise unsatisfactory performance.

The transition from high-tempo ska to the less frantic and slower rocksteady rhythm led to a period of mid-1960s dominance for Treasure Isle that Reid would never match in the subsequent reggae era. Singer Alton Ellis's appropriately

Low Down Dirty Girl
(LAUREL AITKEN)
LAUREL AITKEN

Music by Duke Reid and his group

MANUFACTURED BY FEDERAL RECORD MFG CO LTD. JAMAICA W.I.

A key figure in Jamaican music, Duke Reid went from sound-system operator to successful label boss. The frequently armed former police officer scored big in the mid-1960s, when his Treasure Isle label ruled the rocksteady scene.

titled "Rock Steady" (1966 on Treasure Isle) was one of the first songs to feature the new rhythm. Reid's rocksteady reign was due largely to his talented and industrious session musicians, especially the innovative Trinidadian guitarist Lynn Taitt. As a member of one of Reid's house bands, the Supersonics, which also featured saxophonist Tommy McCook, Taitt gave studio directions that helped create the rocksteady rhythm.

In 1967, what began as a short-lived custom imprint for Reid became the England–based Trojan Records label, issued through the B&C (Beat & Commercial) company. Following a split between major B&C investor Chris Blackwell—founder of Island Records—and B&C's accountant Lee Gopthal, the latter reactivated the dormant Trojan label in 1968, adopting the name that had initially appeared only on Reid productions.

By 1968, Reid had hired the engineer known as King Tubby, who would soon become famous for his 1970s dub remixes, as a disc cutter at Treasure Isle. Thanks in part to Tubby's experimental leanings, Reid unknowingly laid some of the crucial foundations for dub and DJ music, both of which pushed reggae to new creative levels in the 1970s. The pioneering DJ known as U-Roy used many of Treasure Isle's rocksteady rhythm tracks in crafting his seminal "toasting" (Jamaican rapping) records and for his early 1970s hits like "Wake the Town" and "Rule the Nation." In addition, the label played a critical—if unintentional—role in creating the "version." This came about in 1967, when sound-system operator Ruddy Redwood received an acetate, or "dubplate," of the Paragons' "On the Beach" that had accidentally been stripped of vocals.

In the late 1960s Reid's success was hampered by his dislike of Rastas and refusal to work with them, an attitude that largely left the Treasure Isle label on the commercial sidelines. Despite Jamaican hits in 1970 with DJ U-Roy ("Wake the Town" and "Rule the Nation"), Reid's influence on the island's changing soundscape rapidly diminished. The Treasure Isle catalog was sold in 1974 to producer Sonia Pottinger, one of the few women in the Jamaican industry wielding financial and decision-making control at that time. After battling cancer, Reid died in 1975, but his name remains central in Jamaican popular music history.

JUNIOR REID

YEARS ACTIVE: 1970S-PRESENT

Vocalist Junior Reid has been an irrepressible independent force in reggae, persevering as both a solo artist and group member in Black Uhuru in circumstances that might have broken the resolve of others. His lyrical style is very much in the roots reggae tradition of raising spiritual and political awareness with no-holds-barred condemnation of Babylonian wickedness. He also has one of the genre's most distinctive voices.

Delroy "Junior" Reid was born in 1963 in Kingston, Jamaica. In a 1995 interview, he recalled how the young producer Hugh Mundell spent his own money to finance Reid's first recording when he was about fifteen or sixteen years old, in 1978, demonstrating a faith in his talent and potential. Before Mundell's shooting death in 1983—a killing Reid witnessed, as he was in the same car—the young singer worked as songwriter and performer with the vocal group Voice of Progress. The group released a 1982 album titled *Mini Bus Driver*, featuring instrumental backing by ace Jamaican rhythm duo Sly & Robbie.

Reid attracted greater attention in 1985, when his solo album *Original Foreign Mind* was released on the independent Black Roots label. The same year, Reid was invited to replace the recently departed Michael Rose on lead vocals in Black Uhuru, the band that won the first Grammy for best reggae recording in 1985 with their *Anthem* album. He then appeared on the Grammy-nominated albums *Brutal* (1986) and *Positive* (1987). In an interview, he noted that group member Puma Jones was diagnosed with breast cancer before recording began for *Positive*, which prevented her from appearing on the album and her absence from Black Uhuru unsettled him. Although Jones had been replaced, Reid said, her vibe had not.

The disruption of the group's lineup also coincided with his problems obtaining a US visa, which affected his ability to tour. The Jamaican police apparently seized Reid's passport, and the visa cancellation was unexplained, since no criminal charges were filed against him. In a 1993 *Reggae Report* magazine interview, he surmised that this was some sort of deliberate political conspiracy to undermine reggae's subversive momentum and Black Uhuru's presence as heirs to the reggae throne in the wake of Bob Marley's death. Reid blamed his passport troubles on music-business politics and political intrigue in Jamaica.

Of course, this travel obstacle limited his impact in—and income from—America, as he was unable to promote his records with live shows. However, Reid continued performing and recording in Jamaica while reaping some publishing income from songs written for and with Black Uhuru. He also handled his international distribution independently, and having cut the tracks in his own studio, he was able to make direct deals with foreign outlets. With this kind of proactive approach to the music business, he ensured he would live to fight many more days.

He is also quick to note that while it's normal for lead singers to quit groups and go solo, his process was the reverse, since he abandoned a solo career to join a group. His preexisting career meant there was still demand for Reid as a solo artist, evidenced by his British chart success with "Stop This Crazy Thing," which reached #21 in 1988. This reportedly upset Black Uhuru leader Duckie Simpson and contributed to their eventual falling out. Strictly speaking, the song was performed by the British pop and hip-hop remix duo Coldcut and only featured Reid, but as it turned out, the real craziness was just beginning. Reid's support of the single meant leaving a Black Uhuru tour stop in Germany to fly to London for a *Top of the Pops* TV appearance. The performance never actually materialized because Reid was informed that the record charted below the #19 cut-off point, and only

Junior Reid (right) lights up with John Wayne in 1985, the year he was asked to join Black Uhuru.

Techniques

2 Chancery Lane
Kingston, Jamaica.

SHE IS A REGULAR
J. REID
JUNIOR REID

Produced by
W. Riley

92-26832

acts charting higher would be asked to appear on the show.

The deterioration of relations between Simpson and Reid continued after the group's return to Jamaica, as Reid began cutting tracks he had invited the band to play on. No such involvement was forthcoming, partly because Simpson did not welcome the idea of Reid having a solo career parallel to the group's existence. *One Blood* (1990), issued in the United Kingdom on the independent Big Life label (soon absorbed into PolyGram), was the solo Reid record that emerged from the sessions, and its title track is one of his best. Though critically acclaimed, the album never received adequate promotion, and Reid made no money from the deal, thus deepening his disillusionment with the music business. He also felt that Big Life—run by Jazz Summers, manager of the pop group Wham!—could have exercised more influence to resolve his ongoing visa problem. In 1990, Reid also scored a top-five hit in Britain, collaborating with the Soup Dragons on the Rolling Stones cover "I'm Free," and released the album *Long Road*.

The inevitably titled *Visa* (1994) had little distribution in the United States, the country targeted in the title track, but it did advertise his immigration plight, and the actual cancellation stamp from Reid's passport appears on the album cover. The next record, *Junior Reid and the Bloods* (1995), was a collaboration with multiple artists, including Michael Rose (many incorrectly assumed Reid was at odds with Rose, since both had sung lead in Black Uhuru). By 1997, when he released *True World Order* on his own JR label, Reid had finally resolved his visa problems. In the decade that followed, he spent time consolidating his reputation while also promoting young artists. In 2007, Reid achieved some much-deserved attention by collaborating with the R&B singer Alicia Keys on the reggae remix of her #1 single "No One."

SELECT DISCOGRAPHY: *Original Foreign Mind* (Black Roots, 1985); *One Blood* (Big Life/Mercury, 1990); *Progress* (Wing, 1990); *Long Road* (Cohiba, 1991); *Big Timer* (VP, 1993); *Visa* (RAS, 1994); *Listen to the Voices* (RAS, 1996); *True World Order* (JR, 1997); *Rasta Government* (Jet Star, 2003)

REVOLUTIONARIES
YEARS ACTIVE: 1970s

The Revolutionaries were a fluid studio outfit who worked at the highly influential Channel One studio in the 1970s with its founders, the Chinese Jamaican Hoo-Kim brothers. The band arguably upgraded the style and sound of reggae during an intensely competitive decade among Jamaican studios and labels. Although the musicians were both individually and collectively members of other session bands, the Hoo-Kim brothers' emphasis on high sound quality and clarity helped make the Channel One imprint more distinctive. The lineups inevitably varied, but whenever musicians performed in recording sessions at other studios, top-notch substitutes would step in.

The group exemplified the musicianship that characterized the best of roots reggae, while shaping the sound and contributing key innovations. Drummer Sly Dunbar, who arrived from the club band Skin, Flesh and Bones, had an illustrious stint at Channel One. He is credited with creating the so-called Rockers rhythm, which featured persistent kick drum on each bar beat. He also developed a double-drumming style that infused the music with extra intensity. Around 1975, Dunbar developed a creative chemistry with bassist Robbie Shakespeare, with whom he later formed the Sly & Robbie team. By the early 1980s, the duo were producing other artists' records as well as creating their own. Their interlocking drums and bass became essential to the Revolutionaries' much-imitated sound.

As a unit, the group likely performed on more records than have been adequately documented, providing the quintessential roots sound of the mid- to late 1970s. But it was the Revolutionaries' dub releases—more than thirty remixed by the various label producers, including the 1978 releases *Earthquake Dub* and *Jonkanoo Dub*—that truly showcased the band's full instrumental quality.

By the early 1980s, Sly & Robbie were presented with lucrative opportunities to tour with former Wailers singer Peter Tosh in his backing band Word, Sound & Power, and later with the 1985 reggae Grammy winning band Black Uhuru, thus bringing the dominance of the Revolutionaries and Channel One to a close.

MEMBERS: **Sly Dunbar** (drums); **Carlton "Santa" Davis** (drums); **Bertram "Ranchie" McLean** (bass); **Robbie Shakespeare** (bass, rhythm guitar); **Radcliffe "Duggie" Bryan** (lead guitar); **Earl "Chinna" Smith** (lead guitar); **Tony Chin** (rhythm guitar); **Ansel Collins** (keyboards); **Bernard "Touter" Harvey** (keyboards); **Ossie Hibbert** (keyboards); **Noel "Scully" Simms** (percussion); **Uziah "Sticky" Thompson** (percussion); **Herman Marquis** (alto saxophone); **Tommy McCook** (tenor saxophone); **Vincent Gordon** (trombone)

SELECT DISCOGRAPHY: *Aggrovators Meets The Revolutionaries at Channel One* (Third World, 1977); *Earthquake Dub* (Joe Gibbs, 1978); *Jonkanoo Dub* (Channel One, 1978); *Revolutionaries Sounds Vol.2* (Ballistic, 1979); *Drum Sound* (Pressure Sounds, 2007)

The Revolutionaries, Channel One's house band in the 1970s, featured dynamic drum-and-bass duo Sly & Robbie.

CHANNEL ONE
Maxfield Avenue Breakdown
Dubs and Instrumentals
1974 - 79
pressure soUnds 31

WINSTON RILEY

YEARS ACTIVE: 1970s-2012

Born in 1946 in Kingston, Jamaica and trained as a nurse, Winston Riley grew to become a doctor of song and sound. By his own account, he formed the Techniques group with vocalists Slim Smith, Franklyn White, and Frederick Waite in either 1962 or 1964, depending on the source. The group made its recording debut at Kingston's Federal Studio, cutting "No One" in a session organized by conservative Jamaica Labour Party (JLP) politician and recording entrepreneur Edward Seaga, in whose district they were based. The group's mid-1960s string of rocksteady hits for Duke Reid's Treasure Isle label encouraged Riley to establish the Techniques label in 1968. Originally intended as a vehicle for Techniques recordings (often using different group names), the label soon took on other acts, like singer Johnny Osbourne, and by 1969, it had begun licensing material to the British independent soul and reggae label Pama Records for release in England.

Riley scored his first hit as a producer with Osbourne's sociopolitical commentary "Warrior" around 1970, but his first real success followed a deal that same year with Trojan Records that allowed him to create a UK Techniques imprint. The label carried the Jamaican duo Dave & Ansell Collins to the top of the British charts in 1971 with "Double Barrel." Following the record's success, Riley sent the group on a tour of England to capitalize on the hit. In 1974, the Techniques label ceased to exist, but it was around this time that Riley produced the "Stalag 17" rhythm track (1973) featuring Collins on organ, which roots reggae and dancehall artists have continually rerecorded. Riley never left the production realm and survived the decline of roots reggae's popularity in

Jamaica to become a force in the digital dancehall era, working with DJs Super Cat, Tenor Saw, and Buju Banton, and singer Frankie Paul, among many others.

The 1997 release of the *Techniques in Dub* album by Britain's Pressure Sounds label was a powerful reminder of the high quality of Riley's production work in the 1970s. In 2008, in a historical preservation effort, Riley started redeveloping the Techniques Records and studio site on Orange Street in Kingston to transform it into a Jamaican music museum. He received a series of setbacks in 2011 when, according to *Billboard* magazine, he was shot in August, stabbed in September, and then shot in the head and arm in November, with all of these events taking place in Kingston. Each act of violence remains unexplained and the crimes unsolved. After laying in a coma since the November shooting, Riley succumbed to his injuries and died in mid-January 2012.

SELECT DISCOGRAPHY: *Techniques in Dub* (Pressure Sounds, 1997); *Quintessential Techniques* (VP, 2009)

Winston Riley, the man behind the Techniques label and record shop, 1986.

ROCKSTEADY

In 1966, the arrival of rocksteady on the Jamaican music scene marked a departure from the manic pace of ska, offering a generally slower rhythm with more expressive bass phrasing. It was a sound that dancers could literally rock "steady" to and that vocalists could sing over more easily. The slower rhythm also had sociopolitical implications, reflecting the nation's collective introspection as the expected economic fruits of independence failed to appear. Some writers have also partly attributed rocksteady's reduced rhythmic pace to the especially hot weather the island experienced in 1966.

Not surprisingly, many artists claim to have invented the rocksteady rhythm. Jamaican singer Alton Ellis's 1966 hit single "Rock Steady" is considered the first song to include the name of the new beat in its title. Ellis strongly asserted that he alone was responsible for the innovation, but singer Hopeton Lewis claims that rocksteady began in October 1966 with his classic recording "Take It Easy." Lewis cut the single for producer Ken Khouri and was backed by such ace session musicians

as guitarists Ernest Ranglin and Lynn Taitt, the latter of whom is seen as a major instrumental influence on the genre's sound. To deliver his vocals properly, Lewis felt that he needed the band to slow down, and the groove they settled into created an important Jamaican hit. Because rocksteady required fewer musicians than ska, which had featured horns that were largely stripped away in the new style, it also proved more financially viable.

Rocksteady's first major UK hit was Desmond Dekker's "007 (Shanty Town)," which recounted the social misconduct of the "rude boys," the young, frustrated, knife-wielding urban youths of Kingston. Despite the rhythm's association with the rise of an outlaw criminal element, rocksteady was dominated by love songs. The producer most clearly associated with the sound is Duke Reid, and it might be argued that his intense commitment to rocksteady releases on his Treasure Isle label made him slow to respond to the rapid changes that came later in the decade with the introduction of reggae and its dub

offshoot. One of the label's key acts, the vocal group the Paragons, recorded "The Tide Is High," which was later covered by the American new wave group Blondie, topping the UK singles chart in 1980

and the US charts in early 1981. Other rocksteady vocal acts—among them the Heptones, who recorded at producer Coxsone Dodd's Studio One in Kingston in the mid-1960s—continued well into the reggae era, adapting their sound accordingly.

By 1968, reggae had taken control in an almost imperceptible transition, although rocksteady rhythms repeatedly reemerged in the following years, exemplifying Jamaica's musical recycling process.

For a variety of reasons—some musical, others sociopolitical—rocksteady replaced ska around 1966, allowing artists like the Maytals and Paragons to explore slower tempos.

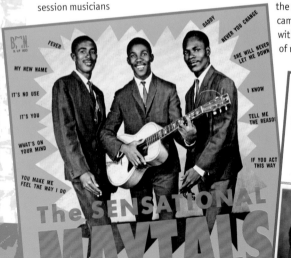

RICO RODRIGUEZ

YEARS ACTIVE: 1950s–2000s

Born Emmanuel Rodriguez in Cuba in 1934, the trombonist who would become known as Rico was one of the many graduates of the Alpha School for Boys in Kingston, Jamaica, where learning the rudiments of music provided both temporary refuge from the deprivations of economic poverty and creative survival tools for overcoming it. Initially tutored by fellow trombonist Don Drummond, a fellow Alpha School student and later a member of the Skatalites, Rico started working for Studio One in 1956, playing on founder Coxsone Dodd's first session. He also played on Jamaican pianist Theophilus Beckford's proto-ska hit "Easy Snappin'" (1959), a crucial record in Jamaica's process of reinterpreting American R&B influences and fusing them with local rhythmic and stylistic accents. Rico's personality as a player was affected by his time spent living in Rastafarian drummer Count Ossie's camp near Wareika Hills. This Rasta gathering point attracted many of Jamaica's top musicians and encouraged artistic and philosophical freedom that was distinctly anticolonial.

Having worked for the island's top producers, including Duke Reid and Leslie Kong, Rico left Jamaica for England in December 1961 and began working as a freelance session man for the Blue Beat and Pama record companies, two of the earliest labels making recordings in Britain for the West Indian community. Contrary to dates given in some sources, Rico's Pama LP debut, *Reco in Reggaeland* (with his name misspelled), was released in 1969. Produced by Bunny Lee and Rico with Jamaican rhythm tracks overdubbed in England, this was the fourteenth album release in Pama's Economy label series (recorded in mono), and one of several tributes to former Skatalites trombonist, Don Drummond that Rico recorded. Later that year, *Blow Your Horn*, credited to Rico & the Rudies, was issued on Trojan Records, one of the biggest

Trombone titan Rico Rodriguez debuted at the dawn of ska and continued blowing well into the twenty-first century.

British reggae labels of the era. The album was again characteristic of early instrumental reggae, but Rico worked in more jazz licks and arrangements than the average player.

One of Rico's career highlights was the 1976 *Man from Wareika* album, released by Island Records and produced by the versatile Karl Pitterson. With its title reaffirming the artist's cultural, physical, and spiritual Rasta roots, the instrumental record is often cited as a pivotal connection between jazz and the Jamaican popular music recordings that it influenced. The album was licensed for release on Blue Note Records, a legendary American jazz label, though the LP wasn't issued in the United States until 1977. While the original album potentially bridged gaps between audiences, its progressive alter ego, *Wareika Dub* (1977), was a thoroughly roots-oriented product unlikely to cross over and appeal to listeners of other genres. In any event, this mighty dub version remained a limited-edition white-label release (a promotional

release without a printed commercial label) until September 2004, when a Japanese reissue emerged.

Rico's profile went from marginal to almost mainstream when he opened shows for Bob Marley & the Wailers on the European leg of their 1977 *Exodus* tour. Once the British 2 Tone ska revival took off in the late 1970s, stimulating fresh audience interest in 1960s Jamaican music, Rico's playing was inevitably in demand, and he eventually joined the British ska outfit the Specials for their recordings and tours. He capitalized on his popularity with a new audience with the albums *That Man Is Forward* (1981) and *Jama Rico* (1982), both released on the 2 Tone record label at the tail end of the revival. The sets ran the gamut from ska and reggae to Afro-jazz, and encapsulated much of his career as an instrumentalist.

After a decade-long hiatus during which he lived in Jamaica, Rico recorded *Rising in the East* (1994) in Tokyo, a testament to how far his musical impact

extended beyond Jamaica's Wareika Hills. On subsequent recordings, he has continued to explore the musical territories on which his top-grade performance reputation was built. The records may not sell in large quantities, but his appearance in 2009 at concerts in London celebrating the fiftieth anniversary of Island Records showed that live audiences still appreciate his roots artistry.

SELECT DISCOGRAPHY: *Reco in Reggaeland* (Pama, 1969); *Blow Your Horn* (Trojan, 1969); *Man from Wareika* (Island, 1976); *Wareika Dub* (Island, 1977); *That Man Is Forward* (2 Tone, 1981); *Jama Rico* (2-Tone, 1982); *Rising in the East* (Jove, 1994); *Roots to the Bone* (Universal, 1995); *Rico's Message: Jamaican Jazz* (Culture Press, 1998); *Togetherness* (Jama, 2005); *Trombone Man: Anthology 1961–1971* (Sanctuary, 2005); *Wareika Vibes* (Jamdown, 2006)

LET THE POWER FALL

DYNAMIC
DY3313
STEREO

MAX ROMEO

MAX ROMEO
YEARS ACTIVE: 1960s–PRESENT

Born Maxwell Livingston Smith in 1947 in the parish of St. Ann, Jamaica, the future Max Romeo moved to Kingston at age ten and eventually ran away from home at age fourteen to escape domestic conflicts. In 1965, after working as a record deliveryman, he recorded his debut single, "Buy Me a Rainbow," with producer Ken Lack, who was one of the first producers to recognize his singing talent. He sang briefly with the all-male vocal group the Emotions, but they soon split up over leadership issues, so he formed an important alliance with Bunny Lee, then on the verge of becoming a producer.

Lee reputedly gave Romeo his stage name because of the singer's appeal to women; he was also responsible for Romeo's biggest-selling record, "Wet Dream." After several other vocalists, including Slim Smith and John Holt, rejected the song's smutty lyrics—

penned by Romeo—the singer himself agreed to cut a version, singing over the rhythm track from Derrick Morgan's "Hold You Jack." The single, which was the third release on Lee's Unity imprint, leaped to #10 on the British pop charts in 1969 despite an airplay ban by the British Broadcasting Corporation (BBC). "Wet Dream" shaped the salacious image of Romeo held by the wider, whiter mainstream audience that bought the record. It was also the kind of song that led to reggae's being incorrectly labeled as novelty music unworthy of the full-length album format. Nonetheless, after six months on the charts, the song had sold an estimated 250,000 copies and put Romeo on the map.

His 1970 album *A Dream* was one of the earliest reggae albums to be largely recorded in London with Britain-based musicians. Tours of Britain followed, but "Wet Dream" was Romeo's only international pop hit. The singer soon shifted focus, possibly in an effort to move on from the limiting identity shaped by the hit,

and his series of albums that followed in the 1970s took on a decidedly more serious tone. The 1970 Jamaican hit "Macabee Version" clearly foreshadowed the artist's philosophical path, and *Let The Power Fall* (1971) featured songs full of sociopolitical reality and biblical allusions projected through a Rastafarian prism.

When Jamaica's People's National Party (PNP), led by Michael Manley, adopted Romeo's massive Jamaican hit "Let the Power Fall On I" for its 1972 election campaign, it pushed his work even further into a serious direction. That single was also tangibly linked to the revivalist church songs and rhythms that were such an integral part of Jamaican popular music. The success of Manley's populist appeal and the movement of Rastafari to the musical foreground meant that many imitators wearing dreadlocks and professing devotion to Jah were attracted to the movement. This phenomenon led Romeo to record the ironically drum-free "Rasta Band Wagon" (1972) as a critique of the "baldheads" who jumped on board but shared nothing in common with Rasta. Romeo's music also reflected the first signs of disillusionment with the

new government, and "No Joshua No" (1973) referred to the characterization of Manley as a new version of the biblical figure Joshua. By accepting this persona of the Israelite leader who led his people into the Promised Land and out of captivity, Manley assumed enormous responsibility for leading Jamaica and its Rastas, among whom he'd gathered support towards greater social justice and prosperity. Romeo's "No Joshua No" reflected a growing dissatisfaction with Manley among Jamaicans, whose expectations of significant social and economic change were not being met.

By 1975, Romeo's material had found consistent popularity with the roots crowd, evidenced by the reggae market success of *Revelation Time* (1975), featuring "Open the Iron Gate." 1976's *War Ina Babylon,* produced by Lee Perry under his exclusive deal with Island Records, was one of the label's high-profile releases that year and became an iconic reggae album. Released as a single in Jamaica a year earlier, the title track had originally been called "Sipple Out Deh," roughly meaning "slippery and dangerous out there." Because the phraseology did not translate easily into the rock market—and because Island

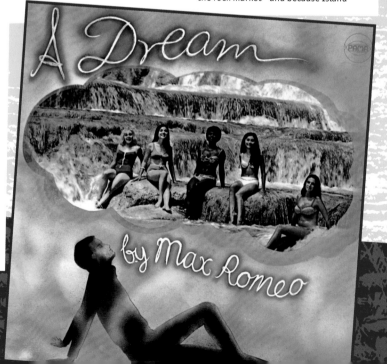

A Dream by Max Romeo

had its own ideas about how the mix should sound—the label revamped the same record as "War Ina Babylon," a commentary on the 1976 election, the chaotic economic conditions in Jamaica, and the unfulfilled hopes of Manley's term in office from 1972.

War Ina Babylon garnered critical acclaim, but after Perry began exhibiting increasingly erratic behavior, Romeo ventured into self-production for 1977's *Reconstruction*. A decade-long hiatus followed as dancehall took hold of Jamaica's music and as the Jamaica Labour Party (JLP), which Romeo did not support, took charge of the government. After a stint living in New York City in the 1980s, he began working with the British Jah Shaka sound system. On his return to recording, marked by 1992's *Fari Captain of My Ship*, Romeo was singing over the kind of digitally propelled rhythm tracks that were by then becoming generic. However, this material—as well as his later work with the hit London production duo Mafia & Fluxy— helped restore his artistic profile and credibility in a marketplace already full of compilations of his 1960s and 1970s recordings. He continues performing live at major international reggae festivals.

SELECT DISCOGRAPHY: *A Dream* (Pama, 1969); *Let the Power Fall* (Dynamic, 1971); *Revelation Time* (Sound Tracs, 1975); *War Ina Babylon* (Island, 1976); *Reconstruction* (Mango, 1977); *Fari Captain of My Ship* (Greensleeves, 1992); *Open the Iron Gate 1973–77* (Blood & Fire, 1999); *The Coming of Jah: Anthology 1967–1976* (Sanctuary, 2002)

A year before releasing his masterful *War Ina Babylon* (1976), Max Romeo readies for battle at Lee Perry's Black Ark studio.

"As a matter of fact, when people ask me about my education, I always tell them that I go to SWU—Sidewalk University, Kingston, Jamaica, that's where I acquire my education."
—MAX ROMEO, on growing up on the streets of Kingston

developed into a touring act backing other reggae artists. Roots Radics' skills as a live act kept them busy touring distant parts of the globe. They are the backing band seen in vocal group Israel Vibration's *Reggae in Holyland*, a 1996 documentary that contains rare footage of the singers in rehearsal with Roots Radics.

Lamont died on December 31, 1993, from prostate cancer, placing the band's future in doubt. They opted to continue, primarily as a live backing act, and in a 1996 *Reggae Report* magazine interview prior to another tour with Israel Vibration, guitarist Dwight Pinkney (formerly of 1970s reggae band Zap Pow) noted that there was still demand for live roots reggae since few dancehall acts could consistently sell out concert venues.

Roots Radics released albums of their own, but the records they made backing such artists as Bunny Wailer and their various dub albums may well stand as the best examples of their work. The core members remain connected to the music business, and Roots Radics backed Israel Vibration on a 2008 tour of Israel. Tragically, former keyboard player Steely died of a heart attack in New York on September 1, 2009, at the age of forty-seven.

MEMBERS: Ansel Collins (keyboard); Carlton "Santa" Davis (drums); Errol "Flabba" Holt (bass); Wycliffe "Steely" Johnson (keyboard); Eric "Bingy Bunny" Lamont (rhythm guitar); Dwight Pinkney (guitar); Earl "Chinna" Smith (guitar)

SELECT DISCOGRAPHY: *Forward Ever, Backward Never* (Heartbeat, 1991); *World Peace III* (Heartbeat, 1991)

The versatile Roots Radics in 1983, unfazed by reggae's shift from roots to dancehall.

ROOTS RADICS
YEARS ACTIVE: 1979–2000s

Roots Radics became one of the most popular studio session units in the days of early 1980s dancehall, recycling rhythms of the not-so-distant past. Errol "Flabba" Holt (bass) and Eric "Bingy Bunny" Lamont (rhythm guitar) formed the outfit in 1979 after leaving Morwells, a Jamaican roots reggae band that had achieved only moderate success. In addition to working as a freelance producer, Lamont had been a member of the all-star Revolutionaries, the house band at Channel One studio in Kingston.

The disintegration of the Channel One band in the late 1970s created commercial opportunities for session bands at other studios, and Roots Radics was frequently hired by emerging dancehall producer Henry "Junjo" Lawes. Working with singer Barrington Levy on such albums as *Bounty Hunter* (1979), Lawes first brought together the key members of what would become Roots Radics, though they had also recorded for producer Errol "Don" Mais's Roots Tradition label. Roots Radics' rotating roster of musicians reflected their informal origins as a loose collective of active studio players. Veteran drummer Carlton "Santa" Davis was among the early contributors, before the outfit was officially formed, as was keyboardist Wycliffe "Steely" Johnson, who later found success in Steely & Clevie, one of the most in-demand reggae production duos of the late 1980s and 1990s. Other well-known members of Roots Radics at one time or another included keyboardist Ansel Collins and guitarist Earl "Chinna" Smith.

As was typical for the most in-demand musicians, Roots Radics' credits were seemingly endless and included work with a wide range of producers. They were one of the few bands that easily negotiated the transition from roots reggae to dancehall, demonstrating ample capability with both musical styles. They came to wider attention as the backup unit on Gregory Isaacs's hugely successful *Night Nurse* album (1982), and toured with the singer. While the influx of digital music technology by the mid-1980s spelled the end of the band's studio supremacy, as producers could program machines instead of hiring musicians, Roots Radics then

MICHAEL ROSE

YEARS ACTIVE: 1970s–PRESENT

According to the artist himself, "Even though they may know his music, a lot of people don't know Michael Rose. They know Black Uhuru." Such is the central dilemma facing Rose, who made his name as the lead singer for one of reggae's best-known Rastafarian-promoting acts, Black Uhuru. That group successfully fused the style of 1970s roots reggae with the sound of the technology-infused 1980s, and won the first-ever Grammy award for best reggae recording in 1985 for their 1983 album, *Anthem*.

Rose was born in Kingston, Jamaica, in 1957. In 1972, he recorded "Dreadlocks Coming to Dinner," produced by Niney the Observer. This was an early version of the 1979 Black Uhuru single "Guess Who's Coming to Dinner," produced by the drum and bass team of Sly & Robbie on their Taxi label. Black Uhuru singer Derrick "Duckie" Simpson drafted Rose and Errol Nelson, who had been members of the vocal group the Jays, to join the band in the mid-1970s. In 1977, they recorded Black Uhuru's debut album, *Love Crisis* (1977), which marked the start of a fruitful phase for Rose in Black Uhuru that ended with the conclusion of the band's contract with Island Records in 1985. That year Rose left the group, later stating in *Reggae Report* that his eventual departure was a logical development, since they "couldn't do business no more. I just had to move on."

After leaving Black Uhuru, Rose continued recording in Jamaica, though for the next decade none of his records were released in the United States. During this post–Black Uhuru phase, he worked as a farmer at his coffee plantation just outside of Kingston, and decided to change the spelling of his name temporarily to Mykal Roze "because it's more cultural," as he explained to *Reggae Report* magazine in 1995. "The spelling is more African." He later

returned to the original spelling, citing audience confusion over whether he was the same singer who had fronted Black Uhuru, though his official website uses a hybrid form—Mykal Rose. Thankfully, as a vocalist responsible for influencing many younger reggae singers, his identity is more clearly defined.

Rose's first solo album, *Proud*, emerged in 1990. It was released on RCA Records in Britain and Japan and was only available in the United States as an import. *Bonanza* (1992), on the other hand, was a Japanese-market exclusive. For his self-titled mid-1990s set *Michael Rose* (1995), he was reunited with Niney the Observer and Sly & Robbie, producers who had played pivotal roles in his musical development; the US label Heartbeat Records, which released the album, gave Rose a renewed presence in the American market.

Since the mid-1990s, Rose has been fairly prolific, recording for a variety of labels. Several of his albums have been issued in dub versions, including *African Roots* (2005) and *Warrior* (2006). These were produced and remixed by the Holland–based guru Ryan Moore (who also records under the name Twilight Circus), whose high-quality recordings echo the vintage mixing style of dub reggae icon King Tubby. These latter-day dub albums have reinforced Rose's solid roots credentials at a time when dub has generally been on the margins of reggae culture. He continues to tour internationally, spreading his music and the philosophical messages of Rastafari.

SELECT DISCOGRAPHY: *Michael Rose* (Heartbeat, 1995); *Be Yourself* (Heartbeat, 1996); *Nuh Carbon* (RAS, 1996); *Dance Wicked* (Heartbeat, 1997); *Dub Wicked* (Heartbeat, 1997); *Selassie I Showcase* (Celluloid, 1998); *Bonanza* (Heartbeat, 1999); *African Roots* (M Records, 2005); *African Dub* (M Records, 2005); *Warrior* (M Records, 2006); *Warrior Dub* (M Records, 2007); *Great Expectations* (Rhythm Club, 2008); *Dub Expectations* (Rhythm Club, 2008)

Michael Rose rocks England's Glastonbury festival in 1982, several years before leaving Black Uhuru to forge a solo career.

OVAL

© 1976 DEB/ Morpheus/ Oval Records Ltd

Morpheus Music

OVAL 1008A

distributed by Virgin Records Ltd

time 2.40

ALL RIGHTS OF THE MANUFACTURER AND OF THE OWNER OF THE RECORDED WORK RESERVED · UNAUTHORISED PUBLIC PERFORMANCE BROADCASTING AND COPYING OF THIS RECORD PROHIBITED

GUESS WHO'S COMING TO DINNER
(M. Rose)
MICHAEL ROSE
produced by Niney the Observer with Castro & Dennis Brown

SANCTUARY RECORDS

Sanctuary Records, which owned the Trojan Records catalog for six years in the mid-1990s, grew out of Smallwood-Taylor Enterprises, which was established in 1976 in England by Rod Smallwood and Andy Taylor. Sanctuary began as an artist management enterprise with roots in heavy metal. After signing Iron Maiden in 1979 and turning that group into a major rock act, the company branched out into booking and merchandising. In the early 1980s, they established Sanctuary Records.

The label entered the reggae market in 2001, spending more than £10 million ($14.5 million) for the Trojan Records catalog, which comprised more than ten thousand titles by many of the reggae era's icons, including Bob Marley & the Wailers, Jimmy Cliff, Desmond Dekker, Lee Perry, Augustus Pablo, Toots & the Maytals, and John Holt. Established in 1968, Trojan was one of the first reggae labels based in the UK, releasing and distributing records on custom imprints through licensing deals with Jamaican producers before signing domestic acts in the early 1970s. By 1969, Trojan had penetrated the British pop charts, and the label continued to score more mainstream hits than competing reggae labels like Pama Records. Trojan represents a crucial phase in reggae history, a period when the music was being established commercially in Britain and crossing over to mainstream audiences. Despite these successes, Trojan first filed for bankruptcy in 1975, and despite attempts to reactivate it, large portions of the catalog seemed destined for oblivion.

Sanctuary reissued some key albums with extra tracks, but since the original releases from Trojan's heyday in the late 1960s and early 1970s are long out of print, compilations have dominated Sanctuary's output. In 2003, an American branch of Sanctuary was established, facilitating the release of many Trojan titles that were never previously issued in the United States. In 2007, amid major financial problems at Sanctuary (highlighted by a 97 percent decline in share value from the previous year), Universal Music Group bought the company for approximately $88 million, ousting the owners and their staff in the process. Universal has since solidified Trojan's historical significance, and September 2011 saw the release of the five-disc, 123-track set *The Story of Trojan Records*.

SCIENTIST
YEARS ACTIVE: 1970s–PRESENT

Overton H. Brown, better known by his recording name, Scientist, is renowned for his creative engineering and mixing talent as well as several albums of his own mixes bearing madcap titles and comic book–style cover designs. It was during his spell as an apprentice of the renowned dub remixer King Tubby that Brown became Scientist, so named because of his prescient ideas about creating automated, motorized faders for mixing consoles, well before such technology became a recording industry standard.

Born on April 18, 1960 in Kingston, Jamaica, Brown developed an interest in electronics as a youth, partly because his father was a repair technician. He began building amplifiers while working as a welder, and started his engineering career at Coxsone Dodd's Studio One in 1978. He soon became a teenage apprentice of King Tubby, and began developing his mixing after Tubby challenged him to tackle a song in the absence of fellow trainee Prince Jammy. Under Tubby's mentoring, Scientist was never allowed to rest on his mixing laurels and was continually encouraged to improve his skills.

Various sources present conflicting time lines for Scientist's career, but after developing a reputation as a creative engineer at King Tubby's studio, in late 1979 he moved to Channel One, which by

Sanctuary Records was not exactly modest about its series *This is Crucial Reggae.*

then was one of Kingston's most popular recording spots. Scientist soon became the engineer of choice for producer Henry "Junjo" Lawes's predigital dancehall production squad, which included the Roots Radics session band. Like Tubby, the young Scientist released albums of his own mixes to build an identity. Most of them featured absurdly colorful titles, such as *Scientist Rids the World of the Evil Curse of the Vampires* (1981), and outlandish cover designs. In 1982, Scientist shifted to Tuff Gong Studios, where he worked with engineer Errol Brown, and three years later, he headed for the United States.

In recent years, Scientist has spoken harshly of record companies, among them Blood & Fire, Trojan Records, and Greensleeves Records. Scientist alleges that these labels have illegally released material without permission from the artists, producers, or engineers whose names are associated with the records. He also claims that they have not paid royalties. In 2002, Scientist filed a copyright infringement lawsuit against Greensleeves for licensing tracks to the 2001 video game *Grand*

Theft Auto III. Ironically, the works in question were taken from *Scientist Rids the World of the Evil Curse of the Vampires*, an album that many fans cite as one of the best dub releases ever. Due to differences in American and British laws (relevant because of former colonial British rule) and the absence of Jamaica's own copyright laws until 1993, a New York district court jury ruled against Scientist in April 2005. The case just scratched the surface of the copyright crises within the realm of Jamaican popular music. At the time of the verdict, Scientist vowed to continue relentless international pursuit of compensation from Greensleeves, which was bought by VP Records in 2008.

OPPOSITE AND LEFT: Half the fun of owning Scientist records is marveling at the comic book–style titles and artwork.

ABOVE: Scientist faces off against Mad Professor at a "dubclash" in Amsterdam, 2001.

SELECT DISCOGRAPHY: : *Scientist Meets the Space Invaders* (Greensleeves, 1981); *Scientist Rids the World of the Evil Curse of the Vampires* (Greensleeves, 1981); *Scientist Wins the World Cup* (Greensleeves, 1981); *Dub in the Roots Tradition* (Blood & Fire, 1996); *Scientist Launches Dubstep into Outer Space* (Tectonic, 2010)

EDWARD SEAGA

Edward Seaga is best known as a former Prime Minister of Jamaica (1980–1989), but his political career also overlapped with his direct involvement in Jamaica's music business in the 1960s as the owner of a record company and as a record producer. Born in Boston to Jamaican parents in 1930, Seaga was one of the few Jamaican politicians who had studied the roots of the island's music. He researched Jamaican spiritual rituals retained from African culture including Kumina/Pukkumina. After graduating from Harvard University in 1952, Seaga recorded the music on the 1956 release of *Folk Music of Jamaica* for the United States–based Folkways Records label, which has since issued a CD version of the album. Seaga notes that he was drawn to the music business through efforts to distribute this release. Jamaican record sellers asked if he could import other music for them, and he soon became the local agent for most of the major American labels.

Seaga established West Indies Records Limited (WIRL) in Kingston in 1958, and although he had not originally planned on venturing into production, he scored a major Jamaican hit in 1960 with "Manny O," performed by the singing duo Higgs & Wilson. Around the same time, another future mainstay of the Jamaican music business, Byron Lee & the Dragonaires, also scored their first hit single with "Dumplins" on the WIRL label. Seaga's only notable competition at the time was producer Ken Khouri of Federal Records, who was then focused on selling calypso and mento records to tourists.

In 1962, Seaga became the minister of development and welfare under the conservative Jamaica Labour Party (JLP) government and was elected to the House of Representatives as Member of Parliament for Western Kingston. As he moved into politics, he had less time to devote to music, and he left his father and cousin in charge of WIRL. Despite his withdrawal from the business, Seaga

LEFT: Supporters of Edward Seaga, Jamaica's prime minister from 1980 to 1989, keep the faith at a 1988 rally.
RIGHT: Seaga joins a dominoes game in Kingston, early 1980s.

played a pivotal role in assembling an entourage to promote Jamaican music at the 1964 World's Fair in New York City. Among Seaga's collaborators on this project were Khouri and Ahmet Ertegun, the cofounder of Atlantic Records, which released *Jamaica Ska* that same year. In selecting musicians for the New York trip, Seaga and his team created a fair bit of controversy. They passed on selecting ska architects the Skatalites—a band that included Rastas—and instead chose the more clean-cut Byron Lee & the Dragonaires. Many musicians felt that class, race, and anti-Rastafarian attitudes influenced the decision to present a more easily acceptable face and sound of Jamaica to the world. Seaga suggests that his familiarity with Lee, as well as the band's versatility and awareness of showbiz norms, made them more suitable for the task. During the mid-1960s, Seaga also played a key role in freeing singer Derrick Morgan from his exclusive recording contract with the British label Blue Beat Records.

Around 1966 the Jamaica Labour Party decided to remove Kingston's Back-O-Wall slum, located in Seaga's district, with bulldozers—an action that displaced a considerable number of musicians in that downtown community. The Back-O-Wall ghetto was home to many Rastafarian groups, so many Jamaicans viewed this demolition

as a means of dispersing the area's Rasta concentration. The rebuilt area became known as Tivoli Gardens, a section of the city that was initially dominated by JLP supporters. Tivoli Gardens gained international notoriety in 2010 as civil unrest related to the proposed extradition of alleged gang leader Christopher "Dudus" Coke to the United States transformed the area into a battleground. Coke was accused of various drug and firearms offences involving trafficking between Jamaica and America.

The ongoing political conflict between the conservative JLP and the democratic, socialist People's National Party (PNP) shaped the harsh social and economic conditions under which roots reggae was created during the 1970s. Even in his nonmusical role (if such a thing really exists in Jamaica) as a party leader, Seaga wielded indirect influence on the music scene. His ascension to the position of prime minister after bloody elections in 1980 also seemed to usher in a new musical era—one in which the spiritual and revolutionary incisiveness that characterized reggae's lyrics gave way to more material concerns. At the same time, the music became gradually less progressive and transitioned into dancehall.

JAMAICAN POLITICS & POPULAR MUSIC

In Jamaica, politics has often been literally a matter of life and death. Given the violence that has plagued elections since the 1940s, musicians must give careful thought to declaring their allegiance to parties or candidates—particularly when they do so in song. Alert politicians, meanwhile, have learned to gauge the mood of the electorate by listening for lyrical themes and philosophical ideas in popular songs. These are just two of the many examples of the close connection between Jamaican music and politics.

Despite colonial oppression, the strength of African cultural legacies in Jamaica ensured that music would play a pivotal social role. Still, few would have predicted the ways in which dissatisfaction with Jamaica's political situation would fuel revolutionary feeling and action on an international level. In the early twentieth century, the black-liberation ideologies promoted by Marcus Garvey created a kind of political foundation for Jamaica's future leaders. However, Garvey died in 1940 and did not live long enough to see his dreams of global black political and economic independence move closer to fruition. As the twentieth century progressed, Jamaica and the African diaspora continued to struggle with colonialism's legacies of race and class preoccupations. Jamaica, under British control from 1655 to 1962 (though Britain's official rule began in 1670), and other Anglo-Caribbean societies were shaped by the racial prejudice that facilitated slavery. Britain's rigid class system also offered few opportunities for economic and social advancement for those not born into wealth.

By the late 1930s, Alexander Bustamante (born William Alexander Clarke in 1884) had become a leading voice for the country's working-class masses. He established the Bustamante Industrial Trade Union (BITU)—reputedly the Caribbean's first trade union—to mobilize workers. Large-scale unemployment arising from the Great Depression had created serious discontent, and in 1938, due to his role in organizing strikes, Bustamante was detained at "His Majesty's Pleasure"—an imperialistic euphemism for serving jail time—though the charges were later dropped. Bustamante's cousin, Norman Manley, entered politics in 1937, and a year later he formed the People's National Party (PNP). Initially, Bustamante backed this movement, but he defected in 1943 to form his own party, the Jamaica Labour Party (JLP), which

MARCUS GARVEY

A PEOPLE WITHOUT THE KNOWLEDGE OF THEIR PAST HISTORY, ORIGIN AND CULTURE IS LIKE A TREE WITHOUT ROOTS.

I KNOW NO NATIONAL BOUNDARY WHERE THE NEGRO IS CONCERNED. THE WHOLE WORLD IS MY PROVINCE UNTIL AFRICA IS FREE

ARTIST JahBobby

first came to power in 1944. By this time, the kind of politically motivated violence that would mar elections in the 1970s and 1980s had already begun.

The PNP first assumed the reins of government in 1955, and as it sought greater autonomy for the island from Britain, the party developed more left-leaning ideologies. By the late 1950s, Jamaica's government was managing the island's internal affairs, making the quest for full political independence the next logical step. In a 1961 referendum, Jamaica rejected the idea of remaining in the West Indies Federation, the organization formed in 1958 to unite the region's British colonial territories. The JLP adopted the song "Freedom" (1961) by singer and songwriter Clancy Eccles to promote its opposition to the West Indies Federation, and Bustamante helped lead the island into independence in 1962. The song, however, had not been written in support of either political party; it was instead an Afrocentric Rastafari contemplation. This is one of the early instances of locally recorded popular music being used in a Jamaican political campaign. It is ironic then, that Bustamante's apparent right-wing alignment with British colonial policies soon manifested itself in his own assaults against Rastafari.

One of Jamaica's earliest record labels, West Indies Records Limited (WIRL), was established in 1958 by Edward Seaga, who would later go on to become a JLP government minister in the early 1960s and eventually Jamaica's prime minister in 1980. A decade before Jamaica gained its independence, Seaga obtained an anthropology degree from Harvard University, where his studies centered on traditional Jamaican cultural practices. In future JLP campaigns, he would make effective use of his understanding of music's role in Jamaican society. The PNP, meanwhile, proved equally aware of music's power to garner votes. Further underscoring the relationship between music and politics was the career path of Vincent Edwards: from his days as King Edwards, one of the "big three" sound-system operators of the late 1950s (along with Coxsone Dodd and Duke Reid), he proceeded to earn a seat in parliament, where he represented the PNP.

In the post-independence era, choosing a political party and/or candidate became a choice between survival and starvation—life and death.

OPPOSITE: Early twentieth-century black nationalist leader Marcus Garvey is considered a religious prophet by Rastafarians.

RIGHT: Rastafarians await the arrival of Ethiopian emperor Haile Selassie (whom they believe to be the messiah) in Kingston, Jamaica, 1966.

Both parties recruited "rude boys" (violent youths) from Kingston's gangland to serve as enforcers, and political violence intensified with the rising economic stakes. These were the seeds of the bloody warfare that characterized elections in the next two decades, as rampant poverty provided an environment in which such discord could flourish.

As social suffering deepened, anguish and frustration surfaced more frequently in Jamaican music. During this time, it became increasingly clear that, despite their social marginalization, the nation's recording artists had become a type of collective political force. In 1968, the Ethiopians released "Everything Crash," a searing statement of acute social disillusionment and despair that was promptly banned by Prime Minister Hugh Shearer's ruling JLP government. The following year, Desmond Dekker sang of the sufferer's harsh economic plight in his international hit "Israelites," although his message may have been lost on those listeners who embraced the song more for its rhythmic qualities than for its lyrical power.

After succeeding his father as leader of the PNP, the socialist-leaning Michael Manley rose to power in 1972, defeating the Shearer-led JLP. Manley's ascent was partly due to image management, as he capitalized on the sentiments of Rastafari and the poor. In fact, 1972 marks a watershed for politicians using reggae while evoking elements of Rasta

culture. In an astute tactical move, Manley visited Ethiopia in the early 1960s, well aware that cordial interaction with Emperor Haile Selassie, the Rasta religious icon seen as God incarnate, could attract new constituents. Manley's use of the so-called Rod of Correction, a wooden staff given to him by Selassie, helped him solicit Rastafarian support for his election campaign. His supporters compared him to the biblical Joshua, who led his people out of captivity, and this became his nickname in both day-to-day conversation and popular songs.

Reggae became an active campaign element for Manley's PNP, which co-opted Delroy Wilson's "Better Must Come" (1971) as a theme song and slogan, even though Wilson asserted that his song protested unfair record industry practices rather than politicians. Among the other artists who released music of sociopolitical relevance was singer Junior Byles, whose 1972 singles "Joshua's Desire" and "Pharaoh Hiding" referred to the biblically inspired nicknames of Jamaica's two leading politicians. The PNP also adopted Eccles's affirmative "Rod of Correction" (1971) and his up-tempo single "Power for the People" (1971), which featured speech fragments from Manley, as well as Eccles's own spoken-word introduction of the politician and his party. It is safe to say that "Power for the People" rates as one of the boldest political endorsements in the history of Jamaican popular music. As a supporter of Manley's democratic socialism, Eccles took an active role in the election campaign, even though he was not an official PNP member. After the administration came to power, he served as one of several unpaid cultural advisers.

To capitalize fully on the connection between music and disenfranchised voters, the PNP established a reggae entourage unofficially referred to as the musical bandwagon, which literally gave reggae acts a platform to perform at various rallies. Organized by Eccles, the bandwagon launched in late 1971, shortly before the February 1972 election. The idea of reaching out to the poor and dispossessed

with roots music—a sound that came from their own environment—captured the mood of the times. Jamaica's first decade of independence had been unfulfilling, and public pressure for change was mounting. Around 1977, Manley said, "I listen carefully to the new reggae songs because they

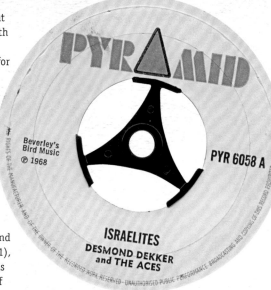

remind me that the slums are still there." While Manley's campaign was successful, his party's association with popular music was a double-edged sword. When the government fell short of its promises, musicians responded in song. Junior Byles's "When Will Better Come" (1972) and Max Romeo's "No Joshua No" (1973) are often cited as prime examples of the disillusionment with Manley and the PNP.

The 1973 oil crisis sent Jamaica into a financial downward spiral, forcing the government to borrow money from the International Monetary Fund (IMF). These loans were accepted despite the IMF's unrealistic loan repayment conditions, which were comparable to those of loan sharks. This situation essentially crippled the already struggling island. The impact was such that one otherwise anonymous studio session unit appeared on dub B-sides of various singles during the 1970s and into the 1980s as the IMF Players. Further tensions resulted from the creation of the Gun Court in 1974, established by the government to curb rapidly increasing gun crimes and arms violations. The court dispensed

Michael Manley, leader of the People's National Party and former prime minster of Jamaica, in the mid-1980s.

harsh penalties—including indefinite detention—to those caught with firearms, ammunition, or even used bullet cartridges. Not surprisingly, this policy ultimately proved ineffective. The flow of weapons into the island continued, and the situation became fodder for additional social commentary in song.

By this time, reggae and the politics of liberation were quite inseparable. This was especially true of Jamaica's ties with American nemesis Cuba and alignment with that country's support for Angola's leftist revolutionary MPLA (Popular Movement for the Liberation of Angola)—then embroiled in a conflict with South African troops. This connection to armed revolutionary struggle in Africa, after much of the continent had already achieved political independence in the previous two decades, allowed America to characterize Jamaica as a Marxist communist state. Reggae DJ Tappa Zukie's 1976 hit "MPLA" and its "Dub MPLA" version demonstrated the extent to which reggae musicians were conscious of the political struggle. The same was true of the Revolutionaries' 1979 *Revolutionaries Sounds Vol. 2* album cover featuring a large illustrated image of iconic Cuban revolution rebel Che Guevara. By 1976, mounting economic disarray and internal political violence in Jamaica had created such turbulent instability (believed by many to have been instigated by America's Central Intelligence Agency) that Manley was forced to declare a state of emergency. According to reports, the murder rate had practically doubled between 1974 and 1976, making an official declaration of national crisis a mere formality. Inevitably, music mirrored the situation, and Max Romeo's "War Ina Babylon" is among the era's more memorable songs.

In 1976, some reggae songs were banned in the run-up to the elections won by Manley's PNP. Ironically, some writers suggest that under Manley, disenchantment with the PNP among the ghetto population increased the ranks of Rastafari, one of the very constituencies that helped sweep Manley into office. The attempted assassination of Bob Marley in December 1976 unambiguously demonstrated a fear and recognition that music had the power to move the people in one direction or another. At 1978's One Love Peace Concert in Kingston, Marley succeeded in bringing Manley and Seaga onstage for a fleeting and symbolic moment of "reconciliation." This again demonstrated that music was a path to the people that politicians could not afford to ignore.

Bob Marley and Edward Seaga at the One Love Peace Concert held in Kingston, Jamaica on April 22, 1978.

As the PNP asserted its brand of democratic socialism, it was undermined by the oil crisis, a global decline in demand for bauxite (Jamaica's major mineral resource), and America's anticommunist paranoia, which ultimately led to direct subversive political interference in Jamaica. The government's inability to cope with such an avalanche of destructive events propelled inflation to new levels. The tourism industry also faltered, putting additional pressure on Jamaica's poor. The economic deprivation and waves of horrific violence that followed were naturally translated into popular music, as artists articulated the people's plight and the nation's desperate need for peace.

The exodus of Jamaica's middle and upper classes to North America in the 1970s brought members of the Chin family—famous for the Randy's record shop, record label and recording studio, all in Kingston—to New York, where they founded VP Records in 1979. Their label became a major force in reggae's dancehall era. Studio One's Coxsone Dodd also fled Jamaica's social decay for New York City in 1980, as many killings were attributed to political election warfare that year.

After regaining power in 1980, the conservative Seaga-led JLP overturned the socialist policies of the Manley government, replacing them with free-market capitalism. The bloody gang violence that characterized the 1980 election campaign inevitably affected the music being made. At the same time, Jamaica's drug culture shifted from ganja to cocaine, infusing the era's digital dancehall with an unfiltered sonic harshness that unfortunately reflected the sociopolitical attitudes of the day.

The ties between politicians, dons (informal rulers of specific urban areas), and musicians in the dancehall era extended the practices of earlier decades. Most notably, in 2010, amid US efforts to extradite Christopher "Dudus" Coke, reggae musicians publicly supported the alleged crime boss and drug kingpin. Bunny Wailer's pro-Dudus "Don't Touch the President," released in late 2009 and written ahead of the social unrest that would grip Kingston, was one of the popular songs during this crisis. It confirmed that Jamaican music remained as relevant to politics as ever.

HAILE SELASSIE
(1892-1975)

Haile Selassie, born in 1892, was no ordinary political or religious figure. Despite his diminutive physical stature, the long-running Ethiopian emperor was declared a god by some Jamaicans and is still worshipped by many (though not all) Rastafarians. Bearing the titles King of Kings, Lord of Lords, Conquering Lion of the Tribe of Judah, Elect of God, and Light of the World, Selassie remains the guiding light of Rastafarian philosophy.

He ascended to the Ethiopian throne in November 1930, bearing the imperial title Ras, signifying his spiritual leadership, with Tafari Makonnen as his family name. Claiming to have descended from the biblical King Solomon, a figure renowned for his wisdom, he adopted the title of Haile Selassie, meaning "Power of the Trinity." In Jamaica, where black-liberation icon Marcus Garvey had spread his teachings and biblical reinterpretations in the 1920s, Selassie's coronation assumed enormous significance. To many, it was the fulfillment of biblical prophecy: Selassie was seen by poverty-stricken, colonially exploited Jamaicans as a black messiah. Following a fruitless plea to the League of Nations for help in repelling Italy's invasion of Ethiopia in 1935, Selassie fled to England. His exile angered Garvey, who condemned Selassie's flight from his homeland in 1936, though any sense of conflict between these historical figures is rarely apparent in reggae lyrics. The Western allies of the Second World War ended Italy's occupation of Ethiopia and restored Selassie's rule in 1941.

When Michael Manley of Jamaica's People's National Party (PNP) astutely visited Ethiopia in the early 1960s, he acquired the Rod of Correction, a wooden staff given to him by Selassie. That the rod—thought to contain Selassie's aura—became a crucial symbol in Manley's successful 1972 election campaign demonstrated how the emperor was perceived in Jamaica. Selassie's three-day visit to the island in 1966 sparked scenes of adulation, particularly among Rastafarians, who emerged from the social margins to mark his arrival. Since Rastas were included in the official welcoming delegation, Selassie's visit increased their credibility in Jamaican society.

Selassie's reign in Ethiopia ended in 1974, following a military coup triggered by his authoritarian rule and the government's apparent indifference to a debilitating famine. He died in captivity in 1975 in the Ethiopian capital city of Addis Ababa, though some Rastas—viewing him as the living god of biblical prophecy—assert his immortality. This belief is demonstrated in such songs as Bob Marley & the Wailers' defiant single "Jah Live" (1976). Selassie's name has been invoked in countless reggae recordings and become an integral part of the music's philosophy. His image, meanwhile, has adorned numerous album covers and is one of reggae culture's most enduring and powerful symbols.

Deified by Rastas, Ethiopian emperor Haile Selassie fled his country in 1936 to escape invading Italian forces.

shows by reggae artists Prince Far I and Creation Rebel the previous year, he set up On-U Sound, a sound system that would later become a record label.

Sherwood eventually took the production helm of his own studio bands using a variety of names, including Dub Syndicate, New Age Steppers, African Head Charge, and Revolutionary Dub Warriors. In 1986, he collaborated with one of his idols, legendary producer Lee Perry, to record *Time Boom X De Devil Dead* (credited to Lee "Scratch" Perry & Dub Syndicate), an album not released outside of Britain until 1987. They added Perry's album *From the Secret Laboratory* to their collaborations in 1990, but due to Perry's infamous behavioral eccentricities, their subsequent professional dealings were fraught with instability and occasional discord.

One of Sherwood's most important achievements was establishing the Pressure Sounds record label in 1994. The reissue label is devoted to rescuing roots reggae rarities and has become well known among aficionados. Sherwood's later freelance production and remixing projects have not been entirely restricted to reggae—he has also worked in rock and electronic pop.

Sherwood's music reached cinema screens through the sound track for 2010's *Fire in Babylon*, a documentary about the seemingly invincible West Indies cricket team of the 1970s. Often the subject of academic theorizing about modern dub, Sherwood may yet have many more chapters to write in his musical journal.

SELECT DISCOGRAPHY: Dub Syndicate: *Fear of a Green Planet* (Shanachie, 1998); **Revolutionary Dub Warriors:** *State of Evolution* (On-U, 1994); **Adrian Sherwood:** *Never Trust a Hippy* (Real World, 2003); *Becoming a Cliché* (Real World, 2006); **with Lee Perry:** *From the Secret Laboratory* (Mango/Island, 1990); *Dubsetter* (On-U Sound, 2010)

ADRIAN SHERWOOD

YEARS ACTIVE: 1970s-PRESENT

Adrian Sherwood's multiple music enterprises are an example of the powerful impact of dub on Britain. Sherwood, founder of the Pressure Sounds label, has worked in licensing and distribution, as a sound system operator, and as a producer. He was born in 1958 in London, and his adventures as a teenage DJ in the early 1970s, as well as his awareness of multicultural issues as a result of close friendships with West Indians, gave Sherwood a framework for his later involvement in the music business.

He was a partner and cofounder in J&A Distribution from 1975 through 1977. After that enterprise dissolved due to financial problems, he served short stints with other licensing and distribution companies specializing in reggae. In 1980, having seen British

LEE 'SCRATCH' PERRY DUB SYNDICATE

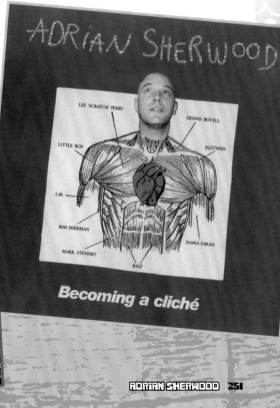

Becoming a cliché

LEROY SiBBLES

YEARS ACTIVE: 1960s–PRESENT

One of reggae's less heralded figures, Leroy Sibbles, born in 1949 in Kingston's Trench Town, was one of the multitalented individuals who helped make legendary producer Coxsone Dodd's Studio One record label and recording facility in Kingston such a creative force. Sibbles led the Heptones, a vocal group that debuted on producer Ken Lack's Caltone label in 1966 with "Gunmen Coming to Town." They later signed with Studio One, where they thrived during the rocksteady era. Their biggest hit, "Fattie Fattie" (1966), was extremely popular with audiences despite being banned from Jamaican radio because of its suggestive lyrics.

During the rocksteady period, Sibbles began playing electric bass. He came to the instrument almost by accident, when Jackie Mittoo, the former keyboardist for ska instrumental giants the Skatalites, drafted him for a club gig even though Sibbles had no experience on bass. He learned quickly and became a fixture at Studio One, where he played bass on such Jamaican hits as "Queen of the Minstrel" (1969) by the vocal group the Eternals, which featured vocals by falsetto singer Cornell Campbell. More notably, he was the bassist on the Abyssinians' vocal anthem "Satta Massa Gana" (1971).

After Mittoo moved to Canada (sources differ regarding the dates of his departure), Sibbles became Studio One's musical director, and his arranging and producing roles expanded significantly. Disillusioned by Dodd's underpayment, Sibbles as an individual and the Heptones as a group left the label in 1971, and Sibbles briefly immigrated to Canada. He returned to spearhead the Heptones' revival under a 1975 deal with Island Records, which was actively promoting its many reggae signings—such as Bob Marley & the Wailers—in the international market. Sibbles stayed with the group through *Better Days* in 1978, when it became clear that better days and bigger things would not arrive as a result of the Island deal. After a second stay in Canada, he returned to his central singer-songwriter role with the Heptones in the mid-1990s. Sibbles also recorded several solo albums between the late 1970s and the 1990s.

The hits Sibbles played on are at the core of reggae culture, but despite the constant reuse of the rhythms by other artists, he receives no composer royalties for his early work with Dodd. This has left him with a lingering sense of bitterness. In 2011, he performed live in Jamaica and abroad in preparation for the projected release of a solo album.

SELECT DISCOGRAPHY: *It's Not Over* (VP, 1997); *Come Rock with Me* (Heartbeat, 1999); *On Top* (ERNI, 1999)

Heptones leader and Studio One musical director Leroy Sibbles never served in the Army, but he played on a legion of albums.

Prod./Compiled by Phill Pratt Dist. by Pama Records

SS10 A

SWEAT FOR YOU BABY
(Heptones)
LEROY SIBBLIES AND THE HEPTONES
REAL COOL
U.ROY

DANNY SIMS

Easily one of the more controversial businessmen in reggae history, entrepreneur-manager Danny Sims has the unfortunate reputation of being the man who attempted to steer Bob Marley in a more commercial direction, and who then profited on numerous occasions from Marley's resistance. Even in an industry rife with exploitative characters, critical consensus regarding Sims's allegedly unethical dealings makes him a unique figure.

Born in Mississippi in 1936, Sims entered the music business around 1960 after running the successful Sapphire's black supper club in New York City's Harlem neighborhood. He was hired by Texas pop singer Johnny Nash to manage a tour of the Caribbean, and the fruitful business relationship led to Sims's full immersion in musical entertainment. Initially, he promoted appearances by American soul acts, including singer Otis Redding, before forming JODA Records with Nash in 1964. The label had a brief run of minor Hot 100 singles in the United States in 1965 and 1966 with both Nash and the R&B duo Sam & Bill before going bankrupt two years later. Sims made the adventurous move of relocating both himself and Nash to Jamaica in 1966. Through previous promotional activities, Sims recognized the depth of Jamaica's musical talent and the potential to profit from it. Nash soon nabbed a major transatlantic hit with the reggae-flavored 1968 single "Hold Me Tight," which reached #5 in both America and Britain.

Nash brought Marley to Sims's attention after the two singers were introduced at a Kingston Rasta gathering in January 1968. Sims promptly signed the young Jamaican artist—and according to some accounts, also fellow Wailers vocalists Peter Tosh and Bunny Wailer—to recording and publishing contracts. The deals came after the Wailers had consulted their Rasta manager and spiritual mentor Mortimer Planno. These moves, especially the publishing deal with Sims's Cayman Music, would take on greater commercial significance in just a few years, as the Wailers' popularity increased. The group had no way of knowing that the dozens of tracks—possibly eighty songs—they recorded for Sims in the late 1960s would be repackaged and recycled for decades to come, much like those they would later cut for Jamaican producer Lee Perry in 1970 and 1971. Sims used Jamaica as an international base of operations, and in 1969 he established JAD Records, a label still releasing Marley's music in the twenty-first century.

By 1970, Sims and Nash had traveled to Europe to work on a commercially unsuccessful Swedish film project. They soon focused on getting Nash a deal with CBS Records in England. They involved Marley in their ongoing songwriting and recording plans and in 1971 summoned the rest of the Wailers to England to work on Nash's next record. Sims also secured a CBS deal for Marley, and the label released the rock-leaning 1972 single "Reggae on Broadway." The song met with indifference in the marketplace, but Nash's 1972 pop-reggae album *I Can See Clearly Now*, which included four songs written by Marley, was a smash hit. Sims had helped to push reggae into the international mainstream, but the diluted, pop-oriented sound trapped the music in a novelty category. In late 1972, Sims and Nash fled the frigid bleakness of London and went to America to further promote *I Can See Clearly Now*.

Their departure left the Wailers in England without immediate touring prospects or a record label until they negotiated a deal with Island Records head Chris Blackwell that same year. Blackwell secured the band's release from Sims's recording contracts and the CBS deal. At this point, Sims used his ample leverage to secure a £5,000 payment, 2 percent of the revenue from the band's first six Island releases, and continued control—through October

1976—of Marley's publishing through his own Cayman Music company. This situation would allegedly lead Marley to credit his compositions to other songwriters to avoid generating income for his former business associate. Oddly, Island later hired Sims as a radio promoter to support "Could You Be Loved," a single from Marley's 1980 *Uprising* album.

Uprising was Marley's final album and his last under contract with Island. In 1980, Sims allegedly proposed to broker an improved deal—one reportedly worth at least $10 million—between Marley and his Tuff Gong label and what was then PolyGram Records. But Marley didn't live long enough to see this deal come to fruition. Ironically, PolyGram went on to buy Island in 1989, gaining control of the Marley catalog before being absorbed into the Universal Music Group in the 1990s.

Not long after Marley's death in 1981, Sims released *Chances Are*, a collection of rough-sounding remixes of the artist's earlier recordings from different sessions, on Cotillion Records.

Critics and fans alike met the album with cynicism and resentment. The memory of Marley's untimely death was still fresh, and the material was far below the songwriting and sound quality Marley had achieved by the end of his life. Seen as an exploitative capitalist—the very type Marley decried in his songs—Sims was permanently tainted with a negative aura, though this had no impact on his ability to manage his business effectively. He was quoted in Stephen Davis's 1990 book *Bob Marley* as saying that "the only thing I didn't get part of was the [Marley] tour money."

In 1984, Sims filed a $6 million suit against Marley's estate, claiming that the superstar had violated his Cayman Music deal by fraudulently crediting songs to others. Among the estate's counterclaims was the argument that the statute of limitations had expired on Sims's allegations. After US court proceedings that lasted three years, Cayman's suit was dismissed, and by the early 1990s, Sims had based himself in South Africa. In January 2004, twenty years after the lawsuit was filed, Sims's

JAD Records reached a ten-year exclusive licensing deal with the Universal Music Group for the release of about 211 vintage Marley recordings. The exact financial terms were not disclosed, but given the wealth of Marley recordings Universal already owned, the agreement gave the label unprecedented access to nearly all of the superstar's catalog. Undoubtedly, it also earned Sims millions of dollars in the process.

Many fans and music journalists have looked with unambiguous disdain on Sims's penchant for exploiting Marley's output. A 1998 *Billboard* magazine review of *The Complete Bob Marley & the Wailers 1967-1972 Part II* summarized the collection as such: "JAD continues to set new standards of commercial contempt for both the posthumous memory of a great artist and the pocketbooks of his unsuspecting audience." Sims continues to be vilified for capitalizing on Marley's recordings, and his decisions to release unfinished songs have threatened to diminish the artist's creative legacy.

SKA

As a uniquely local reinterpretation of R&B rhythms from America's South, ska became synonymous with Jamaica in the early 1960s and was the island's musical trademark until the arrival of rocksteady around 1966. With its intense rhythmic pace, ska never became an international commercial phenomenon, but it played a significant role in the development of Jamaican popular music.

As with many styles of music, ska's origins have long been subject to debate. Renowned Jamaican guitarist Ernest Ranglin asserts with great conviction that the music resulted from a conscious effort at Kingston's Studio One record label to change the rhythmic emphasis of R&B and augment the traditional shuffle signature. However, various other musicians— among them, bassists Byron Lee and Clue J, aka Cluett Johnson—are credited in different sources with either inventing the style or having direct knowledge of how it emerged. Legendary Skatalites saxophonist Tommy McCook pointed to Clue J as the

inventor of ska in part because Clue J frequently used the word "skavoovie" to greet his colleagues. Producer Bunny Lee concurs: he has said that Clue J made key musical innovations that led to the invention of ska before people like Studio One owner and producer Coxsone Dodd began recording it. However, Clue J's role is complicated by the fact that his band, Clue J and His Blues Blasters, included Ranglin and was one of Dodd's earliest session outfits in the late 1950s. Finally, pianist and singer Theophilus Beckford's "Easy Snappin'" is acknowledged by many as the first ska release; it was recorded in 1956 but not released until 1960. No one should expect a satisfactory resolution to this historical debate any time soon.

Ska and its musicians were rooted in Kingston's ghettoes, but the music would escape those urban confines as it gained popularity overseas. In the hands of the dominant sound-system operators who later became

In 1968, after relocating to Jamaica with manager Danny Sims, Johnny Nash hit #5 in America and Britain with this disc's title track.

The Specials, leaders of Britain's brief 2 Tone ska revival, barrel through one of their punk-infused numbers, 1980.

Jamaican dancers at the Drake Hotel in New York City during the ska boom, 1964.

significant studio and record-label owners (particularly Dodd and rival Duke Reid), ska developed a strong local following. But in order to thrive and develop, ska needed to become a viable export. As early as 1959, the new Jamaican music had appeared in Britain on the Blue Beat Records label owned by London-based businessman Emil Shalit. In time, ska became so strongly identified with the label that many British listeners knew it simply as "blue beat." In 1964, a year that proved crucial in ska's evolution, the documentary *This Is Ska* was made, though the extent of its exposure at the time is uncertain. The film featured performances by singer Jimmy Cliff, who was just two years into his recording career, with Byron Lee & the Dragonaires as the backing band. Atlantic Records, meanwhile, had enough interest in the music to release a various artist compilation album called *Jamaica Ska* (1964) in America. The record came complete with detailed dance instructions on the back of the cover. This was also the year (though some sources estimate 1965 instead) that the Skatalites, the genre's prime instrumental practitioners, are thought to have recorded the classic "Guns of Navarone," although the song did not become famous until it achieved hit status in Britain in 1967.

Also in 1964, Jamaican singer Millie Small scored an international smash with "My Boy Lollipop," which peaked at #2 on both the British and American charts and sold a reported six million copies worldwide. Arranged by Ranglin, this pop-crossover hit was recorded with mainly English musicians, and it featured a less bass-heavy sound than was typical of Jamaican ska songs. The less refined "Simmer Down," released in 1963 by vocal group the Wailers (which included future reggae superstar Bob Marley), was a better example of the Kingston ska sound of the time, but given its lack of production gloss, it only garnered Jamaican airplay. Sensing that the market would be more receptive to a commercialized version of ska, Island Records founder Chris Blackwell had the idea of remaking "My Boy Lollipop," an R&B song originally recorded by American singer Barbie Gaye in 1956. Licensing the song to Fontana Records, which had better distribution than Island, Blackwell's earnings from the hit helped him to develop his company.

The 1964 World's Fair in New York City presented an opportunity to capitalize on ska's success and broaden interest even further. Edward Seaga, a Jamaican government minister who had been a music producer and record company owner, coordinated a promotional excursion by a group of Jamaican musicians to the fair. While the event was a major step in making the music an international commodity, his decision to send the "uptown," or middle-class, group Byron Lee & the Dragonaires as ska's representative backing band produced a degree of controversy because ska's roots were deeply rooted in the ghettoes of Kingston. Critics charged that by passing up the dynamic and creative Rasta musicians in the Skatalites, Seaga had undermined the music's authenticity. By contrast, Lee noted in an interview that his group was already scheduled to be in New York, played for free, and was then Jamaica's most popular live backing band.

Many reasons have been given for ska's ultimate demise. Some say the music's frenetic pace and Jamaica's stifling heat made dancing exhausting. Others insist that the lack of any post-independence prosperity in Jamaica changed the national mood and led to slower music. Another explanation is that ska's downfall was the result of the Skatalites' disbanding in 1965. In effect, each of these factors played some part in the end of ska, but they were not the only ones. Skilled musicians need compositions that allow them to exercise their creative capabilities, and the additional rhythmic possibilities afforded by rocksteady, the slower sound that took hold in the wake of ska, provided such space.

In the late 1970s and early 1980s, Britain's 2-Tone label ushered in a ska revival, launching a new wave of disciples that included the Specials, the Selecter, and Madness. While 2-Tone's popularity proved fleeting, ska maintains a cult following across Europe and in Japan. There was also what became known as the "Third Wave" of ska, an international resurgence in the 1980s and 1990s. Ironically, ska has no real presence in modern-day Jamaica.

SKATALITES
YEARS ACTIVE: MID-1960s

Despite the Skatalites' remarkably short life span—the original incarnation of the group lasted from only 1964 to 1965—this powerhouse instrumental unit made a distinct mark on Jamaican popular music. Featuring a fluid lineup that included many of Jamaica's prime musical talents, the Skatalites were ska's seminal group, and one of the genre's few acts whose reputation grew even after they had disbanded and the style was no longer popular.

The scope of the Skatalites' influence should not be underestimated, since they backed numerous singers as session musicians and, even after the band's demise, many members played together in different studio groups. The Skatalites also made their own records, many of which were credited to individual members rather than the full band. One example is "Silver Dollar," a song produced by Treasure Isle studio and label owner Duke Reid and released under the name of Skatalites saxophonist Tommy McCook.

Well versed in jazz and American R&B, the Skatalites found ways to translate their influences into a uniquely Jamaican sound. One explanation for the group's chemistry is the fact that several members had performed together in other bands—among them Eric Dean's Orchestra, popular in Jamaica in the 1940s and 1950s—dating back to their teenage years, more than a decade before the Skatalites were officially formed. McCook, trombonist Don Drummond, alto saxophonist Lester Sterling, and trumpeter Johnny "Dizzy" Moore were all graduates of the Alpha Boys' School in Kingston, an institution that unwittingly built the musical foundation of the Jamaican recording industry. A Catholic institution that sought to educate underprivileged black boys, the school focused on specific subjects, music being one of its specialties. As a result of this musical education, the Skatalites members who were Alpha graduates were knowledgeable in music theory and played from formally notated sheets and charts.

Accounts of when the Skatalites formed vary, but some suggest they came together in 1963. The band officially debuted when they assembled at producer Coxsone Dodd's Studio One in Kingston in 1964—where guitarist Ernest Ranglin served as Dodd's arranger—to back Jackie Opel, a Barbadian singer who occasionally substituted for Skatalites bassist Lloyd Brevett. Although the Skatalites recorded mostly for Studio One, they were free to freelance with other producers and labels. As McCook recalled, this side work was a matter of economic necessity. The long list of producers that the Skatalites worked with includes Treasure Isle's Duke Reid; Prince Buster, who recorded frequently for Britain's Blue Beat Records label; and Justin Yap, who ran Top Deck Records. The band's Top Deck recordings—made at Studio One between 1964 and 1965—are considered by some fans to be their best work, in part because the musicians were able to record multiple takes. This rare luxury was made possible by Yap's

Skatalites sax greats Tommy McCook (left) and Roland Alphonso both died in 1998.

financial investment in the group's projects that allowed them more studio time, and undoubtedly enhanced the quality of the music.

As McCook remembered in a 1994 *Reggae Report* interview, "Whoever brought the composition to the studio was recognized as the composer and arranger and got credit for the recording." He said, "The arranger got £5 for the song, and we got £1 to £2 for performing. At that time £1 was about $4. That was good money at that time. You could buy a lot of things."

The Skatalites were perhaps a logical choice to be part of the promotional entourage sent by Jamaica to the 1964 World's Fair in New York City, but the fact that they were Rastafarians might have discouraged the tour's organizer, the producer and politician Edward Seaga, from presenting them as the face or sound of Jamaica. Instead, Seaga opted for the more conventional Byron Lee & the Dragonaires, who played a diluted version of ska and lacked the urban friction of the Skatalites in full swing.

Many link the end of ska to the breakup of the Skatalites, which occurred after Drummond murdered his common-law wife, Marguerite Mahfood, on New Year's Day in 1965. Drummond suffered from mental illness, and his erratic and unstable behavior had sometimes resulted in him missing gigs. He was subsequently committed to Kingston's Bellevue mental hospital, where he committed suicide on May 6, 1969. According to McCook, "We never used a substitute for Don—we left his space open." He added, "There was nobody around who could fit his space."

At the time, the Skatalites were already facing challenging business issues and personal disputes, and the murder incident proved too much for the group to withstand. They split up in August 1965, and tenor saxophonist Roland Alphonso's new Studio One session crew included former Skatalites members Moore, keyboardist Jackie Mittoo, and bassist Brevett. McCook later said that Alphonso's

decision to stay with Dodd to form the Soul Brothers session band deepened rifts among the now former Skatalites.

After the breakup, McCook became the most notably successful ex-Skatalite. He served as arranger and leader of Reid's Treasure Isle studio session band, the Supersonics, which also included Moore and former Skatalite Lloyd Knibb, who has been called the most important drummer in Jamaica's history. After their dissolution, the Skatalites scored a mainstream British hit in 1967, when the instrumental party anthem "Guns of Navarone," recorded in late 1964, reached #36 on the pop charts.

In 1975, the Skatalites recorded a reunion album, released on the Tropical Soundtracs label, and have subsequently reformed numerous times. Over the years, their sporadic output and touring momentum has been interrupted by disagreements and the deaths of band members. McCook and Alphonso both died in 1998, and cancer took the lives

of Moore and Knibb in 2008 and 2011, respectively. Among the highlights of their later output is the 1975 recording *Heroes of Reggae in Dub: The Skatalites Meet King Tubby*, a strong dub collection that is now quite rare and expensive. The work that established the group's reputation exists on a variety of compilations documenting their creative achievements.

MEMBERS: Roland Alphonso (tenor saxophone); **Lloyd Brevett** (bass); **Don Drummond** (trombone); **Jerome "Jah Jerry" Hines** (guitar); **Lloyd Knibb** (drums); **Tommy McCook** (tenor saxophone); **Jackie Mittoo** (piano); **Johnny "Dizzy" Moore** (trumpet); **Lester Sterling** (alto saxophone)

SELECT DISCOGRAPHY: *Ska Authentic* (Studio One, 1967); *Greetings from Skamania* (Shanachie, 1996); *Heroes of Reggae in Dub: The Skatalites Meet King Tubby* (Motion, 1999); *Occupation Ska!: The Very Best of the Skatalites* (101 Distribution, 2009)

SOUL SYNDICATE

YEARS ACTIVE: 1960s-1980s

Soul Syndicate released few albums under their own name, but as a backing group for other artists, they were central to the roots reggae era. Founded by bassist George "Fully" Fullwood, who was born in Kingston, Jamaica, in 1950, the band began recording in the early 1970s. In a 1980 film interview for the documentary *Word, Sound and Power* (DVD release, 2005), Fullwood and rhythm guitarist Tony Chin noted that their combined individual and collective Jamaican recording sessions accounted for more than 90 percent of the music that came out of the island during the 1970s. Their estimate is no exaggeration: Soul Syndicate played innumerable studio sessions under a variety of pseudonyms, including the Aggrovators, the All Stars, the Upsetters, the Professionals, the Observers, and the Impact All Stars. These names varied according to studio and producer.

The group formed in the early 1960s as the Rhythm Raiders. Fullwood's father financed and organized the unit, whose initial lineup differed from what would become Soul Syndicate's. The Rhythm Raiders played at local clubs in Kingston and did not change their name until around 1968. The decision to become Soul Syndicate—a reference to "the syndicate," the criminal organization in the early 1960s television series *The Untouchables*—stemmed from a conversation between Fullwood and his brother, Leonard. Initially, the band focused on live performances, playing at hotel and dance hall venues in Kingston and backing such singers as Roy Shirley. The group had not planned on recording, but in 1970, producer Bunny Lee offered the opportunity for session work, possibly with singer Delroy Wilson. Later that year, their work on such

Jamaican hits as Max Romeo's "Macabee Version" and Niney the Observer's "Blood and Fire" quickly enhanced their reputation. Unfortunately, increased notoriety did not always bring financial reward, and in a typical session of twenty songs, Fullwood recalls, they would get paid for only a few.

Soul Syndicate backed such major reggae artists as Burning Spear, Augustus Pablo, Jimmy Cliff, Dennis Brown, Johnny Clarke, Gregory Isaacs, and the Mighty Diamonds. Consequently, they also worked for most of Jamaica's top producers, including the aforementioned Lee, Joe Gibbs, Niney the Observer, Keith Hudson, Harry J, Jo Jo Hoo-Kim, Duke Reid, and Lee Perry. The legendary

ABOVE: Formed by bassist George "Fully" Fullwood (back row, second from left), prolific session band Soul Syndicate was responsible for much of the roots reggae that emerged in the 1970s.

LEFT: Soul Syndicate initially focused on live performances, publicized on flyers such as these.

WAS, IS & ALWAYS

Soul Syndicate

era, into the twenty-first century.

By December 1973, when a newspaper ad described Soul Syndicate as the "best recording band" in Jamaica, numerous lineup changes had taken place. Guitarist Earl "Chinna" Smith had replaced Cleon Douglas, who moved to the United States in 1970. Drummer Carlton "Santa"` Davis joined in 1970 after playing marching drums in his youth and performing in bands that backed such Jamaican singers as Alton Ellis and Ken Boothe. Another legendary reggae drummer, Leroy "Horsemouth" Wallace, had briefly preceded him in the group. After a few years, Davis left to join singer Jimmy Cliff's band and was replaced by Max Edwards. Fullwood and Chin were reunited with Davis in 1981, when they joined the drummer as members of Tosh's Word, Sound & Power backing band.

In the midst of Soul Syndicate's prolific 1970s studio work, Jamaica was plagued by political violence connected to the 1976 and 1980 elections. This increasingly drove the group's members to seek overseas touring opportunities, and in the early 1980s, Fullwood and Chin relocated to California. In 1987, when assassins entered Tosh's home, killing three people, including the former Wailer, Davis was also shot. He recovered from his injuries, and by the early 1990s, he, too, had moved to California.

While Soul Syndicate released few albums of their own, reggae fans who have noticed the musicianship and read the credits on classic roots releases know

that the band's sound supported a vast number of major performers. In the era following Fullwood's move to the United States, the band ceased to function as a recording entity. They did, however, continue to perform live and appear at various high-profile international reggae festivals, including 1986's Japansplash (a major annual Japanese event), 2006's Ja Sound Festival in the South of France, and 2010's Sierra Nevada World Music Festival in California. Fullwood also produced *Make Place for the Youth*, a 1989 album by Andrew Tosh, Peter's son. The collection earned a Grammy nomination for best reggae recording. The bassist continues to tour with the Fully Fullwood Band, whose lineup always includes Chin and occasionaly Santa Davis. Working with his wife, Frances Fullwood, who shared writing and production duties, Fullwood has independently released two solo double CDs in America. Both of these—*For All Time* (2003) and *Fully Loaded* (2011)—have received high critical praise.

MEMBERS: George "Fully" Fullwood (bass); Tony "Valentine" Chin (rhythm guitar); Cleon Douglas (guitar); Earl "Chinna" Smith (guitar); Leroy "Horsemouth" Wallace (drums); Carlton "Santa" Davis (drums); Max Edwards (drums); Keith Sterling (keyboards); Richard "Jahmaka" Johnson (keyboards) Leslie Butler (keyboards); Enroy "Tenor" Grant (tenor sax); Derrick Hinds (trombone); Arnold Breckenridge (trumpet); Donald Greaves (trumpet); Donovan Carless (vocalist); Freddie McGregor (vocalist); Dennis Brown (vocalist)

SELECT DISCOGRAPHY: *Harvest Uptown* (Epiphany, 1977); *Was Is & Always* (Epiphany, 1979); *Moodie in Dub Vol. 1: Black Slate Meets Soul Syndicate* (Moodie Music, 1978); *Freedom Sounds in Dub* (w. King Tubby) (Blood & Fire, 1996); *Niney the Observer Presents Soul Syndicate Dub Classics* (Jamaican, 2006)

engineer King Tubby also remixed several Soul Syndicate rhythm tracks in dub, dropping elements in and out of the song, expanding their impact with effects, and emphasizing bass. These sessions did not always include the entire group, but in most instances, they featured at least three members. This was yet another reason Soul Syndicate was able to play on so many recordings and have such a broad impact on Jamaican music.

As far as many reggae fans are concerned, Soul Syndicate's most pivotal work came in 1970, when they backed the Wailers on sessions produced by Perry. At the time, group members

Bunny Wailer, Peter Tosh, and Bob Marley had not yet emerged as international stars. The sessions yielded the local hits "Sun Is Shining" and "Mr. Brown," and Soul Syndicate's sterling contributions earned them work with other producers. Fullwood's memorable bass lines anchor many of reggae's most versioned rhythms, including the one heard on the instrumental "Stalag 17," a 1974 Jamaican hit for organist Ansel Collins. Furthermore, Fullwood also created the bass line for Little Roy's "Phrophecy" (1977, on the Morwell Esq. label) that would eventually be called the "taxi" rhythm when Sly & Robbie re-recorded it on their Taxi Records label in the early 1980s. That bass line hook has been recut hundreds of times in the dancehall

Hot sounds for the Cold War—Steel Pulse brings the sound of Birmingham to Berlin.

STEEL PULSE
YEARS ACTIVE: 1975–2000s

When he first heard of the group Steel Pulse, a perplexed Bob Marley asked, "What kind of name is that?" But really, it made perfect sense for a band brought up in the industrial English Midlands. Steel Pulse formed in the Handsworth area of Birmingham, England, in January 1975. The city's auto industry had fallen into

steep decline, and Britain's economy was imploding, severely hampering what limited opportunities existed for the second generation of black British youth, children of the first major wave of West Indian immigrants that arrived in Britain in the 1950s and 1960s. Steel Pulse's reputation centers on three trilogies of studio albums recorded for three different labels. These collections essentially take them full circle in terms of career evolution.

The group's leader, guitarist, principal songwriter, and lead vocalist, David Hinds, was born in Birmingham in 1958 to Jamaican parents. As a teenager, Hinds was exposed to black-liberation politics in several ways: through learning about the American civil rights movement in the 1960s, his community's exposure to Rastafarianism, and the blatant racism of the deceptively named National Front in Britain—all of which provided motivation that translated into music. Hinds learned to play guitar

by listening to reggae, blues, and funk records. He also received tutelage from school friend and future Steel Pulse guitarist Basil Gabbidon. The group made its live debut in 1975, by which time the lineup had grown to include keyboardist Selwyn Brown, bassist Ronnie McQueen, and drummer Colin Gabbidon.

In 1976, Steel Pulse released their debut single, the Afrocentric "Kibudu-Mansatta-Abuku," a self-produced effort issued on the independent

STEEL PULSE

punk bands and gaining plaudits from the rock audience, they were signed by Island Records in 1978. That same year, they released their full-length debut, *Handsworth Revolution*, produced by Karl Pitterson, who had recently worked as an engineer with Bob Marley & the Wailers, as well as with former Wailers singer-songwriters Bunny Wailer and Peter Tosh. The album yielded the band's first hit single, "Ku Klux Klan," a scathing attack against Britain's racist neo-Nazis. During live performances, the musicians wore adapted white pillowcases on their heads to reinforce the message. On the strength of its assured rhythmic edge and pointed political focus—as well as Island's promotional efforts—the song reached #41 on the British pop charts.

beyond began to embrace the group, and this alienated some fickle fans in the roots reggae community. Luckily, just as critics were challenging Steel Pulse's authenticity, the group landed an opening slot on Bob Marley & the Wailers' 1978 European tour. This gave them the kind of indispensible stamp of approval they needed.

With their 1979 sophomore album, *Tribute to the Martyrs*, Steel Pulse established philosophical connections to such black political pioneers as Patrice Lumumba, the first Prime Minister of the Republic of Congo, and Jamaican black liberation advocate Marcus Garvey. While the songs on this album worked well collectively, the singles were perhaps less memorable than those from *Handsworth Revolution*. *Tribute to the Martyrs* did, however, yield the minor UK hit "Sound System," which stalled at #71 in Britain and was Steel Pulse's final pop chart single there. The album also failed to match the success of *Handsworth Revolution* and peaked at #49 on the British charts.

Neither of their first two albums made any impact on America, and Hinds was quoted in a 1986 *Reggae Report* magazine interview as saying that *Tribute to the Martyrs* received little promotion from Island. He also said that by the time of the follow-up, 1980's *Reggae Fever* (titled *Caught You* in the UK), Island had come to fear the band's militancy. Believing that British audiences had become detached from reggae's political side, Steel Pulse focused on building its continental European following. *Caught You/Reggae Fever* was made against a backdrop of growing friction with Island. Karl Pitterson, who had produced the first two albums, was unavailable, and the experienced Del Newman, who had created strings arrangements in the 1970s for rock artists such as Elton John and Cat Stevens, was hired as a replacement. Despite lacking any reggae background, Newman had a good relationship with the band, but Island fired him because of a clash with a label executive. Oddly, Newman's production

Concrete Jungle label. As part of the leading edge of British reggae, the group performed "Nyah Love" on a talent show. The performance led to a record deal with Anchor Records, which had scored a #1 hit in the United States in 1975 with "How Long" by the British pop band Ace. Steel Pulse went on to record a version of "Nyah Love" with Barbadian-born, London-based musician and producer Dennis Bovell, and while it failed to cross over to the pop charts, the nationally released single helped introduce the band.

A series of lineup changes followed, as Steve Nesbitt replaced Colin Gabbidon on drums, and Alphonso Martin and Mykaell Riley joined the band as percussionists and vocalists. By the end of the 1980s, Riley had gone on to form the Reggae Philharmonic Orchestra, a group of mostly black, classically trained musicians, and the string arrangements

he wrote for that ensemble played a pivotal role in the breakthrough transatlantic success of Soul II Soul, one of the first British R&B groups to have a major commercial impact on the American market.

In the late 1970s, as punk rock propelled itself into Britain's mainstream consciousness, gaining exposure partly through the Rock Against Racism events started in 1976 to counter the fascist National Front political party, Steel Pulse proved themselves onstage in the company of acts like the Stranglers. According to one writer, they were the first reggae band to play an otherwise all-punk bill. Holding their own with

A few months later, the band scored a #35 hit with "Prodigal Son," another one of their live staples. "Prodigal Son" captures the essence of early Steel Pulse and establishes a sonic template for their future classics.

As *Handsworth Revolution* climbed to #9 on the UK album charts, introducing the band's logo on its cover, many were caught off guard by the warm commercial and critical reception, since British reggae bands had not previously achieved much album success. White audiences in the United Kingdom and

of the song "Reggae Fever" later ended up on the finished LP. Island ultimately hired producer Geoffrey Chung to complete the album—a collection that failed to chart and yielded no hit singles. This commercial decline prompted Island to prematurely drop Steel Pulse during their debut American tour in 1980.

Following a memorable appearance at Jamaica's annual Reggae Sunsplash festival in 1981, Steel Pulse began recording a new album with renewed vigor. Restoring the trusted Pitterson to the production helm, the band decamped to the unlikely locale of Aarhus, Denmark, and made what is

generally considered their best studio album, 1982's *True Democracy*. Allegedly completed in a mere twenty-five days, the album combined all of the positive creative elements heard in varying degrees on the three previous albums. Steel Pulse achieved a commercially appealing sound without undermining their roots credibility; outstanding tracks include the spiritual invocation "Chant a Psalm," the Marcus Garvey tribute "Rally Round," and the single "Your House." One of their most appealing introspective songs, "Your House," can be interpreted as a statement of either religious belief or romantic love.

Issued on Elektra Records in the United States and on the band's own Wise Man Doctrine imprint in Britain, *True Democracy* also served as an effective act of revenge on Island, which had discarded the group as its finest moment was imminent. Although the album peaked at #120 in America and failed to chart in Britain, its poor initial sales in no way represented the high-quality songwriting, performances, and production. The album proved influential in the long run, however, and in July 2004, some twenty-two years after its initial release, it finally attained gold status in America, reaching sales of five hundred thousand copies.

Also certified gold in the United States in 2004 was the 1984 follow-up, *Earth Crisis*, produced by Jimmy "Senyah" Haynes, a Barbadian guitarist based in Britain. Haynes had previously worked with another premier British reggae band, Aswad, which also signed with Island in the 1970s. The album featured suitably apocalyptic artwork by Neville Garrick, who had designed most of Bob Marley & the Wailers' album covers. For *Earth Crisis*, Garrick created a collage featuring US President Ronald Reagan, Soviet leader Yuri Andropov, and Pope John Paul II— figures representing political and religious establishment control and repression,

In the 1970s, Steel Pulse's strong rhythms and political lyrics won them fans in the punk community.

which Rasta often subsumed under the derisive description "Babylon." (British Prime Minister Margaret Thatcher was surprisingly absent.) The artwork also depicted war, hunger, and poverty—the consequences of the leaders' perceived moral misdeeds. Garrick's art was the perfect counterpart to the title track, a condemnation of the global political situation and its negative impact on the so-called third world. The song also seemed to be the sound track to the end of the world as prophesied in the book of Revelation.

However political, the record was not without its commercial compromises. In a 1993 *Reggae Report* interview, Hinds recalled that Elektra specifically instructed the band to emulate the pop-reggae style of Eddy Grant's 1982 hit "Electric Avenue." The single "Steppin' Out" was recorded to meet this requirement, yet despite this and other major-label interventions, Steel Pulse has never scored a hit single in the prized American market. While the "Steppin' Out" single received a Grammy nomination for best reggae recording, Elektra's meddling marked the beginning

of the end of the label's relationship with the band. This period also saw the departure of bassist McQueen before the release of the *Earth Crisis* album, although he played on that record.

Ironically, at this complex juncture, Steel Pulse became the first non-Jamaican act to win the Grammy award for best reggae recording. That honor came in 1987 for *Babylon the Bandit* (1986), another collection released by Elektra and produced by Haynes. The album featured a decidedly digital sound, and despite the strength of the songwriting, the electronic drums (played, not programmed) gave off a less organic vibe. The title track exemplified Steel Pulse's new sound, and Haynes's rock guitar proved particularly effective. Yet there was a feeling among some fans that the anti-imperialist lyrics were being undermined by the group's instrumental concessions to "Babylon," as evidenced by the digital

production flourishes. Whatever the critical view, the Grammy win brought the group higher visibility, though the album never reached the American charts. Hinds felt that the album suffered from Haynes's dedication to perfectionism and desire to surpass the creative achievements of *Earth Crisis*.

In 1988, Steel Pulse opened on multiple tours for INXS, Robert Palmer, and Bob Dylan, all in North America,

ABOVE: Designer Neville Garrick's cover for 1984's *Earth Crisis* took aim at the world leaders of "Babylon."
LEFT: British rock singer Tom Robinson (center) and two members of Steel Pulse prepare to blast fascists at a 1978 Anti-Nazi League rally in London.

further promoting their music to the rock world. That year also saw the band signed by MCA Records, which unfortunately followed in Elektra's footsteps in terms of interfering with Steel Pulse's sound. The band made its MCA debut with the aptly titled *State of Emergency* (1988), an album that chronicled the group's identity crisis as it sought a stronger commercial presence. Intended as a pop crossover, the album

contained numerous dance-oriented R&B tracks and love songs—material that compromised the reggae foundation on which Steel Pulse had built their reputation. The album peaked at #127 on the US album charts, and as low sales in the decades since its release attest, it lacked the impact, influence, and ingenuity of the three Elektra records.

In a 1993 *Reggae Report* interview, Hinds insisted that MCA wanted the funky R&B tracks—songs American audiences could more easily identify with—placed at the beginning of the ironically titled *Victims* (1992) album. He said, "Our popularity went down among our hardcore fans and we weren't happy about that . . ." This relegation of reggae to the background further eroded the band's cultural relevance. It also resulted in an uninspired record that tried too hard to appeal to diverse audiences. Upset by blatant discrimination against Rastas and blacks in general, the band rebuked New York City's cabbies with the stinging critique "Taxi Driver" as a single from *Victims*. Martin quit the band around this time, leaving a core triumvirate of Hinds, Brown, and Nesbitt, and in subsequent years, even with the ongoing contributions of other players, these three would collectively remain the face and voice of Steel Pulse.

In 1992, as Steel Pulse attempted to return to roots reggae territory while reemphasizing their continued global currency, MCA released *Live in Paris: Rastafari Centennial*. The band's prestige got another boost in 1993, when they performed by special invitation at Bill Clinton's presidential inauguration.

With 1994's *Vex*, symbolically recorded in Jamaica, Steel Pulse seemed cognizant of how detrimental their commercial compromises had been. In "Back to My Roots," Hinds unambiguously sings, "So we took that commercial road / searching for some fame and gold / and gained the whole wide world / and almost lost our souls." Those revealing and confessional lines support the claim that Steel Pulse had detoured too far from their original path. While the band seemed to take notice on "Back to My Roots," in contradictory fashion, they unwittingly confirmed that same overt commercialization by including many hip-hop elements on the album's other tracks. The vexation that thematically drove the album deepened when MCA dropped the band from the label. As Brown recalled in a 1995 interview, "We reached a stage with the albums where we tried and tried . . . this crossover thing and basically got tired of it."

This was a turning point for Steel Pulse. Inevitably, their forays into R&B, pop, and even dancehall drew criticism from roots fanatics, whose perceptions of the band were built on the uncompromising militancy of their early albums. Personal and health issues also took their toll, as Hinds suffered a torn shoulder tendon that left him unsure of whether he would play again.

Rastanthology, consisting of rerecorded versions of the band's greatest hits, emerged in 1996 on Steel Pulse's Wise Man Doctrine label, giving the group a greater economic stake in their catalog. They returned in 1997 with *Rage and Fury*, recorded at their own Dub Factory studio in Birmingham. On this somewhat uneven transitional record, Steel Pulse attempted to incorporate dancehall rhythms and DJs and add hip-hop flavor to their trademark roots sound. That the album includes a remake of the early hit "Ku Klux Klan," as well as an electronic music remix, suggests that little creative progress was being made. The band also remade America singer Billy Paul's R&B single "Am I Black Enough for You" (1973), updating it with a rap segment. In an effort to sound contemporary, the group again tried to incorporate a range of styles, but this multigenre approach left *Rage and Fury*—as well as the band itself—without a clearly defined identity.

The 1999 live album *Living Legacy*, recorded in France, Puerto Rico, and Holland, found the group in fine form

and garnered a much-deserved Grammy nomination. Still, in light of Elektra's release of *Smash Hits* in 1993, this was their fourth compilation release of the 1990s, and the implication was that Steel Pulse's best days were behind them.

Following a hiatus from studio recording, they released *African Holocaust* through Sanctuary Records in 2004. The album did not make any new musical statements, but it went some way toward repairing the damage the band had done with its overly commercial MCA material in the previous decade. With 2006's *Rastanthology II: The Sequel*, the band again rerecorded tracks from previous albums, though the collection was far less effective than was its predecessor. As long as there are live audiences hungry for the Steel Pulse sound, the group is unlikely to vanish from the reggae landscape. Nevertheless, fans eagerly await a full-fledged return to the classic sound.

MEMBERS: **David Hinds** (lead vocals & guitar); **Steve "Grizzly" Nesbitt** (drums); **Selwyn "Bumbo" Brown** (keyboards & vocals); **Basil Gabbidon** (lead guitar), Handsworth Revolution to True Democracy; **Colin Gabbidon** (drums), "Nyah Love" single; **Alphonso "Phonso" Martin** (vocals & percussion), Handsworth Revolution to Victims; **Ronnie "Stepper" McQueen** (bass), Handsworth Revolution to True Democracy; **Mykaell Riley** (vocals & percussion), Handsworth Revolution

SELECT DISCOGRAPHY:
Handsworth Revolution (Island, 1978); *Tribute to the Martyrs* (Island, 1979); *Caught You/Reggae Fever* (Island, 1980); *True Democracy* (Elektra, 1982); *Earth Crisis* (Elektra, 1984); *Babylon the Bandit* (Elektra, 1985); *Reggae Greats* (Island, 1985); *State of Emergency* (MCA, 1988); *Victims* (MCA, 1992); *Live in Paris: Rastafari Centennial* (MCA, 1992); *Smash Hits* (Elektra, 1993); *Vex* (MCA, 1994); *Rastanthology* (Wise Man Doctrine, 1996); *Rage and Fury* (Mesa, 1997); *Living Legacy* (Wise Man Doctrine, 1999); *African Holocaust* (Sanctuary, 2004); *Rastanthology II: The Sequel* (Wise Man Doctrine, 2006)

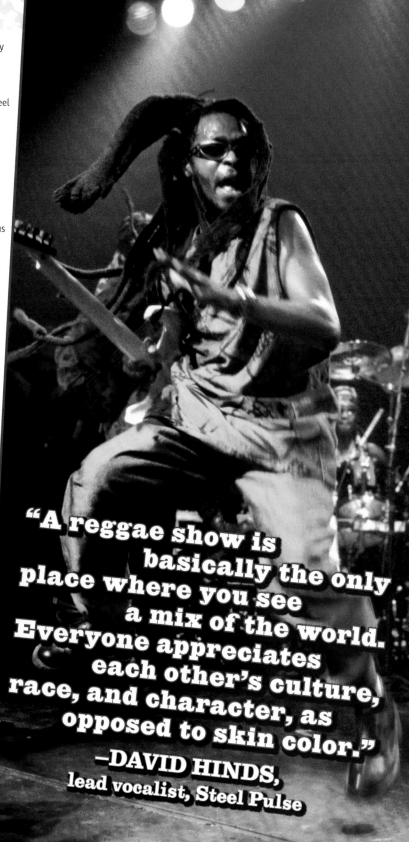

"A reggae show is basically the only place where you see a mix of the world. Everyone appreciates each other's culture, race, and character, as opposed to skin color."
—DAVID HINDS, lead vocalist, Steel Pulse

David Hinds energetically leads Steel Pulse at Irving Plaza in New York City, 2000.

STUDIO ONE

Few Jamaican labels possess the legendary aura of Studio One, often referred to by Jamaican musicians as the university of reggae. Based in Kingston, the joint studio-label operation grew out of owner Coxsone Dodd's Downbeat sound system, which he began in 1954. Dodd was born in 1932 in Kingston, and developed his ability to please the public at a young age, selecting American R&B records played at his mother's liquor store to attract customers.

Dodd made his first recordings for his Downbeat system in 1956, and around 1959, Studio One began selling records to the Jamaican public. It soon established itself at the center of the island's popular music, and throughout the 1960s, it played a key role in the transitions from ska to rocksteady to reggae.

Jamaican pianist Theophilus Beckford's 1960 single "Easy Snappin'" was one of the label's most notable early releases. At the time, such records were made for sound-system purposes without any thought given to developing a local consumer market. It was only after noting the public's enthusiasm for the music that Dodd was encouraged to start selling records. The decision to release Beckford's recording, which had been played on the

Downbeat system for at least two years prior, was a major catalyst for Studio One. The response to "Easy Snappin'" immediately revealed to Jamaican producers the commercial viability of selling records.

Before establishing his own recording facility, Dodd used other Kingston studios. At some point between 1961 and 1963—the date varies depending on the source—he established a humble single-track operation at Brentford Road. By 1967, he had upgraded to a two-track setup. This move toward independence allowed Dodd to work at his own pace and record multiple takes of songs without paying for additional studio time. This fostered the creativity of artists like the Skatalites, who functioned as a Studio One session band and emerged in the early 1960s as Jamaica's prime exponents of ska—the up-tempo Jamaican fusion of R&B and local rhythms that dominated the island in the early 1960s. As Dodd recalled in later years, musicians earned higher weekly wages at Studio One than they would have playing for tourists on the hotel circuit.

After the Skatalites dissolved in 1965, some of their members formed the Soul Brothers, Studio One's next session unit. The group played an active role in the mid-1960s transition from ska to rocksteady, helping to shape the sound of the new style with their innovative musicianship. The Soul Brothers morphed into the Soul Vendors and backed singer Alton Ellis on a 1967 British tour.

Studio One's next session unit, Sound Dimension, formed around 1967, at the tail end of rocksteady, and played through the start of the reggae era in 1968. Members included former Skatalites keyboardist and arranger Jackie Mittoo, who played with the group before moving to Canada, as well as guitarist Eric

"Rickenbacker" Frater and bassist Earl "Bagga" Walker. Studio One's subsequent house band, the Soul Defenders, played together from 1970 to 1976, led by multi-instrumentalist Vin Morgan. Through the remainder of the decade, that group performed under a variety of alternate names, including Sound Dimension, Studio One All-Stars, Brentford Road All-Stars, Brentford Disco Set, and Underground Vegetables.

Engineer Sylvan Morris, who joined Dodd's enterprise around 1966, played a

pivotal role in establishing Studio One's distinctive sound. Applying his electronics knowledge and creative instincts, Morris manipulated tape heads to create delay effects and boost bass frequencies. He also experimented with cutting exclusive "dubplate" versions—soft wax acetate test discs also referred to as specials—of rhythm tracks for sound systems, thus contributing to the development of dub,

If Studio One was the "university of reggae," founder Coxsone Dodd was its dean.

STUDIO
1
MADE IN JAMAICA
Jamrec Music
UNFAITHFUL BABY
(K. PATRICK)
LORD CREATOR
BY JAMAICA RECORDING STUDIO 13 BRENTFORD ROAD

which features often radically remixed versions of recordings.

Amid shifts in Jamaica's social and musical conditions, Studio One began recording roots-oriented Rasta acts, the Abyssinians being a classic example. Although Dodd was willing to work with such artists, he sometimes failed to recognize the potential of their better material. Case in point: the Abyssinians' iconic "Satta Massa Gana," was recorded in 1969 but not released until 1971, after the group had purchased the master tapes. In addition, many acts became disgruntled with Dodd's business practices, claiming that if and when he compensated his musicians, payments were often inequitable and inconsistent.

Through its famous Sunday auditions, Studio One unearthed a wealth of local talent. Newcomers had the benefit of honing their skills with the help of such in-house artists as Leroy Sibbles, a member of the Heptones, whose hands-on ability to write, arrange, sing, play bass, and produce had a tremendous impact on the songs. Dodd, meanwhile, performed a more directorial role. Like other heads of studio-centered enterprises, Dodd released music on various side imprints, among them Port-O-Jam and Coxsone Records.

While Studio One was responsible for mountains of music by a multitude of artists, the label is perhaps best known for a series of early releases by the Wailers: Bob Marley, Peter Tosh, and Bunny Wailer. Made from about 1964 to 1966, these recordings sharpened the talents of the three young singers, prepping them for later international success. The group ultimately grew unhappy with Studio One's financial arrangements and sought other recording opportunities, but the music they made for Dodd helped to solidify both their own reputation and the importance of the label.

Studio One was directly influential at the dawn of reggae, using tape echo and delay to add extra rhythmic punctuations on guitar and keyboards. Vocalist Larry Marshall's "Nanny Goat" (1968) is one of the earliest examples of this, though singer Horace Andy's "Skylarking" (1969) is likely better known. The late 1970s signaled a major shift in Jamaica's music culture. Under Dodd's supervision, DJs such as Sugar Minott began "toasting," or rapping, over old Studio One rhythm tracks, heralding the start of the dancehall era.

This practice underscored the value of the label's vintage catalog. The label's records now hold a central place in the history of Jamaican music, and these recycled rhythms are still being used.

Dodd moved to New York City in 1980 after the Studio One building was robbed. Upon establishing his new studio in the 1980s, he soon reissued catalog releases, licensed tracks to other labels, and occasionally recorded newer artists. The original Jamaican studio resumed operation in 1998, when Dodd returned to Jamaica, and continued until May 2004, when he died of a heart attack at age seventy-two. Jamaican newspapers reported in late 2011 that Studio One was due to resume activities in early 2012, with Coxsone's son Courtney Dodd and other siblings at the helm.

LYNN TAITT
YEARS ACTIVE: 1950s–1960s

Nearlynn Taitt's name has been spelled and abbreviated in a variety of ways (Nearlin, Nearlyn, Lyn, Lynn), but one thing is certain: the guitarist made critical contributions to Jamaican music during the rocksteady era of the mid-1960s. Born in San Fernando, Trinidad, in 1934, Taitt developed a playing style that mirrored the staccato percussive qualities and melodic resonance of the steel pan, a popular instrument in his homeland. Taitt began playing the steel pan at the age of ten, and in 1956 he won a national prize for his soloing skills. He later taught himself guitar, learning on an instrument stolen by friends from a drunken sailor. After playing in the Dutchey Brothers band in Trinidad in the late 1950s, he formed his own group, the Nearlyn Taitt Orchestra, in 1960.

In 1962, Taitt and his band traveled to Jamaica to back touring Trinidadian calypso musicians hired by established Jamaican bandleader Byron Lee. Due to either a dishonest promoter or the calypso performers, Taitt and his crew were not paid for their efforts. Stranded as a result, their planned two-week stay turned into an extended visit. Basing himself in Kingston, Taitt joined the Sheiks, later formed the Cavaliers with ace keyboardist Jackie Mittoo and occasionally served as a substitute guitarist for the influential Skatalites, the leading instrumental exponents of ska who were also a session backing band. He played on trumpeter Baba Brooks's 1965 instrumental hit in Jamaica, "Shank I Sheck," a song that has since been rerecorded by numerous artists. Taitt formed the Comets in 1964, and thanks to his arranging and performance skills, he made an impact on the ska era. Well regarded in Jamaica, the Comets traveled to England in 1967 and spent four months backing the singer and producer Prince Buster.

Later that year, the artistically restless guitarist formed Lynn Taitt and the Jets and played on some of the earliest rocksteady releases, including "Take It Easy" by singer Hopeton Lewis in 1966. Taitt's band recorded extensively at Federal Studio and at West Indies Records Limited (WIRL) studio—both located in Kingston—and worked with a wide range of Jamaica's top producers. He also became a key member of the Supersonics, a group that featured ex-Skatalites and served as Treasure Isle boss Duke Reid's house band in the mid-1960s. Among the most widely heard records to feature Taitt's percussive, rhythmic picking style was Desmond Dekker's 1967 UK hit "007 (Shanty Town)." Taitt also appeared on Johnny Nash's 1968 smash "Hold Me Tight." During this productive mid-1960s period, Taitt also cut solo albums on various labels, including 1968's *Rock Steady Greatest Hits* for Merritone, deepening his imprint on Jamaican music.

Taitt settled in Canada after touring that country in 1968. He based himself in Montreal and worked extensively with Mittoo and fellow Jamaican immigrants. He also performed with a newer generation of Canadian ska, rocksteady, and reggae musicians, among them Jason Wilson. Taitt died on January 20, 2010, and while musicians acknowledge him as one of rocksteady's crucial instrumental architects, his contribution has yet to be fully recognized by listeners.

SELECT DISCOGRAPHY: *Lynn Taitt & the Jets: Hold Me Tight: Anthology 65–73* (Sanctuary, 2005)

Lynn Taitt was an influential rocksteady guitarist who based his sound on the steel pan, an instrument popular in his native Trinidad.

THE TECHNIQUES
YEARS ACTIVE: 1960s–1970s

The Techniques were a ska-era vocal group formed at some point between 1962 and 1964, depending on the source. They were among the star acts at producer Duke Reid's Treasure Isle studio-label in Kingston, which ruled the rocksteady roost in the mid- to late 1960s. While the Techniques had a core group of singers, members such as Bruce Ruffin and Dave Barker had transient spells in the unit. The group made its debut with "No One," recorded at Federal Studio in sessions organized by Edward Seaga, the record producer and label owner who became a politician and eventual Prime Minister of Jamaica with the Jamaica Labour Party (JLP). The single was released in England, possibly in 1963, though there is no definitive source for the release date.

Later hits like "Little Did You Know" and "Queen Majesty" made the Techniques hot property in Jamaica, though two members, Slim Smith and Franklyn White, split around 1966 and later formed the Uniques. By 1968, the Techniques had left Reid's stable. They continued to record sporadically in other configurations, but their peak had passed. Riley established the Techniques record label in 1968 and achieved his biggest commercial success with 1971's "Double Barrel," a #1 British hit for the Jamaican duo Dave & Ansel Collins.

The Techniques' "You Don't Care" (1967) was one of the first songs with a proto-dub B-side, with the remix created by later dub pioneer King Tubby. In the second half of the 1970s, vocalist Winston Riley worked on *Meditation Dub*, a little-known set reconfigured by the Pressure Sounds label in the 1990s and released as the compelling *Techniques in Dub*. In 1972, after a spell as a solo artist, Smith was held at the infamous Bellevue mental

Winston Riley, founder of the Techniques vocal group and later its namesake label, 2005.

health institution in Jamaica, which had also housed legendary Skatalites trombonist Don Drummond. Tragically, Smith committed suicide in 1973, but few reliable details are available about these concluding episodes in his life.

Techniques singer Frederick Waite left Jamaica in 1966 and immigrated to the English Midlands. He went on to manage the short-lived yet surprisingly successful pop-reggae band Musical Youth, which featured two of his sons,

Patrick and Junior. The group scored an international hit with 1982's "Pass the Dutchie" but experienced a rapid decline in popularity after their first album. In another case of tragedy befalling musicians associated with the Techniques, Patrick died in 1993 of heart failure at age twenty-four. At the time, he was facing drug charges, and his brother Junior is under medical supervision for mental health problems. Winston Riley died in January 2012 after being shot in the previous November.

MEMBERS: Winston Riley (vocals); **Slim Smith** (lead vocals); **Frederick Waite** (vocals); **Franklyn White** (vocals)

SELECT DISCOGRAPHY: *Little Did You Know* (Treasure Isle, 1965); *Unforgettable Days* (Techniques, 1981); *Run Come Celebrate: Their Greatest Reggae Hits* (Rounder, 1995); *Techniques in Dub* (Pressure Sounds, 1997)

THIRD WORLD

**YEARS ACTIVE:
1970s–PRESENT**

Few reggae bands have matched the longevity and global impact of Third World, though the band's career has seen its share of commercial peaks and valleys. Artistically, the sustained popularity of the group's recordings during their tenure with Island Records has proved to be the foundation of Third World's staying power. Originally (and briefly) called Sons of the Third World, the group was the result of a split within Jamaican pop-reggae outfit Inner Circle in 1973. Four of the departing members helped form Third World: guitarist Stephen "Cat" Coore, keyboardist Michael "Ibo" Cooper, vocalist Milton "Prilly" Hamilton, and percussionist Irvin "Carrot" Jarrett.

The fact that each of Third World's core members had received some degree of formal musical education made them rare in the reggae world, where artists have historically grown up facing economic hardship. The band's name was itself a statement of cultural experience, political status, and musical eclecticism. Cat Coore's father served as minister of finance in Michael Manley's People's National Party (PNP) government, which ruled Jamaica from 1972 to 1980, when the island experienced its most turbulent social and economic crises. As a result, guitarist Coore was well positioned to articulate the island's angst.

Third World's self-released debut single, "Railroad Track" (1975) didn't stimulate much commercial interest from record labels, but by traveling to England and playing shows there that same year, the group came to the attention of Island Records head Chris Blackwell. Island signed the band and hired them as the opening act for Bob Marley's 1975 European tour. Considering that Third World had yet to release their debut album, these were impressive achievements. When their self-titled full-length debut appeared

the following year, it announced the group's arrival and served as a statement of their potential. Containing a version of the Abyssinians' 1971 Rasta anthem "Satta Massa Gana," the album was an intriguing preview of a career that would include forays into multiple genres. But it was the next album, *96° in the Shade* (1977), that really made people take notice.

In 1976, after seeing the band perform at the Bottom Line in New York City during their first American tour,

vocalist William "Bunny Rugs" Clarke joined the lineup. He added a soulful dynamism that helped define Third World's sound. Both he and drummer Willie Stewart also came on board in time to play on *96° in the Shade*. With its stylistic fusion and chilling historical tale of colonial treachery and murder, the album's title track, "1865 (96° in the Shade)," remains one of the classics in Third World's repertoire.

Released in 1978, *Journey to Addis* yielded the biggest international hit

of the Third World's career, "Now That We Found Love," a dance-friendly pop-reggae remake of a song recorded in 1973 by American R&B group the O'Jays. The album was Third World's highest-charting release in America, where it peaked at #55, and its lead single became their only American pop hit, reaching #47. "Now That We Found Love" cracked the top-ten in Britain, where the market proved more receptive to their music. Third World released three more albums before their deal with Island ran out. While none of these collections broke much

musical ground, they helped to solidify the group's fan base. Interestingly, Third World's string of album covers from the eponymous 1976 debut through 1979's *The Story's Been Told* also presented a visual narrative that thematically linked the records. What's more, the 1980 live album *Prisoner in the Street* reminded audiences that Third World was a killer live act, not just a studio outfit.

The end of the band's deal with Island roughly coincided with the death of Bob Marley, which signaled a turning point

for reggae. In 1981, they began a new story with Columbia Records, for whom they would record a series of five albums. These collections, significantly more commercial and generic-sounding than their previous work, never quite crossed over to wider audiences or endeared the group to fans of traditional roots reggae.

The 1982 single "Try Jah Love" featured a guest appearance by American R&B great Stevie Wonder, with whom Third World had recently toured. The song was the closest they would get to another breakout single; despite gaining airplay on black radio, the group failed to score a major pop hit during its Columbia run. By 1988, they had reached another career crossroads. Suggesting that you sometimes can judge a record by its cover, the band's Columbia-era album covers featured photographs rather than the kinds of illustrations used during their Island days. This was yet another sign that the band was moving toward a new level of commercial visibility.

Some of the band members were unhappy with the level of support from Columbia, and when the deal had run its course, Third World enthusiastically moved to PolyGram Records. Unfortunately, history repeated itself, and despite their commercial potential, the band failed to achieve mainstream success. Their most popular single in this period, 1989's "Forbidden Love," featured an appearance by rapper Daddy-O, a member of the hip-hop group Stetsasonic. Although the band had always drawn from a wide palate of influences, some listeners felt they were trying too hard to cross over. When the PolyGram deal ended in the early 1990s, they returned to a more independent path. They also weathered lineup changes, as Willie Stewart and Michael "Ibo" Cooper left after the 1998 album *Worl'ers*. While subsequent releases have been less frequent, Bunny Rugs has released several solo albums since 1995.

In 2011, Third World released its twenty-third album, *Patriots*, featuring a host of guest appearances by artists such as Stephen and Damien Marley, Gregory

Isaacs, and Sly & Robbie, spanning the reggae and dancehall eras. According to data published in *Billboard* magazine, they sold 779,000 albums in America between 1991 and 2010 and landed ten of their albums in the *Billboard* 200.

In a 1987 interview, Cooper suggested that negative perceptions regarding Third World's roots reggae credentials had been influenced by critics' views of the group's middle-class backgrounds. While few bands, reggae or otherwise, have rivaled their musicianship, Third World's ability to cross musical borders has worked both for and against them.

MEMBERS: Michael "Ibo" Cooper (keyboards and vocals), *Third World* to *Worl'ers*; **Stephen "Cat" Coore** (guitar); **Richie Daley** (bass); **Milton "Prilly" Hamilton** (vocals), Third World; **William "Bunny Rugs" Clarke** (vocals), *96° in the Shade* to *Patriots*; **Irvin "Carrot" Jarrett** (percussion), *Third World* to *Hold on to Love*; **Carl Barovier** (drums), 1973; **Cornel Marshall** (drums), *Third World*; **Willie Stewart** (drums), *96° in the Shade* to *Worl'ers*; **Norris "Noriega" Webb** (keyboards and vocals), *Patriots*; **Lenworth "Ruption" Williams** (drums), *Generation Coming* to *Patriots*; **Rupert Bent Jr.** (guitar & keyboards), *Generation Coming*; **Leroy "Baarbe" Roman** (keyboards & flute), *Generation Coming*; **Maurice Gregory** (keyboards), *Patriots*; **Herbie Harris** (keyboards and vocals), *Ain't Givin' Up* to *Black, Gold & Green*

SELECT DISCOGRAPHY: *Third World* (Island, 1976); *96° in the Shade* (Island, 1977); *Journey to Addis* (Island, 1978); *The Story's Been Told* (Island, 1979); *Arise in Harmony* (Island, 1980); *Prisoner in the Street* (Island, 1980); *Rock the World* (Columbia, 1981); *You've Got the Power* (Columbia, 1982); *All the Way Strong* (Columbia, 1983); *Sense of Purpose* (Columbia, 1985); *Hold on to Love* (Columbia, 1987); *Serious Business* (Mercury, 1989); *Committed* (Mercury, 1992); *Live It Up* (Third World, 1995); *Worl'ers* (Koch, 1998); *Generation Coming* (I-Man, 1999); *Ain't Givin' Up* (Shanachie, 2003); *Black, Gold & Green* (Shanachie, 2005); *Patriots* (VP, 2011)

OPPOSITE: The title track of this 1977 album is perhaps Third World's best-known song.

RIGHT: Third World in Jamaica, 1975: (front, l–r) Michael "Ibo" Cooper and Stephen "Cat" Coore; (back, l–r) Richard Daley, Irvin "Carrot" Jarrett, and Willie "Root" Stewart.

One-hit wonder Nicky Thomas reached #9 on the UK charts with 1970's "Love of the Common People."

NICKY THOMAS
YEARS ACTIVE: 1960s-1970s

Born in Portland, Jamaica, in 1949, singer Nicky Thomas had his first real hint of success as the vocalist on 1969's "Run Nigel Run," produced by veteran singer and label owner Derrick Harriott and credited to the Chuckles. Thomas later worked with hit Jamaican producer Joe Gibbs, a collaboration that yielded "Love of the Common People," which reached #9 on the British pop charts in 1970. It was the only time the singer breached the walls of the British Broadcasting Corporation (BBC), and during his career peak, he also released "BBC," a song dedicated to the institution's lack of reggae airplay.

Released on Trojan Records, "Love of the Common People" was a classic example of the label's questionable penchant for layering pop-styled orchestral strings on Jamaican rhythm tracks in an effort to gain airplay from mainstream radio stations like the BBC. In this case, the formula worked, and the single reportedly sold more than 175,000 copies.

Thomas settled in England after touring in the wake of his hit single's success. While he undoubtedly would have faced financial challenges as a reggae artist regardless of where he was based, the fact that he had already proven himself successful in the British market raised hope that he might sustain a career there. Unfortunately, Thomas's run as a hit artist in Britain began and ended with "Love of the Common People." Frustrated with a lack of airplay, he decided in 1974 to focus on the black ethnic market. Unfortunately, this strategy failed to boost his popularity, as many reggae fans reached for a deeper roots sound. Having fallen out of the limelight, Thomas died in 1990.

SELECT DISCOGRAPHY: *Love of the Common People* (Trojan, 1970); *Love of the Common People: The Best of Nicky Thomas* (Sanctuary, 2003)

ERROL THOMPSON
YEARS ACTIVE: 1968-1980s

Recording engineer Errol Thompson's work at Randy's, one of the hit recording studios in Kingston, has led many critics to label him one of reggae's best engineers of the roots reggae era. While Thompson's early dub experiments were somewhat less radical than those undertaken by the master remix engineer King Tubby, he helped lay the foundation for the experimental subgenre. Born in 1948 in Kingston, Thompson had a background in electronics and in building amplifiers, and got his start at producer Coxsone Dodd's Studio One in Kingston in 1968. He initially worked with recording engineer Sylvan Morris, though friction between the two reportedly led Thompson to Randy's in 1969, a year after the studio was established by Vincent "Randy" Chin.

Among Thompson's earliest engineering assignments was singer Max Romeo's "Wet Dream" (1969). Despite being banned by the British Broadcasting Corporation (BBC), the suggestive song became a top ten hit in Britain. Thompson also engineered the Wailers' (Bob Marley, Peter Tosh, and Bunny Wailer) early sessions with producer Lee Perry. These recordings brought the band notoriety in Britain and drew attention to Thompson's studio skills. He later worked on melodica instrumentalist Augustus Pablo's 1972 album *Java Java Java Java*, an early dub hit in Jamaica, and the following year engineered on Big Youth's *Screaming Target*, now recognized as one of the first major DJ albums. Thompson bolstered his growing engineering reputation with work on roots singer Burning Spear's internationally successful *Marcus Garvey* album, released in 1975.

After leaving Randy's in 1976, Thompson went to work for producer Joe Gibbs, with whom he had collaborated on the 1974 album *Dub Serial*. That album, now seen as a seminal dub release, featured remixed rhythm tracks issued under Joe Gibbs's name. Thompson engineered and frequently coproduced albums at Gibbs's studio, and highlights of his tenure include four volumes of the *African Dub* series, as well as the Jamaican band Culture's acclaimed 1977 album *Two Sevens Clash*. Having formed a production team billed as the Mighty Two, Gibbs and Thompson released "Uptown Top Ranking" (1977), a #1 British hit for the Jamaican schoolgirl singing duo Althea & Donna.

As the dancehall era emerged in the early 1980s, Thompson demonstrated his continuing engineering enterprise on releases by dancehall DJ Yellowman, who was one of the genre's first major-label acts, signing with CBS Records in 1984. Following the closure of Joe Gibbs's Studio—largely the result of fallout from a copyright infringement lawsuit—Thompson found himself working in Gibbs's grocery store until 1993, when the producer reopened the studio. But by the 1990s, Thompson's heyday had passed. While his talent may have remained intact, he recorded only sporadically. After suffering serious heart problems, he died in 2004 at the age of fifty-five.

Errol Thompson's dubs were not as radical as King Tubby's, but he is remembered as one of the best engineers of the roots era.

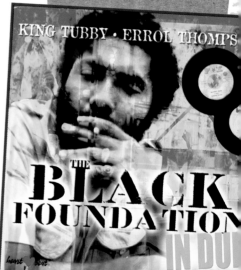

KING TUBBY · ERROL THOMPS[ON]
THE BLACK FOUNDATION IN DU[B]

LINVAL THOMPSON MEETS KING TUBBYS
"INA REGGAE DUB STYLE"
"DIS A YARD DUB"

RIGHT: King Tubby's mixing of Linval Thompson's rhythms made for a collection of classic dub.

FAR RIGHT: Roots hero Thompson in 2005, well after he had left reggae to focus on real estate.

LINVAL THOMPSON

YEARS ACTIVE: 1970s-1980s

Born in Kingston, Jamaica, around 1954, Linval Thompson found himself in New York City in the early 1970s, when he joined his parents, who had immigrated to America. Thompson spent two years living in the boroughs of Brooklyn and Queens. It was during this period in the United States that he made his recording-engineering debut around 1974 on "There is No Other Woman in This World," sung by "Bunny Rugs" Clarke, future lead vocalist of the reggae band Third World. This formative period did not yield any hits, but it proved creatively important, preparing him for success in Jamaica, where he returned later that year. Through his friend Johnny Clarke, the Jamaican singer known for hits like 1975's "Move Out of Babylon," he met producer Bunny Lee, for whom he recorded his first real hit, "Don't Cut Off Your Dreadlocks" (1976).

Thompson recorded several singles for Lee during the reign of the "flying cymbal" sound typified by repetitive, disco-styled hi-hat cymbal playing. In 1976, he branched out into self-production. That year he cut Jamaican hits like the roots reggae anthems "I Love Marijuana" and "Train to Zion,"

both recorded at Kingston's popular Channel One studios run by the Chinese Jamaican Hoo-Kim brothers. After licensing his first self-produced solo album, *I Love Marijuana* (1978), to the British reggae label Trojan Records, Thompson turned to production and achieved greater success in that arena than he had as a singer. He worked with such roots vocalists as Freddie McGregor and Gregory Isaacs in the early predigital phase of dancehall. Thompson justifiably credits himself with having introduced top dancehall producer Henry "Junjo" Lawes to the music business. But by the early 1980s, Thompson had withdrawn from the business. Personal financial troubles, political instability in Jamaica, and apparent disillusionment with dancehall's overwhelming digitization each played a part in his decision.

After leaving the production arena, Thompson found a second career by developing a real estate business in Jamaica in Stony Hill, on the outskirts of Kingston, where Thompson moved in 1979. He occasionally emerges for recordings and live appearances, but Thompson's name will likely remain linked to the roots reggae era.

SELECT DISCOGRAPHY: *Ride On Dreadlocks 1975-77* (Blood & Fire, 2000); *Linval Thompson Anthology: Don't Cut Off Your Dreadlocks* (Trojan, 2004)

"And if you singin' a song for me, I kinda know what I want before you even start to sing....Maybe I don't know everyt'ing, but I have an idea."

—LINVAL THOMPSON, on his production style

TOOTS & THE MAYTALS

YEARS ACTIVE: 1960s–EARLY 1980s; EARLY 1990s–PRESENT

Never a big album-selling group, Toots & the Maytals epitomize the live energy of Jamaican music, its connection to American soul, and its ancestral ties to the rituals and rhythms of the revivalist Baptist church. Around 1961, Frederick "Toots" Hibbert, whose birth date in the mid- to late 1940s varies by source, moved from the parish of Clarendon, Jamaica, to Kingston. There, he soon connected with future Maytals colleagues Jerry Mathias and Raleigh Gordon, though sources differ on whether this was in 1961 or 1962. Before long, they began cutting tracks at producer Coxsone Dodd's Studio One, singing with a vocal style rooted in the church. Like so many other Studio One artists, however, they could not live with Dodd's low payments, and they moved on in 1963. In fact, in a 2007 interview, Toots said Dodd never paid him for singing and explained

that many producers would assign themselves whole or partial ownership of songs they had not written. Toots also noted that Leslie

Kong, head of Beverley's Records, was one producer who would not stiff or underpay his musicians.

Celebrating their escape from Dodd's clutches, the Maytals (as they were still known at the time) spontaneously recorded their first post–Studio One hit, 1964's "Broadway Jungle," for producer and singer Prince Buster, with the Skatalites as their backing band. In 1966, the Maytals won the Jamaica Festival Song

Riding resurgent popularity brought on by UK ska bands, Toots & the Maytals take Europe, 1981.

Competition with "Bam Bam." Recorded under the supervision of musician and producer Byron Lee, the song consolidated their status as Jamaica's top recording artists. That same year, on the eve of an English tour, Toots was arrested for marijuana possession, and his subsequent prison sentence disrupted the Maytals' success. Following his release in 1967, Toots wrote "54-46 (That's My Number)," a reference to his prison stint, claiming that he had been framed by a producer. Kong produced the song and it became a massive Jamaican hit in 1968. Also in 1968, the Maytals recorded the first song to use the word *reggae* in the title, though the track, "Do the Reggay" used a spelling different from the one that is now familiar. In the 1977 book *Reggae Bloodlines* by American music journalist and historian Stephen Davis, Toots said that he had invented reggae by drawing on his experiences in the ghetto. During this period the

band rode a hot streak, and in 1970 they turned their Jamaican hit "Monkey Man" into their only British hit, reaching #47 on the pop charts. Kong's sudden death in 1971 left the group adrift until they teamed with the Dynamic Sounds label and caught the ear of Island Records founder Chris Blackwell. Thanks to its inclusion on Island's 1972 sound track to the film *The Harder They Come*, the Maytals' song "Pressure Drop" became an instant classic. Such British artists as Robert Palmer, the Clash, and the Specials would later cover the song. These versions expanded the Maytals' audience and boosted their credibility.

The Maytals' 1975 album *Funky Kingston* was their first to be released in America—it was originally issued in Jamaica in 1973—even though they were already veterans of the Jamaican scene. The album was actually a compilation of tracks that had been recorded between 1970 and 1974 and released in Jamaica on Byron Lee's Dragon label, a subsidiary of Dynamic. During the late 1970s, as the 2 Tone label spearheaded a UK ska revival, additional bands covered Maytals material. Among them were the Specials, who cut a version of "Monkey Man." These endorsements from younger artists did not lead to any major surge in record sales, but they did help Toots & the Maytals maintain their popularity on the global concert circuit until

the group disbanded in the early 1980s. For the remainder of the decade, Toots became an intermittently active solo artist who topped off the decade by earning a Grammy nomination for best reggae recording for the 1988 album *Toots in Memphis*. The

Maytals reassembled in the early 1990s but concentrated on touring rather than on recording.

The 2004 album *True Love*, a collection of new versions of Maytals classics recorded with famous guest stars, was released on the major label V2/ BMG Records and greatly raised the band's profile. Although this did not translate into outstanding sales, *True Love* earned the Grammy Award in 2005 for best reggae album. Characterized in one review as a "country music set," the record featured

legendary rock guitarists Eric Clapton, Jeff Beck, and Keith Richards, as well as country great Willie Nelson and pop-rock superstar Bonnie Raitt. *True Love* also had its share of established reggae collaborators, among them Bunny Wailer, Shaggy, U-Roy, and the Skatalites. Toots and the Maytals continue to record new material, and in 2010, the *Flip and Twist* album was released.

MEMBERS: Frederick "Toots" Hibbert (lead vocals); Jerry Mathias (vocals); Raleigh Gordon (vocals)

SELECT DISCOGRAPHY: *Funky Kingston* (Island, 1975); *Reggae Got Soul* (Island, 1976); *Toots in Memphis* (Mango, 1988); *Ska Father* (Artists Only, 1999); *Pressure Drop: The Definitive Collection* (Trojan, 2005)

Toots Hibbert shows a fan some love while dressed in his most glittery attire in New York City, 1981.

GANJA

With the title track of his 1978 album *Kaya*, Bob Marley popularized yet another term for marijuana or cannabis, also commonly referred to as *ganja*, or the wisdom weed. The word *ganja* had long been used in Jamaica, where other nicknames for the plant (also sometimes referred to as hemp, a multipurpose fiber) include *sensimilla*, *lamb's bread*, *ishence*, *kali*, *collie*, and *the healing of the nations*. These and other terms have surfaced repeatedly over the years in popular reggae songs. Rastafarians, meanwhile, treat marijuana as a holy herb—a sacramental saving grace that, with its medicinal qualities, was placed on earth by Jah (the Rasta incarnation of God) for the physiological, psychological, and spiritual benefit of the human race.

Ganja has been used for centuries in a variety of forms. Consumed in tea, used as a food additive, and smoked in cornhusks, pipes, papers, and various other suitable materials, marijuana has also held tremendous economic significance for Jamaica. In the twentieth century, however, its connection with Rastafarian culture—often in the contexts of radical social revolution and popular music—made it even more suspiciously perceived by "Babylon," or the establishment. As a lucrative yet illegal underground export, it generates solid income in a perpetually unstable economy. America's Drug Enforcement Administration, actively involved in ganja crop eradication with Jamaican authorities, remains unimpressed.

In Western popular culture, the consumption of marijuana is usually treated with comic disregard or sheer horror, but for the Rastafari communities, the preparation of the herb is a very serious ritual with direct implications for the smoker's spirituality and consciousness. Ganja's cultural centrality in Jamaica as a vital life force is reflected in the reggae music promoting its use. Nonetheless, not every Rasta is a smoker, and there is some reticence within the Jamaican musical community about the negative implications of ganja's strong connection to reggae. While pro-ganja messages may have helped record sales, marijuana consumption has undoubtedly played a major role in reggae's musical transformations, particularly during the 1970s. It's ironic that the British colonial authorities who criminalized ganja consumption in Jamaica in the early twentieth century had previously imported and sold it regularly to indentured Indian workers in the Caribbean.

Researchers rarely attempt to pinpoint an exact time at which Rastafarians began the ritual smoking of ganja. There are well-founded claims that "the herb" was used centuries ago in Africa (particularly central Africa), and that this was a primary channel through which it arrived in Jamaica. Other historians suggest that, prior to Spain's

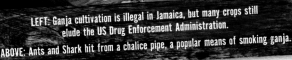

LEFT: Ganja cultivation is illegal in Jamaica, but many crops still elude the US Drug Enforcement Administration.
ABOVE: Ants and Shark hit from a chalice pipe, a popular means of smoking ganja.

In the 1960s, an international wave of black sociopolitical consciousness hit Jamaica. Despite the Jamaican government's best efforts to bring down this movement—efforts that included barring a radical University of the West Indies professor, Walter Rodney, from reentering the country in 1968 because of his pro-Rasta ideologies—the climate of change helped usher in a musical era where artists could speak openly about herb. Since the dawn of the 1970s, Jamaican music has never lacked paeans to ganja, but few of those songs achieved widespread international exposure, and none of them charted on either side of the Atlantic. The 1972 film *The Harder They Come* had its cult college audiences in America, but there weren't many Rastas in the film, and the songs on its sound track were not dedicated, or in Rasta terms, "livicated," to ganja. Of course, urban marijuana subcultures existed long before the rise of reggae, but as larger record labels like Island and Columbia began spreading the music, it accelerated global awareness of ganja consumption.

colonization of Jamaica in the fifteenth century, the indigenous Arawak Indians used it. Whether or not that's true, ganja certainly entered the country via East Indian indentured servants, who consumed it and also used it to make rope. To muddy the historical waters even further, the term *ganja* has Hindi origins. As some research has suggested, there is no indication that Jamaica's marijuana consumers regularly used the term before British colonial authorities—in their zeal to outlaw the plant—adopted it. In 1913, as part of an offensive against any black communal activity perceived as threatening to planters' continual flow of sugar profits, the herb was officially banned in Jamaica.

In the 1930s, selling herb was a well-known means of survival for many in the struggling black masses. Although marijuana has subsequently worked its way up the social ladder, it remains connected to struggle in the face of poverty. Ironically, black-liberation crusader and Rastafari icon Marcus Garvey was opposed to the use of ganja by black people in any context, whether religious or secular, and castigated the use of

herb as a major source of degeneration in Jamaican society. And yet roots reggae artists integrated ganja into the political and artistic frameworks of their music, pairing pro-marijuana anthems with songs referencing Garvey's powerful proclamations of self-determination for African people. The connection is so established that few can imagine any contradiction.

In the late 1940s, police stepped up their activity against Rastas, making the activities of cultivation, possession, or sale of ganja highly dangerous and liable to bring about harassment or imprisonment. The typical Rastafarian physical appearance alone would have guaranteed marginalization in a conservative colonial society, but ganja triggered an ongoing paranoia among the general public, accenting the fear of Rastas that persisted as Jamaican popular music evolved in the 1950s and 1960s.

The Wailers made a graphic statement with the back cover of their 1973 *Burnin'* album, which depicted Bob Marley smoking a joint. The same type of image resurfaced on the second cover that was designed for the preceding *Catch a Fire* LP (1973), replacing the flashy Zippo lighter jacket that opened to reveal an illustrated flame and the record itself. Designed by artist Neville Garrick, the jacket for Bob Marley & the Wailers' 1976 album

Rastaman Vibration had a corrugated, burlap-like texture that proved useful for preparing to smoke marijuana. The material held the herb in place as the seeds rolled away, leading an enthusiastic Marley to comment, "Ratit boy, dis good fe cleaning herb." Those words resonated with Island Record founder Chris Blackwell, who insisted that an equivalent statement be placed on the gatefold jacket's interior. The album achieved international success and broke into the American top ten, spreading both Marley's music and all of its accompanying messages to places that otherwise might have been less accessible to reggae artists. Marley's gold-selling *Kaya* was named for yet another of the herb's nicknames, and the back cover featured a colorful illustration of a large burning joint (or spliff) sprouting its own ganja leaves.

Marley was not the only artist acting as a ganja advocate at the time. In a typically bold countercultural statement, former Wailers member Peter Tosh released 1976's *Legalize It* with an album cover unambiguously featuring him smoking a pipe in the midst of marijuana plants. The title track's chorus proclaimed, "Legalize it, and I will advertise it." Inevitably, such herb-related album covers became either inflammatory or objects of celebration, depending on your perspective. The mere presence of a ganja plant—whether photographed or illustrated—or telltale chalice pipe and accompanying clouds of smoke made a rebellious statement. The latter half of the 1970s also witnessed herbal hurrahs from artists less widely known in the international market. Horace Andy's "Better Collie" (1975), Jacob Miller's "Tired Fe Lick Weed in a Bush" (1976), Culture's "International Herb" (1979), Sylford Walker & Welton Irie's "Lamb's Bread International" (1978), and Black Slate's "Legalise Collie Herb" (1980) are just a few examples

from the avalanche of songs released during the decade dominated by roots reggae. Rarely in popular music have spiritual, visual, commercial, ideological, and narcotic elements been so closely aligned for so long and with such effectiveness.

Reggae artists fought against a system in which marijuana possession was—and still is—a criminal act, and many musicians were victims of

Peter Tosh burns one in New York City's Central Park, 1979.

the Jamaican legislation and its enforcement. In some instances, as was the case with Toots Hibbert of Toots & the Maytals, the "possession" was fabricated by police to justify incarceration. Others, like Tosh, received brutal police beatings for their willful association with the herb.

Despite the widespread, mostly Western preconceptions regarding connections between ganja and dub—reggae's most futuristic manifestation—genre-defining engineers such as

King Tubby and Errol Thompson were known within Jamaica's studio community for *not* smoking weed, or anything else for that matter. Making spacey dub mixes that, paradoxically, were both coherent and abstract required extraordinary levels of concentration, particularly in light of the day's technological limitations. Mental and physical agility and focus remain essential tools of the engineering trade.

By the early 1980s, social, political, and musical changes in Jamaica gave rise to a cocaine culture, while American drug-enforcement initiatives involved curbing the flow of marijuana from the island. On 1983's "Police in Helicopter," singer John Holt captures popular sentiment in his lyrics as he threatens to revolt against the destruction of herb fields. Nonetheless, given the passing of the roots era and changes in drug culture, herbal imagery has become less prevalent in reggae album art, having been replaced by materialistic symbols such as gold chains and expensive cars.

Ganja-inspired designs have not disappeared completely, however. The illustrated cover of country singer Willie Nelson's 2005 reggae tribute album *Countryman*, for example, existed in two versions: one with the touristic palm tree, the other featuring a marijuana leaf. The album topped the *Billboard* reggae chart, and the refusal of some retailers to sell the ganja-promoting version (which necessitated the two different covers) pushed the connection between cannabis and reggae back into the mainstream spotlight. Ziggy Marley's tellingly titled 2011 release *Wild and Free* features Hollywood actor and hemp advocate Woody Harrelson singing about "marijuana trees blowing in the breeze" on the album's title track. Interestingly, the song also restates arguments about the economic benefits of selling hemp, promoting its versatility, and touting it as an organic product. The roots of both reggae and the collie weed are destined to remain intertwined for a long time to come.

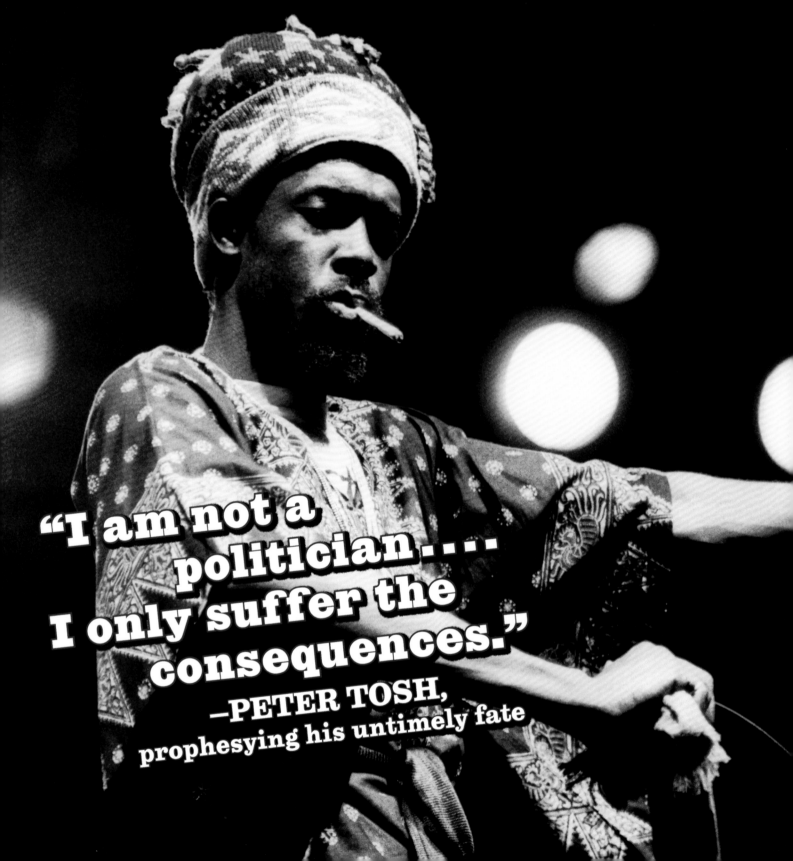

"I am not a politician.... I only suffer the consequences."

—PETER TOSH, prophesying his untimely fate

PETER TOSH
YEARS ACTIVE: 1960s-1987

Peter Tosh was the establishment's most fiercely militant musical adversary. With his uncompromising Pan-Africanist and pro-marijuana views, he was also one of reggae's most openly political artists. By playing a guitar shaped like an M16 rifle, he guaranteed conflict with what he scathingly referred to as the "shitstem." He also regularly rode a unicycle (as depicted on the cover of the 1996 compilation *The Best of Peter Tosh: Dread Don't Die*), perhaps symbolizing the challenging and unlikely balancing act Tosh aimed for in his career but never quite achieved. The politics of confrontation did not always blend well with the pitfalls of commercialization.

Born Winston Hubert McIntosh on October 19, 1944, in Westmoreland, Jamaica, he spent much of his childhood living with an aunt who eventually moved with him to the Denham Town section of west Kingston. After his aunt's death, he went to live with an uncle in Trench Town, Kingston's housing-project ghetto for Jamaica's poor, dispossessed, and the socially outcast Rastafarians. During his youth, Tosh learned to play guitar (on his own)

and piano (taught by an aunt), key tools of his future trade. In 1963 Tosh, Bob Marley, and Bunny Wailer formed the Wailers, the vocal group that would globalize roots reggae throughout the 1970s, though with different members; after 1973, all three original members would continue careers as solo artists. During his well-documented stint with the group, Tosh cowrote with Marley the 1973 resistance anthem "Get Up, Stand Up" and developed his songwriting skills, stage persona, and spiritual identity. By late 1973, Tosh, like bandmate Bunny Wailer, had reached a point where forging a solo career seemed the only viable option, since Island Records head Chris Blackwell was focusing on Marley's talents. Although the Wailers were on the brink of a breakthrough, Tosh was dissatisfied with the circumstances surrounding the group.

Tosh's pro-marijuana single "Legalize It," first released in Jamaica in 1975, achieved predictable success in the streets, despite an equally foreseeable airplay ban. Lack of money limited Tosh's recording, but he secured deals

with Columbia Records in America and Virgin Records in Britain and released the *Legalize It* album in 1976. With its unambiguous title track and cover photo of Tosh smoking in a field of ganja, the album appealed to college students around the world, as well as to Jamaica's constituency of herbal devotees. While *Legalize It* became Tosh's only album to chart in Britain, it was more of an underground phenomenon in America. After peaking at #199 on the *Billboard* Top 200, however, the album continued to sell slowly and consistently. It eventually went platinum in 1999, reaching sales of more than one million, and became Tosh's most commercially successful album in America.

His next album, 1977's *Equal Rights*, is often described as Tosh's definitive musical, ideological, and personal statement. It was recorded in Jamaica—primarily at Randy's in Kingston—and

defined himself as a cutting edge, slicing through "downpression" (the Rasta term for "oppression"). Less obviously related to ganja than was its predecessor, *Equal Rights* failed to chart on either side of the Atlantic. It did, however, resonate strongly with revolutionary-minded music lovers. The commercial failure led to a new label connection when Tosh signed to Rolling Stones Records, the famous British rock group's custom imprint. The leaders of the band, Mick Jagger and Keith Richards, were frequent visitors to Jamaica.

The ultratight Word, Sound & Power touring band that Tosh assembled included the acclaimed drum-and-bass duo Sly & Robbie, American guitarists Al Anderson and Donald Kinsey, and keyboardist Earl "Wire" Lindo, all of whom had played with Bob Marley & the Wailers. Appearing at the One Love Peace Concert held at Kingston's National Stadium in April 1978, Tosh and his group showcased their collective talents for a local audience, but the event is far more infamous for nonmusical reasons. In an outburst of Rastaman rhetoric, Tosh called for fire and brimstone to rain down on Michael Manley and Edward Seaga, the leaders of the nation's warring People's National Party and Jamaica Labour Party, respectively. Tosh blamed the politicians—both of whom were in attendance—for the nation's sustained poverty and flawed spiritual condition. This rant, as well as his endorsement of herb, made Tosh even more of a marked man. His language at the concert was naturally far less than diplomatic, and laced with expletives. In

September 1978, he received a vicious beating from the police—not his first—that injured his skull and no doubt left even deeper psychological lesions. In an interview in the chilling 1993 documentary *Stepping Razor: Red X*, Tosh said that he knew there was a "direct connection" between the beating and his verbal assault on Jamaica's politicians at the One Love Peace Concert. "They know that I speak the truth, and the truth is destructive to the functioning of lies and corruption," he asserted. If anything, the unsavory event reinforced the message in the opening lines of "Equal Rights": "Everyone is crying out for peace / None is crying out for justice."

At least one good thing came of the One Love Peace Concert, however. Jagger reportedly attended and recognized Tosh's potential appeal to a wider audience. The deal Tosh signed with Rolling Stones Records, which had a distribution arrangement with the major label EMI Records, greatly improved his chances of reaching wider markets. At the time, Tosh looked at the alliance as a divine opportunity to spread his message to those who appreciated and respected the music. *Bush Doctor* (1978) was the first fruit of the deal, and the lead single, "(You Gotta Walk and) Don't Look Back," featured a duet between Tosh and Jagger. Tosh had previously recorded the song with the Wailers during the group's 1960s Studio One years, under the guidance of that label's owner, Coxsone Dodd, but the decision to remake it with Jagger did not pay off. It stalled at #81 on America's *Billboard* Hot 100 and reached only #43 in Britain. The album did not break any sales records either, but that was not of primary importance to Tosh, who saw the music as a means of spreading his antiestablishment ideas. If the idea of spearheading an album with a love song like the Jagger duet seemed inconsistent with Tosh's political goals, he likely viewed it as a way to attract new listeners and gain airplay.

mixed in Miami. His revival of "Get Up, Stand Up" and another Wailers-era song, "400 Years," cowritten by Marley, was a clear signal of Tosh's sustained militancy. He took a confrontational stance on the title track, condemned South Africa's institutional racism on "Apartheid," and emphasized the international connection of all black people on "African." With these three historical narratives, Tosh sang of the present as he looked ahead to a "Babylon"-free future, giving the album political weight. On "Stepping Razor," written by Joe Higgs, the Trench Town musical mentor who was the Wailers' first vocal coach, Tosh appropriately

TOP: In 1975, Peter Tosh's message was a hit with college students everywhere.

ABOVE: Tosh's final studio album came out in 1987, the same year he was gunned down in his home.

Tosh's next two albums, *Mystic Man* (1979) and *Wanted Dread & Alive* (1981), were his last for the Rolling Stones' label; his alliance with the group was increasingly plagued by his dissatisfaction with the promotion of his records. Up to the time of Marley's death in 1981, Tosh's overall commercial reception had been lukewarm, and he moved fully to EMI for his next three albums. With his career seemingly in stasis, even though he continued to give electrifying live appearances, Tosh embarked on what would be his final studio album, 1987's *No Nuclear War*, written in the shadow of the ongoing Cold War between the United States and the Soviet Union.

Tosh was assassinated on September 11, 1987, when three gunmen invaded his house, killing two others and injuring four. *No Nuclear War* earned him a posthumous Grammy Award for best reggae album, but this was a sad postscript to a life in which just career desserts arrived a little too late. The documentary *Stepping Razor: Red X*, featuring privately recorded audiotapes documenting Tosh's thoughts and feelings, demonstrated how persecution affected his life. His radical politics of liberation and righteousness still have an audience, as evidenced by the 2011 expanded reissues of *Legalize It* and *Equal Rights*. Andrew Tosh, his eldest son (born in 1967), has continued the legacy by recording a few albums since the late 1980s, and in 2011, he remade his father's "Lessons in My Life," recording the track with another famous reggae son, Ky-Mani Marley.

SELECT DISCOGRAPHY: *Legalize It* (Columbia/Virgin, 1976); *Equal Rights* (Columbia/Virgin, 1977); *Bush Doctor* (Rolling Stones, 1978); *Mystic Man* (Rolling Stones, 1979); *Wanted Dread & Alive* (Rolling Stones/EMI America, 1981); *Mama Africa* (EMI America, 1983); *Captured Live* (EMI America, 1984); *No Nuclear War* (EMI America, 1987); *Honorary Citizen* (Columbia, 1997)

TREASURE ISLE RECORDS

Ex–police officer Arthur "Duke" Reid founded Treasure Isle Records in the early 1960s as an extension of the liquor store he had operated in Kingston, Jamaica, since the early 1950s. Prior to establishing the label and studio, which occupied the space above his storefront, Reid ran his own sound system called the Trojan. He earned a reputation as a ruthless boss, and his rabid local following included crews of henchmen he would dispatch to disrupt rival dances. In a bid to promote his system and dominate the scene, Reid bought radio airtime in the early 1950s and hosted the program *Treasure Isle Time*.

Around 1962, having spent the latter years of the previous decade recording at the West Indies Records Limited (WIRL) studio in Kingston, owned by entrepreneur-turned-politician Edward Seaga, Reid opted to set up his own operation. It was a very basic facility, but the longevity of the rhythms he would record there suggests that the musical quality transcended the limited technology. "Carry Go Bring Come" by Justin Hinds & the Dominoes (1964) was one of the early hits that set the label on the path to success and foreshadowed the prominence of vocal groups on Treasure Isle. Inevitably, Reid shared musicians with other local producers, but his fluid session bands included some of Jamaica's best players, among them members of the Skatalites, those pioneers of ska excellence. Accounts suggest that Reid knew what type of sound he wanted from his musicians, and when he was dissatisfied, the armed producer could apparently be quite intimidating.

Treasure Isle reached its peak in the rocksteady era of the mid-1960s, when Reid's productions ruled the sound systems. Among the illustrious members of the Supersonics, the house band that carried Treasure Isle

at this point, were former Skatalites saxophonist Tommy McCook, innovative guitarist Lynn Taitt, and unheralded bassist Jackie Jackson. During this time, Reid successfully licensed material to fledgling British independent labels—Trojan Records and Pama Records—selling Jamaican music to mainly West Indian audiences. As rocksteady gave way to reggae, Treasure Isle lost its dominance and scored only occasional hits. Reid was out of step with the emerging musical directions, and in the early 1970s, his acute distaste for Rastafarians kept the label from capitalizing on the public's growing appetite for antiestablishment, religious, and political expression through popular music. Given these circumstances, it was somewhat unexpected that Reid found commercial success on his imprint with seminal DJ U-Roy on the 1970 singles "Wake the Town" and "Rule the Nation," and the 1971 Treasure Isle label LP *Version Galore*. On his early Treasure Isle records, the pioneering DJ recycled older rhythms, blazing a trail for a generation of "toasters,"

the chatting, rapping and singing DJs who were the forerunners of America's 1970s rap movement.

Ultimately, however, it was a false dawn for Treasure Isle. Apart from continuing to sell its back catalog, the label was unable to reestablish itself as a major player in the reggae music world. Reid died in 1975, a year after becoming seriously ill with cancer. Before his death, Reid had sold the Treasure Isle catalog to leading female producer Sonia Pottinger, who ran hit labels of her own such as High Note and Tip Top. As was the case with most Jamaican labels, Treasure Isle had an unfortunate reputation for not sharing the wealth with the artists who made its success possible. The resulting bitterness among musicians in its former stable continues to resonate.

SELECT DISCOGRAPHY: *Duke Reid's Treasure Chest: Treasure Isle Rock-Steady* (Heartbeat, 1994); *Ska All Mighty: Classics from the Treasure Isle Label* (Heartbeat, 2002); *The Story of Treasure Isle* (Metro, 2004)

Established by Duke Reid c. 1962, Treasure Isle peaked during the mid-1960s rocksteady period.

TROJAN RECORDS

Trojan Records played a crucial role in establishing reggae's international popularity. It was especially important in Britain, where the label scored thirty hit singles between 1969 and 1975, when the label folded. Had Trojan not pushed reggae into the mainstream, such pop-reggae groups as UB40 might never have achieved their massive crossover success, and the music might have remained an underground phenomenon.

The label began as a short-lived custom imprint for material licensed by the Jamaican label Treasure Isle, whose boss, Duke Reid, was nicknamed Trojan. The first release bearing the Trojan name was issued on July 28, 1967. After a brief dormant spell, Trojan Records Ltd. was created in 1968 by the B&C (Beat & Commercial) Company in partnership with Chris Blackwell's Island Records. Trojan was initially one of many UK subsidiaries established by B&C's owner, Lee Gopthal—a Jamaican Indian—and several partners to release records that were made in Jamaica.

In 1968, Gopthal commissioned a survey to help explain why the label's few full-length releases had sold so poorly compared to its singles. The results suggested that compilations rather than single-artist albums better suited the audience's needs. Thus, Trojan's budget-priced *Tighten Up* compilation series was conceived. The concept was to compile hit reggae songs so that there would be a ready-made market for the LP product. The formula worked, as was evidenced by the solid sales of the first three installments, released between 1969 and 1970. The *Tighten Up* collections propelled Trojan into the public consciousness, and while the music was undoubtedly popular, the scantily clad women often pictured on the album covers may also have been a factor.

In 1969, hits such as as Desmond Dekker's # 1 UK single "Israelites" (released on the subsidiary Pyramid imprint), and Jimmy Cliff's "Wonderful World, Beautiful People" (later released by Island) made Trojan a commercial force on the British charts. The label got an additional—and somewhat unexpected—boost when members of the white middle-class skinhead subculture embraced reggae. The label dealt in both imported and domestic reggae, but according to a former Trojan staffer, material of Jamaican origin almost always outsold British recordings. As Trojan expanded its audience, sales skyrocketed. Whereas a single that was popular among West Indian immigrants might sell between 2,500 and 5,000 copies, one that penetrated the pop mainstream might sell between 40,000 and 200,000—possibly more, depending on chart longevity. The label reached its commercial peak in 1970, when West Indians, skinheads, and pop-music consumers purchased a combined 500,000 Trojan singles.

In some respects, the large number of subsidiaries under Trojan's corporate umbrella obscured the label's commercial impact in the United Kingdom and Europe. There were as many as fifty such subsidiaries, though by 1972, the number had dipped to twenty. "Double Barrel" by Dave & Ansel Collins was issued in 1971, becoming Trojan's only #1 UK hit on Jamaican producer Winston Riley's Techniques imprint. Featuring an instrumental rhythm overdubbed with DJ vocals but no actual singing, "Double Barrel" was an unlikely hit. Even Trojan's own song pluggers (who worked to get songs radio airplay) had been reluctant to approach the British Broadcasting Corporation (BBC) with the track.

Trojan had a habit of adding pop-style string arrangements to their songs, and while this helped its singles gain radio airplay, it weakened the label's credibility in the reggae market. The label preferred familiar, accessible music: as an example, one of its most successful UK singles, Ken Boothe's "Everything I Own" (1974), was a cover of a 1972 hit by the American rock band Bread. To some degree, the strategy paid off, and by 1974, Trojan had come to control an estimated 75 percent of the British reggae market. However, thanks in part to those radio-friendly string arrangements, the label's lightweight pop-reggae crossover songs alienated younger members of reggae's core West Indian audience, possibly contributing to Trojan's demise. What's more, the company apparently underestimated the threat posed by smaller labels that no longer saw Trojan as the first choice among licensees and distributors.

In 1972, further foreshadowing the label's financial decline, Chris Blackwell ended his involvement with the company. Despite its success exporting music to other European countries, the label folded in 1975 when its parent company went bankrupt. The label was sold for a reported £32,000 to Saga Records, which had no prior background in the sale, production, or licensing of reggae. Following the sale, Trojan's new owners undertook a reissue strategy, enlisting expert reggae journalists to provide historical focus and ensure the commercial viability of the releases. In 2011, Sanctuary Records, an imprint that had been bought by the Universal Music Group in 2007, paid in excess of £10 million ($14 million) for Trojan's rich catalog of more than ten thousand titles. Sanctuary subsequently released a series of theme-oriented multidisc compilations that have placed Trojan's music in the hands of both old and new collectors.

Thanks in part to radio-friendly string arrangements, Trojan brought reggae to the UK mainstream, scoring thirty hit singles between 1969 and 1975.

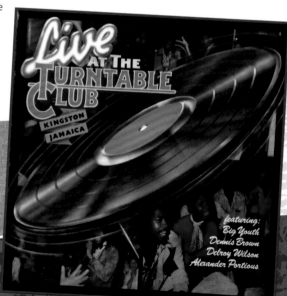

U-ROY

YEARS ACTIVE: 1970s–2000s

U-Roy was not the first Jamaican DJ to appear on record (Sir Lord Comic and King Stitt were among those who came first), but none matched his far-reaching influence in the form of records U-Roy made for Treasure Isle Records in the early 1970s. Born Ewart Beckford, he got his start with the Home Town Hi-Fi sound system founded by King Tubby, who later became a renowned dub remix engineer. U-Roy established himself as a key DJ with the system. Occasionally listed as Hugh Roy, he had little success with his early recording attempts, and

the 1969 singles "Dynamic Fashion Way" and "Earth's Rightful Ruler" produced by Keith Hudson and Lee Perry, respectively, both missed their commercial targets.

U-Roy's big break came soon enough, however, when Treasure Isle boss Duke Reid tapped into the label's ample archives of rhythms and gave the DJ a foundation for his "toasting," a Jamaican style of rapping over instrumental tracks. In 1970, U-Roy ruled the Jamaican scene with three rapid-fire releases: "Wake the Town," "Rule the Nation," and "Wear You to the Ball," the latter a remake of a 1967 hit for the vocal group the Paragons. U-Roy's 1971 debut album, *Version Galore*, was essentially a collection of toasted B-sides that nonetheless proved to be one of the first serious DJ albums to achieve any market impact. U-Roy

has often recalled how shocked he was by his sudden success, though overnight stardom did not bring him much financial reward. Reid provided some payments, but insufficient compensation may have contributed to U-Roy's decision to leave Treasure Isle and work with other producers, among them Lloyd Daley, a former sound system operator.

U-Roy cashed in on the mid-1970s reggae gold rush, signing with Virgin Records for his most prolific phase of full-length album output. Even as other DJs moved into the spotlight, tracks like

U-Roy's most crucial records came in the 1970s, but the trailblazing DJ has kept on toasting into the twenty-first century.

1975's "Chalice in the Palace" helped U-Roy maintain his role as innovator. Influential as both a DJ and as the owner of the Stur-Gav sound system, which he had founded by the mid-1970s, he remained active through the dancehall explosion of the 1980s and has continued into the twenty-first century. Despite his longevity, fans seeking the classic U-Roy sound—one that carved out a bigger niche for DJs in reggae—must reach back to his 1970s catalog.

SELECT DISCOGRAPHY: *Version Galore* (Treasure Isle, 1971); *U-Roy* (Trojan, 1974); *Dread in a Babylon* (Virgin, 1975); *Natty Rebel* (Virgin, 1976); *Rasta Ambassador* (Virgin, 1977); *Version Galore* (Virgin Front Line, 1978); *Jah Son of Africa* (Virgin Front Line, 1978); *With Words of Wisdom* (Virgin Front Line, 1979); *Love Is Not a Gamble* (State Line, 1980); *Foundation Skank* 1971–1975 (Sound System, 2009)

UB40

YEARS ACTIVE: 1979-2000s

Formed in the Midlands city of Birmingham, England, in the late 1970s and featuring singer Ali Campbell, UB40 quickly became the world's biggest-selling reggae band since Bob Marley & the Wailers. Due to the unusual spectacle of white musicians playing actual roots-oriented reggae—as opposed to the pop-reggae hybrids favored by such British rock bands as the Police—the multiracial outfit has inspired both fervor and skepticism throughout its long career.

In 1979 UB40, named for Britain's unemployment benefit form, got a huge boost in exposure when they landed a slot as the opening band for popular rock act the Pretenders, who were on tour. UB40's appeal became even more evident when the band scored a surprise hit with their 1980 debut album, *Signing Off*, released on the independent Graduate Records label. The album peaked at #2 in the United Kingdom, while the double-A-side single "King/Food For Thought" made the top five on the pop charts. Despite reggae's cult appeal, it rarely sold to the mainstream in significant numbers, so UB40's chart success was truly unusual. The debut album did not come out in America until 1994, when it was released as *The UB40 File*. The delay was

likely due to the absence of any US distribution for the band when the record was first issued.

After Graduate omitted the finger-pointing antiapartheid song "Burden of Shame" from the South African version of *Signing Off*, UB40 formed its own label, DEP International. Given UB40's later commercial success, Graduate's inability to retain the band was a major mistake. The group's follow-up album, *Present Arms*, released on DEP in 1981, featured the single "One in Ten" and displayed a more cohesive sound. The album cracked the top five in Britain and spawned the remixed *Present Arms in Dub*, which reached the UK album charts in 1981, becoming the first dub album to do so, though it lacked the radical remixing characteristic of Jamaican dub.

While UB40 were well on their way to becoming an international phenomenon, they had yet to establish a commercial presence in America. The turning point came with their remake of Neil Diamond's "Red Red Wine," originally an American hit in 1968. UB40's version topped the British charts in 1983, and while it cracked the American Top 40 the following year, it wasn't until its rerelease in 1988 that it became a gold-certified #1 hit there as well. "Red Red Wine" appeared on *Labour of Love*, which featured remakes of reggae songs from the 1960s and 1970s. The album eventually went platinum in both

Britain and the United States, and later led to three other *Labour of Love* cover albums. Throughout the series, UB40 has both paid homage to the reggae songs and artists that inspired them and revamped pop songs in a reggae style. Notably, all four of their top-ten US singles have been covers of previous pop hits.

In response to conservative policies that many in Britain deemed destructive, UB40 was among the reggae acts that opposed the reelection of British Prime Minister Margaret Thatcher in 1983. Thatcher's policies led to massive blue-collar unemployment following her government's mass privatization of industries and sustained conflict with labor unions. Her rule was also characterized by racist anti-immigration policies that marginalized non-whites, and a refusal to tackle South Africa's segregationist apartheid laws. (She branded that country's imprisoned black anti-government leader, Nelson Mandela, a "terrorist.") The band gave voice to their feelings on the 1984

album *Geffery Morgan*. The British top-ten single "If It Happens Again" offered direct commentary on the need for a change in British government, echoing the strident "Stand Down Margaret," recorded by fellow Birmingham band the Beat in 1980.

On the eve of a major 1988 tour, just as the group was enjoying the success of 1987's *Rat in the Kitchen*, tragedy struck. Driving while intoxicated, bassist Earl Falconer crashed his car and killed his brother Ray, UB40's live sound engineer. The incident led to a six-month prison sentence for Falconer the following year. More legal problems arose during a tour in 1990, when police in the Seychelles Islands off the coast of Africa allegedly discovered ganja in band members' hotel rooms. The group was deported, and while this was not a great outcome, it was much better than serving mandatory three-year jail sentences.

In 1993, succeeding at a level that most reggae groups had not, UB40 again hit #1 in both America and Britain, topping the charts with their unlikely remake of Elvis Presley's 1961 single "Can't Help Falling In Love." Included on the soundtrack for the film *Sliver*, it sold more than a million copies in America and became the group's biggest-selling single. Its accompanying album, *Promises and Lies* (1993), also went platinum. This marked UB40's career peak: no further major hits have emerged since then, though their albums continued to reach charts in Britain and across Europe.

The band maintained its international profile through consistent touring, but lead singer Ali Campbell's 1995 solo album *Big Love* foreshadowed his eventual departure. This came in January 2008, after the singer had worked on that year's *24/7* album, his final recording with the group. After twenty-eight years in UB40, Campbell allegedly informed his bandmates of his decision via a solicitor. Financial issues played a significant role in the conflict with the band and its management,

who he claimed pushed him out. He was quoted in the British press as saying, "I will never again play with the remaining members of UB40 while I live and breathe." Meanwhile, in British newspaper reports, Campbell's former bandmates insisted that he left entirely of his own accord, and that they were unhappy with the bitter circumstances of the split, which Ali's brother Robin Campbell described as a divorce. British reggae singer Maxi Priest temporarily fronted the band until Ali's other brother, Duncan, took over as singer.

In March 2008, just weeks after Ali Campbell's departure, keyboardist Michael Virtue also left due to management and money issues. He went on to join the band Campbell had formed to support his solo career. UB40 continued to tour, capitalizing on past commercial success, but their future was cast into doubt in October 2011,

when a British court declared the group bankrupt. The declaration stemmed from monies owed by their DEP International record label. Though it's unlikely that any band members will find themselves seeking state assistance and filling out the unemployment forms for which the group is named, the bankruptcy was a bitterly ironic turn of events.

UB40's long-term success has caused some disquiet in the reggae world, as some artists and managers claim that because they are a multiracial outfit fronted by a white singer, they have been more heavily promoted than all-black groups of equal talent. Certainly, no other reggae group in the post–Bob Marley era has matched UB40's platinum sales, and this has raised unavoidable questions regarding the role of race

in popular music. Stylistically, UB40's ability to bridge gaps between roots reggae, dancehall, and pop has been at the heart of their commercial conquest.

MEMBERS: Ali Campbell (lead vocals & rhythm guitar); **Earl Falconer** (bass); **Jim Brown** (drums); **Brian Travers** (saxophone); **Norman Hassan** (percussion); **Robin Campbell** (lead guitar & vocals); **Michael Virtue** (keyboards); Astro (DJ vocals)

SELECT DISCOGRAPHY: *Signing Off* (Graduate, 1980); *Present Arms* (DEP International, 1981); *Present Arms in Dub* (DEP International, 1981); *The Singles Album* (Graduate, 1982); UB44 (DEP International, 1982); *UB40 Live* (DEP International, 1983); *Labour of Love* (DEP International/A&M, 1983); *Baggariddim/ Little Baggariddim* (DEP International/ A&M, 1985); *Rat in the Kitchen* (DEP

OPPOSITE (BOTTOM): This record sleeve features the British unemployment form from which the band took its name.

ABOVE: The members of UB40—a multiracial outfit that would become the world's biggest reggae act since Bob Marley—out for a stroll in their native Birmingham, England, 1981.

International/A&M, 1986); *CCCP: Live in Moscow* (DEP International/A&M, 1987); *UB40* (DEP International/A&M, 1988); *Labour of Love II* (DEP International/ Virgin, 1989); *Promises & Lies* (DEP International/Virgin, 1993); *Guns in the Ghetto* (DEP International/Virgin, 1997); *Labour of Love III* (DEP International/ Virgin, 1998); *Cover Up* (Virgin, 2001); *Homegrown* (DEP International, 2003); *Who You Fighting For* (DEP International, 2005); *24/7* (Reflexmuzic, 2008); *Dub Sessions* (Reflexmuzic, 2009)

DANCEHALL

Dancehall—the DJ-centered Jamaican music most associated with the digital era of the 1980s and later—is the most controversial and contentious branch of reggae. From its unfiltered portrayal of hard-core subject matter to its current digitally centered studio production, dancehall is very much a catalyst for heated debate. Some writers have suggested that it is simply another phase in the continuum of Jamaican popular music, but that view is challenged by a genuine division between the fans of roots reggae and dancehall.

The differences between these two branches of reggae can easily be oversimplified, but some distinctions are quite apparent. Roots reggae's heyday was the 1970s, when lyrics of cultural, social, and political significance (alongside lots of love songs) were anchored by rhythm track performances emphasizing the drums and bass. While much of that music came out of Jamaica, its themes were globally accessible and relevant. Dancehall's lyrics, especially during its mid-1980s explosion, might be seen as less obviously sociopolitical and spiritual—less directly concerned with black liberation struggles and social justice—and focused more on material matters (guns, girls, cars). Dancehall's commercial presence also signaled an important shift in the sound of reggae, as digitally programmed instruments replaced the organic performances of ace studio session musicians.

The concept of the physical spaces referred to as dance halls (open-air settings for dancing to and listening to music dating back to the 1940s) clearly predates the musical style bearing the same name. Without the dance hall as a venue, sound systems (mobile record-playing hi-fi systems with live DJs and large speakers) would have lacked reasons to exist and the ability to generate income, and the entire history of Jamaican popular music would have been radically altered. While ska, rocksteady, and reggae were part of the culture of the dance hall through which "toasting" DJs such as U-Roy and Big Youth emerged, the music that followed those styles developed distinctly different sonic features.

The vocal improvisations of roots-era Jamaican DJs such as U-Roy and Big Youth in the early 1970s helped spark American rap after Jamaican sound-system culture traveled to New York with immigrant DJ Kool Herc. The sound of his massive speakers and his outdoor dual-turntable skills—both inspired by Jamaican dance halls—emphasized the instrumental breaks on dance records, creating the beat-driven sound track over which American rappers could emulate the vocal feats of their Jamaican counterparts. The chants of Jamaican DJs were an extension of African oral traditions in which information is transmitted by voice rather than via written word, and rap became a further extension of this practice.

The first transition toward dancehall in Jamaica occurred in the late 1970s, when Sugar Minott sang over old Studio One–recorded rhythms. He

ABOVE: Dancehall star Nitty Gritty on his Honda S90 outside King Jammy's studio, 1985.
RIGHT: Eek-A-Mouse onstage at Paradiso in Holland, 1985, putting the "arrr!" in reggae.

Lt. Stitchie, the first major-label DJ of the digital dancehall era, commands the stage in Amsterdam, 1989.

worked under the supervision of that studio's head, Coxsone Dodd, creating what some have described as "proto-dancehall." Political turmoil was the chaotic backdrop to this musical evolution, as Jamaicans' dreams of liberation, equality, prosperity, and spiritual righteousness seemed increasingly unlikely to materialize, and new music was needed to match the country's altered mood.

When the conservative Jamaican Labour Party (JLP) won the 1980 election, the change in government signaled the beginning of broader cultural changes. Spearheaded by producer Henry "Junjo" Lawes, the dancehall DJ style gained greater popularity in songs by genre performers such as the albino Yellowman, including relevant lyrics about social encounters at the outdoor dancehall events. Using the Roots Radics studio session band (a rotating roster of studio musicians formed in 1979), Lawes established an early dancehall template on which the next wave would be built. Major labels began taking notice, and in 1983 Yellowman signed an ultimately short-lived contract with CBS Records.

By the early 1980s, digital music technology had become reasonably affordable for small-scale producers, and drum machines, synthesizers, and sequencers could be synchronized, giving individual producers complete pre-production control. Freed from the traditional fees for session musicians, producers could generate more material at less expense. With this change in the economics of record production, however, it soon became apparent that the sonic texture of dancehall was very different from that of the preceding era's roots reggae. The turning point of digital adoption was 1985, when Wayne Smith's "Under Mi Sleng Teng" was created around a Japanese-made Casio keyboard with a generic preset rhythm. The song swept away all domestic competition and boosted dancehall's international profile (ironically, it was produced by King Jammy, one of the pioneers of roots reggae in the 1970s). The track has since been covered more than four hundred times. In 1987, the commercial attention generated by dancehall encouraged Atlantic Records to sign Jamaican performer Lt. Stitchie as the first major-label DJ of the digital dancehall era.

The commercial success of the dancehall movement had a flip side, however. The ease of digital production meant that standard musicianship wasn't finding its way onto most dancehall releases; furthermore, the global economic hardships of the late 1980s didn't foster much innovation in dancehall or the promotion of non-materialistic values or ideals. The change in Jamaica's drug culture affected the music, too: as cocaine replaced marijuana as the general drug of choice, the harsh high end of the sonic spectrum vanquished the formerly prominent bass. It would be a mistake to assume that the act of embracing digital music technology alone led to a creative decline in reggae culture. For example, the productions of Gussie Clarke, whose career took off in 1973 with DJ Big Youth's *Screaming Target* LP, demonstrated how sonic craftsmanship, good songwriting, and high-tech equipment could readily coexist and be very commercially successful during the digitally dominated 1980s in Jamaica and among reggae audiences around the world. But Clarke's records weren't typical of the dancehall era.

Lyrically, dancehall was associated with "slackness"—meaning its songs focused on sex and gun violence rather than on the spirituality that had been at the heart of the Rasta-driven roots

Wayne Smith, whose "Under Me Sling Teng" featured a preset Casio keyboard rhythm, hangs at Channel One, 1984.

reggae. It's true that slackness did not suddenly appear with dancehall; there was plenty to be found in Jamaica's folk-oriented mento music of the 1940s and 1950s, and in fact, every era of the island's popular music has had its notorious and popular songs about lust. What shocked some people was the blatant presentation in dancehall, usually without the double entendre subtleties that had sometimes characterized older records (with notable exceptions like Prince Buster's totally X-rated "Big Five" in 1967). In addition, performers such as Lady Saw and Patra removed the exclusive rights to raunchiness from the male domain and offered their own salacious narratives from the female perspective.

Sex-related controversies didn't end there. Many songs—and the dancehall music culture in general—were openly and aggressively homophobic, though in some cases, foreign critics failed to grasp the cultural contexts of Jamaican society and language. Nonetheless, songs like Buju Banton's 1992 hit "Boom Bye Bye" drew fire from gay-rights groups, which effectively pressured some artists, promoters, and record companies into adopting more conciliatory stances. Understandably, many in the reggae world viewed this as another instance of the white Western establishment forcing people to "bow" in the face of ungodly immorality. Dancehall acts were encouraged by gay-rights groups to sign the Reggae Compassionate Act, a pledge (though not legally binding) introduced in 2007 by a gay-rights coalition to renounce lyrics encouraging hatred or violence. Since the act's introduction, such performers as Capleton, Sizzla, Buju Banton, and the extra-controversial king of dancehall merchandising, Vybz Kartel, have signed it, but the campaign is ongoing.

In 1994, the Jamaican police issued a decree that essentially banned gun lyrics due to rapidly rising crime, which included the murder of dancehall performers such as DJ Dirtsman—brother of the better-known DJ Papa San—who was killed by gunshot in 1993. But the dancehall-related gun violence wasn't limited to Jamaica, as demonstrated by the killing of DJ Tenor Saw in Texas in 1988. And historically, such murders didn't begin with dancehall. Many roots-reggae figures, like Jamaican singers Hugh Mundell and Peter Tosh and dub remix engineer King Tubby, met their demise in Jamaica in gun-related incidents. The dancehall-related killings had the effect of stimulating (or at least contributing to) a wave of Rasta-related socially conscious lyrics in dancehall. These elements had always been present, but proponents like the vocalists Tony Rebel or the late Garnett Silk were very much in the minority. Buju Banton was on the leading edge of a broader change denouncing violence with the song "Murderer" (1993) and later the album *Til Shiloh* (1995), which encompassed Rastafarian social consciousness. Notably, though, these weren't the kinds of dancehall records that usually had significant chart impact outside of Jamaica, so it is possible that they did little to change the Western mainstream perception of the genre. While dancehall became an international chart fixture through hit records by Shaggy, Shabba Ranks, Beenie Man, and Sean Paul, these performers adopted crossover strategies—such as fusing their sound with R&B and hip hop—that mirrored some of the commercial compromises made by roots reggae artists.

In 2010, when a dispute arose between the Jamaican and United States governments regarding the extradition of alleged gangster Christopher "Dudus" Coke, dancehall became a political pawn, and several acts had their US visas canceled. Beenie Man, Bounty Killer, and Mavado all lost lucrative performance opportunities as a result. It remains to be seen whether dancehall will tap further into the philosophies and musical artistry of roots reggae as it seeks to sustain itself in the twenty-first century.

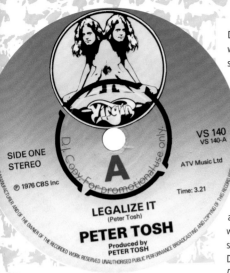

SIDE ONE
STEREO

VS 140
VS 140-A

℗ 1976 CBS Inc

A

ATV Music Ltd

Time: 3.21

LEGALIZE IT
(Peter Tosh)

PETER TOSH

Produced by
PETER TOSH

VIRGIN RECORDS

The foundation of British billionaire entrepreneur Richard Branson's eventual empire was a mail-order record business that became a record label in 1973, scoring an immediate transatlantic hit with a progressive-rock blockbuster titled *Tubular Bells*, by British multi-instrumentalist Mike Oldfield. By the middle of the decade, the label had signed British punk rockers the Sex Pistols, tapping into their commercially lucrative disrepute, and begun augmenting its existing repertoire of alternative and progressive rock acts (including German synth band Tangerine Dream) with punk releases. Given the rising profile of Bob Marley and the inroads Island Records had made selling reggae to young white rock fans, it was only a matter of time before the genre caught Branson's attention.

In the wake of Bob Marley's mid-1970s commercial breakthroughs, Virgin signed former Wailers singer Peter Tosh (already with CBS Records in the United States), producer and artist Keith Hudson, and the DJ U-Roy. In an effort to capitalize on reggae's growing popularity in Britain and Africa, Branson went to Jamaica with Sex Pistols singer Johnny Rotten (an avowed fan of the music) and consultant

Don Letts (a reggae DJ who had worked with British punk rockers the Clash) to sign more acts. To achieve its objective, the company reportedly spent more than $100,000 on the trip.

Virgin staked its claim in the reggae market with the specialist Front Line imprint, established in 1978, though Virgin (and its Caroline Records subsidiary label) had already been releasing records by some reggae artists like U-Roy from as early as 1975. Among the artists who released music on Front Line were vocal group the Mighty Diamonds, singer Johnny Clarke, and DJ Big Youth. Dub poet Linton Kwesi Johnson's 1978 *Dread Beat An' Blood* album was a record that gave Front Line real credibility. This was a far cry from the lightweight, string-laden, pop-style reggae that characterized Trojan Records, which had been a leading British label just a few years earlier, and arguably contributed to that company's financial demise. Front Line's signature logo, a bleeding black fist clenching barbed wire, spoke to the ways in which reggae and revolutionary struggles were seen as part of the same continuum. The image was ideal for the substantial African market, though sales fell when the Nigerian government changed hands and the country declared a freeze on foreign exchange. In addition to giving reggae musicians larger platforms for disseminating their antiestablishment ideologies, Front Line offered attractive advances and the promise of actually receiving royalties. These financial rewards were important, as many artists sought to escape a Jamaican industry that had repeatedly left them victimized.

Virgin's Front Line arguably overstocked its roster and issued records at a rate that far outpaced the audience's appetite, rather like a buffet with too many options. By 1980, Virgin had ended its flirtation with reggae, but not before leaving behind some fine records. In the early 1990s, the Virgin subsidiary Caroline Records, began reissuing key releases from the catalog.

VP RECORDS

Like Motown Records is to 1960s soul, VP Records is synonymous with dancehall reggae. The label originated with Randy's Record Mart, founded in 1958 in Kingston, Jamaica, by Vincent "Randy" Chin and his wife Pat. In 1979, after moving to the United States, the family established a retail and distribution operation in New York City. This led to the almost inevitable launch of VP Records around 1991, with the involvement of sons Christopher and Randy. Another son, Clive, had been a producer in the 1970s for Randy's studio and record label established in 1968.

VP Records had established a large retail outlet in New York by the mid-1990s, while Vincent and Pat Chin's daughter was running the company's wholesale operation in Miami. In 2002, VP signed a distribution deal with the major label Atlantic Records that enabled VP to push dancehall performers such as Sean Paul into the international pop mainstream. Looking ahead to what the deal might mean for reggae, an Atlantic executive

in 2002 compared its potential impact to what Chris Blackwell achieved with Island Records in the 1970s, breaking reggae acts like Bob Marley & the Wailers into the pop mainstream.

In May 2008, VP expanded its reggae empire with the $6.2 million purchase of Greensleeves Records, a Britain-based record and publishing company founded as a record shop in 1975. This acquisition effectively made VP reggae's biggest single label. At the end of 2009, VP had seven of *Billboard* magazine's top-ten reggae albums of the year, demonstrating the dominant role that independent labels continue to play in the genre.

In 2011, the label was rocked by the murder of thirty-five-year-old A&R (Artists and Repertoire) director Joel Chin outside his home in Jamaica.

TOP LEFT: Virgin's roster in the mid-1970s included Peter Tosh, the former Wailer.

RIGHT: Christopher Chin in the mid-1980s, before helping his family launch VP Records in the United States, a successor to Randy's in Jamaica.

BUNNY WAILER

YEARS ACTIVE: 1960s-2000s

Born Neville O'Riley Livingston on April 10, 1947, in the Trench Town district of Kingston, Jamaica, Bunny Wailer is one of reggae's most enduring artists. Throughout his career, he has stayed true to the spirit of the roots era, carrying themes of social and political consciousness into decades when they were no longer as popular. In 1963, he formed the Wailers with fellow singers and future reggae superstars Bob Marley and Peter Tosh, recording the ska hit "Simmer Down" for Coxsone Dodd's Studio One label. Despite scoring other Jamaican hits such as "I'm Still Waiting" and "Put It On," both in 1965, the Wailers' paltry earnings did not match their rapid musical progress in these early years.

After Bob Marley left Jamaica in 1966 on a brief trip to the United States to live with his mother, Bunny Wailer was imprisoned the following year for marijuana possession. That experience would later inspire the song "Fighting Against Conviction" from Bunny's 1976 debut solo album, *Blackheart Man*. Before that solo career began, he continued to work with the Wailers, recording with the group during its stints with producers Leslie Kong (upon whom Bunny allegedly placed a deadly curse) and Lee Perry. Kong's productions began reaching the British charts in 1967 with Desmond Dekker's "007 (Shanty Town)," and Perry scored a 1969 UK hit for The Upsetters with "Return of Django," so both producers were well positioned to boost the Wailers' career. However, neither of these connections fulfilled their promise, with both Kong and Perry releasing material against the group's wishes. The Wailers seized the opportunity to record *Catch a Fire* in 1972 for international release on Chris Blackwell's Island Records. After that record and its 1973 follow-up,

Burnin', Bunny's dissatisfaction with the business and its touring rituals—and the need to record more of his own songs—led to his departure from the band. Tosh left the Wailers at the same time for similar reasons.

Bunny signed a distribution deal with Island as a solo artist shortly after he left the group. He insisted that his contract include a release clause freeing him from contractual obligations to the label in the event of Blackwell's death. Through his own Solomonic label—an imprint established in 1973 and used mainly for his own releases in Jamaica—he began licensing material to Island. 1976's *Blackheart Man*, the first such release, was warmly received, and heralded as a reggae landmark. It included the classic song "Dreamland," but despite its critical success, the album was not a big

seller. Similarly, his next two politically centered LPs for Island (*Protest* in 1977, and *Struggle* in 1978) were critically well received, but not commercially successful. However, 1980's *Bunny Wailer Sings the Wailers* was just the sort of record that Island had in mind, since Bob Marley's rise to reggae superstardom by this time had sparked greater interest in his (mostly) pre-Island vocal trio collaborations with Tosh and Wailer. "Cool Runnings," from the *Rock 'n' Groove* album (1980), was an enormous hit throughout the Caribbean,

BUNNY WAILER

WIP 6347-A
WIPX 1630

℗ 1978 Island International Ltd

ATV Music Ltd

DREAM LAND
(Bunny O'Riley)

PRODUCED, ARRANGED AND DIRECTED BY
BUNNY WAILER
From the album "Blackheart Man"—
JLPS 9415

In 1978, Bunny Wailer (left) and Peter Tosh had long since left the Wailers, but they still shared a certain spark.

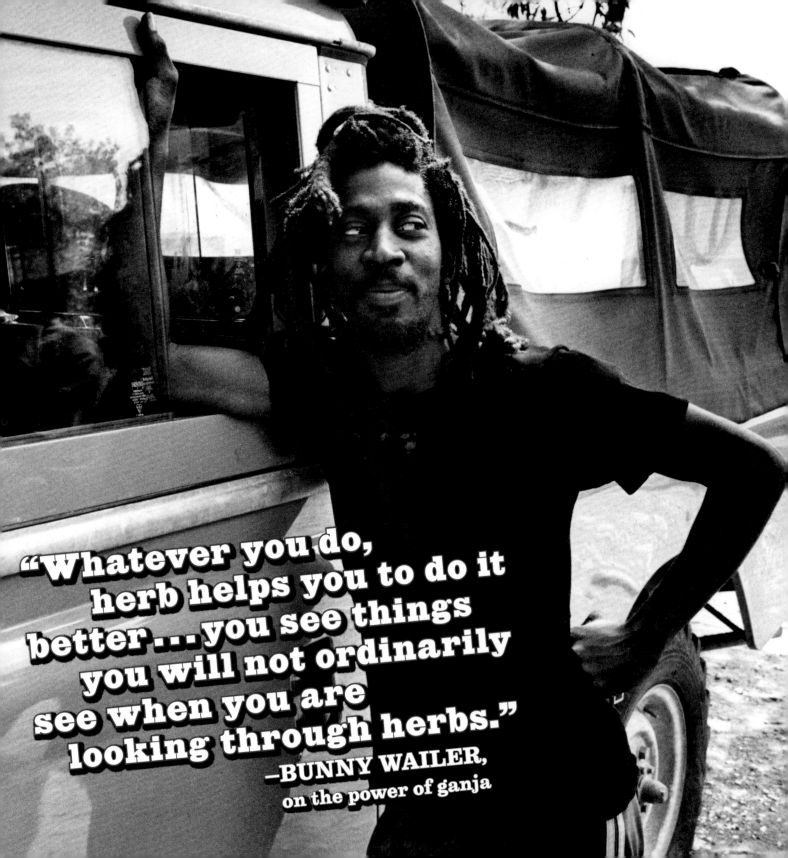

"Whatever you do, herb helps you to do it better ... you see things you will not ordinarily see when you are looking through herbs."

—BUNNY WAILER,
on the power of ganja

Bunny Wailer sings *The Wailers*

DANCING SHOES

"Love Fire") is a classic representation of the vital sound that had become marginal and dispensable in the reggae market with the rise of dancehall.

Other activities would soon demand Wailer's attention, as he formed his own political party, the United Progressive People (UPP), in 2000. This was an unprecedented move for a Jamaican musical artist, and unlike the island's two major political organizations, the UPP promoted the decriminalization of marijuana as a means of effecting social stability and boosting the economy through hemp manufacturing.

In October 2009, Wailer released "Don't Touch the President," supporting the practice of giving back to the community by alleged drug lord Christopher "Dudus" Coke, who was extradited to the United States in 2010. As the last surviving member of the original group the Wailers, he holds tremendous symbolic significance in the reggae world and remains an active, visible, and artistically successful link between generations of Jamaican musicians and audiences around the world. His legacy also continues through his daughter, Ngeri Livingston, who has started a singing career under the name Cen'C Love.

SELECT DISCOGRAPHY: *Blackheart Man* (Mango/Island, 1976); *Protest* (Mango/Island, 1977); *Struggle* (Mango/Island, 1978); *Rock 'n' Groove* (Solomonic, 1980); *In I Father's House* (Solomonic, 1980); *Bunny Wailer Sings the Wailers* (Mango/Island, 1980); *Tribute* (Solomonic, 1981); *Liberation* (Solomonic, 1989); *Time Will Tell: A Tribute to Bob Marley* (Shanachie, 1990); *Marketplace* (Shanachie, 1991); *Crucial! Roots Classics* (Shanachie, 1994); *Hall of Fame: A Tribute to Bob Marley's 50th Anniversary* (Shanachie, 1996); *Dubd'sco: Volumes 1 & 2* (Solomonic 1999); *Communication* (Solomonic, 2000); *World Peace* (Solomonic/Tuff Gong, 2003)

but Bunny's other 1980s releases are difficult to find. This scarcity suggests that the albums he released during the rise of dancehall were not as cohesive. Wailer might have achieved more success had he toured in support of his albums, but he preferred to remain near his Jamaican home base, and it was not until 1988 that he embarked on his first American concert tour.

In a seemingly uncharacteristic bid for mainstream success, Wailer collaborated with I-Threes vocalist Marcia Griffiths—part of the female vocal trio that replaced Tosh and Wailer after their departure from the Wailers—on "Electric Boogie," which broke into the American *Billboard* Hot 100 in 1989, years after its initial 1982 release. Wailer wrote, produced, arranged, and sang background vocals on the track.

In the decade that followed, he earned three Grammy Awards, winning best reggae album for *Time Will Tell: A Tribute to Bob Marley* (1991), *Crucial! Roots Classics* (1995), and *Hall of Fame: A Tribute to Bob Marley's 50th Anniversary* (1997). The fact that Bunny rerecorded classics for those albums suggests both that the songs firmly stood the test of time and that the state of reggae in the 1990s was not particularly healthy, largely lacking innovation. The Grammy-winning records overshadowed the 1999 release of the ambitious *Dubd'sco: Volumes 1 & 2*, which brought the deep "dubwise" (dub-oriented) roots flavor back into the spotlight, however briefly. The excellent "Burning Dub" (a remix of his 1978 song

OPPOSITE: Bunny Wailer looks pretty lighthearted in 1976, the year he released his landmark *Blackheart Man*.

ABOVE AND RIGHT: Bunny has released many records on his Solomonic label, established in 1973.

THE WAILERS

**YEARS ACTIVE: 1960s-1973
(THE WAILERS)
1974-1981 (AS BOB MARLEY
& THE WAILERS)
1981-2000s (AS THE WAILERS
BAND)**

As a platform for the emergence of Bob Marley, Peter Tosh, and Bunny Wailer as solo acts, the Wailers were a vehicle for reggae's international popularity. More than any other group, they are associated with giving reggae credibility in the rock market, even after Tosh and Wailer left the band in 1973. Following this split, the renamed Bob Marley & the Wailers broke through commercial barriers to establish reggae as an album-oriented music form during the remainder of the decade. The instrumentalists left behind after Marley's tragic death in 1981 continued to perform and record as a unit, The Wailers Band.

The original members of the Wailers were initially taken in by Studio One founder Coxsone Dodd, who helped them develop their sound, and the band scored their first hit with 1963's "Simmer Down." This was one of the many singles they would record about the era's "rude boys," whose knife-wielding, Kingston gangster activity became a featured topic in Jamaican songs, particularly in the mid-1960s. The song called for an end to their violent behavior. Under the tutelage of musician Joe Higgs—who had been one-half of Higgs & Wilson, a duo best known for the 1959 Jamaican hit "Manny-O"—the Wailers refined their harmonic vocal blend. The group actually transitioned through several names, including the Teenagers, Wailing Rudeboys, and, at the suggestion of Dodd, the Wailing Wailers. At this stage, they were not a self-contained band. On many of their early hits—including the original version of "One Love" (1965), a song Marley later made famous as a solo artist—they were backed by members of the legendary Skatalites, top Jamaican session musicians whose playing is considered the best in the ska era. Some of the singles even predate that band's formation.

In addition to the well-known triumvirate of Bob Marley, Bunny Wailer, and Peter Tosh, the early Wailers featured three other singers. Junior Braithwaite left the outfit in the summer of 1965, and backup singers Beverly Kelso and Cherry Smith departed the following year as the group struggled with paltry earnings.

Marley spent most of 1966 (from February to October) in the United States, living with his mother and working factory jobs, and this effectively placed the group on hiatus. Upon returning to Jamaica, he reunited with Tosh and Wailer. Partially due to Dodd's distaste for the Rastafarian faith all three had adopted, they left Studio One in 1966 and formed their own record label—the short-lived Wail 'N' Soul—the following year.

After that independent enterprise stalled, in 1969 the Wailers recorded for Leslie Kong at Beverley's Records, for whom Marley had cut "Judge Not" and "One Cup of Coffee" in 1962 as a solo singer. Against the group's wishes, Kong later compiled several singles recorded during this time and released them as 1970's *The Best of the Wailers*. Bunny Wailer declared that Kong would die as punishment for this betrayal—a pronouncement that seemed powerfully mystical in 1971, when Kong suffered a fatal heart attack. The next phase for the band involved collaborating with the enigmatic producer Lee Perry, also in 1969. Perry captured the edgier aspects of the Wailers' vocals while stripping down the rhythm tracks to the bare essentials, giving the group an earthier sound and more distinct identity. Unfortunately, the musical progress would be tainted by claims surrounding Perry's business dealings. Legend has it that the producer allegedly sold the session master tapes to the English label Trojan Records unbeknownst to the group, though Perry accused Trojan of misconduct. These recordings were released in Britain in various forms and under numerous album titles—*Soul Rebels* (1970), *Soul Revolution* (1971), and *African Herbsman* (1973) being key examples—for years to come. Perry's underhanded sale was one key impetus for the Wailers' to push their own Tuff Gong Records imprint, which they had established in 1965, according to some sources.

In 1972, the Wailers traveled to London to play a series of shows with singer Johnny Nash. When the gigs did not materialize, they found themselves stranded in England. To add insult to injury, CBS Records ignored Marley's "Reggae on Broadway" single (produced by Nash), producing further discouragement within the group. In desperation the Wailers arranged to meet Island Records founder Chris Blackwell, who recalls that his investment in the group was a leap of faith, since he had not heard any of their demos or seen them play live. By this time, the group had assembled its own Jamaican rhythm section, enlisting brothers Aston "Family Man" Barrett and Carlton Barrett, who had played bass and drums, respectively, in Perry's Upsetters studio band.

Blackwell signed the Wailers to Island with the intent of presenting them in the image of a black rock group, and after spending £4,000

on recording sessions at Dynamic Sounds in Kingston, he hired American session men Wayne Perkins and John "Rabbit" Bundrick to overdub rock guitar and keyboards in London. When the resulting album, *Catch a Fire*, was released (1972 in Britain, 1973 in America), its sales impact was initially minimal, but the positive critical response was enough to justify a groundbreaking tour in Britain and another one in America, where they supported a relatively unknown Bruce Springsteen. *Catch a Fire* did not simply contain elements of rock music. The album sleeve resembled an oversized Zippo lighter, and this unique packaging mimicked the style-conscious record jacket concepts of the rock world, making mainstream music fans curious about the music within. In addition to the core Wailers members, Jamaican session musicians played on the album. Among them was now-famous bassist Robbie Shakespeare, who appears on the opening track, "Concrete Jungle." The group's 1973 appearance on the British Broadcasting Corporation (BBC) television rock show *The Old Grey Whistle Test* was vital in bringing them greater attention and promoting their debut.

Released a mere six months later, 1973's *Burnin'* would be the final Wailers album to include Peter Tosh and Bunny Wailer, both of whom departed the following year. *Burnin'* contained Marley's "I Shot the Sheriff," which rock guitarist Eric Clapton covered in 1974, scoring a major hit. 1974 also saw the release of the *Natty Dread* album, which was the first credited to Bob Marley & the Wailers. The departures of Tosh and Wailer left a harmonic void filled by the I-Threes, a trio of female backup singers comprising Marcia Griffiths, Judy Mowatt, and Marley's wife, Rita. While the I-Threes were a new addition to the band, Rita Marley and Griffiths had provided backing vocals on *Catch a Fire*. The subsequent tour once again included dates in America, and this time, Marley and company were tapped to support the popular American soul-funk group Sly &

the Family Stone, who peaked musically in the late 1960s and early 1970s. They were ultimately removed from the bill in October 1973 after only a few shows— allegedly for upstaging the headline act.

As with the two previous albums, the principal tracking sessions for *Natty Dread* took place in Kingston at Harry J's studio. The record found the I-Threes fully blended into the musical mix and featured the blues-rock guitar

of American musician Al Anderson. Initially a session player, Anderson became a full-fledged band member, and he credits Marley with helping him

In 1972, at the start of their Island Records run, the Wailers consisted of (l–r) Bunny Wailer, Bob Marley, Carlton Barrett, Peter Tosh, and Aston "Family Man" Barrett.

adopt a healthier lifestyle. During this time, the guitarist gave up alcohol and meat and adopted the "Ital" Rastafarian vegetarian diet and fitness regimen that Marley valued so highly.

The Wailers were quite good on record, but their live performances truly defined their relationship with audiences. The 1975 concert album *Live!*, recorded in London, captured some of their onstage energy and arguably boosted their status in the United Kingdom. The following year's *Rastaman Vibration* album represented a commercial turning point for the band. A top-ten hit in

LEFT: *Burnin'* (1973), the final album to feature Bunny Wailer and Peter Tosh, included "I Shot the Sheriff," later a hit for rocker Eric Clapton.

ABOVE: American guitarist Al Anderson joined the Wailers in 1974.

America, the album featured a more commercially calculated production style, much smoother than the earlier *Catch a Fire*, and revealed a group whose chemistry had been honed through persistent touring.

A relatively stable Wailers lineup supported Marley through the acclaimed 1977 *Exodus* album (compiled during his London exile following an assassination attempt in Jamaica in late 1976), the following year's not-so-acclaimed *Kaya*,

and the double live album *Babylon by Bus*, also released in 1978. Interestingly, Marley chose Steel Pulse, a reggae group from Birmingham, England, as the opening act for his European tour supporting *Exodus*, boosting the credibility of British reggae in the process.

In 1980, the group traveled at its own expense to perform at Zimbabwe's independence celebrations, underlining the link between reggae's

revolutionary-themed lyrics and their manifestation in the form of political action. As world-conquering touring continued that year, the Wailers filled a football stadium in Milan, Italy, playing to one hundred thousand fans. They also performed at New York City's storied Madison Square Garden. Not long after, Marley fell ill, and in May 1981, he died of cancer in Miami.

In the years that followed, legal problems limited the ability of the remaining members to perform under the Wailers name. In 1987, having been a part of the operation since 1970, Carlton Barrett was shot and killed in Kingston at the age of thirty-five. In a bizarre conspiracy, his wife and a taxi driver with whom she was romantically involved were arrested and charged with the murder. In 1989, nearly a decade after Marley's passing, the Wailers Band, as they had become known, released their debut album, *I.D.* Although they remained musically tight and active on the global touring circuit, they never stepped out of Marley's shadow. As the

1990s progressed, more original members left the fold. In light of the ongoing personnel changes, *I.D.* seemed an ironic title for their debut album. Most audiences remain unfamiliar with the post-Marley incarnations of the band and will always associate the Wailers with Bob's identity.

In a strange postscript, Aston Barrett sued Marley's estate in 2006 for £60 million in damages for unpaid royalties. Barrett claimed that he was not merely a band member or a session player, but that he was in fact the cowriter of many of Marley's biggest hits. The case was dismissed the same year, as the defense cited a 1994 agreement in which all of Barrett's claims were reportedly settled for "several hundred thousand dollars." Instead of receiving a massive payout, the bass-playing father of fifty-two children found himself saddled with about £2 million in legal costs.

MEMBERS: **Bob Marley** (vocals, guitar & percussion); **Bunny Wailer** (vocals & percussion), *Catch a Fire* to *Burnin'*; **Peter Tosh** (vocals & keyboards), *Catch a Fire* to *Burnin'*; **Junior Braithwaite** (vocals), left in 1965; **Aston "Family Man" Barrett** (bass), *Catch a Fire* to *Uprising*; **Carlton Barrett** (drums & percussion), *Catch a Fire* to *Uprising*; **Al Anderson** (lead guitar), *Natty Dread* to *Rastaman Vibration*, *Babylon by Bus*, *Survival*, *Uprising*; **Donald Kinsey** (guitar), *Rastaman Vibration*; **Earl "Chinna" Smith** (lead & rhythm guitar), *Rastaman Vibration*; **Julian "Junior" Marvin** (guitar), *Exodus* to *Uprising*; **Tyrone Downie** (keyboards, percussion & backing vocals), *Natty Dread* to *Uprising*; **Earl "Wire" Lindo** (keyboards), *Burnin'*, *Babylon by Bus*, *Survival*, *Uprising*; **Alvin "Seeco" Patterson** (percussion), *Burnin'* to *Uprising*; **Beverley Kelso** (vocals), 1963–1966; **Cherry Smith** (vocals), 1963–1966

SELECT DISCOGRAPHY: *Bob Marley and the Wailers: Trench Town Rock: The Anthology 1969-78* (Sanctuary/Trojan, 2002); *One Love at Studio One 1964-1966* (Heartbeat/Studio One, 2006) *1969-78; the Wailers Band: I.D.* (Atlantic, 1989); *Majestic Warriors* (Tabu, 1991); *Jah Message* (RAS, 1996)

DELROY WILSON
YEARS ACTIVE: 1960s–1995

Singer Delroy Wilson's name runs through multiple streams of reggae history, but his career is another tragic example of an undervalued and exploited young talent falling short of his potential and dying at a relatively early age. Wilson was born in 1948 in Kingston, Jamaica. In 1961, when he was just thirteen, he signed with producer Coxsone Dodd; his first Jamaican hit single, "Spit in the Sky" (written by Dodd), was released the following year.

Such songs recorded by the young Wilson were a product of the fierce competition between Dodd and his sound system- and-record producing rival (and former employee) Prince Buster. Wilson later recalled that he was used as "the missile that could get rid of Prince Buster." Although this period marked the start of an influential career, it was also the beginning of Wilson's blatant exploitation at the hands of producers who would pay him poorly and claim ownership of songs he had written.

Besides working on his own recordings for Dodd, Wilson sang on early solo recordings by Leonard Dillon, who would go on to form the vocal group the Ethiopians in the mid-1960s. Wilson scored a major Jamaican hit in 1966, "Dancing Mood," as the rocksteady era took hold. Spurred by a lack of financial compensation for the hits he had performed on, Wilson left Dodd around 1967 and embarked on the customary "producer tour," seeking an improved situation. After forming the short-lived W&C label with fellow singer Stranger Cole, Wilson entered into a series of abortive relationships with other labels and artists. He settled for a time with Sonia Pottinger's stable of performers, but Wilson's best career run came under the guidance of producer Bunny Lee, who had promoted records for established producers Duke Reid and Leslie Kong in the early 1960s. One of Wilson's biggest hits, 1971's "Better Must Come," was adopted as a campaign song in Jamaica by the then-opposition People's National Party (PNP), led by Michael Manley. Jamaican poverty was deepening, and as economic decline set in, a sense of social injustice became more acute. While "Better Must Come" must have seemed a fitting piece of sociopolitical commentary, Wilson claimed to have written the song about the Jamaican recording industry's unfair treatment of artists and his own poverty in the midst of global reggae success.

Although Wilson scored big Jamaican hits with the upbeat likes of "Dancing Mood," his vocal tone was also ideal for singing about anguished circumstances, as was evidenced by "Trying to Wreck My Life" (1973), "Have Some Mercy" (1974), and "I'm Still Waiting" (1976). After reaching his peak in the 1970s, he continued to record sporadically into the next decade, but the rise of dancehall largely consigned him to the nostalgia circuit. He developed a drinking problem and died of liver failure in March 1995. According to 1960s-era Jamaican singer Patsy Todd, the real cause of Wilson's death was the broken heart he suffered after failing to fully achieve his dream of international stardom.

SELECT DISCOGRAPHY: *Better Must Come: The Anthology* (Trojan, 2004); *Bunny Lee Presents Delroy Wilson* (Reggae Champs, 2011)

Exploited by producers, Delroy Wilson was an influential singer who never quite reached his potential.

XTERMINATOR RECORDS

Established in Kingston, Jamaica, in 1989, Xterminator Records became a standard-bearer for "cultural" reggae in the dancehall era, rejecting themes of violence and overt sexuality in favor of more uplifting ideals. Phillip "Fattis" Burrell, who was born in 1954 in the Trench Town area of Kingston but raised in England until his teenage years, founded the combined label and studio operation. Prior to forming Xterminator, Burrell's first Jamaican production on his Kings & Lions label was singer Sugar Minott's 1984 single "More Dogs to the Bone." He also released music via his custom Vena label, established in 1987.

After its debut, Xterminator was a critical and commercial success through the following decade, releasing music

Xterminator owner Phillip "Fattis" Burrell (left) hangs tough with dancehall artist Half Pint in London's Brixton district, 1986.

by such Jamaican singers as Beres Hammond, Luciano, Cocoa Tea, and dancehall star Sizzla. Burrell created a sound that successfully fused digital dancehall elements with roots reggae style, as was superbly demonstrated on the 1999 multiartist remix album *MLK Dub*. Xterminator productions frequently utilized top session players rather than total digital programming and were known for their sonic polish, clarity, and positive lyrical content. Easily one of the most talented Jamaican reggae producers to emerge since the 1980s, Burrell died in Kingston in December 2011 at age fifty-seven.

YABBY YOU
YEARS ACTIVE: 1970s–2000s

Controversial because of his religious beliefs, Vivian Jackson, better known as Yabby You, was one of the artists who embodied the classic roots reggae aesthetic. He became a walking paradox, wearing natty dreadlocks—hallmarks of Rastafarianism—while making no secret of his commitment to the Christian faith. He rejected the divinity of Rastafarian icon Haile Selassie, and due to his contrasting image and beliefs, he was often referred to as Jesus Dread.

As befit his unusual life, Yabby You chose unconventional pathways to enlightenment. Accounts of his birth date in Kingston, Jamaica, vary between 1946 and 1950. Spiritually compelled to leave home at age twelve, he literally wandered across the land, seeking religious "reasonings" (religious and philosophical discussions) and direction. He eventually settled back in Kingston, where he earned a living from metalwork. He suffered from malnutrition, stomach ulcers, and arthritis that badly affected his legs. These afflictions left him reliant on crutches and inevitably limited his career as a live performer.

Yabby You's first record, "Conquering Lion," was recorded in 1970 and first released in 1972, and credited to Vivian Jackson & the Ralph Brothers. It proved to be a career-defining track, not only because of its contemplative religious message, but also because its enigmatic chorus refrain, "Yabby yabby you," led audiences to give him his stage name. The artist's health and finances were so precarious prior to cutting the record that it almost didn't get made. He had recently left the hospital following a stomach operation and was unable to perform any work beyond providing racetrack betting advice for a nominal fee. As a result, he barely scraped together enough money for studio time and tape. In what some might consider divine intervention, a group of session musicians (including bassist Aston "Family Man" Barrett and guitarist Earl "Chinna" Smith) gathered by Leroy

CONQUERING LION
-VIVIAN JACKON

(YABBY YOU)

"Horsemouth" Wallace convened at Kingston's Dynamic Sounds and willingly cut the rhythm track for "Conquering Lion" for free. The ever-innovative engineer King Tubby tracked the vocals, finding the song creatively stimulating. Unfortunately, two years would pass before Yabby You could afford to press copies for release and sale. Even with an initial pressing of only one hundred copies, the artist's limited finances meant that sales from each batch of pressings had to finance the next one. Uncertain of how the record might be received because he was unknown, Yabby You initially attributed credit to the better-known King Tubby. He need not have worried, as demand for "Conquering Lion" led to successive pressings, establishing the song in both the marketplace and Rastafarian consciousness.

After a series of successful follow-up singles, some of which continued

to bear his birth name, Yabby You released the album *Conquering Lion* in 1977; it essentially made his name in roots reggae. Such songs as "Love Thy Neighbour" and "Run Come Rally" were spiritual calls to arms, though the grammatical flaws in the album's liner notes read like an incomplete translation from another language. Later, he occasionally produced other artists, including Trinity, Dillinger, and the Prophets. After landing two songs on the 1980 sound track to the film *Babylon*, he spent much of the decade sidelined by his infirmities. He reemerged occasionally, releasing such albums as the 1993 collaboration *Yabby You Meets Mad Professor & Black Steel in Ariwa Studio*.

In 2002, the British reissue label Blood & Fire collected his prime vocal and production work, as well as King Tubby's dub mixes, and issued the *Dub it to the Top 1976–1979* compilation. Given Yabby You's biblically informed lyrics, use of top-class session players, and frequent collaborations with the

engineering genius of King Tubby, it's easy to argue that he was on the cutting edge of the Rasta roots reggae sound. He died January 12, 2010, from a brain aneurysm.

SELECT DISCOGRAPHY: *Conquering Lion* (Prophet, 1977); *Jesus Dread* (Blood & Fire, 1997); *Dub It to the Top 1976–1979* (Blood & Fire, 2002)

Yabby You, a devout Christian with Rasta locks, 1979.

TAPPA ZUKIE
YEARS ACTIVE: 1970s–1990s

Tappa Zukie began his career as a "toaster" and later worked as a producer. Reversing the career path taken by most international reggae artists, he rose to prominence in the United Kingdom before finding fame in Jamaica. Zukie was born David Sinclair on July 2, 1955, in Kingston, Jamaica. His mother sent him to England at age seventeen, and he quickly established himself as a hit toaster in London, recording the album *Man a Warrior*, released in Jamaica in 1973 and in Britain two years later. The title track featured instrumentation based on "Papa Was a Rollin' Stone," a 1972 hit for the American R&B group the Temptations.

He returned to Jamaica in 1974 and became a bodyguard for hit producer Bunny Lee. Despite this connection, he did not go directly back into the recording studio. A rift developed between Tappa (as he was generally known) and Lee, reportedly over Lee licensing the song "Natty Dread Don't

Cry" to the British reggae label Trojan Records. When the dispute was patched up, Lee provided the rhythm tracks for what became 1976's *MPLA* album in Jamaica. Quickly recorded, the album saw release on Virgin Records in the UK two years later. The Virgin deal also yielded *Peace in the Ghetto* (1978), and generated money that allowed Tappa to build a community center in the Trench Town section of Kingston. That short-lived Virgin alliance disintegrated over allegations Tappa had heard that money from sales of his records in apartheid South Africa was being used by that country's government to quell black discontent there.

One of his best-known albums is

Tappa Zukie in Dub (1976), which features the engineering talents of Philip Smart, also known as Prince Philip, a trainee of master dub engineer King Tubby. The album is also notable because it was never released in Jamaica; and in the UK, only a few hundred copies were initially issued. This made it an instant collector's item.

By 1978, when Tappa's X-rated "She Want a Phensic" was a Jamaican hit and popular within the UK reggae community, he had become increasingly popular among Britain's punk rockers, many of whom were reggae fans. Further boosting his international street credibility was the enthusiastic endorsement of American poet and rock singer Patti Smith, who went so far as to take Tappa on tour as a supporting act. Tappa also worked as a producer, and artists who benefited from his production skills include the unheralded Jamaican vocal group Knowledge, whose debut album, *Hail Dread*, was released in 1978 by A&M Records. Duly ignored by the mainstream audiences at whom it was directed, the album was reissued in Jamaica that same year as *Words, Sounds & Power* on Tappa's Stars label.

In the 1980s, after shifting his home base back to Jamaica, he focused on community activities. Meanwhile, the dancehall artists he had inspired moved to the fore by using digital technology. By the mid-1990s, Tappa Zukie had established his own pressing plant and retail outlet in Kingston. He had also returned to the studio and produced such works as the vocal group the Heptones' 1995 reunion album *Pressure*.

SELECT DISCOGRAPHY: *Man a Warrior* (Mer, 1973); *MPLA* (Klik, 1976); *Tappa Zukie in Dub* (Klik, 1976); *Escape from Hell* (Stars, 1977); *Peace in the Ghetto* (Front Line, 1978)

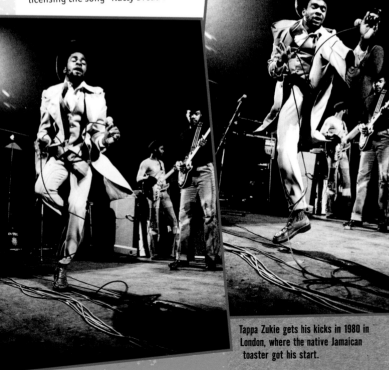

Tappa Zukie gets his kicks in 1980 in London, where the native Jamaican toaster got his start.

★FURTHER★
ENLIGHTENMENT

REGGAE BEST-OF LISTS

The individuals, albums, and other subjects in the following lists are *not* ranked by preference but instead are placed in chronological or alphabetical order. While these lists take key aspects of reggae history into account, they are also largely subjective, reflecting the author's viewpoint. These are not intended to be thoroughly definitive judgments, but they will provoke thought about your own reggae favorites.

TOP 25 ESSENTIAL ROOTS REGGAE ALBUMS

These albums represent aspects of roots reggae's core sound, listed in chronological order. While these are certainly not the only records typifying the roots style, they collectively provide an overview that defines roots in ways that words alone cannot ever achieve. This list does not include compilations, and instead focuses on original album releases. At the very least, this is a great starting point for further exploration.

1. Various Artists: *The Harder They Come* (Island, 1972)
2. The Wailers: *Catch a Fire* (Island, 1972)
3. Lee Perry: *Blackboard Jungle Dub* (Upsetter, 1973)
4. The Abyssinnians: *Satta Massagana* (aka *Forward on to Zion*) (Jam Sounds, 1976)
5. Bunny Wailer: *Blackheart Man* (Island, 1976)
6. Burning Spear: *Marcus Garvey* (Mango/Island, 1976)
7. Augustus Pablo: *King Tubby Meets Rockers Uptown* (Island, 1976)
8. Peter Tosh: *Legalize It* (Columbia, 1976)
9. Max Romeo: *War Ina Babylon* (Island, 1976)
10. Rico: *Man from Wareika* (Island, 1976)
11. The Congos: *Heart of the Congos* (Black Ark, 1977)
12. Third World: *96° in the Shade* (Island, 1977)
13. Peter Tosh: *Equal Rights* (Columbia, 1977)
14. Bob Marley & the Wailers: *Exodus* (Island, 1977)
15. Culture: *Two Sevens Clash* (Lightning, 1977)
16. Junior Murvin: *Police and Thieves* (Island, 1977)
17. Keith Hudson: *Rasta Communication* (Greensleeves, 1978)
18. Ijahman: *Haile I Hymn* (Island, 1978)
19. Linton Kwesi Johnson: *Dread Beat An' Blood* (Virgin Front Line, 1978)
20. Dr. Alimantado: *Best Dressed Chicken in Town* (Greensleeves, 1978)
21. Ijahman: *Are We a Warrior* (Island, 1979)
22. Bob Marley & the Wailers: *Survival* (Island, 1979)
23. Steel Pulse: *True Democracy* (Elektra, 1982)
24. Black Uhuru: *Anthem* (Island, 1983)
25. Jackie Mittoo: *The Keyboard King at Studio One* (Universal Sound, 2004)

TOP 10 SONGS ABOUT GANJA

Legal disclaimer: This list is not designed to encourage ganja consumption! These songs are not all just about the artists' personal marijuana experiences, but they also tackle inextricably related social, political and medical stigmas and events. The songs also provide a useful cross-section of the many other slang descriptive terms for ganja.

1. "Legalize It" by Peter Tosh: *Legalize It* (CBS, 1976)
2. "Tired Fe Lick Weed in a Bush" by Jacob Miller (Neville King, 1976)
3. "Kaya" by Bob Marley & the Wailers: *Kaya* (Island, 1978)
4. "International Herb" by Culture: *International Herb* (Virgin, 1979)
5. "Sinsemilla" by Black Uhuru: *Sinsemilla* (Island, 1980)
6. "Legalise Collie Herb" by Black Slate: *Amigo* (TCD, 1980)
7. "One Draw" by Rita Marley: *Who Feels It Knows It* (Shanachie, 1981)
8. "Pass the Kouchie" by Mighty Diamonds: *Changes* (Music Works, 1981)
9. "Police in Helicopter" by John Holt: *Police in Helicopter* (Greensleeves, 1983)
10. "Lamb's Bread International" by Welton Irie: *Lamb's Bread International* (Blood & Fire, 2000)

TOP 15 DUB ALBUMS

Arguably reggae's most powerful and pervasive contribution to popular music, dub is one of the few subgenres that always sounds futuristic. With so many high quality vintage dub albums, including some underrated compilations of otherwise unavailable material, this is likely to be one of the most contentious lists. While some of the early 1970s dub albums were less radical than the decade's later offerings, those foundation releases remain artistically important.

1. Herman Chin Loy: *Aquarius Dub* (Aquarius, 1973)
2. Lee Perry: *Blackboard Jungle Dub* (Upsetter, 1973)
3. King Tubby: *Dub from the Roots* (Total Sounds, 1974)
4. Keith Hudson: *Pick a Dub* (Atra, 1974)
5. Augustus Pablo: *King Tubby Meets Rockers Uptown* (Island, 1976)
6. Lee Perry: *Super Ape* (Island, 1976)
7. Horace Andy: *In the Light (Dub)* (Hungry Town, 1977)
8. Keith Hudson: *Brand* (Pressure Sounds, 1977)
9. Gregory Isaacs: *Slum: Gregory Isaacs in Dub* (Burning Sounds, 1978)
10. Inner Circle: *Heavyweight Dub/Killer Dub* (Top Ranking Sounds, 1978)
11. Linton Kwesi Johnson: *LKJ in Dub* (Island, 1980)
12. Scientist: *Scientist Rids the World of the Evil Curse of the Vampires* (Greensleeves, 1981)

13. Glen Brown and King Tubby: *Termination Dub: 1973–1979* (Blood & Fire, 1996)
14. Ja-Man All Stars: *In the Dub Zone* (Blood & Fire, 2003)
15. The Revolutionaries: *Drum Sound: More Gems from the Channel One Dub Room—1974 to 1980* (Pressure Sounds, 2007)

TOP 10 BEST ALBUM COVERS

The beauty of the album cover is very much in the eye of the beholder, and connected to its relevance to the record's musical content. These illustrated and photographic covers include powerful images evoking consciousness of African roots, ranging from daily street life in Jamaica to international politics and religion. Some simply represent memorable and imaginative design interpretations of the artists and their work.

1. The Wailers: *Burnin'* (Island, 1973)
2. Jimmy Cliff: *Struggling Man* (Island, 1973)
3. Bob Marley & the Wailers: *Live* (Island, 1975)
4. Various Artists: *The Front Line* (Virgin, 1976)
5. Max Romeo & the Upsetters: *War Ina Babylon* (Island, 1976)
6. Steel Pulse: *Tribute to the Martyrs* (Island, 1979)
7. Black Uhuru: *Anthem* (Island, 1983)
8. Steel Pulse: *Earth Crisis* (Elektra, 1984)
9. The Reggae Philharmonic Orchestra: *The Reggae Philharmonic Orchestra* (Mango/Island, 1988)
10. King Tubby: *Dub Gone 2 Crazy* (Blood & Fire, 1996)

TOP 10 BEST DREADLOCKS ON ALBUM COVERS

Besides images of marijuana, the reggae album cover's biggest selling point has been the display of dreadlocks, whether subtle or spectacular. Though it's worth emphasizing that not every picture of a dreadlocked artist or group on an album cover automatically means it's a reggae release, locks have nonetheless been an enduring symbol of a roots sound and philosophy. These covers prove it.

1. Big Youth: *Dread Locks Dread* (Klik, 1975)
2. Bob Marley & The Wailers: *Live!* (Island, 1975)
3. The Congos: *Congo* (CBS, 1979)
4. Fred Locks: *Black Star Liner* (Vulcan, 1976)

5. Ijahman: *Are We a Warrior* (Island, 1979)
6. Bunny Wailer: *Rock 'N' Groove* (Solomonic, 1981)
7. Rita Marley: *Who Feels It Knows It* (Shanachie, 1981)
8. Peter Tosh: *Wanted Dread & Alive* (Rolling Stone, 1981)
9. Black Uhuru: *Liberation: The Island Anthology* (Island, 1993)
10. Burning Spear: *Calling Rastafari* (Burning Music, 1999)

TOP 25 REGGAE EXECUTIVE PRODUCERS/STUDIO & LABEL OWNERS

The economics of Jamaican music production meant that many figures who bankrolled recording sessions and releases became producers by default. Still, even those who weren't very hands-on possessed an acute awareness of what the public wanted or could be persuaded to buy. In many ways, these were reggae's biggest risk takers, on the cutting edge of either stylistic or technological innovation. Ultimately, the producers became reggae's most influential tastemakers.

1. Chris Blackwell
2. Dennis Bovell
3. Glen Brown
4. Geoffrey Chung
5. Gussie Clarke
6. Tommy Cowan
7. Coxsone Dodd
8. Clancy Eccles
9. Joe Gibbs
10. Harry J
11. Keith Hudson
12. Ken Khouri
13. King Jammy
14. King Tubby
15. Leslie Kong
16. Bunny Lee
17. Mad Professor
18. Sylvan Morris
19. Lee "Scratch" Perry
20. Duke Reid
21. Winston Riley
22. Scientist
23. Edward Seaga
24. Leroy Sibbles
25. Sly & Robbie

TOP 10 REISSUE ALBUMS

Historical perspective and hunger for original roots have led to dozens of reissues, some with great attention to discographical detail and liner notes. Some labels have also been busy compiling previously scattered singles and "dubplates" (for example, the UK's Pressure Sounds imprint), but this list mainly includes rereleases of single artist albums. Each year reveals new reissues, so this list is one of many possible gateways.

1. Horace Andy: *In the Light/In the Light (Dub)* (Blood & Fire, 1977)
2. The Congos: *Heart of the Congos* (Blood & Fire, 1996)
3. Inner Circle: *Heavyweight Dub/Killer Dub* (Blood & Fire, 1999)
4. Various Artists: *The Story of Jamaican Music: Tougher Than Tough* (Mango/Island, 1993)
5. King Tubby & Soul Syndicate: *Freedom Sounds in Dub* (Blood & Fire, 1996)
6. Sugar Minott: *Ghetto-ology + Dub* (Easy Star, 2000)
7. The Wailers: *Catch a Fire (Deluxe Edition)* (Universal, 2001)
8. Various Artists: *This is Reggae Music: The Golden Era 1960–1975* (Trojan, 2004)
9. Lee Perry: *I Am the Upsetter: The Story of the Lee "Scratch" Perry Golden Years* (Trojan, 2005)
10. The Joe Gibbs: *African Dub: Chapters 1, 2, 3, & 4.* (VP, 2007)

CULTURE CLUB

DO YOU REALLY WANT TO HURT ME

TOP 10 REGGAE SONGS BY NON-REGGAE ARTISTS

No, these are not necessarily the best reggae songs by pop artists, but they are among the best known to mainstream audiences, mostly because of their global chart success. It's true that applying the term "reggae" to some of these records certainly stretches its definition, but in each case the reggae influence is undeniable. Despite usually being shadows of the roots sound, these records still raised awareness of reggae's commercial appeal.

1. "Stir It Up" by Johnny Nash: *I Can See Clearly Now* (Epic, 1972)
2. "Mother and Child Reunion" by Paul Simon: *Paul Simon* (CBS, 1972)
3. "I Shot the Sheriff" by Eric Clapton: *461 Ocean Boulevard* (RSO, 1974)
4. "Boogie on Reggae Woman" by Stevie Wonder: *Fulfillingness' First Finale* (Motown, 1974)
5. "Hotel California" by the Eagles: *Hotel California* (Asylum, 1976)
6. "Police and Thieves" by The Clash: *The Clash* (Epic, 1977)
7. "Walking on the Moon" by the Police: *Reggatta De Blanc* (A&M, 1979)
8. "Dreadlock Holiday" by 10cc: *Bloody Tourists* (Mercury, 1978)
9. "Do You Really Want to Hurt Me" by Culture Club: *Kissing to Be Clever* (Epic, 1982)
10. "All That She Wants" by Ace of Base: *The Sign* (Arista, 1993)

TOP 10 SONGS BY REGGAE ARTISTS COVERING ROCK-POP SONGS

The reggae influence on the pop world usually stands out more than when reggae acts cover pop-rock staples, but such covers always bring some new flavor to the songs. There have been entire reggae tribute albums to rock icons like Bob Dylan and the Police, demonstrating the broad scope of the practice. And yes, we know the Jolly Boys are really a mento band, but what an unusual cover.

1. Aswad: "Don't Turn Around" (written by Albert Hammond and Diane Warren, originally recorded by Tina Turner)
2. Black Uhuru: "Hey Joe" (Jimi Hendrix)
3. Bob & Marcia- "Young, Gifted & Black" (Nina Simone)
4. Chalice: "Paint it Black" (Rolling Stones)
5. Jimmy Cliff featuring Tim Armstrong: "Guns of Brixton" (The Clash)
6. Dubxanne: "Message in a Bottle" (The Police)
7. Easy Star All-Stars: "Breathe" (Pink Floyd)
8. Inner Circle: "The Bed's Too Big Without You" (The Police)
9. The Jolly Boys: "Rehab" (Amy Winehouse)
10. Jackie Mittoo: "Summer Breeze" (Seals and Crofts)

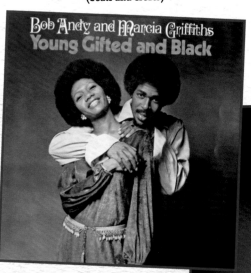

Bob Andy and Marcia Griffiths
Young Gifted and Black

TOP 10 FEMALES IN REGGAE

This list does extend beyond the boundaries of roots reggae into the dancehall era in an effort to include a broad cross-section of high-impact women in reggae. While there are many more female artists who scored hit singles, comparatively few enjoyed full-fledged careers inclusive of sustained international success. This list combines singers whose success was mainly in Jamaica with those with noteworthy audiences beyond the island.

1. Phyllis Dillon
2. Hortense Ellis
3. Marcia Griffiths
4. Sandra "Puma" Jones
5. Lady Saw
6. Rita Marley
7. Judy Mowatt
8. Patra
9. Sonia Pottinger
10. Millicent "Patsy" Todd

TOP 20 RECORD LABELS

With Jamaica's large number of imprints, compiling this list was hardly straightforward. It mainly consists of the most frequently occurring hit labels for both albums and singles, and some that were perhaps more influential than commercially successful. Blue Beat Records was a major pre-reggae label, and Beverley's Records also existed in the early 1960s ska era, though it lasted long enough to be part of the transition from rocksteady into reggae.

1. Beverley's Records
2. Black Ark
3. Blood & Fire
4. Blue Beat Records
5. Greensleeves Records
6. Harry J
7. Island Records
8. Pama Records
9. Pressure Sounds
10. Randy's Records
11. RAS Records
12. Studio One
13. Techniques
14. Top Ranking Sounds
15. Treasure Isle
16. Trojan Records
17. Tuff Gong Records
18. Virgin Records
19. VP Records
20. WIRL (West Indies Records Limited)

TOP 10 UNDERRATED ARTISTS

There certainly are enough underrated reggae acts to fill a page, as the genre witnessed a speedy turnover of hit artists. The acts listed here have all enjoyed critical acclaim to one degree or another, and even varying limited measures of commercial success, but the creative contributions of these artists are too often overlooked when considering quality and/or innovation in roots reggae.

1. Black Slate
2. Glen Brown
3. Chalice
4. Keith Hudson
5. Ijahman Levi
6. Misty in Roots
7. Mystic Revealers
8. Reggae Philharmonic Orchestra
9. Soul Syndicate
10. Twilight Circus Dub Sound System

TOP 10 UNUSUAL ALBUMS

Quite a few oddities here, including a dub version of a dub album based on a rock record, and a classically influenced reggae album. The Mystic Revelation of Rastafari's *Grounation* was a triple album when it was originally released, at a time when few non-rock acts would issue music on such a scale. As for *Pure Reggae*, including Eric Clapton and soca star Arrow raises serious questions about the title's accuracy.

1. The Mystic Revelation of Rastafari: *Grounation* (Ashanti, 1973)
2. Judge Dread: *Bedtime Stories* (Catcus, 1975)
3. Jacob Miller: *Natty Christmas* (Joe Gibbs, 1978)
4. Reggae Philharmonic Orchestra: *Reggae Philharmonic Orchestra* (Mango/Island, 1988)
5. Dread Zeppelin: *Un-Led-Ed* (I.R.S., 1990)
6. Various Artists: *Rock 'n' Reggae* (PolyGram, 1996)
7. Various Artists: *Pure Reggae* (PolyGram, 1998)
8. Willie Nelson: *Countryman* (Lost Highway, 2005)
9. Ziggy Marley: *Family Time* (Tuff Gong, 2009)
10. Easy Star All-Stars: *Dubber Side of the Moon* (Easy Star, 2010)

AUGUSTUS PABLO

IN FINE STYLE

ORIGINAL ROCKERS
7" and 12" selection 1973 - 1979 · pressure sounds 38

TOP 50 REGGAE SINGLES

The following singles are from the reggae era (or the cusp of it) only, in keeping with the book's main theme and primary time frame. Some were not big sellers but are included anyway because of the excellent performance and/or production that made them great records. So, this list is based partly on historical importance but largely on personal preference. These are listed alphabetically by artist—numerical ranking proved impossible!

1. The Abyssinians: "Satta Massa Gana" (Clinch, 1971)
2. The Abyssinians: "Declaration of Rights" (Clinch, 1972)
3. Althea & Donna: "Uptown Top Ranking" (Lightning, 1977)
4. Aswad: "Don't Turn Around" (Mango/Island, 1988)
5. Big Youth: "S 90 Skank" (Down Town, 1972)
6. Black Slate: "Legalise Collie Herb" (Ensign, 1980)
7. Black Uhuru: "Guess Who's Coming to Dinner" (Taxi, 1979)
8. Bob & Marcia: "Young, Gifted and Black" (Trojan, 1970)
9. Dennis Brown: "Money in My Pocket" (Lightning, 1979)
10. Burning Spear: "Marcus Garvey" (Island, 1975)
11. Dennis Bovell: "Brain Damage" (Fontana, 1981)
12. Johnny Clarke: "None Shall Escape the Judgement" (Explosion, 1974)
13. Jimmy Cliff: "The Harder They Come" (Island, 1972)
14. Jimmy Cliff: "Wonderful World, Beautiful People" (Trojan, 1969)
15. Dave & Ansel Collins: "Double Barrel" (Techniques, 1971)
16. Desmond Dekker: "(007) Shanty Town" (Pyramid, 1967)
17. Desmond Dekker: "Israelites" (Pyramid, 1969)
18. Doctor Alimantado: "Reason for Living" (Greensleeves, 1977)
19. Eric Donaldson: "Cherry Oh Baby" (Dynamic, 1971)
20. Alton Ellis: "I'm Still in Love with You" (Studio One, 1967)
21. Harry J All Stars: "Liquidator" (Harry J, 1969)
22. John Holt: "Police in Helicopter" (Greensleeves, 1983)
23. Ijahman: "Jah Heavy Load" (Island, 1978)
24. Gregory Isaacs: "Night Nurse" (Mango/Island, 1982)
25. Bob Marley & the Wailers: "No Woman, No Cry" (Live) (Island, 1975)
26. Bob Marley & the Wailers: "Redemption Song" (Island, 1980)
27. Rita Marley: "One Draw" (Shanachie, 1981)
28. The Melodians: "Rivers of Babylon" (Beverley's, 1969)
29. Mighty Diamonds: "Bodyguard" (Front Line, 1979)
30. Junior Murvin: "Police and Thieves" (Island, 1976)
31. Mystic Revealers: "Remember Romeo" (RAS, 1993)
32. Augustus Pablo: "King Tubby Meets the Rockers Uptown" (Island, 1976)
33. The Paragons: "The Tide Is High" (Treasure Isle, 1967)

34. Reggae Regular: "Black Star Liner" (Greensleeves, 1978)
35. Max Romeo: "War Inna Babylon" (Island, 1976)
36. Steel Pulse: "Prodigal Son" (Island, 1978)
37. Steel Pulse: "Your House" (Elektra, 1982)
38. Third World: "Now That We Found Love" (Island, 1978)
39. Toots & the Maytals: "Pressure Drop" (Pyramid, 1969)
40. Toots & the Maytals: "Funky Kingston" (Dragon, 1973)
41. Toots & The Maytals: "54-46 That's My Number" (Trojan, 1971)
42. Peter Tosh: "Legalize It" (CBS, 1976)
43. Peter Tosh: "Equal Rights" (CBS, 1977)
44. Twin Roots: "Know Love" (Black Ark, 1977)
45. The Upsetters: "Return of Django" (Upsetter, 1969)
46. Bunny Wailer: "Love Fire" (Solomonic, 1977)
47. The Wailers: "Get Up, Stand Up" (Island, 1973)
48. Delroy Wilson: "Better Must Come" (Attack, 1971)
49. Yabby You with Trinity: "Jah Vengeance" (Grove Music, 1977)
50. Tappa Zukie: "MPLA" (Klik, 1976)

REGGAE TIME LINE

in the island's lengthy political struggle, the other being the more conservative Jamaica Labour Party (JLP).

1945 Bob Marley (Nesta Robert Marley) is born to a white Jamaican soldier in his fifties, Norval Marley, and a nineteen-year-old black Jamaican woman, Cedella Malcolm, in the St. Ann parish of Jamaica.

1838 Slavery is abolished in Jamaica.

1914 Marcus Garvey launches the United Negro Improvement Association in Kingston.

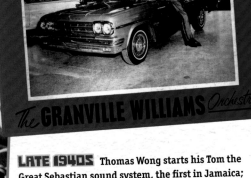

PRE-1494 Arawak tribe inhabits Jamaica.

1494 Columbus sights Jamaica on his second voyage to the New World.

1503-1504 Columbus is stranded on Jamaica (third voyage).

1509 Spanish settle in Jamaica and use it as a base for their privateer raids on English and Dutch shippers. Spanish Town serves as Jamaica's capital from 1534 to 1872.

1655 England invades Jamaica.

1670 Jamaica is formally ceded to Great Britain in the Treaty of Madrid.

1930 Ras Tafari Makonnen is crowned Emperor of Ethiopia, assuming the name Haile Selassie. Some Rastas will later declare that he is a living god.

1938 Rising unemployment and resentment toward British racial policies result in deadly riots against British rule.

— The People's National Party (PNP) is founded in Jamaica by Norman Manley, father of Michael Manley. The PNP becomes one of the two antagonists

LATE 1940S Thomas Wong starts his Tom the Great Sebastian sound system, the first in Jamaica; Ken Khouri sets up one of the earliest recording studios in Jamaica.

EARLY 1950S Stanley Motta's MRS Records label records mento and calypso singer Lord Fly, producing the first mento recording and the first Jamaican domestic commercial release.

1954 Coxsone Dodd sets up his Downbeat sound system, with Count Machuki as his DJ.

— Ken Khouri establishes Federal Records, which runs Jamaica's first record-pressing plant

1958 Chris Blackwell founds Island Records in Jamaica and releases the label's first LP—an album of jazz standards by blind pianist Lance Haywood.

— Edward Seaga opens the WIRL (West Indies Records Limited) studios, recording Jamaican acts.

1959 OR 1960 The Folkes Brothers' single "Oh Carolina" features Count Ossie's Rastafarian drumming group, a significant cultural and musical breakthrough at the time.

1960 Blue Beat Records is established in Britain and becomes synonymous with Jamaican ska music.

1962 Chris Blackwell establishes Island Records in the United Kingdom with an investment of $5,300.

— Jamaica gains full independence from Great Britain but remains a member of the British Commonwealth. Alexander Bustamante of the JLP become Jamaica's first Prime Minister.

— Jimmy Cliff, working for Leslie Kong's Beverley's Records label, unearths the talent of Bob Marley and Desmond Dekker, helping both artists cut their first recordings.

— Peter Tosh and Junior Braithwaite join Bob Marley and his childhood friend Neville Livingston (Bunny Wailer), along with backup singers Beverly Kelso and Cherry Smith, to form the Wailers, under the guidance of Joe Higgs.

— The first ska recordings are released by the Studio One house band.

1963 Coxsone Dodd opens Studio One in the back of his family's record shop in Kingston.

— The Wailers' first single, "Simmer Down," released on Studio One, goes to #1 in Jamaica.

1964 Tommy McCook, Roland Alphonso, Lloyd Brevett, Lloyd Knibb, Lester Sterling, Don Drummond, Jerome "Jah Jerry" Hines, Jackie Mittoo, and Johnny "Dizzy" Moore form the Skatalites in Kingston.

— Millie Small scores an international hit with the ska-pop "My Boy Lollipop."

— Politician Edward Seaga selects Jimmy Cliff, Byron Lee & The Dragonaires, and others to represent Jamaican music at the 1964 World's Fair in New York City.

1966 Rocksteady emerges as the dominant music from Kingston. Its slower rhythm is a change of pace from the frantic ska beat.

— Ethiopian emperor and Rastafarian icon Haile Selassie visits Jamaica on April 21; enthused Rastas break down police barriers and surround his plane. Selassie waits forty-five minutes before emerging from the cabin, but is moved to tears by the reception.

— Bob Marley moves to the United States, settles in Delaware, and takes a job on the night shift in a Chrysler factory.

1967 The Paragons release the rocksteady classic "The Tide is High."

— The Cimarons, later considered the first British reggae group, form in London to back touring rocksteady artists.

— The "version" (a precusor to dub) is born when engineer Byron Smith at Treasure Isle studio accidentally omits the vocals on the Paragons' 1966 song "On the Beach."

1968 Coxsone Dodd visits the United Kingdom and brings back an Echoplex delay box, paving the way for reggae and dub.

1969 Desmond Dekker's "Israelites" tops the UK pop charts [and reaches #9 in the United States], a first for a reggae single.

— Lee "Scratch" Perry releases "The Upsetter."

1970 Wailers release "The Best of the Wailers."

1971 Leslie Kong dies of a heart attack. A curse had been famously put on him a year prior by Bunny Wailer, who was upset about recordings Kong released by the Wailers.

▬ The Wailers' label, Tuff Gong Records (after Bob Marley's street name) becomes fully commercially active.

▬ Dave & Ansel Collins's single "Double Barrel" goes to #1 in the United Kingdom.

▬ The Abyssinians release "Satta Massa Gana" two years after recording it for Coxsone Dodd, who refused to release it.

1972 Michael Manley of the PNP becomes the prime minister of Jamaica in an impressive victory.

▬ The reggae film *The Harder They Come* is released and becomes a genre-defining favorite. The sound track is released on Island Records.

▬ The Wailers sign with Island Records.

▬ Channel One Studios, run by the Hoo-Kim brothers, opens its doors.

1973 The Wailers' *Catch a Fire*, with the Rod Dyer–designed Zippo cover, is released in the United States.

▬ DJ Big Youth reportedly becomes the first reggae star to appear onstage with Rastafarian dreadlocks.

▬ Lee "Scratch" Perry opens Black Ark studio.

1974 *Dub from the Roots*, King Tubby's first dub effort, is released.

▬ Bob Marley re-forms the Wailers as a backing group for himself as a solo artist, a year after Peter Tosh and Bunny Wailer leave the group. Marcia Griffiths, Judy Mowatt, and Rita Marley are his backup singers. *Natty Dread*, an unabashedly political album, is released.

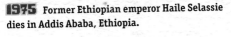

1975 Former Ethiopian emperor Haile Selassie dies in Addis Ababa, Ethiopia.

▬ After a violent election, the PNP wins a second term and nationalizes key Jamaican industries.

1976 Burning Spear's seminal album, *Marcus Garvey*, is released.

▬ Bob Marley's *Rastaman Vibration* is released. It becomes Marley's only top-ten album in the United States, and the first reggae album to chart so successfully.

▬ Mikey Dread's influential radio show *Dread at the Controls* debuts in Jamaica.

1977 Culture releases its album *Two Sevens Clash*. The title references the date July 7th, 1977, when many Jamaicans believed Armageddon would occur.

▬ Bob Marley & the Wailers' *Exodus* is released on Island Records. *Time* magazine later names it album of the century.

▬ Dennis Bovell establishes the Lover's Rock record label as the reggae subgenre of the same name flourishes in the United Kingdom.

1978 Rastafarian gang members supporting the then-minority Jamaica Labour Party are lured to the Green Bay Artillery Range with the promise of guns and money; there they are ambushed by Jamaican Defence Force soldiers. Five are killed in what becomes known as the Green Bay Massacre—the high-water mark for government mistrust and politically sanctioned violence in Jamaica.

— The One Love Peace Concert is held in the National Stadium in Kingston in an attempt to reconcile Jamaica's increasingly violent political conflict. Bob Marley succeeds in getting the rival leaders, Edward Seaga and Michael Manley, to publicly join hands onstage.

— Bob Marley receives the United Nations Peace Medal.

1980 Former reggae producer Edward Seaga of the JLP becomes prime minister and privatizes key Jamaican businesses; he receives substantial aid from the US government.

— Dancehall begins to emerge as a reggae offshoot that first began in the late 1970s, incorporating rapping over hyped-up rhythms.

1981 Bob Marley succumbs to cancer.

1983 Lee Perry's Black Ark studio is burned down—allegedly by Perry himself.

1984 King Tubby releases the first all-digital reggae tune, "Tempo," by Anthony Red Rose.

1985 Black Uhuru wins the first Grammy for best reggae recording for their album *Anthem*.

— Wayne Smith's "Under Mi Sleng Teng," produced by King Jammy, ignites the digital dancehall trend when it becomes a massive hit in Jamaica.

1986 Judy Mowatt becomes the first female vocalist to be nominated for a Grammy in the best reggae album category.

1987 Steel Pulse becomes the first (and still only) non-Jamaican act to win the Grammy for best reggae recording, for their 1986 album *Babylon the Bandit*.

— Peter Tosh is murdered in his home during an attempted robbery

1988 Hurricane Gilbert devastates Jamaica.

1989 King Tubby is murdered outside of his home in Kingston.

1990s Reggaeton, combining reggae, dancehall, and Latin rhythms, enters the scene.

1992 Shabba Ranks wins a Grammy for "As Raw As Ever," becoming the first dancehall performer to win the best reggae album award.

1994 Blood & Fire is established in England and becomes one of the most important labels in reissuing reggae albums

— Bob Marley is inducted posthumously into the Rock & Roll Hall of Fame.

1999 Jamaicans violently protest a 30 percent increase in fuel prices.

2001 Chris Blackwell is inducted into the Rock & Roll Hall of Fame.

2004 Hurricane Ivan destroys thousands of homes and causes millions of dollars in damage in Jamaica.

— *Rolling Stone* names Lee "Scratch" Perry number 100 on their list of "100 Greatest Artists of All Time."

2008 Tommy Cowan is awarded the Order of Distinction medal; Byron Lee is awarded the Order of Jamaica medal.

2010 Jimmy Cliff is inducted into the Rock & Roll Hall of Fame

— Widespread violence in Kingston occurs as Jamaican soldiers try to capture drug king Christopher "Dudus" Coke and extradite him to the United States.

2011 Dennis Brown is awarded the Jamaican Order of Distinction

2012 Coxsone Dodd's son, Courtney, reopens Studio One.

RASTA REGGAE GLOSSARY

A Partial Look at the Language

BABYLON a term used in reggae music to describe the corrupt establishment; the "system"

BALDHEAD a straight person; one without dreadlocks; one who works for Babylon

BASHMENT a great event or happening; a dance hall; a party

BLUNT a type of marijuana joint where the wrapping is a tobacco product, often from a cigar

CHALICE a type of bong or pipe used to smoke marijuana; a ceremonial cup in religious contexts

DANCEHALL DJ-centered Jamaican music most associated with the digital era of the 1980s and beyond

DOWNPRESSION the Rastafarian term for "oppression"

DREAD person who has dreadlocks; a Rasta; a greeting to a friend

DREADLOCKS hair that is neither combed nor cut and often associated with Rastafari

DUB a roots electronic music created by skillful, artistic re-engineering of recorded tracks, often with all vocal elements taken out or creatively fragmented

DUBPLATE an acetate disc that was made as a pre-release of a specific record and often exclusively for a specific sound system

DJ a person who sings or toasts over instrumental music (often dub music); DJs became popular in reggae during the early 1970s and were soon firmly associated with dancehall from the 1980s onward

FLYING CYMBAL a sound that was developed by producer Bunny Lee and drummer Carlton "Santa" Davis by alternately opening and closing the hi-hat on a drum set; it was introduced to reggae music in 1974 and was inspired by protodisco American releases of that era

GANJA a slang term (of Sanskrit origin) for "marijuana;" the term came into use in Jamaica with the influx of East Indian contract laborers

I AND I "you and me" and/or "the almighty and me;" Rasta speech eliminates divisive words like *you, me, we,* and *they* and replaces them with the more communal *I and I*

IRIE excellent, cool, highest; state of feeling great

JAH God, shortened from *Jehovah*

JAMAICAN LABOUR PARTY the main conservative political party in Jamaica; it was founded in 1943 and first came to power in 1944; its most famous leader, Edward Seaga, won the prime minister election in 1980

JAMDOWN a slang term for "Jamaica"

LOVERS ROCK a form of reggae that was popularized in Britain in the 1970s and that centers around songs filled with lyrics about love and equally syrupy rhythms; a large number of lovers rock artists were female

MENTO a style of Jamaican folk music that was popular in the 1950s; it draws on African musical traditions and is often considered a direct predecessor to the ska and reggae sounds that would become popularized in the following decade

MODS a British white subculture that embraced Jamaican ska music and was known for its fashion (often featuring tailor-made suits) and for driving scooters

NATTY a person with dreadlocks

OBEAH the witchcraft or spiritual science native of Africa; a type of voodoo in Jamaica and across the Caribbean

ONE DROP a rhythm in which a snare-and-kick-drum accent is placed on the third beat of each bar; popularized by Carlton Barrett of Bob Marley and the Wailers, it is a major part of reggae music's sound

PEOPLE'S NATIONAL PARTY a social democratic and liberal Jamaican political party that was founded by Norman Manley in 1938; Manley's son Michael was elected prime minister of Jamaica in 1972

RASTA a follower of Marcus Garvey's philosophies and one who usually worships the Almighty in the person of Haile Selassie

RIDDIM the Jamaican patois pronunciation of *rhythm,* referring to the instrumental accompaniment to a song

ROCKSTEADY a music genre (originated in Jamaica in 1966) that slowed down the rhythm and hectic pace of ska

ROD OF CORRECTION a gift that was given to People's National Party leader Michael Manley by Ethiopian emperor Haile Selassie; the walking stick was used as a prop by Manley during the 1972 prime minister elections to appeal to Rastafarian voters

ROOTS conscious, Rasta reggae; a fellow Rasta

RUDE BOYS Jamaican youth gangsters who came out of the Kingston suburban ghettoes in the 1960s and who were known for their violent ways

SELECTOR the DJ/toaster who operates a sound system and selects which artists and songs get played; selectors are often vocal and help keep the crowd engaged with the music

SING-JAY a DJ who utilizes melody in combination with toasting and/or talking

SKA a Jamaican style of music that was popularized in the early 1960s and is known for its emphasis on the offbeat and for its intense rhythmic pace

SKINHEADS a subculture of British white working-class youth that embraced reggae in the late 1960s but that was also known for its racist neo-Nazi fascism and violent behavior toward West Indians

SLACKNESS refers to song lyrics that focus on sex and gun violence and that are often misogynistic or homophobic in nature

SOUND SYSTEMS stereo setups manned by top disc selectors who hosted open-air dances where people could come to hear the top tracks of the era

SPLIFF a cone-shaped cigarette for smoking marijuana; a joint

SUFFERATION major suffering and poverty, often in Jamaican ghettos

TOASTING improvised rapping or talking over instrumental tracks, made famous by sound-system DJs in the early 1970s

VERSION the instrumental track of a song that was separated from the vocals and often used in sound systems for DJs to toast, or rap, over; the version helped lead to the dub style of music that was popularized in the mid-1970s

YARD home; Jamaica

ZION a Rastafarian term for "Africa," more specifically "Ethiopia" as the original birthplace of mankind

★ BIBLIOGRAPHY ★

This is not an exhaustive listing of all of the sources used for this book, nor does it represent all of the significant material available on the subject. Instead, it provides various starting points for further reading.

BOOKS

Alleyne, Mike. "Positive Vibration? Capitalist Textual Hegemony & Bob Marley." In *Caribbean Romances: The Politics of Regional Representation*. Edited by Belinda J. Edmondson (Charlottesville: University Press of Virginia, 1999), 92–104.

—. "The Digital Imprint on Caribbean Music." In *Culture and Mass Communication in the Caribbean: Domination, Dialogue, Dispersion*. Edited by Humphrey A. Regis (Gainesville: University Press of Florida, 2001), 125–137.

—. "International Crossroads: Reggae, Dancehall & the U.S. Recording Industry." In *Globalization, Diaspora & Caribbean Popular Culture*. Edited by Christine Ho & Keith Nurse (Kingston: Ian Randle Press, 2005), 283–296.

Allsopp, Richard. *Dictionary of Caribbean English Usage*. New York: Oxford University Press, 1996.

Baker, Stuart. *The Album Cover Art of Studio One Records*. London: Soul Jazz Books, 2011.

Barrett, Leonard E. *The Rastafarians*. Boston: Beacon, 1997.

Barrow, Steve, and Peter Dalton. *The Rough Guide to Reggae*. 3rd ed. London: Rough Guides, 2004.

Bradley, Lloyd. *Bass Culture: When Reggae Was King*. New York: Penguin, 2001.

—. "Roots-Rock Reggae." In *The Story of Island Records: Keep On Running*. Edited by Suzette Newman and Chris Salewicz (New York: Universe Publishing, 2010), 90–96.

Campbell, Horace. *Rasta and Resistance: From Marcus Garvey to Walter Rodney*. Trenton, N.J.: Africa World Press, 1987.

Chang, Kevin O'Brien; and Wayne Chen. *Reggae Routes: The Story of Jamaican Music*. Philadelphia: Temple University Press, 1998.

Chevannes, Barry. *Rastafari: Roots and Ideology*. Syracuse, N.Y.: Syracuse University Press, 1994.

Collingwood, Jeremy. *Lee "Scratch" Perry: Kiss Me Neck: The Scratch Story in Words, Pictures and Records*. London: Cherry Red Books, 2011.

Davis, Stephen, and Peter Simon. *Reggae Bloodlines: In Search of the Music and Culture of Jamaica*. New York: Da Capo Press, 1992.

de Koningh, Michael, and Laurence Cane-Honeysett. *Young, Gifted, and Black: The Story of Trojan Records*. London: Sanctuary Publishing, 2003.

de Koningh, Michael, and Marc Griffiths. *Tighten Up!: The History of British Reggae*. London: Sanctuary Publishing, 2004.

Foster, Chuck. *Roots Rock Reggae: An Oral History of Reggae Music from Ska to Dancehall*. New York: Billboard Books, 1999.

Grishin, Yuri. *The Famous British Collectable Record Labels: Island Records 1962–1977*. Moscow: Yuri Grishin, 2006.

Hill, Donald R. *Calypso Calaloo: Early Carnival Music in Trinidad*. Gainesville, Fla.: University Press of Florida, 1993.

Katz, David. *Solid Foundation: An Oral History of Reggae*. New York: Bloomsbury, 2003.

—. *People Funny Boy: The Genius of Lee "Scratch" Perry*. London: Omnibus Press, 2006.

King, Stephen A. *Reggae, Rastafari, and the Rhetoric of Social Control*. Jackson, Miss.: University Press of Mississippi, 2002.

Lesser, Beth. *King Jammy's*. Toronto: ECW Press, 2002.

Lewin, Olive. *Rock It Come Over: The Folk Music of Jamaica*. Kingston: The University of the West Indies Press, 2000.

Manuel, Peter, Kenneth Bilby, and Michael Largey. *Caribbean Currents: Caribbean Music From Rumba to Reggae*. Philadelphia: Temple University Press, 1995.

Morrow, Chris. *Stir It Up: Reggae Album Cover Art*. San Francisco: Chronicle Books, 1999.

Murrell, Nathaniel S., William D. Spencer, and Adrian A. McFarlane. *Chanting Down Babylon: The Rastafari Reader*. Philadelphia: Temple University Press, 1998.

Newman, Suzette, ed., and Chris Salewicz, ed. *The Story of Island Records: Keep On Running*. New York: Universe Publishing, 2010.

O'Neil, Thomas. *The Grammys*. New York: Penguin, 1999.

Partridge, Christopher. *Dub in Babylon: Understanding the Evolution and Significance of Dub Reggae in Jamaica and Britain from King Tubby to Post-Punk*. London: Equinox Publishing, 2010.

Pollard, Velma. *Dread Talk: The Language of the Rastafari*. Kingston: Canoe Press, 1994.

Salewicz, Chris, and Adrian Boot. *Reggae Explosion: The Story of Jamaican Music*. New York: Abrams Books, 2001.

Sherlock, Philip, and Hazel Bennett. *The Story of the Jamaican People*. Princeton, N.J.: Markus Wiener Publishers, 1998.

Southall, Brian. *The A–Z of Record Labels*. London: Sanctuary Publishing, 2003.

Stolzoff, Norman C. *Wake the Town and Tell the People: Dancehall Culture in Jamaica*. Durham, N.C.: Duke University Press, 2000.

Veal, Michael E. *Dub: Soundscapes and Shattered Songs in Jamaican Reggae*. Middletown, Conn.: Wesleyan University Press, 2007.

Walker, Klive. *Dubwise: Reasoning From The Reggae Underground*. London: Insomniac Press, 2006.

PERIODICALS

In addition to the specific articles listed below, multiple issues of the following newspapers, magazines, and journals were consulted by the author and are excellent sources of reggae-related information:

Billboard (www.billboard.com)

Caribbean Beat (www.caribbean-beat.com)

Caribbean Quarterly (www.uwi.edu/cq)

Full Watts (www.reggaezine.co.uk/fullwatts.html)

The Guardian (www.guardian.co.uk)

The Jamaica Gleaner (http://jamaica-gleaner.com/)

The Independent (www.independent.co.uk)

Jamaica Journal (http://web1.dloc.com/ufdc/?m=hdBI2&b=UF00090030)

Jamaica Observer (www.jamaicaobserver.com)

The New York Times (www.nytimes.com)

Reggae Report (www.reggaereport.com)

Rolling Stone (www.rollingstone.com)

Waxpoetics (www.waxpoetics.com/magazine)

Alleyne, Mike. " 'Babylon Makes the Rules': The Politics of Reggae Crossover." *Social & Economic Studies* 47, 1 (1998): 65–77.

—. "Globalisation and Commercialisation of Caribbean Music." *Popular Music History* 3,3 (Dec. 2009): 247–273.

—. "Mirage in the Mirror: Album Cover Imagery in Caribbean Music." *Bucknell Review* XLIV, 2: 123–132.

—. "White Reggae: Cultural Dilution in the Record Industry." *Popular Music & Society* 24, 1 (Spring 2000): 15–30.

Atwood, Brett. "Labels Stepping Over Each Other in Race For Kamoze." *Billboard*, November 1994: 10, 109.

Borzillo, Carrie. "Black Uhuru Members Tangle With Label and Each Other." *Billboard*, April 1995: 11, 14.

Bradshaw, Jon. "Blackwell's Island." *Rolling Stone*, May 1982: 23–27.

Campbell, Charles H. E. "Lionesses on the Rise." *Jamaica Journal* 32, 3 (2010): 26–31.

Campbell, Howard. "Chris Blackwell and the Internationalisation of Reggae." *Jamaica Journal* 33, 1 and 2 (2010): 36–39.

Carayol, Seb. "Coxson's Testament: The Legacy of Studio One's Recordings." *Wax Poetics,* no. 16 (2006): 127–132.

—. "Playing in Mr. B's Yard: The Soul Syndicate Rocked Classic Tracks for Reggae's Top Producers." *Wax Poetics,* no. 20 (2007): 53–64.

Gilmore, Mikal. "The Life and Times of Bob Marley." *Rolling Stone*, March 2005: 68–78.

Gurgen, Sara. "Inner Circle: From Bad Bwoys to Soundbwoys." *Reggae Report* 16, 2 (1998): 20–21.

Hutcheon, David. "The Last Crusade." *Mojo*, no. 212 (2011): 82–94.

Katz, David. "The Godfather: Reggae and Dancehall Don Bunny 'Striker' Lee." *Wax Poetics,* no. 23 (2007): 101–106.

—. "Death of a Legend." *Caribbean Beat,* no. 103 (2010): 32.

Ma, David. "Opposites Attract." *Wax Poetics,* no. 43 (2010): 46–50.

Meschino, Patricia. "Ini Kamoze: The Return of the Hotstepper." *Reggae Report* 13, 1 (1995): 16–17.

—. "Come On Over." *Billboard*, July 2011: 33.

O'Neill, Lee. "Joe Higgs: The Teacher Then and Now." *Reggae Report* 13, 7 (1995): 22–23.

Palmer, Bob. "Jimmy Cliff Reggae: Serious." *Rolling Stone*, January 1975: 16–17.

Tulloch, Courtney. "Reggae." *Rolling Stone*, March 1971, 48.

Van Pelt, Carter. "Ijahman Levi." *Reggae Report* 13, 5 (1995): 22–23.

—. "Israel Vibration: Spreading Jah Vibes." *Reggae Report* 13, 10 (1995): 12.

QUOTATION SOURCES

p. 4: Laurel Aitken interviewed in the movie *Skinhead Attitude*, 2003.

p. 11: Big Youth interviewed by Kavelle Anglin-Christie for the *Jamaica Gleaner* newspaper, 2006.

p. 14: Duckie Simpson of Black Uhuru interviewed by Tim Ianna, reprinted online at www.rebelbase.be

p. 32: Burning Spear interviewed by Jason Gross for online magazine *Perfect Sound Forever*, http://www.furious.com/perfect/burningspear.html, September 1997.

p. 49: Jimmy Cliff interviewed by Michele Norris for NPR's *All Things Considered*, 2010.

p. 64: Desmond Dekker interviewed on video by Jett Martin for Dekker's website, www.desmonddekker.com, 2004.

p. 77: Lucky Dube interviewed by Makeda Dread for Reggae Makossa TV, 1992.

p. 86: Marcus Garvey quote on BrainyQuote.com, Xplore Inc, 2012. http://www.brainyquote.com/quotes/quotes/m/marcusgarv201970.html

p. 109: Justin Hinds interviewed by Toby Gohn, 1998, printed online at http://hechicero.vrm.free.fr/james_wilson_bobmarley_supersite/justinhinds.htm

p. 119: Ian Lewis of Inner Circle interviewed by Erik Magni for online reggae magazine *United Reggae*, February 2012, http://unitedreggae.com/articles/n900/022112/interview-inner-circle

p. 159: Bob Marley quote in his biography on IMDb (The Internet Movie Database), http://www.imdb.com/name/nm0002490/bio

p. 207: Lee "Scratch" Perry interviewed by Danny Kelly for *New Musical Express* magazine, November 1984, reprinted online at www.uncarved.org/dub/scratch.html

p. 239: Max Romeo interviewed by Peter I [sic] for online magazine *Reggae Vibes*, www.reggae-vibes.com, 2004.

p. 269: David Hinds of Steel Pulse interviewed by Dan Levy for *Juice* magazine, reprinted online at http://www.juicemagazine.com/steelpulse.html

p. 277: Linval Thompson interviewed by Peter I [sic], reprinted online at http://www.reggae-vibes.com/concert/linthompson/linthompson1.htm

p. 286: Peter Tosh quote on Thinkexist.com, http://thinkexist.com/quotes/peter_tosh/

p. 298: Bunny Wailer interviewed by Chris Simunek for *High Times* magazine, reprinted online at http://www.marleysite.com/interview/wailer.htm

★ INDEX ★

Note: **Boldfaced** page locators refer to main entries in the encyclopedia. *Italics* indicate illustrations.

"007 (Shanty Town)", *64*, 65, 146, 193, 194, 236, 272, 297
"96° in the Shade," 89, 274
2 Tone Records, 5, 196, 210, 219, 257, 259, 279
2 Tone ska revival, 65, 219, 237
1,000 Volts of John Holt, 111
"400 Years," 161, 286

A

A Dream, 238, *238*
Absolute Beginners (film), 5
Abyssinians, the, *2*, **2–3**, 52, 63, 93, 212, 252, 271, 274
Ace of Base, 9, 196
Aces, the, 64
Adams, Glen, 201, 203, 210
Adler, Lou, 199
Africa
  music and dance traditions from, 172–73
  oral traditions from, 172, 292
  Rastafarianism and links to, 89–90, 92
  reggae in, 18, 76
  See also Ethiopia, Haile Selassie
Africa Must Be Free, 189, 202
African Brothers, the, 180
African Disciples, the, 62
African drumming, 84, 155
African Dub series, 95, 276
African Herbsman, 206, 221, 300
African Museum, 11–12, 121, *123*
"After Tonight," 28
Agard, George, 210
Aggrovators, the, **3**, 37, 260, 263
Aitken, Laurel, *4*, **5**, 24, 125, 196, 200, 203, 259
"Al Capone," 24, 219, *219*
album covers, **128–31**
  comic-book, 242, *242*, *243*
  dreadlocks on, 309
  ganja on, *74*, 129, 130, 162, *282*, 282–83
  Island Records and, 126–28, 130–31, 216
  for Steel Pulse, 267–68
  top 10, 309
  for the Wailers, 126, 127, *127*, 128, *129*, 130, *130*
  women on, 129, *154*, 288
albums, best
  dub, 309
  reissue, 310
  roots reggae, 308
  unusual, 312
Alcapone, Dennis, **6**, *6*, 66, 102
Alimantado, Dr., **67**, *67*, 98
"All I Have Is Love," 122
All Stars, the, 263
Alligator Records, 3
Alpert, Herb, 199
Alpha School for Boys, 132, 155, 237, 257
Alphonso, Roland, 63, 155, *257*, 258
Althea & Donna, 83, 95, *215*, *216*, 217, 276
A&M Records, 30, 44, 66, 99, 126, 199, 306
Amalgamated Records, 35, 94
American rap, Jamaican DJs and, 57, 196, 231, 287, 292
American soul, 116, 278
"Amigo," *13*, *13*
Anchor Records, 43, *43*, 266
Anderson, Al, 286, 301, *302*
Anderson, Alpharita (Rita), 158, 167. *See also* Marley, Rita
Anderson, Esther, *127*, 127
Andy, Bob, *6*, **25**, *25*, 100, 114, 204, 216
Andy, Horace, **6–7**, *7*, 19, 68, 75, 110, 138, 186, 271, 283
Another Cycle, 46
Anthem, 16, 150, 217, 233, 241, 261
Anthony B, 193
Anything for You, 156
Aquarius Dub, 39, *39*, 74, 150, 201, 202
Aquarius record shop and label, 39, 101, 212
Arawak Indians, 141, 148, 170, 198, 282
Are We a Warrior, 116, 131, *131*
Ariola Records, 37
Arista Records, 95, 198, 219
Ariwa Sounds, 157
Armond, Wayne, 37, 55
Armstrong, Tim, 48
"Artibella," 26
Ashfield, Tony, 111
Aswad, *8*, **8–10**, *10*, 34, 43, 54, *124*, 126, 154, 163, 166, 196, 267
Atlantic Records, 150, 152, 245, 256, 294, 296
Austin, Peter, 42, 156
Average White Band, 118

B

"Ba Ba Boom," 61
Babcock, Charlie, 108
"Baby, I Love You So," 39, 74, 178, 202
"Baby Come Back," 96
Babylon (film), 8, 28, 305
Babylon by Bus, 163, 302
Babylon the Bandit, 9, 268
Back-O-Wall ghetto (Kingston), 89, 142, 245
"Back to Africa," 63, 83
"Back to My Roots," 268–69
Back to Zion, 109
"Bad Boys," 120
Bad to the Bone, 120
Badarou, Wally, 53, 122
Badu, Erykah, 165
Bafaloukos, Theodore, 52
Bailey, Ras Elroy, 13
"Bam Bam," 278
"Bangarang," 56, 147, 203
Banton, Buju, 100, 235, 295
Banton, Pato, 96, 99
Barbados, reggae in, 97, 98, 200
Barker, Dave, xv, 57
Barnes, Lloyd, 7, 181

Barrett, Aston "Family Man," 85, 112, 190, 206, 260, 300, *301*, 302, 304
Barrett, Carlton, 85, 190, 206, 300, *301*, 302
Barrett, Howard, 204
Barrow, Steve, 19
Bayyan, Khalis, 48
B&C Company, 94, 125, 126, 232, 288
Beat, the, 60, 196, *196*, 219, 290
Beat Down Babylon, 35
Beat Pharmacy, 191
Beatles, the, 11, 194
Beck, Jeff, 279
Beckford, Andrew "Bees," 17
Beckford, Theophilus, **10**, *10*, 68, 210, 222, 237, 254, 270
Beckwith, Martha, 137
Bedward, Alexander, 90
Beenie Man, 22, 23, 30, 99, 100, 295
Belafonte, Harry, 152, 176
"Believe in Yourself," 169
Belnavis, Anita, 166
Beltones, the, 103
Benjamin, Donald, 8, 10
Bennett, Louise, 134
Bennett, Mikey, 43
Bennett, Sydney, 198
Bentley, Kris, 120
Berry, Chuck, 152
Best Dressed Chicken in Town, 67, *67*, 98
Better Mus' Come (film), 37, 55
"Better Mus' Come," 147, 248, 303
Beverley's Records, 26, 39, 44, 46, 65, 146, 158, 185, 200, 210, 300
"Big Five," 135, 219, 295
Big Life label, 234
Big Ship, 156
Big Youth, xv, *11*, **11–12**, *12*, 23, 31, 43, 66, 110, 112, 231, 276, 292, 294, 296
  influence of, 134, 196
Birkin, Jane, 135
"Bit by Bit," 187
"Black and White," 99, *99*
Black Ark Studio, xv, 10, *58*, 59, 60, 75, 85, 122, 149, 198, *205*, 206, *207*, 208, 209, 221
"Black Head Chinaman," 185, 218
Black Liberation Dub, 157
Black Magic, 48
Black Panthers, 133
Black Roots label, 180, 233
Black Roses, 120, *120*
"Black Skin Blue Eyed Boys," 96, 210

Black Slate, **13**, *13*, 283
Black Star Line steamship company, 86–87
Black Uhuru, xv, *14*, **15–17**, 130, 138, 149, 217, 233, 234, 241, 261
Black Woman, 156, 188
Blackboard Jungle Dub, 74, 75, 208
Blackheart Man, 130, 212, 297
Blackwell, Chris, xv, 35, 53, **124–27**, *125*
  and B&C, 232, 288
  and Black Ark studio, 208
  and Bob Marley, 161, 283, 285
  and commercialization of reggae, 128, 194
  and Coxsone Dodd, 68
  and Ernest Ranglin, 222
  and film, 50, 53, 125, 152
  and Ijahman Levi, 116
  and Lee Perry, 60
  and Millie Small, 215, 256, 262
  and Sly & Robbie, 261
  and the Wailers, 103, 163, 300–301
  See also Island Records
Blasted, 37
Blender, Everton, 104
Blissett, Winston, 225
Blondie, 155, 204, 236
Blondy, Alpha, **18**, *18*, 76
Blood & Fire Records, 3, 7, **19**, 131, 213, 243, 305
"Blood and Fire," 110, 263
Bloom, Bobby, 40, 99
Blotta, Luciano, 55
Blue Beat Records, 5, 10, **24–25**, 84, 102, 137, 152, 185, 215, 218, 232, 237, 256, 257, 262
Blue Mountain imprint, 99
Blue Note Records, 237
Blue Wave Studio, 98
Blues Busters, 26
Bob & Marcia, **25**, *25*, 84, 100, 103, 114, 216
Bob Marley & the Wailers, 100, 162–63, 300–2
  album covers for, 126, 127, *127*, 128, *129*, 130, *130*
  and Island Records, 124, 126, 127, 128, 253, 297, 300–1
  and the I-Threes, 100, 114, 167, 188, 189, 216, 301
  and Jacob Miller, 178
  and Sylvan Morris, 186
  and Karl Pitterson, 212, 213
  and Rico Rodriguez, 237
  and Sanctuary Records, 242
  and Danny Sims, 253–54
  and Steel Pulse, 266
Bobby Digital, 138

and Black Uhuru, 15, 16, 241
and Bob Marley, 124, 126, 127,
  158, 161
and Bunny Wailer, 297
and Burning Spear, 33–34, 127
and the Clarendonians, 42
and Derrick Harriott, 102
and Desmond Dekker, 65
and Dillinger, 66
and Dr. Alimantado, 67
early releases, 5, 215, 222
vs. Greensleeves Records, 99
and Gregory Isaacs, 122
and Greyhound, 99
and the Heptones, 106, 252
and Ini Kamoze, 136
and Inner Circle, 118
and Jackie Edwards, 80
and Jimmy Cliff, 44, 46, 47, 48
and Joyce Bond, 128, 203
and Justin Hinds, 108
and Karl Pitterson, 212
and Lee Perry, 127, 208–9
and Leslie Kong, 149
and Linton Kwesi Johnson,
  134, 135
and Max Romeo, 238–39
and the Maytals, 279
and the Pioneers, 210
and Sly & Robbie, 261
and Steel Pulse, 40, 127,
  266–67
50th anniversary celebration,
  127, 237
and Third World, 274
and the Wailers, 124, 126, 127,
  253, 297, 300–301
Israel Vibration, *132*, **132–33,**
  240
"Israelites," 65, *65*, 146, 194, 248,
  248, 259
Issels, Dr. Josef, 163
"It Mek," 65
Ital diet, 93, 124, 301
Italy
  invasion of Ethiopia, 92, 250
  reggae festival in, 23
  the Wailers in, 163, 302

J
Ja-Man All Stars session band, 38
Jackson, Jackie, 3, 193, 287
Jackson, Michael, 181
Jackson, Siggy, 24, 25
Jackson, Vivian. *See* Yabby You
JAD Records, 193, 253, 254
Jagger, Mick, 99, 166, 286
Jah Bull, *202*
Jah Glory, 18

Jah is Real, 34
"Jah Jah Dub," 202
"Jah Live," 93, 114, 189, 250
Jah Shaka sound system, 239
Jahugliman (publication), *92*
Jah Works, 192
Jamaica Broadcasting
  Corporation (JBC), 68, 71
Jamaica Festival Song
  Competition, 70, 117, 153,
  278
Jamaica Film Festival, 55
Jamaica Labour Party (JLP), 78,
  83, 144, 147, 235, 239, 245,
  246–47, 248, 249, 294
Jamaica Recording and Publishing
  Company, 68
Jamaica Song Festival, 147
Jamaican popular music,
  evolution of, xviii, 142–43,
  172–73
Jamaicans, the, 61
James, Lloyd. *See* King Jammy
James Bond (film), 125, 128,
  152, 216
Japan, reggae in, 20, 23, 43, 202,
  237, 264
Jarrett, Irvin "Carrot," 117, 274,
  275
Java Java Dub, 221
"Java Java Java," 201, 202, 221,
  276
Jay-Z, 227
Jays, the, 15, 241
jazz, 222, 237, 257
"Je T'Aime," 135
Jeffreys, Garland, 28, 135
Jenkins, Arthur, 193
Jet Star Phonographics, 203
Jets, the, 215
Jezebel, 108, 108–9
Jiving Juniors, the, 102
Jobson, Brian, *198,* 199
Jobson, Diane, 198
Jobson, Dickie, 52, 198
Jobson, Wayne, xviii, 54, *198,*
  198–99, *199*
JODA Records, 253
"Jogging," 156
Johnson, Carl "Sir JJ," 83
Johnson, Cluett "Clue-J," 10,
  222, 254
Johnson, Harry. *See* Harry J
Johnson, J.J., 70
Johnson, Linton Kwesi, 23, 27, 28,
  104, *133,* **133–35,** *134,* 175,
  191, 296
Johnson, Roydel, xviii, 59–60
Johnson, Tony, 20

Johnson, Wycliffe "Steely," 138,
  240
Jolly Boys, the, 176
Jones, Desi, 37
Jones, Grace, 261
Jones, Sandra "Puma," *14,* 15, 16,
  217, 223, 233
Jonkanoo, 172, 175
Jordan, Louis, 5
Journey, 118
Journey to Addis, 131, 274
Judge Dread, **135,** *135*
"Judge Dread," 206, 219
"Judge Not," 146, 149, 300
Jump Up label, 200
"Just Don't Want to Be Lonely,"
  156

K
Kalypso label, 137
Kamoze, Ini, *136,* **136–37,** 261
Katz, David, 125
Kay, Janet, 28, 154, 217
Kaya, 163, 212, 281, 283, 302
Kelly, R., 22, 227
Kelso, Beverley, 158, 300
Kenya, Mau-Mau guerrillas in,
  33, 92
Kenyatta, Jomo, 33
Kevorkian, François, 75
Keys, Alecia, 234
Khouri, Ken, 5, 24, 78, **137,** 175,
  188, 236, 245
Killer Dub, 118, *120,* 138
Killer on the Rampage, 97, *98*
Kilowatts, the, 70
Kimsey, Chris, 48
King Edwards, 63, 230, 231, 232,
  247
King Jammy (Prince Jammy), 7,
  15, 74, *75,* 121, 122, **138,**
  138, 186, 189, 294
  studio of, *72–73*
King Jammy's (book), 138
King Pioneer Ska Productions, 10
King Stitt, 220, 230, 289
King Tubby, 3, 7, 74–75, *139,*
  139–40, 197, 213, 283, 295
  and Augustus Pablo, 201
  and Bunny Lee, 147
  and Burning Spear, 34
  and Derrick Harriott, 102
  and Duke Reid, 140, 232
  and Glen Brown, 31
  and Inner Circle, 118
  and Johnny Clarke, 43
  and King Jammy, 140
  and Lee Perry, 208
  and Lloyd Daley, 63

and Mikey Dread, 71
and the Morwells, 187
and "Niney the Observer," 110
and Scientist, 242
and Soul Syndicate, 264
and sound systems, 74, 113,
  140, 231, 289
and Sugar Minott, 181
and the Techniques, 272
and Yabby You, 305
"King Tubby Meets Rockers
  Uptown," 39, 74, 178, 202
Kingston, Jamaica, **141–43**
  Back-O-Wall ghetto in, 89,
    142, 245
  recording studios in, 103, 137,
    142, 143, *143–44,* 146, 149,
    156, 221, 235, 287, 304
  See also Trench Town
Kingstonians, the, 102
Kinsey, Donald, 286
Kirton, David, 224
Klash (film), 55
Knibb, Lloyd, 61, 155, 258
"Know Love," 209
Knowledge (group), 306
Kong, Leslie, 5, 26, 39, 111, **146,**
  149
  and Bob Marley, 44, 146, 149,
    158
  and Desmond Dekker, 44, 46,
    65, 146, 149
  and Jackie Opel, 200
  and Jimmy Cliff, 44, 46, 146
  and the Melodians, 174
  and the Pioneers, 210
  song mocking, 185, 218
  and Toots & the Maytals, 278
  and the Wailers, 161, 297, 300
  See also Beverley's Records
Kool & the Gang, 48
Kool Herc (DJ), 292
"Ku Klux Klan," 266, 269
Kumina, 90, 92, 143, 172, 245

L
Labour of Love, 174, 290
Lack, Ken, 42, 105, 147, 210, 238,
  252
Lady Saw, 55, 217, 295
Lamont, Eric "Bingy Bunny," 187,
  240
Land of Look Behind (film), 191
Landis, Joya, 216
Lawes, Henry "Junjo," 98, 111,
  133, 190, 240, 243, 277,
  294, *295*
Lawrence, Beryl, 188

Lee, Bunny "Striker," 7, **146–47,**
  147, 254
  and the Aggrovators, 3
  and Cornell Campbell, 36–37
  and Dave & Ansel Collins, 57
  and Delroy Wilson, 303
  and Dennis Alcapone, 6
  and Derrick Morgan, 147, 185
  and Dillinger, 66
  and flying-cymbal sound, 260
  and Inner Circle, 117
  and John Holt, 111
  and Johnny Clarke, 43
  and King Tubby, 140
  and Lee Perry, 206
  and Linval Thompson, 277
  and Max Romeo, 238
  and Mighty Diamonds, 176
  and Pama Records, 203
  and Randy's Records, 221
  and Rico Rodgriguez, 237
  and Soul Syndicate, 263
  and Tappa Zukie, 306
Lee, Byron, 150, *152,* **152–53,**
  200, 254, 257, 272, 278.
  See also Byron Lee & the
  Dragonaires; Dynamic
  Sounds
Legacy, 150
Legalize It, 130, 283, 285, 287
Legend, 47, 127, 164
Lennox, Annie, 48
Let It Play, 37
"Let the Power Fall On I," 238
"Let Your Yeah Be Yeah," 46, 210
Letts, Don, 66, 296
Levan, Larry, 75
Levi, Ijahman. *See* Ijahman Levi
Levine, Steve, 169
Levy, Barrington, 240
Levy, Ray, 198
Lewis, Hopeton, 25, **153,** 236, 272
Lewis, Ian "Munty," 117, *117,* 118,
  120, 132
Lewis, Roger, 117, 118, 120, 132
Life and Debt (film), 55
Lindo, Earl "Wire," 286
Lindo, Willie, 101
"Liquidator," 103, *103,* 174
Little Richard, 184, 193
"Little Sheila," 5
Live!, 162, 302
Live and Direct, 9, *9*
Live at Stubb's, 197
Live at the Roundhouse, 41
Live Loving, 180, *181*
Living Legacy, 34
"Living on the Front Line," 97
Livingston, Ngeri, 299
Lizzy (DJ), 6

PHOTO CREDITS

© **Lee Abel**
x, 62, 76–77, 157 right, 192 top, 244–245, 257, 311 top right, 312 top

Art Resource, NY
© Knud Petersen: 314

Collection of Toula Ballas
65 right, 196 right

© **Janette Beckman**
4, 291

Bridgeman Art Library
© Harry Hamilton Johnston/Royal Geographical Society, London, UK: 173

Collection of Timothy Collins
140 top, 154 bottom right, 183, 201 bottom, 205 bottom, 206 top, 215 left, 234 right, 277 left, 306 top

Corbis
© Lynn Goldsmith: 17; © Alain Le Garsmeur: 72–73, 144–145; © David J. & Janice L. Frent Collection: 87 top; © Daniel Lainé: 91, 170 inset; © Patrick Chauvel/Sygma: 144 top left, 316 left; © David Bergman: 227 bottom; © Underwood & Underwood: 314 center; © Esther Anderson: 319

© **David Corio**
xvi bottom left & right, 8 bottom, 20–21, 37 right, 64 left, 68–69, 82, 85 right, 97 bottom, 98 bottom, 110 left, 116, 117, 124–125, 138 left, 150 left, 178–179, 184 left, 189 left, 191, 201 top, 217 right, 241 top, 246, 273 top, 277 right, 304 left, 307, 311 bottom right

Collection of David Corio
2 right, 3 center, 6 top right, 7 top, bottom left, 8 top, 12 left, 15 right, 16 center, 25 top, 26 inset & right, 30 bottom left, 31 top right, 33 right insets, 34 top left, bottom, 35 top, 36 inset, 37 left, 42 bottom right, 44 left, 60, 63 left, 64 right, 67 left, 68 bottom left, 79 right, 104 top, 105 bottom, 106, 107 left, 110 right, 111 top, 112 center & bottom right, 113 left, 123 bottom, 147 bottom left, 156 right, 161, 181, 184 right, 187 left, 204 bottom, 206 bottom, 234 left, 236 top, 241 bottom, 252 right, 259 left, 270 left, 271 bottom & top, 297 bottom, 304 right, 305 bottom left & top

© **James Crowley**
48–49, 168–169, 214

© **Rico D'Rozario**
xi, 29 left, 114–115, 132, 208, 237, 292–293, 294 top

Everett Collection
44–45, 52 left, 52–53; © New Yorker Films: 50–51, 54 bottom; © Ronald Grant/Mary Evans Picture Library: 52 inset; Library of Congress: 86; © Music Mirrorpix: 315 top center

Courtesy of Fully Fullwood
263 left & center; 263 right © Genie Polos

Getty Images
© Michael Ochs Archives: vi–vii, 57 bottom, 90 top, 152 right, 158 left, 172, 175 top, 204 top, 247, 301, 315 bottom; © Lee Jaffe: xiv–xv, 18 left, 107 right, 158–159, 162 bottom, 167, 212 top, 261 right, 285 left inset, 302 top, 308 right; © Charlie Gillett

Collection/Redferns: 6 top left, 155 right; © Jose Jordan/AFP: 20 inset; © John Lynn Kirk: 23 left inset; © Chris Walter/WireImage: 25 bottom; © David Redfern/Redferns: 26 left; © Fin Costello/Redferns: 27 right, 154 bottom left; © GAB Archive/Redferns: 34 top right, 112 left; © Echoes/Redferns: 41 left, 177 top, 253, 276 left; © Lynn Pelham/Time & Life Pictures: 92 left, 93 left; © Chris Morphet/Redferns: 118–119; © Gems/Redferns: 135; © Ian Dickson/Redferns: 160; © Virginia Turbett: 182 left; © Rob Loud: 197 bottom; © Michael Bezjian/WireImage: 199 right; © Jodi Cobb/National Geographic: 245 right; © Universal History Archive: 250; © Terrence Spencer/Time Life Pictures: 259 right; © Evening Standard/Hulton Archive: 262 left, 268 bottom; © Dimitrios Kambouris: 317 right

© **Kim Gottlieb–Walker/www.Lenswoman.com**
xvi top, 32–33, 42 top right, 66 right, 103 top, 109, 125 right, 127 top, 143 bottom, 147 bottom right, 164, 193, 205 top, 223 top, 239, 252 left, 275, 286 top

© **Kim Gottlieb–Walker from her book "Bob Marley and the Golden Age of Reggae"**
78–79, 126 bottom, 298

© **Bob Gruen**
47 bottom right, 284–285

Collection of Miles Hare/www.xraymusic.co.uk
3 top, 12 right, 16 left & top, 29 center, 30 right, 59 right, 71 inset, 74 left, 75 right, 83 top, 95 top left & right, 125 bottom center, 126 top, 139 bottom, 146 right, 147 top left & right, 157 left, 163, 177 bottom, 178 left, 185 bottom right, 190 bottom, 202 bottom, 209 right, 210, 212 bottom, 219 top & bottom right, 220 right, 222 top, 248 right, 266 right, 278 bottom, 286 bottom, 288, 290, 299 top, 303 left, 313, 316 center

© **LOisa Haun**
133

© **Dave Hendley**
31 top left, 67 right, 113 right, 121, 139 top, 305 bottom right

© **Brian Jahn**
xii, xvii top right, xix, 43 bottom, 165 bottom, 186, 230 left, 243 top, 282 top

Kobal Collection
© Phillip Lynch: 55 top

Library of Congress
143 top

Landov
© PA Photos: 24 bottom left

© **Beth Lesser**
inside front cover, xvii top left & bottom, 7 bottom right, 10 right, 29 right, 35 bottom, 38, 56 top, 75 left, 92 right, 123 top, 136, 138 right, 141, 187 right, 202 top, 220 left, 221, 228 inset, 230 right, 233, 235, 240, 248 left, 260 right, 261 left, 281 inset, 289 left, 292 center, 294 bottom right, 295, 296 right, 303 right, 316 bottom, 317 left, inside back cover

London Features
211, 218

Mary Evans Picture Library
National Archives: 90 bottom left; 90 bottom right

Collection of Josh Mrvos
154 top, 209 left, 215 right, 219 bottom left, 254 right

© **Mystic Seaport Collection, Mystic, Conn.**
87 bottom

Collection of Laurent Pfeiffer
27 left, 54 top, 55 bottom, 74 right, 112 top right, 140 bottom, 223 bottom, 292 left

Photoshot
© Starstock: 256 top left

Redux
© Angel Franco/New York Times: 150–151

Retna Ltd.
© Jay Blakesberg: 197 top; © Jeff Davy: 251 top

Rex USA
© Bill Zygmant: 96; © Ray Stevenson: 267

© **Ebet Roberts**
vi top & bottom left, 14–15, 36 left, 100, 101, 166, 169 right, 195 bottom, 217 left, 249, 269, 279 bottom, 283, 316 top center

© **Peter Simon**
xx–xxi, 40, 46, 93 right, 165 top, 270 top right, 280–281

urbanimage.tv
© Adrian Boot: viii, ix, 1 right, 2 left, 10 left, 13 bottom, 23 right, 58–59, 61, 70–71, 80–81, 88, 89, 94, 105 top, 111 bottom, 134 left, 144 bottom left, 148–149, 156 left, 162 top, 170–171, 180 top 190 top, 196 left, 207, 216, 222 bottom, 225, 228–229, 231, 255, 265, 278 top, 297 top, 306 bottom, 310 bottom left & top, 317 center; © Johnnie Black: 22–23

Courtesy of urbanimage.tv
3 bottom, 5 bottom, 6 bottom, 19, 24 top, bottom right, 31 bottom right, 41 right, 42 left, 43 top, 48 top, 50 inset, 65 left, 66 left, 68 top left, 80 top, 83 bottom, 95 bottom right, 97 top, 102, 103 bottom, 108, 122, 124 top, 127 bottom left & right, 128, 129, 130, 131 right, 149 bottom inset, 152 left, 174 left, 175 bottom, 176, 180 bottom, 182 right, 185 top & bottom left, 188 left, 200, 203, 232, 236 bottom, 238, 242 top, 243 bottom, 256 top right & bottom, 260, 262 right, 266 left, 271 center right, 273 bottom, 274, 279 top, 282 bottom, 285 right, 287, 289 right, 292 right inset, 294 bottom left, 296 top, 299 center & bottom, 300 right, 302 bottom, 308 left, 309 left & center, 314 right, 315 top right, 316 right